Handbook of
Aging and the Social Sciences

The Handbooks of Aging
Consisting of Three Volumes

Critical comprehensive reviews of
research knowledge, theories, concepts, and issues

Editor-in-Chief
James E. Birren

Handbook of the Biology of Aging
Edited by Edward J. Masoro and Steven N. Austad

Handbook of the Psychology of Aging
Edited by James E. Birren and K. Warner Schaie

Handbook of Aging and the Social Sciences
Edited by Robert H. Binstock and Linda K. George

Part Two
Aging and Social Structure

Contents

Part One
Theory and Methods

To Martha, Jenny, Ruth, and R. C. Binstock
—R.H.B.

To my mentors and dear friends: Bob Atchley, George Maddox, and Jim House
—L.K.G.

The sponsoring editor for this book was Nikki Levy, the production editor was Rebecca Orbegoso, and the copyeditor was Eileen Favorite. The cover was designed by Amy Stirnkorb. Composition was done by Kolam Information Services in Pondicherry, India, and the book was printed and bound by Maple-Vail in Binghamton, New York.

Cover photo credit: © 2001 Corbis Images.

This book is printed on acid-free paper. ∞

Academic Press
A Harcourt Science and Technology Company
525 B Street, Suite 1900, San Diego, California 92101-4495, USA
http://www.academicpress.com

Academic Press
Harcourt Place, 32 Jamestown Road, London NW1 7BY, UK
http://www.academicpress.com

Library of Congress Catalog Card Number: 00-111075

International Standard Book Number: 0-12-099194-2

PRINTED IN THE UNITED STATES OF AMERICA
01 02 03 04 05 06 MB 9 8 7 6 5 4 3 2 1

Handbook of
Aging and the Social
Sciences

Fifth Edition

Editors
Robert H. Binstock and Linda K. George

Associate Editors
Victor W. Marshall, Angela M. O'Rand, and James H. Schultz

ACADEMIC PRESS
A Harcourt Science and Technology Company

San Diego San Francisco New York Boston London Sydney Tokyo

Part Three
Social Factors and Social Institutions

Part Four
Aging and Social Intervention

Contributors and Editors

Numbers in parentheses indicate the pages on which the author's contribution begin.

Duane F. Alwin (22), Department of Sociology and Institute for Social Research, University of Michigan, Ann Arbor, Michigan 48106–1248

Cynthia M. Beall (125), Department of Anthropology, Case Western Reserve University, Cleveland, Ohio 44106

Vern L. Bengtson (295), Andrus Gerontology Center, University of Southern California, Los Angles, California 90089

Robert H. Binstock (333), School of Medicine, Case Western Reserve University, Cleveland, Ohio 44106

Richard T. Campbell (22), Department of Sociology, University of Illinois at Chicago, Chicago, Illinois 60607

William H. Crown (352), The MEDSTAT Group, Cambridge, Massachusetts 02140

Stephen J. Cutler (462), Department of Sociology, University of Vermont, Burlington, Vermont 05405

Dale Dannefer (3), Margaret Warner Graduate School of Education and Human Development, University of Rochester, Rochester, New York 14627

Judy Feder (387), Institute for Health Care Research and Policy, Georgetown University, Washington, DC 20007

Kenneth F. Ferraro (313), Department of Sociology and Gerontology Program, Purdue University, West Lafayette, Indiana 47907

Linda K. George (217), Center for the Study of Aging and Human Development, Duke University, Durham, North Carolina 27710

Roseann Giarrusso (295), Andrus Gerontology Center, University of Southern California, Los Angeles, California 90089

Gunhild O. Hagestad (3), Graduate Program in Human Development and Social Policy and Department of Sociology, Northwestern University, Evanston, Illinois 60208; and Agder University College, Kristiansand, Norway 4604

Tamara K. Hareven (141), Departments of Individual and Family Studies and History, University of Delaware, Newark, Delaware 19176

Mark D. Hayward (69), Population Research Institute and Department of Sociology, Pennsylvania State University, University Park, Pennsylvania 16802–6210

Jon Hendricks (462), University Honors College, Oregon State University, Corvallis, Oregon 97331–2221

John C. Henretta (255), Department of Sociology, University of Florida, Gainesville, Florida 32611–7330

Charlotte Ikels (125), Department of Anthropology, Case Western Reserve University, Cleveland, Ohio 44106

Robert L. Kane (406), School of Public Health, University of Minnesota, Minneapolis, Minnesota 55455

Rosalie A. Kane (406), School of Public Health, University of Minnesota, Minneapolis, Minnesota 55455

Eric R. Kingson (369), School of Social Work, Syracuse University, Syracuse, New York 14244

Harriet L Komisar (387), Institute for Health Care Research and Policy, Georgetown University, Washington, DC 20007

Neal Krause (272), Department of Health Behavior and Health Education, School of Public Health, University of Michigan, Ann Arbor, Michigan 48109–2029

Charles F. Longino, Jr. (103), Department of Sociology, Wake Forest University, Winston-Salem, North Carolina 27109

Joanne Lynn (444), Center to Improve Care of the Dying, RAND Corporation, Arlington, Virginia 22202

J. Beth Mabry (295), Andrus Gerontology Center, University of Southern California, Los Angeles, California 90089

George L. Maddox (426), Center for the Study of Aging and Human Development, Duke University, Durham, North Carolina 27710

Victor W. Marshall, Institute on Aging, University of North Carolina, Chapel Hill, North Carolina 27599

Amy E. McLaughlin (238), Department of Sociology, University of Maryland, College Park, Maryland 20742

Phyllis Moen (179), Departments of Human Development and Sociology, Cornell University, Ithaca, New York 14853

Marlene Niefeld (387), Institute for Health Care Research and Policy, Georgetown University, Washington, DC 20007

Angela M. O'Rand (197), Department of Sociology, Duke University, Durham, North Carolina 27708

Leonard I. Pearlin (238), Department of Sociology, University of Maryland, College Park, Maryland 20742

Mark F. Pioli (238), Department of Sociology, University of Maryland, College Park, Maryland 20742

Jill Quadagno (333), Pepper Institute on Aging and Public Policy, Florida State University, Tallahassee, Florida 32306

Carol D. Ryff (44), Department of Psychology, University of Wisconsin, Madison, Wisconsin 53706

James H. Schulz, Florence Heller Graduate School, Brandeis University, Waltham, Massachusetts 02254

William J. Serow (86), Center for the Study of Population, Florida State University, Tallahassee, Florida 32306

Burton Singer (44), Office of Population Research, Princeton University, Princeton, New Jersey 08544

Anne M. Wilkinson (444), Center to Improve Care of the Dying, RAND Corporation, Arlington, Virginia 22202

David R. Williams (160), Department of Sociology, and Institute for Social Research, University of Michigan, Ann Arbor, Michigan 48106

John B. Williamson (369), Department of Sociology, Boston College, Chestnut Hill, Massachusetts 02467

Colwick M. Wilson (160), Department of Sociology, and Institute for Social Research, University of Michigan, Ann Arbor, Michigan 48106

Zhenmei Zhang (69), Department of Sociology, Pennsylvania State University, University Park, Pennsylvania 16802–6210

Foreword

This volume is one of a series of three handbooks on aging, *Handbook of the Biology of Aging*, *Handbook of the Psychology of Aging*, and *Handbook of Aging and the Social Sciences*. The series is in its fifth edition, which reflects the growth of research and publication on aging.

The handbook series is used by research personnel, graduate students, and professional personnel for access not only to the rapidly growing volume of literature, but also to the perspectives provided by the integration and interpretations of the findings by experienced and well-informed scholars. The subject matter of aging has matured and expanded in recent years, with much research and education being conducted. It has become a mainstream topic in the sciences, ranging from the biological to the social, and also in the many professions that serve older persons.

A product of this exponential growth of research literature on aging and the speed of access in the information age is that an overwhelming amount of information is quickly available to individuals. One result of such information overload can be an adaptive narrowing of interests and scope. This is particularly relevant to understanding a complex field such as aging, in which many factors interact. More than ever, students of aging need integration and interpretations from experts in subtopics adjacent to their special interests. The handbook series provides the opportunity to read not only a topic of special interest but also adjacent subject matter that may have important implications. This opportunity is particularly significant in aging, which is not a lock-and-key issue solved by one discipline, one study, or one insight.

Rapid changes in the 20th century provided evidence that environmental factors can contribute much to both the length and the quality of life. Aging is a dynamic process, with shifts in the magnitude of what contributes to the aging process. There is little doubt that our genetic background as a species and our individual heredity contribute to our prospects for length of life and life-limiting and disabling diseases. We can expect much more understanding of the genetic factors in aging as contemporary research continues to expand. However, environmental factors, both physical and social, and our behavior modulate the expression of our genetic predispositions. In a broad perspective, aging is a product of ecological forces. For this reason researchers and students of aging must be aware of diverse factors contributing to the phenomena of aging. The handbook series makes available interpretations of a vast literature and contributes to the integration of a highly complex but vital subject matter.

Public interest in aging has grown along with the impressive increases in life expectancy and in the numbers and proportion of older persons. This interest presumably has led to the increased support of research and scholarship by governments and foundations. Aging has become a topic of daily life discussions. Further improvements in our life expectancy and reductions in limitations on the quality of life with advancing age may be expected to emerge from the efforts of those who have written chapters for the series of handbooks on aging.

Without the intense efforts and cooperation of the editors and associate editors of the individual volumes, the series would not be possible. I thank Edward J. Masoro and Steven N. Austad, the editors of the *Handbook of the Biology of Aging*, and their associate editors, Judith Campisi, George M. Martin, and Charles V. Mobbs; Robert H. Binstock and Linda K. George, editors of the *Handbook of Aging and the Social Sciences*, and their associate editors, Victor W. Marshall, Angela M. O'Rand, and James H. Schulz; K. Warner Schaie, my co-editor of the *Handbook of the Psychology of Aging*, and the associate editors, Ronald P. Abeles, Margy Gatz, and Timothy A. Salthouse.

I also express my appreciation to Nikki Levy, Publisher at Academic Press, whose long-standing interest and cooperation have facilitated the publication of the series of handbooks on aging.

James E. Birren

Preface

This fifth edition of the *Handbook of Aging and the Social Sciences* provides extensive reviews and critical evaluations of research on the social aspects of aging. It also makes available major references and identifies high-priority topics for future research.

To achieve these purposes, the handbook presents knowledge about aging through the systematic perspectives of a variety of disciplines and professions: anthropology, demography, economics, epidemiology, history, medicine, political science, policy analysis, social psychology, social work, and sociology. Building upon four previous editions (1976, 1985, 1990, and 1996), this handbook reflects the tremendous growth during the past five years of ideas, information, and research literature on the social aspects of aging.

The handbook is intended for use by researchers, professional practitioners, and students in the field of aging. It is also expected to serve as a basic reference tool for scholars, professionals, and others who are not currently engaged in research and practice directly focused on aging and the aged.

When the first edition of this handbook was being prepared by Bob Binstock and Ethel Shanas in the early 1970s, only a small number of social scientists were equipped to address any specific topic in a first-rate fashion. More than a quarter of a century later, the field has burgeoned in such quality and quantity that a great many scholars would be outstanding contributors for each of the various subjects chosen for this volume.

Accordingly, this fifth edition was planned and implemented to enlist predominantly new contributors from among the rich variety of distinguished scholars and path-breaking perspectives now constituting the field. Of the 42 authors and coauthors in this edition, 25 are contributing to the handbook for the first time. Only 2 authors have contributed to all five editions, 1 is contributing for the fourth time, 4 are contributing for the third time, and 10 are contributing for a second time.

In several respects the contents of this fifth edition are also substantially different from those of its predecessors. Eleven chapters address subjects not covered in the fourth edition. Ten topics maintained from the previous volume have been addressed by different authors, who bring their own perspectives to bear upon the subject matter. The other four chapters have been substantially revised and brought up-to-date, one of them with a new coauthor.

Topics chosen for this volume that were not in the fourth edition include the following chapters: "Person-Centered Methods for Understanding Aging: The Integration of Numbers and Narratives" (Chapter 3); "Demography of Aging: A Century of Global Change, 1950–2050" (Chapter 4); "Geographical Distribution and Migration" (Chapter 6); "Historical Perspectives on Aging and Family Relations" (Chapter 8); "The Social Psychology of Health" (Chapter 12); "Social Support" (Chapter 15); "The Aging Self in Social Contexts" (Chapter 16); "Aging and Role Transitions" (Chapter 17); "Emerging Issues in Chronic Care" (Chapter 22), "The End of Life" (Chapter 24); and "Emerging Social Trends" (Chapter 25).

Many continuing topics dealt with by new authors are treated from viewpoints rather different from those in previous editions. Chapter 7, "Age, Aging, and Anthropology," for example, departs from the familiar approach of comprehensively reviewing the place of age and aging in anthropological research to examine broader contexts that have influenced the current state of the field—changes in the global and national political environments, changes within the discipline of anthropology itself, and changes within the subspecialty of the anthropology of age and aging. Another example is Chapter 23, "Housing and Living Arrangements," which, unlike recent handbook treatments of the topic, addresses the topic in terms of a theory-driven research agenda for developing interventions that might beneficially modify aging processes and the experience of aging.

As implied by this design to have continuing topics addressed from new but complementary perspectives, the editors and associate editors regard the earlier editions of the handbook as part of the active literature in the field. These volumes remain important reference sources for topics and perspectives not represented in this fifth edition. Indeed, because of the ongoing life of those earlier chapters, it was feasible to introduce new dimensions within the limited space available in the present volume. Some of the present chapter authors, in fact, build explicitly and actively upon the work of their predecessors in the earlier editions. By the same token, it seemed reasonable not to allocate space in this volume to updating certain subjects that were treated in excellent chapters published in the fourth edition only 5 years ago.

The 25 chapters of this fifth edition are organized in four sections: Part One, Theory and Methods; Part Two, Aging and Social Structure; Part Three, Social Factors and Social Institutions; and Part Four, Aging and Social Intervention. Each chapter was conceived and written specifically for this volume. The book includes a thorough subject index and a comprehensive bibliography on the social aspects of aging. The research literature cited and referenced in each chapter is also indexed by author at the end of the volume.

The contributors to this fifth edition successfully met a number of challenges. They organized their chapters in terms of analytical constructs that enabled them to sift through a great deal of literature bearing upon their topics. They provided historical perspectives on these subjects, drawing upon classic and contemporary references in the field, and constructed their presentations to ensure that the usefulness of the volume would not be limited by specific time referents. Most impressively, they were able to present their knowledge and viewpoints succinctly and to relate their treatments to those of their fellow authors.

In developing the subject matter for this volume and in the selection of contributors, the editors were assisted by three associate editors: Victor W. Marshall, Angela M. O'Rand, and James H. Schulz. They also helped the editors in the process of editorial review in which critical comments and suggestions were forwarded to the authors for their consideration in undertaking revised drafts. Jim Schulz has been an associate editor throughout four editions of the handbook and has authored various chapters since the first edition; we take this opportunity to express our great appreciation and admiration for his outstanding contributions over a quarter of a century.

We sadly report that George C. Myers, associate editor for the second, third, and fourth editions, died several months before this volume went to press. George was a pioneering leader in demographic and sociological research on aging, as well as a superb associate editor of and contributor to various editions of the handbook. He was also a great teacher, colleague, and friend. We, and the field of gerontology, will sorely miss him.

The success of this volume is due primarily to the seriousness with which the chapter authors accepted their assignments and to the goodwill with which they responded to editorial critiques and suggestions. To these colleagues, the editors and associate editors express their special appreciation. Linda George thanks Bob Binstock for taking on, and discharging magnificently, more than his share of the editorial work for this edition.

Robert H. Binstock
Linda K. George

About the Editors

Robert H. Binstock

is professor of aging, health, and society at Case Western Reserve University. A former president of the Gerontological Society of America (1976) and chair of the Gerontological Health Section of the American Public Health Association (1996–1997), he has served as director of a White House Task Force on Older Americans for President Lyndon B. Johnson and as chairman and member of a number of advisory panels to the United States government, state and local governments, and foundations. Professor Binstock is the author of over 200 articles and book chapters, most of them dealing with politics and policies related to aging. His 22 authored and edited books include *Home Care Advances: Essential Research and Policy Issues* (2000); *The Lost Art of Caring: A Challenge to Health Professionals, Families, Communities, and Societies* (2001); and five editions of the *Handbook of Aging and the Social Sciences*. Among the honors he has received for contributions to gerontology and the well-being of older persons are the Kent and the Brookdale Awards from the Gerontological Society of America, the Key Award from the American Public Health Association, the American Society on Aging Award, and the Arthur S. Flemming Award from the National Association of State Units on Aging.

Linda K. George

is professor of sociology at Duke University, where she also serves as associate director of the Duke University Center for the Study of Aging and Human Development. She is a fellow and past president of the Gerontological Society of America. She is currently chair of the Aging and Life Course Section of the American Sociological Association. She is former editor of the *Journal of Gerontology, Social Sciences Section*. She currently serves on the editorial boards of the *Journal of Gerontology: Social Sciences*, the *Journal of Aging and Health*, and the *Journal of Health and Social Behavior*. Professor George is the author or editor of seven books and author of more than 200 journal articles and book chapters. She co-edited the third and fourth editions of the *Handbook of Aging and the Social Sciences*. Her major research interests include social factors and illness, stress and coping, and the aging self. Among the honors Professor George has received are Phi Beta Kappa, the Duke University Trinity College Distinguished Teaching Award, the W. Fred Cottrell Award for Outstanding Achievement in the Field of Aging, and the Mentorship Award from the Behavioral and Social Sciences Section of the Gerontological Society of America.

Victor W. Marshall

is professor of sociology at the University of North Carolina at Chapel Hill and director of the University of North Carolina Institute on Aging. Prior to 1999 he directed the University of Toronto Institute for Human Development, Life Course and Aging. He is a founding member and former vice-president of the Canadian Association on Gerontology, and former editor of the *Canadian Journal on Aging*. He chairs the Fellowship Committee of the Gerontological Society of America and is a member of the Board of the Southern Gerontological Society. He is on the editorial boards of *Ageing and Society*, *The Journal of Aging and Health*, and *Social Forces*. As director of the Canadian Aging Research Network, he developed an extensive research program on the aging of the labor force. Current research investigates the health consequences of disrupted labor force participation of older workers, retirement of Canadian Forces veterans, and well-being in later life. His most recent books are C. Ryff and V. Marshall (Eds.), *The Self and Society in Aging Processes* (1999), and V. Marshall and others (Eds.), *Restructuring Work and the Life Course* (2001).

Angela M. O'Rand

is professor of sociology at Duke University, where she has been on the faculty since 1979. She is affiliated at Duke with the Center for Aging and Human Development and with the Center for Demographic Studies. Her research interests have centered on life course transition patterns from midlife to retirement. These studies have spanned topics focused on midlife divorce, educational reentry, and alternative pathways to retirement. They have also embedded these life course processes in family and labor market structures, with a concern for identifying gender stratification in adulthood trajectories. One stratification emphasis throughout her work has been on pensions and their effects on labor mobility, labor exit, and retirement income inequality. Numerous publications have appeared in *American Sociological Review*, *Social Forces*, *Sociological Forum*, *The Gerontologist*, *Journal of Gerontology*, *Research on Aging*, *Social Science Research*, *Sociological Quarterly*, among other journals and anthologies. She and John C. Henretta have recently published a book titled *Age and Inequality: Diverse Pathways to Retirement*.

James H. Schulz

is professor emeritus, Brandeis University. He is an economist (Ph.D., Yale, 1966) specializing in the economics of aging, pension and retirement policy, and international aging issues. A former president of the Gerontological Society of America, he received the society's 1983 Kleemeier Award for outstanding research in aging, the 1998 Clark Tibbitts Award for contributions to the field of gerontology, and a 1999 Testimonial Award from the United Nations Secretary General for his international aging research and other activities related to the "International Year of Older Persons." His books include *Providing Adequate Retirement Income*, *The World Ageing Situation, 1991*, *Economics of Population*

Aging, When "Life-Time" Employment Ends: Older Worker Programs In Japan, and *Social Security in the 21st Century.* His most recent research is on social security privatization issues and includes *Older Women and Private Pensions in the United Kingdom.* His best known book is *The Economics of Aging* (which has been translated into Japanese and Chinese and is currently available in its seventh edition).

Part One

Theory and Methods

One

Concepts and Theories of Aging

Beyond Microfication in Social Science Approaches

Gunhild O. Hagestad and Dale Dannefer

I. Aging and the Social Sciences: Theoretical Challenges

Our goal in this chapter is not to provide a comprehensive overview of orientations, traditions, or key prophets in social theories of aging. Several such pieces have been published recently (e.g. Bengtson & Schaie, 1999; George, 1995; Hendricks, 1992; Lynott & Lynott, 1996; Marshall, 1995). Here, we encourage metatheoretical reflection on what the study of aging has contributed to social science understanding, and how social science might have shed light on age and aging. Agreeing with the concern that the field lacks theoretical impetus, we suggest that theoretical efforts could benefit from engaging in two sets of ongoing conversations. One set addresses societies under conditions of late modernity, including the volatile political contexts of welfare states in transition. To such conversations must be added the fact that these societies are also aging. A second group of conversations is spurred by the growing body of work on the life course. An examination of this perspective confronts social scientists interested in aging with some critical issues. In our view, creative dissent,

or what Bourdieu (1991) calls "working dissensus" around these issues would spur theoretical advances. In particular, such discourse may help us re-engage in basic questions about age and social life and reverse a strong trend towards *microfication*. As we elaborate below, microfication entails a focus on individuals in their micro-worlds and a neglect of the wider social context.

A. About Theoretical Understanding

While we cannot address the extensive literature on social theory, some orienting comments will be useful. First, theory implies explanation; it must do more than simply describe. Finding explanations means "moving up" in generality, subsuming what we are seeking to understand under a more general principle. Empirical research involves a movement between theory and observation, an inductive–deductive cycle. Researchers choose different entry points in the cycle when they initiate inquiry. Second, the adequacy of an explanation is partly specified by its generality across settings and historical periods. A goal of theoretical work is to apprehend the conditions

Handbook of Aging and the Social Sciences, Fifth Edition

under which explanations are and are not applicable.

A third principle concerns the position of the researcher. Even when lost in a dust-cloud of empiricism, researchers whose work appears atheoretical necessarily operate with some implicit theory, which may simply stem from their own experiences and taken-for-granted life world (Hacking, 2000). The social context shapes individual aging, including that of gerontologists and their questions. Although reflexivity is now being called necessary as a general social practice (Beck, Giddens, & Lash, 1994), it is an enduring imperative of social science that its practitioners consider how their role in knowledge production is shaped by their own political, cultural, and biographical locations.

B. The Leisure of the Theory Class?

In a somewhat flippant twist to the title of a classic book by Veblen (1912), *The Theory of the Leisure Class*, some commentators have suggested that theory is a luxury, which cannot be prioritized when a research community is under strong pressures to produce "facts" and constantly refine the tools for their production. Such pressures give rise to concerns about the long-term direction and purpose of our work.

Over the last couple of decades, a number of authors have expressed alarm about the lack of theoretical rigor in the social scientific study of aging. Indeed, earlier editions of this handbook have characterized social science work in aging as atheoretical and descriptive (Maddox & Campbell, 1985; Myers, 1996). Despite such warnings, things do not seem to be improving. In the recent *Handbook of Aging Theory*, Bengtson, Rice, and Johnson (1999) contend that the general state of affairs can now be described as a "disinheritance of theory." A related analysis (Bengtson, Burgess & Parrot, 1997) found that 80% of articles in key journals included no reference to theory. The neglect of theory not only represents a loss to the study of aging; it also deprives base disciplines of new insight.

The social sciences have lacked a productive dialogue between data and theory related to aging. In psychology, by contrast, aging research has contributed to a new rigor and to revisiting the "big questions" of the discipline. For example, the issues of stability and change in development, fundamental questions about the nature and stability of intelligence and personality, and the challenges of the age-period-cohort conundrum have all been informed by research in aging, as exemplified in the work of Baltes and Schaie (e.g., Baltes & Smith, 1999; Schaie, 1996). Perhaps one reason why psychology seems to have gained from the study of aging is that the individual is taken to be its proper analytical focus. But the individual has also been the primary unit of analysis in much sociological work on aging, to the neglect of age-related social dynamics. Indeed, compared with the early days of gerontology, recent decades seem to have brought a persistent tendency toward microfication in social science approaches to aging.

C. Increasing Microfication?

Microfication refers to a trend in the substantive issues and analytical foci, what we might call the ontology of social research in aging. Increasingly, attention has been concentrated on psychosocial characteristics of individuals in microinteractions, to the neglect of the macrolevel. Apart from population characteristics, macrolevel phenomena of central interest to social scientists, such as social institutions, cohesion and conflict, norms and values, have slipped out of focus or been rendered invisible.

As Riley has consistently emphasized, age is a feature of social structure as well as of individuals. With the exception of her own work (e.g., Riley, Foner, & Riley, 1999) and the contributions of authors taking a political economy perspective (e.g. Minkler & Estes, 1991, 1998; Myles, 1989; Phillipson, 1982; Walker, 1981), few systematic efforts to develop a general approach for conceptualizing age beyond the individual level can be found.

Microfication probably has multiple interrelated causes. One is the general *zeitgeist* of late modernity, with an emphasis on individual agency (see section II.C). Other factors are a "medicalization" of old age (Estes & Binney, 1989; Phillipson, 1982), and a tendency to treat aging in problem-focused terms. Definitions of gerontology have increasingly tended to include the word *problem* (Achenbaum & Levin, 1989). Often, such a "misery perspective" (Tornstam, 1992) may stem from good intentions, focusing on troubled segments of the older population in order to give decision makers a basis for making sociopolitical changes or aiding medical professionals. A final force in the microfication process and the emphasis on problems is the structure of research funding, which, in turn, reflects the complex of factors mentioned above.

D. Themes from the Field: A Look at Recent Journal Articles

The problem-centered microfocus in approaches to aging is reflected in scientific output. Participants at national and international meetings can seemingly spend full days in sessions on dementia and caregiver burden. On the other hand, they may have ample free time if they look for discussions of structural changes in aging societies, relationships between age groups, or age and inequality. To match such impressions against some concrete evidence, we carried out a content analysis of the 1995–1999 volumes of two key journals in the field: *Journal of Gerontology/Social Sciences* (JG) and

Ageing and Society (A&S). We first turned our attention to article titles, on the assumption that they give an indication of central topics in the field. In both journals, titles centered on illness and impairment appeared most frequently. In A&S, the top ranking was shared with family networks and intergenerational relations, which was the second most common topic in JG. Two other topics were among the "top five" in both journals: caregiving and work/retirement.

When articles included empirical data, we categorized the levels of analysis for dependent and independent variables: individual (physical, psychological, social-contextual characteristics of individuals); micro (relationships in primary groups); meso (relationships/characteristics of secondary groups, such as organizations, communities); macro (culture, social structure, population). An article was coded according to the "highest" level used.

In JG, 94% of the articles had dependent variables on either the individual or microlevel. For A&S, the figure was 77%. Only 3% of the JG articles focused on a macrolevel dependent variable; 17% did so in A&S. The figures for independent variables suggest that researchers also tend to search for explanations on a microlevel. In JG, 77% of the articles had independent variables on an individual or microlevel. The figure for A&S was 55%. The latter journal was more likely to include macrolevel independent variables (32% versus 12%). There seems to be an unspoken assumption that the older individuals get, the less important are what epidemiologists Link and Phelan (1995) call "basic social conditions" on the macrolevel. We would concur with O'Rand and Campbell (1999), who comment on the near absence of structural variables in current aging research.

The bulk of articles take a social-psychological approach, with both dependent and independent variables on an individual or microlevel. Although the social psychology of aging constitutes an important meeting ground between psychology and sociology (George, 1996a), it leaves some fertile soil for social science understanding untilled. Our analysis also points to a neglect of age on a mesolevel, as a dimension of communities and social organizations. In other social science inquiry, the significance of community and neighborhood characteristics has been highlighted recently (e.g., Sampson, Raudenbusch & Earls, 1997). To our knowledge, no one has examined relationships between community age structure and such phenomena as social cohesion and conflict. Lawrence (1996) documents the neglect of age in studies of organizations: "there is little research and even speculation on how age might influence other organizational phenomena besides individual behavior" (p. 43). She suggests attention to the relationship between age and organizational processes such as change, innovation, and inertia—factors highlighted by Davis and Combs (1950) half a century ago.

E. An Eclipse of a Social Science Legacy?

Taking a longer view suggests that the current situation represents something of a regression. A search for structural understanding of age has not always been so rare in the social sciences (Reinharz, 1987). Long before gerontology was a recognized field, the founding fathers of social inquiry pondered the connection between age and social structure. Comte reflected on progress and its connection to generational succession and longevity. Marx and Engels considered how industrialization might affect the significance of age as well as gender. Durkheim explored links between age and social integration.

When gerontology emerged as an organized field in the mid-20th century,

the implications of dramatic shifts in the age structure of society were being recognized. Davis and Combs (1950) anticipated issues posed by graying populations. Although some of their hypotheses have not been supported, their analysis pointed to the urgency of considering the age composition of populations and its possible relation to social structure. Similar concerns were evident in the first *Handbook of Social Gerontology*, assembled by Clark Tibbitts (1960). The subtitle, *Societal Aspects of Aging*, clearly distinguished it from the companion volume, *Handbook of Aging and the Individual: Psychological and Biological Aspects* (Birren, 1959). In his preface, Tibbitts (1960) stated that social gerontology separates out phenomena of aging that are related to humans as members of social groups and of society, as well as aging in society itself.

Fundamental shifts have taken place in the field of aging since the pioneering publications. Handbooks since then have not used the term *social gerontology*. Instead, aging has been the key word. Aging has increasingly been viewed as an individual-level, life-long process, and the key social-science task has been defined as examining effects of social contexts on this process. A number of authors have suggested that in mastering this task, the life-course perspective represents an especially promising tool (Bengtson, Parrott & Burgess, 1996; George, 1996a; Settersten, in press).

II. Understanding Age, Aging, and the Old: The Promises and Problems of a Life-Course Perspective

The growing scholarship on the life course has nurtured awareness of old age as part of a long life journey, of individual lives as embedded in a changing social context, and hence, of the complex interplay between biographical time and historical time (Hareven, 1982). This very focus on dynamism across levels faces researchers with some fundamental analytical issues. We focus on three interrelated issues: questions of stability and change, the problem of levels, and views of aging individuals as social actors.

A. Stability and Change: Interplay of Individual and Sociohistorical Context

Life-course analysis has been rightly credited with demonstrating the power of social conditions and social change to shape the outlooks, health, choices, and activities of developing individuals. Elder's (1974, 1998) work on consequences of the Depression in the United States and Mayer's (1988) studies of the effects of World War II in Germany (see also Maas, Borchelt & Mayer, 1999) are prime examples of how historical circumstances and events shaped the life trajectories of individuals who experienced them. Clearly, life-course research has increased awareness of the dynamic interplay between macrolevel social change and patterns of individual lives. At the same time, as Riley and Riley (1999) warn, focusing on the life course without an explicit recognition of social structures and processes can lead to what these authors call life-course reductionism. Such reductionism can take many forms. Dannefer and Uhlenberg (1999) contend that much research conducted within the life-course framework—for all the fruit it has borne—lacks a clear conception of social structure and represents a prime site of microfication. Their seemingly counterintuitive claim is based on a probing of how issues of time and timing interact with the issue of levels in longitudinal work on the life course.

Some of the best known work on the life course is based on events and circumstances in the first decades of life, such as Elder and associates' intricate linking of later life consequences to childhood deprivation and family disorganization (see Elder, 1974; 1998). This work constitutes a critical contribution towards identifying what is known and what needs to be known about life-course dynamics. Yet, from the vantage point of a structural treatment of age and aging, it has been limited by its own problems of temporality. We point to three interrelated issues, all of which can lead to an astructural, individualistic bias.

1. The Time 1 Problem

Although "social-structural" variables (e.g., social class, military conscription) are prominent in Elder (1974) and co-workers' studies of Depression effects, they are often systematically considered only at the initial observation period. When social-structural characteristics are considered only at Time 1, social structure at subsequent time periods is unmeasured, and thereby treated as given. Thus, Dannefer and Uhlenberg (1999) argue that Time 1 context becomes transformed into a characteristic of the individual. The focus on early–late life connections comprises a form of microfication whenever it leads to a neglect of social-structural factors encountered after Time 1. A corollary of the Time 1 problem is the idea that effects of social and historical change depend on its timing in the life course— what Elder calls "the life stage principle."

2. The Life Stage Principle: "Formative Years"?

Elder's (1974) work on the Depression found that, on some key dimensions, individuals who were children at the time of economic deprivation and family disruption were more affected than those who were teens at the time. Although we are not aware of Elder having discussed it, one important question to pose is whether we assume that the younger individuals are when historical change hits, the more likely the change is to leave permanent marks. Most of the psychodynamic tradition in psychology built from this premise. Recently, Stewart (e.g., Stewart & Healy, 1989) has presented an argument for why historical events leave more of an impact if they happen in a phase of life which she labels "identity formative." Mannheim's (1952/1928) classic work on generations also views youth as "formative years." In today's society, life's first decades are "transition dense," a time which presents ample data grit for life-course data mills.

It is possible that a view of early life as the domain "where the action is" survives more easily in societies or historical periods which, comparatively speaking, do not present that much action. O'Rand and Campbell (1999) describe differences in national contexts during the 20th century: "Indeed, if one thinks about the life of a citizen in 20th century Ukraine as akin to sailing through a hurricane in a rowboat, Americans have faced a thunderstorm from the comfort of a yacht" (p. 71). In many regions of the world, events in recent turbulent years have provided ample opportunities to explore the life stage principle through empirical work. Did the movement from the old GDR to a united Germany have more profound effects among retired officers who lost more than a third of their pension income, midadult single mothers who no longer had support guaranteed through social policy, or young people who found that their Ph.D. diplomas were not worth the paper on which they were engraved? When major "frame conditions" of life crumble on the macrolevel, reverberations are most likely felt on all other levels, and individuals have multiple experiences of "failed contracts,"

to use Foner's (1993) term. It would seem reasonable to expect that the failure of a contract after a long life of investment in it is likely to be more disruptive than when there is still time to explore other opportunities.

The movement of individuals through social structure inevitably raises the third issue: social change.

3. The Change Assumption

The excitement over cohort analyses of life-course patterns under conditions of social change has often led to an additional problem: a tendency to assume that effects of social context on individuals are more readily discernible in times of major change, and that such analysis is a sufficient test of the impact of social forces on aging. If no cohort differences are found, it is taken as an indication that the process being studied is a "true age effect" which, when the logic is pressed, ultimately means it is somehow rooted in an organismic process, or otherwise in the essence of "normal" or "natural" aging. On the other hand, if cohort differences are found, they are assumed to index the magnitude of the social.

In either case, the interpretation involves serious analytical omissions. It neither recognizes intracohort processes of social stratification (e.g., O'Rand & Henretta, 1999), nor the basic processes of social reproduction that constantly reconstitute the entire field of relationships and culture in which actors operate and are themselves constituted. Organisms do not become human actors apart from the constantly recurring, constitutive forces of social dynamics on micro-, meso-, and macrolevels. These pervasive social processes cannot be discerned through "cohort effects." Indeed, they constantly reconstitute the stability of the social order. Thus, they are no less potent in constituting human aging in times of stability than they are in times of change

(Dannefer & Uhlenberg 1999). The real difference is that, in times of stability, such social forces can be ignored, as their effects are reappropriated into the discourse of ontogenetic outcomes. This practice does not completely avoid consideration of contextual effects, but gets by "cheap," testing the force of the environment by measuring single dimensions of a complex, multileveled environment (i.e., the cohort effect), and assuming that whatever variation is not accounted for by that test can be attributed to intraindividual processes. Ironically, however, the regular, systematic effects of relentlessly recurring social processes can be most readily discerned under regular and predictable social conditions.

Caspi and Moffitt (1993) challenge the change assumption from a psychological perspective. They use a similar, counterintuitive logic to assert a complementary proposition: that the robustness of individual characteristics is most evident during times of change. If a sustained and pervasive change of experience, such as trauma and deprivation, does not alter one's personality, few would disagree with the claim that this is indeed a stronger test than that offered by experience under normal conditions. Again, however, this assertion avoids, and obscures, the equally central question of the importance of the social under conditions of stability (Dannefer, 1993). The effects of social forces are perhaps most potent when they are unnoticed, as in the pervasive, taken-for-granted realities of a stable and unremarkable societal period.

B. The Problem of Levels

1. Lives through a Macrolens

As we mentioned above, the life-course perspective has encouraged a view of old age as a part of a long life journey. Although such a longer view is essential,

it is also important not to forget that lives should not only be addressed with individuals as units. Social scientists must also seek to describe and understand lives on a macrolevel. Several traditions have addressed this level, including sociodemographic work, which characterizes populations, and constructivist approaches that have analyzed the structure and images of the life course as artifacts of broader institutional forces.

The sociodemographic approach focuses on "statistical histories of birth cohorts" (Winsborough, 1980). An impressive body of work, especially in North America, has followed Ryder's (1965) call for using the cohort as a unit in the study of social change. Such studies use measures of heterogeneity (Dannefer, 1988; O'Rand and Henretta, 1999) to explore patterns of inequality, or parameters for prevalence, duration, and spread to compare the transition patterns and life-course trajectories of cohorts (e.g., Hogan, 1981; 1999; O'Rand & Henretta, 1999; Uhlenberg, 1996; Uhlenberg & Miner, 1996). Recently, such an approach has been used to explore how the baby boom cohorts fare as they approach early old age (e.g., Cornman & Kingson, 1996).

Other macroperspectives emphasize the social construction of age, including old age (e.g., Phillipson, 1998). A political economy perspective (Minkler & Estes, 1991, 1998) emphasizes structural factors, and sees age in interaction with gender, class, and ethnicity. In a related approach, European scholarship has elaborated a concept of the life course as a social institution, constituted by the market and the nation-state (Esping-Andersen, 1997; Kohli, 1986; Kohli & Meyer, 1986; Leisering & Walker, 1998; Mayer & Müller, 1986). Leisering and Leibfried (1999) devote a chapter to "Life course as politics," while Walker (1999) reminds readers that the "social construction of old age, through public policy, is derived from theoretical perspectives even if these are not explicit or conscious in the policy process" (p. 362). Several authors (e.g., Minkler, 1996) draw a distinction between a political economy perspective and a humanist or cultural perspective on age. The latter is seen as concentrating on cultural meanings. Yet, recent work shows the necessity of linking these perspectives. For example, one lesson from the comparative project AGE is that the cultural idea of life as an age-linked pathway is linked to economic institutions. Such a notion is an "epiphenomenon" of a market economy and a "waged life course" (Fry, 1992). Discussions of age and gender (e.g., Arber & Ginn, 1997; Walker, 1993) have illustrated how cultural ideals and social policy with regard to gender roles are mutually reinforcing.

Deepened insight into the contours of lives on a macrolevel and the social forces that shape them could be gained though strengthened collaborative and comparative efforts, especially by merging distinct strengths of research communities in Europe and North America. As we shall see in the next section, recent developments in tools and databases make international collaboration especially necessary.

2. "The Rest of the Story": Making Links across Several Levels

Life-course studies make bold attempts to grasp connections across micro- and macrolevels, by many called the most important theoretical challenge facing the social sciences (e.g., Alexander, Giesen, Münch, & Smelser, 1987; Giddens, 1984; Reinharz, 1987). In much of the work by Elder and associates, effects of massive changes on the macrolevel are seen as mediated through meso- and microlevels, which give meaning to the new conditions (Elder & Caspi, 1990). *Meaning* includes the interpersonal significance of altered resource constellations and interpretations of change. Elder and co-

workers suggest a two-step explanation: Macrolevel change creates new opportunities or constraints on meso- and microlevels, such as community and family. In turn, these more microconditions affect individual development. This notion has important ramifications, often overlooked.

If we start with individual level phenomena, we may indeed find plausible ways to account statistically for variability in such outcomes by invoking meaning construction, resources, and so forth on a micro- or mesolevel. However, there is a bigger story to be told, one linking proximal social contexts to more distal, macrolevel factors. All too often, we fail to look for this part of the story, because it requires analysis of dynamics that appear elusive, and it calls for comparison, either diachronically though history, or synchronically, across states or cultures.

Recent studies illustrate the fruitfulness of seeking the rest of the story, a macrolink. Considerable research has focused on loneliness among old people. Typically, this individual-level phenomenon is linked to characteristics of social networks. However, recent comparative work has shown the importance of making one more connection, to a cultural level. Identical networks have strikingly different personal significance across contexts. Jylhä and Jokela (1990) found that old people living alone in a "gregarious" culture, Greece, were more likely to feel lonely than were old Finns, embedded in a culture which may define being alone as "solitude." Similar contrasts emerged in de Jong Gierfeld and van Tilburg's (1999) Dutch–Italian comparison. Torres (1999) proposes a conceptual framework for considering cultural values, for instance, regarding relationships as mediating between social systems and individual aging.

An established research tradition has provided solid evidence of the connection between personal networks and individuals' health (e.g. George, 1996b; Thoits, 1995). Several researchers have recently echoed Link and Phelan's (1995) warning against "psychologizing" such health-predictive factors without considering the wider societal context for them. On a macrolevel, strong associations have been found between societal income inequality, morbidity, and mortality rates (Kawachi, Kennedy, & Wilkinson, 1999). We now need links between the micro- and macrohealth stories. For example, is economic inequality negatively related to a culture of trust, and consequently, to cohesion and network building, in turn affecting individual health and well-being (Kawachi, Kennedy, Lochner, & Prothow-Stith (1999)?

We presently have available new statistical tools to permit exploration of linkages across levels, from individuals, to family units and communities, to nations (O'Rand & Campbell, 1999; Riley & Riley, 1999). In addition, there are rapidly growing databases on multiple aspects of aging in many societies. The present offers unprecedented opportunities for understanding aging across multiple levels of social reality.

3. Interdependence: Overcoming Level Centrism

A central concept in the life course perspective has been interdependence among lives. Much attention has been given to interdependence of role trajectories on an intraindividual level, such as between women's work and family careers. Inter-individually, the focus has been on interwoven lives, such as parents and children sharing resources and stresses, married individuals coordinating trajectories (Moen, 1996; O'Rand & Henretta, 1999), or individuals facing "countertransitions" created by others' life changes (Hagestad, 1991). As can be seen, all these examples pertain to individual or microlevels.

Elias (1978) would likely argue that such "level myopia" limits our understanding of contemporary life. He contends that in modernity, "chains of interdependence become more differentiated and grow longer; consequently they become more opaque and, for any single group or individual, more uncontrollable" (p. 68).

The family is not only a primary group, but also a social institution that shapes social ties in powerful ways. Policies often create a web of contingencies across institutional domains and among family members (Hagestad, 1992). Parents have a legal duty to support children until they reach the age of 18, but often, social policies maintain parental responsibility much longer (Marin, 2000). Women's entitlements, such as pensions or unemployment benefits, are often profoundly affected by care responsibilities that are reinforced through social policy (Walker, 1993). The fates of individuals in disparate age groups are intricately interconnected in the institution of the family (Heclo, 1988). For example, care leaves alleviate stress for adults, whereas they create security for children and vulnerable old people, and reduce the need for costly services for the aged.

4. Beyond Time and Space?

Discussions of late modernity have moved beyond Elias's account of interdependence, using such terms as "time–space distentiation" (Giddens, 1991). A process of globalization, accelerated by communication technology, disembeds individuals from anchorings in local contexts (Gergen, 1991). Using the concept of "imagined communities," Calhoun (1991) explores shifts in how recent cohorts of adults spend their time communicating with people whom they will never meet face-to-face. Illustrations of his points are readily available. In Norway, a midwife recently established an information-sharing website for expectant mothers. Quickly, one-third of first-time mothers were using it. In a number of countries, there are reports of pensioners who communicate with school children on the Internet, sometimes across national boundaries. Our guess is that in the near future, sizable vanguards of old people will communicate and relate in ways that challenge the persistent microlocal perspectives on social ties in later life. How new modes of relating will affect contact and influence across age and cohort lines is an open question.

5. Age Segregation: Separation and Segmentation

Relationships among members of different age groups outside the family have received scant attention in social research on aging. One lens for examining this phenomenon is the issue of age segregation. Conceptually, it is useful to separate between spatial, institutional, and temporal segregation, all of which are connected to key dimensions of modern society.

If our interest is spatial segregation, we examine residential patterns for age homogeneity. Demographers use an "index of dissimilarity," a tool also used to address racial patterns, to measure residential segregation by age (e.g., Smith, 1998). Available databases show that gerontology has mostly focused on this type of segregation. Spurred by Rosow's work on integration (e.g., Rosow, 1973), researchers have examined possible relationships between the age homogeneity of residential units, quality of interpersonal networks, and social support. In the United States, age-segregated settings have been reported to facilitate interactions and the provision of social services, which in turn, may improve well-being (e.g. Lawton, Moss, & Moles, 1984). Such findings would clearly have to be interpreted in a cultural context, as old people in a number cultures would be

aghast at the very notion of age-segregated living, especially settings in which no children are allowed.

An institutional perspective on age segregation entails a more macro view. As classic social science scholars argued, modernization entails increased social differentiation. Often, age serves as a basis of society's division of labor, through age-related roles (Cain, 1964; Neugarten & Hagestad, 1976; Riley, Johnson, & Foner, 1972; Reinharz, 1987). In most industrialized societies, the young have roles embedded in educational institutions; adults are tied into economic and political institutions, the old into pension systems and leisure. Often, social policies for the old and the young originate and are implemented in separate government agencies. Spatial and institutional segregation could be labeled *separation*, because physical or symbolic barriers divide age groups. These forms of segregation also have a temporal dimension, through the life course. Under modern conditions, the social differentiation has undergone a "temporalization" (Kohli, 1986). Contrasting institutional anchorings are part of the "tripartite life course," a sequence of segmented roles and activities, which channel age groups into distinct meso- and microlevel settings. Sociologist Simmel (1955), and more recently, historian Ariès (1978) point out that modern social differentiation has a spatial component that goes beyond the issue of residence. Individuals lead their lives on many, separate "islands," to use Ariès's metaphor. Such islands are often age-homogeneous, for instance residential areas, work organizations, schools and arenas for leisure activities.

Discussions of age segregation have a point–counterpoint quality similar to that found in the general discourse on modernity (see the next section). Although Simmel (1955) links modern differentiation and segmentation to individuation and freedom, Ariès focuses on risks, suggesting that the spatial separation of age groups creates new vulnerabilities, especially among the young. Based on her cross-cultural perspective on old age, Keith (1994) warns that "we should be vigilant to question age separation wherever it occurs, no matter how 'natural' it seems" (p. 214).

Riley and co-workers (Riley, Foner, and Riley, 1999), in their discussions of structural lag, have expressed concern that increases in longevity have been so dramatic and rapid that modern society has not kept up, leaving a vital population of new old people marginalized. This represents a risk to individuals in the form of social exclusion and life-course discontinuity; a cost to society because vast human resources are underutilized. Similar ideas were prominent in the framework for the United Nations' International Year of Older Persons (Hagestad, 1998; United Nations, 1999). The UN has several times warned against age segregation. A 1989 resolution warned that age segregation, combined with sexism, often creates social and economic deprivation for older women. The UN here recognizes the structural basis of ageism. When individuals in different life phases and historical generations are ensconced on different age-homogeneous islands, they have little chance to know each other, a situation that creates fertile ground for stereotypes and misunderstandings.

We are now touching on central issues regarding socialization. Our literature search shows that when the key words "age segregation" appear in publications on youth, they are typically found in discussions of delinquency and mental health problems. Authors worry that separation from a spectrum of adults deprive children and youth of valuable socialization experiences. Coleman (1982) presents a clear statement of concerns about youth. Until late 20th century, he notes, young people were largely integrated into the productive activities of everyday life. Now they are segregated from adults, in mesolevel settings focused solely on education, while adults spend a great deal of time in settings where there are no children. Consequently, adults become less understanding of children, while children do not know adults and their lives.

Under late modern conditions, individuals turn 70 in a society that is dramatically different from the society in which they turned 7. Adults become "immigrants in time" (Mead, 1970) and need continuous socialization to update orientations, language, and skills. Some of this learning, inevitably, requires help from the young (Hagestad, 1998). Age segregation creates socialization deficits for members of all age groups. Coleman urges the creation of "age-balanced organizations" that mirror the age structure of society at large. In such organizations, persons would spend some time working, some time learning, and some time teaching. His recommendation is remarkably similar to some of Riley's (Uhlenberg & Riley, 2000) suggestions for age integration, fueled by a concern for new generations of old.

C. Individuals as Actors: Structure and Agency Revisited

Recent discussions of development and aging have increasingly emphasized agency and choice. Individuals are seen as "architects of their own lives" (George, 1996a); they "must produce, stage and cobble together their biographies themselves" (Beck, 1994, p. 13). Giddens (1991) asserts that "strategic life planning becomes a way to reflexively organize the future, to colonise it" (p. 85). At the same time, both Beck and Giddens warn against taking what Settersten (1999) calls an "agency without structure" view; both emphasizing that autonomy and choice are themselves culturally defined, and the conditions that regulate their expression are closely tied to social structure.

North American life-course scholars have also emphasized individual agency (e.g. Elder, 1998; Clausen, 1995). And yet, the perspective has also been accused of taking an oversocialized view of individuals (George, 1996a; Marshall, 1999), a "structure without agency" view (Settersten, 1999). Earlier, the age-stratification framework (Riley et al., 1972) was attacked on similar grounds, for seeing individuals as passive role incumbents.

Recently, a number of authors have advocated an "agency within structure view" (Settersten, 1999) that seeks to understand how individuals shape or change structures, as well as the reverse (Alwin, 1995; Mayer & Tuma, 1990; Riley et. al., 1999). Taking agency within structure seriously will require that we attend carefully to the issue that many scholars consider the central unresolved theoretical problem in the social sciences (e.g., Giddens, 1994), what Hendricks and Leedham (1991) call "the self-structure dialectic."

In the field of aging, as elsewhere, efforts to grapple with agency have yet to confront several issues, including (a) the definition of action, (b) the constitutive nature of action for both self and society, and (c) the asymmetrical force of agentic power. These issues inevitably confront us with the "darker sides" of agency and choice, such as risk, stress, and uncertainty.

Few gerontological discussions of agency or action include an explicit definition, although it is often equated with choice and self-expression and sometimes with efficacy. In its classic formulation, human action or agency refers to the purposeful behavior of human beings (Weber, 1964). This seemingly simple definition has far-flung implications, linking action to meaning and to the self, and hence to culture.

Society is not simply influenced through the actions of human beings; it is *constituted* through agentic human action (Baars, 1991). Action produces not just effects, but situations and relationships (Dannefer, 1999; McMullin & Marshall, 1999). These fundamental principles have not yet been integrated into discussions of structure and action in social gerontology.

That human action is irreducibly purposeful and agentic does not mean that it is an expression of freedom, or that it has any efficacy in producing desired change. There is an *asymmetry in power* between the agency of individual actors and of systems (Dannefer, 1999). This has long been emphasized by scholars working within the political economy tradition. However, the dimension of power is hardly limited to the political sphere or the macrolevel. Studies of microinteraction have shown power to be ubiquitous, affecting individual life chances in such diverse settings as work (e.g., Kanter, 1977), nursing homes (e.g., Kuypers & Bengtson, 1984), and schools (Gubrium, Holstein, & Buckholdt, 1994). Recognition of such asymmetries requires acknowledgment that agency is expressed within the context of resilient social dynamics. Kohn and associates (e.g., Kohn & Slomczynski, 1993) have shown that work organizations provide sharply different degrees of autonomy. Over time, these experiences produce a divergence in members' abilities and their values, along class lines. The long-term effects of such contrasts can be observed in retirement, as demonstrated in a classic study of French pensioners (Guillemard, 1982). It is thus clear why a large proportion of an individual's "agentic expression" reproduces existing patterns of behavior, whether imposed, as in army boot camps, or encouraged, as in the manipulation of consumption through advertisement. Such reproduction is an integral aspect of agency within structure.

Even Beck (1994) has warned against an "individualization of the social," emphasizing that most risks have a so-cial-structural base beyond the control of actors. Despite his emphasis on choice, he worries that societal crises, such as unemployment and poverty, become cast as personal failures. Internalization of choice and responsibility can constitute an assault on the self, one of risk's truly dark sides.

In a discussion of individuation among British youth, Furlong and Cartmel (1997) point to "paradoxical socializa-tion." Youth are socialized into an ideo-logy of choice, while structural conditions pose severe constraints. They argue that a sense of choice may have increased in areas such as leisure, but that fundamen-tal patterns of social reproduction along class lines remain. Of course, this process is not limited to youth or the British Isles. Recognizing the neglect of such issues in the field of aging, Phillipson (1994) warns that "we must guard against the re-inventing of gerontology which, in elevat-ing personal meaning and the inventive-ness of everyday life, ignores the basic social divisions which continue to dis-em-power significant groups of elders" (p. 8). For both young and old, the combination of enduring processes that preserve classic patterns of inequality with a somewhat illusory sense of choice and personal effi-cacy raises anew the dangers of what Ryan (1976) called blaming the victim.

III. Concluding Remarks

A. Summing Up

In a review of the 1985 edition of this handbook, Walker (1987) reflected on how North American social science ap-proaches to aging appeared to have aban-doned macrotheory in favor of a focus on aging individuals. As we have seen, his reflections were timely. Research has in-creasingly centered on individual aging, especially its problematic aspects. In add-

ition, the search for explanations often stops at the microlevel, with a strong focus on the immediate social worlds of aging individuals. Even mesolevel social contexts, such as organizations and com-munities, are typically overlooked. This trend towards microfication is not lim-ited to North America, but can also be observed in European work. We suggest that microfication has multiple causes: late modernity's emphasis on individuals and their agency, a steady medicalization of old age, strong pressures from problem-oriented professions and politicians.

The costs of the microfocus are signifi-cant. It hampers our ability to address the aging society in the context of global eco-nomic and technological change. It limits our capacity to provide new twists to old questions in our home disciplines. Ex-amples of such questions are many: do dramatically altered age structures of populations and the explosion in long-evity call for new ways to think about social differentiation, both in terms of division of labor and inequality, and its links to age? Do current institutional ar-rangements provide adequate socializa-tion for long lives? How does the age–cohort composition of communities, orga-nizations, and primary groups affect social cohesion, level of conflict, creativity, and innovation? How are attitudes, motives and well-being of individuals affected by membership in different age structures, on micro- meso- and macrolevels?

The life-course approach has often been seen as a panacea for rediscovering the social. We argue that, despite the notable substantive and theoretical contributions of this framework, it has only to a limited degree taken us beyond the individual level, especially in North American scholarship. The life-course perspective confronts us with many thorny issues re-garding interconnections between levels, timing and temporality, and fundamental assumptions about human action. We have warned that a tendency to equate the significance of macrolevel forces with times of change implies that they have little relevance in times of stability; that the current celebration of agency may lead to a neglect of powerful structural constraints that organize lives. In our view, it is only by a sustained, multilevel emphasis that the attention to individual outcomes, including choice and decision making, be balanced with the necessary attention to the continued power of social forces to organize and define the structure and meaning of individual lives.

B. Final Reflections

Our brief "theoretical credo" early in the chapter included the imperative of reflexivity. As researchers, we need an ability to reflect on our own role in meaning production, the implicit working assumptions we bring to our research, and the constraints presented by the power structures within which our work is embedded.

Giddens (1984) discusses "a double hermeneutic." As social scientists, we not only formulate statements about society's meaning systems, but our statements become a part of the systems we describe. Bourdieu (1990) urges us to be aware that we are engaged in a battle over common sense, a war in which words are key weapons. Gerontology has a proud heritage of challenging myths about aging and providing solid information about the circumstances of the old. And yet, as our analysis of article titles shows, researchers may not be without blame if the general public associates aging with dependency and illness. Research language may indeed reify and reproduce a view of aging and old people of which we, upon reflection, would not want to be part. Being reflective on the science we practice confronts us with an unsettling question: Is the image of aging presented in research one to which aging researchers can subscribe for themselves?

In studies of aging, we are not only limited by the visors of culture and personal experience. We are also under considerable pressure from the implicit theories of medical professionals, funders, and politicians. The latter create policies that shape the structure and quality of lives, and they prioritize research questions through decisions about funding for scientific work.

The early versions of this chapter had the tentative heading "Getting back to where we once belonged." Using a Beatles title from our student days, we were ready to continue the nostalgia by calling for a rekindling of the social science legacy of aging studies in the mid-20th century. As we struggled with a bundle of issues, it became clear that we wanted to call for a future-oriented, expanded horizon. It struck us that the social "disembedding" of 21st-century life offers new freedom and opportunities to transcend some of the limitations of scientific home bases. Cross-national conversations and collaboration across communities that face different opportunities and constraints and possess contrasting skills and strengths may force aging researchers to move up in levels of generality, recognize their own basic social conditions, and move beyond implicit theories—their own as well as those of policy makers and funders. Such intensified dialogues may help us move beyond microfication, and create a bigger social science story of aging.

References

Achenbaum, W. A., & Levin, J. S. (1989). What does gerontology mean? *Gerontologist, 29*, 393–400.

Alexander, J. C., Giesen, B., Münch, R., & Smelser, W. J. (1987). *The micro-macro link*. Berkeley, CA: University of California Press.

Alwin, D. (1995). Taking time seriously: Studying social change and human lives. In

P. Moen, G. H. Elder, Jr., & K. Lüscher (Eds.), *Examining lives in context: Perspectives on the ecology of human development*. Washington, DC: American Psychological Association.

Arber, S., & Ginn, J. (Eds.). (1997). *Connecting gender and ageing: A sociological approach*. Buckingham, PA: Open University Press.

Ariès, P. (1978). The family and the city. In A. S. Rossi, J. Kagan, & T. K. Hareven (Eds.), *The family* (pp. 227–235). New York: Norton.

Baars, J. (1991). The challenge of critical gerontology: The problem of social constitution. *Journal of Aging Studies, 5,* 219–243.

Baltes, P. B., & Smith, J. (1999). Multilevel and systemic analyses of old age: Theoretical and empirical evidence for a fourth age. In V. L. Bengtson & K. W. Schaie (Eds.), *Handbook of theories of aging: In honor of Jim Birren* (pp. 153–173). New York: Springer Publishing Company.

Beck, U. (1994). *Ecological enlightenment: Essays on the politics of the risk society*. Atlantic Highlands, NJ: Humanities Press.

Beck, U., Giddens A., & Lash, S. (1994). *Reflexive modernization: Politics, tradition and aesthetics in the modern social order*. Stanford, CA: Stanford University Press.

Bengtson, V. L., Burgess, E. O., & Parrott, T. M. (1997). Theory, explanation and a third generation of theoretical development in social gerontology. *Journal of Gerontology, Social Sciences, 52B,* S72–S88.

Bengtson, V. L., Parrott, T. M., & Burgess, E. O. (1996). Progress and pitfalls in gerontological theorizing. *Gerontologist, 6,* 768–772.

Bengtson, V. L., Rice, C. J., & Johnson, M. L. (1999). Are theories of aging important? Models and explanations in gerontology at the turn of the century. In V. L. Bengtson & K. W. Shaie (Eds.), *Handbook of theories of aging: In honor of Jim Birren* (pp. 3–20). New York: Springer Publishing Company.

Bengtson, V. L., & Schaie, K. W. (Eds.). (1999). *Handbook of theories of aging: In honor of Jim Birren*. New York: Springer Publishing Company.

Birren, J. E. (Ed). (1959). *Handbook of aging and the individual: Psychological and Biological aspects*. Chicago: University of Chicago Press.

Bourdieu, P. (1990). *In other words: Essays towards a reflexive sociology*. Stanford, CA: Stanford University Press.

Bourdieu, P. (1991). Epilogue: On the possibility of a field of world sociology. In P. Bourdieu & J. S. Coleman (Eds.), *Social theory for a changing society* (pp. 373–387). Boulder, CO: Westview Press.

Cain, L. D. (1964). Life course and social structure. In R. E. L. Faris (Ed.), *Handbook of modern sociology* (pp. 272–309). Chicago: Rand McNally

Calhoun, C. (1991). Indirect relationships and imagined communities: Large-scale social integration and the transformation of everyday life. In P. Bourdieu & J. S. Coleman (Eds.), *Social theory for a changing society* (pp. 95–121). Boulder, CO: Westview Press.

Caspi, A., & Moffitt, T. E. (1993). When do individual differences matter? A paradoxical theory of personality coherence. *Psychological Inquiry, 4,* 247–271.

Clausen, J. (1995). *American lives: Looking back at the children of the Great Depression*. New York: Free Press.

Coleman, J. S. (1982). *The asymmetric society*. Syracuse, NY: Syracuse University.

Cornman, J. M., & Kingson, E. R. (1996). Trends, issues, perspectives and values for the aging of the Baby Boom cohorts. *Gerontologist, 36,* 15–26.

Dannefer, D. (1988). Differential gerontology and the stratified life course: Conceptual and methodological issues. In G. L. Maddox & M. P. Lawton (Eds.), *Annual review of gerontology and geriatrics, 8* (pp. 3–36). New York: Springer Publishing Company.

Dannefer, D. (1993). When does society matter for individual differences? Implications of a counterpart paradox. *Psychological Inquiry, 4,* 281–284.

Dannefer, D. (1999). Freedom isn't free: Power, alienation and the consequences of action. In J. Brandstädter & R. M. Lerner (Eds.), *Action & self-development: Theory and research through the life span* (pp. 105–131). Thousand Oaks, CA: Sage.

Dannefer, D., & Uhlenberg, P. (1999). Paths of the life course: A typology. In V. L. Bengtson & K. W. Schaie (Eds.), *Handbook of theories of aging: In honor of Jim Birren* (pp. 306–326). New York: Springer Publishing Company.

Davis, K., & Combs, J. W., Jr. (1950). The sociology of an aging population. In D. B. Armstrong (Ed.), *The social and biological challenge of our aging population* (pp. 146–170). New York: Columbia University Press.

de Jong Gierveld, J., & van Tilburg, T. G. (1999). Living arrangements of older adults in the Netherlands and Italy: Coresidence values and behaviour and their consequences for loneliness. *Journal of Cross-Cultural Gerontology, 14*, 1–24.

Elder, G. H. Jr. (1974). *Children of the Great Depression: Social change in life experience.* Chicago: University of Chicago Press.

Elder, G. H. Jr. (1998). The life course and human development. In R. M. Lerner (Ed.), *Handbook of child psychology: Vol. 1. Theoretical models for human development* (pp. 939–991). New York: John Wiley & Sons.

Elder, G. H., Jr., & Caspi, A. (1990). Studying lives in a changing society: Sociological and personological exploration. In A. I. Rabin (Ed.), *Studying persons and lives: The Henry A. Murray lectures in personality* (pp. 201–247). New York: Springer Publishing.

Elias, N. (1978). *What is sociology?* New York: Columbia University Press.

Esping-Andersen, G. (1997). Welfare states at the end of the century: The impact of market, family and demographic change. In P. Hennesy & M. Peersen (Eds.), *Family, market and community: Equity and efficiency in social policy* (pp. 63–76). Paris: OECD, Social Policy Studies. No. 21.

Estes, C., & Binney, E. (1989). The biomedicalization of aging: Dangers and dilemmas. *Gerontologist, 5*, 587–598.

Foner, N. (1993). When the contract fails: Care for the elderly in nonindustrial cultures. In V. L. Bengtson & W.A. Achenbaum (Eds.), *The changing contract across generations* (pp. 101–117). New York: Aldine De Gruyter.

Fry, C. L. (1992). Changing age structures and the mediating effects of culture. In Van den Heuvel, W. J. A. Illsley, R., Jamiesen, A., & Knipscheer, C. P. M. (Eds.), *Opportunities and challenges in an ageing society* (pp. 29–43). Amsterdam: Royal Academy of Sciences.

Furlong, A., & Cartmel, F. (1997). *Young people and social change: Individualization and risk in late modernity.* Buckingham, UK: Open University Press.

George, L. K. (1995). The last half-century of aging research—and thoughts for the future. *Journal of Gerontology, 50B*, S1–S3.

George, L. K. (1996a). Missing links: The case for a social psychology of the life course. *Gerontologist, 36*, 248–255.

George, L. K. (1996b). Social factors and illness. In R. H. Binstock & L. K. George (Eds.), *Handbook of aging and the social sciences* (4th ed.) (pp. 229–252). San Diego, CA: Academic Press.

Gergen, K. J. (1991). *The saturated self: Dilemmas of identity in contemporary life.* New York: Basic Books.

Giddens, A. (1984). *The constitution of society: Outline of a theory of structuration.* Berkeley, CA: University of California Press.

Giddens, A. (1991). *Modernity and self-identity: Self and society in the late modern age.* Cambridge, UK: Polity Press.

Giddens, A. (1994). *Beyond left and right.* Stanford, CA: Stanford University Press.

Gubrium, J. F., Holstein, J. A., & Buckholdt, D. R. (1994). *Constructing the life course.* Dix Hills, NY: General Hall.

Guillemard, A-M. (1982). Old age, retirement, and the social class structure: Analysis of the structural dynamics of the later stage of life. In T. Hareven & K. Adams (Eds.), *Aging and life course transitions: An interdisciplinary perspective* (pp. 221–243). New York: Guilford.

Hacking, I. (2000). *The social construction of what?* Cambridge, MA: Harvard University Press.

Hagestad, G. O. (1991). Trends and dilemmas in life-course research: An international perspective. In W. R. Heinz (Ed.), *Theoretical advances in life-course research*: Vol. I (pp. 22–57). Weinheim: Deutscher Studien Verlag.

Hagestad, G. O. (1992). Assigning rights and duties: Age, duration and gender in social institutions. In W. R. Heinz, (Ed.), *Theoretical advances in life course research* (Vol. III, pp. 261–279). Weinheim: Deutscher Studien Verlag.

Hagestad, G. O. (1998). Towards a society for all ages: New thinking, new language, new conversations. *Bulletin on Aging, 2/3*, 7–13.

Hareven, T. K. (1982). *Family time and industrial time*. Cambridge, UK: Cambridge University Press

Heclo, H. (1988). Generational politics. In J. L. Palmer, T. M. Smeeding, & B. B. Torrey (Eds.), *The vulnerable* (pp. 381–411). Washington, DC: Urban Institute Press.

Hendricks, J. (1992). Generations and the generation of theory in social gerontology. *International Journal of Aging and Human Development, 35*, 31–47

Hendricks, J., & Leedham, C. A. (1991). Dependency or empowerment? Toward a moral and political economy of aging. In M. Minkler & C. Estes (Eds.), *Critical perspectives on aging: The political and moral economy of growing old* (pp. 51–64). Amityville, NY: Baywood Publishing Company.

Hogan, D. (1981). *Transitions and social change: The early lives of American men*. New York: Academic Press

Jylhä, M., & Jokela, J. (1990). Individual experiences as cultural: A cross cultural study on loneliness among the elderly. *Ageing and Society, 10*, 295–315.

Kanter, R. M. (1977). *Men and women of the corporation*. New York: Basic Books.

Kawachi, I., Kennedy, B. P., Lochner, K., & Prothrow-Stith, D. (1999). Social capital, income inequality, and mortality. In I. Kawachi, B. P. Kennedy, & R. G. Wilkinson (Eds.), *The society and population health reader, Vol. I: Income inequality and health*. New York: New Press.

Kawachi, I., Kennedy, B. P., and Wilkinson, R. C. (1999). *The society and population health reader, Vol. I: Income inequality and health*. New York: New Press.

Keith, J. (1994). Old age and age integration: An anthropological perspective. In M. W. Riley, R. L. Kahn, & A. Foner (Eds.), *Age and structural lag* (pp. 197–216). New York: Interscience.

Kohli, M. (1986). The world we forgot: An historical review of the life course. In V. W. Marshall (Ed.), *Later life* (pp. 271–303). Beverly Hills, CA: Sage Publications.

Kohli, M., & Meyer, J. W. (1986). *Social structure and the social construction of life stages. Human Development, 29*, 145–149.

Kohn, M. L., & Slomczynski, K. M. (1993). *Social structure and self-direction: A comparative analysis of the United States and Poland*. Cambridge, MA.: Blackwell.

Kuypers, J., & Bengtson, V. L. (1984). Perspectives on the older family. In W. H. Quinn & G. A. Houston (Eds.), *Independent aging: family and social systems perspectives* (pp. 3–21). Rockville, MD: Aspen Publications.

Lawrence, B. (1996). Interest and indifference: The role of age in the organizational sciences. *Research in Personnel and Human Resources Management, 14*, 1–59.

Lawton, M. P., Moss, M., & Moles, E. (1984). Suprapersonal neighborhood context of older people: Age heterogeneity and well-being. *Environment and Behavior, 16*, 89–109

Leisering, L., & Leibfried, S. (1999). *Time and poverty in western welfare states: United Germany in perspective*. Cambridge, UK: Cambridge University Press.

Leisering, L., & Walker, R. (1998). *The dynamics of modern society*. Bristol, UK: The Policy Press.

Link, B. G., & Phelan, J. (1995). Social conditions as fundamental causes of disease. *Journal of Health and Social Behavior (special issue)*, 80–94.

Lynott, R. J., & Lynott, P. P. (1996). Tracing the course of theoretical development in the sociology of aging. *Gerontologist, 36*, 749–760.

Maas, I., Borchelt, M., & Mayer, K. U. (1999). Generational experiences of old people in Berlin. In P. B. Baltes & K. U. Mayer (Eds.), *The Berlin aging study. Aging from 70 to 100* (pp. 83–110). Cambridge, UK: Cambridge University Press.

Maddox, G. L., & Campbell, R. T. (1985). Scope, concepts, and methods in the study of aging. In E. Shanas & R. H. Binstock (Eds.), *Handbook of aging and the social sciences* (2nd ed.) (pp. 3–28). New York: Van Nostrand Reinhold.

Mannheim, K. (1952). The problem of generations. In K. Mannheim(Ed.), *Essays on the sociology of knowledge* (pp. 276–322). London: Routledge & Kegan Paul. Original work published 1928.

Marin, M. (2000). Generational relations and the law. In S. Arber & C. Attias-Donfut (Eds.), *The myth of generational conflict: The family and state in ageing societies* (pp. 100–114). London: Routledge.

Marshall, V. W. (1995). The last half-century of aging research—and thoughts for the past. *Journal of Gerontology, 50B*, S131–S133.

Marshall, V. W. (1999). Analyzing social theories of aging. In V. L. Bengtson & K. W. Schaie (Eds.), *Handbook of theories of aging: In honor of Jim Birren* (pp. 434–455). New York: Springer Publishing Company.

Mayer, K. U. (1988). German survivors of World War II: The impact on the life course of the collective experience of birth cohorts. In M. W. Riley (Ed.), *Social structures and human lives* (pp. 229–246). Newbury Park, CA: Sage Publications.

Mayer, K. U., & Müller, W. (1986). The state and the structure of the life course. In A. B. Sörensen, F. E. Weinert, & L. Sherrod (Eds.), *Human development and the life course: Multidisciplinary perspectives* (pp. 217–246). Hillsdale, NJ: Lawrence Erlbaum.

Mayer, K. U., & Tuma, N. B. (1990). Life course research and event history analysis: An overview. In K. U. Mayer & N. B. Tuma (Eds.), *Event history analysis in life course research* (pp. 3–20). Madison, WI: University of Wisconsin Press.

McMullin, J. A., & Marshall, V. W. (1999). Structure and agency in the retirement process: A case study of Montreal garment workers. In C. D. Ryff & V. W. Marshall (Eds.), *The self and society in aging processes* (pp. 305–338). New York: Springer.

Mead, M. (1970). *Culture and commitment: A study of the generation gap*. Garden City, NJ: Natural History Press.

Minkler, M. (1996). Critical perspectives on ageing: New challenges for gerontology. *Ageing and Society, 16*, 467–487.

Minkler, M., & Estes, C. (Eds.) (1991). *Critical perspectives on aging: The political and moral economy of growing old*. Amityville, NY: Baywood Publishing Company.

Minkler, M., & Estes, C. (Eds.) (1998). *Critical gerontology: Perspectives from political and moral economy*. Amityville, NY: Baywood Publishing Company.

Moen, P. (1996). Gender, age, and the life course. In R. H. Binstock & L. K. George (Eds.), *Handbook of aging and the social sciences* (4th ed.) (pp. 171–187). San Diego, CA: Academic Press.

Myers, G. C. (1996). Aging and the social sciences: Research directions and unre-solved issues. In R. H. Binstock & L. K. George (Eds.), *Handbook of aging and the social sciences* (4th ed.) (pp. 1–11). San Diego, CA: Academic Press.

Myles, J. (1989). *Old age in the welfare state*. Lawrence, KS: University Press of Kansas.

Neugarten, B. L., & Hagestad, G. O. (1976). Age and the life course. In R. H. Binstock & E. Shanas (Eds.), *Handbook of aging and the social sciences* (pp. 35–55). New York: Van Nostrand Reinhold Co.

O'Rand, A. M., & Campbell, R. T. (1999). On reestablishing the phenomenon and specifying ignorance: Theory development and research design in aging. In V. L. Bengtson & K. W. Schaie (Eds.), *Handbook of theories of aging: In honor of Jim Birren* (pp. 59–78). New York: Springer Publishing Company.

O'Rand, A. M., & Henretta, J. (1999). *Age and inequality: Diverse pathways through later life*. Boulder, CO: Westview Press.

Phillipson, C. (1982). *Capitalism and the construction of old age*. London: Macmillan.

Phillipson, C. (1994). *Modernity, post-modernity and the sociology of ageing: reformulating critical gerontology*. Paper presented at XII World Congress of Sociology, Bielefeld, Germany, July.

Phillipson, C. (1998). *Reconstructing old age. New agendas in social theory and practice*. London: Sage Publications.

Reinharz, S. (1987). The embeddedness of age: Toward a social control perspective. *Journal of Aging Studies, 1*, 77–93.

Riley, M. W., Foner, A., & Riley, J. W. (1999). The aging and society paradigm. In V. L. Bengtson & K. W. Schaie (Eds.), *Handbook of theories of aging: In honor of Jim Birren* (pp. 327–343). New York: Springer Publishing Company.

Riley, M. W., Johnson, M. E., & Foner, A. (1972). *Aging and society, vol. III: A sociology of age stratification*. New York: Russell Sage.

Riley, M. W., & Riley, J. W. (1999). Sociological research on age: Legacy and challenge. *Ageing and Society, 19*, 123–132.

Rosow, I. (1973). The social context of the aging self. *Gerontologist, 13*, 82–87.

Ryan, W. (1976). *Blaming the victim*. New York: Vintage Books.

Ryder, N. (1965). The cohort as a concept in the study of social change. *American Sociological Review, 30,* 843–861.

Sampson, R. J., Raudenbush, S. W., & Earls, F. (1997). Neighborhoods and violent crime: A multi-level study of collective efficacy. *Science, 277,* 918–924.

Schaie, K. W. (1996). *Adult intellectual development: The Seattle Longitudinal Study.* New York: Cambridge University Press.

Settersten, R. (1999). *Lives in time and place: The problems and promises of developmental science.* Amityville, NY: Baywood Publishing Company.

Settersten, R. A., Jr. (Ed.) (in press). *Invitation to the life course: Towards new understandings of old age.* Amityville, NY: Baywood Publishing Company.

Simmel, G. (1955). *Conflict and the web of group affiliations.* Translated by K. H. Wolff and R. Bendix. New York: Free Press.

Smith, G. C. (1998). Change in elderly residential segregation in Canadian metropolitan areas, 1981–91. *Canadian Journal on Aging, 17,* 59–82.

Stewart, A. J., & Healey, J. M. (1989). Linking individual development and social changes. *American Psychologist, 44,* 30–42.

Thoits, P. A. (1995). Stress, coping and social support processes: where are we, what next? *Journal of Health and Social Behavior, 36,* 53–79.

Tibbitts, C. (1960). Origin, scope and fields of social gerontology. In C. Tibbitts (Ed.), *Handbook of social gerontology: Societal aspects of aging* (pp. 3–26). Chicago: University of Chicago Press.

Tornstam, L. (1992). The quo vadis of gerontology: On the scientific paradigm of gerontology. *Gerontologist, 32,* 318–326.

Torres, S. (1999). A culturally-relevant theoretical framework for the study of successful ageing. *Ageing and Society, 19,* 33–51.

Uhlenberg, P. (1996). Mutual attraction: Demography and life course analysis. *Gerontologist, 36,* 681–685.

Uhlenberg, P., & Miner, S. (1996). Life course and aging: A cohort perspective. In R. H. Binstock & L. K. George (Eds.), *Handbook of aging and the social sciences* (4th ed.) (pp. 208–228). San Diego, CA: Academic Press.

Uhlenberg, P., & Riley, M. W. (2000). Essays on age integration. *Gerontologist, 40,* 261.

United Nations (1989). *Elderly women.* Resolution No. 44/76. General Assembly. New York: United Nations.

United Nations (1999). *International Year of Older Persons, 1999: Activities and legacies.* Report of the Secretary General. Item 107 of the provisional agenda, 54th session. New York: United Nations.

Veblen, T. (1953[1912]). *The theory of the leisure class: An economic study of institutions.* New York: New American Library.

Walker, A. (1981). Towards a political economy of old age. *Ageing and Society, 1,* 73–94.

Walker, A. (1987). Aging and the social sciences: The North American way. *Ageing and Society, 2,* 235–241.

Walker, A. (1993). Intergenerational relations and welfare restructuring: The social construction of an intergenerational problem. In V. L. Bengtson & A. W. Achenbaum (Eds.), *The changing contract across generations* (pp. 141–165). New York: Aldine De Gruyter.

Walker, A. (1999). Public policies and theories of aging: constructing and reconstructing old age. In V. L. Bengtson & K. W. Schaie (Eds.), *Handbook of theories of aging: In honor of Jim Birren.* New York: Springer Publishing Company.

Weber, M. (1964). *The theory of social and economic organization.* (A. M. Henderson & T. Parsons, trans.) New York: Free Press.

Winsborough, H. (1980). A demographic approach to the life-cycle. In K. W. Back (Ed.), *Life course: Integrative theories and exemplary populations* (pp. 65–75). Boulder, CO: Westview Press.

Two

Quantitative Approaches

Longitudinal Methods in the Study of Human Development and Aging

Duane F. Alwin and Richard T. Campbell

I. Introduction

There is a virtual consensus among quantitative social scientists that one of the most productive approaches to the study of aging and human development (hereafter, simply aging) involves the collection and analysis of longitudinal data. This is borne out by the vast number of research projects over the past few decades that pay attention to the location and measurement of events and processes *in time* (see Young, Savola, & Phelps, 1991). Indeed, students of aging are fast approaching the point where they will have, for some content domains, from a number of societies, a collection of several longitudinal data sets that will permit them to study patterns and processes of aging in different historical and cultural contexts. For example, in the United States, the series of panel surveys known as the Health and Retirement Study (HRS) will provide a series of replicated longitudinal studies of a sequence of birth cohorts currently and in the future. The first of these began in 1992 as a panel survey of persons from cohorts born in 1931

through 1941 and reinterviewed in 1994, 1996, 1998, and 2000 (Juster & Suzman, 1995). The idea for the HRS derived from a growing awareness of the inadequacy of data available from the Retirement History Survey that began in 1969 and followed a set of cohorts of men and unmarried women born in 1906 through 1911 for 10 years. Basing one's inferences about processes of aging, it was argued, on such a limited spectrum of historical cohorts had obvious limitations, given, for example, the growing participation of women in the labor force and related changes in the family. The collection of data on health and other antecedents of work and retirement decisions for more recent cohorts was viewed as essential to understanding experiences related to processes of aging in the more contemporary social context.

The assessment of change over time is fundamental to the quantitative study of aging, and longitudinal designs are vastly superior to cross-sectional studies in their ability to reveal causal influences in social processes because they can better pinpoint the temporal order of events,

Handbook of Aging and the Social Sciences, Fifth Edition

conditions, and experiences. For example, consider the explosion of research interest in the relationship between socioeconomic status (SES) and health. Many of the existing studies on this topic are cross-sectional and not necessarily suited to the kind of causal analysis that is necessary to understand the SES–health connection. In cross-sectional studies it is possible to observe a substantial association between indicators of SES and measures of health, but this research strategy is quite limited because it ignores the dynamic processes of social stratification. For example, few studies measure both health in old age and health status at earlier points in the life cycle; therefore it is difficult to know the extent of *intraindividual change* in health status, or how stable *interindividual differences* in health are over the life span. Studies that measure health at midlife or old age rarely include measures of early health status, or of early socioeconomic life experiences and family background. It is well known, for example, that early educational attainment, which is influenced by parental socioeconomic characteristics, shapes later life occupational opportunities as well as the economic consequences of those attainments (Sewell & Hauser, 1975). Using a life-course perspective, along with longitudinal data that measure early family background and relevant childhood socialization experiences, it would be possible to better sort out the extent to which the SES–health linkage is largely causal, or in part spuriously due to a range of "selection" factors that index events and experiences occurring earlier in the life course (see House, Kessler, & Herzog, 1990).

As we will argue below, even the best longitudinal data are unlikely to firmly resolve many substantive issues of this sort, in that there will still be relevant variables that are omitted from the data, limitations of sampling, measurement imperfections, and other impediments to drawing confident causal inferences. On the other hand, longitudinal data permit one to address far more interesting questions than is possible with cross-sectional data. For example, continuing with the SES–health linkage, how do early health deficits affect life-long socioeconomic outcomes? Do the advantages and disadvantages linked to one's family background differentially affect current health status, and by what processes are these effects transmitted? Does the linkage between SES and health change over historical time (e.g., are younger cohorts less disadvantaged by early health deficits)? Do changes in (physical and mental) health status contribute to the loss of social status or social capital? Do changes in cognitive and/or emotional well-being shape decisions to exit the labor force, or retire, and therefore impact one's social status? These are just some of the types of questions that could be answered with data from longitudinal designs, about which one can only speculate from relationships observed in cross-sectional designs.

Longitudinal data are also essential for examining issues linked to life-course theory, which focuses primarily on the developmental or age related patterns of change over the life span that are embedded in social institutions and subject to historical variation and change (e.g. Elder, 1992; Elder & O'Rand, 1995; O'Rand & Campbell, 1999). However, in research on aging and the life course, there are several major impediments to drawing inferences about change and its sources. Perhaps the most fundamental of these is to be able to locate events and processes in time and specify their causal relation to consequences or outcome variables, while taking other causal factors into account. Thus, in research on aging, virtually all the best designs for studying life-course phenomena are *longitudinal* because they allow one to more accurately conceptualize the nature of the substantive phenomenon and locate lives in time. This requirement strongly implies the need for repeated longitudinal studies based on sequences of birth cohorts. In what follows, we review what we consider to be the major advantages of longitudinal designs and the major difficulties in drawing inferences from longitudinal data, reviewing some of the available solutions to these problems. By drawing attention to problems of integrating theory, design, and analysis, we return to many of the same themes covered in our previous handbook chapter (see Campbell & Alwin, 1995), but here we focus explicitly on quantitative methods in longitudinal research.

II. Elements of Longitudinal Research Design

If one takes a life-course perspective with respect to the study of processes of aging and recognizes that human lives are embedded in social and historical contexts, it is clear that a range of ontogenic and sociogenic factors impinge on people's lives in ways that affect their well-being (Featherman & Lerner, 1985). From this perspective the "life course" consists of a complicated set of interlocking trajectories or pathways across the life span that are marked by sequences of events and/or social transitions that impact upon individual lives. Capturing these events and relating them to measures of health and functioning (among other things), as well as linking them to underlying social processes, is an important focus of a great deal of research on aging, and these are the major theoretical concerns that drive the present discussion of longitudinal methods.

A. Longitudinal Research Designs

Any research design that locates and measures events and processes in time is referred to as *longitudinal* (Campbell, 1992). This includes everything from complicated life-history calendars, which go to great lengths to date events, their timing, and duration (see Freedman, Thornton, Camburn, Alwin, & Young-DeMarco, 1988), to life histories presented in narrative form. As Featherman (1980) suggested some 20 years ago, it is important to distinguish between longitudinal *data* and longitudinal *designs* for gathering such data. The most common contrast for discussing longitudinal designs is between those that collect data on the life course *prospectively* and those that collect it *retrospectively*. Although these pure types are often contrasted, the two types are increasingly combined within the same overall design (Scott & Alwin, 1998). It is perhaps most useful to contrast the principal types of "design elements" in terms of the overall aims of the research, and in this sense "longitudinal designs" usually include one or more of the following: repeated cross-sections, event history measurement, panel studies, and retrospective measurement (Campbell & Alwin, 1995; Duncan & Kalton, 1987).

Repeated cross-sectional sample surveys focus on aggregate changes in a given population and are used to assess *net changes* in frequencies, averages, proportions, and rates, as well as studying processes of cohort replacement and change (Firebaugh, 1997; Firebaugh & Haynie, 1997). We include repeated surveys as a type of longitudinal design because they locate events and experiences in time, and although they do not measure the same individuals over time they do follow the same birth cohorts. *Panel studies* focus on microlevel change or *gross change* in individuals or households within a given population, and permit the investigation of factors affecting individual or household change. Both repeated cross-sections and panel studies are inherently prospective in nature, although respondents can be asked for information from the past. *Event history designs* focus explicitly on the plan to obtain the timing and sequences of events in biographical time for some population of interest. Event history data permit the study of onsets, durations, and sequences of events and their causes for individuals. *Retrospective* designs include the use of diaries, letters, life stories, biographies, memoirs, and any other kind of data obtained by asking people to report on events, states, and circumstances that existed in the past (Clausen, 1998). We return briefly to the issue of retrospective measurement below. As we noted, it is not uncommon for these types of "design elements" to all be incorporated into the same overall design; for example, panel studies and event history measurement are often combined, and it is increasingly recognized that all are to some extent necessary to understand the nature of the life course (see Giele & Elder, 1998).

B. Research Design Criteria

Kish (1987) codified three major criteria for evaluating research designs, which vary according to research objectives: representation, randomization (or control), and realism. These design criteria are especially important in the evaluation of longitudinal designs. *Representation* is critical if the goal of research is to draw inferences beyond the data at hand to the universe from which the data presumably come. For decades now, it has been an unquestionable tenet of social science methodology that the key to representation lies in the use of probability sampling and inferential statistics. Here the methodological issues are straightforward, whether one is estimating properties of the general population or specific age groups within the population. The main objective, in addition to valid and reliable measurement, is to develop practical sampling techniques that will produce representative samples of those populations or subpopulations with efficient estimates of sampling variability.

Although representation is often of critical importance, in other circumstances *randomization* or *control* is the critical design feature. Here the concern is not necessarily to generalize to a population of interest, but to a causal process (see Campbell & Stanley, 1963). Experimental or quasi-experimental approaches involve "manipulation" of variables with random assignment of individuals (or a controlled approximation) to conditions of the treatment variable. Here the investigator seeks to attribute changes in mean levels of specified variables to an experimental manipulation, so as to arrive at a causal inference. Interest in the case of the *true experiment* is primarily in ruling out the possibility that chance determined the experimental or treatment effects observed. Hence the emphasis is on randomization, on the assumption that the *only* way to draw a causal inference is under strict conditions of the control of all extraneous variables. This is the case if the goal of the research is to make strong causal inferences about the effect of X on Y, where generalization is to a theory or a hypothesis, under some set of scope conditions (Holland, 1986).

In the latter case, where experimentation is the main feature of the design, investigators are rarely interested in estimating population or subpopulation parameters (e.g., means, proportions, rates, and variances); however, there are instances in which both randomization and representation are important, for example, the New Jersey Income Maintenance experiment (Hannan, Tuma, & Groeneveld, 1978) or the Salk Polio vaccine trial (Meier, 1972). Experimental manipulation is virtually impossible in the study of many of the issues of concern to students of aging, so the experimental design serves mainly as a "model" to emulate rather than one to be routinely employed (Kish, 1987). Some nonexperimental research is based on "controlled investigations," in which some type of quasi-experimental control can be introduced to approximate the kind of control achievable via randomization.

Finally, it is often not possible to optimize either representativeness or control through randomization. There are many examples of nonrepresentative, nonexperimental methods that involve ethnographic or qualitative studies. Also included are historical studies, either of individuals' lives, through oral histories, or the historical analysis of archives of populations, or nations, or social movements (see Thompson, 1978). These types of researches satisfy the design criterion of *contextual realism*, although they cannot be considered "statistical" designs. There is renewed interest in the interface between qualitative and quantitative data, and this provides an opportunity to place greater emphasis on this type of design criterion (see Laub & Sampson, 1998; also see Singer & Ryff, chapter 3 this Volume).

C. Longitudinal Design and the Measurement of Change

Appropriate elements of longitudinal design often depend on the conceptual requirements of the particular substantive problem and its specific aims. These matters will, in theory, determine the kinds of data that are optimally appropriate for studying these issues and the appropriate statistical analysis methods to use in drawing inferences about the causal processes of interest. For many studies of aging, the *measurement of change* is of critical importance, and longitudinal designs provide a number of options for assessing change. Equally important, but less often studied, are the complementary concepts of continuity and stability (see Alwin, 1994; Brim & Kagan, 1980). Once the nature of change and stability, or

both, has been assessed, it is then necessary and desirable to be able to examine the causes of events and processes in people's lives and the social experiences that have shaped their life outcomes.

The concept of *transition* is one of the most useful for describing change in people's lives (e.g., the transition to widowhood, retirement, or movement to an assisted-care facility). The prediction of the movement in and out of various "states" of existence is the focus of survival or hazard models, (a.k.a. event history models), which focus on the factors that predict the likelihood that such events will occur and such transitions will be made given they have not happened up to that point. However, some states are more difficult to assess than others, and in many instances it is difficult to identify the transition from one state to another. This is the case with various cumulations of experiences, such as health status, levels of job experience, socioeconomic statuses, and psychological attributes (e.g., levels of anxiety or depression or changes in memory) that are thought to be measured on a continuous scale. For these types of variables, it is possible to employ models based on the concepts of *growth* and *decline*. The study of both discrete and continuous models for the analysis of change in research on aging is necessary and useful, and we focus this chapter on the application of these tools.

To usefully employ concepts of change, however, it is necessary to know something beforehand about the appropriate interval of time to observe to be able to detect change. The observation plan will normally specify the rationale for the periodicity of measurement as well as articulate the timing of measurement with respect to the changes happening in the lives of individuals and households. Following our brief discussion of the design criterion of *control* mentioned above, it is particularly important that the observation plan specify those factors relevant to the process that occur at earlier points in the life course. Thus, the research design should be driven by theoretical considerations with respect to what is known about the nature of the phenomenon of stability and change. The dilemma here is that in order to properly design longitudinal studies, it is important to know a considerable amount about the very thing that is the object of research. Various conceptual or theoretical choices, such as how likely causal factors are to change over the course of time, or the nature of the selection processes at work, not only affect the design of the research and its articulation with life-course processes, but also affect the appropriateness of the statistical procedures. When these three aspects of problem solving—conceptualization, design, and analysis—are out of synch, inevitable compromises result (Campbell, 1988; Campbell & Alwin, 1995, pp. 32–33). Compromise is a characteristic ingredient of science, and some have argued that research design involves a sequence of compromises (Kish, 1987). It is rarely possible to avoid compromises, and rather than avoiding them altogether, the goal is to appreciate their implications and to know when particular compromises are devastating to the research objectives.

D. Measurement Issues

In its most general sense, measurement represents the link between theory and the analysis of data. Whether the data are qualitative or quantitative, or both, linking theory and research via measurement is critical to longitudinal research. To connect earlier and later events and experiences within individual lives or show the evolving nature of developmental or aging processes, we need valid and reliable reports about people's lives over time. In many longitudinal designs measurement is *prospective*. Prospective mea-

surement has both advantages and disadvantages. From the life-course perspective, which emphasizes the importance of the conditioning influences of prior life events and experiences, it is important to track individual trajectories of experience against the background of many of the causal antecedents across time. Many of the causal antecedents of later behavior or events in people's lives can only be measured concurrently, that is, at the time they occur (Featherman, 1980). The events and experiences that occur in people's lives over time are often a very complex mixture of things, and a distinct advantage of the prospective measurement design is that the intricate sequence of these events and experiences can be monitored. Prospective designs also have important disadvantages: they tend to be very expensive, and panel attrition and missing observations due to nonresponse can present serious problems.

As noted earlier, the alternative is to collect data retrospectively, asking people to reconstruct their past life experiences (Schwarz & Sudman, 1994). Among other things, researchers routinely question people concerning their social background or early life history (e.g., father's and mother's occupations, educational levels, native origins, marital status). In other cases researchers are also interested in people's perceptions of past events and social changes. In the latter type of study there is no way to measure the veridicality of perceptions, unless they can be validated by existing data, and perceptions of past events are often biased (see Alwin, Cohen, & Newcomb, 1991).

In research on aging, retrospective measurement has two major problems—differential survival and reliability of recall. Cross-sectional retrospective studies can, by definition, investigate only the life histories of survivors, and thus, social processes that are linked to differential survivorship are poorly represented by retrospective data (Featherman, 1980). For example, studying the determinants of marital satisfaction using retrospective data on marital histories by looking only at current intact marriages would be very misleading. A second problem with retrospective data is that they tend to contain considerable error. Human memory can access past events and occurrences, and in general, the longer the recall period, the less reliable are retrospections (Dex, 1995). In addition, several factors affect people's abilities to recall the timing of past events. For example, one such factor is *telescoping*, reporting events as happening more recently than they actually did. Also, more recent experiences may bias people's recollections about their earlier lives, threatening their validity (Scott & Alwin, 1998).

Some phenomena are clearly not amenable to valid and reliable retrospective measurement. For example, Kessler, Mroczek, and Bell. (1994) suggested that although it might be possible to obtain some long-term memories of salient aspects of childhood psychiatric disorders, many childhood memories are lost due to either their lower salience or active processes of repression. Despite their difficulties, retrospective measurement can be very valuable, especially in the measurement of event histories. One quite useful application of the technique of retrospective measurement is the *life-history calendar*, an approach which employs detailed reports, often on a monthly basis, of transitions occurring across a number of life domains, for example, living arrangements, marital status, and educational status (see Freedman et al., 1988).

Issues of measurement are intimately linked to the analysis and interpretation of data. Most social data contain *errors of measurement*, even when special efforts are undertaken to maintain high levels of data quality. Obtaining accurate and complete data on people's lives has its challenges, and some of them may vary by the age of the respondent. For example, as persons age, their responses to standard measurement tools may be affected by various kinds of cognitive and physical impairment (e.g., Schwarz, Park, Knauper, & Sudman, 1999). If so, what can be done to offset some of these problems? Two things can be done: the first is to improve the quality of data collected through enhanced techniques of interviewing or improved follow-up approaches. The second is to model the sources of error, their magnitudes, and to take measurement errors into account in the analysis of the data.

There is a vast literature on improving the quality of survey data generally (Alwin, 1991), and current theorizing suggests the possibility that either the methods of data collection in the aging population may have to be altered, or special techniques may need to be used (see Schwarz et al, 1999). Current reviews of the cognitive abilities literature suggest that, although decline in some cognitive functions is evident in old age, it is probably not as universal, nor as inevitable as is normally assumed (Hertzog & Schaie, 1988, p. 128). Although there is the possibility of a relationship between chronological age to factors that affect survey reporting, for example, comprehension, accessibility to information retrieval and assessment, and communication, the evidence for this is weak (Alwin, 1999). Support for this conclusion exists in the work of Rodgers and Herzog (1992), who collected systematic data that permitted them to compare survey reports and administrative records. They found few age differences in the accuracy in self-reports of factual material (e.g., voting behavior, value of housing, and characteristics of neighbors).

It is important to reduce preventable measurement errors, such as taking precautions in reducing the likelihood of bias in reports given by older respondents, but some errors can be taken into account in the modeling of the data. Structural equation models (SEM) permit assessment of relationships among theoretical constructs, while controlling on measurement errors, when there are multiple measures of concepts (Bollen, 1989). This multiple indicator approach is essentially an embodiment of simple notions of factor analysis, where one has multiple measures of a common factor. If such a measurement design is available, then there are a number of currently available computer programs (e.g., AMOS, EQS, LISREL, M-Plus) that can perform the necessary statistical estimation (see Arbuckle & Wothke, 1999; Bentler, 1995; Jöreskog & Sörbom, 1996; Muthén & Muthén, 1998; see also West, 1999, for a comprehensive discussion of available SEM software).

E. Sampling

The concept of population is very important in the study of aging, and investigators should always define the population of interest, regardless of the research question. Certainly, the design of efficient sampling methods for representing populations of interest is of critical importance if the investigator wishes to generalize beyond his own data. We normally construe our "samples" to be true samples in the sense that their existence is governed by a probability process that selects cases from a population or universe. Even when we cannot, because of the use of study participants from nonrandom samples (e.g., volunteer subjects), there is an urge to generalize to a broader group of people. There is, of course, no way to demonstrate the external validity of the research, without meeting some basic requirements of sampling. Apart from the appeal to some method of probability sampling, one cannot know how generalizable are their results.

The data used in research on aging increasingly come from complex multistage national samples. Traditional sampling methods employ geographic clustering to reduce costs. As a result, subjects within clusters are more homogeneous than they would be if drawn under simple random sampling, and between-cluster variance is introduced. Telephone survey methods offer some promise of avoiding these issues, but unfortunately "random digit dialing" does not completely solve the problem because most such sampling schemes are clustered at the level of the telephone exchange. Statistical analyses that compute standard errors based on simple random sampling will usually produce incorrect estimates. Calculating correct standard errors requires both the application of survey weights and the ability to take the sample design into account. In general, this requires information on Primary Sampling Unit (PSU) membership, at least in the form of "pseudo PSUs" to protect confidentiality, for each subject.

Until very recently, routines for the correct computation of standard errors were unavailable in standard software packages. Recently, several ways of dealing with this problem have become available, and increasingly, journal editors and reviewers, particularly in the health sciences, are insisting on correct estimates of standard errors. First, stand-alone software packages for most standard statistical routines that take the sampling design into account have become available, particularly SUDAAN (Shah, Barnwell, Hunt, & LaVange, 1993) and STATA (Stata Corporation, 1998). Second, multilevel models, as described below, are a way of dealing with a complex sampling design. Finally, the most recent version of SAS includes some procedures for analyzing multistage samples, and SPSS markets WESVAR, a package for the analysis of complex surveys that will read SPSS files.

F. Selection Issues and Missing Data

Any longitudinal study has to deal with missing data issues. No study, particularly one based on older populations, will retain all of its subjects over time. Attrition occurs due to death and incapacity, residential mobility, fatigue and sometimes because gatekeepers refuse to give access to subjects. Even when subjects are retained, they sometimes cannot or will not respond to specific items or sets of items on surveys. Until just a few years ago, these issues were largely ignored by researchers, but in recent years, an enormous amount of work has been done on this problem. In longitudinal studies of aging, the missing data problem takes three forms: (a) *non-response*, in which subjects selected to participate do not, either because of refusal or because they cannot be located; (b) *loss to follow-up*, in which individuals drop out of panel studies after having participated in one or more waves, and (c) *item nonresponse*, in which respondents fail to answer one or more items in a particular data collection phase.

Little and Rubin (1987) distinguish among three classes of missing data: (a) data missing completely at random (MCAR), (b) data missing at random (MAR), and (c) nonignorable missing data. These are somewhat complex definitions, which only make sense in the context of a specific model for a particular outcome. If the presence or absence of data on a given variable is completely independent of either the true value of that variable or any other variable, the data are considered MCAR. Suppose instead, that the variable in question is MAR conditional on the value of some other variable. For example, less educated respondents might be less willing to answer questions about voting behavior, *regardless of how they actually voted*. In that case, after controlling for education, the data are MAR, as Little and Rubin refer to this.

Here it is theoretically possible to handle the problem by controlling on the relevant variables. A third type of missing data—*nonignorable missing data*—is one in which the data are missing because the true value of the variable causes the data to be absent, and controlling for another variable will not make the problem disappear. For example, if people with high incomes will not report the true value of their incomes, we cannot assume that the data are MAR, conditional on some other variable, say education. The key point of course is that it is rarely possible to know if data are missing nonignorably.

There are three well-known strategies for dealing with missing data in longitudinal research: (a) weighting adjustments, (b) imputation, and (c) direct analysis of the observed data (Little & Schenker, 1995). Historically, weighting adjustments have been commonly used with survey data to deal with both selection issues and attrition. For example, if one knows that certain kinds of subjects are less likely to agree to participate in particular studies, it is possible to develop weights to compensate for the undersampling. Similarly, if certain kinds of subjects are more likely to drop out of studies, one can develop weights to correct for differential loss to follow-up. The problem with this approach is that one must have a good model for the weights, and the weights add complexity to the analysis. Imputation, or "estimating" the actual values is often a viable option. Imputation can be done in a number of ways that we will not cover here, except to say that one desirable feature of an imputation procedure is that it should not affect the variance of a variable or its covariances with other variables in major ways. In order to accomplish this, most imputation methods include a random error component attached to some sort of regression or maximum likelihood estimator. This procedure reduces the efficiency of sample estimates, but the loss of efficiency can be compensated for by doing multiple imputations (Schafer, 1997).

There are also emerging methods for analyzing the data without imputation but that control statistically for missing data. In longitudinal studies, assuming unbiased sampling at baseline, data on a specific outcome at earlier time points can often be used to control for attrition at later time points. Little (1993) refers to these methods as "pattern mixture models" (see also Hedeker & Gibbons, 1997). A second and somewhat related approach involves the analysis of incomplete data via SEMs. Allison (1987) showed how to do this by factoring a data set into groups of subjects based on missing data patterns and then doing SEM using a "multiple groups" approach. An SEM package named AMOS generalizes this approach to allow for any patterns of missing data, but requires that the dependent variable be normally distributed. (Arbuckle & Wothke, 1999). Somewhat similar group-based missing data methods are possible for certain kinds of logistic regression models using categorical data methods (Agresti, 1990). Missing data methods depend heavily on intensive computations, some of which outstrip the capacity of even the fastest desktop computers even for relatively small problems. Missing data routines in standard statistical packages are still quite primitive. On the other hand, new methods and algorithms are constantly being developed, and this is an area that researchers need to watch carefully.

III. Aging, Development, and Time Dependence

As we noted at the outset, human development and aging happen in time; therefore, research that is focused on these processes must grapple with time and the conceptualization of development and change in person's lives (Campbell & O'Rand, 1988). Even the simplest cross-sectional comparison of age groups implies a developmental or time-based biographical perspective, that is, continuity and change at the level of the individual. In such a case, differences among age groups are thought to be a result of processes that vary as a function of where the person is along a continuum of biographic time (Riley, 1973). We focus here on *biographic* or *individual* time, as opposed to *historical* time, although as we point out later, an interest in aging and development often necessitates an awareness of history and historical events (Elder, 1994; Hareven, 1982; Ryder, 1965). As we noted earlier, when conceptualizing what we mean by *change*, the concept of *transition* is useful for describing some aspects of changes in people's lives, but we also mentioned that for continuous variables we needed alternative concepts of change (e.g., *growth* or *decline*). In both cases the precise measurement of change is an essential ingredient to studying the role of aging in processes of change.

For purposes of organizing a discussion of research approaches that deal with the time-dependent nature of aging processes, we distinguish between *event-based* and *process-based* research strategies. Event-based research focuses on the discrete changes or transitions in people's lives, whereas in process-based research change is thought of as continuous and gradual. If we cross-classify whether research strategies are (a) event-based versus process-based, and (b) whether they focus on causes or consequences, we can distinguish between four types of approaches to the study of aging: (1) research concerned with *predicting the occurrence of an event*, or the transition from one state or another; (2) strategies where the main concerns involve determining the *consequences of an event or a set of related events*; (3) *studies of intraindividual change*, where change is assessed in terms of growth or development, and where the main objective is the prediction of initial levels and rates of change; and (4) strategies that focus on *the change and stability of interindividual differences* and their consequences. Obviously, some research includes a simultaneous concern with one or more of these strategies, but normally one will use a different set of statistical tools for analyzing the different aspects of the problem. All of these approaches are multivariate in orientation, but look at different kinds of data, and within each approach there is a typical kind of model that is of interest, in some cases estimable by more than one analysis framework.

A. Causes of Events and Transitions

Since the infusion of Cox regression models into the social sciences nearly three decades ago, researchers have focused considerable attention on predicting events, or more precisely the transitions between states (Cox, 1972). The basic model, as described by Allison (1984) is for the hazard, loosely thought of as the probability of making a transition from state *I* to state *j* given that the transition has not taken place to time *t* (see also Allison, 1995; Teachman, 1983; Tuma & Hannan, 1984). In this sense these models may be viewed as an extension of the methods of life table analysis. Survival models result from regressing the *hazard rate* on a set of predictor variables, and given the regression framework the same logic applies to the interpretation of coefficients as "causal" effects, as is the case with ordinary regression analysis. To be specific, users of event history models face the same set of challenges as do users of other multivariate statistical techniques, especially with regard to the specification of causal ordering, the control of confounded extraneous variables, the biasing effects of measurement error, and multicollinearity.

One of the most prominent examples of hazard-rate models in research on aging is in the study of mortality and morbidity (see Manton, 1990). These are the kinds of problems for which such models were invented and the subject matter is directly linked to the substantive issues of aging. There are many other examples in research on aging where these models are particularly appropriate—one example is in the study of transitions from paid employment to retirement (Henretta, 1997). A typical study in the retirement literature would consist of a cross-sectional sample in which (a) all persons have left the labor force, and (b) we have the exact date of withdrawal, then we might simply regress the log of time on some set of predictors. But there are several things that are problematic with applying this approach. First, how do we think of the X's? Are they constant over time? Suppose we want to use income as a predictor? Which income? At the time of retirement, prior to retirement, or what? Secondly, suppose all members of the sample have not left the labor force, or suppose some have reentered? Another approach to the study of retirement would be to employ longitudinal data, such as the HRS, that tracks respondents from approximately age 50 through time, including age as a predictor (see Bound, Schoenbaum, Stinebrickner & Waidmann, 1999).

B. Consequences of Events and Transitions

One of the most common types of research in social sciences is to ask what effects being in a particular state has on the well-being of individuals. For example, what are the consequences to individuals of marriage, parenthood, divorce, widowhood, or particular health shocks? Indeed, one of the most common approaches to research on mental health is to identify risk factors associated with major life events and experiences. Beginning in the late 1970s, there has been a veritable industry that has grown up around studying the impact of (especially negative) life events on mental health outcomes. In such research the outcome variables can be either transition rates, or continuous-level measures of states, and there are many different analytic approaches that can obviously be used. One of the most difficult problems in studying the consequences of events is that the experience of events is often confounded with other "selection" factors that also contribute to variation in the outcome variables of interest. This is a problem that has plagued the study of the impact of divorce on children, for example, since many of the outcome variables of interest are also dependent upon the set of factors that selected the family into divorce.

From the point of view of design, the key to studying the consequences of events is to be able to study individuals over time, prior to the occurrence of the event, and then following them over time. This approximates one of Campbell and Stanley's (1963) classic "quasi-experimental" designs. One example of this kind of study is a prospective study of a large probability sample of married individuals age 65 and older developed by Jim House, Ron Kessler, and Camille Wortman (Carr et al., 2000). In this study, called the CLOC (Changing Lives of Older Couples) study, the investigators obtained a cross-sectional sample of the population in a geographically restricted area (in this case Detroit), oversampling older respondents, and then checked death registers in order to identify sample members who experienced widowhood and then returned to those individuals for an interview. These data have some desirable qualities; in particular that there are baseline measures of mental health, and therefore changes in mental health may be prospectively studied. A recent report from this work (Carr et al., 2000) examined the extent to which differences in marital quality condition differences in the linkage between the experience of widowhood and mental health. Because they were able to assess both marital quality and mental health at baseline, it is possible to link independent variables to changes in the dependent variable, assessing the effects of marital quality differences, net of the widowed's level of mental health at the time. The findings contradict the widespread belief that grief is greater if the marriage is conflicted. Carr and her collaborators show the opposite is true; that is, widowed persons who were conflicted at baseline exhibited better subsequent psychological well-being.

C. Intraindividual Rates of Growth and Decline

Some of the most important quantitative developments in recent years for the study of aging are the advances that have been made in the modeling of growth (and decline) curves, which allow researchers to study *intraindividual change* and its causes. Growth curve analysis grew out of the tradition in psychology of studying change scores, and although there are admittedly problems with the study of change scores between two points in time, growth curve approaches focus on trajectories of change across many observations, typically three or more points in time (see Rogosa, Brandt, & Zimowski 1982). The application of the growth curve approach now includes the ability to model *intraindividual change* in latent variables while taking errors of measurement into account (McArdle & Anderson, 1990; McArdle & Epstein, 1987; Willett & Sayer, 1994). The basic approach involves modeling the initial levels (or intercepts) and rates of change (or slopes) in a set of unobserved variables referred to as latent growth curves. These models are closely related to *multilevel* models in which observations over time are considered to be nested within individuals (see Muthén, 1994).

Latent growth curve models fit the study of aging well because they focus on continuous processes of change while allowing for measurement errors in the variables over time. These models should be distinguished from more common *autoregressive* SEMs (see Alwin, 1988); however, the two types of model are not incompatible. The latter type of model focuses on changes in *interindividual* differences over time, sometimes referred to as *differential stability*, whereas latent growth curve models focus on absolute levels of *intraindividual* change (growth or decline), and the study of *individual differences in intraindividual change* (rates of growth and decline) (Buss, 1979). The sets of models provide different information about the processes involved and both rely on SEM techniques to estimate the parameters involved. In order to illustrate the application of these models to the study of aging, we present estimates for a set of models in which determinants (age and education) of levels and changes in tests of immediate recall are studied over time in an older population (see Table 2.1). These estimates are based on the Assets and Health Dynamics Among the Oldest Old (AHEAD) study, companion to the original HRS and now a part of the HRS, which collected data on 8222 Americans who were at least age 70 in 1993 (or the spouses of the persons at least 70) (see Alwin, Wray, & McCammon, 2000, for details of the study). The results in Table 2.1 illustrate how processes of decline in mental function in old age can be studied using latent growth curve models. There is a significant overall decline in immediate word-recall abilities in this population over the time period studied. Here age is negatively associated with both the intercepts and slopes of the latent growth curves, indicating a significant decline in memory with age. Education, on the other hand, is unrelated to interindividual

Table 2.1
Latent-Growth Models for Immediate Word Recall: AHEAD Data[a]

Parameter	Model 1	Model 2	Model 3	Model 4	Model 5
μ_1	4.855***	4.855***	4.855***	4.855***	4.855***
μ_S	−0.061***	−0.061***	−0.061***	−0.061***	−0.061***
σ_I^2	1.546***	1.546***	1.546***	1.546***	1.546***
σ_S^2	0.017***	0.017***	0.017***	0.017***	0.017***
σ_{IS}	0.029***	0.029***	0.029***	0.029***	0.029***
$\sigma_I^2|X$		1.066***	1.326***	1.232***	1.066***
$\sigma_S^2|X$		0.016***	0.016***	0.017***	0.016***
$\sigma_{IS}|X$		0.023**	0.019*	0.033***	0.023**
γ_{Iage}		−0.084***	−0.096***		−0.084***
γ_{Sage}		−0.005***	−0.005***		−0.005***
γ_{Ieduc}		0.154***		0.169***	0.154***
γ_{Seduc}		−0.003		−0.002	
r_I^2		0.311***	0.142***	0.203***	0.311***
r_S^2		0.038***	0.033***	0.003	0.033***
χ^2	50.162	60.496	54.143	56.376	63.143
df	3	7	5	5	8
χ^2/df	16.721	8.642	10.829	11.275	7.893

[a]All models use respondents age 70 and older, listwise present (n = 3,987), interviewed in 1993, 1995 and 1998. (From Alwin, Wray, & McCammon, 2000).

differences in slopes, but is significantly and powerfully related to differences in intercepts. The relative unimportance of age as a predictor in these models is not an indication that aging is not an important factor in cognitive functioning. Rather, it suggests that among the AHEAD sample (age 70+), not much of the interindividual variation in decline in word recall over time, as evidenced by the true slope, may be attributed to the aging of the sample. Thus, these findings could be interpreted as indicating that beyond age 70, word recall declines at roughly the same rate per year, regardless of differences in absolute age.

If we look at these same three-wave data using autoregressive models of changes in individual differences over time, we obtain a more complete version of the picture. These models are often referred to as *simplex models* in the psychometric literature, and can be estimated in either standardized or unstandardized form (see Alwin, 1988; Heise, 1969; Jöreskog, 1978; Wiley & Wiley, 1970). The results for the measures of immediate recall are given in Table 2.2, which display estimates of both reliability and (standardized) stability parameters in the autoregressive form of the model. These estimates indicate that independent of levels of growth or decline in word recall, individual differences are

becoming more stable with time, suggesting that in older age the factors contributing to decline in memory levels do not disturb more stable individual differences (see Alwin et al., 2000).

D. The Consequences of Change in Interindividual Differences

Perhaps the most common strategy for research in aging, as well as social science generally, involves correlational and regression-type studies in which the focus is on inferences about how the effects of changes in individual differences lead to changes in other variables. Thus, we often encounter the putative assertion that "a change in X leads to a change in Y." In research on aging, inclusion of "age" in a regression model for some outcome would be interpreted in this fashion. However, until such inferences are based on true "aging" (that is, inferences drawn from observing what happens as people age) in longitudinal studies and not just from cross-sectional age differences, these types of conclusions should be considered mainly speculative. Given the increasing prevalence of longitudinal data with repeated measures for both dependent and independent variables (i.e., time-varying covariates), plus the existence of many analytic devices (i.e., event history models, growth curve models, or SEMs)

Table 2.2
Simplex Models for Immediate Word Recall: AHEAD Data[a]

Model	Variable	Stability coefficients			Reliability
		IREC93	IREC95	IREC98	
Heise	IREC93	1.000			0.546
	IREC95	0.855	1.000		0.546
	IREC98	0.830	0.970	1.000	0.546
Wiley &	IREC93	1.000			0.557
Wiley	IREC95	0.847	1.000		0.546
	IREC98	0.790	0.932	1.000	0.591

[a]For sample description see Table 2.1. (From Alwin, Wray, & McCammon, 2000).

for incorporating change in individual differences into the model, we will in the future begin to see much stronger inferences about the effects of aging. There is a large number of social processes where questions about changes in social experiences and the effects of the passage of time on outcomes are of particular interest, but owing to limitations of space we do not consider them further here. Suffice it to say that as researchers include predictor variables, such as health, disability, occupation, and cognitive functioning, as time-varying covariates, assessing the consequences of their change rather than simply their initial levels assessed at some arbitrary point in time, our knowledge of the processes of aging will be greatly enhanced.

IV. Cohort Differences and Historical Time

Human development and aging happen within a particular cultural and historical context. If people change as they develop and age, and if they do so in part through the influences of the historical time period, then the study of social change is important to researchers interested in aging and human development. On the one hand, period factors are interesting in their own right at a macrolevel because "history" is a factor in the life of the society. At the same time, because of the linkage between individual change and social change, period factors are important sources of explanation in models of individual change and stability. In the research on the Bennington women and their political development over their lives, for example, it was argued that in order to understand the persistence of their political views from their years at Bennington during the influence of the New Deal, it was necessary to consider the impact of their children's political development during the anti-Vietnam

War and Civil Rights movements of the 1960s (Alwin, Cohen, & Newcomb, 1991).

Even in relatively stable societies, each generation has its unique problems and themes that produce the differences in experience that we often summarize using the concept of *cohort* (Ryder, 1965). In modern industrial society, where there is a high degree of technological change and vast changes occurring to the family, new generations regularly face situations dramatically different from those confronted by their parents (Clausen, 1986). As we highlighted at the beginning of this chapter, most of our inferences about aging and about factors contributing to change in individuals and the consequences of that change are based on studies of particular cohorts or sets of cohorts coming from a given time period. Therefore, inferences about aging or its consequences need to include caveats regarding the possibility of cohort differences that result from the socialization effects or environmental constraints of previous time periods.

Social scientists often turn to repeated cross-sectional surveys (an important form of longitudinal design) for purposes of identifying cohort effects on mean levels (e.g. Campbell, Abolafia, Maddox, 1985), but this is not the only source of inferences about cohorts. Even in repeated surveys of this sort, where cohort membership is highly confounded with age, it is often impossible to disentangle the effects of age versus cohort. Moreover, single cohort studies that trace individuals' lives over time completely confound *biographic* and *historic* time, and it is virtually impossible to separate the effects of aging from historical or period effects in such studies (see Mason & Fienberg, 1985). In general, using any of these kinds of designs it is nearly impossible to identify the separate effects of *aging, cohort,* and *period* in any exploratory fashion. One needs to turn to supplementary types of data and invoke theory and common sense to produce "side information," that is, assumptions about the nature of certain historical and generational processes that can form the basis for identifying some of the effects. Increasingly, researchers are turning to the examination of *aging* and *cohort* influences on parameters other than mean levels (e.g., parameters expressing patterns of stability of individual differences) (see Alwin, 1994, 1995).

Ordinarily the types of data available to distinguish "cohort effects" from the effects of aging are not adequate, and theoretical knowledge is not strong enough to place many constraints or assumptions on the data. Very often we are forced into a situation where we must entertain alternative explanations. Although it rarely possible to identify the unique effects of this tripartite set of time-based explanations, it is possible to identify *two* fundamental properties in the data—*cohort replacement* and *intracohort change* (Firebaugh, 1997). Thus, it is possible to partition social change into these two parts— the part arising from the *stability of individuals* (cohort replacement) and the part that arises from *individual change* (intracohort change). The latter part, the extent of individual change, still confounds aging and period influences, and the former still confounds the possibility of cohort and aging effects. However, if one is willing to make certain assumptions about these various inferences, it is possible to creatively interpret repeated cross-sectional survey data (e.g., Alwin & McCammon, 1999). Repeated measures of the same individuals (i.e., panel data) are required to ascertain information on gross rates of constancy and change.

V. Spatiality and Context

If we conceptualize aging and human development within a life-course pers-pective, then people whose lives are developing also move across space as well as time. Although the concept of *place* is time-honored in social science, methods are emerging that respond to the need to consider *spatiality* in peoples' lives (see Raudenbush & Sampson, 1999). Data are increasingly collected and analyzed with space in mind, but to this point very little research has been undertaken that incorporates space as well as time into models of interest. Recently, under the rubric of "multilevel models" (also known variously as "random coefficient," "mixed," "hierarchical," and "random effects" models) statisticians have significantly advanced our ability to deal with these issues. The basic idea behind multilevel models is fairly straightforward, although the statistical work is somewhat complicated. Multilevel models deal with two seemingly different situations—the "nesting" of individuals in contexts and (optionally) repeated measures over time. Several excellent statistical introductions are available, particularly Bryk and Raudenbusch (1992), Snijders and Boskers (1999), and Kreft and de Leeuw (1998), and there are an increasing number of examples in the literature (e.g., see Campbell, 1998; Firebaugh & Haynie, 1997; Hedeker & Gibbons, 1994). Recently, these models have been extended to include not just intervally measured outcomes but the whole range of variable types covered under the rubric of the generalized linear model including dichotomous, ordered, and polytomous outcomes, as well as count variables with Poisson or negative binomial distributions. Software is now widely available in SAS and STATA for the full range of multilevel models and in several excellent stand-alone packages including HLM, Mln, and Don Hedeker's MIX series (see Hedeker, 1998a, 1998b).

Multilevel models treat coefficients at one level of analysis as dependent variables at a higher level. Suppose, for example, we have a sample of fifty nursing homes with a sample of subjects in each. Within each home, we run a regression equation relating a general measure of adaptation to characteristics of the individual, such as level of activities of daily living (ADL) impairment. Note, for future reference, that each subject is measured *once*. We would find, in all likelihood, that the 50 sets of regression coefficients showed a great deal of variation across facilities. Now suppose we treated those coefficients, including the intercept, as dependent variables in a regression at the aggregate level, treating characteristics of the facilities, such as type of ownership and organizational arrangements, as predictors. This analysis would permit us to link institutional factors to effects at the individual level. For example, one might find that individuals admitted to privately funded homes have higher intercepts and lower slopes.

Or, consider a longitudinal study in which we were looking at the process of adaptation to the nursing home at the individual level. Note here that we have data on a single nursing home. For each subject, we might have data at 30-day intervals for a year beginning at entry. If we were to plot the regression of each individual's score on time, we would have what Rogosa (1988) refers to as a "collection of individual growth curves." Conventional methods of analyzing such data, such as multivariate analysis of variance (MANOVA) attends to the *average curve*, but not to variation about it; indeed, variation about the curve is treated as error. Moreover, conventional approaches make it difficult to deal with time-varying independent variables and suffer badly when subjects are not observed at particular time periods. Data are in this case nested within individuals, and multilevel analysis allows one to ask how variation in the individual curves can be explained by characteristics of individuals, such as le-

vels of chronic disease, family support, and the like.

Finally, consider the same longitudinal study of adaptation carried out in multiple nursing homes. In such a case, data now exist at three levels. First, the time data are nested within individuals, and second, the individuals are nested within nursing homes. Here the coefficients of the individual growth curves can be related to both the characteristics of the individuals and the characteristics of the homes. For example, one might find that high initial levels of adaptation (the intercepts) are associated with family structure, that rates of change over time are associated with both individual characteristics, such as chronic disease, and with organizational variables, such as staff training. It is important to note that these models cannot be estimated by standard regression methods because those methods assume the regression coefficients to be fixed rather than random.

VI. Conclusions

The growing use of longitudinal data in research on aging is clearly a positive development. Such data permit inferences about the dynamic processes that shape the experiences of individuals and increasingly produce valuable results. Thus, our discussion of quantitative methods in research on aging has focused primarily on longitudinal research because we think that the very nature of the field requires most research to be longitudinal. Although the models of change and stability that are envisioned using longitudinal data are good in theory, in practice there are several impediments to obtaining the data that are necessary for drawing inferences about the causes and consequences of events and processes in people's lives. This chapter has focused on some of the challenges that face quantitative approaches to the study of aging and development, including the design of longitudinal studies, the measurement of critical quantities, the formulation of models that describe the dynamic processes involved, and the ability to generalize from one's results. We have reviewed what we consider to be the major difficulties in drawing inferences from longitudinal data and some of the contemporary solutions to these problems.

In addition to the advantages longitudinal data provide for studying the nature of processes linked to aging in present-day society, there are also advantages to having data that span more than one period of historical time and more than one cultural and/or institutional context. Again, using the HRS as an example, these data used in conjunction with other U.S. longitudinal studies, such as the National Longitudinal Study of Labor Market Experience, the Longitudinal Surveys of Aging (LSOA I and II), and other surveys, such as the Panel Study of Income Dynamics, the potential now exists for some domains of content for examining life-course differences across different historical periods (Campbell, 1994). The same is true for capturing variation in patterns and processes of aging across societies, where different cultural, institutional, and policy factors affect patterns and processes of aging.

Ultimately the examination of these types of questions would require what we call "parameterized models," by which we mean models that are sufficiently comparable across data sets in terms of measurement and analysis so that one can seriously compare coefficients (see Campbell & Alwin, 1995, p. 47). Attaining this level of quantification requires detailed attention to issues of conceptualization, design, measurement, and analysis, and in order to develop such models we need to move toward greater standardization in many domains of measurement. As philo-

sophers of science point out, the principle of "standardization"—that units of measurement have some constancy across time and space—is particularly relevant. We believe that future emphases in the quantitative study of aging will pay greater attention to issues of standardization of procedure, because in the end historical and cross-cultural comparisons are the most fruitful way to understand the processes of aging across a variety of different cultural, institutional, and historical contexts.

Acknowledgments

Support for this research was provided by federal grants HHS-AG15890 (Campbell) and NIA-AG04743–09 and NIA-AG015437–02 (Alwin). We also acknowledge the research assistance of Ryan McCammon and the helpful suggestions of Linda Wray and Debby Carr.

References

Agresti, A. (1990). *Categorical data analysis.* New York: Wiley.

Allison, P. D. (1984). *Event history analysis: Regression for longitudinal event data.* Beverly Hills: Sage Publications.

Allison, P. D. (1987). Estimation of linear models with incomplete data. In C. C. Clogg (Ed.), *Sociological methodology 1987* (pp. 71–103). Washington DC: American Sociological Association.

Allison, P. D. (1995). *Survival analysis using the SAS system: A practical guide.* Cary, NC: SAS Institute.

Alwin, D. F. (1988). Structural equation models in research on human development and aging. In K. W. Schaie, R. T. Campbell, W. Meredith, & S. C. Rawlings (Eds.), *Methodological issues in aging research* (pp. 71–170). New York: Springer.

Alwin, D. F. (1991). Research on survey quality. *Sociological Methods & Research, 20,* 3–29.

Alwin, D. F. (1994). Aging, personality and social change: The stability of individual differences over the adult life-span. In

D. L. Featherman, R. M. Lerner, & M. Perlmutter (Eds.), *Life-span development and behavior* (Vol. 12, pp. 135–185). Hillsdale, NJ: Lawrence Erlbaum Associates.

Alwin, D. F. (1995). Taking time seriously: Social change, social structure and human lives. In P. Moen, G. H. Elder, Jr., & K. Lüscher (Eds.), *Linking lives and contexts: Perspectives on the ecology of human development* (pp. 211–262). Washington, DC: American Psychological Association.

Alwin, D. F. (1999). Aging and errors of measurement: Implications for the study of life-span development. In N. Schwarz et al. (Eds.), *Cognition, aging, and self-reports* (pp. 365–385). Philadelphia, PA: Psychology Press.

Alwin, D. F., Cohen, R. L., & Newcomb, T. M. (1991). *Political attitudes over the life-span: The Bennington women after fifty years.* Madison, WI: University of Wisconsin Press.

Alwin, D. F., & McCammon, R. J. (1999). Aging vs. cohort interpretations of differences in GSS vocabulary scores. *American Sociological Review, 64(2),* 272–286.

Alwin, D. F., Wray, L. A., & McCammon, R. J. (2000). *Aging, sensory impairment and cognitive functioning.* Paper presented at the annual meetings of the Gerontological Society of America, November, Washington, D.C.

Arbuckle, J. L., & Wothke, W. (1999). *AMOS users' guide. Version 4.0.* Chicago, IL: Smallwaters Corporation.

Bentler, P. M. (1995). *EQS Structural equations program manual, version 5.7.* Encino, CA: Multivariate Software.

Bollen, K. A. (1989). *Structural equations with latent variables.* New York: Wiley.

Bound, J., Schoenbaum, M., Stinebrickner, T. R., & Waidmann, T. (1999). The dynamic effects of health on the labor force transitions of older workers. *Labour Economics, 6,* 179–202.

Brim, O. G., Jr., & Kagan, J. (1980). *Constancy and change in human development.* Cambridge, MA: Harvard University Press.

Bryk, A. S., & Raudenbush, S. W. (1992). *Hierarchical linear models: Applications and data analysis methods.* Beverly Hills: Sage Publications.

Buss, A. R. (1979). Toward a unified framework for psychometric concepts in the multivariate developmental situation: Intraindividual change and inter- and intraindividual differences. In J. R. Nesselroade & P. B. Baltes (Eds.), *Longitudinal research in the study of behavior and development* (pp. 41–59). New York: Academic Press.

Campbell, R. T. (1988). Integrating conceptualization, design, and analysis in panel studies of the life course. In K. W. Schaie, R. T. Campbell, W. Meredith, & S. C. Rawlings (Eds.), *Methodological issues in aging research* (pp. 43–69). New York: Springer.

Campbell, R. T. (1992). Longitudinal research. In E. F. Borgatta & M. L. Borgatta (Eds.), *Encyclopedia of sociology* (vol. 3, pp. 1146–1158). New York: Macmillan.

Campbell, R. T. (1994). A data-based revolution in the social sciences. *ICPSR Bulletin, 14,* 1–4.

Campbell, R. T. (1998). Editor's introduction: Why this issue? *Research on Aging, 21,* pp. 131–43.

Campbell, R. T., Abolafia, J., & Maddox, G. L. (1985). Life-course analysis in social gerontology: Using replicated social surveys to study cohort differences. In A. S. Rossi (Ed.), *Gender and the life course* (pp. 301–318). San Drego: Aldine.

Campbell, R. T., & Alwin, D. F. (1995). Quantitative approaches: Toward an integrated science of aging and human development. In R. H. Binstock & L. K. George (Eds.), *Handbook of aging and the social sciences* (pp. 31–51). San Diego: Academic Press.

Campbell, R. T., & O'Rand, A. M. (1988). Settings and sequences: The heuristics of aging research. In J. E. Birren & V. L. Bengtson (Eds.), *Emergent theories of aging* (pp. 58–79). New York: Springer.

Campbell, D. T., & Stanley, J. C. (1963). Experimental and quasi-experimental designs for research on teaching. In N. L. Gage (Ed.), *Handbook of research on teaching.* Chicago: Rand McNally. (Also published as *Experimental and quasi-experimental designs for research.* Chicago: Rand McNally, 1966).

Carr, D. S., House, J. S., Kessler, R. C., Nesse, R. M., Sonnega, J. & Wortman, C. (2000). Marital quality and psychological adjustment to widowhood among older adults: A longitudinal analysis. *Journal of Gerontology: Social Sciences, 55B,* S197–207.

Clausen, J. A. (1986). *The life course: A socio-logical perspective.* Englewood Cliffs, NJ: Prentice-Hall.

Clausen, J. A. (1998). In J. Z. Giele & G. H. Elder, Jr. (Eds.), *Crafting life studies: Intersection of personal and social history* (pp. 189–212). Newbury Park, CA: Sage Publications.

Cox, D. R. (1972). Regression models and life tables. *Journal of the Royal Statistical Society*, Series B, *34*, 187–202.

Dex, S. (1995). The reliability of recall data: A literature review. *Bulletin de Methodologie Sociologique, 49*, 58–89.

Duncan, G. J., & Kalton, G. (1987). Issues of design and analysis of surveys across time. *International Statistical Review, 55*, 7–117.

Elder, G. H., Jr. (1992). Life course. In E. F. Borgatta & M. L. Borgatta (Eds.), *Encyclopedia of Sociology* (Vol. 3, pp. 1120–1130). New York: Macmillan.

Elder, G. H., Jr. (1994). Time, human agency, and social change: Perspectives on the life course. *Social Psychology Quarterly, 57*, 4–15.

Elder, G. H., Jr., & O'Rand, A. M. (1995). Adult lives in a changing society. In K. S. Cook, G. A. Fine, & J. S. House (Eds.), *Sociological perspectives on social psychology* (pp. 452–475). Needham Heights, MA: Allyn and Bacon.

Featherman, D. L. (1980). Retrospective longitudinal research: Methodological considerations. *Journal of Economics and Business, 32*, 152–169.

Featherman, D. L., & Lerner, R. W. (1985). Ontogenesis and sociogenesis: Problematics for theory and research about development and socialization across the lifespan. *American Sociological Review, 50*, 659–676.

Firebaugh, G. (1997). *Analyzing repeated surveys.* Thousand Oaks, CA: Sage Publications.

Firebaugh, G., & Haynie, D. L. (1997). Using repeated surveys to study aging and social change. In M. A. Hardy (Ed.), *Studying aging and social change: Conceptual and methodological issues.* Thousand Oaks, CA: Sage Publications.

Freedman, D., Thornton, A., Camburn, D., Alwin, D. F., & Young-DeMarco, L. (1988). The Life History Calendar: A technique for collecting retrospective data. In C. C. Clogg (Ed.), *Sociological methodology* (pp. 37–68). Washington, DC: American Sociological Association.

Giele, J. Z., & Elder, G. H., Jr. (1998). *Crafting life studies: Intersection of personal and social history.* Newbury Park, CA: Sage Publications.

Hannan, M. T., Tuma, N. B., & Groeneveld, L. P. (1978). Income and independence effects on marital dissolution: Results from the Seattle and Denver income maintenance experiments. *American Journal of Sociology, 84*, 611–633.

Hareven, T. (1982). *Family time and industrial time.* Cambridge, UK: Cambridge University Press.

Hedeker, D. (1998a). *MIXNO: A computer program for mixed-effects nominal logistic regression.* Technical Report, School of Public Health, University of Illinois at Chicago.

Hedeker, D. (1998b). *MIXPREG: A computer program for mixed-effects Poisson regression.* Technical Report, School of Public Health, University of Illinois at Chicago.

Hedeker, D. R., & Gibbons, R. D. (1994). A random-effects ordinal regression model for multilevel data. *Biometrics, 50*, 933–944.

Hedeker, D. R., & Gibbons, R. D. (1997). Application of random-effects pattern-mixture models for missing data in longitudinal studies. *Psychological Methods, 2*, 64–78.

Heise, D. R. (1969). Separating reliability and stability in test–retest correlation. *American Sociological Review, 34*, 93–101.

Henretta, J. C. (1997). Changing perspectives on retirement. *Journal of Gerontology: Social Sciences, 52B*, S1–S3.

Hertzog, C., & Schaie, K. W. (1988). Stability and change in adult intelligence: Simultaneous analysis of longitudinal means and covariance structures. *Psychology and Aging, 3*, 122–130.

Holland, P. (1986). Statistics and causal inference. *Journal of the American Statistical Association, 81*, 945–60.

House, J. S., Kessler, R. C., & Herzog, A. (1990). Age, socioeconomic status, and health. *Milbank Quarterly, 68(3)*, 383–411.

Jöreskog, K. G. (1978). Structural analysis of covariance and correlation matrices. *Psychometrika, 43*, 443–477.

Jöreskog, K. G., & Sörbom, D. (1996). *LISREL8: User's reference guide.* Chicago: Scientific Software International.

Juster, F. T., & Suzman, R. (1995). An overview of the Health and Retirement Study. *Journal of Human Resources, 30,* S7–S56.

Kessler, R. C., Mroczek, D. K., & Belli, R. F. (1994). Retrospective adult assessment of childhood psychopathology. In D. Shaffer & J. Richters (Eds.), *Assessments in child and adolescent psychopathology.* New York: Guilford.

Kish, L. (1987). *Statistical design for research.* New York: Wiley.

Kreft, I. G. G., & de Leeuw, J. (1998). *Introducing multilevel modeling.* Thousand Oaks, CA: Sage Publications.

Laub, J. H., & Sampson, R. J. (1998). Integrating quantitative and qualitative data. In J. Z. Giele & G. H. Elder, Jr. (Eds.), *Crafting life studies: Intersection of personal and social history* (pp. 213–230). Newbury Park, CA: Sage Publications.

Little, R. J. (1993). Pattern-mixture models or multivariate incomplete data. *Journal of the American Statistical Association, 88,* 125–134.

Little, R. J., & Rubin, D. B. (1987). *Statistical analysis with missing data.* New York: Wiley.

Little, R. J., & Schenker, N. (1995). Missing data. In G. Arminger, C. C. Clogg, & M. E. Sobel (Eds.), *Handbook of statistical modeling for the social and behavioral sciences* (pp. 39–75). New York: Plenum Press.

Manton, K. G. (1990). Mortality and morbidity. In R. H. Binstock & L. K. George (Eds.), *Handbook of aging and the social sciences,* 3rd ed. (pp. 64–90). San Diego: Academic Press.

Mason, W. M., & Fienberg, S. E. (1985). *Cohort analysis in social research: Beyond the identification problem.* New York: Springer-Verlag.

McArdle, J. J., & Anderson, E. (1990). Latent variable growth models for research on aging. In J. E. Birren & K. W. Schaie (Eds.), *Handbook of the psychology of aging,* 3rd ed. (pp. 21–44). San Diego: Academic Press.

McArdle, J. J., & Epstein, D. (1987). Latent growth curves within developmental structural equation models. *Child Development, 58,* 110–133.

Meier, P. (1972). The biggest public health experiment ever: The 1954 field trial of the Salk poliomyelitis vaccine. In J. M. Tanur et al. (Eds.), *Statistics: A guide to the unknown* (pp. 2–13). San Francisco: Holden-Day.

Muthén. B. O. (1994). Multilevel covariance structure analysis. *Sociological Methods & Research, 22,* 376–398.

Muthén, L. K., & Muthén, B. O. (1998). *Mplus—The comprehensive modeling program for applied researchers. User's guide.* Version 1.02. Los Angeles: Muthén & Muthén.

O'Rand, A. M., & Campbell, R. T. (1999). On reestablishing the phenomenon and specifying ignorance: Theory development and research design in aging. In V. L. Bengtson & K. W. Schaie (Eds.), *Handbook of theories of aging* (pp. 59–78). New York: Springer.

Raudenbush, S. W., & Sampson, R. J. (1999). Ecometrics: Toward a science of assessing ecological settings, with application to the systematic social observation of neighborhoods. *Sociological Methodology* (Vol. 29, pp. 1–41). Washington, DC: American Sociological Association.

Riley, M. W. (1973). Aging and cohort succession: Interpretations and misinterpretations. *Public Opinion Quarterly, 37,* 35–49.

Rodgers, W. L., & Herzog, A. R. (1992). Collecting data about the oldest old: Problems and procedures. In R. M. Suzman, D. P. Willis, & K. G. Manton (Eds.), *The oldest old* (pp. 135–156). New York: Oxford University Press.

Rogosa, D. (1988). Myths about longitudinal research. In K. W. Schaie, R. T. Campbell, W. Meredith, & S. C. Rawlings (Eds.), *Methodological issues in aging research* (pp. 171–209). New York: Springer.

Rogosa, D., Brandt, D., & Zimowski, M. (1982). A growth curve approach to the measurement of change. *Psychological Bulletin, 92,* 726–748.

Ryder, N. B. (1965). The cohort as a concept in the study of social change. *American Sociological Review, 30,* 843–861.

Schafer, J. L. (1997). *Analysis of incomplete multivariate data.* New York: Chapman & Hall.

Schwarz, N., Park, D., Knäuper, B., & Sudman, S. (Eds.) (1999). *Cognition, aging and self-reports.* Philadelphia, PA: Psychology Press.

Schwarz, N., & Sudman, S. (Eds.). (1994). *Autobiographical memory and the validity of self-reports*. New York: Springer-Verlag.

Scott, J., & Alwin, D. F. (1998). Retrospective vs. prospective measurement of life histories in longitudinal research. In J. Z. Giele & G. H. Elder, Jr. (Eds.), *Crafting life studies: Intersection of personal and social history* (pp. 98–127). Newbury Park, CA: Sage Publications.

Sewell, W. H., & Hauser, R. M. (1975). *Education, occupation and earnings: Achievement in the early career*. New York: Academic Press.

Shah, B. V., Barnwell, B. G., Hunt, P. N., & LaVange, L. M. (1993). *SUDAAN User's manual: Release 6.0*. Research Triangle Park, NC: Research Triangle Institute.

Snijders, T. A. B., & Bosker, R. J. (1999). *Multilevel analysis: An introduction to basic and advanced multilevel modeling*. Thousand Oaks, CA: Sage Publications.

Stata Corporation. (1998). *User's guide version 6*. College Station, TX: Stata Corporation.

Teachman, J. (1983). Analyzing social processes: Life tables and proportional hazards models. *Social Science Research, 12,* 263–301.

Thompson, P. (1978). *The voice of the past: Oral history*. Oxford: Oxford University Press.

Tuma, N., & Hannan, M. (1984) *Social dynamics: Models and methods*. Orlando, FL: Academic Press.

West, J. (1999). *Structural equation software*. URL: http://www.gsm.uci.edu/~joelwest/SEM/ Software.html.

Wiley, D. E., & Wiley, J. A. (1970). The estimation of measurement error in panel data. *American Sociological Review, 35,* 112–117.

Willett, J. B., & Sayer, A. G. (1994). Using covariance structure analysis to detect correlates and predictors of individual change over time. *Psychological Bulletin, 116,* 363–381.

Young, C., Savola, K., & Phelps, E. (1991). *Inventory of longitudinal studies in the social sciences*. Newbury Park, CA: Sage.

Three

Person-Centered Methods for Understanding Aging
The Integration of Numbers and Narratives

Burton Singer and Carol D. Ryff

I. Introduction

Extensive empirical evidence documents associations between early and midlife risk factors and later life chronic disease and disability (Arneson & Foredahl, 1985: Barker & Osmond, 1986; Power & Mathews, 1998; Wadsworh & Kuh, 1997). These findings generate considerable interest in understanding the subtle nuances of life histories that might explain how such outcomes come about. Broad-gauged interest in successful aging (Baltes & Baltes, 1990; Rowe & Kahn, 1998), with particular emphasis on how some individuals manage to effectively adjudicate multiple difficult challenges also suggests in-depth comparative studies of life histories. Detailed accounts of whole lives have previously been studied primarily as individual cases (Clausen, 1993: Kleinman, 1988, 1995; McAdams, 1993, 1994), with evidence frequently presented in the form of narratives. These range from rich ethnographies (Kleinman, 1995) to a diversity of focused interviews and, in a medical context, to open-ended responses to inquiries by clinicians.

Complementing such narrative accounts of life histories are structured longitudinal surveys that contain—for each individual—hundreds, or even 1000+, responses to questions about experiences over time and across multiple life domains (Glueck & Glueck, 1968; Hauser et al., 1993; Power, Manor, & Fox, 1991; Wadsworth & Kuh, 1997). In principle, those interested in the impact of multiple facets of life histories on a given outcome(s), should be able to construct representations of whole lives from the survey responses. Despite considerable interest in this task across multiple disciplines (Elder, 1974; Glueck & Glueck, 1968; Vaillant, 1983), there has been a dearth of analytic strategies for producing representations of whole lives and for aggregating them into meaningful taxonomies that facilitate the understanding of how given outcomes come about.

Furthermore, large groups of investigators from diverse fields of inquiry (Coleman, 1996; Kleinman, 1995) have expressed strong preference for *either* narrative evidence *or* quantitative structured survey data as the preferred source of empirical data about the human condition. We take the position that there is much to be gained from a flexible integration of qualitative and quantitative evidence on the same groups of people. Systematic strategies for doing this are in their infancy; however, notable examples are evident over the past 40+ years (Elder, 1974; Glueck & Glueck, 1968; Sampson & Laub, 1993). The lack of systematic integration strategies has been accompanied by incomplete understanding of the nature of the knowledge acquisition process (i.e., how phenomenological theories of knowledge relate both to processes of data analysis, broadly conceived, and even modern neuroscience).

With these observations in mind, our primary objective is to demonstrate how to integrate narrative and numerical evidence in large data sets, where the individual history—or major segments of a whole life—is the basic unit of analysis. En route, we will also demonstrate the following:

1. How to construct narratives from numerical survey responses and utilize them as part of an analytical strategy to understand "whole lives"
2. How to construct taxonomies of histories—or profiles—to represent complex pathways to diverse health outcomes
3. How to identify subgroups of heterogeneous populations for which in-depth qualitative studies could facilitate the understanding of how complex health outcomes come about

We exhibit a range of methodologies via three case studies. In the first two, there is a specific question addressed that is best answered by integrating both numerical and narrative information. The third case study shows how to systematically identify subgroups of large populations within which combined narrative and numerical evidence could then be usefully assembled to facilitate the construction of pathways to particular outcomes. Methodologies, in our view, are communicated most convincingly by showing how they provide answers to questions that were not answerable without them. Via such demonstrations, we then describe broad sets of questions that could be answerable with the same techniques. In addition, we indicate how each technique relates to other methods that might plausibly be applied to address similar questions.

In the first case example, the empirical data are approximately 13,000 pages of transcribed text from focused interviews with physical and biological scientists. The analytical objective is to characterize their life histories, emphasizing the principal features that are associated with gender differences in cumulative publication profiles over entire careers. Starting with interview data, the findings are distilled to a quantitative model of the productivity process. This case study is grounded in the sociology of science, although the analytical strategy has broad applicability. Furthermore, the conceptual emphasis on cumulative adversity relative to advantage and the focus on managing multiple challenges over the life course are core aspects of human experience relating to diverse health outcomes at later ages.

The second case example illustrates the use of rich longitudinal survey data to construct taxonomies of life histories to explain how specific mental health outcomes come about. Narratives are developed—by the investigators—for a subsample of the full quantitative response vectors of individuals in the survey. The narrative constructions are, thus, part of the data analytic strategy. The basic idea is that the structure of whole lives can be better grasped in story form than via long symbol lists (i.e., raw response vectors, even when they are partitioned by life domain and particular themes). The narratives then serve as guides to a sequential process of constructing composite variables and identifying subsets of the original variables to represent life histories for the full population via responses to targeted select variables. In this process, we make explicit the inevitable tensions between nuanced descriptions of whole lives and the abstractions of them necessary to aggregate histories into distinct groups of lives. The narrative descriptions of the profiles then form the basis for an explanation of how given health outcomes come about.

In the final example, we explain grade-of-membership (GoM) models as a means to identify subgroups within heterogeneous large populations that are good candidates for focused interviews and more in-depth surveys. The generic problem in this instance is one of understanding how important gross population trends come about over time. The specific example that we examine is the widely documented, and controversial, decline in disability among the age 65+ population over the past 18 years. Because of the enormous variation in the mix of disabilities among the elderly, a difficult problem, *a priori*, is simply identification of a meaningful taxonomy of groups—indexed by clusters of disabilities—for which narrative histories could usefully shed light on the paths to such disability profiles. We describe a sophisticated quantitative methodology that identifies from a large survey of data where the most informative fine-grained qualitative and quantitative evidence could be usefully assembled.

II. Case Example 1: Gender Differences in Scientific Productivity

A. Background and Measurement

In studies of elite groups of scientists from the 1920s to the present, it has been found that males publish more papers than females and that the disparity between them increases with number of years elapsed since completion of the Ph.D degree (Cole & Zuckerman, 1987). Historically, there has been no association between sex status and (a) admission to graduate schools of varying prestige or assessed quality; (b) receipt of post-doctoral fellowships; (c) acceptance or rejection of manuscripts submitted for publication; (d) success rates for grant applications; and (e) number of early career honorific awards received. *A priori*, one might expect important disparities by sex in early career experiences that would translate to productivity differences within a few years of Ph.D completion. These disparities, in turn, would be expected to reveal themselves in multiple short longitudinal surveys (e.g., surveys covering the 5-year post-Ph.D period). Clear disparitites could also be expected in later-career 5-year periods. However, as noted, this is not what occurs. Hence, we are left with an unresolved productivity puzzle that encompasses large segments of scientific careers.

To get to the roots of the productivity disparities, 123 extended interviews were conducted with men and women scientists, many of whom had been elected to the National Academy of Sciences (Cole & Zuckerman, 1987). Prior to the interviews, an elaborate chronological chart was prepared for each interviewee. The chart was a pictorial version of the main features of the person's curriculum vitae. It identified major publications, publication totals for each year post-Ph.D, major personal events such as marriages and births of children, honorific awards, changes of institution of employment, and a research grant history, when it was available. The chronological charts acted as aids to facilitate recall of experiences that each scientist regarded as important for his or her career development. The scientists were encouraged to elaborate on key aspects of their lives, frequently with detailed anecdotal stories. The interviews typically lasted between 2 and 2.5 hours. The transcribed text of the full set of interviews ran to approximately 13,000 pages.

B. Analytical Strategy

Text analysis consisted of initially coding each interview such that paragraphs describing experiences that, *a priori*, were thought to influence productivity were identified, labeled by topic, and transferred to a master file. The Generalized Automated Text Organization and Retrieval System, GATOR, (Giordano, Cole, & Zuckerman, 1988) was originally developed for this project and utilized in a heavily interactive mode to store and retrieve blocks of labeled text. The system was designed to facilitate inquiry with statements such as "what did the women who worked in basic biology laboratories say about the impact of children on the pace and advancement of their research when they were in the age range 30–40 years?" A coding system for the original text was utilized so that key labels such as [woman], [biology/lab], [children], [30–40 years of age] were attached to appropriate blocks of text. The question posed above thus corresponded to a logical AND statement involving the four labels, [woman], [biology/lab], [children], and [30–40 years of age]. The logical AND statement was then used by GATOR (an early precursor of NUDIST; Richards, 1997) to retrieve the relevant labeled text for all individuals described by the AND statement from a master file and display it sequentially so that commonalities and/or differences in experience across individuals became transparent.

The initial coding of text was guided by the extant literature on plausible explanations for productivity patterns (see Cole & Singer, 1991, pp. 285–288 for a review).

Many inquiries at the first stage of text examination—analogous to the four-component AND statement described above—suggested new questions to ask. The initial inquiries also identified anticipated modes of explanation that were not supported by the extended interviews. This led the investigators to recode major portions, or even all, of the original text such that new Boolean questions were posed to the freshly coded text so as to reveal previously unsuspected commonalities across individuals.

For example, all scientists experience rejection of grant proposals central to keeping their research programs going. Some scientists reacted to this negative challenge by saying, in effect, "I'll show them," and then produced revised grant submissions that eventually succeeded. Others got discouraged, and their negative reactions to this negative challenge actually slowed down the pace of work in their laboratories, even if only for a short period of time. Coding the interviews to identify [grant proposal experience], [man (or woman)], [within 10 years post-Ph.D] allowed investigators to isolate blocks of text that pertained to this kind of experience and to sequentially examine these experiences for multiple individuals, while comparing the reports of men and women separately. It is important to emphasize that *whole paragraphs* and often *multiple paragraphs* were labeled by the coding scheme; this was NOT labeling key words and phrases. It was the full story that counted.

The net result of this process was the identification of a *small difference* between men and women that could be consequential for productivity differentials over a career, particularly if the experience *occurred multiple times*. The salient point was that a somewhat higher fraction of women scientists had negative reactions (i.e., discouragement) to grant rejections than their male counterparts, and this generated soul searching by them about their ability to succeed in the highly competitive world of high-technology science. The successful male scientists had sufficient self-confidence to pass off the rejection and continue their work at full pace. This finding was one of several similar important clues about the sources of male–female productivity differentials revealed by the extensive comparative examination of blocks of coded and recoded text looking across individuals.

A fundamental methodological point is that, although software such as GATOR, ETHNOGRAPH (Seidel, Kjolseth, & Seymour, 1988), and NUDIST afford filing and retrieval tools, the iterative process of coding and recoding text is highly labor intensive and does not lend itself to automated text analysis strategies. Indeed, the coding must be driven by a set of *organizing principles* and prior literature. Furthermore, searching text by key words and phrases does not identify whole stories that are both idiosyncratic to an individual and exhibit sufficient commonality across individuals that patterns can be discerned. The tension between the idiosyncrasies of an individual and abstractions of multiple cases represent a common, unavoidable issue in the early stages of comparing relatively unstructured texts across individuals.

C. Key Findings

As documented in detail in Cole and Singer (1991), disparities between men and women only emerged gradually. They revealed themselves in *cumulative* numbers of publications, *total* citations to published work, promotion to tenured positions at the most prestigious science departments, and receipt of top honorific recognition, such as Nobel Prizes, Fields Medals, and Lasker Awards. Observations of small fragments in time of male and female careers whose initial starting conditions were roughly the same, revealed

virtually no distinctions in productivity by sex. It was, rather, the *cumulative long-term* nature of productivity and, in turn, reward differentials that was revealed by the more fine-grained text analyses.

Cole and Singer (1991) summarized these findings with the "theory of limited differences" that emphasized the following points. Individuals are exposed to a sequence of events of many different types, some or all of which may occur more than once, depending upon the substantive context. Associated with each individual is an outcome variable(s) (e.g., manuscript completions and manuscript publications in a science career setting; annual wages and /or annual income). A "kick-reaction" pair is associated with each event. In the context of science careers, examples of kicks (which may be positive, neutral, or negative) are acceptance or rejection by a top Ph.D institution; positive and/or negative funding decisions on grant applications; positive and/or negative publication decisions based on manuscript submissions: marriage to a spouse who either hinders or facilitates the scientists' career. Associated with each kick is a positive, neutral, or negative reaction by the person who experiences it. This reaction acts with other kicks and reactions to influence the outcome variable(s).

The evolution of events, their associated kick-reaction pairs, and changes in levels of outcome variables are characterized as a vector stochastic process where the conditional probabilities of current state occupancy or changes in state are based on the individual's prior history. Kick-reaction sequences tend to determine the outcome histories, and over short time intervals, the outcome of any single kick-reaction pair will be small (or "limited"). Although nearly all kick-reaction pairs influence durations to future events by small amounts, there are a *few* special events for which the probability of a negative reaction to a negative kick for women exceeds the corresponding probability men. The downstream consequence of all these processes is the slower publication output for women than men.

When applied to science careers, this general framework implies that cumulative productivity differentials between men and women scientists are the result of small—or limited—differences in their reactions to a limited set of kicks. It is the cumulative effect of these small differences that produce, analogous to a "multiplier effect," major productivity differentials between men and women over a career. Details about the specific nature of the differentials, as they apply to science careers, are given in Cole and Singer (1991). The essential point here is that the framework outlined above was developed from the prolonged iterative examination of multiple blocks of coded—and recoded—segments of text. Based on the text analysis described above, the centrality of reactions became transparent. They clarified why analyses of extant longitudinal surveys of scientists could not reveal a major source of productivity differentials.

Limited differences and cumulation are by no means restricted to the study of productivity differentials in science careers. The same phenomenon may be present in pathways to the onset of chronic disease, to breakdown in functioning of the hypothalamic–pituitary–adrenal (HPA) axis, to immune system impairment, and so on. This is not to say that single major challenges do not have long-lasting effects. However, the great plasticity of human mental and physical functioning, and the ability to adapt in response to challenge, suggests that many physiological system breakdowns may be caused by cumulating "limited differences." Thus, characterizing pathways to diverse health outcomes at older ages calls for in-depth focused inter-

views—constrained by organizing principles—and adaptive analytical strategies that facilitate *discovery* of subtle underlying mechanisms.

III. Case Example 2: Narratives as Part of an Analytical Strategy

A. Understanding Psychological Resilience

Among those who experience major episodes of depression in adult life, or earlier, some manage to subsequently regain high levels of well-being—that is, they demonstrate resilience. We asked whether those who show such recovery have particular features that distinguish them from those who continue to suffer from depression. An affirmative answer could suggest prevention strategies which, if applied early in life, might serve to by-pass episodes of depression or minimize their severity and facilitate recovery from them. Developing a taxonomy of life histories of the resilient and distinguishing them from histories of the depressed is usefully implemented with a person-centered analytical strategy. We applied this perspective to data from the Wisconsin Longitudinal Study (WLS). Our analyses focused exclusively on women, who are at greater risk for depression than men.

B. Longitudinal Data

The WLS began with a random sample of 10,317 men and women who graduated from Wisconsin high schools in 1957. Survey data were collected from the original respondents in 1957, 1975, and 1992/93. Telephone interviews were conducted during 1992/93 with 8020 of the 1975 respondents, 6535 of whom also responded to a mail survey. Data have been collected on respondents' family background, starting resources, academic abilities, youthful aspirations, social support, social comparisons, and the timing and sequencing of adult educational and occupational achievements, work events and conditions, family events, and physical and mental health. The present illustrative analyses focus on a subset of the 5009 primary respondents who participated in all three waves of the WLS and who responded to questions assessing affective disorder and well-being in the most recent survey. The affective disorder questions were administered to a randomly selected 80% of respondents (Hauser et al., 1993). For each individual, there were responses on 1000+ variables covering all three waves of the survey and information across the multiple life domains indicated above.

At age 52–53, individuals were classified as depressed/unwell if they had a prior episode(s) of serious depression and also lacked high current levels of psychological well-being. They were called resilient if they had a prior history of depression, but reported high levels of current well-being. Depression was assessed in a telephone interview using a subset of questions from the Composite International Diagnostic Interview (CIDI) (Witchen et al., 1991) measure of major depression (MDE) as defined in the DSM-III-R (APA, 1987). Respondents who reported any episode of depressed affect and who experienced three or more of a series of seven symptoms during the two weeks prior to the interview were classified as "ever depressed".

Psychological well-being was assessed using Ryff's scale (Ryff, 1995; Ryff & Keyes, 1995), which measured the six dimensions of autonomy, environmental mastery, personal growth, purpose in life, positive relations with others, and self-acceptance. High well-being is operationalized as agreeing or strongly agreeing with six or more of the seven items on each of the six well-being scales. Low well-being is defined as strongly disagreeing, disagreeing, or neither agreeing nor disagreeing with five or more of the seven items on each of the six well-being scales.

The resilience criteria were satisfied by 168 women, and there were 59 women who satisfied the depressed/unwell criteria. The analytical task required developing a taxonomy of life histories for each group such that the characterization of any history is sufficiently nuanced to capture the richness of individual experience, but not so detailed as to represent only very few women. The person-centered strategy described below is one response to this challenge.

C. A Person-Centered Strategy

Construction of an empirical taxonomy of life histories requires a set of organizing principles—based on prior literature—that constrain the distillation of 1000+ responses for each individual into composite variables. Such composites are the basis for the ultimate representations of categories of histories. The following five principles were used to specify combinations of individual characteristics essential to explain how the outcomes came about.

1. Adversity and its cumulation over time has negative mental health consequences.
2. Advantage and its cumulation over time has positive mental health consequences.
3. Reactions to adversity or advantage influence the impact of life experiences.
4. Position in social hierarchies has consequences for mental health.
5. Social relationships influence the impact of life experiences and enduring conditions.

These propositions are not new to the social sciences, mental health, or aging fields. What is new is the integration of them into an analytic strategy to guide life history analysis. The methodology is usefully decomposed into five principal steps: (a) guided by the organizing principles, life history narratives were constructed for a subsample of cases from each outcome group (i.e., resilient and depressed/unwell); (b) abstracted chronological charts, each one representing a synthesis of several narratives, were constructed; (c) reduced response vectors, **b**, consisting of composite variables suggested by the chronological charts and individual variables whose rationale derives from the organizing principles, were specified; (d) aggregates (categories) of histories, in terms of response vectors judged to be close to one another, were specified; and (e) tests of distinguishability were conducted. Step (e) reduces to ascertaining whether or not the categories of histories characterizing the resilient women occur with low frequency in the depressed/unwell group, and conversely, whether histories characterizing the depressed/unwell women occur with low frequency among the resilient women. If the taxonomies of histories are to be a basis for explanation of the mental health outcomes, there should be distinguishability of categories of histories between the two groups.

1. Construction of Life History Narratives

A small random sample ($6 < n < 10$) of cases was selected from each outcome group, and a narrative biographical story was written for each individual. We adopted Stone's (1979) conception of narrative, defined as "the organization of material in a chronological sequential order and the focusing of the content into a single coherent story, albeit with subplots" (p. 3). Our rationale for writing narratives based on survey data (with 1000+ responses per individual) is that the human mind has difficulty processing enormous amounts of information in parallel (i.e., long lists of responses representing a single life), although it is well suited to process a coherent story (i.e., a written narrative about a life) (Turner, 1996). Our use of narratives here is qualitatively different from their role in the previous example. Specifically, the construction of narratives—by the analyst and starting with numerical response data—is part of an analytical strategy. The narratives do not represent empirical data derived from focused interviews, recorded conversations, or text written by the respondents, but stories written by investigators to describe "whole lives through time."

In generating the narratives, responses selected for inclusion were those expected to impact mental health, based on prior theoretical and empirical literature. Our goal was to tell a life story in such a way that omitted information made little or no difference for understanding the relevant life experiences preceding and predicting midlife mental health outcomes. Each narrative included information on the respondent's IQ and high school class rank, detailed educational and work histories, marital history (including dates of marriages and divorces), deaths in the family, number of children, quality of interpersonal relationships, and physical health, including drinking and smoking behavior. The narratives facilitated comprehension of whole lives of unique individuals as a prelude to generating aggregates of lives for each mental health outcome group. The narratives essentially told a story of how the individual's life unfolded across time, and thereby helped in the formulation of hypotheses about how work, family, and social background, organized according to the guiding conceptual principles, impact midlife mental health outcomes.

We view the crafting of whole life stories as fundamental to comprehending pathways to health outcomes. New insight is acquired as detailed information about real people comes into focus. This point has long been appreciated by life history researchers of the idiographic, case study variety (McAdams, 1994; Mishler, 1997). Portraying whole lives as an initial step in the analysis of surveys is not an end in itself, but a crucial beginning to the generation of ideas— what McAdams (1994) refers to as the "context of discovery"—that will guide subsequent formulation of aggregates for nomothetic analyses. Preserving the individual as the unit of analysis is of fundamental importance in this person-centered strategy.

2. Abstract Chronological Charts

Two life histories can be aggregated and called similar, or even approximately indistinguishable, when the response vectors representing them are very similar. At the level of individual cases, represented by raw response data on 1000+ variables or by narratives, there is so much idiosyncratic detail that meaningful aggregation seems almost hopeless. However, via the organizing principles, it is possible to start with sets of three or four narratives and begin specifying composite variables that ultimately lead to the specification of response vectors, some of which are sufficiently similar that they can be aggregated into a common category.

To illustrate how this is done, consider a large table where the rows are identified by the organizing principles and the columns correspond to age intervals. For each individual narrative, the cells of the table are filled by verbal descriptions of experiences that, for example, contribute to cumulation of advantage (organizing principle (ii)) in the age range 36–52. For one individual, we may find the entries: (a) confides in a spouse and a close friend, (b) actively participates in her church, (c) has been persistently active on the local school board. For a second individual we may find (a') very close with spouse; (b')

active in local bowling league; (c') long-term volunteer worker in environmental activist group; (d') weekly visits with friends. The beginning of a composite variable, focused on cumulative social relationships, is suggested by combining condition (b) for the first person and conditions (b') and (c') for the second person into the more abstract condition, "long-term participation in civic organizations." This abstract condition can then be combined with the other responses in a single composite response that *captures both individuals; to wit, let $a = 1$ if at least 3 of the 4 social relationship conditions holds (i) regular visits with friends; (ii) at least one close confidant; (iii) persistent participation in civic organization; (iv) regular participation in religious organization/church. Otherwise, set $a = 0$.* The composite variable, a, should be viewed as one of what may be several cumulative advantage variables in a single cell of what we refer to as an abstract chronological chart. It is a five-row (corresponding to the five organizing principles) by four-column (corresponding to the age intervals: < 18, 18–36, 36–52, 52+) table whose entries are variables, such as a above that represent a synthesis of information from several narratives. Observe that variables such as a represent multiple individuals with cumulative positive relationship experience when $a = 1$, and several individuals without such advantage when they satisfy $a = 0$.

The composite variables are the initial basis for revised response vectors for all individuals that need to satisfy two criteria. First, the revised response vector for a given individual should provide for a nuanced summary of the person's life history as it relates to mental health outcomes. Second, the response vector should not be too idiosyncratic. This latter condition is essential if we are to aggregate life histories—represented as reduced response vectors—so that individuals with "similar" response vectors can be grouped into common categories of histories. Our construction of the variable **a**, above, illustrates—at the most primitive level—how to remove idiosyncrasy and still retain nuance of description.

3. Specification of Reduced Response Vectors

Guided by the abstract chronological charts, we specify a provisional reduced vector of variables, whose values for a single individual define the person's reduced response vector. The provisional reduced vector of variables will, clearly, represent all persons for whom we have constructed narratives. However, this is only a small subsample of a much larger population. We augment this group with 10–15 new cases for whom we do not have narratives. Their provisional reduced response vectors augmented by responses on additional variables that are clearly linked to the organizing principles are displayed. Visual examination of these augmented response vectors for the new cases AND those for which there are narratives serves to suggest new composite variables and revisions of those specified for the provisional reduced vector of variables. The result of this visual inspection and judgment is a new second-stage reduced vector of variables. We continue bringing in blocks of 10–15 new cases at a time, repeating the above step, and thereby iteratively refining the reduced vector of response variables until all cases for a given mental health outcome group have been examined. The final reduced vector of response variables, **b**, is the basis for initiating the formal specification of a taxonomy of histories. In particular, for the 168 resilient women in WLS, their response vectors on the variables in **b** are the input to an aggregation strategy delineated in the next subsection.

4. Aggregation of Reduced Response Vectors: Pathway Specification

We begin by binary coding all variables in **b**. If, for example, a given variable can assume five possible values, labeled 1, 2, 3, 4, and 5, then we replace it by five dummy variables, each taking on the value 1 if a particular response level—say, for example, level 3—is attained and 0 otherwise. A single individual will have a 1 for only one of these dummy variables, and a 0 for the rest of them. With this binary coding at hand, the response vector for each person can be represented as a logical AND statement, the components of which are descriptions of the responses on each of the binary coded variables. In several applications of this methodology to-date (Peikes, 2000; Singer, Ryff, Carr, & Magee, 1998; Zhao, McLanahan, Brooks-Gunn, & Singer, 1999), the binary coded reduced vector of variables had between 18 and 26 components, depending upon the particular study.

Next, we identify the longest AND statement common to at least 20 individuals. This identifies a set of response vectors—equivalently, a set of life histories—that exactly match one another on the components of the AND statement. If the components of the AND statement are distributed across the whole lives *and they are interpretable as meaningful pathways to a given mental health outcome*, then we have succeeded in aggregating a set of life histories into a well defined group. For the resilient women in WLS, the binary coded version of **b** had 17 components, and the longest AND statement common to at least 20 individuals had 7 components. Actually 26 women out of the 168 who comprised the resilient group were in this aggregate. Based on the seven component AND statement, these women can be described by the following brief narrative (paraphrased) (Singer, et al., 1998).

The women grew up in households where neither parent was a high school graduate. There was no chronic alcoholism in their childhood homes, and they never lived with an alcoholic during adulthood. No woman in this group ever had the experience of being a single parent. They all experienced upward mobility in the workplace, from their first post-high-school job until they were surveyed again at age 36. They experienced further upward occupational mobility through age 52. All women compared themselves favorably with their parents and siblings in terms of educational, occupational, and financial achievements. These largely positive features, in terms of an absence of adversity and presence of cumulative advantage, describe some core ingredients that could facilitate recovery from episodes of depression. An important experience indicating a possible route to episodes of depression was the death of at least one parent for all of these women. Moving to information outside of the AND statement formally identifying this group, we find that 73% of the women participated in caregiving for an ill person or had at least one chronic health problem themselves. Approximately half of these women had two or more chronic health conditions. These represent additional possible precipitating circumstances for depressive episodes. Returning to the positive experiences that could have long-term impact to facilitate recovery, it is worth noting that 85% of the women in this group were in the top third of their high school class in terms of *both* grades and IQ. This is a facilitating factor for the occupational success experienced by all of these women.

With an initial aggregate of histories at hand, we eliminate this group from further consideration and identify the longest possible AND statement characterizing at least 20—and hopefully more—of the remaining women. In the WLS resilient women, this did not lead to a long enough AND statement that was sufficiently nuanced to characterize possible routes into episodes of depression, as well as the cumulation of advantage that would promote recovery. This led to specification of more complex Boolean statements that were both consistent with our organizing principles and represented the life histories of a substantial number of women. At least two strategies can be used for this specification. First, *visual inspection* of the 17-component response vectors revealed a group of 48 women, all of whom grew up in a household with at least one alcoholic parent, AND who had a diversity of different forms of compensating advantage in adulthood (represented by logical OR statements).

A more formally mechanized approach to this step—using, for example, Ragin's QCA software (Ragin, 1987)—would be to minimize the Boolean expression representing all women who are not in the first group identified via the "longest possible AND statement criterion." The resulting minimal Boolean expression would, hopefully, have clearly interpretable components that would represent distinct pathways—hence, additional members of the desired taxonomy of life histories—to given mental health outcomes. Although the analysis in Singer et al. (1998) proceeded beyond the first specification of an initial group by visual inspection and judgment, linked to organizing principles, we recommend application of both strategies en route to a final taxonomy. Indeed, as illustrated in Ragin (1987), minimal Boolean expressions that are not readily interpretable on a first pass through reduced response vectors often suggest recoding and construction of alternative composite variables that ultimately lead to a useful taxonomy.

5. Tests of Distinguishability

Having constructed a taxonomy of pathways for each outcome category—resilient and depressed/unwell in the present example—it is necessary to demonstrate that the routes to any one outcome differ in important ways from the set of routes to a different outcome. To this end, we first ask whether the aggregate pathways for the resilient women differ from the pathways for the depressed/unwell population. In particular, we tabulate the frequency with which the resilient pathways occur in the depressed/unwell population. Conversely, we take the aggregate pathways representing the depressed/unwell women and tabulate the frequency with which those pathways actually occur among the resilient women. We expect to find that the resilient pathways are rare in the depressed/unwell population and also that the depressed/unwell pathways are rare in the resilient population. For example, 16% of the resilient women are on the pathway indicated above by the seven-component logical AND statement. Only 9% of the depressed/unwell have the same pathway $(p < .10)$. Twenty percent of the resilient women are on the pathway where at least one parent is a chronic alcoholic AND there are a diversity of compensating positive experiences in adulthood. This pathway only occurs for 5% of the depressed/unwell population $(p < .05)$. Sharper discrimination occurs depending upon the particular application (see, e.g., Zhao et al., 1999). The central point, however, is that assessment of distinguishability is important for making the case that there are, as hypothesized, qualitatively different routes to distinct mental health outcomes.

IV. Case Example 3: Identifying Subpopulations for In-Depth Study

A. A Generic Problem

Elderly populations at the level of communities contain many people who have multiple disabilities and multiple chronic conditions, no combination of which occurs at high frequency. This makes classification of the age 65+ population into disability/chronic condition groups particularly problematic. Indeed, simply describing the joint distribution of comorbid conditions is an unwieldy and difficult task.

Accompanying this distributional difficulty is the empirical finding of an overall decline in disability from 1982–1994, as ascertained in the National Long Term Care Survey (NLTCS) (Manton, Corder, & Stallard, 1997; Singer & Manton, 1998) and over longer time horizons as ascertained in the Framingham Heart Study (Allaire et al., 1999). To obtain a more nuanced picture of disability decline, it would be useful to track the change over time in membership in different disability categories that represent meaningful partitions of the age 65+ population. Longitudinal studies of subsamples within such disability categories could usefully clarify disability/chronic condition histories and related psychosocial and medical histories that comprise pathways to diverse health outcomes. Such longitudinal assessments should be both quantitative and qualitative in character. Structured interviews of work and family life histories, psychological and social factors related to them, and mental and physical health histories would thus augment the extant NLTCS instruments. In addition, focused interviews identifying salient life experiences, reactions to them, life outlooks, major disappointments, and significant achievements would facilitate nuanced characterizations of pathways to health outcomes at later ages. Pathway constructions for these enriched longitudinal subsamples of the NLTCS could proceed via the methodology described for case 2, above.

A useful quantitative statistical methodology that facilitates identification of an interpretable taxonomy of disability groups involves fitting the family of GoM models to a multidimensional table of counts of joint occurrences of people's inability to perform a diverse set of activities of daily living (ADLs), tests of physical functioning, or both. We describe and illustrate this methodology on data from the NLTCS. The central point of introducing this quantitative technique is that it clearly identifies where—in a very heterogeneous large population narrative and numerical data should be assembled to facilitate understanding variations of pathways to diverse later life disability profiles.

B. What Does Grade of Membership Do?

A GoM representation of the joint distribution of persons along J dimensions identifies each individual with a point in a unit simplex (see Figure 3.1). The vertices of the simplex correspond to extreme (or ideal) profiles of conditions. In the context of disability, these will be extreme profiles of impairments. Edges of the simplex correspond to sets of conditions, some of which are from one vertex and the remainder from the second vertex at the terminal points of the edge. Thus, a person identified with an interior point on an edge has a sufficiently heterogeneous set of disabilities that components from two profiles (corresponding to the vertices) are necessary to represent his

or her response vector. The interiors of the faces of the simplex correspond to sets of conditions, some of which are from each of the three vertices of the triangle defining the face. More complex sets of conditions are identified with points in subsimplices defined by four or more vertices.

The relationship of this geometrical structure to individual discrete-valued response vectors, $\mathbf{X} = (X_1, X_2, \ldots X_J)$, can be seen from the following considerations. For a population of I individuals, their responses can be summarized by counts in a J-dimensional contingency table containing $L_1 \times L_2 \times \ldots \times L_J$ cells, where $L_j =$ number of possible response levels (categories) associated with the variable, X_j. The typically strong dependence among the components of $\mathbf{X}$ can be represented by identifying a vector $\mathbf{g}$ such that conditional on $\mathbf{g}$, $X_1, X_2, \ldots, X_J$ are statistically independent. That such a representation

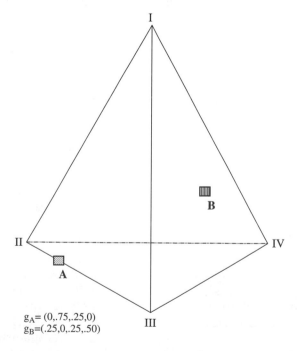

$g_A = (0,.75,.25,0)$
$g_B = (.25,0,.25,.50)$

Note: Person A shares conditions with profiles II and III
        Person B shares conditions with profiles I, III, and IV
Figure 3.1   GoM Simplex with four profiles.

is always possible for finite contingency tables was established by Woodbury, Tolley, and Manton (2000). They also demonstrated that $\mathbf{g} = (g_1, \ldots, g_K)$ was a set of nonnegative weights such that $g_1 + g_2 + \ldots + g_K = 1$. Furthermore, the conditional probability that each response variable X_j takes on the level l_j given $\mathbf{g}$ can be represented as a linear combination of the components, g_k, of $\mathbf{g}$ multiplied by the probability that an ideal-type-k individual had response level l_j on the jth variable. It is precisely this representation that identifies individuals with points in a unit simplex. In particular, the simplex has K vertices, and g_k for an individual—referred to as the person's GoM score for the kth profile—indicates what fraction of that individual's responses are members of the kth ideal profile. The number of profiles, K, and the response probabilities for type-k individuals are all estimated by fitting the GoM model to the J-dimensional response vectors. Technical details of the estimation process are described in Berkman, Singer, and Manton (1989) and Manton, Woodbury, and Tolley (1994).

C. Application to the National Long-Term Care Survey

The NLTCS consists of list-based samples of approximately 20,000 persons age 65+ drawn from Medicare enrollment files in the years 1982, 1984, 1989, and 1994. These persons were screened initially for chronic ADLs and instrumental ADLs (IADL) disability. Operationally, chronic meant that an ADL or IADL condition lasted, or was expected to last, 90 days or more. To ensure a national sample of the age 65+ population at each survey date, a fresh supplementary list sample of 5000 persons age 65–69 was drawn from Medicare enrollment files in 1984, 1989, and 1994. A detailed description of the NLTCS is given in Corder, Woodbury, and Manton (1993).

A battery of 27 ADL, IADL, and functional impairment measures—listed in Table 3.1—was selected to represent a comprehensive set of measures of functioning (Manton, Corder, & Stallard, 1997).

Best fitting GoM models for each of the survey years revealed that K = 6 profiles were identified for the community population and that there was very little variation in the ideal profiles over time. Independent of the model, a seventh profile was added for the elderly institutionalized population. This group is quite homogeneous, having an average of 4.8 ADLs chronically impaired. The full set of profiles is listed in Table 3.2.

Profiles I–III represent persons who are generally functionally intact. In contrast, Profiles IV–VI identify persons with significant physical or cognitive impairment. Heterogeneity within the functionally intact group is represented by persons who share conditions with pairs of profiles I, II, and III. Such people have GoM scores, at a given survey, with non-zero entries for precisely two profiles; for example, $\mathbf{g} = (.3, .7, 0, 0, 0, 0)$ is the GoM score vector for a person whose responses on ADL, IADL, and physical functioning are closer to profile II (a weighting of .7) than to profile I (a weighting of .3).

We will denote the category of functionally intact persons by *C(1–3)*. They are persons with response vectors exactly at one of the profiles I, II, or III, supplemented by persons who share conditions with any pair of them. Geometrically, persons in *C(1–3)* are either at one of the vertices in the unit simplex, defined by GoM scores, and labeled I, II, or III, or they are on one of the edges that link pairs of these vertices.

Heterogeneity in the severely disabled group, called *C(4–6)*, is represented by persons who are either at profiles IV, V, or VI or share conditions with pairs of them. A different form of heterogeneity, *C(int)*, is designated for persons who are on edges

Table 3.1
Activities of Daily Living and Measures of Physical Functioning assessed in the
National Long Term Care Survey[a]

ADL Items: Needs help with	(IADL Items: Needs help with)
Eating	Heavy work
Get in/out of bed	Light work
Getting about inside	Laundry
Dressing	Cooking
Bathing	Grocery shopping
Using a toilet	Getting about outside
	Traveling
Are you	Managing money
Bedfast	Taking medicine
Using a wheelchair	Telephoning
Restricted to no inside activity	

Can you
See well enough to read a newspaper
How much difficulty do you have: None, Some, Very difficult, Cannot at all

Climbing 1 flight of stairs
Bending for socks
Holding a 10=lb. package
Reaching over head
Combing hair
Washing hair
Grasping small objects

[a]From Manton, Stallard, and Corder (1997).

connecting one of the vertices {I, II, III} to one of the vertices in the set {IV, V, VI}. Finally, a more extreme form of heterogeneity, designated by *C(res)*, is represented by persons who share conditions with three or more profiles. Geometrically, they are identified with points in the faces of the unit simplex (K = 6) or in its interior. The partitioning of the age 65+ population into the four disability categories defined above, augmented by the institutionalized population, identifies clearly distinct groups that should be subsampled for in-depth focused interviews.

D. What Has Been Learned and Next Questions

The GoM methodology facilitated the partitioning of the heterogeneous aging population into different subgroups, differentiated by their profiles of functional independence/impairment. However, this analysis does not clarify how these profiles come about i.e., what are the pathways to disability outcomes and the factors responsible for variation in disability decline over time across these groups?

Concerning disability decline, published analyses based on the NLTCS indicate that a 1.5% per annum decline in the proportion of the age 65+ population that is chronically disabled has occurred over the time period, 1982–1994 (Manton, et al., 1997; Singer & Manton, 1998). This population-wide trend masks the variation in change in percent chronically disabled that occurs in the subgroups defined by the GoM partitioning of the age 65+ population. Table 3.3 demonstrates this

Table 3.2
Disability Profiles[a]

I	Active, no functional impairment
II	Very modest impairment, *some* difficulty climbing stairs, lifting a 10=lb. package, and bending for socks [No ADL or IADL]
III	Moderate physical impairment, *great* difficulty climbing stairs, lifting 10=lb. package, reaching over head, etc. [No ADL or IADL]
IV	*All* IADLs, great difficulty climbing stairs, lifting 10-lb. package
V	Some ADLs AND IADLs AND difficulty climbing stairs, *cannot* lift 10=lb. package
VI	*All* ADLs AND *all* IADLs AND *all* tasks [High percentage in wheelchairs]
VII	Institutionalized

[a]ADL, activities of daily living, IADL, Instrumental ADLs. From Manton and Singer (2000).

Table 3.3
Percent per Annum Changes in Prevalence of Chronic Disability From 1982–1994 × Age × Gender[a]

Disability category	Men age 65–84	Women age 65–84	Men age 85+	Women Age 85+
C(1–3)	+0.209	+0.30	+1.45	+0.25
C(4–6)	−2.78	−5.31	−2.65	−2.91
C(int)	−2.11	−0.74	+4.08	−0.155
C(res)	1.05	−1.01	−3.13	+0.048
Inst.	−1.60	−1.71	−0.94	+0.158

[a]From: Manton and Singer (2000).

variability, further subdividing the elderly population by age and gender.

A nuanced understanding of percent per annum changes in each cell of this table, and of the variation across groups and how it comes about, requires in-depth quantitative and qualitative analyses from each subgroup. Both retrospective and prospective assessments of cumulative adversity, reactions to and management of life challenges, and psychological well-being and the underlying basis for it should be carried out with a combination of structured survey instruments and focused interviews. A synthesis of the analytical strategies presented in case examples 1 and 2, above could be used to construct the requisite pathways and, hence, account for the percent per annum changes in Table 3.3.

V. Implications

A central task for persons working with longitudinal studies of aging is the integration of cross-time, multidomain data to explain how a broad range of outcomes (e.g., mental or physical health) come about. We have discussed two methodological strategies for constructing life history representations to answer how particular outcomes come about. In case 1, we used narrative data derived from focused interviews to describe life history representations that account for differential scientific productivity between men and women. In case 2, we used longitudinal survey data to describe a methodology for aggregating fine-grained individual histories into a taxonomy of pathways to account for psychological resilience (i.e., recovery from depression) given mental health outcomes. The common denominator in both strategies is that they begin with idiosyncratic individual histories, and the analytical steps then identify important commonalities and differences across lives, leading to aggregation of histories into relatively homogeneous groups.

Both examples provide instances of what we can regard as *bottom-up analytical strategies*. They are person-centered in the sense that the individual life history is the unit of analysis, and the aggregation process itself operates on whole lives. In contrast, there are what can be regarded as *top-down analytical strategies*. What they have in common is a set of techniques for partitioning a heterogeneous population of individuals into progressively more homogeneous subgroups. Case 3 illustrates one kind of top-down partitioning strategy (i.e., GoM analysis), but only carries the analysis to the identification of subgroups on whom refined life history data could be used to depict pathways to these heterogeneous later life health profiles.

We would like to summarize the important points from the three case examples. Beginning with long narratives as data, case example 1 emphasizes that all questions and lines of analysis en route to life history representations cannot, at the outset, be fully anticipated. Coding and recoding of blocks of text from each fine-grained record, guided by organizing principles, is thus central to the inductive process of identifying common themes and important differences across lives that will enter into the ultimate life history representations. A software system, such as NUDIST or GATOR, that facilitates open-ended inquiry and allows for continuing additions and changes to coding schemes is a critical tool for establishing different files of text that an investigator can examine comparatively. A basic theme in developing life history representations from narratives is that the investigator must be highly interactive with each stage of analysis and the final product. The many stages of judgment by the investigator that precede the final product raise important questions about the effect of personal biases that may enter coding decisions. Two responses are relevant. First, software systems such as NUDIST render the coding decisions *transparent* to any critic who may, in turn, want to develop alternative coding schemes leading to possibly different life history representations. Second, any given set of life history representations (e.g., the simulation model in the science careers example) can, in principle, be tested on other comparable populations to ascertain whether or not pathways representing one population can be replicated or generalized.

Case 2 illustrates how to integrate cross-time and multidomain longitudinal survey data to obtain taxonomies of life histories that describe how a given outcome comes about. The first step in the analysis, construction of narratives *by the investigator* as a means to understand whole lives, represents an unorthodox use of survey data, deserving some comment. We subscribe to the view that human thought processes involved in explaining how something "came about" tend generally to construct a narrative path from a prior understood state to the state we need to explain. That is, we engage in a process of projecting one story onto another, and this process is at the core of how human minds actually construct meaning (Turner, 1996). Simply put, we naturally grasp ideas in terms of stories. The lists of raw numerical responses from longitudinal surveys are in a form overly remote from the narrative path that facilitates understanding. For this reason, we initiate the analysis of longitudinal survey data with the construction of narratives from randomly selected cases. For a particularly lucid exposition of literary mental powers as the basis of everyday thought, including connections to cognitive neuroscience and the nature and origin of language, see Turner (1996).

Following the construction of narratives, the remaining inductive steps in developing life history representations involve the same high degree of cognitive involvement by the investigator as the coding and recoding of text in case 1. Judgment about specification of composite variables—guided by organizing principles—and repeated appeal to what has been learned from individual narratives and integration of them in the form of abstract chronological charts, is fundamental to creating the life history representations. The extent to which the entire process can be fully automated is, in our opinion, an open question. The strategies we present are heavily interactive between the investigator and computer-generated displays of selected blocks of numerical responses for multiple persons. This makes the construction of taxonomies of life histories labor intensive and intellectually demanding. It has the advantage, however, of giving the investigator an active role in tuning the trade-offs between nuance of fine-grained individual histories and more coarse-grained aggregation into groups regarded as having equivalent histories.

The GoM methodology, described in case 3, represents the first stage of a top-down strategy for partitioning a heterogeneous population into homogeneous subgroups. GoM is equivalent to crisp clustering when each individual is represented by a single ideal profile. Life histories can be linked to a GoM-based construction if there is a set of variables not used to construct the ideal profiles and that are ascertained by longitudinal survey or as the result of coding narratives. Then, for each individual, there would be a GoM score history and more nuanced life history information. Such data could then be analyzed using a synthesis of the methods in cases 1 and 2.

Two bottom-up analytical strategies that might serve as alternatives to what we have put forth are optimal matching (Abbott & Barman, 1997; Abbott & Hrycak, 1990) and event structure analysis (Griffin, 1993). Optimal matching, which derives from the literature on comparison of DNA sequences, takes univariate time series for individuals and groups them together into sets of what are regarded as equivalent histories. The grouping requires the availability of a metric on the space of possible sequences (histories), and two sequences are defined to be members of the same group if their distance apart—in terms of the metric—is sufficiently small. To apply the automated optimal matching technique requires that input data be in the form of what

we have called "reduced response vectors." The analogue of steps leading from more complex longitudinal data to this stage, as we have described in case 2, must still be carried out for univariate time series prior to carrying out the formal aggregation step (Abbott & Hrycak, 1990). Although optimal matching is a natural way to proceed in the construction of a taxonomy of histories, the problem with its implementation on cross-time, multidomain data is that there is no obvious metric yet developed that is suited to the complex multidimensional time series corresponding to individual histories (as discussed in case 2). Furthermore, a single measure of distance between two multidimensional histories seems too coarse for decisions about what should constitute equivalent histories. Our strategy for aggregation of reduced response vectors—step (4), case 2—uses information about multiple features of life histories. This suggests that any automated aggregation technique, analogous to optimal matching, should be based on a multidimensional measure on the space of possible histories.

Event structure analysis (ESA) (Griffin, 1993) is a more organized strategy for the analysis of narratives than what we described in case 1. The final output of ESA, in the form of a detailed tree-like graphical display of a full history, was implicitly carried out en route to summarizing the essential features of science career histories. However, Griffin's strategy yields a more comprehensive summary of an individual narrative. It is also substantially more labor intensive than what we described. It would be useful to employ Griffin's methodology in a reanalysis of the science career interviews to ascertain whether or not important—and previously unnoticed—sources of male–female differences in productivity could be identified.

Concerning top-down person-centered analytical strategies, there is a considerable diversity of them. A valuable review of both concepts and methods is contained in Cairns, Bergman, and Kagan (1998). One common strategy focuses on clustering techniques, where a critical input to the algorithms is a metric on the space of histories. Not surprisingly, applications of these techniques, which partition a heterogeneous population into relatively homogeneous clusters, have been restricted to low-dimensional data and rather simple summaries of histories. To get to the level of nuance and multidomain representations of the kind we have discussed requires a quite different set of measures of similarity of histories be constructed than heretofore. This is an important research topic for the future.

Recursive partitioning (RP) classification (Breiman et al., 1984; Zhang & Singer, 1999) is an automated procedure that fits trees to multidimensional longitudinal data such that pathways down the tree to a given outcome identify homogeneous subpopulations with common histories. Trees are constructed with the objective of maximizing ability to predict membership in the outcome categories. Each pathway down the tree ending in a given terminal node (identified with a health outcome) corresponds to a logical AND statement incorporating information across multiple life domains. Two or more pathways into the same terminal node are identified with a logical OR statement describing how that particular outcome came about. The *judgment* of the investigator is required to determine whether all pathways to the nodes identified with a given outcome should be summarized by a single complex Boolean expression, or partitioned into two or more sets of pathways defining qualitatively different kinds of histories. Recursive partitioning (RP) algorithms could accept either the original raw response vectors or reduced response vectors, as described in case example 2, as input.

From our perspective, a limitation of RP for generating a taxonomy of life histories is the fact that the performance criteria and the splitting rules for tree construction are not constrained by substantive knowledge from any field of scientific inquiry (e.g., a set of organizing principles). Thus, the pathways down the best predictive trees are not always interpretable within the knowledge of a given field. This disjunction between statistical performance criteria, based solely on numerical goodness-of-fit, and constraints on tree structures and splitting rules derived from extant scientific knowledge have proven problematic in past applications of RP. Levy et al. (1981, 1985), for example, applied RP to neurological assessments of comatose patients to predict which patients were likely to recover with moderate disabilities as opposed to remaining vegetative or dying within 1 year of hospital admission. The numerically best predictive trees were virtually *never* neurologically interpretable. Rather, inspection of 20+ nearly optimal trees led to selection, based on scientific judgment, of a prognostic tree that had interpretable pathways. For a start at more interactive (i.e., allowing the investigator to modify trees during the construction process on the basis of organizing principles) and flexible strategies based on RP technology, the reader should consult Zhang and Singer (1999).

In addition to our focus on person-oriented data-analytic techniques, it is also important to underscore the advantages of having both qualitative and quantitative data on the same individuals. Indeed, much of the subtlety about lives through time is revealed through focused interviews, while broader sociodemographic characteristics and facets of lives ascertainable with psychometric scales are measurable with structured longitudinal surveys. It is still relatively rare to find both kinds of evidence on the same population in the study of life histories. Exemplary examples, however, are the investigations of criminal careers by Sampson and Laub (1993), study of the impact of war mobilization on the lives of men in L. Terman's longitudinal study (Elder & Clipp, 1988; Elder, Pavalko, & Clipp, 1993; Giele & Elder, 1998), and the classic investigations of children growing up during the Depression of the 1930s (Elder, 1974). The effective integration of qualitative and quantitative evidence via person-centered methods is, despite these examples, still a topic in need of further methodological development. Our case examples illustrate new strides in this direction.

From the perspective of understanding aging processes, there are a host of outcomes that could be usefully illuminated by person-centered life history blends of numbers and narratives across multiple life domains. For example, it would be important to characterize pathways to dementia and distinguish them from life history representations of persons who remain cognitively intact. A common feature of illness among the elderly is the presence of multiple co-occurring chronic conditions. The availability of nuanced life history representations accounting for co-morbidity, and distinguishing them from pathways of resilient persons who remain healthy practically until death, would be suggestive of primary prevention strategies to reduce co-morbidity in younger cohorts.

References

Abbott, A., & Barman, E. (1997). Sequence comparison via alignment and Gibbs sampling: A formal analysis of the emergence of the modern sociological article. In A. E. Raftery (Ed.), *Sociological Methodology, 1997* (pp. 47–87). Washington, DC: American Sociological Association.

Abbott, A., & Hrycak, A. (1990). Measuring resemblance in sequence data: An optimal matching analysis of musician's careers. *American Journal of Sociology, 96,* 144–185.

Allaire, S., LaValley, M., Evans, S., O'Connor, G., Kelly-Hayes, M., Meenan, R., Levy, D., & Felson, D. (1999). Evidence for decline in disability and improved health among persons aged 55 to 70 Years: The Framingham Heart Study. *American Journal of Public Health, 89,* 1678–1683.

American Psychiatric Association (APA). (1987). *Diagnostic and statistical manual of mental disorders* (3rd ed.). Washington, DC: American Psychiatric Association.

Arneson, E., & Foredahl, A. (1985). The Tromso Heart Study: coronary risk factors and their association with living conditions during childhood. *Journal of Epidemiology & Community Health, 39,* 210–214

Baltes, P., & Baltes, M. (1990). *Successful aging: Perspectives from the behavioral sciences.* Cambridge, UK: Cambridge University Press.

Barker, D., & Osmond, C. (1986). Infant mortality, childhood nutrition, and ischaemic heart disease in England and Wales. *Lancet, I,* 1077–1081.

Berkman, L., Singer, B., & Manton, K. (1989). Black/white differences in health status among the elderly. *Demography, 26*(4), 661–678.

Breiman, L., Friedman, J., Olshen, R., & Stone, C. (1984) *Classification and regression trees.*Belmont, CA: Wadsworth.

Cairns, R., Bergman, L., & Kagan, J. (Eds.). (1998). *Methods and models for studying the individual.* Thousand Oaks, CA: Sage Publications.

Clausen, J. (1993). *American lives: Looking back at children of the great depression.* Berkeley: University of California Press.

Cole, J., & Singer, B. (1991). A theory of limited differences: Explaining the productivity puzzle in science. In H. Zuckerman, J. Cole, & J. Bruer (Eds.), *The outer circle: Women in the scientific community* (pp. 277–323 & 338–340), New York: W.W. Norton.

Cole, J., & Zuckerman, H. (1987). Marriage, motherhood, and research performance in science. *Scientific American, 255*(2), 119–125.

Coleman, J. S. (1996). A vision for sociology. In J. Clark (Ed.), *James S. Coleman* (pp. 343–349). London: Falmer Press.

Corder, L., Woodbury, M., & Manton, K. (1993). Health loss due to unobserved morbidity: A design based approach to minimize nonsampling error in active life expectation estimates. In J. Robine, C. Mathers, M. Bone, & I. Romieu (Eds.), *Calculation of health expectancies* (pp. 217–232). Colloque INSERM, 226. London: John Libbey Eurotext Ltd.

Elder, G. (1974). *Children of the great depression: Social change in life experience.* Chicago: University of Chicago Press.

Elder, G., & Clipp, E. (1988). Wartime losses and social bonding: Influences across 40 years in men's lives. *Psychiatry, 51,* 177–198.

Elder, G., Pavalko, E., & Clipp, E. (1993). *Working with archival data: Studying lives.* Newbury, CA: Sage Publications.

Giele, J., & Elder, G. (Eds.) (1998). *Methods of life course research: Qualitative and quantitative approaches.* Thousand Oaks, CA: Sage Publications

Giordano, R., Cole, J., & Zuckerman, H. (1988). Text retrieval on a microcomputer. *Perspectives in computing, 8*(1), 52–60

Glueck, S., & Glueck, E. (1968). *Delinquents and non-delinquents in perspective.* Cambridge, MA: Harvard University Press.

Griffin, L. (1993). Narrative, event structure analysis, and causal interpretation in historical sociology. *American Journal of Sociology, 98,* 1094–1133.

Hauser, R., Carr, D., Hauser, T., Hayes, J., Krecker, M., Kuo, H., Magee, W., Presti, J., Shinberg, D., Sweeney, M., Thompson-Colon, T., Uhrig, S., & Warren, J. (1993). *The class of 1957 after 35 years: Overview and preliminary findings.* Working paper 93–17. Madison, WI: Center for Demography and Ecology, University of Wisconsin-Madison.

Kleinman, A. (1988). *The illness narratives: Suffering, healing, and the human condition.* New York: Basic Books.

Kleinman, A. (1995). *Writing at the margin: Discourse between anthropology and medicine.* Berkeley, CA: University of California Press.

Levy, D., Bates, D., Caronna, J., Cartlidge, N., Knill-Jones, R., Lapinski, R.,Singer, B., Shaw, D., & Plum, F. (1981). Prognosis in nontraumatic coma. *Annals of Internal Medicine, 94,* 293–301.

Levy, D., Caronna, J., Singer, B., Lapinski, R., Frydman, H., & Plum, F. (1985). Predicting outcome from hypoxic-ischemic coma. *Jour-*

nal of American Medical Association, 253, 1420–1426.

Manton, K., Corder, L., & Stallard, E. (1997). Chronic disability in elderly United States populations: 1982–1994. *Proceedings of National Academy of Sciences, 94,* 2593–2598.

Manton, K. & Singer, B. (2000). Variation in disability decline and medicare expenditures. *Proceedings of National Academy of Sciences.*

Manton, K., Stallard, E., & Corder, L. (1997). Changes in the age dependence of mortality and disability: Cohort and other determinants. *Demography, 34*(1), 135–157.

Manton, K., Woodbury, M., & Tolley, H. D. (1994). *Statistical applications using fuzzy sets.* New York: John Wiley.

McAdams, D. (1993). *The stories we live by: Personal myths and the making of the self.* New York: William Morrow.

McAdams, D. (1994). *The person: An introduction to personality psychology* (2nd ed.). New York: Harcourt Brace.

Mishler, E. (1997). Missing persons: Recovering development stories/histories. In R. Jessor, A. Colby, & R. Shweder (Eds.), *Ethnography and human development* (pp. 73–99). Chicago: University of Chicago Press.

Peikes, D. (2000). *"Pathways of Resilience and Vulnerability in Health"* Ph.D. Dissertation, Princeton University.

Power, C., Manor, O., & Fox, A. (1991). *Health and class: The early years.* London: Chapman and Hall.

Power, C., & Matthews, S. (1998). Accumulation of health risks across social groups in a national longitudinal study. In S. Strickland & P. Shetty (Eds.), *Human biology and social inequality* (pp. 36–57). Cambridge, UK: Cambridge University Press.

Ragin, C. (1987). *The comparative method: Moving beyond qualitative and quantitative strategies.* Berkeley: University of California Press.

Richards, T. (1997). *QSR NUD*IST* (version 4.0; computer software). Victoria, Australia: Qualitative Solutions and Research.

Rowe, J., & Kahn, R. (1998) *Successful aging.* New York: Pantheon Books.

Ryff, C. (1995). Psychological well-being in adult life. *Current directions in psychological science, 4,* 99–104

Ryff, C., & Keyes, C. (1995). The structure of psychological well-being revisited. *Journal of Personality and Social Psychology 69,* 719–727.

Sampson, R., & Laub, J. (1993). *Crime in the making: Pathways and turning points through life.* Cambridge, MA: Harvard University Press

Seidel, J., Kjolseth, R., & Seymour, E. (1988). *The Ethnograph: A users guide.* Littleton, CO: Qualis Research Associates.

Singer, B., & Manton, K. (1998). The effects of health changes on projections of health service needs for the elderly population of the United States. *Proceedings of the National Academy of Sciences, 95,* 15618–15622.

Singer, B., Ryff, C., Carr, D., & Magee, W. (1998). Linking life histories and mental health: A person-centered strategy. In A. Raftery (Ed.), *Sociological methodology, 1998* (pp. 1–51). Washington, DC: American Sociological Association.

Stone, R. (1979). The revival of narrative: Reflections on a new old story. *Past and Present, 85,* 3–24.

Turner, M. (1996). *The literary mind.* New York: Oxford University Press.

Vaillant, G. (1983). *The natural history of alcoholism.* Cambridge, MA: Harvard University Press.

Wadsworth, M., & Kuh, D. (1997). Childhood influences on adult health: A review of recent work from the British 1946 national birth cohort study, the MRC national survey of health and development. *Pediatric Perinatal Epidemiology, 11,* 2–20.

Wittchen, H., Robins, L., Cottler, L., Sartorius, N., Burke, J., & Reiger, D. (1991). Cross-cultural feasibility, reliability and sources of variance of the composite international diagnostic interview (CIDI). *British Journal of Psychiatry, 159,* 645–653.

Woodbury, M., Tolley, H. D., & Manton, K. (2000). Grade of membership analysis: Models to analyze categorical data based on a convex geometry. *Proceedings of National Academy of Sciences.*

Zhang, H., & Singer, B. (1999). *Recursive partitioning in the health sciences.* New York: Springer-Verlag.

Zhao, H., McLanahan, S., Brooks-Gunn, J., & Singer, B. (2000). Studying the real child rather than the ideal child: Bringing the person into developmental studies. In L. Bergman, R. Cairns, L-G. Nilsson & L. Nystedt (Eds.), *Developmental science and the holistic approach* (pp. 393–419). Mahwah, NJ: Lawrence Erlbaum.

Part Two

Aging and Social Structure

Four

Demography of Aging

A Century of Global Change, 1950–2050

Mark D. Hayward and Zhenmei Zhang

The Baby Boom cohort in the ethos of the United States has come to signify a rapid and imminent aging of the population. Media reports abound emphasizing the impending challenges to Social Security and Medicare once the Baby Boom enters prime retirement ages at the middle of the next decade. Explosive growth in the size of the elderly population is juxtaposed with concerns about whether elders will also be living longer in better or worse health. The challenges of population aging to American social institutions are mirrored in the perceptions and expectations of everyday Americans. Many Americans lack confidence that Social Security will provide for them in old age, anticipating a breakdown in the social contract between their parents and grandparents and the federal government (e.g., Roper Starch Worldwide, 1999). Population aging frequently is seen and portrayed as the demographic villain disrupting basic social institutions and the social contracts linking individuals to these institutions (Schulz, Borowski, & Crown, 1991).

Despite news media stories and popular perceptions, the American experience with population aging is neither unique nor extreme in the context of other countries' experiences with population aging (Easterlin, 1991; Schulz et al., 1991). Here, our basic goal is straightforward—to demonstrate that many countries will experience levels and rates of population aging unlikely to be experienced in the United States. How these countries face this demographic challenge may have implications for adapting pension and health care policy in the American context. In addition, we emphasize that population aging has become a worldwide phenomenon. The prior 50 years—the period since 1950—was the period in which demographic changes spanning at least 100 years resulted in relatively mature populations in Europe and Northern America. The next 50 years, however, are likely to bring extraordinary changes in age of populations in the developing nations—the pace of which is unprecedented in world history. The fertility and mortality revolutions that have spawned population aging will occur at a much more rapid pace in developing countries than in the developed nations that have led the trend. (For a review of the mortality and fertility revolution worldwide, see Easterlin, 1997.) As we show here, there is

Handbook of Aging and the Social Sciences, Fifth Edition

evidence pointing toward a worldwide convergence in population aging, characterized by populations containing large numbers of older persons and relatively stable in size. Whether this trend also foretells a parallel trend in the extension of the years persons can expect to live in good health is also considered.

I. Population Aging: An International Demographic Phenomenon

The year 1999 marked the period of time in world history in which the six billionth person was added to the world's population. Not surprisingly, much of the media attention was directed at the world's growing population and the comparatively high rates of fertility in developing nations. The population problem of the year, according to a variety of media, was burgeoning and young populations—especially in developing parts of the world.

Although the world added its sixth billionth citizen, a relatively quiet demographic revolution has been occurring worldwide. It is the revolution from a demographic regime of high fertility and relatively low mortality to a regime of low fertility and low mortality. Demographic regimes with high fertility and low mortality give rise to fast-growing, young populations. Demographic regimes with low fertility and low mortality result in slow growing or stable populations with a comparatively old age structure. As we will illustrate later, a number of European nations have had a demographic regime of low fertility and low mortality in place for some time, resulting in very slow growing and aged populations.

The significance of the spread of the demographic revolution from developed to developing nations was recognized by the United Nations in its declaration of

1999 as the International Year of Older Persons. Thus, while 1999 saw the addition of its six billionth citizen, this year also marked the recognition that the world as a whole is entering a phase in which populations are maturing. The United Nations designation recognized a

' "society for all ages," in recognition of humanity's demographic coming of aging and the promise it holds for maturing attitudes and capabilities in social, economic, cultural and spiritual undertakings, not least for global peace and development in the next century'. (United Nations, 1992, 47/5 annex)

These themes were also echoed in the United Nation's Programme of Action of the International Conference on Population and Development in 1994 (United Nations, 1994).

As we suggest in this chapter, what some demographers might consider to be the last demographic revolution (i.e., the transition to a mature and stable population) is projected to occur at a pace in developing nations in the next 50 years never experienced by the developed nations who led the revolution. We illustrate past and expected future patterns of the demographic revolution worldwide by comparing demographic changes in developed and developing nations for two periods—the prior 50 years of experience and the next 50 years of projected experience. We make use of demographic data and demographic projections provided by the United Nations (United Nations, 1996a, 1996b) for the 100-year period.

Understanding the portents of the demographic revolution, particularly the declines in mortality, for international trends in the health and functioning of the older population is vital for anticipating the global demands on health-care systems and health-care costs (Robine & Romieu, 1998; Waidmann & Manton, 2000; World Health Organization, 2000). A guiding aim of the United Nations Principles for Older Persons is "to add life to the years that have been added to life" (United Nations, 1991). Does declining mortality over a number of decades within a country signify that members of population are living longer healthier lives? Or does the mortality revolution foster the lengthening of ill health prior to death? What can we learn from the experiences of developed nations in the past 50 years that can be projected to developing nations who will be aging in the next 50 years?

The answers to these questions are not as straightforward as one might presume. Conceptually, the correspondence between mortality changes and morbidity in a population is ambiguous (see Crimmins, 1996, for an overview). If mortality declines because diseases are prevented or their onset is delayed, population health will improve with the change in mortality. However, if mortality declines occur because of declines in the mortal consequences of diseases, population health is expected to decline (Crimmins, Hayward, & Saito, 1994). This idea was the impetus for Verbrugge's (1989) conceptual model to account for an apparent rise in mild disability in the United States during the 1970s—a period in which mortality was falling. Complicating this relationship between mortality and morbidity, however, is the fact that population health is multidimensional. Much of disability, for example, is a product of nonfatal chronic conditions such as arthritis and vision impairment. Among Americans at older ages, for example, about 50% of disability is an outcome of nonfatal conditions (Verbrugge & Patrick, 1995). Understanding historical changes in disability thus necessitates attention to changes in the mix of fatal and nonfatal conditions experienced by the population, and it requires knowledge of where in a disease process improvements in health are occurring.

Another important component in understanding the conceptual link between population-level mortality and morbidity is the differential progress in understanding the etiology of various diseases and associated lifestyle changes and medical interventions in disease diagnosis and treatment. Progress in one disease sphere need not be mirrored by progress in all disease spheres. Indeed, this is what should be expected given the societal decisions about the allocation of health-care resources, scientific discoveries that aid in fighting one disease but not others, and changes in population composition. These factors, as well as other sociopolitical forces, contribute to uneven changes in disease and disability prevalence in a population—changes that need not be uniformly downward (Bonneux, Barendregt, Meeter, Bonsel, & van der Maas, 1994).

Further clouding our understanding of the relationship between morbidity and mortality changes is the lack of consistent, high-quality, and nationally representative health data for a lengthy time period. The United States has the longest times series—over three decades—of the prevalence of chronic conditions available for a national population, the National Health Interview Survey (NHIS). However, changes in survey design and methodology have challenged researchers' ability to use these data to document historical trends in population health within the United States. Similar time series are unavailable for other countries. Since the 1980s, a number of longitudinal studies of health have also been fielded within the United States (e.g., the National Long-Term Care Survey, the Longitudinal Study of Aging, and the Health and Retirement Survey). These surveys are characterized by substantial differences in survey design, content, and health measurement, making it difficult to develop a precise picture of recent changes in population health. At a very general level, the bulk of these studies point to a decline in the prevalence of disability in the population during the 1980s and 1990s accompanying mortality declines for the period (Crimmins, 1998; Crimmins, Saito, & Ingegneri, 1997; Freedman & Martin, 1998; Manton, Stallard, & Corder, 1995), although the magnitude and origins of the decline remain ambiguous.

Internationally, there is growing attention to the implications of long-term declines in mortality for the health of the surviving population (e.g., Murray & Lopez, 1996; Robine & Romieu, 1998). Similar to the problems discussed above for the United States, international differences in survey design, content, the measurement of health, and calculation methods have frustrated international comparisons of population health—particularly comparisons based on the expected number of years lived in good or bad health—an indicator of population health that integrates the mortality and morbidity experiences of a population. Although a growing number of countries are calculating these types of measures, efforts to institutionalize ongoing monitoring of changes in population health are thus far largely restricted to the developed nations (e.g., Robine, Jagger, & Egidi, 2000). In large part, these efforts have been sparked by the International Network on Healthy Life Expectancy (REVES). Recognized officially by the World Health Organization (WHO), REVES is an independent organization of scholars and policymakers dedicated to promoting international consistency in the design, measurement, and calculation of health expectancy measures used in monitoring population health. An alternative approach is that by the Global Burden of Disease Group—a collaborative effort between Harvard University, WHO, and the World Bank (e.g., Murray & Lopez, 1996). This latter approach focuses more on the use of vital statistics data and demographic modeling techniques in assessing cross-national differences in

population health (see Waidmann & Manton, 2000, for a more comprehensive review).

In some sense, these efforts to document the association between changes in mortality and the health of the surviving population have produced some important lessons for anticipating how global changes in population aging will influence the health of surviving populations (Crimmins, 1996). Foremost is the recognition that methodological factors are likely to cloud assessments of changes in population health—particularly when making cross-national comparisons. Methodological issues aside, international differences in health-care systems, public health goals and policies, and progress in disease fighting are likely to result in a high degree of cross-national variability in trends in population health (Murray & Lopez, 1996; World Health Organization, 2000). These factors, in combination, make it difficult to project future population health; such estimates are likely to be even more unreliable than mortality projections. Later in the discussion we review the available evidence to assess the general implications of projected trends in cross-national differences in mortality for cross-national differences in the health of the surviving population.

II. Fertility and Mortality Data for United Nations Estimates and Projections

The population estimates and projections referenced in our discussion of population aging were obtained using two educational software packages, DemoGraphics '96 and DemoTables '96. These software packages are an educational tool from the United Nations Population Fund (UNFPA), developed in association with the Netherlands Interdisciplinary Demographic Institute (NIDI) by Gerhard K.

Heilig (IIAASA), Vienna, Austria (Heilig, 1998a, 1998b). The data for the two software packages were provided by the Population Division of the United Nations Department for Economic and Social Information and Policy Analysis, and are from the *United Nations World Population Prospects, The 1996 Revision* (United Nations, 1996a, 1996b). A 1998 revision became available in 1999. Although some of the estimates differ slightly between the two revisions, the population aging trends shown here are unaffected.

We focus primarily on two major regions of the world to compare historical changes in population aging—more developed regions and less developed regions. More developed regions encompass Europe, Northern America, Japan, Australia and New Zealand. Less developed regions include all countries of Africa, Latin America and the Caribbean, Asia (excluding Japan), Melanesia, Micronesia, and Polynesia. We also provide region-specific estimates (e.g., Africa and Europe) and subregion information to demonstrate how international differences in population aging shift over the historical period 1950–2050. When pertinent to the discussion, we provide demographic estimates and projections of specific national populations.

Our analyses make use of demographic estimates of population age structures and vital rates to document the historical record since 1950. Changes in the demographic estimates over an approximately 50-year period are used to reference changes in population aging, and the sources of these changes. United Nations projections of population structure and vital rates are used to describe population aging as it is expected to be in the year 2050. Comparisons of the demographic estimates for 1995 and the projected estimates for 2050 provide the basis for making inferences about changes in population aging over the next (approxi-

mately) 50-year period. Details regarding the quality of the demographic estimates and the ways in which the projections were made can be found in *United Nations World Population Prospects, The 1996 Revision* (United Nations, 1996a, 1996b). Although the United Nations projections provide low, middle, and high variant estimates, all of our analyses in this chapter make use of the middle variant population projections for 2050.

Analysts must always approach demographic projections with skepticism. The fact that the United Nations projections were recently mirrored in projections made by the United States Census Bureau (U.S. Bureau of the Census, 1999) suggests the use of similar assumptions and data inputs rather than the calculation of reliable forecasts. Missing in the two sets of projections is a sense of the likelihood of one demographic future over another. Lee and Carter (1992) have developed a stochastic approach that provides upper and lower bounds for projections, although their approach has not been applied to the problem of forecasting global population aging into the next century. Lee and Tuljapurkar (1994) discuss the differences between their stochastic approach and the idea of uncertainty expressed in the demographic tradition of high, medium, and low variant projections. In the context of this recent methodological work, our use of the middle variant projection should not be interpreted as the most likely demographic future. It represents one of many possible futures. (Unanticipated epidemics, for example, have the potential to alter the demographic future. The HIV epidemic has led the United Nations to reduce projected declines in mortality in countries with high sero-prevalence of HIV. It is important to recognize, however, that these adjustments were done based on a strong set of assumptions rather than on a scientific model of the association between HIV prevalence and age-specific mortality rates. The anticipated increase in life expectancy in sub-Saharan Africa, for instance, could well be lower than projected—or higher.)

III. Population Age Structures around the World

In 1950, the world's population reached 2.5 billion people (see Table 4.1). The world was a place populated largely by children and adolescents—almost 44% of the total population was less than 20 years of age. Approximately 8% was 60 years of age and older, and only about 3% were 70 years of age and older. Worldwide, the elderly constituted only a small fragment of the world's population.

In 1950, however, the world was far from homogeneous with respect to population aging. The data in Table 4.1 show a number of substantial differences across countries and regions in terms of the percentage of a population that was older. More developed regions (i.e., Europe, Northern America, Japan, and Australia and New Zealand) had significantly more elderly persons in their populations relative to less developed regions (persons 60 years and older constituted 11.7% of the population in more developed regions compared to 6.4% in less developed regions).

By 1995, roughly the midpoint in the 100-year span of time we are considering, the percent of the world's population ages 60 years and older had grown only slightly from 8.1% to 9.5%. What had grown markedly since 1950, however, was the cross-national gap in population aging. Persons ages 60 years and older constituted 18.3% of the population in developed countries in 1995 compared to 11.7% in 1950—an increase of about 56%. Less developed regions, however, had aged only slightly. The percentage of persons younger than 20 years of age in 1995 was 44%—down from about 48% 50

years earlier. The percent of persons ages 60 years and older changed hardly at all—from 6.4% to 7.3%.

These figures underscore why population aging is currently viewed primarily as a social problem of developed nations. Historically, over much of the 20th century, population aging has been concentrated in more developed regions of the world. Within the more developed regions, Europe especially shows evidence of the demographic revolution to a mature population. Approximately 20% of Western and Southern Europe's populations in 1995 were 60 years of age or older. On a worldwide basis, Greece had the greatest percentage of persons older than age 60 in 1995—22.1% (results not shown). Sweden and Italy followed closely behind with 21.8% of their populations aged 60 years and older. Canada and the United States lagged significantly behind Europe—about 16% of the North American population was 60 years of age and older in 1995.

Projections to 2050 show that the percent of the world's population aged 60 years and older is expected to be about 21%—about the level of Europe presently. The percent of older persons in developed nations is expected to grow over a 50-year period from 18.3% to 31.2%—almost a third of the population. The elderly population in the United States is projected to comprise 27.1% of the nation's total population, indicating that the United States will experience much less extreme population aging compared to the majority of developed nations. The percent of older persons in developing nations is expected to grow from 7.3% to 19.2% over the same period. Less developed parts of the world in 2050 will have populations that have roughly the same age structure as developed nations in 1995 have. Developed nations are moving toward having very old populations while less developing nations are moving toward old populations.

Table 4.1

Population Distribution by Age Groups, 1950, 1995, and 2050[a]

Geographic area	Population (1000s) Total	1950 (% of total population)					1995 (% of total population)					2050 (% of total population)				
		0–19	20–59	60+	70+	80–	0–19	20–59	60+	70+	80+	0–19	20–59	60+	70+	80+
World total	2,523,878	43.9	48.0	8.1	2.9	0.5	40.4	50.1	9.5	4.0	1.1	27.4	51.9	20.7	10.4	3.4
More developed regions	812,687	35.7	52.5	11.7	4.8	1.0	26.5	55.2	18.3	8.9	3.0	22.6	46.2	31.2	18.6	8.0
Less developed regions	1,711,191	47.8	45.8	6.4	2.1	0.3	44.0	48.8	7.3	2.7	0.6	28.0	52.7	19.2	9.2	2.8
Least developed countries	197,572	51.2	43.4	5.4	1.8	0.3	54.4	40.8	4.8	1.7	0.3	32.8	55.6	11.6	4.5	1.0
Africa	223,974	52.7	42.2	5.1	1.7	0.3	54.3	40.7	5.0	1.8	0.3	32.7	55.6	11.8	4.8	1.1
Asia	1,402,021	45.6	46.5	6.7	2.2	0.3	41.0	50.8	8.2	3.1	0.7	26.4	51.7	21.9	10.8	3.4
Eastern Asia	671,156	44.0	48.5	7.4	2.3	0.3	33.3	56.4	10.3	4.1	0.9	24.4	48.7	26.9	14.5	5.0
Europe	547,318	34.6	53.3	12.1	5.1	1.1	26.1	55.0	18.9	8.9	3.0	21.6	45.6	32.8	19.2	7.9
Southern Europe	109,012	35.9	51.5	11.3	4.7	1.1	24.4	55.4	20.2	9.5	3.1	19.5	43.3	37.2	24.3	10.6
Western Europe	140,916	30.6	54.4	15.0	6.2	1.2	23.5	56.4	20.1	10.3	3.8	21.0	44.7	34.2	21.4	10.1
Latin America and Caribbean	166,337	49.8	44.2	6.0	2.1	0.4	44.0	48.5	7.5	3.1	0.8	26.8	50.9	22.2	11.7	4.0
Northern America	171,617	34.4	53.2	12.4	4.8	1.1	28.6	55.0	16.3	8.8	3.0	24.7	47.9	27.4	16.1	7.4
Australia/New Zealand	10,127	33.8	53.6	12.6	4.9	1.1	28.8	55.7	15.5	7.9	2.4	24.5	47.8	27.7	16.6	7.1

[a]From United Nations (1996a, 1996b).

This point can be seen in Figures 4.1, 4.2, and 4.3 which show the age–sex pyramids (age–sex structures) for more developed regions and less developed regions of the world for 1950, 1995, and 2050. The young age of the population in less developed nations in 1950 is indicated by the pyramid's broad base in Figure 4.1. Note also that the pyramid quickly tapers with age, indicating proportionately fewer people at adult ages in the population—particularly past age 60. The pyramids for 1995 in Figure 4.2 show the relatively mature population of the more developed nations. The pyramid has achieved a squared look compared to that for 1950. The size of the very young age groups no longer exceeds the sizes of the prime adult population and in fact is smaller than these age groups. The pyramid for the less developed regions, however, remains distinctly broad based much like that shown for 1950.

By 2050, the pyramid for the more developed regions (see Figure 4.3) shows a projected completion of the demographic revolution as indicated by the relatively square age–sex structure. Although not indicated in Table 4.1, many countries in more developed regions are projected to stabilize and then lose population in the next 50 years. This pattern is expected to characterize countries such as the United Kingdom, Spain, Greece, Germany, the Netherlands, France, and Finland. Note that this is only a partial list. Note also that population loss will be confined nearly exclusively to Europe. The American population is expected to continue to grow, although relatively slowly during the next 50 years. By 2050, the American population is projected to be 347.5 million people—up from 267 million in 1995.

Although the projected population pyramid for less developed regions in 2050 does not match the squared shape of that for the more developed regions, its shape nonetheless indicates the remarkable achievement of a mature population.

Note particularly the squared base extending into prime adult ages. The shape of the pyramid is reminiscent of that for more developed nations in 1995. Clearly, these projections reinforce the idea that the demographic revolution toward an older and more stable population will no longer be confined to more developed countries.

IV. Fertility and Mortality Changes Driving Changes in Age Structure

World fertility levels in 1950 were very high as indicated by a total fertility rate (TFR) of 5.0 (see Table 4.2). The TFR can be roughly translated as the expected number of children in a completed family. Mortality rates were also relatively high in 1950 as indicated by life expectancies at birth of 45.1 years for males and 47.6 years for females. Approximately 156 infants died out of 1000 births at that point in history.

More developed nations in 1950 were already in the midst of the fertility and mortality revolutions, having relatively low fertility and mortality rates. More developed regions had an expected completed family size of 2.8 in comparison with 6.2 in less developed regions. Life expectancy differences across the two regions also were stark. Male life expectancy in more developed regions was 63.9 and female life expectancy was 69.0. These expectancies exceeded those for less developed regions by 23.8 and 27.2 years respectively!

By 1995, world fertility had dropped precipitously with an expected completed family size of three children. Mortality also dropped considerably over the 50-year period. Life expectancy increased considerably on a worldwide basis to 62.2 years for males and 66.5 years for females. When comparing the major regions of the world, one can observe that

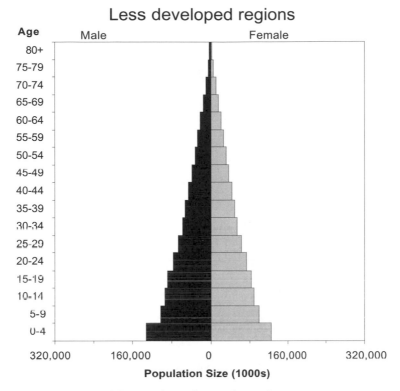

Less developed regions

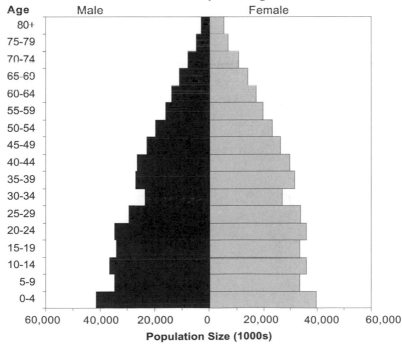

More developed regions

Figure 4.1 Estimates of population by age groups and sex, 1950. (From United Nations, 1996a, and 1996b.)

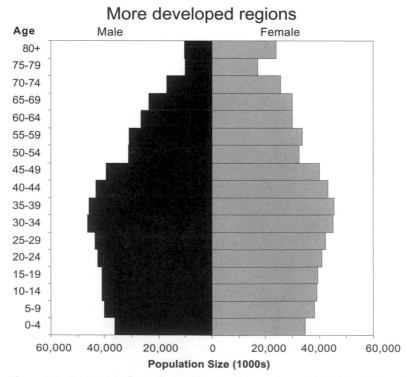

Figure 4.2 Estimates of population by age groups and sex, 1995. (From United Nations, 1996a, 1996b.)

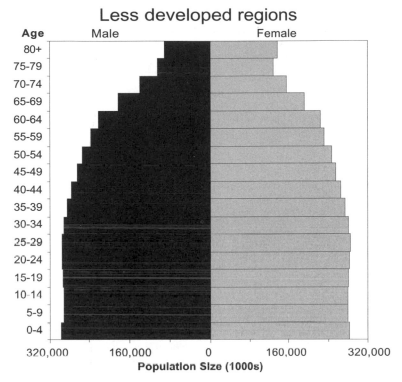

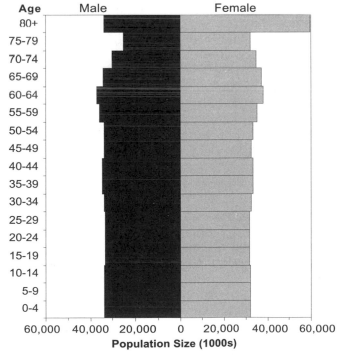

Figure 4.3 Projections of population by age groups and sex, 2050, medium variant. (From United Nations, 1996a, 1996b.)

Table 4.2
Vital Rates, 1950, 1995, and 2050[a]

Geographic area	1950–1955				1990–1995				2045–2050			
	TFR	IMR	e(0)M	e(0)F	TFR	IMR	e(0)M	e(0)F	TFR	IMR	e(0)M	e(0)F
World total	5.0	156.0	45.1	47.8	3.0	62.0	62.2	66.5	2.1	16.0	74.2	79.1
More developed regions	2.8	58.0	63.9	69.0	1.7	11.0	70.4	78.0	2.1	5.0	78.0	84.0
Less developed regions	6.2	179.0	40.1	41.8	3.3	68.0	60.6	63.7	2.1	17.0	73.6	78.2
Least developed countries	6.5	194.0	34.9	36.2	5.5	109.0	48.7	50.8	2.1	25.0	69.9	73.5
Africa	6.6	185.0	36.4	39.2	5.7	94.0	50.4	53.3	2.1	22.0	70.4	74.5
Asia	5.9	180.0	40.6	42.0	2.8	62.0	63.2	66.0	2.1	15.0	74.8	79.3
Eastern Asia	5.7	181.0	41.4	44.6	1.9	41.0	67.6	71.9	2.1	7.0	76.4	81.1
Europe	2.6	72.0	63.4	68.5	1.6	13.0	68.5	76.9	2.0	5.0	76.9	83.3
Southern Europe	2.7	76.0	61.5	65.1	1.4	11.0	72.7	79.3	2.0	6.0	79.1	85.0
Western Europe	2.4	45.0	65.1	69.9	1.5	7.0	73.2	80.2	2.0	5.0	79.1	85.5
Latin America and Caribbean	5.9	126.0	49.8	53.1	2.9	40.0	65.3	71.8	2.1	10.0	75.2	81.5
Northern America	3.5	29.0	66.2	71.9	2.0	9.0	72.8	79.5	2.1	5.0	79.1	84.7
Australia/New Zealand	3.3	24.0	67.0	72.3	1.9	7.0	74.5	80.3	2.1	5.0	79.9	85.4

[a]TFR, total fertility rate. IMR, infant mortality rate. e(0)M and e(0)F reference the life expectancy at birth of males and females, respectively. From United Nations (1996a, 1996b).

the fertility and mortality declines were greatest in less developed countries. Fertility rates almost halved, and more than 20 years were added to life expectancy in less developed countries. Declines in fertility and mortality were also experienced in more developed countries although to a lesser extent. The TFR in developed countries was 1.7—a fertility rate significantly below that needed for population replacement and life expectancy grew to over 70 years for both males and females. Fertility and mortality rates of this magnitude account for the advanced aged structures of more developed countries, and in some instances the expected declines in the overall size of these nations' populations between 2025–2050. Note that among the developed nations, the TFR for North America was 2.0 in 1995—slightly higher than most European countries.

By 2050, the TFR is projected to be 2.1 worldwide. Note that the projection implies *no differences separating the fertility experiences of more and less developed regions of the world*. Note, also, that although a mortality gap is expected to exist between more and less developed regions of the world, the mortality of less developed countries in 2050 is expected to be lower than that experienced by developed nations in 1995! Not surprisingly, therefore, the expected age structures of less developed countries in 2050 are indicative of mature populations converging on those of more developed nations (see Figure 4.3).

Assuming the plausibility of the projected vital rates, the pace of change in the vital rates for the less developed region of the world over the 100-year period is extraordinary given the fertility and mortality rates of 1950. In the projection shown here, fertility rates are expected to drop from 6.2 to 2.1 between 1950 and 2050, and life expectancy is expected to grow from about 40 years to about 74 years for males and 78 years for females.

If this demographic future occurs, or one similar, these revolutionary demographic changes will foretell dramatic shifts in the age structure of the world's population over time.

The pace of expected change in the vital rates in more developed regions is also noteworthy although much less dramatic. Fertility between 1950 and 2050 is expected to decline somewhat, from 2.8 to 2.1; this relatively small change is due primarily to the already low fertility in 1950. Note also the expected rebound in fertility by 2050 from the very low rates experienced in the 1990s. Mortality over the same 100-year period also declines, but again, the declines are not expected to be of the magnitude experienced in less developed countries. This is due, however, primarily to a key assumption in the projection (i.e., that mortality has far less to fall in developed nations). The idea behind this assumption has generated considerable debate in the demographic literature (see Manton, Stallard, & Tolley, 1991; Olshansky and Carnes, 1994; Wilmoth, 1997) and there is little consensus. The key lesson from the estimates is that the demographic revolutions going on in less developed countries are already dramatic, and, assuming that the trend continues, will exert profound effects on the age structures of those countries. The demographic revolution occurring in more developed countries, although no less important, is much quieter and part of a longer historical trend that began well before 1950.

V. Implications of the Demographic Revolution for Population Health

The prior discussion regarding the ambiguous link between mortality changes and the health of the surviving population makes clear the difficulty in making projections of population health. This most likely explains the paucity of population health projections in the demographic and public health literatures. Kinsella (2000) and Waidmann and Manton (2000) review the available evidence on cross-national differences in "trends" in population health, relying typically on estimates from two points in time to make inferences about the general patterns of health changes in the population. These two studies are careful to note the limitations of these data (i.e., two points in time do not necessarily imply a trend). Based on available evidence, it appears that there is a generally positive association between improvements in life expectancy and the years individuals can expect to live in good health. The data for eleven developed nations indicate either improvements or relative stagnation in healthy life expectancy as overall life expectancy has improved; no countries experienced a decline in healthy life expectancy with improved life expectancy. Nonetheless, the scarcity of estimates points to the difficulties in making strong inferences about the relationship between mortality changes and future changes in population health.

Murray (1997; Murray & Lopez, 1996) has developed projections of population health for a 40-year period (1990–2020) based on a measure called disability-adjusted life years (DALYs). The DALY measure references the years of life lost in a population from premature mortality combined with the years of life lost due to disability. (The conceptual framework behind the DALY, as well as a discussion of its computation, can be found in Murray & Lopez, 1996.) Increases in the value of DALYs over time denote a decline in the health of a population, (i.e., this denotes an increased departure from life in perfect health). Declines in the value of DALYs reference improvements in the health of the population. Murray (1997) discusses the procedures used to make the projections, with careful attention given to the assumptions made in developing the projections.

Summarizing Murray's results, there is no clear pattern of change in overall levels of population health for the 1990–2020 period. DALYs in which all major conditions (i.e., communicable diseases, noncommunicable diseases, and injuries) are grouped are expected both to increase and decrease, depending on the region of the world. European nations, for example, are expected to experience very little change in population health, while improving health is expected in India and Asia (except China). Worse population health is anticipated in the remaining parts of the world.

Increases in DALYs for noncommunicable diseases (e.g., the major chronic diseases) are projected by Murray's approach for much of the world; the lone exception is the developed countries where chronic diseases currently represent the vast majority of health problems in the population. Much of the expected increase in the DALYs caused by noncommunicable diseases is due to the aging of the population into the high-risk ages for these diseases. The forces of population aging (i.e., changes in the age structures of populations) appear to outweigh epidemiological improvements (i.e., pathological changes in the aging process at the individual level)—at least in this model.

We suggest a cautious approach in interpreting Murray's projections, and Murray himself agrees with our concern. Moreover, we think it worthwhile to develop projections of health expectancies along the lines proposed by REVES such as disability-free life expectancy and life free of functional limitations. These expectancies are based on the International Classification of Diseases and Disability (ICIDH) and avoid the sometimes controversial assumptions that go into constructing DALYs. The health expectancies also are less subject to the effects of changing population composition, providing for a cleaner assessment of the association between changes in overall life expectancy and expectancies of the years individuals will experience major health problems.

VI. Summary

Many Americans view population aging as a uniquely American experience. Frequently cast as a social problem, population aging is seen as the culprit threatening Social Security and Medicare. The phenomenon of the "sandwich generation," middle-aged and older persons providing care to very elderly parents, has also been laid at the feet of population aging. Demographic determinism rather than the inadequacies of social, economic, and political policy garners much of the public's attention.

Here, we have shown that the United States experience parallels that of more developed nations. And, in fact, the population of the United States is expected to be younger than many European countries and continue to grow over the next 50 years. In stark contrast, among the more developed countries, most European populations will stabilize (i.e., the number of deaths will roughly equal the number of births), and some European countries will experience a decline in population size as the number of deaths in the aged populations exceeds the number of births. Some scholars have characterized this trend as "a profound development in industrial societies" (Davis, Bernstam, & Ricardo-Campbell, 1987, p. x). As Davis (1987) observes,

Looked at in the long-run perspective of human evolution, the below-replacement fertility now characterizing most of the industrial countries is anomalous. Never before in recorded history—not in the Great Depression, not in the eighteenth and nineteenth centuries, and not in ancient times—has fertility been so low for whole societies as it is now in the industrial world. And never has it been so low during the millions of years of hominid evolution. (p. 48)

Others have cast a more negative spin on this development, inferring "disastrous demographic consequences" and "population 'implosion'" (Bourgeois-Pichat, 1987, p. 25). This perception has contributed in no small degree to the plethora of pronatalist policies in many European countries—none of which appear to have substantially altered the trend of below-replacement fertility.

Until recently, much of the demographic community's attention was directed at population aging in more developed nations, frequently characterized as industrialized nations. Viewed in a larger historical context, however, the demographic experience of the more developed nations can more accurately be viewed as the leading edge of a worldwide demographic revolution. In general, the mortality revolution began in more developed nations in the mid-19th century with the advent of disease-control technologies (Easterlin, 1997). With the noted exception of France, sustained fertility declines began in Western European countries in the latter part of the 19th century. With the spread of the mortality and fertility revolutions in the 20th century to Latin America, the Middle East, Asia and lastly to Sub-Saharan Africa, the estimates shown here illustrate that the large gap in fertility rates and life expectancy eroded somewhat between 1950 and 1995. This erosion is expected to continue such that by 2050 very few international differences in fertility and mortality are likely to remain. At the end of the 100-year period, therefore, current projections indicate that the demographic revolution to older, stable populations will be very close to completion. Globally, the elderly will constitute a significant portion of the overall population, with few substantial differences expected in this pattern across national populations.

Current projections of future trends in population health point to an optimistic future for some countries and a somewhat less optimistic future, in terms of the burden of disease, for other countries. Although these population health projections are clearly preliminary, one characteristic of these projections will almost certainly characterize future trends in population health—cross-national variability. Over an extended period of time, it is likely that we will observe a variety of changes in population health. Some countries might well experience improvements, subsequent declines, and then future gains, while other countries will experience completely different patterns of change. National differences in public health priorities, health-care infrastructure, population composition, and progress in disease fighting will almost certainly lead to different rates of improvement, and perhaps declines, in population health.

Neither improvements nor declines in population health necessarily imply success or failure in improving the health of a population. This point is important to underscore, since indicators of population health are frequently used to assess the population's demand for health-care services, evaluate the effectiveness of health-care infrastructures, and gauge progress toward public health goals. Under conditions of falling mortality, a decline in population health, for example, is an

expected epidemiological stage that can occur when increases in life expectancy are greater than reductions in the incidence of health problems. In addition, at any one time we are likely to see improvements in some indicators of health and not others, and improvements in some age groups and not others. (Crimmins, 1996, p. S224.)

Success in improving health is most appropriately gauged by using a range of indicators of population health that encompass changes across the various domains of health.

Some individuals might question the inevitability of the demographic changes described above. Our reasoning is based on the fact that fertility and mortality changes are sweeping the world. No part of the world is untouched, and no return to the patterns of high fertility and mortality is anticipated. The universality of the demographic changes and their lack of reversibility do not stem from some intrinsic demographic law. Rather, the mortality and fertility revolutions driving population aging are "rooted in breakthroughs in human knowledge about methods of . . . disease control, and, short of a global catastrophe, this knowledge will not be lost" (Easterlin, 1997 p. 145). Seen in this context, the worldwide march toward an older population marks the triumph of scientific contributions in enhancing the health and well-being of individuals, and symbolizes the demographic coming of age on a global scale.

Acknowledgment

Partial support for this research was provided by grants from the National Institute on Aging (R01 AG 11758) and the National Institute of Child Health and Human Development (5 P30 HD28263).

References

Bonneux, L., Barendregt, J. J., Meeter, K., Bonsel, G. J., & van der Maas, P. J. (1994). Estimating clinical morbidity due to ischemic heart disease and congestive heart failure: The future rise of heart failure. *American Journal of Public Health, 84,* 20–28.

Bourgeois-Pichat, J. (1987). The unprecedented shortage of births in Europe. In K. Davis & M. S. Bernstam, & R. Ricardo-Campbell (Eds.), *Below-replacement fertility in industrial societies* (pp. 3–25). New York: Cambridge University Press.

Crimmins, E. M. (1996). Mixed trends in population health among older adults. *Journal of Gerontology: Social Sciences, 51B,* S223–S225.

Crimmins, E. M. (1998). Is disability declining among the elderly? Defining disability and examining trends. *Critical Issues in Aging, 2,* 10–11.

Crimmins, E. M., Hayward, M. D., & Saito, Y. (1994). Changing mortality and morbidity rates and the health status and life expectancy of the older population. *Demography, 31,* 159–175.

Crimmins, E. M., Saito, Y., & Ingegneri, D. (1997). Trends in disability-free life expectancy in the United States. *Population and Development Review, 23,* 555–572.

Davis, K. (1987). Low fertility in evolutionary perspective. In K. Davis, M. S. Bernstam, & R. Ricardo-Campbell (Eds.), *Below-replacement fertility in industrial societies* (pp. 48–65). New York: Cambridge University Press.

Davis, K., Bernstam, M. S., & Ricardo-Campbell, R. (1987). *Below-replacement fertility in industrial societies.* New York: Cambridge University Press.

Easterlin, R. A. (1991). The economic impact of prospective population changes in advanced industrial countries: An historical perspective. *Journals of Gerontology, 46,* S299–S309.

Easterlin, R. A. (1997). *Growth triumphant, the twenty-first century in historical perspective.* Ann Arbor: The University of Michigan Press.

Freedman, V. A., & Martin, L. G. (1998). Understanding trends in functional limitations among older Americans. *American Journal of Public Health, 88,* 1457–1462.

Heilig, G. K. (1998a). *Demographics '96.* New York: Netherlands Interdisciplinary Demographic Institute and the United Nations Population Fund.

Heilig, G. K. (1998b). *Demotables '96.* New York: Netherlands Interdisciplinary Demographic Institute and the United Nations Population Fund.

Kinsella, K. (2000). Demographic dimensions of global aging. *Journal of Family Issues, 21,* 541–558.

Lee, R. D., & Carter, L. (1992). Modeling and forecasting the time series of U.S. mortality. *Journal of the American Statistical Association, 87,* 659–671.

Lee, R. D., & Tuljapurkar, S. (1994). Stochastic population forecasts for the U.S.: Beyond high, medium, and low. *Journal of the*

American Statistical Association, 89, 1175–1189.

Manton, K. G., Stallard, E., & Corder, L. S. (1995). Changes in morbidity and chronic disability in the U.S. elderly population: Evidence from the 1982, 1984, and 1989 National Long Term Care Surveys. *Journal of Gerontology: Social Sciences, 50B,* S194–S204.

Manton, K. G., Stallard, E., & Tolley, H. D. (1991). Limits to human life expectancy: Evidence, prospects, and implications. *Population and Development Review, 17,* 603–657.

Murray, C. J. L. (1997). Alternative projections of mortality and disability by cause 1990–2020. *Lancet, 349,* 1498–1504.

Murray, C. J. L., & Lopez, A. D. (1996). *The global burden of disease.* Cambridge, MA. Harvard University Press.

Olstansky, S. J., & Carnes, B. A. (1994). Demographic perspectives on human senescence. *Population and Development Review, 20,* 57–80.

Robine, J. M., Jagger, C., & Egidi, V. (2000). *Selection of a coherent set of health indicators: A first step towards a user's guide to health expectancies for the European Union.* Montpellier, France: Euro-REVES.

Robine, J. M., & Romieu, I. (1998). *Healthy active ageing: Health expectancies at age 65 in the different parts of the world.* Paper presented at the World Health Organization Expert Committee on Determinants of Healthy Ageing, Geneva, Switzerland.

Roper Starch Worldwide. (1999). *Baby boomers envision their retirement: An AARP segmentation analysis.* Washington, DC: Roper Starch World Wide, Inc. and AARP.

Schulz, J. H., Borowski, A., & Crown, W. H. (1991). *Economics of population aging.* New York: Auburn House.

U. S. Bureau of the Census (1999). *World population profile: 1998* (WP/98). Washington, DC: U.S. Government Printing Office.

United Nations. (1991). *United Nations principles for older persons* (Resolution 46/91). New York: United Nations.

United Nations. (1992). *Proclamation on aging* (A/RES/47/5). New York: United Nations Division for Social Policy and Development.

United Nations. (1994). *The programme of action of the international conference on population and development* (United Nations Publication No. E.95.XIII.18). New York: United Nations Department of Economic and Social Affairs.

United Nations. (1996a). *World population prospects: The 1996 revision. Annex i: Demographic indicators.* New York: Department for Economic and Social Information and Policy Analysis, Population Division.

United Nations. (1996b). *World population prospects: The 1996 revision. Annex ii and iii: Demographic indicators by major area, region, and country.* New York: Department for Economic and Social Information and Policy Analysis, Population Division.

Verbrugge, L. M. (1989). Recent, present, and future health of American adults. In L. Breslow & J. E. Fielding & L. B. Love (Eds.), *Annual Review of Public Health* (Vol. 10, pp. 333–351). Palo Alto, CA: Annual Reviews Inc.

Verbrugge, L. M., & Patrick, D. L. (1995). Seven chronic conditions: Their impact on U.S. adults' activity levels and use of medical services. *American Journal of Public Health, 85,* 173–182.

Waidmann, T. A., & Manton, K. G. (2000). *Measuring trends in disability among the elderly: An international review.* Washington, DC: Urban Institute.

Wilmoth, J. R. (1997). In search of limits. In K. W. Wachter & C. E. Finch (Eds.), *Between Zeus and the salmon* (pp. 38–44). Washington, DC: National Academy Press.

World Health Organization. (2000). *The world health report 2000.* Geneva, Switzerland: World Health Organization.

Five

Economic and Social Implications of Demographic Patterns

William J. Serow

I. Introduction

The aim of this chapter is to review the economic and social consequences of the aging of human populations. Its focus is on the macroeconomy or society. This perspective excludes individual-level biological or economic changes, except when such changes are likely to have aggregate-level implications.

The chapter begins with an overview of the role that each of the three components of population change—fertility, mortality, and migration—play in societal aging. This approach allows some consideration of the economic and social consequences of aging within nations. The next section is the heart of the chapter. It deals with the implications of changes in overall population age structure and anticipated changes in the age structure of the older population itself. This line of thought is continued in the next section, which focuses on the two principal issues that have captured the attention of most researchers in this subject area—pensions and retirement income in general, and the financing of health care. Finally, the chapter attempts to place all of these issues into a broader

socioeconomic framework by speculating how aging will affect and be affected by globalization and the potential expansion of free trade.

II. Demographic Determinants of Population Aging

As is now well established, the aging of populations is brought about by sustained low fertility rates, reinforced by declining levels of mortality at all ages. At the level of large political entities, migration behaviors would only rarely affect the aggregate aging of the population and not in any theoretically predictable way. As the size of the geographic unit of analysis grows smaller, though, the potential role of migration as an important determinant of population aging increases. The outcome of interplay between these factors in influencing population aging, especially low fertility and declining levels of mortality, have been widely studied and need not be considered here in any detail (see, e.g., the classic paper by Coale, 1956, and the more recent work of Calot & Sardon, 1999). What is critical here is an awareness of past and prospective trends in fertility and mortality as well as their implications for the age structure of a population.

A. Fertility Levels

It is now generally recognized that reductions in the level of fertility have been primarily responsible for the current aging of populations throughout the industrialized world. Decreases in the absolute number of children in the population have the immediate effect of increasing the proportion of all other age groups. Depending on previous demographic behaviors, the aging that immediately occurs with fertility reduction may well have quite favorable economic outcomes since increases in the relative size of the working age population are both highly probable and usually highly desirable outcomes (Freidlander & Klinov-Malul, 1980).

Although there have been in the past and will continue to be in the future occasional rises in period fertility, the norms for completed fertility by cohorts seem to be well established. Fertility levels throughout the industrialized world have been at or below the replacement level for a generation or more at present, and it is difficult to find any evidence suggesting any significant increase in the foreseeable future.

In terms of population aging, the effects of past and prospective changes in fertility are in a real sense quite well known and predictable. Unless there is a dramatic reversal of the long secular trend towards the one-to-two child norm, there is no doubt that the aging "from the bottom" will persist. The impact of this outcome is (barring other demographic shifts) an extended period of time characterized by some as being a "demographic gift" (Bloom & Williamson, 1998). Evenson (1999) characterizes this period as when the labor force grows, but the number of prelabor force consumers declines.

Although most explicitly related to fertility declines in developing countries, the principle would seem to apply equally in advanced nations. In this context, it should perhaps be restated as the period when changes in the relative size of the labor force exceed those of other portions of the population. In the context of developing nations, the focus is placed on differences between the working age and younger segments of the population; in the context of advanced nations, the point of contrast is typically between working age and older segments.

Throughout this and much of the rest of the discussion of population forecasts in this chapter, it is well to recall the inherent degree of uncertainty in any population projection (Friedland & Summer, 1999). This uncertainty increases as both the size of the population in question and the proximity of the projection date to the present diminish (Ahlburg & Land, 1992). It is *not* the intention here to argue that these (or any) projections are statements of absolute fact. They are rather chosen to illustrate the most probable course of demographic events and to suggest the type of policy and other responses that would seem appropriate. It is critical for policy makers to monitor demographic behaviors over time and alter policy choices accordingly. With particular regard to the older population, it is well to bear in mind that there is less uncertainty regarding their future numbers than is true for younger components of the population. If we accept age 60 as the lower threshold of "the older population," then it is the case that everyone who will attain this age for the next 60 years has already been born. Absolute numbers will depend on future courses of mortality and, depending on geographic considerations, possibly migration, but not on fertility. However, relative numbers (that is, the proportion of total population represented by persons aged 60 and over) are dependent on all three components of population change.

To illustrate the role that fertility levels and changes may play in the process of population aging, consider the data shown in Table 5.1. These show past and forecasted fertility levels (here, the net reproduction rate or the number of surviving daughters a woman would expect to bear over her lifetime) as well as broad age groups of the population for Australia, Hong Kong, and Sweden. The data are from 1950 through 2050 and are taken from the United Nations' (1998) *World Population Prospects: The 1996 Revision*. The countries were chosen because they represent three quite different paths to low fertility and are suggestive therefore of demographic consequences owing to differences in both timing and extent of fertility decline.

Hong Kong began the post World War II era with high and rising fertility levels, a phenomenon by no means uncommon in the early stages of the so-called demographic transition. In approximately one generation, between the 1960–1965 and 1980–1985 quinquennia, effective fertility plummeted to levels below replacement. The U.N. demographic staff forecasts that such subreplacement levels will persist throughout the projection period, although gradually rising after the first quarter of the 21st century. Hong Kong's political status has, of course, recently changed, and it is now a "Special Administrative Region" of the People's Republic of China. Accordingly, projections are even more uncertain than usual here, owing to the possibility of changes in regulations governing migration to Hong Kong from the rest of China.

In Sweden, by way of contrast, fertility has been quite near replacement from both a retrospective and a prospective point of view. Other than a "baby-bust"

Table 5.1
Fertility and Demographic Indicators: Australia, Hong Kong, and Sweden, 1950–2050[a]

Year	Australia				Hong Kong				Sweden			
		Percent aged				Percent aged				Percent aged		
	NRR	0–14	15–59	60+	NRR	0–14	15–59	60+	NRR	0–14	15–59	60+
1950	1.5	27	60	13	1.9	30	66	4	1.0	23	62	15
1955	1.6	29	59	12	2.1	35	61	4	1.1	24	60	16
1960	1.5	30	58	12	2.4	41	54	5	1.1	22	61	17
1965	1.4	30	58	12	1.8	40	54	6	1.0	21	61	18
1970	1.2	29	59	12	1.4	37	56	7	0.9	21	59	20
1975	1.0	28	59	13	1.1	30	61	9	0.8	21	58	21
1980	0.9	25	61	14	0.9	26	64	10	0.8	20	58	22
1985	0.9	24	61	15	0.7	23	66	11	0.9	17	59	24
1990	0.9	22	62	16	0.6	22	65	13	1.0	18	59	23
1995	0.9	22	62	16	0.6	20	66	14	0.9	19	59	22
2000	0.9	21	63	16	0.6	17	68	15	0.9	19	58	23
2005	0.9	20	63	17	0.7	16	68	16	0.9	18	59	23
2010	1.0	20	61	19	0.7	14	68	18	1.0	18	57	25
2015	1.0	20	60	20	0.7	14	64	22	1.0	17	57	26
2020	1.0	19	59	22	0.8	14	59	27	1.0	18	55	27
2025	1.0	19	57	24	0.8	13	55	32	1.0	18	54	28
2030	1.0	19	56	25	0.8	13	52	35	1.0	18	53	29
2040	1.0	18	55	27	0.9	13	49	38	1.0	18	53	29
2050		18	54	28		14	47	39		18	53	29

[a]NRR, net reproduction rate is for 5- and 10-year periods, beginning with year stated. From United Nations (1998).

decade from the mid-1970s through the mid-1980s, fertility levels have not, nor are they forecasted to, deviate by more than 10% from replacement over any given 5-year period.

Australia effectively combines fertility behaviors with similarities to the experiences of both Hong Kong and Sweden. At the beginning of the projection period, in 1950, fertility was relatively high and rose somewhat, reflecting the post-World War II "baby boom" characteristic of many economically advanced nations. Fertility declined to slightly below replacement in recent years, but like Sweden, Australia's fertility is expected to regain the replacement level in the immediate future and then remain at that level throughout the projection period.

The phenomenon of a demographic gift due to fertility patterns can be seen quite clearly in the Hong Kong age structure data. Coinciding with the onset of low fertility, there is an extended period— from 1980 through 2020—when roughly two-thirds of the population is between the ages of 15 and 59. Certainly there is a reversal in the composition of the other components of the population, but nonetheless these numbers suggest a nontrivial advantage over this period relative to those of Australia and Sweden, where the proportions hover at about 60% through 2020. It is the long-term changes that are perhaps most striking, though also the most temporally remote. The ultimate effect of sustained subreplacement fertility in Hong Kong is suddenly realized in the year 2020 and beyond, when the relative number of persons of working age begins to decline precipitously. Such a decline is present, but much more gradual, in the cases of Australia and Sweden.

In sum, the effect that changes in fertility eventually have on the process of population aging depend greatly upon the magnitude and tempo of fertility changes. Unquestionably, fertility at or below the replacement level if sustained over time will, other things being equal, lead to substantial increases in the relative number of older persons in a population. An abrupt decline in fertility from initially high levels can lead to a relatively long period in the immediate future of favorable (from the perspective of age structure) economic outcomes, followed by a sudden reversal of fortunes. Conversely, constant or more gradual fertility reductions may be lacking the "demographic gift," but are also unlikely to be characterized by dramatic and potentially adverse changes in age structure. Consequently, assessment of the economic implications of such behavior depends in considerable part on the time preferences of the analyst. The greater the relative preference for the present and near term future over the longer term, the greater one would favor the precipitously declining and very low fertility behavior of Hong Kong. However, it should be recalled that the "demographic gift" is very much a transitional state and the momentum effect identified by Keyfitz (1971) applies in reverse when fertility persistently remains below the replacement level (Kim & Schoen, 1997). In the case of contemporary Europe, for example, Preston and Guillot (1997) find that constant fertility at the current level would ultimately decrease the population by about one fourth, versus only 2% if replacement fertility were immediately realized.

B. Mortality Levels

The impact of reductions in mortality upon age structure depends on the specific ages at which they occur. Typically, mortality reductions are greatest at the ages where mortality levels are the highest, that is, at the beginning and end of life. Reductions in mortality that are concentrated among infants and children have the demographic consequence identical to an *increase* in fertility, namely an upsurge in the number of young persons in the population.

Using the United States as a representative example of mortality changes in economically advanced nations, overall longevity (as measured by life expectancy at birth) has increased by 55% during the present century. As illustrated by the data in Table 5.2, the greatest increases (50% or more) in life expectancy (and therefore the greatest reductions in mortality) have occurred at the first year of life and at all ages from 70 on. By partitioning overall mortality change into two approximately equally long periods (1900 to 1951 and 1951 to 1997), we can also see that the reductions in mortality among the elderly are concentrated in the more recent decades, while infant and childhood reductions largely occurred prior to World War II. Although comparative studies generally find that mortality at older ages is low in the United States relative to that of other economically advanced countries (Himes, 1994; Manton & Vaupel, 1995), there is no reason to doubt that this same generic pattern applies elsewhere.

Similarly, recent U.S. Census Bureau projections (Day, 1993) of the population assume that although life expectancy at birth will increase by about 8% between 1995 and 2050, life expectancy at age 65 is projected to rise by 31% during this same interval. Life expectancy is forecast to rise by a total of six years overall during this period; the Bureau projects that five of these six years will occur at ages 65 and over.

The extent to which future changes in mortality may result in a substantially greater expectation of life at birth than is now found in Japan (currently 81 years),

Table 5.2

Changes in Longevity, by Age: United States, 1900–1997[a]

Age	Life expectancy at this age			Percent change		
	1900–1902	1949–1951	1997	1900–1995	1900–1951	1951–1997
0	49.2	68.1	76.5	55.4%	38.2%	12.4%
1	55.2	69.2	76.1	37.9%	25.3%	10.0%
5	55.0	65.5	72.2	31.3%	19.2%	10.2%
10	51.1	60.7	67.2	31.4%	18.8%	10.6%
15	46.8	55.9	62.3	33.1%	19.4%	11.4%
20	42.8	51.2	57.5	34.4%	19.7%	12.3%
25	39.1	46.6	52.8	35.0%	19.0%	13.4%
30	35.5	41.9	48.1	35.5%	18.0%	14.8%
35	31.9	37.3	43.4	36.0%	16.9%	16.3%
40	28.3	32.8	38.7	36.6%	15.8%	18.0%
45	24.8	28.5	34.1	37.7%	15.0%	19.7%
50	21.3	24.4	29.7	39.7%	14.8%	21.7%
55	17.9	20.6	25.4	42.1%	15.0%	23.5%
60	14.8	17.0	21.4	45.0%	15.4%	25.6%
65	11.9	13.8	17.7	49.2%	16.6%	28.0%
70	9.3	10.9	14.3	53.8%	17.4%	31.0%
75	7.1	8.4	11.2	58.2%	18.6%	33.3%
80	5.3	6.3	8.5	60.4%	19.6%	34.1%
85	4.0	4.7	6.3	59.1%	18.4%	34.3%

[a]Computed from National Center for Health Statistics, *Vital Statistics of the Unit*, Volume II, Mortality, Part A, Section 6: Life Tables. PHS 98–1147, and *United States Life Tables*. National Vital Statistics Reports, 47, (28) Hyattsville: NCHS, 1998.

for example, has been a topic of consider-able controversy in the scientific litera-ture (Manton, Stallard, & Tolley, 1991; Vaupel, 1997, 1998; Wilmoth, 1997). There is no need to repeat this debate here. At present, the consensus of scho-lars is that the current demographic dy-namics of the United States and many other nations strongly favor a situation wherein the older population will itself gradually become older over the course of time. This phenomenon may be termed "aging from the top."

To illustrate the effects of actual mor-tality changes on age structures within the older population, *independent of any simultaneous effects from fertility or mi-gration*, the data in Table 5.3 present add-itional information from the same U.S. life tables used in Table 5.2. These data arc completely independent of fertility and migration levels; the comparisons made over time in Table 5.3 reflect how age structure is impacted solely by changes in mortality in the United States over the course of the 20th century. The data presented show (left-hand column for each year) the proportion of the total

life table population in each 5-year age group from 60–64 through 80–84, as well as the open-ended interval starting at age 85. Thus, the hypothetical share of the American population aged 60 and above has risen from 14.4% consistent with the mortality experience of 1900 through 19% at midcentury to 22.1% at present. For current purposes, more important are the data shown for each year in the right-hand column, which are the shares of the older population to be found in each age group. Here, a substantial aging of the older population is revealed. The median age among persons 60 and over climbs from 68.6 to 69.6 to 70.8 from the earliest to the latest of the three data points. The share aged 85 and over within these hypo-thetical populations increases by a factor of 2.5.

C. The Role of Migration

Most analyses of the demography of aging pay little attention to the role that migra-tion plays in the underlying demographic dynamics of growth and decline and, of course, the determination of population

Table 5.3
Share of Population at Older Ages: United States Life Tables, 1900, 1950, and 1997[a]

Year	1900–1902		1949–51		1997	
	Total population (%)	60+ population (%)	Total population (%)	60+ population (%)	Total population (%)	60+ population (%)
60–64	4.52%	31.47%	5.28%	27.79%	5.48%	24.78%
65–69	3.73%	25.97%	4.59%	24.14%	4.94%	22.32%
70–74	2.81%	19.59%	3.72%	19.56%	4.21%	19.02%
75–79	1.84%	12.84%	2.69%	14.16%	3.30%	14.94%
80–84	0.97%	6.75%	1.64%	8.64%	2.28%	10.30%
85+	0.49%	3.38%	1.09%	5.72%	1.91%	8.64%
Total	14.37%	100.00%	19.01%	100.01%	22.12%	100.00%
Median age of those 60+:		68.6		69.6		70.8

[a]Computed from National Center for Health Statistics, *Vital Statistics of the United States, 1995*. Vol. II, Mortality, Part A. Section 6: Life Tables, and *United States Life Tables, 1997*.

age structure. Migration tends to be more volatile and perhaps less predictable than are the other components of population change. Certainly, particularly for migration between countries, many of the biological or behavioral parameters within which fertility and mortality are typically analyzed are absent. Instead, levels and sometimes even sources of migration are determined as matters of public policy. Nonetheless, migration can have a measurable impact on the size, growth rate, and even the age and ethnic structure of a population.

1. At the National Level

At the national level, the lessened importance of migration generally makes sense, since the contribution of international migration to population change is negligible in most cases. Even when sustained immigration or emigration are characteristic of a national population, only rarely does either phenomenon represent a direct increment or decrement to the current size of the older population. An interesting exception to this generalization might be noted among countries where relatively large numbers emigrate at the beginning of working life, spend years abroad in a foreign labor force, and then return home for what may be a relatively comfortable retirement (Borjas & Bratsberg, 1996; Dustmann, 1996; Thomas-Hope, 1999).

There seems to be a great renewal of interest in immigration issues in aging societies, even research considering the interplay between immigration and fertility (Teitelbaum & Winter, 1998). A few studies deal with the possibility of changing immigration policy in order to compensate for low birth rates (Heer, 1986), although most authors suggest this is unlikely to become a widespread policy choice (Golini, 1999). However, studies that link these two demographic phenomena are scarce and deal with

household and living arrangements of elderly immigrants (Boyd, 1991; Glick, Bean, & van Hook, 1997) or with their internal redistribution (Rogers & Raymer, 1999).

2. At the Subnational Level

The past two decades have seen a considerable increase in research interest in the internal migration of older persons. Although much of the research has been focused at the descriptive level, considering stability and change in patterns of movement (Longino, 1982), there is also a substantial line of research that focuses upon the determinants of such moves. Important work in this context has stemmed from the recognition that there is considerable heterogeneity in the motivations for moving, focusing upon distinct types of elderly movers (Speare & Meyer, 1988; Wiseman & Roseman, 1979). Bean, Myers, Angel, and Galle (1994) summarize much of this literature.

Our attention here is more properly directed towards consideration of the consequences of such internal migration. Although most of the focus will be placed on consideration of the consequences of migration at the place of destination, some consideration needs be paid to the effects at the place of origin as well. Migration of older persons is often dichotomized into those seeking amenities and those seeking support (see chapter 6 by Longino, this volume). One could suggest that the within the former type, the same positive selectivity of migration customarily encountered in the analysis of any long-distance move applies. That is, amenity-seeking older movers are drawn from a more affluent population of older persons; these individuals are frequently stereotyped (correctly) as being relatively young and healthy and usually move as an intact couple. Conversely, movers seeking support tend to be older, less affluent, widowed, and generally less well off economically.

Estimates of the fiscal magnitude of retiree migration were developed from 1980 U.S. Census of Population data by Longino and Crown (1990). Their results, at the state level, indicate the amount of annual income "transferred" between states as a result of migration of persons aged 60 and over between 1975 and 1980. The data show a range from an increase of annual personal income in Florida of about $3.5 billion to a loss of nearly $2.0 billion for the state of New York.

Income shifts of this magnitude, combined with the realization that expenditures from income can lead to even greater increases in income and employment opportunities, have fostered the emergence of state and local economic development policies based on attracting retirees (Reeder, 1998). After all, mobile retirees are usually comparatively affluent individuals who will spend at the local level, but who will require comparatively little in the way of local-level publicly provided services (Serow & Haas, 1992).

Little attention has been paid to more long-term issues associated with the phenomenon. Following on the seminal work of Litwak and Longino (1987), Serow (1990) concludes that

> The primary areas of destination [for elderly migrants] may be viewed as "winning" in at least two fundamental respects. First, they benefit economically from the presence of younger elderly migrants who move at or shortly after the time of retirement.... Second, these areas are spared the public costs associated with demand for much of the care and support services needed at the end of life, if, as a consequence of bereavement and/or failing health, these older persons chose to move [away from their retirement site] to areas where family and friends may be found. (pp. 462–463).

Much more research needs to be done on the economic, social, and demographic consequences of this latter sort of move.

III. The Critical Variable: Age Structure

With the exception of nations that serve as destinations for substantial numbers of international migrants—the United States, Canada, Australia—most economically advanced countries are at the end of the demographic transition. The nations of Europe, North America, Oceania, and, increasingly much of Southeast Asia and portions of Latin America, are characterized by minimal rates of population growth, resulting from low and fairly stable levels of fertility and low and declining rates of mortality. For these nations, the issues of the consequences of the age structure of the population growth have come to the fore.

There is a substantial intellectual history devoted to this topic. The so-called stagnation thesis of the period between the two world wars argued that aggregate demand was tied to the growth of population and that as demographic growth diminished and the pace of population aging accelerated, overall economic growth would suffer (Hansen, 1939; Keynes, 1937). Much more attention is now being paid not to the concern for economic disaster as a simple consequence of demographic aging, but rather to questions of the economic well-being of individuals within the population, especially from the perspectives of differences among cohorts and between age groups (Disney 1996). By beginning with the individual as the unit of analysis, much current work deals with intergenerational differences; the comparisons of economic well-being across generations owe much to the seminal work of Easterlin (1968, 1987) and colleagues (Easterlin, Schaeffer, & Macunovich, 1993).

A. The Concept of "Dependency"

The dramatic increase in dependency is one of the most frequently expressed issues concerning aging and changes in population structure, in some cases leading to rather alarmist conclusions. The concept of dependency consists of the relative number of persons who would not usually contribute to the productive potential of a nation and, hence, are viewed as being "dependent" for their support on those who do so contribute. Typically, one will encounter the so-called "dependency-ratios," which are simply the number of persons in the "dependent" ages (0–14, 0–17, or 0–19; 60 or 62 or 65 and over) per 100 persons in the "productive" age groups (the residual from the above ages). There are obviously many problems with this measure: not all persons below and above the "productive" ages fail to make an economic contribution. Similarly, not all working-age persons are economically active. Ideally,

one would wish to use nonlabor force to labor force ratios, but for simple descriptive statements the dependency ratio concept is useful. This is particularly true when making intertemporal and/or cross-national comparisons.

All too often, the tendency is to concentrate on the dramatic increase in the relative and (usually) absolute increases in the upper ends of the age structure, without paying much heed to changes at the lower end. We can illustrate this point by considering the population changes projected to occur in the same three countries discussed previously when considering the role played by fertility changes over time: Australia, Hong Kong, and Sweden. Table 5.4 shows the current (1995) and projected (to 2050) populations for these three entities.

Table 5.4
Projections of Population by Age in Australia, Hong Kong, and Sweden: 1995–2050[a]

	1995	2000	2025	2050
Australia				
Total	17,866	18,838	23,931	25,286
0–14	3,846	3,956	4,650	4,639
15–59	11,234	11,878	13,654	12,203
60+	2,786	3,004	5,627	7,089
Persons 0–14 per 100 15–59	34.2	33.3	34.1	38.0
Persons 60+ per 100 15–59	24.8	25.3	41.2	58.1
Total	59.0	58.6	75.3	96.1
Hong Kong				
Total	6,123	6,373	6,503	5,618
0–14	1,196	1,096	863	792
15–59	4,072	4,324	3,533	2,631
60+	855	953	2,107	2,195
Persons 0–14 per 100 15–59	29.4	25.3	24.4	30.1
Persons 60+ per 100 15–59	21.0	22.0	59.6	83.4
Total	50.4	47.4	84.1	113.5
Sweden				
Total	8,788	8,898	9,511	9,574
0–14	1,653	1,698	1,738	1,720
15–59	5,215	5,282	5,131	5,072
60+	1,920	1,919	2,642	2,782
Persons 0–14 per 100 15–59	31.7	32.1	33.9	33.9
Persons 60+ per 100 15–59	36.8	36.3	51.5	54.9
Total	68.5	68.5	85.4	88.8

[a]From United Nations, Department of Economic and Social Affairs (1997).

In terms of the overall level of dependency, there is substantial change in the first quarter of the century, with the total number of "dependents" in these three nations rising from levels of 50–69 per 100 persons of "prime working age" (ages 15 to 59) in 1995 to levels of 89–114 at the end of the projection period. What differentiates this prospective experience from that of the past is the shift in the composition of the dependent population. Although there is little change in the so-called youth dependency ratio anywhere, that portion of dependency ascribable to those aged 60 and over rises appreciably, more than doubling in Australia, quadrupling in Hong Kong, and increasing by 50% in Sweden. It is this rising level of old-age dependency and the prospective burden on the working age population that forms the core of the current interest in the economics of slowing population growth. Collectively, these three geopolitical entities capture well the range of experience that is likely to occur in presently industrialized nations. Sweden reflects the European model of low and stable fertility, low and moderately declining mortality, and minimal immigration over the long term. Australia reflects the North American–Oceania model of moderately low and stable fertility, low and declining mortality, and significant immigration over the long term. Hong Kong represents well the case of newly industrialized nations, most easily characterized by low and rapidly declining fertility as well as low and moderately declining mortality.

B. Age–Cost Profiles

In the aggregate, a declining number of young dependents and their associated costs is likely to partially compensate for the rising number and costs of the elderly. This leads to the possibility that the rising pension and health-care expenditures associated with an increase in the number and proportion of older people may be offset in some fashion by the declining need for educational expenditures for the young. The complete economic costs must be divided between public and private expenditures; one also needs to consider the long-run implications of what might be viewed as maintenance or consumption expenditures—associated with pensions—versus the human-capital forming nature of educational expenditure. One must go beyond the simple counting of young and old heads; rather, the real costs of maintaining "dependents" of various ages must be considered.

Easterlin's (1991) review of this issue suggests that total costs per dependent do not vary that much, according to age, and that the shift in the composition of dependency should not have that great an effect on the ability of the economy to sustain growth. Similarly, Schulz, Borowski, and Crown (1991) argue that "the total dependency ratio will not be higher when members of the baby boom retire than when they were children in the 1950s, 1960s and early 1970s" (pp. 337–338). Although this is true in the aggregate, there is also a wide divergence in the nature of institutional arrangements present in various nations, and one must be very careful about drawing conclusions for a specific nation from such general conclusions. The real issue ultimately becomes a political one—how to persuade the working population that because less of their own income will be needed to support their own (young) dependents, some of these savings will need to be captured via taxation to pay the public costs of the older population. In principle, this should be easy since ultimately everyone would benefit, but the issues of equity between generations—which have become a major concern in the United States and elsewhere (Behrman, Pollak, & Taubman, 1995; Logan & Spitze, 1995)—will need to be addressed.

C. The Age Structure of the Older Population

An important aspect of the aging of populations and its health-care consequences that is frequently overlooked is the aging that is likely to occur within the older population itself. The World Health Organization (1995) points to three specific issues that will become increasingly relevant under these demographic conditions: (a) the possibility of further decreases in mortality at the expense of increased morbidity; (b) increased incidence of debilitating, expensive, and thus far untreatable conditions such as Alzheimer's disease and other forms of dementia; and (c) long-term care of the frail elderly.

Although there exists a considerable body of data arguing that age-specific rates of frailty and disability are decreasing over time (Alter & Riley, 1989; Manton, Stallard, & Liu, 1993; Olshansky & Ault, 1986; Weiss, 1990), there is little doubt that mortality and disability are positively associated with old age, especially at advanced old ages. Thus, the aging of the older population is apt to increase the absolute number of ill and disabled persons, even though age-specific rates may be decreasing. Binstock (in press) demonstrates that within the older population, health-care utilization rises monotonically with age. For example, average annual physician contacts number 10.2 for those aged 65 to 74 but 13.7 for those aged 75 and older. Similarly, the number of days of hospital care and the number of hospital discharges are (on a per person basis) some 52% and 41% greater, respectively, among the latter age group.

To illustrate how the older population itself will age in coming years, data from Australia, Hong Kong, and Sweden are once again useful because they are representative cases of most of the experiences that are likely to occur throughout the presently industrialized world. As shown in Table 5.5, there is a modest change through the year 2020 in the proportion of persons aged 80 and over within the universe of those aged 60 and over. In these cases, and again in most other demographically similar places, this proportion decreases around the year 2020, as the large number of persons born in the 1950s and 1960s attain their sixtieth birthday. After the passage of this "baby boom" group into the ranks of those aged 60 and over, there is a considerable upsurge in the aging of the older population through the end of the projection period in 2050. By this point in time, the proportion of the older population in these entities aged at least 80 has risen from about one in five or six (Sweden, Australia) or one in nine (Hong Kong) in 1995 to slightly more than one in four in Australia and about three in ten in Sweden and Hong Kong. At the beginning of the period there was wide variation in the number of persons aged 60–64 for each 100 individuals aged 80 and over: 1 to 1 in Sweden, 1.5 to 1 in Australia, 2.5 to 1 in Hong Kong. After the temporary upsurge in the first decades of the century, this level gradually declines so that by 2040 there would be absolutely more persons aged 80+ than there would be aged 60–64. This is particularly important because so much caregiving is actually provided by the youngest elderly to the oldest elderly (Coward, Horne, & Dwyer, 1992).

This sort of age structural change will be characteristic of all presently industrialized and many presently industrializing nations over the course of the next half-century. The three issues raised by WHO point to the economic and ethical issues that need to be faced. More resources will be required to meet the acute and chronic health care and long-term care needs of larger and older elderly populations. In addition, extending life expectancy when the additional years are characterized by physical illness, mental illness, and/or institutionalization is

Table 5.5
Projections of the Older Population by Age in Australia, Hong Kong and Sweden: 1995–2050[a]

	1995	2000	2010	2020	2030	2040	2050
Australia							
Total 60+	2,786	3,004	3,856	5,028	6,087	6,739	7,089
60–64	688	770	1184	1375	1,450	1,393	1,446
65–69	679	646	865	1184	1,379	1,452	1,380
70–74	586	607	655	1020	1,197	1,272	1,236
75–79	395	485	488	668	936	1,109	1,189
80+	438	496	664	781	1,125	1,513	1,838
% 80+	15.72%	16.51%	17.22%	15.53%	18.48%	22.45%	25.93%
Hong Kong							
Total 60+	855	953	1,186	1,791	2,242	2,290	2,184
60–64	255	249	378	589	465	429	370
65–69	222	238	218	454	561	419	409
70–74	166	198	208	322	510	407	381
75–79	113	139	179	167	358	453	343
80+	99	129	203	259	348	582	681
% 80+	11.58%	13.54%	17.12%	14.46%	15.52%	25.41%	31.18%
Sweden							
Total 60+	1,920	1,919	2,267	2,519	2,744	2,787	2,782
60–64	402	435	618	553	606	505	562
65–69	400	377	524	528	563	548	477
70–74	404	358	373	538	488	540	454
75–79	319	335	290	415	427	463	458
80+	395	414	452	485	660	731	831
% 80+	20.57%	21.57%	20.03%	19.25%	24.05%	26.23%	29.87%

[a]From United Nations, Department of Economic and Social Affairs (1997).

questionable both economically and ethically. This recalls the ongoing discussion concerning the "rectangularization" or compression of mortality (Myers & Manton, 1984; Wilmoth & Horiuchi, 1999), which argues that at least during the present century death has been increasingly postponed, but possibly at the cost of greater years of morbidity.

It is also of course the case that the gender mix of the older population changes with age, becoming increasingly female. This is largely due to biology, although there is some speculation that differences in labor force behaviors are also involved in excess male mortality (Vallin, 1999). This has particular importance to what we view as the primary economic issues associated with the aging of populations, namely the funding and security of pensions and all other retirement income

sources. The economic circumstances of older women, especially widows, have generally been poor when compared with those of older men (see chapter 19 by Crown, this volume).

IV. Some Economic Questions and Current Answers

No one issue associated with population aging has elicited as much attention as the ability of societies to ensure the economic well-being of their older population. Current policy discussion in many nations emphasizes the burdens and trade-offs involved for the rest of society in order to ensure the well-being of the large post-World War II birth cohorts in their old age. The reason for this concern is both simple and by now very well known: most public pension schemes are funded on a "pay-as-you-go" basis, that is, the contributions to the system of the currently employed are used to provide the benefits provided to the currently retired. Implicit in the arrangement is the understanding that each successive generation supports its predecessor(s) and, in turn, is supported by the succeeding generation(s). In principle, this arrangement works well so long as the relative size of the generations change but little and other features of the scheme (age and other criteria for eligibility, real benefit level, etc) remain invariant. A similar statement can be made for the financing of health care and indeed any other program in which the entitlement is financed by means of intergenerational transfers of income.

A. Public Pensions and Retirement Income

The institutional parameters underlying public pension systems vary considerably from country to country, and there is no obvious means of generalizing about them. Nonetheless, the basic elements of the programs tend to follow the broad outlines suggested above. Although there is certainly a trend away from the unfunded pension liability scheme we have identified here—it is especially frequent, if not yet the norm, in newly industrialized nations (Bravo, 1999)—this remains the basic framework confronting policy makers as they struggle to cope with the actual or prospective aging populations. Certainly, a wide variety of solutions may be considered. At the simplest level, one may simply "tinker" with the parameters of the system by changing such things as the age at eligibility for full pensions or the rate at which earnings are replaced. Similarly, changes in regulations governing the amount of earnings a pensioner might accumulate or the extent to which pension income is subject to

taxation could, on the margin, have an impact on the labor force participation of pension program participants. (See chapter 20 by Kingson and Williamson this volume, for further elaboration of these issues.)

B. Health Care and Social Support

Much more difficult to deal with, over the long term, will be costs and funding mechanisms for the health care of an aging population. The prime issue of population aging that must be faced in industrialized nations, from both an economic and a sociodemographic perspective, is health care and its costs. In general, there have been substantial increases in longevity in much of the industrialized world (see chapter 4 by Hayward & Zhang, this Volume), although important exceptions to this generalization can be found in portions of Eastern Europe (Cockerham, 1997; Velkoff & Kinsella, 1993). As noted above, older persons consume health-care resources to a degree much disproportionate to their numbers (see also the chapter 21 by Feder, Komisar, & Niefeld, this Volume).

The costs of providing health services to older persons will probably be the major policy question that will need addressing in these countries over the next quarter century. It does not appear that the simple solutions proffered for pension reform (such as delaying age of eligibility) would be as efficacious in the health-care arena (see, e.g., Wittenburg, Stapleton, Scrivner, & Hobbie, 1999).

The aging of the older population will have a disproportionately larger impact on health-care demand and its costs than on public pension systems and their costs. It is difficult to escape the conclusion that substantially increased health-care costs follow from the aging of populations. Ultimately, the choice may come down to restricting access to care or increasing tax revenues to cover those costs.

V. Summary and Conclusions: How the Free-Market Economy Will Respond to Population Aging

Although growing public expenditures for pensions and health do imply increased tax revenues, they need not necessarily imply an increase in taxes as a share of total output and income. Projections by the Organisation for Economic Cooperation and Development (1988), for example, suggest that only modest increases in real (adjusted for inflation) earnings—less than 1% per year through 2040—coupled with constant tax rates will maintain the level of taxes per employed person at the 1980 level. More controversially, the World Bank (1994) argues for the abolition of social insurance, replacing it with a "multipillar" system, incorporating (a) a mandatory tax-financed public pillar designed to alleviate poverty; (b) a mandatory funded, privately managed pillar (based on personal accounts or occupational plans) to handle people's savings; and (c) supplemental voluntary pillar (again based on personal saving or occupational plans) for people who want more protection (p. 292).

If the aging of a population really does adversely affect economic growth, then increased pressure for expenditures on pensions and health care would have calamitous effects. Disney (1996) finds no such effect, and Schulz (1999) asserts that population aging has much less effect on economic growth than well-established factors such as technological change, entrepreneurship, capital formation, and labor force participation. Public policy can certainly encourage growth through these factors.

Although uncertainty always exists in such matters, there is considerable reason to be optimistic regarding the long-range trend in real wages and income levels in industrialized societies. Although there are short-run problems associated with the transition from secondary (manufacturing) to tertiary ("service") activity, these are independent of demographic issues. The population dynamics of the industrialized world are such that an aging of the labor force is inevitable for about the next 25 to 30 years. After that it will probably start to become somewhat younger. Much of the concern with an aging labor force revolves around the fear of declining labor productivity and subsequent decline or stagnation in earnings and income. However, with the transition in the means of production, there is less of a premium on strength and more of a premium on experience. Hence, having relatively more workers in the 50–59 age range and relatively fewer aged 20–29 does not bode poorly for productivity per worker and consequently for wage levels. It is also important to bear in mind that we have become accustomed to regarding each new generation of workers as being better educated and therefore (potentially) more productive than its predecessors. However, educational attainment seems to have reached an upper asymptote in many developed countries (Serow & Sly, 1992).

From an economic growth perspective, though, these issues underscore the difficult nature of the choices that will need to be faced in the process of resource allocation. The current evidence suggests that the availability of resources to allocate is probably not going to be a problem. Easterlin (1994) argues that alarmist views (e.g., Wattenberg, 1987) that foresee a dire outlook for economic growth due to demographic change on developed countries are likely to be off the mark. A question unanswered here, but one which will command increasing amounts of scholarly and policy-making attention in the future, is how all these issues will play out through the aging process of developing countries. Although there is increasing research in this field (Treas &

Logue, 1986; Martin & Kinsella, 1994; Vanderleyden & Schoenmaeckers, 1999), our present state of recognition of the scope and magnitude of the issues is in its infancy.

References

Ahlburg, D. A., & Land, K. C. (1992). Population forecasting: Guest editors' introduction. *International Journal of Forecasting, 8*, 289–299.

Alter, G., & Riley, J. C. (1989). Frailty, sickness, and death: models of morbidity and mortality in historical populations. *Population Studies, 43*, 25–45.

Bean, F. D., Myers, G. C., Angel, J. L., & Galle, O. R. (1994). Geographic concentration, migration, and population redistribution among the elderly. In L. G. Martin & S. H. Preston (Eds.), *Demography of aging* (pp. 319–355). Washington, DC: National Academy Press.

Behrman, J. R., Pollak, R. A., & Taubman, P. (1995). *From parent to child: Intrahousehold allocations and intergenerational relations in the United States.* Chicago: University of Chicago Press.

Binstock, R. H. (in press). Health care: Organization, use and financing. In G. L. Maddox (Ed.), *Encyclopedia of aging* (3rd ed.). New York: Springer Publishing Company.

Bloom, D. E., & Williamson, J. G. (1998). Demographic transitions and economic miracles in emerging Asia. *World Bank Economic Review, 12*, 419–456.

Borjas, G. J., & Bratsberg, B. (1996) Who leaves? The outmigration of the foreign-born. *Review of Economics and Statistics, 78*, 165–176.

Boyd, M. (1991). Immigration and living arrangements: elderly women in Canada. *International Migration Review, 25*, 4–27.

Bravo, J. (1999). Fiscal implications of ageing societies regarding public and private pension systems. In R. Cliquet & M. Nizamuddin (Eds.), *Population ageing: Challenges for policies and programmes in developed and developing countries* (pp. 141–153). New York: UN Fund for Population Activities and Brussels: Population and Family Study Centre.

Calot, G., & Sardon, J. -P. (1999). Les facteurs du vieillissement demographique. *Population, 54*, 509–552.

Coale, A. J. (1956). The effects of changes in mortality and fertility on age composition. *Milbank Memorial Fund Quarterly, 34*, 79–114.

Cockerham, W. C. (1997). The social determinants of the decline of life expectancy in Russia and Eastern Europe: A lifestyle explanation. *Journal of Health and Social Behavior, 38*, 117–130.

Coward, R. T., Horne, C., & Dwyer, J. W. (1992). Demographic perspectives on gender and family caregiving. In J. Dwyer & R. Coward (Eds.), *Gender, families and elder care* (pp. 18–33). Newbury Park, CA: Sage.

Day, J. C. (1993). *Population projections of the United States, by age, sex, race, and Hispanic origin: 1993 to 2050.* Washington, DC: U.S. Bureau of the Census, Current Population Reports, P25–1104.

Disney, R. (1996). *Can we afford to grow older?* Cambridge, MA: The MIT Press.

Dustmann, C. (1996). Return migration: The European experience. *Economic Policy, 22*, 215–250.

Easterlin, R. A. (1968). *Population, labor force and long swings in economic growth: The American experience.* New York: Columbia University Press.

Easterlin, R. A. (1987). *Birth and fortune: The impact of numbers on personal welfare.* Chicago: University of Chicago Press.

Easterlin, R. A. (1991). The economic impact of prospective population changes in advanced industrial countries. *Journal of Gerontology: Social Sciences, 46*, S299–S309.

Easterlin, R. A. (1994). The birth dearth, aging and the economy, In S. Asefa & W-C. Huang, (Eds.), *Human capital and economic development* (pp. 11–34). Kalamazoo, MI: W.E. Upjohn Institute.

Easterlin, R. A., Schaeffer, C. M., & Macunovich, D. J. (1993). Will the baby boomers be less well off than their parents? Income, wealth, and family circumstances over the life cycle in the United States. *Population and Development Review, 19*, 497–522.

Evenson, R. E. (1999). Global and local implications of biotechnology and climate change for future food supplies. *Proceedings of the*

National Academy of Sciences of the United States of America, 96, 5921–5828.

Friedland, R. B., & Summer, L. (1999). *Demography is not destiny.* Washington, DC: National Academy on an Aging Society.

Freidlander, D., & Klinov-Malul, R. (1980). Aging of Populations, dependency and economic burden in developed countries. *Canadian Studies in Population, 7,* 49–55.

Glick, J. E., Bean, F. D., & van Hook, J. V. (1997). Immigration and changing patterns of extended family household structure in the United States: 1970–1990. *Journal of Marriage and the Family, 59,* 177–191.

Golini, A. (1999). Population ageing in developed countries: Lesson learnt and to be learnt. . In R. Cliquet & M. Nizamuddin (Eds.), *Population ageing: Challenges for policies and programmes in developed and developing countries* (pp. 49–84). New York: UN Fund for Population Activities and Brussels: Population and Family Study Centre.

Hansen, A. S. (1939). Economic progress and declining population growth. *American Economic Review, 29,* 1–15.

Heer, D. M. (1986). Immigration as a counter to below-replacement fertility in the United States. *Population and Development Review, 12,* (suppl.), 262–269.

Himes, C. L. (1994). Age patterns of mortality and cause of death structures in Sweden, Japan and the United States. *Demography, 31,* 633–650.

Keyfitz, N. (1971). On the momentum of population growth. *Demography, 8,* 71–80.

Keynes, J. M. (1937). Some economic consequences of a declining population. *Eugenics Review, 29,* 13–17.

Kim, Y. J., & Schoen, R. (1997). Population momentum expresses population aging. *Demography, 34,* 421–428.

Litwak, E., & Longino, C. F., Jr. (1987). Migration patterns among the elderly: A developmental perspective. *The Gerontologist, 27,* 266–272.

Logan, J. R., & Spitze, G. D. (1995). Self-interest and altruism in intergenerational relations. *Demography, 32,* 353–364.

Longino, C. F., Jr. (1982). Changing aged nonmetropolitan patterns, 1955–60 and 1965–70. *Journal of Gerontology: Social Sciences, 37,* S228–S234.

Longino, C. F., Jr., & Crown, W. H. (1990). Retirement migration and interstate income transfers. *The Gerontologist, 30,* 784–789.

Manton, K. G., Stallard, E., & Liu, K. (1993). Frailty and forecasts of active life expectancy in the United States. In K. G. Manton, B. H. Singer, & R. M. Suzman (Eds.), *Forecasting the health of elderly populations* (pp. 159–81). New York: Springer-Verlag.

Manton, K. G., Stallard, E., & Tolley, H. D. (1991). Limits to human life expectancy: Evidence, prospects, and implications. *Population and Development Review, 17,* 603–637.

Manton, K. G., & Vaupel, J. W. (1995). Survival after the age of 80 in the United States, Sweden, France, England, and Japan. *New England Journal of Medicine, 333,* 1,232–1,235.

Martin, L. G., & Kinsella, K. (1994). Research on the demography of aging in developing countries. In L. G. Martin & S. H. Preston (Eds.), *Demography of Aging* (pp. 356–403). Washington, DC: National Academy Press.

Myers, G. C., & Manton, K. G. (1984). Compression of mortality: myth or reality? *The Gerontologist, 24,* 346–353.

Olshansky, S. J., & Ault, A. B. (1986). The fourth stage of the epidemiologic transition: The age of delayed degenerative diseases. *Milbank Memorial Fund Quarterly, 64,* 355–391.

Organisation for Economic Cooperation and Development (1988). *Aging populations: The social policy implications.* Paris: OECD.

Preston, S. H., & Guillot, M. (1997). Population dynamics in an age of declining fertility. *Genus, 53,* 15–31.

Reeder, R. (1998). *Retiree-attraction policies for rural development* (Agricultural Information Bulletin no. 741). Washington, DC: U.S. Department of Agriculture.

Rogers, A., & Raymer, J. (1999). The regional demographics of the elderly foreign-born and native-born populations in the United States since 1950. *Research on Aging, 21,* 3–35.

Schulz, J. H. (1999). Population ageing: Economic growth and generational transfers (labour, productivity and saving issues). In R. Cliquet & M. Nizamuddin (Eds.), *Population ageing: Challenges for policies and programmes in developed and developing* countries (pp. 123–140). New York: UN Fund for Population Activities and Brussels: Population and Family Study Centre.

Schulz, J. H., Borowski, A., & Crown, W. H. (1991). *Economics of population aging: The "graying" of Australia, Japan and the United States.* New York: Auburn House.

Serow, W. J. (1990). Economic implications of retirement migration. *Journal of Applied Gerontology, 9,* 452–463.

Serow, W. J., & Haas, W. (1992). Measuring the economic impact of retirement migration: The case of western North Carolina. *Journal of Applied Gerontology, 11,* 200–215.

Serow, W. J., & Sly, D. (1992). Economic aspects of structural change in the older population of the United States: 1980–2020. In G. Stolnitz (Ed.), *Demographic causes and economic consequences of population aging* [Economic Commission for Europe, Economic Studies No. 3] (pp. 203–213). New York: United Nations.

Speare, A., & Meyer, J. (1988). Types of elderly residential mobility and their determinants. *Journal of Gerontology: Social Sciences, 43,* S74–S81.

Teitelbaum, M. S., & Winter, J. (1998). *A question of numbers: High migration, low fertility, and the politics of national identity.* New York: Hill and Wang.

Thomas-Hope, E. (1999). Return migration to Jamaica and its development potential. *International Migration, 37,* 183–207.

Treas, J., & Logue, B. (1986). Economic development and the older population. *Population and Development Review, 12,* 645–673.

United Nations, Department of Economic and Social Affairs (1997). *The sex and age distribution of the world populations: The 1996 revision.* New York: United Nations.

United Nations, Department of Economic and Social Affairs (1998). *World population prospects: The 1996 revision.* New York: United Nations.

Vallin, J. (1999). *Mortalité, sexe et genre.* Liege: Union Internationale pour l'Etude Scientifique de la Population.

Vanderleyden, L., & Schoenmaeckers, R. (1999). Population ageing: Key issues and recommendations for action. In R. Cliquet

& M. Nizamuddin (Eds.), *Population ageing: Challenges for policies and programmes in developed and developing countries* (pp. 267–288). New York: UN Fund for Population Activities and Brussels: Population and Family Study Centre.

Vaupel, J. W. (1997). Trajectories of mortality at advanced ages. In K. W. Wachter & C. E. Finch (Eds.), *Between Zeus and the salmon: The biodemography of longevity* (pp. 17–37). Washington, DC: National Academy Press.

Vaupel, J. W. (1998). Demographic analysis of aging and longevity. *American Economic Review, 88,* 242–247.

Velkoff, V. A., & Kinsella, K. (1993). *Aging in eastern Europe and the former Soviet Union.* Washington, DC: U.S. Bureau of the Census.

Wattenberg, B. (1987). *The birth dearth.* New York: Pharos Books.

Weiss, K. M. (1990). The biodemography of variation in human frailty. *Demography, 27,* 185–206.

Wilmoth, J. R. (1997). In search of limits: what do demographic trends suggest about the future of human longevity? In K. W. Wachter & C. E. Finch (Eds.), *Between Zeus and the salmon: The biodemography of longevity* (pp. 38–64). Washington, DC: National Academy Press.

Wilmoth, J. R., & Horiuchi, S. (1999). Rectangularization revisited: Variability of age at death within human populations. *Demography, 36,* 475–495.

Wiseman, R. F., & Roseman, C. C. (1979). A typology of elderly migration based on the decision-making process. *Economic Geography, 55,* 324–337.

Wittenburg, D. C., Stapleton, D. C., Scrivner, S., & Hobbie, R. A. (1999). *The impacts of an increase in the Social security retirement age and the Medicare eligibility age on Social Security, Disability Insurance, Medicare, and employment.* Washington, DC: AARP.

World Bank (1994). *Averting the old age crisis: Policies to protect the old and promote growth.* New York: Oxford University Press.

World Health Organization (1995). *The World Health Report 1995: Bridging the gaps.* Geneva: WHO.

Six

Geographical Distribution and Migration

Charles F. Longino, Jr.

I. Introduction

The public appetite for new information about the geographical distribution and migration of the older population during the past two decades has been amazing, far out of proportion to its importance to the academic research community. It is not difficult to understand how this can happen, however. Population shifts, or their anticipation, easily rub up against a number of policy issues concerning re sources, markets, and economic development, which are important both to governments and significant sectors of the American business community.

The study of geographical distribution first gained some practical policy import- ance with the passage of the Older Ameri- cans Act (OAA) in 1965. The interstate distribution of OAA funds is based on the size of the older population within each state. In addition, the intrastate distribu- tion of OAA funds has often reflected the geographical distribution of population within and between service districts.

The study of migration, on the other hand, first attracted interest simply be- cause of the intellectual interest of re- searchers. Knowledge about retirees who move was a curiosity, not a necessity. During the past decade, however, this situ- ation has changed. An increasing number of states have begun deliberately, and sometimes vigorously, to recruit retirees from outside their borders as a part of their economic development policies. Other states have been very interested in the successes and failures of these efforts.

Because the topic crosses several discip- linary lines, and because many different conceptual perspectives are involved, findings on the same topics are some- times difficult to integrate. So researchers in different disciplines, interested in the same issues, may sometimes not know about the other's work. This chapter will move a step or two toward overcoming the isolation of those sharing in a com- mon endeavor.

This chapter is limited almost entirely to a review of the literature during the decade of the 1990s. A similar chapter in the 1990 edition of this handbook re- viewed the literature from the 1970s and 1980s. Research articles have increased substantially in volume over the past dec- ade, however. As a result, there is rela- tively little overlap between the two chapters.

Handbook of Aging and the Social Sciences, Fifth Edition
Copyright © 2001 by Academic Press.
All rights of reproduction in any form reserved.

The second part of this chapter is devoted to the topic of geographical distribution. It includes state variations and distributions of the older population in rural and urban places.

The third section of the chapter focuses on migration. The theoretical approaches used during the decade are summarized, and the research is guided by these approaches. Then updated migration trends are described. There is a brief discussion of the characteristics of migrants, followed by a more involved discussion of types of cyclical migration. Finally, the issue of migration impact is addressed, focusing on the economic, political, and social dimensions of impact.

II. Geographical Distribution

A. State Variations

Only 13% of the national population is 65 or over in 2000. Figure 6.1 depicts the most recent (1998) geographic distribution. If one expects to find a high concentration of older persons in those states to which they tend to migrate, then the map in Figure 6.1 makes little sense. Why should North and South Dakota, Nebraska, and Maine be in the same category with Florida? State variation in the distribution of the older population is striking. Fourteen states have proportions of 13.7% or over, and an equal number of states have proportions under 12%. Why such extreme variation between states? The answer to these questions is not straightforward. Several different answers are possible.

Morrison (1990) reminds us that a concentration of older residents in a state may result from three different processes:

- *Accumulation* occurs when older residents remain behind when younger residents leave. Historically, this pattern has been experienced throughout the

Plains states, including North and South Dakota and Nebraska.

- *Recomposition* occurs when older migrants are drawn to an area that younger residents are leaving. This process is more likely to occur in those rural areas where economic opportunities cannot support the younger population, but where scenic beauty and low cost of living can still attract older migrants. Population changes in the Missouri and Arkansas Ozarks region, the Pennsylvania Poconos, the West Virginia Panhandle, and in some Atlantic coast counties in North and South Carolina demonstrate this process.
- *Congregation* occurs when migrants of all ages are attracted to an area, but older migrants arrive at a faster pace than others do. Examples are Florida, Arizona, North Carolina, and Oregon.

Some researchers have shown (Frey, 1993) that during the 1970s there was an increase in the number of states fitting the congregation pattern and a decrease fitting the accumulation pattern.

These distinctions, however, tend to minimize the complexity of the geography of population aging. A shift in what Frey calls "new elderly births," or aging in place, may be accomplished through the rapid immigration of working-aged persons in previous decades (Frey, 1995). Paying close attention to where baby boomers move during their working years will forecast population aging in the 2020s and beyond (Frey, 1992a). They have tended to move, for example, from the metropolitan cities of Midwestern states to the big suburbs of small central cities in Sunbelt states. This pattern should continue to fuel the aging of the Sunbelt in the early decades of the 21st century (Frey, 1999).

B. Rural and Urban Variations

A metropolitan county contains a central city of 50,000 or more. Nearly three-

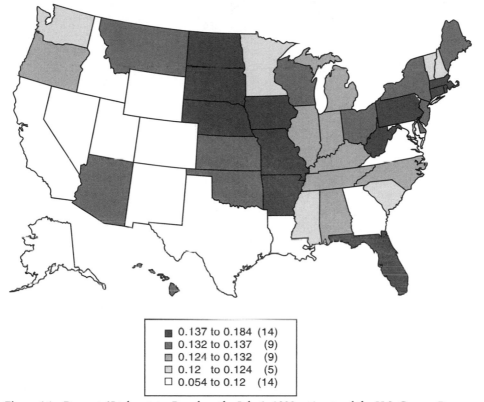

Figure 6.1 Percent 65+ by state. Based on the July 1, 1998 estimate of the U.S. Census Bureau.

0.137 to 0.184 (14)
0.132 to 0.137 (9)
0.124 to 0.132 (9)
0.12 to 0.124 (5)
0.054 to 0.12 (14)

quarters (74%) of the older U.S. population lives in metropolitan counties, a similar proportion to that of the total population (77%). Because of this fact, it becomes important to understand how population is distributed *within* these urbanized places (Golant, 1990a, 1992). For example, there has apparently been some displacement of the inner city elderly population due to "gentrification" (Singelakis, 1990). Since 1950, those aged 65 and older have gradually, and increasingly, lived in the suburbs. In 1977 for the first time a majority of metropolitan dwellers in this age group were suburbanites, and in 1990, 60% of white residents aged 65 and older lived there. This shift is less due to late-life moves to the suburbs than to aging in place (Frey, 1999).

Metropolitan deconcentration (the movement out of the big cities to smaller,

but not necessarily rural, places) is another macrolevel process that affects population redistribution in our time (Longino & Haas, 1992). Many nonmetropolitan counties experienced a slowing of population decline in the 1960s; in the 1970s, their net migration rates climbed above the break-even point, signaling a genuine and widespread metropolitan–nonmetropolitan turnaround. Older people seemed to have been in the vanguard of migration to nonmetropolitan counties. The turnaround happened for them in the 1960s, not the 1970s. Mounting evidence now indicates that by the late 1980s, metropolitan counties were once again outgrowing nonmetropolitan ones (Fuguitt & Beale, 1993). So although the greater net growth in rural counties was widespread, it was not long lasting. The slight reverses of balance between rural and urban growth over the past four decades should not obscure the tendency of migrants of all ages, and especially those of retirement age, to move down the metropolitan hierarchy, to destinations with somewhat smaller populations than their original locales (Frey, 1992b; Longino, 1995).

Only part of the growth of a metropolitan or nonmetropolitan older population is due to migration. Nonetheless, the migration component is interesting by itself. About half of older migrants in the 1970 and 1980 censuses moved from one metropolitan county to another. A much smaller proportion, from one-tenth to nearly one-quarter, was moving about outside of metropolitan areas. About one-third of elderly migrants were moving between metropolitan and nonmetropolitan counties, and they were shifting the balance from metropolitan to nonmetropolitan locations (Longino, 1990b; Longino & Haas, 1992).

III. Migration

A.   Conceptual Models

The 1990s saw a steady advancement of conceptual models in the study of retirement migration. They do not compete directly with one another, but instead have different types of starting points: the life course, the migration decision process, housing disequilibrium, and place identity.

1. The Life-Course Models

One line of theoretical development has tended to make the life course of migrants its central focus, emphasizing those triggering mechanisms associated with life events and probabilities. This conceptualization draws from demographic and human-development perspectives and is congenial with other concerns of gerontological research. Warnes (1992), for example, developed a long list of life-course events that occur, on average, at different ages. He sequenced them and discussed the housing needs and mobility patterns associated with them. In later life, the list includes retirement, bereavement, and frailty.

Litwak and Longino (1987) presented a developmental context for the patterns of elderly interstate migration commonly reported from demographic studies. They argue that the nature of modern technology puts the kinship structures of older people under pressures to make three basic types of moves. The first type involves persons who are recently retired, a second type includes persons who are experiencing moderate forms of disability, and a third type is an institutional move when health problems overwhelm the capability of the family to care for older relatives at home. The pressure may be slight for the first type of move, but it may increase for the second type and again for the third.

a. The First Move   When retirees have intact marriages, are relatively healthy, and have enough income in retirement, there are social pressures for some of them to relocate for lifestyle or amenity reasons. Personal characteristics predict the expectation of migration as well as its timing, but so do ties to the current community of residence and ties to other persons, especially family members. Some retirees have planned their move for years and have vacationed at, and visited, the new locations many times in anticipation of the move. The reasons for relocation are complex and have to do with the attraction of amenities, friendship network maintenance, and the ability to make a psychological shift of identity from one place to another (Longino, 1995). At this stage of retirement, however, kinship functions can be managed over considerable distances, although it would be a mistake to assume that no recent retirees move closer to their children or other relatives.

b. The Second Move The pressure for the second type of move occurs when older people develop chronic disabilities that make it difficult to carry out everyday household tasks (Longino, Jackson, Zimmerman, & Bradsher, 1991; Miller, Longino, Anderson, James, & Worley, 1999), a situation often compounded by widowhood (Bradsher, Longino, Jackson, & Zimmerman, 1992; Chevan, 1995). Migrants who move away from their children when they are healthy and married may later move back toward them when, as type-two migrants, they are disabled and/or widowed (R. Clark & Wolf, 1992; Lin & Rogerson, 1995; Moss & Moss, 1992; Silverstein, 1995; Speare & McNally, 1992).

c. The Third Move Limited kin resources is the motive for the third basic type of move from more or less exclusive kin care. Most third types of move are local rather than long-distance (McAuley, Pecchioni, & Grant, 1999), usually to an assisted living facility or nursing home. When older persons suffer from more severe forms of chronic disability or do not have children who can and will help them, then institutional care is crucial (Silverstein & Zablotsky, 1996; Speare, Avery & Lawton, 1991).

De Jong, Wilmath, Angel, and Cornwell (1995) and Choi (1996) argue effectively that poor health, reduced social affiliation, economic insecurity, having functional limitations, and getting on with life after a family crisis, are all adequate reasons for moving. The life-course model merely arranges some of these motivations around a type of move.

2. The Migration Decision Models

A second line of theoretical advancement in the 1990s built upon migration decision-making theory (Wiseman, 1980) to delineate person–environment adjustment processes by which the elderly decide whether or not and where to move. Wiseman had argued that moves were triggered by push and pull factors, such as climate, environmental hassle level, or cost of living, and facilitated or hampered by indigenous filters such as personal resources or the housing market. Once the decision to move is made, the selection of a destination follows. Only then can the migration outcome be considered. There are feedback loops in Wiseman's model. People who do not decide to move, or cannot successfully choose a destination, may adjust to their present location through various mechanisms in order to avoid feeling trapped there. Furthermore, over time, migration outcomes that initially may be improvements generate new pushes and pulls that may eventually trigger another move. This model is well adapted to framing survey research questions, although it is never ideal to study processes at only one point in time (W. Clark, 1992).

Cuba (1991), studying migrants to Cape Cod, challenged Wiseman's assertion that the decision to move preceded the selection of a destination. Most had not considered other places and knew they wanted to live on the Cape before they had worked out the final decision to move.

Haas and Serow (1993) elaborate on the Wiseman model, fitting it to the circumstance of the recently or nearly retired amenity migrant. They add to the model "remote thoughts" or daydreams about moving (Longino, 1992) that precede the formal process, and the information sources that make the actor aware of push–pull factors. Another important addition to the original decision model, following the move, is developing ties within the community. Community adjustment has been understudied (Serow, 1992). The Haas–Serow model was tested successfully on retired interstate migrants to Idaho. (Carlson, Junk, Fox, Rudzitis, & Cann, 1998). Further, using 1990 census data, Clark, Knapp, and White (1996) found that the location of retirement moves can be explained less well by push or pull factors taken separately than by a balance between such factors, consistent with the decision model. And, finally, Kallan (1993) suggests that although individual-level variables are stronger predictors of the migration of older adults, contextual variables and multilevel interactions improve the explanatory power of the models. The influence of some contextual variables, such as climate, crime rates, and cost of living, varies among elderly subgroups.

3. The Housing Disequilibrium Model

Economic incentives due to housing assets may be assessed within the context of the migration decision model. When they are the focus, however, the resulting model is better described as a housing disequilibrium model (Fournier, Rasmussen, & Serow, 1988). The housing disequilibrium model, as applied to older migrants (Clark & White, 1990), received a lot of attention from researchers in the early 1990s. The push to move from less affordable rental housing tends to motivate central city moves, while the pull to more appropriate, owned, housing tends to motivate suburban moves.

A study conducted by Steinnes and Hogan (1992) supported the hypothesis that elderly migration to Arizona, both seasonal and permanent, results, in part, from the economic gains made in the housing markets from which migrants move. Americans experience relatively little geographic mobility in the 15 years or so leading up to retirement. As a consequence, they tend to gain through the appreciation of their residential property. Selling a house in California, for example,

can net a surplus that can be "spent" on seasonal migration or a move to a more affordable housing market.

4. The Place Identity Model

A final conceptual framework emerging during the 1990s may be called the place identity model. Cuba (1989) argues that 'selves' as well as 'bodies' can be mobile. Moving oneself physically to another community does not necessarily mean that one also moves emotionally. There are some migrants who never put down roots but remain emotionally tied to their former communities. Some of them have problems changing from being a vacationer to being a permanent resident after they arrive in their destination communities. This social psychological approach is interesting and deserves greater study.

Cuba and Hummon (1993a) argue that identification with one's dwelling, one's community, and one's region are arrived at differently. Personal possessions and the dwelling itself fosters identification with the dwelling as "home," especially for older women; social participation and the size of one's friendship network are essential for strong identification with the community. And, finally, younger migrants more often base their identity on affiliations of friendship, family, and emotional self-attributions, whereas older migrants do so in terms of dwelling and prior experience with place (Cuba & Hummond, 1993b). Weak community identity could hinder adjustment and thereby contribute to a second migration decision cycle.

Finally, we confront shifts in place identity throughout our lives and the experience that accrues serves to inform future decisions (Watkins, 1999). Place identity, therefore, must be seen as part of a long-term process of adjustments.

B. Patterns of Migration

1. Destinations

The first way of describing migration destinations is to compare the numbers who moved to different states or counties, ranking the states or counties that received the largest proportions. In 1940, and since 1960, a census item has asked where one lived exactly 5 years before the census: in the same house, in another county in the same state, in another state or abroad. Using this item, the numbers and proportions of interstate and intrastate migrants can be compared over time.

Census microdata are handy for making these comparisons, because it is nearly impossible to study retirement migration by solely relying on the tables printed and distributed by the Census Bureau. A microdata file contains a sample of individual census records (with identifiers removed) and allows the researcher to create new custom-designed tabulations. There is a drawback when using microdata, however, because on the individual records, counties containing fewer than 100,000 persons are clustered together in units called PUMAs (public use microdata areas). This policy responds to a concern that individuals in a small population in a small geographical area could be recognized, thus violating the basic confidentiality promised by the Census Bureau to citizens.

When the top 100 counties or county groups (PUMAs) are ranked in terms of net interstate migration, Florida contains one-third of these destinations for interstate migrants, in keeping with its sovereign status as a retirement state. But perhaps more interesting, the substate destinations are located in coastal, mountain, and desert counties across the United States from seaside New Hampshire to the Puget Sound in Washington. Maricopa County, Arizona (Phoenix), and

Clark County, Nevada (Las Vegas), rank second and fourth, respectively, and are the leading destinations in the West. Riverside County, California, (Palm Springs), ranks 29th and is California's only entry on the list.

Although the Sunbelt pattern generally holds, there is greater variety than is commonly assumed. Some strong regional destinations, such as Cape Cod, do not show up in interstate migration patterns simply because so many of its migrants come from within state (Cuba, 1992). New Jersey, on the other hand, has consistently received enough retirees from New York and Pennsylvania, keeping it among the top ten interstate destination states since 1960. Most regional retirement locations, especially those outside the Sunbelt, only show up when county-level data are used.

Channelization is a nautical term denoting a very busy port; deep channels are dug to accommodate ship traffic. Dechannelization refers to a process leading to the reverse outcome, a gradual silting in of the channels due to less traffic. Retirement migration is a good example of both processes. One of the defining characteristics of interstate retirement migration is that migrants coming from all over the nation have concentrated their destinations in only a few states, forming highly channeled flows into these states. Nearly 60% (56% in 1990) arrive in just 10 states, having lived in other states 5 years before. Florida dominates the scene, attracting about a quarter of all interstate migrants over 60 in all four census decades (Longino & Perricone, 1991).

A new phenomenon occurred in the 1985–1990 migration period. There was a gradual dechannelization of retirement migration—that is, a small decrease in the proportion of migrants received by the major destination states, a gentle spreading out of the flows, as compared with earlier migration periods. This process is very gradual, but as it happens, it is important to note the states that are sliding, inch by inch, losing some of their attractiveness to migrants, and those that are moving up in the rankings. Dechannelization is good news for all of those states interested in attracting migrants that are not already on the top of the list of destinations (Golant, 1990b; Longino, 1994).

As Table 6.1 shows, the leading four destination states—Florida, California, Arizona, and Texas—all had lower percentages in 1990 than in 1980, although they held their same ranking relative to one another in 1990 as in 1980. Although the losses were small, the pattern is clear and persistent. Underscoring the subtlety of this change, most of these declines are not noticeable because there were over a quarter million more interstate in-migrants over 60 in 1980 than in 1990. It would be wrong, for example, to predict the demise of Florida as the leading destination for retired migrants on the basis of

its slight decline in the overall share of migrants during this period. The number of migrants moving into Florida during the migration period reported in 1990 actually increased over that reported in 1980.

Within the broader context of slight declines in market share experienced by the major receiving states, there are some states that could be called "sliders." These are states that have experienced a decline in popularity over several decades. Chief among these is California. It has been ranked second since 1960, but its share of the in-migrant pool has declined in every decade since that time, from 13.6% to 6.9%, or nearly by half. The other sliders are all northeastern states: New Jersey, New York, Illinois, Ohio, and Michigan. By 1990, all but New Jersey and Pennsylvania had dropped completely off the list. These rankings also show the consolidation of the Sunbelt as the major retirement area of the country.

Table 6.1
Ten States Receiving Most In-Migrants Age 60+ in 5 Year Periods Ending in 1960, 1970, 1980 and 1990[a]

Rank	1960			1970			1980			1990		
	State	No.	%	State	No.	%	State	No.	%	State	No.	%
1	FL	208,072	22.3	FL	263,200	24.4	FL	437,040	26.3	FL	451,709	23.8
2	CA	126,883	13.6	CA	107,000	9.9	CA	144,880	8.7	CA	131,514	6.9
3	NJ	36,019	3.9	AZ	47,600	4.4	AZ	94,600	5.7	AZ	98,756	5.2
4	NY	33,794	3.6	NJ	46,000	4.3	TX	78,480	4.7	TX	78,117	4.1
5	IL	30,355	3.3	TX	39,800	3.7	NJ	49,400	3.0	NC	64,530	3.4
6	AZ	29,571	3.2	NY	32,800	3.0	PA	39,520	2.4	PA	57,538	3.0
7	OH	27,759	3.0	OH	32,300	3.0	NC	39,400	2.4	NJ	49,176	2.6
8	TX	26,770	2.9	IL	28,800	2.7	WA	35,760	2.2	WA	47,484	2.5
9	PA	25,738	2.8	PA	28,600	2.7	IL	35,720	2.1	VA	46,554	2.4
10	MI	20,308	2.2	MO	25,300	2.3	NY	34,920	2.1	GA	44,475	2.3
Total interstate migrants	931,012			1,079,200[b]			1,622,120[c]			1,901,105		
% of Total in top 10 states		60.7			60.4			59.5			56.3	

[a]From U.S. Census Bureau.
[b]This figure was derived by extrapolating from a 1 in 100 sample. The actual census count was 1,094,014.
[c]This figure was derived by extrapolating from a 1 in 40 sample. The actual census count was 1,654,000.

Regional destinations attract migrants primarily from adjacent states. Examples are Cape Cod, Massachusetts, the New Jersey shore, the Pocono Mountains of northeastern Pennsylvania, and the Wisconsin Dells, all located outside the Sunbelt. Other locations in the Appalachian mountain chain, the Ozark region of Missouri, and Arkansas are in the noncoastal Sunbelt (Rowles & Watkins, 1993; Watkins, 1990). Southern and western Nevada and areas in the Pacific Northwest are all retirement areas of strong regional attraction (Cuba & Longino, 1991), and areas frequently cited in retirement guides as good placed to retire (Savageau, 2000).

2. State-to-State Streams

Migration stream data are derived from a state origin–destination matrix. Every state sends and receives migrants aged 60 and older, even Alaska. However, the 1990 census showed that only Florida, California, Arizona, Texas, and North Carolina attracted three or more unusually large streams from states outside their regions. Therefore, these may be considered national destination states. If states are ranked by net migration, North Carolina is in third place behind Florida and Arizona. When the state-to-state streams are charted that contain more than 4,000 migrants each, there are only two major patterns. The first contains streams into Florida from states north of North Carolina and east of the Mississippi River. The second contains streams out of California to the states of Oregon and Washington to the north and Nevada and Arizona to the east (Longino, 1994).

3. Substate Analyses of Interstate Out-Migration

It is easy to compare states and streams of migrants between states. There are only 51 units, if the District of Columbia is included. In census microdata, rural counties are combined so that none of these county groupings contain fewer than 100,000 persons. Single counties may also contain large cities. By comparing counties or county groupings, therefore, it is possible to get a much clearer fix on the actual origins and destinations of older migrants.

The top 100 counties *sending* the largest numbers of interstate migrants to other states are the comparatively populous metropolitan or suburban counties. Ten are located in Florida! These are, in descending population size, Pinellas, Broward, Dade, Palm Beach, Pasco, Sarasota, Hillsborough, Volusia, Orange and Lee Counties. These counties receive far more interstate migrants than leave them for counties outside of Florida, but migrants of retirement age do leave Florida, a point often missed by media accounts of retirement migration.

When the 100 largest streams between counties or county groups are arrayed, three general patterns of out-migration can be observed, those typified by the boroughs New York City, Cook County, Illinois, home of Chicago, and Los Angeles County, California. The pattern of migration from the boroughs of New York City shows a favorite national destination and a favorite regional destination. These New York retirees have a long-standing love affair with the state of Florida. Their favorite regional destination is coastal New Jersey.

From Cook County's vantagepoint, the popular Sunbelt destination states all seem about the same distance away, thus they are all fair game. If metropolitan New York loves Florida, Cook County plays the field. Migrants from Wayne County (home of Detroit) in Michigan seem to follow the Chicago pattern.

The pattern for Los Angeles County is very different from the New York City boroughs. From 1985 to 1990, Los

Angeles County sent nine large county to county streams of retirees to counties in three adjacent states: Arizona, Nevada, and Oregon. Adjacency is the heart of the Los Angeles County out-migration pattern.

4. "Migration" to Nursing Homes

Analyses of movement for institutional care is a promising new area of migration research. It typically includes all migrants, those moving across county lines in the same state as well as those moving from a different state. McAuley, Pecchioni, and Grant (1999) employed a conceptual framework based upon migration theory and the long-term care decision process. These researchers compared the distance of the move and characteristics of migrants who moved from other communities into Virginia nursing homes. Most moved from within state. They found that scarcity of supply (i.e., low availability of nursing home beds) in the county of origin is a push factor in the move. Additionally, nursing homes in Virginia with religious affiliations were more likely to attract admissions from other counties, due, presumably, to loyalty to church sponsorship. Chain facilities also drew from greater distances. Finally, Medicaid payment was associated with an increased likelihood of admission from a different country and nonadjacent county, but with a decreased likelihood of admission from another state.

Colsher and Wallace (1990) studied older rural residents, comparing their anticipated and actual relocations. They compared institutional and noninstitutional moves and found a high proportion of health-related moves in both categories. In some ways, those not moving to institutions were in poorer physical and mental health. It is a mistake to think that all health-related moves late in life are to institutions. It is equally false to assume that only the healthy move.

5. Migration from Abroad

Not all older migrants move from one place to another within the nation. Between 1985 and 1990, nearly a quarter-million (236,000) migrants aged 60 and older moved to the United States from abroad. Compared to the nearly two million interstate migrants, their numbers are not great, but they are important in certain regions of the country (Longino, 1995).

In 1975–1980 and 1985–1990, not surprisingly, their settlement focused on states that have major ports of entry (large international sea and airports). These were California, New York, Florida, Texas, Illinois, and New Jersey. The overall volume from abroad increased 31% between those two decades, with California, New York and Florida each receiving over 30,000 migrants. If Florida leads the way in attracting interstate migrants, California has the same honor regarding older migrants from abroad, welcoming one-third of the total, or nearly 78,000, in 1985–1990. New York ranks second, attracting 14%, nearly matched by Florida's 13%.

Studies of Hispanic older migrants find that they tend to move to the destination state nearest to their country of origin (Biafora & Longino, 1990). For example, Cubans and Puerto Ricans tend to move to Florida, Mexicans to Texas and California. Other Hispanics are more evenly distributed between California, Florida, and New York. These stream patterns connect to strong cultural enclaves that have developed within the United States. The enclaves also tend to be attractive to Hispanics who make interstate moves in retirement. Asian migration falls largely on the Pacific Coast for similar reasons. A large minority of these migrants was born in the United States.

6. Cross-National Comparisons

It is not possible to thoroughly survey international research on later life migration in the space that is available. However, some directions can be summarized.

Rogers contributed two important unifying ideas to cross-national comparisons in the 1990s. The first was the mathematical formulation of a common migration age schedule, which enabled him to observe a similarity in all the countries where appropriate data were available. Migration rates are highest among young adults, and their dependents, declining with age to a long low plateau during middle age then rising again slightly following retirement, and finally rising at the end of life. Second, Rogers, Watkins, and Woodward (1990), building upon Rogers' earlier work, compared Japan, Italy, England, and the United States, showing that the mobility of elders seemed to follow a geographic pattern in industrial societies. With the growth of national economic resources, the mobile elderly tended to concentrate in the mildest climactic zones in their countries, which are often coastal areas. Rogers (1992) also edited an influential volume that extended these ideas to other societies and has served to unify international research on this topic.

With the development of the European Union, several barriers to intracontinental mobility have recently fallen. Perhaps the most exciting migration research in Europe today is that focused on international permanent and seasonal migration from Northern to Southern Europe, particularly from the United Kingdom to Portugal, Spain, Greece, and Malta (Williams, King, & Warnes, 1997). The late-life increase in disability seems to be the only factor sufficiently strong to deter continued seasonal migration from the north (Warnes, King, Williams, & Patternson, 2000). Serow, Friedrich, and Haas (1996) suggest that the same seasonal migration pattern may be emerging for Germans traveling to Spain. Within Germany, the dominant influence on all mobility, including that of older Germans, has been the political unification of east and West Germany. Migration flows are predominantly toward the west and south.

C. Migration Selectivity

"Who moves among the elderly?" was the title of the first comprehensive census analysis of the population characteristics of older mover types (Biggar, 1980). Biggar's article made a very strong statement. She was able to show that the distance mobility types (nonmovers, local movers, intrastate migrants, and interstate migrants) among the elderly had distinctive profiles. Local movers were "negatively selected" from among the potential movers at their origin, and migrants were "positively selected." That is, local movers had lower average incomes and were living dependently with others at higher rates than were nonmovers. Interstate migrants were the most positively selected, being younger, more often married, living in their own homes, and having higher average incomes than persons in the other mobility categories. Subsequent studies in the 1980s supported Biggar's initial findings.

There were some important extensions of these findings in the 1990s. Hazelrigg and Hardy (1995) compared the income characteristics of older migrants with nonmigrant age peers at their destinations and found that the migrants were better off. They attributed this to the tendency of migrants to move to locations with a somewhat lower cost of living than at their origin. Cost of living and income are higher in large cities. Second, some important selectivity factors are at work. Moving is costly, and this tends to screen out those who cannot afford to make a move. Further, amenity migrants tend to move soon after retirement, before there is any decay in their retirement income relative to more recent retirees.

D. Cyclical Migration

There are three cyclical patterns of interstate migration that have been identified in the United States over the past 20 years. They are seasonal migration, counterstream migration, and return migration.

1. Seasonal Migration

The Census Bureau does not attempt to directly measure seasonal migration. Although it does keep track of the number of persons who completed their census forms away from home at the time of the census, the data from this set of records have not been broken down by age, so they are difficult to interpret. However, there have been several local surveys—in Texas, Arizona, and Florida—that provide snapshots of seasonal migrants and their destinations, even though they do not represent a national picture (Longino & Marshall, 1990).

Survey results (McHugh & Mings, 1991) have identified seasonal migrants as overwhelmingly white, retired, healthy, married couples largely in their sixties. These are characteristics associated, in other studies, with amenity migration. Another study (Martin, Hoppe, Marshall, & Duciuk, 1992) compared samples of older Canadians who wintered in Florida with U.S. citizens who spend their winters in the Rio Grande Valley of Texas. The aggregate characteristics of the migrants are similar to those studied by McHugh and Mings in Arizona.

Nevertheless, Hogan and Steinnes (1993) argue that seasonal and permanent migrants cannot be estimated well by the same statistical model. And, indeed, the Canadian seasonal migrants in Florida are diverse, as well (Tucker, Mullins, Beland,

Longino, & Marshall, 1992). English-speaking and French-speaking Canadians tend to settle in different parts of the state. The demographic profiles of the residents in these two settlements of seasonal migrants are very similar in many ways. However, the Francophone Canadians are more youthful, have lower levels of education and monthly income, and have larger families, contributing, by their visits, to larger social support networks in Florida.

McHugh and Mings (1991) were the first to emphasize the fact that the colder the climate, the more likely retirees are to migrate seasonally. United States retirees in states along the Canadian border have a greater propensity to migrate seasonally than those in states located further south.

A good deal of research has been devoted to the question of whether seasonal migration is only a stage, that is, a precursor to a permanent move (Longino, Marshall, Mullins, & Tucker, 1991; McHugh, 1990). Whether seasonal migrants settle down at their destination and become permanent residents depends upon the balance between their ties to places and persons at origin and destination, and the shift in these ties over time. Furthermore, seasonal migrants are also encouraged to remain year round by their relatives and friends who have already moved permanently to seasonal destinations. The vast majority of seasonal migrants, perhaps 80%, however, apparently do not relocate permanently. They extend or shorten their visits, and they finally end their extended series of visits when their health forces them to do so.

McHugh and Mings (1994) examined the health care of seasonal residents in Arizona and found that they tend to adjust to health decrements over time. Their major adjustment strategies include reducing the number of side trips during their winter residence, and by giving up their recreational vehicles in favor of renting lodging while in Arizona.

Health issues affect seasonal migration also on a policy level. Canadians wintering in Florida tend to limit their length of stay in response to their nation's national health insurance rules that require them to spend more than half a year in Canada to keep their benefits. These international seasonal migrants undertake a strategic orientation toward the Canadian and U.S. health-care systems. One study (Marshall, Longino, Tucker, & Mullins, 1989) found that most seasonal migrants visited a Canadian doctor for a check-up and stocked up on prescription drugs prior to leaving Canada. One-third left specific instructions with relatives or friends in case of a medical emergency, and four-fifths enrolled in a private health insurance plan to supplement their provincial health plan.

Mings (1997), comparing seasonal migration in the United States, Canada, and Australia, found many similarities. He studied winter visitors in a caravan (recreational vehicle) park in tropical northern Queensland. The demographic profiles of persons in the three national categories were very similar, and all maintained high levels of recreational activities. However, the Australians had traveled longer distances to get to their destination, and had a somewhat lower level of social interaction than Canadian and U.S. seasonal migrants. The result was a lower level of social integration among the Australian seasonal migrants.

McHugh, Hogan, and Happel (1995) argue that temporary residence is much more frequent than we realize. They found that cyclical migration often occurs in stages, beginning with vacationing in midlife and leading to longer stays in the retirement years. Many migrants who had moved permanently to Arizona tended to make extended visits back to their origins when temperatures rose to uncomfortable levels, placing them in the category of cyclical movers as well. When those

who moved to Arizona only in the winter were combined with those who left in the summer, and those who moved within Arizona seasonally, the number was substantial. They estimated that one-fourth of older persons in Arizona fall into one of these categories. Apparently, seasonal migration generates its own lifestyle and culture, different from that of permanent migrants, but equally valuable in its own right. Once having adopted the lifestyle, seasonal migration is likely to last for several years, finally interrupted, and reluctantly terminated.

2. Counterstream Migration

Seasonal migrants are inclined to give their origin, their home base, as their usual residence on the census long form. If they complete the census form during their seasonal visit, it is sent to the enumeration district of their more usual place of residence to be counted. On the other hand, persons who say that they have moved across county or state boundaries in the past 5 years are counted at their destination as permanent migrants.

When the state-to-state streams of older migrants were studied, using 1980 census data, the researchers were not at all surprised to find counterstreams. Counterstream is a term used for streams in the opposite direction from the larger stream in exchanges between pairs of states. The counterstream (for example, from Florida to New York) is, by definition, smaller than the migrant stream (for example, from New York to Florida). These paired exchanges are an expected part of the migration landscape. Furthermore, the researchers found that counterstreams were negatively selective. That is, more of the migrants in the counterstreams had negative characteristics (e.g., they were somewhat older, on average, and were more often widowed and living dependently with relatives) after a counterstream move than were migrants in the stream (Litwak & Longino, 1987). These findings led to the speculation that counterstreams contain a large proportion of retirees who had moved at an earlier time to a popular retirement destination and are later returning to the state from whence they came. Unfortunately, because the census contains no item on individual migration history, there is no way to determine what proportion of counterstream migrants are actually returning. There are some first-time movers in the counterstreams.

Using 1990 census data, and comparing the fifty largest pairs of streams and counterstreams, three geographical patterns were found (Longino, 1995). The first is exchanges between Florida and several of its major partners: New York, Ohio, Pennsylvania, Michigan, Illinois, Massachusetts, Connecticut, Indiana, Virginia, Maryland, and Wisconsin. The streams were *into* Florida, of course, with counterstreams in the opposite direction. The second geographical pattern is exchanges between California and adjacent or regional states: Arizona, Washington, Oregon, Nevada, and Texas. The larger stream, in this pattern, is *out of* California! This pattern of exchanges among adjacent states is clearly regional. The third pattern, also regional, is the Mid-Atlantic exchange system. It includes streams out of New York to three adjacent states, Pennsylvania, New Jersey, and Connecticut, with counterstreams to New York. If it continues to be true that counterstream migrants are older and more dependent than stream migrants, then Florida is in a much more advantageous position than California or New York.

There is only one item in the census that identifies the location of a previous residence. The item asks for one's state of birth. People who move to their states of birth from elsewhere are known among demographers as return migrants. Counterstream migrants are not necessarily returning to their state of birth, although some are.

3. Return Migration

a. The Decline of Return Migration over Time It had been commonly assumed that return migration would be much higher among retirees than others. Serow (1978) was the first to report that 20% of all interstate migrants, regardless of age, are returning to their states of birth.

Rogers (1990) argued that return migration is a dynamic process that changes over time and is difficult to study with single-census "snapshots." When return migration is examined over several decades and projected into the future, Rogers concludes that retirees tend to return to their states of birth at lower rates than younger migrants, and that the gap is widening.

For older people, return migration as a proportion of total migration is, indeed, on the decline. Serow had shown, using 1970 data, that 20.3% of older migrants were returning to their states of birth. The 1980 figure was 18.6%. In 1990, the comparable figure declined further to 17.5% (Longino, 1995).

b. Ethnic Enclave Settlement and Return Migration Regional return migration of African Americans to the South and Southwest involves a historical work cycle. Industrial states recruit workers from rural parts of the country. However, over time, return migration streams develop that carry some of the retired workers back to their states of birth. These return streams build in a delayed but roughly proportional response to the earlier stream development for work. Rogers (1990) is correct in insisting that return migration must be understood in the context of the complex rhythms of rising and falling stream migration throughout the life course.

In this context, it is not surprising to find that a majority of African American migrants age 60 and older are moving into the southern states. Nor is it surprising to find that return migration rates are high among these migrants (Longino & Smith, 1991).

It is too early in the industrial recruitment process to see high rates of return migration among Hispanics from Illinois and Michigan to the Southwest. However, projecting from the African American work and retirement migration patterns, such a development would not be surprising in the future.

c. Subtypes of Return Migration

There are two types of return migration discussed in the literature. The first is "provincial return migration," a subset of amenity migration. It consists of life-style-motivated movers who are choosing to move to their states of birth. They are younger, slightly better educated, more affluent, and far more often married than return migrants in general. The second type, "counterstream return migration," is a subset of dependency migration. It is made up of return migrants found in the counterstreams flowing out of popular destination states, who are presumably returning to their preretirement location after several years. They are making the health-related dependency moves as delineated in the life-course model proposed by Litwak and Longino (1987). They tend to be older, more often widowed, and more often living with relatives or in institutional settings after their move. Using data from the 1980 census, Longino and Serow (1990) found evidence of these two types of return migrants. Interregional migrants returning to their states of birth in the Northeast and Midwest fit the aggregate description of counterstream return migration, and interregional migrants to the South and the Southwest fit the aggregate description of provincial return migration.

E. Migration Impact

1. Economic Impact

The decade of the 1990s began with a spate of articles considering the economic impact of retirees at their destination. Longino and Crown (1990) and Crown and Longino (1991) documented the sizable amount of income that was transferred to and from states due to retirement migration. The 1979 income of migrants who had moved into Florida between 1975 and 1980 amounted to over $4 billion dollars. In the same year, New York state lost over $2.2 billion from out-migration between 1975 and 1980. Ten years later, the income from 1985–1990 in-migrants had doubled to $8.3 billion for Florida. Considering the fact that older migrants are pumping most of their income into the economy through consumption, but not competing for jobs, this was a sizable economic boost to Florida's economy. In the same year, New York lost nearly $4 billion (Longino, 1995). The income figures for other states fell in between Florida and New York.

Serow (1990) analyzed the percent of their incomes that older migrants paid in state and local taxes in Florida and concluded that their economic contribution to the state was substantial. Sastry (1992), using a regional input–output modeling system and data from the Consumer Expenditure Survey, agreed that retirement migration had large, positive, total impacts on the Florida economy. Finally, using data from an expenditure survey of older migrants around Asheville, North Carolina, Serow, Friedrich, and Haas (1992) demonstrated the economic dynamics that produce specific benefits for the local and state economies.

Simultaneously, Glasgow and her colleagues were examining rural retirement counties across the country, and speculating about the positive economic contribution that retirees could make. They showed that these 515 rural counties, where the older population was growing through migration, outperformed nonmetropolitan area averages for job growth (Reeder & Glasgow, 1990). Retirees were said to establish a "mailbox economy" of social security and pensions (Glasgow, 1991). These studies argued that older migrants had not been an excessive burden on local public service expenditures, which tended to be low in any case (Glasgow & Reeder, 1990; Glasgow, 1995), a point echoed by Joseph and Cloutier (1991) concerning rural Canadians. Voss and Fuguitt (1991) showed that in rural low-income counties in the South, new income from migrants only replaced that taken out by out-migrants. These were not the same set of counties, however, that Glasgow called "retirement counties." Hodge (1991) reported data supportive of Glasgow's analysis in his study of smaller communities in the province of British Columbia, Canada. Bennett (1992, 1993), in studying high-amenity retirement counties on the Atlantic seaboard, offered strong support to Glasgow's observations. Schneider and Green (1992), however, noted that the economic success of the retirement counties cannot be attributed simply to retirement migration. Rural counties, when accessible to heavily traveled transportation corridors and abundant with amenities, are attractive to young people as well.

Schneider and Green (1992), Glasgow (1990), and Cook (1990) were early contributors to the discussion of the utility of community policies to attract retirees. Fagan and Longino (1993) demonstrated the benefits to rural retirement counties of diversifying their economic development strategy by adding tourism and active retiree recruitment. Deller (1995) used a regional economic model to simulate the impact of a policy of retirement recruitment on the state of Maine. He argued that the short-run beneficial economic impact of retiree recruitment is significant and warrants serious consideration. Finally, the economic benefits of elderly winter residents to Phoenix (Happel, Hogan, & Pflanz, 1988), and to Arizona generally (Hogan & Happel, 1994), are also now documented.

However, despite the preponderance of evidence, concerns continued to be voiced on the subject of retiree recruitment. Stallmann and Siegel (1995) warned that the long-term effects of aging in place, if retiree recruitment were to fall off, could be negative for rural communities in terms of increased public expenditures for health and long-term care services. This is a concern also shared by Mullins and Rosentraub (1992). Indeed, this anxiety may grow in the years immediately ahead. Due to the long-term effects of fertility decline during and following the Great Depression, the growth of entrants into the retirement years will level off during the early 2000s just before baby boomers retire. This factor alone is likely to produce a greater aging in place effect in retiree communities that are fed by migration but do *not* actively recruit new younger retirees (Longino & Perricone, 1991).

2. Local Political Activism and Support for Public Services

As the 1990s dawned, there was a tentative consensus among students of retirement migration that the political impact of migrants was small to nonexistent. Rosenbaum and Button (1989) studied the political impact of the expanding older population on city and county governments in Florida. Their findings suggested that older Floridians are politically active at the local level but seldom get involved in organized advocacy for the elderly, and they are not against local policies largely beneficial to other groups. They did find a private anxiety among many municipal and county officials, however, that the elderly may someday have a negative political impact on their communities.

This picture seems quite naïve a decade later. Political research of the past decade tells a more complex story. Local voting studies have tended to examine the results of local school budget referenda. Using the results of school district bond elections in Florida, Button (1992) and especially MacManus (1997) found that a higher percentage of elderly residents and voters in a school district are associated with lower support for schools. This finding is consistent with recent research by Simonsen and Robbins (1996), who found that citizens and senior citizens, in particular, were much less supportive of public services that they do not expect to use. This would include schools.

3. Impact on Community Social Structure and Values

Longino (1990a) argued that retirement enclaves in rural counties tend to be worlds unto themselves, relatively unattached to local social structure. Cuba (1992) even argued that on Cape Cod, the distinguishing characteristics of older migrants make them susceptible to scapegoating by nonmigrants and younger migrants.

Later studies have seen migrants as more proactive, as change agents in their communities. Rowles and Watkins (1993), for example, provide case studies of three contrasting Appalachian communities at different stages of development as retirement destinations. They draw from their analysis a temporal model of community development involving overlapping phases of emergence, recognition, restructuring, and saturation. This study is refreshingly insightful because it analyzes retirement migration in a broader social context. *Place identity* theory is also useful as it focuses on adaptive dynamics in retirement communities. For example, middle-class retirees, moving to a small town in the mountains or on the seashore, are likely to band together to protect the environmental ambiance of the community. They may, for instance, oppose the local chamber of commerce as it attempts to develop land for housing or to invite in light industry. Local opinion may see the migrants as selfishly obstructing attempts to create economic opportunities that would raise the standard of living for the next generation of local residents. The lure of economic development through retiree recruitment, in some small towns, could have disappointing consequences for local boosters as the size and power of the older population increases.

IV. Future Research Priorities

The knowledge gains during the 1990s in the study of geographical distribution and migration were substantial. Studies pertaining to the distribution of the older population are necessarily related to policy issues, especially those concerning health and social services. Economic development has been added to that list over the past decade. As the baby boom generation matures, these issues will increase in importance.

The first two decades of migration research, during the 1970s and 1980s, produced many descriptive studies and offered little conceptual development (Serow, 1996). During the 1990s, greater theoretical development took place, now offering researchers a variety of frameworks in which to work. There is likely to be even greater theoretical refinement in the 21st century.

The basic patterns of migration now have been explored. No doubt, these will be updated and refined in the future. But the topic that offers the greatest opportunity for research advances is that of migration selectivity. Except for examinations of where migrants were born, surprisingly little research in the 1990s dealt with the characteristics of various types of migrants and the influence of these characteristics on migrant decisions and behavior.

The study of seasonal migration, especially in Arizona, has generated a serious subfield, with its own emerging theory and research agenda. Work in this area should flower during the next decade. The study of return migration, on the other hand, generated relatively little interest during the later 1990s and may decline further in the next decade.

Migration that is related to early retirement will become visible for the first time in the next decade simply because the early retirees will be baby boomers, thus boosting their numbers. And there will be a high level of anticipation and speculation about the geographical distribution and migratory behavior of this large cohort as it crosses the line into retirement in the following decade (Longino, 1998). Finally, also because of the impending retirement of baby boomers, economic development issues are likely to increase in both importance and research viability during first decade of the 21st century.

References

Bennett, D. G. (1992). The impact of retirement migration on Carteret and Brunswick counties, N.C. *North Carolina Geographer, 1,* 25–38.

Bennett, D. G. (1993). Retirement migration and economic development in high-amenity, nonmetropolitan areas. *The Journal of Applied Gerontology, 12(4),* 466–481.

Biafora, F., & Longino, C. F., Jr. (1990). Elderly Hispanic migration in the United States. *Journal of Gerontology: Social Sciences, 45,* S212–S219.

Biggar, J. C. (1980). Who moved among the elderly, 1965–1970: A comparison of types of older movers. *Research on Aging, 2,* 73–91.

Bradsher, J. E., & Longino, C. F., Jr., Jackson, D. J., & Zimmerman, R. S. (1992). Health and geographic mobility among the recently widowed. *Journal of Gerontology: Social Sciences, 47(5),* S261–S268.

Button, J. W. (1992). A sign of generational conflict: The impact of Florida's aging voters on local school and tax referenda. *Social Science Quarterly, 73(4),* 786–797.

Carlson, J. E., Junk, V. W., Fox, L. K., Rudzitis, G., & Cann, S. E. (1998). Factors affecting retirement migration to Idaho: An adaptation of the amenity retirement migration model. *The Gerontologist, 38(1),* 18–24.

Chevan, A. (1995). Holding on and letting go. *Research on Aging, 17(3),* 278–302.

Choi, N. G. (1996). Older persons who move: Reasons and health consequences. *The Journal of Applied Gerontology, 15(3),* 325–344.

Clark, D. E., Knapp, T. A., & White, N. E. (1996). Personal and location-specific characteristics and elderly interstate migration. *Growth and Change, 27,* 327–351.

Clark, R. L., & Wolf, D. A. (1992). Proximity of children and elderly migration. In A. Rogers (Ed.), *Elderly migration and population redistribution* (pp. 77–96). London: Belhaven Press.

Clark, W. A. V. (1992). Comparing cross-sectional and longitudinal analyses of residential mobility and migration. *Environment and Planning A, 24,* 1291–1302.

Clark, W. A. V., & White, K. (1990). Modeling elderly mobility. *Environment and Planning A, 22,* 909–924.

Colsher P. L., & Wallace, R. B. (1990). Health and social antecedents of relocation in rural elderly persons. *Journal of Gerontology: Social Sciences, 45,* S32–S38.

Cook, A. K. (1990). Retirement migration as a community development option. *Journal of the Community Development Society, 21(1),* 83–101.

Crown, W. H., & Longino, C. F., Jr. (1991). State and regional policy implications of elderly migration. *Journal of Aging and Social Policy, 3,* 185–207.

Cuba, L. J. (1991). Models of migration decision making reexamined: The destination search of older migrants to Cape Cod. *The Gerontologist, 31(2),* 204–209.

Cuba, L. J. (1992). *The Cape Cod retirement migration study: A final report to the National Institute on Aging.* Wellesley, MA: Wellesley College.

Cuba, L. J. (1989). Retiring from vacationland: From visitor to resident. *Generations, 13(2)*, 63–67.

Cuba, L. J., & Hummon, D. M. (1993a). A place to call home: Identification with dwelling, community and religion. *The Sociological Quarterly, 34*, 111–131.

Cuba, L. J., & Hummon, D. M. (1993b). Constructing a sense of home: Place affiliation and migration across the life-cycle. *Sociological Forum, 8(4)*, 547–572.

Cuba, L. J., & Longino, C. F., Jr. (1991). Regional retirement migration: The case of Cape Cod. *Journal of Gerontology: Social Sciences, 46*, S33–S42.

DeJong, G. F., Wilmoth, J. M., Angel, J. L., & Cornwell, G. T. (1995). Motives and the geographic mobility of very old Americans. *Journal of Gerontology: Social Sciences, 50B(6)*, S395–S404.

Deller, S. C. (1995). Economic impact of retirement migration. *Economic Development Quarterly, 9(1)*, 25–38.

Fagan, M., & Longino, C. F., Jr. (1993). Migrating retirees: A source for economic development. *Economic Development Quarterly, 7(1)*, 98–106.

Fournier, G. M., Rasmussen, D. W., & Serow, W. J. (1988). Elderly migration as a response to economic incentives. *Social Science Quarterly, 69*, 245–260.

Frey, W. H. (1992a). Boomer magnets. *American Demographics, 34–37*, 53.

Frey, W. H. (1992b). Metropolitan redistribution of the U.S. elderly: 1960–70, 1970–80, 1980–90. In A. Rogers (Ed.), *Elderly migration and population redistribution* (pp. 123–142). London: Belhaven Press.

Frey, W. H. (1993). U. S. elderly population becoming more concentrated. *Population Today*, April, 6–9.

Frey, W. H. (1995). Elderly demographic profiles of U.S. states: Impacts of "new elderly births," migration, and immigration. *The Gerontologist, 35(6)*, 761–770.

Frey, W. H. (1999). *Beyond social security: The local aspects of an aging America*. Washington, DC: Center on Urban and Metropolitan Policy, The Brookings Institution.

Fuguitt, G. V., & Beale, C. L. (1993). The changing concentration of the older nonmetropolitan population: 1960–1990. *Journal of Gerontology, 48(6)*, S278–S288.

Glasgow, N. L. (1990). Attracting retirees as a community development option. *Journal of the Community Development Society, 21(1)*, 102–114.

Glasgow, N. L. (1991). A place in the country. *American Demographics, 13(3)*, 24–30.

Glasgow, N. L. (1995). Retirement migration and the use of services in nonmetropolitan counties. *Rural Sociology, 60(2)*, 224–243.

Glasgow, N. L., & Reeder, R. J. (1990). Economic and fiscal implications of nonmetropolitan retirement migration. *The Journal of Applied Gerontology, 9(4)*, 433–451.

Golant, S. M. (1990a). The metropolitanization and suburbanization of the U.S. elderly population: 1970–1988. *The Gerontologist, 30(1)*, 80–85.

Golant, S. M. (1990b). Post-1980 regional migration patterns of the U.S. elderly population. *Journal of Gerontology: Social Sciences, 45*, S135–140.

Golant, S. M. (1992). The suburbanization of the American elderly. In A. Rogers (Ed.), *Elderly migration and population redistribution* (163–180). London: Belhaven Press.

Haas, W. H., III, & Serow, W. J. (1993). Amenity retirement migration process: A model and preliminary evidence. *The Gerontologist, 33(2)*, 212–220.

Happel, S. K., Hogan, T. D., & Pflanz, E. (1988). The economic impact of elderly winter residents in the Phoenix area. *Research on Aging, 10(1)*, 199–133.

Hazelrigg, L. E., & Hardy, M. A. (1995). Older adult migration to the sunbelt: Assessing income and related characteristics of recent migrants. *Research on Aging, 17*, 209–234.

Hodge, G. (1991). The economic impact of retirees on smaller communities. *Research on Aging, 13(1)*, 39–54.

Hogan, T. D., & Happel, S. K. (1994). 1993–94 winter residents important to AZ economy. *Arizona Business, 41(7)*, 1–4.

Hogan, T. D., & Steinnes, D. N. (1993). Elderly migration to the Sun belt: Seasonal versus permanent. *Journal of Applied Gerontology, 12*, 246–260.

Joseph, A. E., & Cloutier, D. S. (1991). Elderly migration and its implications for service provision in rural communities: An Ontario perspective. *Journal of Rural Studies, 7(4)*, 433–444.

Kallan, J. E. (1993). A multilevel analysis of elderly migration. *Social Science Quarterly, 74,* 403–416.

Lin, G., & Rogerson, P. A. (1995). Elderly parents and the geographic availability of their adult children. *Research on Aging, 17(3),* 303–331.

Litwak, E., & Longino, C. F., Jr. (1987). Migration patterns among the elderly: A developmental perspective. *The Gerontologist, 27(3),* 266–272.

Longino, C. F., Jr. (1990a). Geographical distribution and migration. In R. H. Binstock & L. K. George (Eds.), *Handbook of aging and the social sciences, third edition* (pp. 45–63). San Diego, CA: Academic Press.

Longino, C. F., Jr. (1990b). Geographic mobility and family caregiving in nonmetropolitan America: Three-decade evidence from the U.S. census. *Family Relations, 39,* 38–43.

Longino, C. F., Jr. (1992). The forest and the trees: Micro-level considerations in the study of geographic mobility in old age. In A. Rogers (Ed.), *Elderly migration and population redistribution* (pp. 23–24). London: Belhaven Press.

Longino, C. F., Jr. (1994). From sunbelt to sunspots. *American Demographics, 16,* 22–31.

Longino, C. F., Jr. (1995). *Retirement migration in America.* Houston: Vacation Publications.

Longino, C. F., Jr. (1998). Geographic mobility and the baby boom. *Generations, 22,* 60–64.

Longino, C. F., Jr., & Crown, W. H. (1990). Retirement migration and interstate income transfers. *The Gerontologist, 30,* 784–789.

Longino, C. F., Jr., & Haas, W. H., III. (1992). Migration and the rural elderly. In C. N. Bull (Ed.), *Aging in rural America* (pp. 17–29). London: Sage Publications.

Longino, C. F., Jr., Jackson, D. J., Zimmerman, R. S., & Bradsher, J. E. (1991). The second move: Health and geographic mobility. *Journal of Gerontology: Social Sciences, 46,* S218–S224.

Longino, C. F. Jr., & Marshall, V. W. (1990). North American research on seasonal migration. *Ageing and Society, 10,* 229–235.

Longino, C. F., Jr., Marshall, V. W., Mullins, L. C., & Tucker, R. D. (1991). On the nesting of snowbirds. *Journal of Applied Gerontology, 10,* 157–168.

Longino, C. F., Jr., & Perricone, P. J. (1991). The elderly population of south Florida, 1950–1990. *The Florida Geographer, 25,* 2–19.

Longino, C. F., Jr., & Serow, W. J. (1990). Regional differences in the characteristics of elderly return migrants. *Journal of Gerontology: Social Sciences, 47,* S38–S43.

Longino, C. F., Jr., & Smith, K. J. (1991). Black retirement migration in the United States. *Journal of Gerontology: Social Sciences, 46,* S125–S132.

MacManus, S. (1997). Selling school taxes and bond issues to a generationally diverse electorate: Lessons from Florida referenda. *Government Finance Review, April,* 17–22.

Marshall, V. W., Longino, C. F., Jr., Tucker, R. D., & Mullins, L. G. (1989). Health care utilization of Canadian snowbirds: An example of strategic planning. *Journal of Aging and Health, 1,* 150–168.

Martin, H. W., Hoppe, S. K., Marshall, V. W., & Daciuk, J. F. (1992). Sociodemographic and health characteristics of Anglophone Canadian and U.S. Snowbirds. *Journal of Aging and Health, 4,* 500–513.

McAuley, W. J., Pecchioni, L., & Grant, J. (1999). Admission-related migration by older nursing home residents. *Journal of Gerontology: Social Sciences, 54B,* S125–S135.

McHugh, K. E. (1990). Seasonal migration as a substitute for, or precursor to, permanent Migration. *Research on Aging, 12,* 229–245.

McHugh, K. E., Hogan, T. D., & Happel, S. K. (1995). Multiple residence and cyclical migration: A life course perspective. *Professional Geographer, 47(3),* 251–267.

McHugh, K. E., & Mings, R. C. (1991). On the road again: Seasonal migration to a Sunbelt metropolis. *Urban Geography, 12,* 1–18.

McHugh, K. E., & Mings, R. C. (1994). Seasonal migration and health care. *Journal of Aging and Health, 6,* 111–122.

Miller, M. E., Longino, C. F., Jr., Anderson, R. T., James, M. K., & Worley, A. S. (1999). Functional status, assistance, and the risk of a community-based move. *The Gerontologist, 39(2),* 187–200.

Mings, R. C. (1997). Tracking "snowbirds" in Australia: Winter sun seekers in far north Queensland. *Australian Geographical Studies, 35,* 168–182.

Morrison, P. A. (1990). Demographic factors reshaping ties to family and place. *Research on Aging, 12(4)*, 399–408.

Moss, M. S., & Moss, S. Z. (1992). Themes in parent–child relationships when elderly parents move nearby. *Journal of Aging Studies, 6(3)*, 259–271.

Mullins, D. R., & Rosenstraub, M. S. (1992). Fiscal pressure?: The impact of elder recruitment on local expenditures. *Urban Affairs Quarterly*, December, 337–354.

Reeder, R. J., & Glasgow, N. L. (1990). Nonmetro retirement counties' strengths and weaknesses. *Rural Development Perspectives, 6(2)*, 12–17.

Rogers, A. (1990). Return migration to region of birth among retirement-age persons in the United States. *Journal of Gerontology: Social Sciences, 45*, S-128–S134.

Rogers, A. (Ed.). (1992). *Elderly migration and population redistribution*. London: Belhaven Press.

Rogers, A., Watkins, J. F., & Woodward, J. A. (1990). Interregional elderly migration and population redistribution in four industrialized countries. *Research on Aging, 12*, 251–93.

Rosenbaum, W. A., & Button, J. W. (1989). Is there a gray peril?: Retirement politics in Florida. *The Gerontologist, 29*, 300–306.

Rowles, G. D., & Watkins, J. F. (1993). Elderly migration and development in small communities. *Growth and Change, 24*, 509–538.

Sastry, M. L. (1992). Estimating the economic impacts of elderly migration: An input-output analysis. *Growth and Change, 23(1)*, 54–79.

Savageau, D. (2000). *Retirement places rated*. New York: Macmillan.

Schneider, M. J., & Green, B. L. (1992). A demographic and economic comparison of nonmetropolitan retirement and nonretirement counties in the U.S. *Journal of Applied Sociology, 9*, 63–84.

Serow, W. J. (1978). Return migration of the elderly in the U.S.A.: 1955–1960 and 1965–1970." *Journal of Gerontology, 33*, 288–295.

Serow, W. J. (1990). Economic implications of retirement migration. *The Journal of Applied Gerontology, 9(4)*, 452–463.

Serow, W. J. (1992). Unanswered questions and new directions in research on elderly migration: Economic and demographic perspec-

tives. *Journal of Aging & Social Policy, 4(3/4)*, 7389.

Serow, W. J. (1996). Demographic and socioeconomic aspects of elderly migration in the 1980s. *Journal of Aging & Social Policy, 8(1)*, 19–38.

Serow, W. J., Friedrich, K., & Haas, W. H. (1992). Measuring the economic impact of retirement migration: The case of western North Carolina. *The Journal of Applied Gerontology, 11(2)*, 200–215.

Serow, W. J., Friedrich, K., & Haas, W. H. (1996). Residential relocation and regional redistribution of the elderly in the USA and Germany. *Journal of Cross-Cultural Gerontology, 11*, 293–306.

Silverstein, M. (1995). Stability and change in temporal distance between the elderly and their children. *Demography, 32(1)*, 29–45.

Silverstein, M., & Zablotsky, D. (1996). Health and social precursors of later life retirement-community migration. *Journal of Gerontology: Social Sciences, 51*, S150–S156.

Simonsen, W., & Robbins, M. (1996). Does it make any difference anymore? Competitive versus negotiated municipal bond issuance. *Public Administration Review, 56(1)*, 57–64.

Singelakis, A. T. (1990). Real estate market trends and the displacement of the aged: Examination of the linkages in Manhattan. *The Gerontologist, 30(5)*, 658–666.

Speare, A., Jr., Avery, R., & Lawton, L. (1991). Disability, residential mobility, and changes in living arrangements. *Journal of Gerontology: Social Sciences, 46(3)*, S133–S142.

Speare, A., Jr., & McNally, J. (1992). The relation of migration and household change among elderly persons. In A. Rogers (Ed.), *Elderly migration and population redistribution* (pp. 61–67). London: Belhaven Press.

Stallmann, J. I., & Siegel, P. B. (1995). Attracting retirees as an economic development strategy: Looking into the future. *Economic Development Quarterly, 9(4)*, 372–382.

Steinnes, D. N., & Hogan, T. D. (1992). Take the money and the sun: Elderly migration as a consequence of gains in unaffordable housing markets. *Journal of Gerontology: Social Sciences, 47(4)*, S197–S203.

Tucker, R. D., Mullins, L. C., Beland, F., Longino, C. F., Jr., & Marshall, V. W. (1992). Older Canadians in Florida: A comparison of Anglophone and Francophone seasonal migrants. *Canadian Journal on Aging, 11,* 281–297.

Voss, P. R., & Fuguitt, G. V. (1991). The impact of migration on southern rural areas of chronic depression. *Rural Sociology, 56(4),* 660–679.

Warnes, A. M. (1992). Migration and the life course. In T. Champion & T. Fielding (Eds.), *Migration processes and patterns* (pp. 175–187). London: Belhaven Press.

Warnes, A. M., King, R., Williams, A. M., & Patternson, G. (2000). The well-being of British expatriate retirees in southern Europe. *Ageing and Society, 19,* 717–740.

Watkins, J. F. (1990). Appalachian elderly migration. *Research on Aging, 12,* 409–429.

Watkins, J. F. (1999). Life course and spatial experience: A personal narrative approach in migration studies. In K. Pandit & S. Davies-Wiothers (Eds.), *Migration and Restructuring in the United States* (pp. 294–312). Boulder, CO: Rowman and Littlefield.

Williams, A. M., King, R., & Warnes, A. M. (1997). A place in the sun: International retirement migration from northern to southern Europe. *European Urban and Regional Studies, 4,* 115–134.

Wiseman, R. F. (1980). Why older people move. *Research on Aging, 2(2),* 141–154.

Seven

Age, Aging, and Anthropology

Charlotte Ikels and Cynthia M. Beall

I. Retrospective and Prospective

Previous editions of this handbook have featured comprehensive reviews of the place of age and aging in anthropological research. These works have documented that early (pre-1970s) anthropological interest in age was largely formal in character (i.e., centered on how age structured social relations). In the kinship domain this interest manifested itself particularly in the study of lineages in which generational age and relative age (birth order) within a single generation defined an individual's rights and duties to other lineage members. In the community domain, interest focused on age grades and age sets, especially as found in East Africa, where they were perceived as mechanisms that, in addition to allocating statuses and roles, served to link horizontally people who were already linked vertically through lineage ties, thereby enhancing societal integration.

Although most early ethnographies contained a descriptive chapter on the life cycle (not the life course), aging as such was seldom directly studied. Instead the reader toured the local cycle of rites of passage that marked major status transitions: birth, puberty, marriage, parenthood, and death. To most researchers how participants experienced or felt about these rites was of less importance than their structure and official significance. In that era older people—the aged—were most visible to anthropologists in their role as informants.

By the 1960s, however, the situation was beginning to change. Like other social scientists, anthropologists realized that the impact on the United States of population aging and of increased numbers of the aged had become a major social issue, and they began to turn their attention directly to the older population. Initially they scoured the ethnographic literature to test hypotheses about the relationship between a set of variables and the status of the aged around the world. Then they moved in on the aged directly—investigating firsthand concentrations of elderly wherever they could find them: settled trailer parks, retirement communities, congregate housing, and nursing homes. Most of these studies, carried out in the 1960s and 1970s, focused on how older people maintained ties with their adult children living elsewhere, developed social relationships in

Handbook of Aging and the Social Sciences, Fifth Edition

the new community, and found valued activities in which to invest themselves.

The last setting mentioned above, the nursing home, inevitably called attention to the fact that aging is often associated with physical decline and disability. Since the 1980s this fact has nearly overpowered all other facts about age and aging for anthropology. The number of anthropologists working on some aspect of age-associated disability, be it on experiencing or interpreting illness, obtaining appropriate health care, or being "burdened" by providing care, is probably about equal to the number working on all other aging-related phenomena. Closely related to this shift within anthropology is another shift: the great increase in the proportion of anthropologists whose primary research area is in the United States and in their own communities. Together these two shifts mean that the nature of the relationships among age, aging, and the field of anthropology in the United States today is very different from what it was just 30 years ago.

In this edition of the handbook, rather than simply limiting ourselves to bringing this research up to date, we intend to examine the broader contexts that have influenced the current state of the field. These contexts include changes in the global and national political environments, changes within the discipline of anthropology itself, and changes within the subspecialty of the anthropology of age and aging. Together these changes threaten to overwhelm the traditional image of anthropology as a holistic, comparative, and cross-cultural endeavor with a new image as a cultural specialty best suited to exercising its expertise in interdisciplinary and applied environments. This transformation had been underway since at least the 1960s, but it accelerated rapidly during the 1970s and 1980s, the very decades that the anthropology of age and aging was maturing as a subfield.

Anthropology, however, is not concerned solely with the cultural dimension of the human experience. Rather, as a field, it has long emphasized the study of humanity in both its sociocultural and biological aspects. Physical anthropologists deal with the biological nature of the aging process and seek to understand why we age as well as the biological, cultural, and environmental factors that influence how we age. From the earliest days, evolutionary theory has played a key role in attempts to answer the fundamental question of why we age. One evolutionary explanation, the mutation accumulation hypothesis, reasons that the frequency of late-acting deleterious mutations has increased over evolutionary time because of weak natural selection at advanced ages. The resultant high frequency of late-acting deleterious genes accounts for biological aging.

Another evolutionary explanation, the antagonistic pleiotropy hypothesis, reasons that a given mutation could have beneficial effects early in the life cycle and detrimental effects later. That is, the effects of such genes are pleiotropic (having more than one effect) and antagonistic (having opposing influences on survival at different stages of the life cycle). Natural selection would increase their frequency due to the survival and/or reproductive benefits early in life despite any later deleterious effects that underlie aging. These two evolutionary hypotheses can explain why there is a late phase of the life cycle characterized by increasing vulnerability (Rose & Mueller, 1998). The emerging consensus among evolutionary theorists is that senescence itself is not an adaptation; that is, it is not the result of natural selection for that trait. Instead it may be an exaptation (a trait serving current beneficial functions that did not evolve that way), a neutral, or even a deleterious trait.

A related evolutionary question is the determination of the length of the life span. Maximum life span, the age at death of the longest-lived member of a species, is a species characteristic even though it is measured in a single individual. Currently it is a little over 122 years for humans. Humans, apes, and elephants are the only species of terrestrial mammals with maximum life spans over 50 years (Comfort, 1979). Comparing many species revealed that maximum life span potential correlates strongly with brain size (Sacher, 1959). Therefore, human maximum life span potential probably has not changed since the emergence of Homo sapiens at least 100,000 years ago when current brain size was attained. Survivorship was low then, and selection would have acted to favor healthy reproductive-age individuals. A by-product (probably largely unexpressed due to low survivorship) of selection for larger brains was relatively high maximum life span potential. Maximum life span is measured in individuals living in favorable environments where predators, disease, and nutrition are well controlled. Human maximum life span may increase even more with future improvements in late life mortality control. However, it seems to be an emergent property of our large brains and intelligence rather than the result of selection for the ability to survive more than 100 years.

Another puzzling phenomenon from the evolutionary perspective is menopause, the universal cessation of reproductive capacity among human females less than half way through the maximum life span potential. Every woman in every population who survives long enough becomes postmenopausal. Physical anthropologists have used several sources of data to address the question of why there is a long postreproductive life for human females. Demographic data from humans, nonhuman primates, and other mammalian species indicate that a young-adult peak reproductive capacity is attained and is followed by a decline with age in female (and male) fertility and fecundity (Finch, 1990; Gage, 1998). Menopause may be a trait that has emerged simply as a result of improved survivorship allowing many females to survive long enough to live beyond the end of the fertility decline caused by the loss of ovarian follicles. If so, then menopause has no special adaptive significance. Alternatively, some hypotheses, including the "grandmother" hypothesis, argue that natural selection favors females who switch from reproducing themselves to caring for the offspring of others. If so, then there would be selection for ending the fertile period (Leidy, 1999).

In summary, the bulk of the theoretical models and demographic evidence indicates that, until recently, just a small proportion of people lived long life spans. As a result, natural selection has been working to produce healthy young adults of reproductive age and probably has not operated strongly on the life span after young adulthood. This interpretation implies that the origins of variation in biological processes during later adulthood may be found at younger ages. Therefore, one aim of contemporary studies is to identify sources of population and individual differences in vulnerability, morbidity, and mortality late in adulthood that have their origins at earlier stages of the life cycle. Another aim of contemporary studies is determining which aging changes are inevitable concomitants of the passage of time and which are subject to environmental influence.

II. Reshaping the Field

Sociocultural anthropology as practiced in the United States into the 1970s historically distinguished itself from sociology primarily in its choice of research sites, scale of society under study, and emphasis on long-term immersion in fieldwork. Generally, unless they intended to become specialists on Native American culture, aspiring anthropologists were expected to conduct fieldwork outside of the United States. Because their aims were generally holistic in nature (i.e., acquiring an understanding of the local "big picture"), they tended to work in small-scale social units such as villages, bands, or neighborhoods where, ideally at least, they could keep track of personnel and activities through long-term participant-observation. As ethnographers their priority was on understanding local culture rather than on direct problem-solving or hypothesis testing, which were seen more as the domain of sociologists. In fact anthropology and sociology have always overlapped to some extent in both disciplinary aims and methods. Applied (i.e., problem-solving) anthropology has long been known as the "fifth" field of anthropology (along with the traditional four fields of archaeology, sociocultural anthropology, physical or biological anthropology, and linguistics). And sociologists have employed participant-observation and other qualitative methods to study immigrants, subcultures, and neighborhoods in the United States.

Probably the most significant difference between the two fields has been the emphasis anthropology places on working with people from a culture different from one's own. For the anthropologist-in-training "going to the field" has constituted the disciplinary rite of passage, complete with its own three phases of separation, liminality, and reincorporation (van Gennep, 1960). In the narrative of this rite, the novice is removed ("separated") from the world as previously known, shorn of the familiar props of everyday life (language, food, comfort, world view, personal associates, etc.), and thrust into somebody else's world. During this sojourn the novice occupies the liminal status of the outsider, pursuing a quest for knowledge and undergoing

trials of all sorts (see Howell, 1990, for the kinds of trials fieldworkers actually face). Finally, mission accomplished, the novice returns to the acclaim of tribal elders (more senior anthropologists) and is reincorporated into the community as one transformed by the experience of "being in the field."

Initial fieldwork is not only about gathering enough data to produce a dissertation; fully as important is its presumed de-centering of the trainee's universe. After fieldwork, one's previous world is no longer seen in the same light; ideally, the anthropologist-in-training has acquired a new perspective on his or her own culture, one that allows the questioning of the once-familiar categories and premises on which that world is built. Most anthropologists (84% in Howell's, 1990 study), conduct off-campus fieldwork of some sort (e.g., excavation, survey, ethnography) though not all of this research involves working in an unfamiliar society nor even in an "ethnic community" within one's home society. In fact the proportion of dissertation (and subsequent) research that is conducted by anthropologists on mainstream Americans within the United States is widely perceived to be increasing. On the one hand this is all to the good. Who could object to the application of anthropology's holistic and cross-cultural approach to the beliefs, practices, and institutions of our own dominant population? On the other hand, this shift has serious implications for the field as a whole and for the subfield of the anthropology of age and aging in particular.

First, fieldwork carried out in one's own language while enjoying all the comforts of home (sleeping in one's own bed, watching one's favorite television programs, keeping up with the happenings in the lives of family and friends) inescapably insulates the fieldworker from the kind of totalizing experience that can de-center one's world. Second, the more anthropologists work in the United States and proportionately less in other societies, the more the data gathered will reflect the situation in the United States and the less opportunity we will have to appreciate the broad range of human adaptability. Third, the more anthropologists work in the United States the more they risk having their research priorities set by others as they are more likely to be employed outside of anthropology departments and to have to justify their research in terms meaningful to their nonanthropologist associates, employers, and funders.

The retreat of anthropology from the wider world has been influenced by both external and internal factors.

A. External Factors

The most important external factors affecting anthropological research have been post-World War II decolonization and the Cold War (Cumings, 1998; Herman, 1998; Nader, 1997). From anthropology's earliest beginnings in the 19th century and regardless of their individual research aims, anthropologists have inevitably been dependent upon the goodwill of the powers that be to carry out their work. During the colonial era, British social anthropologists, for example, relied on their fellow countrymen to maintain order and to require local political subordinates to assure their safety in the field. Some even served in the colonial administration before taking up positions as professional anthropologists. The monographs they wrote on kinship, religion, and political organization could be drawn on by colonial magistrates as they attempted to adjudicate disputes in accordance with customary law.

In the two decades following the end of World War II, most British, French, and Dutch colonies became independent. As sovereign states they now determined the terms under which foreigners were allowed to conduct research on their territory. Much of Africa and South and Southeast Asia became problematic field sites because of political instability, bureaucratic red tape, sensitivities about the past, or suspicions about the true purposes of the proposed fieldwork and the uses to which its findings might be put. According to Chomsky et al. (1997) and Simpson (1998), they were right to be suspicious. The writings of anthropologists along with those of other behavioral scientists became primary sources of data on populations in countries deemed problematic by the United States government and/or military (i.e., those countries currently or potentially experiencing communist insurgencies). When more direct links between fieldwork and the military were revealed first in the early-mid 1960s in Project Camelot, which targeted Latin America (Herman, 1998), and later in work carried out in Thailand, concerned scholars called for a severance of these types of connections. But it was too late. According to Herman (1998) many governments, especially in Latin America, but elsewhere too (Burma, Nepal, Afghanistan, Iran, Pakistan, Iraq, Yemen, Saudi Arabia, Sudan, Egypt, and others), promptly imposed restrictions and in some cases outright bans on foreign scholars for fear they were connected with the Central Intelligence Agency. Fieldwork by American scholars in communist countries or those allied with the Soviet Union was, of course, even less likely.

The Cold War also generated a great interest in development programs and area studies on the part of the American government. Development programs, in which anthropologists played important roles, were intended by the Western nations that sponsored them not simply to raise standards of living or provide markets for their products and services but to create alternate routes out of poverty and, thereby, forestall revolutions. The postwar growth in the field of area studies reflected the government's intent to produce a cadre of regional experts available for consultation. Now that the Cold War is over, the perceived need for regional experts is being replaced by a need for people who can interpret transnational and global contexts and their impact on the interests of the United States, and funding priorities clearly reflect this. The Ford Foundation, for example, has been reorganizing its programs along thematic rather than area concerns. Economists reign supreme during the post-Cold War era of the "free market."

To summarize, anthropological research outside of the United States has become more problematic due to restriction or denial of access to field sites, to anthropologists' own concerns about the possible uses to which their data might be put, and to changing priorities of potential funders. But there are also factors internal to the discipline that have led to increased emphasis on "doing ethnography at home."

B. Internal Factors

1. Factors Internal to the Discipline as a Whole

Decolonization posed not only a political problem for anthropologists but also an epistemological one. Some foreign scholars became extremely uncomfortable when confronted by local scholars with doctoral degrees of their own who were fully competent to carry out research in their own countries. Although some of these scholars were often happy to collaborate with their one-time politically advantaged foreign colleagues on joint projects, others as well as nonscholars resented their continued presence and, particularly, their claim to speak authoritatively for the populations that they studied. Some anthropologists responded to this challenge by writing "multivocal" ethnographies (i.e., including the perspectives and interpretations of members of the local community).

Other anthropologists have been so influenced by recent intellectual trends that they no longer believe anthropology can be—or ever was—a scientific pursuit (e.g, Aunger, 1995; Jaarsma & Rohatynskyj, 2000). For example, both postmodernism and discourse theory challenge the notion that there is a single reality "out there" for the ethnographer to study and describe; therefore, they see little merit in conducting conventional fieldwork and even less in writing the traditional ethnography. This view is far more pervasive in sociocultural anthropology than in the other four fields.

2. Factors Internal to the Subfield

As a subfield the anthropology of age and aging was beginning to emerge in the United States in the late 1970s. Whereas the earliest publications on the topic such as those by Simmons (1945, 1960) were based on secondary data analysis, by the late 1970s enough field studies focused on age and aging had accumulated that within a very short period several cross-cultural collections (Amoss & Harrell, 1981; Fry, 1980, 1981; Myerhoff & Simic, 1978), all touting the special contributions of anthropology to gerontology, appeared. Most of the anthropologists whose works were published in these volumes had worked in isolation from one another, regarded themselves as pioneers, and felt marginalized at gerontology conferences dominated by sociologists, psychologists, and social work professionals whose primary focus was on the United States. As these researchers gradually became aware of each other's work and reached a critical mass, they established The Association for Anthropology and Gerontology (AAGE) in 1978.

Although it has a multidisciplinary membership, AAGE retains its primary identification with anthropology and holds its annual business meeting during the annual meeting of the American

Anthropological Association. In 1986, with the encouragement of AAGE, the Department of Anthropology at Case Western Reserve University founded the *Journal of Cross-Cultural Gerontology* to provide "an international and interdisciplinary...forum for scholarly discussion of the aging process and the problems of the aged throughout the world" (journal self-description, each issue, unnumbered page).

Although intending to emphasize a "holistic, comparative and international perspective," the anthropologists who join AAGE face the same dilemmas as other anthropologists, namely, restrictions on fieldwork, high probability of finding employment outside of traditional anthropology departments, and a need to make their research comprehensible and attractive to researchers, employers, and funders whose first priority is the situation in the United States. Since, in this country, aging and the elderly are first and foremost perceived as financial problems, funding agencies favor research projects and programs that promise to find ways to reduce costs, particularly health-care costs. Thus disproportionate funding has been channeled into such topics as caregiving, long-term care, and cultural factors affecting the receipt or delivery of health care. As a consequence, aging has nearly become a subspecialty of medical anthropology rather than of anthropology as a whole and at a time when the integrity of medical anthropology itself as a discipline is being questioned (Browner, 1999).

III. The New Anthropology of Age and Aging

A. Physical Anthropology and Biological Aging

Consideration of the following topics, changes in blood pressure, bone mass, hearing, and menopause, illustrates the potential of cross-cultural studies of biological aging to offer insights into the intrinsic (perhaps universal) and extrinsic (perhaps population or environment specific) aspects of the aging process.

An age-related increase in blood pressure after young adulthood is so widespread in industrial populations that it has been considered a part of the usual aging process (Finch, 1990). Yet reports of more than 36 nonindustrial populations in which blood pressure remains stable throughout adulthood illustrate that men and women can maintain normal or low normal blood pressure throughout adulthood (James & Baker, 1995). Such studies raise the question of the factors that account for the observations of increase with age in industrialized societies (Pearson, Morrell, Brant, Landis, & Fleg, 1997).

An age-related loss of bone mass after attaining a young adult peak is so widespread that it has been characterized as "a universal phenomenon of human biology that occurs regardless of sex, race, occupation, economic development, geographic location, historical epoch, or dietary habits...." (Parfitt, 1983, p. 1181). Age-related bone loss is associated with an increase in age-related fractures and associated morbidity and mortality. However, the universality of the phenomenon of bone loss is not consistent with findings of low fracture rates among East Asians (Silverman & Madison, 1988) and Mexicans (Martin, Block, Sanchez, Arnaud, & Beyene, 1993). Such findings suggest that other, unidentified factors influence the likelihood of fractures among individuals with low bone mass.

Hearing thresholds increase after young adulthood and the prevalence of hearing loss increases with age in industrial populations (Fozard, 1990). However, the relative contribution of intrinsic biological aging phenomena and longer exposure to everyday noise is uncertain. This question was addressed with a study of natives of Easter Island (Goycoolea et al., 1986). Hearing thresholds for Easter Island residents 45 years of age and older were measured, and islanders were grouped according to inferred noise exposure measured as number of years on "the island of the great silence" or in urban, mainland Chile. Hearing thresholds increased with age least among those with no exposure to urban noise and increased in proportion to the length of time resident in Chile. Those results suggest that higher thresholds reflect an intrinsic aging phenomenon whose rate of change and absolute level can be modified by the ambient noise environment.

Menopausal symptoms are experienced by a large proportion of North American women. For example, nearly half a sample of North American women interviewed in the year prior to menopause reported hot flashes in the two weeks prior to the interview (McKinlay, Brambilla, & Posner, 1992). Yet a comparison of North American and Japanese women between 45 and 55 years of age revealed that North American women reported symptoms such as hot flashes and cold or night sweats at a rate three to four times higher than the Japanese women (Lock, 1998). Nor did Maya women in Mexico report experiencing hot flashes (Martin et al., 1993). This difference in the experience of menopause led to the observation that "Menopause is both an objective hormonal event and a subjectively perceived endocrine transition" (Martin et al., 1993, p. 1839). It also raises the question of the identity of social and biological factors influencing the perception itself.

Many existing cross-cultural studies have shortcomings that somewhat limit confidence in their findings. Virtually none is longitudinal, and nearly all report on small samples that are especially small at the very oldest ages. Many of the findings of population contrasts arise from research conducted in rural villages and towns in developing countries. These sites have small populations and inevitably will have few people of advanced age. For example, a town of 1000 people in a developing country nowadays will likely have just 30–50 people over 65 years of age, and very few will be over 80 years of age (Kinsella & Taeuber, 1992). The possibility for small-sample-size effects to influence the findings is large, especially considering the increasing variance of biological phenomena with age (Comfort, 1979). However, many of the phenomena described above have been reported from multiple research sites and on more than one continent. Those natural experimental replications bolster confidence in the reliability of the findings.

In summary, cross-cultural studies of biological aging reveal that some age-related changes common in industrial societies are not inevitable, that the degree of change may be modulated by the environment, and that the outcome of universal changes may vary. They indicate the potential of cross-cultural research to identify novel factors contributing to successful aging (Rowe & Kahn, 1997).

B. Sociocultural Anthropology and Health Issues

Although physical anthropologists have examined biological processes, sociocultural anthropologists have been more concerned with the experience of illness and the phenomenon of caregiving. Most of these works attempt to explicate the special role of cultural factors in the genesis, experience, and management of age-related changes in health and functionality. Sociocultural researchers investigating the nature of menopause in Newfoundland (Davis, 1997), Greece and Mexico (Beyene, 1989), Japan and North America (Kaufert & Lock, 1992; Lock, 1993), among Indian women in South Africa (Du Toit, 1990), and among Australian women of Italian background

(Gifford, 1994) agree with their physical colleagues that not only are the meanings of the end of the reproductive stage of life culturally constructed but so too are the physiological and psychological symptoms leading up to it.

Anthropologists have taken a special interest in dementia as it is manifested, interpreted, and managed in ethnic communities in the United States (e.g., Cubans and Puerto Ricans—Henderson, 1996, and Chinese—Elliott, Di Minno, Lam, & Tu, 1996) and abroad. In Asia large base populations (in India and China) combined with rapid population aging (in China and Japan) have contributed to substantial local interest in gerontological issues including dementia. Ikels (1997, 1998a) has been conducting a longitudinal study on Chinese elderly in the city of Guangzhou and found dementia to be much less feared than in the United States due to both cultural and situational factors. In his work in Japan, Traphagan (1998) has focused on the strategies elderly Japanese use to avoid becoming demented, while Cohen (1998) uses his work in India to critique the biological reductionism of old age so characteristic in the United States.

Reflecting the broader gerontological interest in the phenomenon of family caregiving, Keith (1992) analyzed the significance of cultural context for understanding patterns of care cross-culturally. She points out that societies differ in the requirements they set for functionality and in the process of designating familial caregivers. If the standards for functionality are physically demanding, requiring, for example, that people be able to walk great distances, disability and the need for caregiving set in much earlier. The selection of an appropriate caregiver is influenced by a society's kinship system; societies practicing unilineal descent usually have more explicit rules than those practicing bilateral descent. Yet even among societies having patrilineal

descent in common, there is substantial diversity. Among the Sherpas of Nepal the youngest son (and his wife) is the designated caregiver, whereas among the pre-World War II Japanese it was the oldest son. In China responsibility for parents was generally divided among all the sons. In bilateral kinship systems, selection criteria are more idiosyncratic, and people need to think strategically about who will care for them in old age.

Comparative studies of caregiving practices and motivation among specific populations include those by Harris and Long (1999) and Hashimoto (1996) on Japanese and Americans, and Sung (1994) on Koreans and Americans. Care-seeking behavior has been studied among the !Kung San in Botswana by Rosenberg (1997) and in Kenya by Cattell (1997), and Hennessy and John (1995) studied caregiver burden among the Pueblos. Beyond care provided by the family, Morgan, Eckert, and Lyon (1995) examined the board- and-care home, a transitional setting that postpones the move to institutional care. The tradition of studying long-term care facilities, the next step in the continuum of care, has been continued in the United States by Shield (1997), in Canada by Woolfson (1997), and in Japan by Kinoshita and Kiefer (1992).

C. Recent Work on Aging and Social Issues

Given anthropology's historically great interest in kinship, it should not be surprising that family roles and dynamics, quite apart from the issue of caregiving, have been a major research focus. During the 1980s, Potash (1986), eschewing the traditional structural-functional mode of analysis, organized a set of papers that took the perspectives of widows themselves, demonstrating the options and the constraints that shaped the possibilities open to them. Without an appreciation of the nature and extent of kin group solidarity, patterns of affinal and consanguineal relationships, variations in household and community organization, the relative importance of male and female economic contributions, the significance of natal group rights, and the nature of marital alliances. (Potash, 1986, p. 43)

Potash argues we cannot really understand the experience of widowhood. This emphasis on the context in which a seemingly abstract role is enacted is echoed more than a decade later by Ikels (1998b) in her discussion of grandparenthood in cross-cultural perspective when she points out the importance of descent systems (unilineal or bilateral), flexibility in the concept of kinship, and household organization and residence patterns as well as the overall position of older people in the wider society. More concrete studies of American Indian grandmothers are presented in Schweitzer (1999).

Anthropologists have paid special attention to the needs of immigrant and refugee elderly. Ikels (1998c) has considered their special health needs, but in addition to physical problems these elders may experience severe disruption in family roles and other aspects of their lives with profound implications for their mental health. These issues are addressed by Becker and Beyene (1999) in their study of elderly Cambodian refugees; Dossa (1999) in her study of elderly Ismaili (Muslim) women who were uprooted from East Africa and resettled in Canada; Frank and colleagues (1998), Kauh (1997), and Pang (1998) in their work with elderly Korean-Americans, and Omidian (1996) in her work among Afghan refugees.

Barresi (1997) correctly points out that researchers working in the field of "ethnogerontology" need to be alert to differences in their depictions of aging in national, racial, and cultural populations. Too often a general account is given that ignores intrapopulation diversity (e.g., north–south divides in culture and/or politics are likely to make for important

distinctions among Irish, Italian, Chinese, Vietnamese, and Korean elders). Furthermore these general accounts are frequently frozen in time and no longer apply to more recent cohorts of immigrants. A third limitation is that, given the problem orientation of much gerontological research, investigators tend to focus on disadvantaged populations or disadvantaged segments of populations.

Beyond the family, anthropologists have investigated social networks and exchange among black and white elderly (Barker, Morrow, & Mitteness, 1998; Groger & Kunkel, 1995), rural American elderly (Shenk, 1998), urban American elderly (Schreck, 1996), and elderly in India (van Willigen & Chadha, 1999). One of the most innovative (and popular) ethnographies of the 1990s is Counts and Counts's (1997) study of North American migratory seniors, winningly titled *Over the Next Hill*, who upon retirement opted to become "gypsies and pioneers" roaming the country in their RVs (recreational vehicles). In a great departure from their previous work on death and dying in the Pacific, Counts and Counts became "Skips" by joining Escapees, an RV club with its own parks for full-timers. The friendship characteristic of such parks creates sibling-like bonds among the temporary residents, providing them a sense of family wherever they go. This is an ethnography about positive, creative, and adventurous elders, and it provides an important antidote to the dismal image of elders with which most of us are familiar.

The issue of resource control and its contribution to the status of the elderly was an important theoretical topic in the anthropology of age and aging in the 1960s and 1970s, but later, at least domestically, it fell by the wayside or was turned over to economists and social policy researchers. Anthropologists working abroad, however, have remained interested in this topic. Smith (1998) studied the impact of the transition to sedentism among former pastoralists in Kenya; this latest test of modernization theory found that although younger people had gained control over the fruits of their own labor, they had not directly challenged the authority of the elders in other domains. He attributes this conservative stance to the continued prestige of the traditional age grade system and to the fact that there is still sufficient land not yet under cultivation that the young are not dependent on the old for land transfers.

Two anthropologists working in Ghana (Stucki, 1992; van der Geest, 1997) have found that respect in old age can no longer be guaranteed; rather, the possession of cash and how it has been used over the life course influence outcomes in old age. In countries with high youth unemployment but social welfare programs that benefit the elderly such as South Africa, older people can become magnets around whom dependent younger kin gather (Moller & Sotshongaye, 1996; Sagner & Mtati, 1999). Although the economic contributions of the elderly are frequently written off by development specialists, the income-earning potential of the rural sector in Jamaica could be enhanced if policymakers developed ways to work with older farmers rather than attempting to make agriculture attractive to younger people (Woodsong, 1994).

Because formal age grades are far more common among men than women, the study of power differentials among women across the life course was relatively neglected by early anthropologists. Brown has been a pioneer in remedying this neglect and in the 1990s, with coeditors, published two cross-cultural collections. The first (Kerns & Brown, 1992) was an update of their earlier (Brown & Kerns, 1985) work on how the status of middle-aged women varies across societies. These two works challenge the popular assumption in the United States that when women lose their youth they essen-tially lose everything. Instead they demonstrate that a variety of factors, including the extent to which younger women are secluded, the severity of restrictions during the menstrual cycle, the availability of roles for older women in the public domain, and the amount of control women exercise over the labor of younger kin, influence whether middle (and early old) age is viewed as a liberating or a depressing time of life. Brown's later work with Dickerson-Putman (Dickerson-Putman & Brown, 1998) goes beyond the analysis of female power across the life course to examine the dynamic of power relations between women of different ages. Other works on gender and aging include an ethnography by Lamb (2000) on India and a collection of African case studies edited by Udvardy and Cattell (1992).

D. Recent Work on Aging and Psychological Issues

Over the past two decades anthropologists have become more interested in the subjective experience of aging. Studies reflecting this interest have taken primarily two tacks: those focused on subjective well-being (and its components) and those focused on the meaning older people ascribe to their personal life story. Keith and associates (1994) report on their cross-cultural attempt to assess both the levels and the content of subjective well-being (or life satisfaction) across the life course in the United States, Ireland, Hong Kong, and Botswana. They found that simply comparing populations on the basis of their average well-being scores would reveal little useful information, as scores are influenced by cohort and period effects as well as culturally appropriate response styles. For example, among the !Kung of Botswana, a discourse of complaint is an acceptable way to mobilize support, but among the Chinese an emphasis on the importance of emotional moderation skews scores towards the middle range.

The emergence of the personal life story as a major focus in aging studies by anthropologists can probably be attributed to two factors: the publication in 1986 of Kaufman's book *The Ageless Self* and the increasing trend to narrative analysis within the field. Kaufman's San Francisco elderly informants refused to conform to the image of old age created by gerontologists. Instead of accepting identities as old people, a category other than "adults," they saw their later years as continuations of the lives they had been living all along. Age affected their energy levels and their options, but it was not an intrinsic aspect of identity; they saw themselves as "ageless." These findings reawakened anthropological interest in the life cycle, reconceptualized as the life course (i.e., the emphasis was not on the rituals that marked transitions but on the content and meaning of what occurred between the rituals). Ethnographers began to use the life course as the primary means of organizing and making sense of their data. For example, in one of a relatively few studies dealing with aging among Islamic populations, Rasmussen (1997) utilized a life-course perspective to examine the changing nature of social participation among the seminomadic Tuareg of Niger, while Hakansson and LeVine (1997) did so among the Gusii of Kenya.

IV. The Future Anthropology of Age and Aging

As has been demonstrated above, in the past few decades anthropologists have moved beyond the agenda that first attracted them to the study of age and aging. That early agenda focused on age as a principle of social organization and emphasized the role of anthropology in providing data that could be used to broaden our knowledge about the range of human behavior and adaptation. By the 1960s these data, at first secondary but increasingly primary in nature, were being used to look for regularities among variables with the aim of uncovering the role of culture in shaping the meaning of age and the experience of aging across particular contexts, (e.g., industrial versus agricultural societies). The 1970s brought both promise and peril to anthropology: Promise because it was a time when anthropologists in the newly emerging subfield of age and aging set out to conduct ethnographic investigations actually organized around the concept of aging, peril because it was a time that paradoxically marked the beginning of the shift within the broader field away from cross-cultural research.

By the 1980s and 1990s this shift was also apparent in the subfield. Increasingly anthropologists of age and aging were conducting much of their research in biomedical and other nontraditional settings within mainstream American society, struggling to justify their research methodology and objectives in terms that non-anthropologist service providers, policymakers, and funders would find acceptable. In the abstract, bringing the anthropological message to people working outside of the discipline is essential and desirable if anthropologists believe in the intrinsic value of an anthropological perspective. In the concrete it should result in greater understanding of the experience of aging within our own society and in the development of programs and policies that are sensitive to the needs of their intended beneficiaries. We have no quarrel with such proselytizing. Rather, our concern is that this mission not replace the earlier one of a holistic, comparative, and cross-cultural orientation to the wider world. It is time for the anthropology of age and aging to reexamine its past and to turn again to theoretical questions about the significance of the physical, social, and cultural environment for the experience and meaning of aging.

References

Amoss, P. T., & Harrell, S. (1981). *Other ways of growing old: Anthropological perspectives*. Stanford, CA: Stanford University Press.

Aunger, R. (1995). On ethnography: Storytelling or science? *Current Anthropology, 36,* 97–130.

Barker, J., Morrow, J., & Mitteness, L. S. (1998). Gender, informal support networks, and elderly urban African Americans. *Journal of Aging Studies, 12,* 199–222.

Barresi, C. M. (1997). Current issues in ethnogerontology. In K. Ferraro (Ed.), *Gerontology: Perspectives and issues* (2nd ed.) (pp. 267–284). New York: Springer Publishing Company.

Becker, G., & Beyene, Y. (1999). Narratives of age and uprootedness among older Cambodian refugees. *Journal of Aging Studies, 13,* 295–314.

Beyene, Y. (1989). *From menarche to menopause: Reproductive lives of peasant women in two cultures*. Albany: State University of New York Press.

Brown, J. K., & Kerns, V. (1985). *In her prime: A new view of middle-aged women*. South Hadley, MA: Bergin & Garvey.

Browner, C. H. (1999). On the medicalization of medical anthropology. *Medical Anthropology Quarterly, 13,* 135–140.

Cattell, M. G. (1997). The discourse of neglect: Family support for the elderly in Samia. In T. S. Weisner, C. Bradley, & P. L. Kilbride (Eds.), *African families and the crisis of social change* (pp.157–183). Westport, CT: Greenwood.

Chomsky, N., Katznelson, I., Lewentin, R. C., Montgomery, D., Nader, L., Ohmann, R., Siever, R., Wallerstein, I., & Zinn, H. (1997). *The Cold War and the university: Toward an intellectual history of the postwar years*. New York: The New Press.

Cohen, L. (1998). *No aging in India: Alzheimer's, the bad family, and other modern things*. Berkeley: University of California.

Comfort, A. (1979). *The biology of senescence*. New York: Elsevier.

Counts, D. A., & Counts, D. R. (1997). *Over the next hill: An ethnography of RVing seniors in North America*. Peterborough, Ontario: Broadview.

Cumings, B. (1998). Boundary displacement: Area studies and international studies during and after the Cold War. In C. Simpson(Ed.), *Universities and empire: Money and politics in the social sciences during the Cold War* (pp. 159–188). New York: The New Press.

Davis, D. L. (1997). Blood and nerves revisited: Menopause and the privatization of the body in a Newfoundland postindustrial fishery. *Medical Anthropology Quarterly, 11,* 3–20.

Dickerson-Putman, J., & Brown, J. K. (1998). *Women among women: Anthropological perspectives on female age hierarchies*. Urbana, IL: University of Illinois Press.

Dossa, P. A. (1999). (Re)imagining aging lives: Ethnographic narratives of Muslim women in diaspora. *Journal of Cross-Cultural Gerontology, 14,* 245–272.

Du Toit, B. M. (1990). *Aging and menopause among Indian South African women*. Albany: State University of New York.

Elliott, K. S., Di Minno, M., Lam, D., & Tu, A. M. (1996). Working with Chinese families in the context of dementia. In G. Yeo & D. Gallagher-Thompson (Eds.), *Ethnicity and the dementias* (pp. 89–108). Washington, D.C.: Taylor & Francis.

Finch, C. E. (1990). *Longevity, senescence, and the genome*. Chicago: Chicago University Press.

Fozard, J. L. (1990). Vision and hearing in aging. In J. E. Birren & K. W. Schaie (Eds.), *Handbook of the psychology of aging* (3rd ed.) (pp. 150–171). San Diego: Academic Press.

Frank, G., Blackhall, L. J., Michel, V., Murphy, S. T., Azen, S. P., & Park, K. (1998). A discourse of bioethics: Patient autonomy and end-of-life decision making among elderly Korean Americans. *Medical Anthropology Quarterly, 12,* 403–423.

Fry, C. L. (Ed.) (1980). *Aging in culture and society*. New York: Praeger.

Fry, C. L. (Ed.) (1981). *Dimensions: Aging, culture and health*. Brooklyn, NY: J. F. Bergin.

Gage, T. B. (1998). The comparative demography of primates: With some comments on
the evolution of life histories. *Annual Review of Gerontology, 27,* 197–221.

Gifford, S. M. (1994). The change of life, the
sorrow of life: Menopause, bad blood and
cancer among Italian-Australian working
class women. *Culture, Medicine and Psychiatry, 18,* 299–319.

Goycoolea, M. V., Goycoolea, H. G., Farfan, C.
R., Rodriguez, L. G., Martinez, G. C., &
Vidal, R. (1986). Effect of life in industrialized societies on hearing in natives
of Easter Island. *Laryngoscope, 96,*
1391–1396.

Groger, L., & Kunkel, S. (1995). Aging and exchange: Differences between black and
white elders. *Journal of Cross-Cultural Gerontology, 10,* 269–287.

Hakansson, N. T., & LeVine, R. A. (1997).
Gender and life-course strategies among
the Gusii. In T. S. Weisner, C. Bradley, &
P. L. Kilbride (Eds.), *African families and
the crisis of social change* (pp. 253–267).
Westport, CT: Greenwood.

Harris, P. B., & Long, S. (1999). Husbands and
sons in the United States and Japan: Cultural expectations and caregiving experiences. *Journal of Aging Studies, 13,*
241–267.

Hashimoto, A. (1996). *The gift of generations:
Japanese and American perspectives on
aging and the social contract.* Cambridge,
UK: Cambridge University Press.

Henderson, J. N. (1996). Cultural dynamics of
dementia in a Cuban and Puerto Rican
population in the United States. In G. Yeo
& D. Gallagher-Thompson (Eds.), *Ethnicity
and the dementias* (pp. 153–166). Washington, DC: Taylor & Francis.

Hennessy, C. H., & John, R. (1995). The interpretation of burden among Pueblo Indian
caregivers. *Journal of Aging Studies, 9,*
215–229.

Herman, H. (1998). Project Camelot and the
career of Cold War psychology. In C. Simpson (Ed.), *Universities and empire: Money
and politics in the social sciences during
the Cold War* (pp. 97–133). New York: The
New Press.

Howell, N. (1990). *Surviving fieldwork.* Washington, DC: American Anthropological Association.

Ikels, C. (1997). Long-term care and the disabled elderly in urban China. In J.Soko-
lovsky (Ed.), *The cultural contexts of aging:
Worldwide perspectives* (2nd ed.) (pp. 452–
471). Westport, CT: Greenwood.

Ikels, C. (1998a). The experience of dementia
in China. *Culture, Medicine and Psychiatry, 22,* 257–283.

Ikels, C. (1998b). Grandparenthood in cross-
cultural perspective. In M.Szinovacz (Ed.),
Handbook of grandparenthood (pp. 40–52).
Westport, CT: Greenwood.

Ikels, C. (1998c). Aging. In S. Loue (Ed.), *Handbook of immigrant health* (pp. 477–491).
New York: Plenum.

Jaarsma, S. R., & Rohatynskyj, M. A. (Eds.)
(2000). *Ethnographic artifacts: Challenges
to a reflexive anthropology.* Honolulu: University of Hawaii Press.

James, G. D., & Baker, P. T. (1995). Human
population biology and blood pressure: Evolutionary and ecological considerations and
interpretations of population studies. In J. H.
Laragh & B. M. Brenner (Eds.), *Hypertension:
Pathophysiology, diagnosis, and management* (pp. 115–126). New York: Raven Press.

Kaufert, P., & Lock, M. (1992). "What are
women for?": Cultural constructions of
menopausal women in Japan and Canada.
In V. Kerns & J. Brown (Eds.) *In her prime:
New views of middle-aged women* (2nd ed.)
(pp. 201–219). Urbana: University of Illinois
Press.

Kaufman, S. R. (1986). *The ageless self:
Sources of meaning in late life.* Madison:
University of Wisconsin Press.

Kauh, T. (1997). Intergenerational relations:
Older Korean-Americans experiences. *Journal of Cross-Cultural Gerontology, 12,*
245–271.

Keith, J. (1992). Care-taking in cultural context: Anthropological queries. In H. L. Kendig & A. Hashimoto (Eds.), *Family support
for the elderly* (pp. 16–30). Oxford: Oxford
University Press.

Keith, J., Fry, C. L., Glascock, A. P., Ikels, C.,
Dickerson-Putman, J., Harpending, H. C., &
Draper, P. (1994). *The aging experience: Di-
versity and commonality across cultures.*
Thousand Oaks, CA: Sage.

Kerns, V., & Brown, J. K (1992). *In her prime:
New views of middle-aged women* (2nd ed.).
Urbana: University of Illinois Press.

Kinoshita, Y., & Kiefer, C. W. (1992). *Refuge of the honored: Social organization in a Japanese retirement community*. Berkeley: University of California Press.

Kinsella, K., & Taueber, C. M. (1992). *An aging world II*. Washington, DC: U.S. Government Printing Office.

Lamb, S. (2000). *White saris and sweet mangoes: Aging, gender, and body in North India*. Berkeley: University of California Press.

Leidy, L. E. (1999). Menopause in evolutionary perspective. In W. R. Trevathan, E. O. Smith, & J. J. McKenna (Eds.), *Evolutionary medicine* (pp. 407–427). Oxford: Oxford University Press.

Lock, M. M. (1993). *Encounters with aging: Mythologies of menopause in Japan and North America*. Berkeley: University of California Press.

Lock, M. M. (1998). Menopause: Lessons from anthropology. *Psychosomatic Medicine, 60*, 410–419.

Martin, M. C., Block, J. E., Sanchez, S. D., Arnaud, C. D., & Beyene, Y. (1993). Menopause without symptoms: The endocrinology of menopause among rural Maya Indians. *American Journal of Obstetrics and Gynecology, 168*, 1839–1845.

McKinlay, S. M., Brambilla, D. J., & Posner, J. G. (1992). The normal menopause transition. *American Journal of Human Biology, 4*, 37–46.

Moller, V., & Sotshongaye, A. (1996). "My family eat this money too": Pension-sharing and self-respect among Zulu grandmothers. *Southern African Journal of Gerontology, 5(2)*, 9–19.

Morgan, L. A., Eckert, J. K., & Lyon, S. M. (1995). *Small board- and-care homes: Residential care in transition*. Baltimore: Johns Hopkins University Press.

Myerhoff, B., & Simic, A. (1978). *Life's career-aging: Cultural variations on growing old*. Beverly Hill, CA: Sage.

Nader, L. (1997). The phantom factor-impact of the Cold War on anthropology. In N. Chomsky, I. Katznelson, R. C. Lewentin, D. Montgomery, L. Nader, R. Ohmann, R. Siever, I. Wallerstein, & H. Zinn, *The Cold War and the university: Toward an intellectual history of the postwar years* (pp. 107–146). New York: The New Press.

Omidian, P. A. (1996). *Aging and family in an Afghan refugee community: Transitions and transformations*. New York: Garland.

Pang, K. Y. C. (1998). Symptoms of depression in elderly Korean immigrants: Narration and the healing process. *Culture, Medicine, and Psychiatry, 22*, 93–122.

Parfitt, A. M. (1983). Dietary risk factors for age-related bone loss and fractures. *The Lancet, 2(8360)*, 1181–1185.

Pearson, J. D., Morrell, C. H., Brant, L. J., Landis, P. K., & Fleg, J. L. (1997). Age-associated changes in blood pressure in a longitudinal study of healthy men and women. *Journal of Gerontology, 52A(3)*, M177–M183.

Potash, B. (1986). *Widows in African societies: Choices and constraints*. Stanford: Stanford University Press.

Rasmussen, S. J. (1997). *The poetics and politics of Tuareg aging: Life course and personal destiny*. Dekalb, IL: Northern Illinois University Press.

Rose, M. R., & Mueller, L. D. (1998). Evolution of human lifespan: Past, Future, and Present. *American Journal of Human Biology, 10*, 409–420.

Rosenberg, H. G. (1997). Complaint discourse, aging and caregiving among the Ju/'hoansi of Botswana. In J. Sokolovsky (Ed.), *The cultural context of aging: Worldwide perspectives* (2nd ed.) (pp. 33–55). Westport, CT: Bergin & Garvey.

Rowe, J. W., & Kahn, R. L. (1997). Successful aging. *The Gerontologist, 37*, 433–440.

Sacher, G. A. (1959). Relation of brain weight and body weight in mammals. In G. E. W. Wolstenholme & M. O'Connor (Eds.), *Ciba Foundation colloquia on ageing* (pp. 115–133). London, UK: Churchill.

Sagner, A., & Mtati, R. Z. (1999). Politics of pension sharing in urban South Africa. *Ageing and Society, 19*, 393–416.

Schreck, H. C. (1996). *The elderly in America: Volunteerism and neighborhood in Seattle*. Lanham, MD: University Press of America.

Schweitzer, M. M. (Ed.) (1999). *American Indian grandmothers: Traditions and transitions*. Albuquerque: University of New Mexico Press.

Shenk, D. (1998). *Someone to lend a helping hand: Women growing old in rural America*. Williston, VT: Gordon & Breach.

Shield, R. R. (1997). Liminality in an American nursing home: The endless transition. In J. Sokolovsky (Ed.), *The cultural context of aging: Worldwide perspectives* (2nd ed.) (pp. 472–491). Westport, CT: Bergin & Garvey.

Silverman, S. L., & Madison, R. E. (1988). Decreased incidence of hip fracture in Hispanics, Asians, and Blacks: California hospital discharge data. *American Journal of Public Health, 78(11)*, 1482–1483.

Simmons, L. W. (1945). *The role of the aged in primitive society*. New Haven, CT: Yale University Press.

Simmons, L. W. (1960). Aging in preindustrial societies. In C. Tibbits (Ed.), *Handbook of social gerontology* (pp. 62–91). Chicago: University of Chicago Press.

Simpson, C. (Ed.) (1998). *Universities and empire: Money and politics in the social sciences during the Cold War*. New York: The New Press.

Smith, K. (1998). Farming, marketing, and changes in the authority of elders among pastoral Rendille and Ariaal. *Journal of Cross-Cultural Gerontology, 13*, 309–332.

Stucki, B. (1992). The long voyage home: Return migration among aging cocoa farmers of Ghana. *Journal of Cross-Cultural Gerontology, 7*, 363–378.

Sung, K. (1994). A cross-cultural comparison of motivations for parent care: The case of Americans and Koreans. *Journal of Aging Studies, 8*, 195–209.

Traphagan, J. W. (1998). Localizing senility: Illness and agency among older Japanese. *Journal of Cross-Cultural Gerontology, 13*, 81–98.

Udvardy, M., & Cattell, M. (Eds.) (1992). *Gender, aging and power in Sub-Saharan Africa: Challenges and puzzles*. Special issue of the *Journal of Cross-Cultural Gerontology, 7(4)*.

van der Geest, S. (1997). Money and respect: The changing value of old age in rural Ghana. *Africa, 67*, 534–559.

van Gennep, A. (1960). *The rites of passage*. Chicago: University of Chicago Press.

van Willigen, J., & Chadha, N. K. (1999). *Social aging in a Delhi neighborhood*. Westport, CT: Bergin & Garvey.

Woodsong, C. (1994). Old farmers, invisible farmers: Age and agriculture in Jamaica. *Journal of Cross-Cultural Gerontology, 9*, 277–299.

Woolfson, P. (1997). *Old age in transition: The geriatric hospital*. Westport, CT: Bergin & Garvey.

Eight

Historical Perspectives on Aging and Family Relations

Tamara K. Hareven

Scholars and policy makers generally focus on old age as a distinctive life stage, isolated from the rest of the life course. Gerontologists have studied aging from several directions: the developmental perspective focusing on biological and psychological changes; the institutional approach stressing the socioeconomic status and the roles of older people; and the cultural perspective concentrating on negative stereotypes and changing images of aging (Achenbaum, 1978). Little effort has been made to integrate these perspectives or interpret them as interrelated processes over the life course. The historical role of the family in relation to old age has received even less attention.

Without denying the unique problems of late life, it is important to interpret it in a life-course and historical context. The "discovery" of old age as a distinct life stage in the 20th century was part of a larger historical process involving the emergence of new stages of life and their societal recognition. It was also part of a continuing process toward age segregation in the family and the larger society (Hareven, 1976). A historical and life-course perspective sheds light on long-term developments affecting "middle" and "old" age and generational relations in the later years of life. This chapter, using a life-course perspective, examines historical changes in generational relations and the family in later years of life.

I. The Life-Course Perspective

A life-course perspective uses both developmental and historical frameworks, focusing on the timing of life transitions and their impact on intergenerational relationships. It enables us to examine how patterns of generational assistance were formed over life and were carried over into the later years; how they were shaped and modified by historical circumstances and by people's cultural traditions; and what strategies individuals and families followed in order to secure future supports for later life. In its emphasis on interaction with historical time, the life-course approach provides an understanding of the location of various cohorts in their respective historical contexts. Specifically, it enables scholars and policy makers to examine the historical conditions that have affected different cohorts over their lives and also helps to explain differences in the experiences shaping their respective life histories (Elder, 1978; Hareven, 1978).

The life-course approach has especially significant implications for understanding the conditions of older people, because patterns of providing support, and expectations for receiving support in old age, are part of a continuing interaction among parents, children, and other kin over their lives as they move through historical time. Relations of mutual support are formed earlier in life and are reshaped over the life course by historical circumstances, including events such as migration, wars, and the decline or collapse of local economies (Elder, 1974; Hareven, 1978). A life-course perspective helps us understand how problems, needs, and patterns of adaptation of older people were shaped by their earlier life experiences and by historical conditions.

The life-course approach emphasizes three types of timing: individual timing of life transitions in relation to historical events; synchronization of individual and family life transitions under varying historical and cultural contexts; and the impact of earlier life events, as shaped by historical circumstances on subsequent ones. The timing of life transitions involves the sequencing of an individual's entry into and exit from different family, work, and community roles over the life course. The pace and definition of "timing" hinge upon the historical, social, and cultural contexts in which people undergo such transitions.

Age is an important determinant of the timing of life transitions, but it is not the only one. Changes in family status, other roles, and life stage are often equally important. Synchronization of individual life transitions with family transitions often involves the juggling of multiple family- and work-related roles over the life course. Individuals live in a variety of familial configurations that change over the life course and vary under different historical and cultural contexts. These changing configurations have a significant impact on who would actually be available to family members in the later years of life (Hareven, 1991a; Uhlenberg, 1978; Hareven & Masaoka, 1988).

Synchronizing individual transitions with familial ones can generate tensions, especially when individual goals conflict with the needs and dictates of the family as a collective unit. The interdependence of earlier life transitions with later ones has a powerful effect on generational relations. The timing of adult children's individual life transitions, such as leaving home or getting married, often conflicts with the demands and needs of aging parents. For example, Hareven (1982) and Hareven and Adams (1996) found that aging parents expected at least one daughter, usually the youngest, to postpone or give up marriage in order to care for them. Hogan, Eggebeen, and Snaith (1996) found that the death of an aging parent enabled caregiving children, who were "young old," to begin preparing for their own old age and for assisting their children or grandchildren.

The life-course approach also emphasizes the cumulative impact of earlier life events on later ones. The "early" or "delayed" timing of certain transitions affects the pace of later ones. For example, Elder (1974) documented the negative impact that the Great Depression had on the transition to adulthood among young men and women in Berkeley and Oakland, California. Hareven (1982) found similar patterns for comparable cohorts in Manchester, New Hampshire.

The impact of historical forces on the life course may continue over several generations. One generation transmits to the next the "ripple effects" of the historical circumstances that shaped its life history (Hareven, 1978; Hareven & Masaoka, 1988). Studying the same cohorts in different communities, Elder (1974) and

Elder and Hareven (1993) found that delays or irregularities in the parents' timing of their work and family careers, resulting from the Great Depression, affected the timing of their children's life transitions. Both studies also emphasized, however, that the impact of historical events on the life course is reversible: military service during World War II and the GI bill of rights enabled young men to partially overcome the negative impact of the Great Depression on their opportunities and achievements.

The life-course perspective provides a framework for understanding variability in both expectations of and patterns of support in later life (Fry & Keith, 1982; Hareven & Adams, 1996; Jackson, Antonucci, & Gibson, 1990; Kohli, 1986; Keifer, 1974). Patterns of generational assistance are shaped by values and experiences that evolve over the life course. For example, in the United States, the premigration history of racial and ethnic groups affects expectations of support in later life, with older cohorts emphasizing support from family members and younger cohorts advocating reliance on societal programs (Hareven & Adams, 1996). The earlier life-course experiences of each cohort, as shaped by historical events, also affect the availability of economic and educational resources and support networks (Elder, 1974; Hareven & Adams, 1996; Sokolovsky, 1990). To understand these differences, both the social milieu at the time at which members of a cohort reach that age and their cumulative experience as shaped by historical events must be considered.

The distinction between "cohort" and "generation" is also critical. "Generation" designates kin relationships (e.g., parents and children). A "cohort" consists of a specific age group that shares a common historical experience that affects the subsequent life course of that group (Bengtson, Rosenthal, & Burton, 1990; Ryder, 1965). Several scholars have warned against confounding the genealogical and cohort meanings of "generation." Kertzer (1983) pointed out that when a population is divided on genealogical principles into various generations, a substantial age overlap across generations will result. A generation might include several cohorts, each of which encountered different historical experiences that have affected its life course. For example, Hareven and Adams's (1996) comparison of assistance patterns of two cohorts of adult children to aging parents in a New England community shows that members of the same generation belonged to two different cohorts. In families with large numbers of children, siblings in the same "generation" were members of two cohorts, who differed in the historical experiences they had encountered and in their attitudes towards generational supports.

A. The Emergence of Discontinuities in the Life Course

In preindustrial society, demographic, social, and cultural factors combined to produce little differentiation in the stages of life. Childhood and adolescence were not distinct stages; children were considered miniature adults, gradually assuming adult roles in their early teens and entering adult life without a moratorium from adult responsibilities. Adulthood flowed into old age without institutionalized disruptions or commemorations such as retirement. In rural communities, the insistence of older people on self-sufficiency and continued control over family estates delayed the assumption of economic independence by adult children and afforded aging parents a bargaining position for support in old age (Greven, 1970; Smith, 1973). Even in the 19th century, parenthood and work generally stretched over an entire lifetime without an "empty nest" and compulsory retirement (Chudacoff & Hareven, 1979). The integration of economic activities with family life also provided continuity in the usefulness of older people, particularly for widows, even when their capacity to work was waning.

In contemporary Western society one is accustomed to thinking of most transitions to family and work roles as individual moves. In the past, however, the timing of individual transitions had to be synchronized with familial ones. The family was the most critical agent in initiating and managing the timing of life transitions. Control over the timing of individual members' transitions was a crucial factor in the family's efforts to manage its resources, especially in balancing members' contributions to the family economy. The absence of a narrow, age-related timing of transitions to adult life allowed more intensive interaction among age groups within family and community, thus providing a greater sense of continuity and interdependence among generations.

One should not idealize, however, the condition of the elderly in preindustrial society. Although the aged were venerated publicly, they were insecure in private life. Signs of this insecurity are reflected in wills, where support for aged parents by their children was mandated (Demos, 1970, 1978). Nevertheless, old people experienced economic and social segregation far less frequently than they do today, and, except for widowhood, they retained their familial and economic positions until the end of their lives (Smith, 1973). In cases of illness or poverty, they were supported by their children or other kin, or were placed by town authorities in the households of neighbors, or even nonrelatives. Institutions served only as a last resort (Demos, 1970; Greven, 1970).

Industrialization led only gradually to differentiation in age groups and a greater specialization in age-related functions. Despite the introduction of compulsory retirement and pension plans by some employers at the beginning of the 20th-century, discontinuities in the life course were still not marked, and age groups were not segregated. For example, parenthood was not segregated in early adulthood. Today, parents generally complete child-rearing with a third of their lives still ahead; in the 19th century, parenthood was a lifelong career. The combination of relatively late marriage, high fertility, and shorter life expectancy rarely allowed an "empty nest." In addition, one parent often died before the end of child-rearing. Because they married earlier and lived longer than men, women were typically the survivors. In their study of 19th-century communities in Essex County Massachusetts and in Providence, Rhode Island, Chudacoff and Hareven (1978, 1979) found an absence of abrupt later life transitions. Except for widows, the continuity in the work life and familial integration of older people suggests that the aged experienced little residential and functional isolation. Widowed or not, however, the extension of motherhood over most of the life course continued to engage women in active familial roles into old age.

Social, economic, and cultural changes of the past century, however, gradually led to a segregation of work from other aspects of life and to a shift from the dominance of familial values to an emphasis on individualism and privacy. Since the mid-19th century, child-labor laws and compulsory school attendance increasingly segregated the young (Bremner, Hareven, Barnard, & Mennell 1970). Similarly, the gradual withdrawal of older people from the labor force at the beginning of the 20th century led to increasing social isolation. Numerous studies document the absence of abrupt retirement for men in the early 20th century (Chudacoff & Hareven, 1978; Dahlin, 1980; Haber & Gratton, 1994; Ransom & Sutch, 1996; Smith, 1979). Compulsory or formal retirement was not the usual mode of exit from the labor force. Instead, inability to continue working in physically demanding tasks forced early retirement or movement into part-time menial jobs. Over time, disability became associated with age and age-segregated groups emerged. The changes discussed above have affected all stages of life, resulting in the segmentation of the life course, the emergence of more uniform transitions between life stages, and the separation of age groups from each other. This separation occurred first in the middle class and later extended to the working class. Patterns still vary among racial and ethnic groups (see Jackson, Jayakody, & Antonucci, 1996; Markides, Costley, & Rodriguez, 1981; Markides & Krause, 1985; Taylor, Chatters, & Jackson, 1993).

B. Historical Changes in the Timing of Life Transitions

In the 19th century, the timing of transitions—to the empty nest, to widowhood, and out of the headship of one's own household followed no ordered sequence and extended over a relatively long time. Older women experienced more marked family transitions than men because of widowhood, although the presence of at least one adult child in the household meant that widowhood often did not result in a dramatic transition into solitary residence (Chudacoff & Hareven, 1979; Hareven & Uhlenberg, 1995; Smith, 1979). Similarly, major transitions into adulthood, such as leaving school, starting work, leaving home, and marrying and having children, were not as structured as they are today. The order in which they occurred varied significantly. Children and youth shuttled back and forth from school to work depending on the seasons, the availability of jobs, and the economic needs of the family. Departure from school did not mark a definite turning point, nor, at a time when child labor was an established practice, did entry

into the labor force necessarily imply the transition to adulthood. Leaving home, a phenomenon typically associated with the commencement of adulthood today, did not have such significance in the preindustrial and early industrial periods (Kett, 1977; Modell, Furstenberg, & Hershberg, 1976).

In the 19th century, later age at marriage, higher fertility, and shorter life expectancy produced family configurations different from those in contemporary society. The time range necessary for a cohort to accomplish these transitions was wider. In the 20th century, transitions to adulthood have become more uniform, more orderly in sequence, and more rigidly defined. The increasing rapidity in the timing of transitions to adulthood, the separation of an individual's family of origin from his or her family of procreation, and conformity to age norms have converged to isolate and segregate age groups and generations within the larger society (Hogan, 1989; Hogan, Eggebeen, & Clogg, 1993; Modell, Furstenberg, & Hershberg, 1976). Importantly, the timing of transitions is now viewed as an individual decision rather than a familial one.

Demographic changes in American society since the late 19th century partly explain the changes in the timing of life transitions. Declines in mortality have dramatically increased the odds of intact survival of the family unit over the lifetime of its members. Except when disrupted by divorce, married couples live together for longer, children grow up with their parents as well as with their siblings, and grandparents survive well into their grandchildren's adulthoods. Now great-grandparenthood has emerged as a common life stage. Longevity and survival to adulthood maximized the opportunity for generational overlap and for available pools of kin, despite the decline in fertility (Cherlin & Furstenberg, 1990; Townsend, 1968; Uhlenberg, 1974, 1978).

The most pronounced discontinuity for couples during the 20th century, especially after World War II, was the empty nest. This stage emerged as a modal pattern of the middle and later years of life as a result of the decline in mortality, the combination of earlier marriage, and the often closely-spaced bearing of fewer children, and the more uniform pattern of children leaving home earlier in their parents' lives. It meant that couples experienced an extended period of life without children. At the same time, women's tendency to live longer than men resulted in a protracted period of widowhood in old age (Glick, 1977; Uhlenberg, 1978). Demographic factors only partially account for the empty nest. Even in the 19th-century, children were old enough to leave when their parents were still alive. The nest was rarely empty, however, because at least one adult child remained at home to care for aging parents if no other assistance was available (Chudacoff & Hareven, 1979; Hareven, 1982; Smith, 1981).

The timing of life transitions to adulthood in the 19th-century was erratic because it was based on family needs, rather than on age norms. Familial obligations, dictated by economic insecurity and by cultural norms of kin assistance, took precedence over age norms. Over the 20th-century, on the other hand, age norms emerged as more important determinants of timing than familial obligations. As Modell, Furstenberg, and Hershberg (1976) concluded: " 'Timely' action to nineteenth century families consisted of helpful response in times of trouble; in the twentieth century, timeliness connotes adherence to a socially-sanctioned schedule" (p. 30).

Since the 1980s, more erratic and flexible patterns in the timing of life-course transitions have appeared again. The movement of young adult children in and out of the parental home has become less predictable (Goldscheider & Goldscheider, 2000). This contemporary pattern, however, differs from that of the past in a fundamental way. In the late 19th-century, children stayed in the parental home or moved back and forth to meet the needs of their family of orientation. In contemporary society, young adult children reside with their parents in order to meet their own needs, because of their inability to develop an independent work career or to find affordable housing.

C. Interaction of Early Life Transitions with Later Ones and Their Impact on Old Age

Historically, early life transitions were bound up with later ones in a continuum of familial needs and obligations. The life transitions of the younger generation were intertwined with those of the older generation. Specifically, the timing of children's leaving home, getting married, and setting up a separate household was contingent on the timing of parents' transitions into retirement or widowhood (Chudacoff & Hareven, 1978; Greven, 1970; Hareven, 1982).

The strategies that parents and children followed in their reciprocal interactions over the life course varied across societies. In Europe, land inheritance was a major factor used by parents to control their young adult children's life transitions (e.g., Fauve-Chamoux, 1996). But parental strategies took different forms for mate selection and the timing of each child's marriage, depending on whether it was the inheriting son or a noninheriting son or daughter. Similarly, Kertzer and Hogan (1996) emphasize the significance of inheritance in regulating coresidence and generational supports in a 19th-century Italian sharecropping village. They found differences between wage earners and sharecroppers in the use of inheritance in exchange for supports in old age and their impact on the familial and economic status of women. In colonial New England, inheritance was used by parents to control the timing of their adult children's transitions out of the parental home and into marriage (Greven, 1970; Smith, 1973). Whether the absence of land holding in urban society diminished parental control over the timing of their children's designation as caretakers for the parents' old age is still an open question.

II. Generational Supports over the Life Course

The supports that older people receive from their adult children and other kin is an important contemporary issue in generational relations. It was also an important issue in the past. Generational relations in later life are interconnected with experiences and transitions from earlier life. The study of generational relations in old age, thus requires a multidimensional approach: externally, an examination of the interaction of individuals and families with social institutions and with the historical processes affecting them; and internally, an examination of these relations within the family and with the wider kin group.

A. Myths about Generational Relations in the Later Years

A major myth about the past is that a golden age once existed during which older generations coresided with their children and other kin, and elderly people were secure in receiving supports from their families. It includes the assumption that industrialization and urbanization led to the emergence of the nuclear household, eroded kinship ties, and diminished generational supports. Historical research over the past three decades has challenged this myth. In reality, the dominant form of household structure in western Europe and in the United States

in the preindustrial period, as well as following industrialization, was nuclear. Elderly parents did not typically live with their adult married children, although they often resided separately nearby and were engaged in a variety of mutual supports (Demos, 1978; Greven, 1970; Laslett, 1977). Older people in Western society never experienced a golden age. Both in preindustrial Europe and in colonial America, aging parents entered into contracts with inheriting sons in order to secure basic supports in old age (e.g., Brandes, 1996; Demos, 1978). In American society, generational assistance and relations with wider kin have been based on voluntary reciprocities rather than on rigidly enforced customs or laws. To understand how these patterns changed over time, it is necessary to take into account the cultural values governing reciprocal relations among the generations and other kin in different time periods and among groups within the same culture.

B. Coresidence

The household arrangements of older people have been a continuing theme in historical research on the family and aging. As a large body of scholarship has demonstrated, nuclear household patterns have predominated since the preindustrial period in the United States and Western Europe. The modal pattern has been one where the younger generation establishes a separate household following marriage. Except for some variation over the life course, elderly couples and aging widows have attempted to maintain independent households for as long as possible. However, households expanded to include other kin in times of need, during periods of accelerated migration, housing shortages or unemployment, and, most notably, to accommodate dependent older family members (Chudacoff & Hareven, 1978; Laslett, 1977; Laslett & Wall, 1972). Despite the predominance of nuclear household arrangements, the most common expansions of households result from including aging, frail relatives.

The fact that aging parents and adult children did not typically coreside does not mean that the generations were isolated from each other. Even in urban areas throughout the 19th century, solitary residence was uncommon for all age groups (Kobrin, 1976). Individuals residing in nuclear households were enmeshed in frequent or continued interactions with children who were not coresiding (Hareven, 1982). The ideal shared by both the older and the younger generations was residing on the same land in rural areas, or in the same building or same neighborhood in urban areas, but not in the same household. "Intimacy from a distance," the preferred mode of generational interaction, has been persistent since the early settlement of North America, and reaches back into the European past (Demos, 1970; Laslett & Wall, 1972).

Dependency during late life, however, often resulted in coresidence with adult children. In fact, the emphasis of historians on the continued nuclearity of the household, in an effort to revise earlier myths, has led to an oversight of both an overall increase in household extension from the late 19th to the early 20th century and an increase in coresidence of aging parents with adult children (Dahlin, 1980; Ruggles, 1987). Coresidence with a child, single or married, was the major solution if aging parents were too frail to live alone, both in Europe and the United States. Alter, Cliggett, and Urbiel (1996) found that coresidence of aged parents with an adult child tended to increase in the later years of life in 19th-century Belgium. Similarly, Guinnane (1996) found high rates of coresidence of elderly parents with adult children in 19th-century Ireland. Whenever possible, however, parents preferred to coreside with an unmarried child. Brandes (1996) found in northern Spain and Portugal that,

although elderly parents had a similar preference for retaining the autonomy of their households, widowed mothers were placed with various children on a "rotation system." In European regions where inheritances were impartible (not divided among children), the inheriting son coresided with aging parents and was expected contractually to be their main supporter. Coresidence of generations frequently occurred in 19th- and 20th-century American communities when elderly parents were unable to live alone (Chudacoff & Hareven, 1978; Hareven, 1991b; Smith, 1981; Zachritz & Gutmann, 1996). In the absence of children, frail elderly people, especially widows, moved in with other relatives or strangers. Hareven and Uhlenberg (1995) found that in parts of the northeastern United States in 1910, more than three-fourths of all older widows were living with their children. Smith (1979) found that of all Americans over age 65 in 1900, one-third lived in households containing three generations.

In urban communities that attracted large numbers of rural migrants and immigrants, coresidence with extended kin increased greatly over the 19th century (Anderson, 1971; Hareven, 1982), but declined dramatically in the 20th. More than 70% of persons age 65 or older resided with kin at the turn of the century; by 1980, only 23% did (Ruggles, 1987). Using 1900 census data, Haber and Gratton (1994) found significant differences in the coresidence of older people by gender, locality, class, and race. Particularly important are their findings of higher coresidence in farm areas and small towns, as compared with urban areas.

During the 19th century, configurations of household members also changed over the life course in relation to the family's economic needs or in response to external opportunities (Chudacoff & Hareven, 1979; Hareven, 1991a). When children were not available, older people, especially widows whose children had left home, shared household space with boarders and lodgers in exchange for services or rent. Sharing household space with such unrelated individuals provided the extra income and sociability some older people, especially widows, needed to maintain their own residence and helped avert loneliness after their children had left home. In some cases older people who could not live alone, but who had no children or relatives, moved into other people's households as boarders (Hareven & Uhlenberg, 1995; Modell & Hareven, 1973).

As commonly thought, in Asian countries there was and is a higher rate of coresidence of elderly parents with adult children than in the West. Coresidence of older people with their offspring was pervasive in Southeast Asia in general (Martin, 1990). In East Asia, patterns were similar. In Korea of the 1980s, 80% of parents over 60 lived with one or more children. In the rural suburbs of Shanghai in 1986, about one-third of people over 60 lived with a married son and 8% lived with a daughter (Gui, 1988). Coresidence with at least one adult child has been the customary pattern for aged parents in Taiwan, Thailand, and Japan, especially among aged widows, for whom coresidence with an adult child is the major form of support. Knodel, Chayovan, and Siriboon (1996) found that in Thailand, the majority of men and women over 65 coreside with a child. Older children move out and set up their own households, but typically one unmarried child coresides with aging parents, especially when they need assistance. The type of supports provided by children who do not coreside depend on their residential proximity to aging parents. Children living closer to their parents are more likely to provide food and clothing, while children living at a greater distance more commonly provide money. In Sri Lanka, supports to aging parents by noncoresi-dent children are limited to financial contributions (Uhlenberg, 1996). In Japan, rates of coresidence are lower than in the other Asian countries; about 60% of people 65 and older coreside with a child. Rates of coresidence declined steadily between 1960 and 1980, a change Morioka (1996) attributes to the disintegration of the traditional *ie* system following World War II, and to the increasing determination of the younger generation to live separately from their parents.

Scholars' understanding of the antecedents, meanings, and consequences of coresidence of older parents and their adult children is severely limited by the use of cross-sectional data. In addition, research is needed that examines specific transmission of exchanges of goods and services, the quality of caregiving, and family interaction patterns (e.g., decision making, conflicts and tensions) in intergenerational households.

C. Life-Course Antecedents Shaping Intergenerational Supports

Despite a strong tradition of kin assistance in American society, spouses and children have been the main caregivers for aging parents. Even in time periods and among ethnic groups where individuals were deeply embedded in reciprocal relations with extended kin, the main responsibility for caregiving, particularly for frail elderly parents, fell on children. Other kin provided sociability and occasional help, but children maintained the day-to-day care. This strong reliance on children as caregivers raises the question of whether higher fertility results in a larger pool of caregivers for older parents. Alter, Cliggett, and Urbiel (1996) report that in 19th-century Belgium, high fertility made a larger number of supporters available to aging parents. In the United States, however, regardless of how many children a couple had, one child usually became the primary caregiver (Chudacoff

& Hareven, 1979; Hareven & Adams, 1996; Smith, 1981). Caregiving for aging parents, however, was related not only to the number of available children, but also to inheritance systems, the cultural values governing generational supports, gender and birth order of the children, and geographic proximity. Even in the United States where only one child became the caregiver, regardless of how many children a couple had, the existence of a larger number of children provided a larger pool from which the caregiving child could be designated.

In American society, both adult children and older parents preferred that the latter remain in their own homes for as long as possible. Children made an effort to have their parents reside nearby, preferably in the same building or the same block, but not in the same household if it could be avoided. In cases of illness or need, children visited their parents on a daily basis, arranged for medical treatment, provided bodily care, prepared meals, and ran errands. In some cases, several siblings contributed jointly by hiring a nurse to take daily care of a frail parent who was still living at home. After the death of one parent, children, especially daughters, took in the surviving parent if he or she was too frail to live alone or needed extensive help with daily activities (Hareven & Adams, 1996).

Daughters fulfilled their caregiving role at a high price to themselves and to their spouses and other family members. Caregiving for aging parents in her own household often disrupted a daughter's career, crowded her residence, caused strain in her marriage, and made it difficult to prepare for her own and her spouse's retirement and old age (Brody, 1990; Cantor, 1983; Hareven & Adams, 1996). Sons were not totally exempt from caregiving duties, but tasks tended to be allocated along gender roles. Men typically performed managerial and maintenance tasks, and provided financial support; women predominantly performed daily hands-on caregiving tasks (Dwyer & Coward, 1991; Dwyer & Seccombe, 1991; Hareven, 1993; Kaye & Applegate, 1990).

Generational supports in old age are part of a life-course continuum of reciprocal relations between the generations. As noted above, in 19th-century Europe, inheritance played a major role in designating the caretaker for aging parents (Brandes, 1996; Ehmer, 1996; Fauve-Chamoux, 1996; Kertzer & Hogan, 1996). In societies where a stem family system predominated, as Fauve-Chamoux and Morioka point out respectively for the French Pyrenees and Japan, the main caregiving responsibility for aging parents fell upon the inheriting son, who continued to coreside with his parents after marriage, while the noninheriting children left home and maintained contact only from a distance. Similarly, in the northern Iberian Peninsula, according to Brandes (1996), in areas with impartible inheritance, the inheriting son was also the caregiver for aging parents. In areas with partible inheritance, patterns of care taking with or without coresidence took different forms.

In European societies with partible inheritance and in landless societies, selection of the caretaking child varied by economic circumstances, life-course antecedents, and cultural prescriptions. In 18th- and 19th-century Central Europe, for example, caregiving for aging parents differed between landholding families and those who engaged in small commodity production in the household because of differences in inheritance practices (Ehmer, 1996). Among landless families, caregiver selection was contingent on arrangements formed between parents and a caregiving child. Clearly, designation of a caregiver was a life-course "imperative" that required advance planning, such as inheritance contracts and other strategies.

In 19th- and 20th-century American society, there was no prescribed rule as to which child would become a "parent keeper." Adult children's involvement with the care of aging parents was closely related to their earlier life-course experiences, their ethnic and cultural traditions, and the historical contexts affecting their lives. Routine assistance from children to aging parents over their life course prepared the children to cope with parents' later life crises, especially widowhood and dependence in old age. If the child was not already residing with the parent, the selection of a child for that role was governed by that particular child's ability and willingness to take the parent in, by the consent or support of the parent keeper's spouse, and by the readiness of the parent to accept the plan. Some children took on this responsibility unexpectedly because of a sudden crisis, such as the onset of widowhood, but most evolved gradually into that role (Hareven & Adams, 1996). Frequently, however, it was the daughter, who had already shouldered the role of kin keeper for her network, who fell into the role of parent keeper.

Morioka (1996) identifies specific phases in generational exchanges over the life course in Japan, in preparation for caregivng. In the early phase, parents extend assistance to their children; in the later phases, the children, especially the inheriting child in the stem family, become caregivers for aging parents. Analyzing the role transitions of five cohorts of parents and children in northern Japan, Masaoka and Fujimi (1996) document variations in the selection of the caregiving child across cohorts and communities. Similarly, in Sri Lanka, Uhlenberg (1996) found a strategy of reciprocity between parents' providing assistance to their children early in life and their receiving support from their children in old age. These types of strong generational reciprocities also have been reported for Thailand

(Knodel et al., 1996) and for Taiwan (Hermalin, Ofstedal, & Chang, 1996).

III. The Role of Extended Kin and Nonkin

As pointed out above, contrary to prevailing popular myths and sociological theories, urbanization and industrialization did not break down traditional ties and reciprocal relations among kin (Anderson, 1971; Hareven, 1978). Whether they resided separately or in the same household, mutual assistance with extended kin was at the base of survival for members of the nuclear family. Kin served as the most essential resource for economic assistance and security and shouldered the major burden of providing supports for individual family members over the life course and in critical life situations, such as unemployment, illness, or death (Anderson, 1971; Hareven, 1982).

Collective family coping and individuals' obligations to their kin were dictated by their culture, which required that individual choices be subordinated to collective familial considerations and needs. Maintaining the autonomy of the family required strong interdependence among kin. Close contact and mutual exchanges among parents, their adult children, and other kin persisted throughout the 19th century and survived into the 20th century in various forms in the lives of working-class and ethnic families in the United States. Societal values rooted in ethnic cultures provided ideological reinforcements for these obligations (Eggebeen & Hogan, 1990; Hareven, 1982). Mutual assistance among kin, although involving extensive exchanges, was not strictly calculative but expressed an overall principle of reciprocity over the life course and across generations. Individuals who subordinated their own careers and needs to those of the family as a collective unit did so out of a sense of responsibility, affection, and familial obligation, rather than with the expectation of immediate or future gain. Such sacrifices were not made without protest, however, and at times involved competition and conflict among siblings as to who should carry the main responsibility of support for aging parents (Hareven & Adams, 1996).

In recent decades, remarriage following divorce has had a significant impact on the availability of kin and on the introduction of a new age diversity within the family. It has re-created kinship configurations that resemble those resulting through remarriage following the premature death of a spouse in the 18th or 19th centuries. Changes in the configurations of kin resulting from the increase in divorce and remarriage rates during the past three decades may have important implications for the availability of kinship pools in late life, as well as for generational boundaries within kinship groups. "Blended families" often exhibit substantial variation in the ages of both spouses and children. Furstenberg (1981) argues that divorce did not deplete kinship ties, and that children's ties with grandparents survived divorce. Because the older generation is likely to invest in child rearing, Furstenberg concludes that children reared within these complex configurations will maintain stronger obligations towards future supports for the older generation. As age again becomes heterogeneous within the family, the salience of generational segregation in the larger society may decline as well.

Nonkin also need to be examined as sources of support and caregiving for older adults. Riley and Riley have observed that "the boundaries of the kin network have been widened to encompass many diverse relationships, including several degrees of stepkin and in-laws, single parent families, adopted and other 'relatives' chosen from outside the family, and many others" (1996, p. 6). They character-

ize these complex kinship and fictitious kinship relations as "a latent web of continually shifting linkages that provide the potential for activating and intensifying close kin relationships as they are needed" (Riley & Riley, 1996, p. 6).

Surrogate kinship networks are not entirely new. In the 19th and early 20th centuries, families in various ethnic groups and in the working class were enmeshed in networks of kin and surrogate kin. Some of these networks stretched across wide geographic regions, linking into one social system migrants or immigrants in their communities of settlement with their kin in their communities of origin. These nonfamily ties were activated by need (Hareven, 1982). The significance of nonkin networks in contemporary society is that they transcend the boundaries of age and generation, which may enhance their flexibility and efficacy. In earlier times, such networks were governed by norms of reciprocity and economic considerations. Further research is needed to identify the rules and principles by which contemporary nonkin networks operate and to follow them longitudinally to determine their durability and effectiveness.

IV. The Impact of Social Change

A. Cohort Differences

Historical changes in generational supports and in attitudes toward receiving and providing such supports are best reconstructed through a comparison of cohorts whose lives were located in different historical contexts. Hareven and Adams (1996) found in Manchester, New Hampshire, significant differences in the attitudes and caregiving practices of two cohorts in relation to their earlier historical experiences. An older cohort (born 1910–1919), who came of age during the Great Depression, and a younger cohort (born 1920–1929), who came of age during World War II, were both the children of textile workers, predominantly from Quebec and Poland, who migrated to Manchester to work in the Amoskeag Mills.

Both cohorts were, to some degree, transitional between a tradition of deep involvement in generational assistance, reinforced by strong family and ethnic values, on the one hand, and the individualistic values and lifestyles that emerged after World War II, on the other hand. Both cohorts were also transitional in that they were still strongly bound by their parents' values and expectations that children should serve as their major caregivers. Both attempted to fulfill this script, often at a high price to their own marriages, to their ability to help their grown children, and to their preparations for their own "old age." Both cohorts were socialized with expectations and ideologies of kin assistance similar to those of their parents, but they implemented those norms under different historical and social circumstances. The older cohorts' lives conformed more closely to the script of their traditional familial and ethnic cultures, while the younger cohort, as it Americanized, was pulled in the direction of individualistic middle-class values. The older cohort was committed to caregiving for aging parents; the younger cohort was ambivalent and felt that bureaucratic agencies should carry the main responsibility (Hareven & Adams, 1996).

The differences between the two cohorts of adult children thus reflect the historical process of increasing individualization in family relationships and reliance on public agencies and bureaucratic institutions to shoulder the responsibilities for the care of dependent elderly. These historical changes have tended to escalate insecurity and isolation for older people, most markedly in areas of need that are not met by public programs. Although some of the historical patterns of intense kin interaction have survived among first-generation African-American immigrant and working-class families, a gradual weakening of mutual assistance among kin has occurred over time (e.g., Burton & Dilworth-Anderson, 1991; Dowd & Bengtson, 1978; Mutran, 1986; Taylor & Chatters, 1991). Sokolovsky (1990) and others have warned against romanticizing the generational interdependence among African Americans and more recent immigrant groups, such as Hispanics and Koreans.

Important elements of support exchanges between older parents and nonresident children remain unknown. Most studies in gerontology and sociology that report the persistence of kin supports for older people in contemporary society have not documented the intensity, quality, and consistency of these supports in meeting the needs of older people, especially of the frail and chronically ill elderly. Earlier studies usually examined social interaction rather than caregiving and other forms of social support. Subsequent studies have provided more systematic evidence of various supports from adult children to aging parents, especially for the "old old" (Brody, 1990; Cantor, 1983). Even in these studies, however, the consistency, intensity, and quality of the support provided were not examined systematically.

Except for members of certain ethnic groups, future cohorts may not have the same strong sense of familial interdependence characteristic of earlier cohorts. They also may lack sufficiently large pools of kin on whom to rely. Rossi and Rossi (1990) found that in Boston, younger respondents expressed a stronger sense of normative obligations to kin than the older ones and concluded that obligations to kin have not declined over the past century. An adequate test of this conclusion, however, would require a comparison of data from multiple cohorts spanning the past century.

B. Changes in the Family

The major changes that have led to the partial isolation of older people in Western society today were rooted not so much in changes in family structure or residential arrangements, as has generally been argued, but rather in the transformation and redefinition of family functions and values. Among these changes, the erosion of an instrumental view of family relationships—and the resulting shift to sentimentality and intimacy as the major cohesive forces in the family—has led to the weakening of an interdependence between members of the nuclear family and extended kin. With the exception of specific ethnic groups, affective relationships have gradually replaced instrumental ones.

The family's retreat from the community and the growing privatization of the modern middle-class family led to the formation of sharper boundaries between family and community and intensified the segregation of different age groups within the family, causing the elimination of older people from viable family roles. The ideology of domesticity that emerged during the first half of the 19th century enshrined privacy as a major value in family life. The home was glorified as a retreat from the world and, at the same time, as a specialized child-nurturing center. This ideological shift first occurred in the urban middle class, but it soon affected the working class and various ethnic groups as well. Since then, the emphasis on domesticity and child-rearing as the major preoccupations of the middle-class family—and especially on the role of women as custodians of the domestic retreat—has tended to insulate middle-class urban families from the influence and participation of aging parents and other relatives. This transition contributed to the weakening influence of older people in the family (Hareven, 1977).

The care of dependent, sick, delinquent, and elderly members of the community, which had been considered part of the family's obligation in the preindustrial period, was gradually transferred to specialized institutions such as asylums, reformatories, and nursing homes. The family ceased to be the only source of support for its dependent members, and the community ceased to rely on the family as the major agency of welfare and social control (Bremner, 1956; Rothman, 1971). This transfer of social welfare functions from the family to public institutions over the past century and a half has not been fully consummated, however. On the one hand, family members increasingly assume that the public sector has a major responsibility for care of the aged; on the other hand, state and the federal governments assume that the family is responsible for some of these areas. This confusion in the assignment of responsibilities often means that old people are caught between the family and the public sector without receiving needed assistance from either.

The expectation that family and kin shoulder the major burden for the care of aged relatives still prevails, but without the structural arrangements (e.g., proximity in residence) that would enable kin to discharge such responsibilities. The decline in instrumental relations among kin and their replacement by an individualistic orientation toward family relations, with sentimentality and intimacy as the major cohesive forces, has led to the weakening of the role of kin assistance in middle-class families in particular, and to an increasing isolation of the elderly in American society (Hareven, 1977). What Guillemard (1996) calls the "deinstitutionalization of the life course" has also had a significant impact on reciprocities between generations. She argues, for example, that the introduction of early retirement in some European countries has resulted in erratic timing of the exit from work and rendered the ability of generations to assist each other less predictable.

Finally, changes in the family must be interpreted in the larger context of social and economic change. Did industrialization and urbanization lead to the dramatic restructuring of generational relations and patterns of mutual assistance? A comparison of the patterns in Europe and the United States with those in East Asia raises important questions about global change. Is the trend toward the residential separation of older people from their children in Asian countries part of a "convergence" process with the West? Are Asian countries changing at a more rapid pace than occurred in Western Europe and the United States? If so, are surface similarities between Asian and Western societies a disguise for more profound cultural differences? For example, do elderly parents now living in nuclear households in Japan and Taiwan interact with adult children in similar ways to those of contemporary Americans living in nuclear families? Cultural traditions have played a major role in shaping patterns of generational assistance and the expectations of generations from each other. What may appear on the surface to be an "isolated" nuclear family in Asia does not mean that elderly parents are isolated from assistance from their children and other kin. Comparative research is needed to broaden our understanding of the relative contributions of transformations resulting from social and economic change and the persistence or modification of cultural traditions to the structure and quality of intergenerational relationships across time and place.

Acknowledgments

I am grateful for the thoughtful suggestions by Carole Haber, the invaluable editorial help provided by Robert Binstock and Linda George, as well as the effective assistance of Ann Garrett and Loren Marks, and the meticulous editing and proofing by Elizabeth Feather.

References

Achenbaum, W. A. (1978). *Old age in the new land: The American experience since 1790.* Baltimore, MD: John Hopkins University Press.

Alter, G., Cliggett, L., & Urbiel, A. (1996). Household patterns of the elderly and the proximity of children in nineteenth century city: Verviers, Belgium, 1831–1846. In T. K. Hareven (Ed.), *Aging and generational relations over the life course: A historical and cross-cultural perspective* (pp. 30–52). Berlin: Walter de Gruyter.

Anderson, M. S. (1971). *Family structure in nineteenth century Lancashire.* Cambridge, UK: Cambridge University Press.

Bengtson, V. L., Rosenthal, C., & Burton, L. (1990). Families and aging: Diversity and heterogeneity. In R. H. Binstock and L. K. George (Eds.), *Handbook on aging and the social sciences* (3rd ed.) (pp. 263–287). San Diego, CA: Academic Press.

Brandes, S. (1996). Kinship and care for the aged in traditional rural Iberia. In T. K. Hareven (Ed.), *Aging and generational relations over the life course: A historical and cross-cultural perspective* (pp. 13–29). Berlin: Walter de Gruyter.

Bremner, R. H. (1956). *From the depths: The discovery of poverty in the United States.* New York: New York University Press.

Bremner, R. H., Barnard, J., Hareven, T. K., & Mennell (Eds.). (1970). *Children and youth in America: A documentary history, Volume, 1, 16–1865.* Cambridge, MA: Harvard University Press.

Brody, E. M. (1990). *Women in the middle: Their parent-care years.* New York: Springer.

Burton, L., & Dilworth-Anderson, P. (1991). The intergenerational family roles of aged black Americans. In S. K. Pifer & M. D. Sussman (Eds.), *Families: Intergenerational and generational connections* (pp. 311–330). New York: Haworth Press.

Cantor, M. H. (1983). Strain among caregivers: A study of experience in the U.S. *The Gerontologist, 12*, 597–624.

Cherlin, A., & Furstenberg, F. (1990). *The new American grandparent.* New York: Basic Books.

Chudacoff, H., & Hareven, T. K. (1978). Family transitions to old age. In T. K. Hareven (Ed.), *Transitions: The family and the life course in historical perspective* (pp. 217–244). New York: Academic Press.

Chudacoff, H., & Hareven, T. K. (1979). From the empty nest to family dissolution. *Journal of Family History, 4*(1), 69–84.

Dahlin, M. R. (1980). Perspectives on the family life of the elderly in 1900. *The Gerontologist, 20*, 99–107.

Demos, J. (1970). *A little commonwealth: Family life in Plymouth Colony.* New York: Oxford University Press.

Demos, J. (1978). Old age in early New England. In J. Demos & S. Boocock (Eds.), *Turning Points: American Journal of Sociology* (suppl.), *84*, S248–S287.

Dowd, J. J., & Bengtson, V. L. (1978). Aging in minority populations: An examination of the double jeopardy hypothesis. *Journal of Gerontology, 33*, 427–36.

Dwyer, J. W., & Coward, R. T. (1991). A multivariate comparison of the involvement of adult sons versus daughters in the care of impaired parents. *Journal of Gerontology: Social Sciences, 46*, S259–S269.

Dwyer, J. W., & Seccombe, K. (1991). Elder care as family labor: The influence of gender and family position. *Journal of Family Issues, 12*, 229–47.

Eggebeen, D. J., & Hogan, D. P. (1990). Giving between generations in American families. *Human Nature, 1*, 211–232.

Ehmer, J. (1996). "The life stairs": Aging, generational relations, and small commodity production in central Europe. In T. K. Hareven (Ed.), *Aging and generational relations over the life course: A historical and cross-cultural perspective* (pp. 53–74). Berlin: Walter de Gruyter.

Elder, G. H., Jr. (1974). *Children of the Great Depression.* Chicago: Chicago University Press.

Elder, G. H., Jr. (1978). Family history and the life course. In T. K. Hareven (Ed.), *Transitions: The family and the life course in historical perspective* (pp. 17–64). New York: Academic Press.

Elder, G. H., Jr., & Hareven, T. K. (1993). Rising above life's disadvantages: From the Great Depression to global war. In J. Modell, G. H. Elder, Jr., & R. Parke (Eds.), *Children in time and place* (pp. 47–72). New York: Cambridge University Press

Fauve-Chamoux, A. (1996). Aging in a never-empty nest: The elasticity of the stem family. In T. K. Hareven (Ed.), *Aging and generational relations over the life course: A historical and cross-cultural perspective* (pp. 75–99). Berlin: Walter de Gruyter.

Fry, C. L., & Keith, J. (1982). The life course as a cultural unit. In M. W. Riley, R. P. Abeles, & M. S. Teitelbaum (Eds.), *Aging from birth to death* (pp. 51–70). Boulder, Colorado: Westview Press.

Furstenberg, F. F., Jr. (1981). Remarriage and intergenerational relations. In R. W. Fogel, E. Hatfield, S. B. Kiesler, & E. Shanas (Eds.), *Aging: Stability and change in the family* (pp. 115–142). New York: Academic Press.

Glick, P. C. (1977). Updating the life cycle of the family. *Journal of Marriage and the Family, 31*, 5–13.

Goldscheider, C., & Goldscheider, F. K. (2000). *The changing transition to adulthood: Leaving and returning home.* Thousand Oaks, CA: Sage Publications.

Greven, P. (1970). *Four generations: Population, land and family in colonial Andover, Massachusetts.* Ithaca, NY: Cornell University Press.

Gui, S. X. (1988). A report from mainland China. *Journal of Cross-Cultural Gerontology, 3*, 149–167.

Guillemard, A. M. (1996). Equity between generations in aging societies: The problem of assessing public policies. In T. K. Hareven (Ed.), *Aging and generational relations over the life course: A historical and cross-cultural perspective* (pp. 208–224). Berlin: Walter de Gruyter.

Guinnane, T. W. (1996). The family, state support and generational relations in rural Ireland at the turn of the twentieth century. In T. K. Hareven (Ed.), *Aging and generational relations over the life course: A historical* and cross-cultural perspective (pp. 100–119). Berlin: Walter de Gruyter.

Haber, C., & Gratton, B. (1994). *Old age and the search for security: An American social history.* Bloomington: Indiana University Press.

Hareven, T. K. (1976). The last stage: Historical adulthood and old age. *Daedalus, 105*(4), 13–27

Hareven, T. K. (1977). Family time and historical time. *Daedalus, 106*(2), 57–70.

Hareven, T. K. (1978). Introduction: The historical study of the life course. In T. K. Hareven (Ed.), *Transitions: The family and the life course in historical perspective* (pp. 1–16). New York: Academic Press.

Hareven, T. K. (1982). *Family time and industrial time.* Cambridge, UK: Cambridge University Press.

Hareven, T. K. (1991a). Synchronizing individual time, family time, and historical time. In J. Bender & D. E. Wellbery (Eds.), *Chronotypes: The construction of time* (pp. 167–184). Stanford, CA: Stanford University Press.

Hareven, T. K. (1991b). The history of the family and the complexity of social change. *American Historical Revue, 96,* 95–124.

Hareven, T. K. (1993, April). *Male caregivers for aged relatives: A life course perspective.* Paper presented a National Institute on Aging conference on "Male Caregivers," Bethesda, MD.

Hareven, T. K., & Adams, K. (1996). The generation in the middle: Cohort comparisons in assistance to aging parents in an American community. In T. K. Hareven (Ed.), *Aging and generational relations over the life course: A historical and cross-cultural perspective* (pp. 272–293). Berlin: Walter de Gruyter and Company.

Hareven, T. K., & Masaoka, K. (1988.) Turning points and transitions: Perceptions of the life course. *Journal of Family History, 13,* 271–289.

Hareven, T. K., & Uhlenberg, P. (1995). Transition to widowhood and family support systems in the twentieth century, northeast U.S. In D. I. Kertzer & P. Laslett (Eds.), *Aging in the past: Society, demography, and old age* (pp. 273–302). Los Angeles, CA: The University of California Press.

Hermalin, A. I., Ofstedal, M. B., & Chang, M. C. (1996). Types of supports for the aged and their providers in Taiwan. In T.K. Hareven (Ed.), *Aging and generational relations over the life course: A historical and cross-cultural perspective* (pp. 411–525). Berlin: Walter de Gruyter.

Hogan, D. P. (1989). Institutional perspectives on the life course: Challenges and strategies. In D. I. Kertzer & K. W. Schaie (Eds.), *Age structuring in comparative perspective* (pp. 95–105). Hillsdale, NJ: Lawrence Erlbaum Associates, Publishers.

Hogan, D. P., Eggebeen D. J., & Clogg, C. C. (1993). The structure of intergenerational exchanges in American families. *American Journal of Sociology, 98,* 1428–1459.

Hogan, D. P., Eggebeen, D. J., & Snaith, S. M. (1996). The well-being of aging Americans with very old parents. In T. K. Hareven (Ed.), *Aging and generational relations over the life course: A historical and cross-cultural perspective* (pp. 327–346). Berlin: Walter de Gruyter and Company.

Jackson, J. S., Antonucci, T. C., & Gibson, R. C. (1990). Cultural, racial and ethnic influences on aging. In J. E. Birren & K. W. Schaie (Eds.), *Handbook of the psychology of aging* (pp. 103–23). San Diego, CA: Academic Press.

Jackson, J. S., Jayakody, R., & Antonucci, T. C. (1996). Exchanges within black American three-generation families: The family environment context model. In T. K. Hareven (Ed.), *Aging and generational relations over the life course: A historical and cross-cultural perspective* (pp. 347–377). Berlin: Walter de Gruyter and Company.

Kaye, L. W., & Applegate, J. S. (1990). *Men as caregivers to the elderly.* Boston: Lexington Books.

Kiefer, C. W. (1974). *Changing culture, changing lives: An ethnographic study of three generations of Japanese Americans.* San Francisco: Jossey-Bass.

Kertzer, D. I. (1983). Generation as a sociological problem. *Annual Review of Sociology, 9,* 130–149.

Kertzer, D. I., & Hogan, D. P. (1996). Relations between older adults and the adult children in a nineteenth-century Italian town. In T. K. Hareven (Ed.), *Aging and generational relations over the life course: A historical and cross-cultural perspective* (pp. 30–52). Berlin: Walter de Gruyter.

Kett, J. (1977). *Rites of passage: Adolescence in America, 1790 to the present.* New York: Basic Books.

Knodel, J., Chayovan, N., & Siriboon, S. (1996). Familial support and the life course of Thai elderly and their children. In T. K. Hareven (Ed.), *Aging and generational relations over the life course: A historical and cross-cultural perspective* (pp. 30–52). Berlin: Walter de Gruyter.

Kobrin, F. E. (1976). The fall of household size and the rise of the primary individual in the United States. *Demography, 13,* 127–38.

Kohli, M. (1986). Social organization and subjective construction of the life course. In A. B. Sorenson, F. E. Weinert, & L. R. Sherrod (Eds.), *Human development and the life course: multidisciplinary perspectives* (pp. 271–292). Hillsdale, NJ: Lawrence Erlbaum Associates.

Laslett, P. (1977). *Family life and illicit love in earlier generations.* Cambridge, UK: Cambridge University Press.

Laslett, P., & Wall, R. (Eds.). (1972). *Household and family in past time.* Cambridge, UK: Cambridge University Press.

Markides, K. S., Costley, D. S., & Rodriguez, L. (1981). Perceptions of intergenerational relations and psychological well-being among elderly Mexican Americans: A causal model. *International Journal of Aging and Human Development, 13,* 43–52.

Markides, K. S., & Krause, N. (1985). Intergenerational solidarity and psychological well-being among older Mexican Americans: A three-generation study. *Journal of Gerontology, 40,* 390–392.

Martin, L. G. (1990). The status of South Asia's growing elderly population. *Journal of Cross-Cultural Gerontology, 5,* 93–117.

Masaoka, K., & Fujimi, S. (1996). Some inter- and intracohort comparisons of generational interactions. From the acquisition of parental roles through postparenthood in Japan, 1914–1958. In T. K. Hareven (Ed.), *Aging and generational relations over the life course: A historical and cross-cultural perspective* (pp. 483–510). Berlin: Walter de Gruyter.

Modell, J., Furstenberg, F., & Hershberg, T. (1976). Social change and transitions to adulthood in historical perspective. *Journal of Family History, 1,* 7–32.

Modell, J., & Hareven, T. K. (1973). Urbanization and the malleable household: Boarding and lodging in American families. *Journal of Marriage and the Family, 35,* 467–479.

Morioka, K. (1996). Generational relations and their changes as they affect the status of older people. In T. K. Hareven (Ed.), *Aging and generational relations over the life course: A historical and cross-cultural perspective* (pp. 411–525). Berlin: Walter de Gruyter.

Mutran, E. (1986). Intergenerational family support among blacks and whites: Response to culture or to socioeconomic differences. In L. E. Troll (Ed.), *Family issues in current gerontology* (pp. 189–203). New York: Springer Publishing Company.

Ransom, R., & Sutch, R. (1996). The impact of aging on the employment of men in American working-class communities at the end of the nineteenth century. In D. L. Kertzer & P. Laslett (Eds.), *Aging in the past: Demography, society, and old age* (pp. 303–327). Berkeley: University of California Press.

Riley, M. W., & Riley J. W., Jr. (1996). Generational relations: A future perspective. In T. K. Hareven (Ed.), *Aging and generational relations over the life course: A historical and Cross-Cultural Perspective* (pp. 526–533). Berlin: Walter de Gruyter and Company.

Rossi, A. S., & Rossi, P. H. (1990). *Of human bonding: Parent-child relations across the life course.* Hawthorne, New York: Aldyne de Gruyter.

Rothman, D. (1971). *The discovery of the asylum: Social order and disorder in the new republic.* Boston: Little, Brown.

Ruggles, S. (1987). *Prolonged connections: The rise of the extended family in nineteenth century England and America.* Madison: University of Wisconsin.

Ryder, N. B. (1965). The cohort as a concept in the study of social change. *American Sociological Review, 30,* 843–861.

Smith, D. S. (1973). Parental power and marriage patterns: Analysis of historical trends in Hingham, Massachusetts. *Journal of Marriage and the Family, 35*, 419–428.

Smith, D. S. (1979). Life course, norms, and the family system of older Americans in 1900. *Journal of Family History, 4*, 285–299.

Smith, D. S. (1981). Historical change in the household structure of the elderly in economically developed societies. In J. G. March, R. W. Fogel, E. Hatfield, S. B. Kiesler, & E. Shanas (Eds.), *Aging: Stability and change in the family* (pp. 91–111). New York: Academic Press.

Sokolovsky, J. (1990). Bringing culture back home: Aging, ethnicity, and family support. In J. Sokolovsky (Ed.), *The cultural context of aging: Worldwide perspectives* (pp. 200–211). New York: Bergin & Garvey Publishers.

Taylor, R. J., & Chatters, L. M. (1991). Extended family networks of older black adults. *Journal of Gerontology: Social Sciences, 46*, S210–S217.

Taylor, R. J, Chatters, L. M., & Jackson, J. S. (1993). A profile of familial relations among three-generation black families. *Family Relations, 42*, 332–342.

Townsend, P. (1968). The emergence of the four-generation family in industrial society. In B. L. Neugarten (Ed.), *Middle age and aging: A reader in social psychology* (pp. 255–257). Chicago: The University of Chicago Press.

Uhlenberg, P. (1974). Cohort variations in family life cycle experiences of U.S. females. *Journal of Marriage and the Family, 34*, 284–292.

Uhlenberg, P. (1978). Changing configurations of the life course. In T. K. Hareven (Ed.), *Transitions: The family and the life course in historical perspective* (pp. 65–97). New York: Academic Press.

Uhlenberg, P. (1996). Intergenerational support in Sri-Lanka: The elderly and their children. In T. K. Hareven (Ed.), *Aging and generational relations over the life course: A historical and cross-cultural perspective* (pp. 462–482). Berlin: Walter de Gruyter.

Zachritz, J., & Gutmann, M. P. (1996). Residence and family support systems for widows in nineteenth- and early twentieth-century Texas. In T. K. Hareven (Ed.), *Aging and generational relations over the life course: A historical and cross-cultural perspective* (pp. 225–253). Berlin: Walter de Gruyter and Company.

Nine

Race, Ethnicity, and Aging

David R. Williams and Colwick M. Wilson

As the elderly population grows in the United States, it will include higher percentages of elders from minority groups. This changing composition of the elderly population calls for increased attention to the needs, challenges, and experiences of these groups. Traditional interest in minority elders has been dominated by studies of black–white differences. There is growing recognition that the minority elderly are racially and ethnically diverse, and there are important intergroup and intragroup differences. This chapter seeks to enhance our understanding of the minority elderly by providing an overview of selected characteristics of this population. We will describe trends in the growth of the elderly, explore differences in their socioeconomic profiles, consider the patterns of and potential explanations for disparities in health status, and describe the social resources of minority and majority elders. Trends that are likely to face the minority elderly in the future will be identified and research needs discussed. Whenever possible, we will utilize data that go beyond black–white comparisons to highlight the heterogeneity that exists within the population of minority elderly. Members of racial groups do not agree on the preferred terminology for referring to themselves. In an effort to respect individual dignity, we will use the most preferred terms for each racial group (Hispanic or Latino, black or African-American, American Indian or Native American) interchangeably (Tucker et al., 1996).

I. Growth of the Minority Elderly

Demographic trends over the latter half of the 20th century clearly indicate that the United States has experienced dramatic growth in both the number and proportion of persons 65 years of age and older (Angel & Hogan, 1991). For example, the number of persons aged 65 and over was 12.3 million in 1950, 20.0 million in 1970, and 31.1 million in 1990. Projections for the first half of the 21st century indicate that older adults will increase from being 12.5% of the total population in 1990 to 20% by the year 2030 and remain that high through 2050 (U.S. Bureau of the Census, 1996). Similarly, the median age of the United States population rose from 29.4 years in 1960 to 32.8 in 1990, and it is projected to climb to 38.1

Handbook of Aging and the Social Sciences, Fifth Edition

in 2020 and 38.8 in 2050 (U.S. Bureau of the Census, 2000a, 2000b). One interesting feature of the increase in the American elderly population is that ethnic minorities are increasing at a faster rate than their majority counterparts. Non-Hispanic whites declined from being 80% of the total elderly population in 1980 to 74% in 1995, and they are expected to be 67% by the year 2050 (U. S. Bureau of the Census, 1993). The black elderly population more than doubled from 1.2 million in 1960 to 2.6 million in 1995, and it is estimated to increase by almost 300% between 1995 and 2050.

Hispanics are expected to outnumber blacks as the largest ethnic minority group of older persons by the middle of the 21st century (Angel & Hogan, 1991). Due to high rates of fertility and immigration, the Hispanic elderly population will increase from 4.5% of the total U.S. elderly population in 1995 (1.5 million) to 17.5% (13.8 million) in 2050. Although the absolute number of older Asian/Pacific Islanders (API) is only larger among minority elders than that of the American Indians, their growth rate will be faster than any other ethnic elderly group in the United States (U.S. Bureau of the Census, 1996). In 1995 they numbered about 600,000 but by the mid-21st century they will increase eightfold to 5 million. There were 129,000 American Indian elders in 1995, but by 2050 this group is projected to more than triple its size to 473,000. However, they will continue to be the smallest ethnic elderly group in the United States, increasing from 0.4% of the total population of persons 65 and older in 1995 to 0.6% by 2050.

II. Heterogeneity of the Minority Elderly

There is considerable heterogeneity within all of the officially recognized racial and ethnic categories. Among Hispanics, Mexican Americans account for approximately 49% of the elderly, 15% are of Cuban nationality, 12% are Puerto Ricans, and the remainder are mainly from Central and South American countries (Markides & Miranda, 1997). The immigration history of the various Hispanic groups is one important reason for the heterogeneity that exists within this population (Cubillos & Prieto, 1987). For example, some Mexican Americans resided in the southwestern region of what is now called the United States as far back as colonial times, while others migrated to the United States between 1942 and 1963, when persons were recruited from Mexico and other countries to fill the need for agricultural workers. Mexican immigrants from these two periods have now reached old age and account for most of the elderly in this ethnic group. In recent times there has also been an influx of both documented and undocumented Mexican immigrants to the United States. This group of recent immigrants will significantly contribute to the rapid growth of the Hispanic elderly population over the next 50 years.

Large numbers of young and middle-aged Cuban professionals migrated to the United States during the 1960s as political refugees. Most of these Cuban immigrants have grown old, and they account for the fact that Cubans are a larger share of the Hispanic elderly than they are of the Hispanic population overall. Most elderly Puerto Ricans resident on the U.S. mainland were born in Puerto Rico. Puerto Ricans did not migrate to the mainland in large numbers until after World War II, and most of those immigrants were young. For example, 70% of most of those who left for the mainland in the 1950s were between the ages of 15 and 39 (Sanchez-Ayendez, 1988). Puerto Rican immigrants to the mainland are distinctive because their status as citizens and their geographical proximity have facilitated relatively frequent back and forth movement between the island and the mainland.

There are 26 API elderly subgroups in the United States (U.S. Bureau of the Census, 1993). The Chinese are the largest group, accounting for 30% of the Asian elderly. The other major groups are Japanese and Filipinos (24% each), Koreans (8%), Asian Indians (5%), and other API groups (5%). Like Hispanics, the immigration history differs for various subgroups of the API population and is one of the key determinants of diversity within this elderly group. Most elderly Chinese Americans are native-born children of young immigrants to the United States in the early 20th century. A higher proportion of Japanese Americans are elderly than any of the other API groups, though their absolute numbers are smaller than the Chinese. Compared to other API subgroups, Japanese Americans have a longer immigration history in the United States and lower rates of recent immigrants (Tanjasiri, Wallace, & Shibata, 1995). In contrast, Vietnamese and Cambodian elderly are relatively recent immigrants who mostly migrated to the United States after the passage of the Hart-Cellar Immigration Reform Act in 1965. This act eliminated the quota system with its racial and geographical biases and thus made it possible for increasing numbers of immigrants from this and other regions to migrate to the United States.

The Native American elderly are a relatively small proportion of the total American Indian population and the U.S. population, more generally. In 1990, American Indian elders' aged 60 or over numbered 166,000, or 9% of the total American Indian population (John, 1996). However, they are a highly diverse group. There are more than 500 federally recognized tribes and entities of American Indians, Eskimos, and Aleuts. Many of these subgroups have their own distinctive history, culture, and language and differ on a broad range of religious, eco-

nomic, and social characteristics, as well as cultural norms. The Native American elderly are also geographically concentrated, with two thirds of this population residing in 10 states (John, 1996). Oklahoma (18%), California (13%), Arizona (9%), and New Mexico (6%) have the largest numbers of American Indian elders. The American Indian elderly are also disproportionately concentrated in rural areas. In 1990, almost half (48%) of all American Indian elders aged 60 and older resided in rural areas (John, 1996). Some urban Indian elders move to reservation environments in order to access care from the Indian Health Service (John, 1996).

III. The Socioeconomic Circumstances of Minority Elders

Table 9.1 indicates that there is considerable racial variation among older persons in years of formal education and poverty, two widely used measures of socioeconomic status (SES). A substantial proportion of the elderly of all racial groups have less than 12 years of formal education. This is true for 31% of whites and 37% of Asians. However, among persons aged 65 and older, almost 6 out of every 10 blacks and 7 out of every 10 Hispanics have not completed high school. Similarly, whites 65 years and older have rates of high school graduation that are more than twice that of Hispanic elders and 1.7 times that of blacks. Elderly whites are also twice as likely as black elders and 2.5 times as likely as Hispanic elders to have acquired a bachelor's degree or more. Interestingly, compared to whites, Asian American elders are overrepresented at both extremes of the educational distribution. The API elderly are both more likely than whites to not have completed 12 years of education and to have a baccalaureate degree or higher. Of all racial groups, the API elderly have the

Table 9.1
Selected Socioeconomic Characteristics by Race at Age 65 and Older

Socioeconomic characteristics	Whites (%)	Blacks (%)	Hispanics (%)	Asian and Pacific Islanders (%)
1. Education[a]				
Less than 12 years	31.0	58.6	69.6	37.2
12 years	36.1	23.5	16.2	27.7
13–15 years	18.1	10.5	8.2	15.3
16 years or more	14.8	7.4	6.0	19.8
2. Poverty[b]				
Percent below poverty	9.0	26.0	23.8	12.3

[a]U.S. Bureau of the Census, 1996.
[b]U.S. Bureau of the Census, 1997.

highest percentage of individuals (20%) who have attained at least 16 years of formal education

The pattern for Hispanics reflects the impact of immigration with large numbers of Latinos being raised outside of the United States in the context of lower educational opportunities compared to their U.S.-born counterparts. The black–white differentials reflect the historical legacy of racism and the unequal educational opportunities and lack of investment in education for blacks that characterized U.S. society when black seniors were growing up. Fischer and colleagues (1996) show that the initial efforts to educate blacks after the Civil War were replaced by Jim Crow laws in the late 19th century that led to a decline in spending on education for blacks, such that one-third of the counties in the South had no high schools for blacks in the 1930s. In 1911, Atlanta had no high school that would accept African Americans. The schools that did exist for blacks were inferior in quality. This lack of educational training and opportunity, combined with discrimination in employment, is reflected in the current economic circumstances of the black elderly.

The lower panel of the table shows poverty status differences by race. Poverty thresholds are established by the federal government every year (adjusted for inflation) and take into account the size, composition, and structure of the household. During the latter half of the 20th century there has been a steady decline in the poverty rates among the aged of all races. At the same time, the data in the lower panel of Table 9.1 show that rates of poverty are still relatively high among the elderly. Roughly one-fourth of black elders and Latino elders, nearly one-tenth of white elders, and about one-eighth of API elders reside in households that fall below the federal poverty line. Other data reveal that the level of poverty for American Indian elders resembles that of blacks (John, 1996). In 1989, 29% of American Indians aged 60 and over lived in poverty, and 39% had incomes that were less than 125% of the poverty line. However, data on poverty tell only a part of the story of economic vulnerability. In addition to persons who actually fall below the poverty line, a large number of persons are only slightly above this level and are at an elevated risk of becoming poor. Data from the 1990 census on older Americans who are economically vulnerable—the poor and near poor (those with annual income above the poverty threshold but less than twice the poverty level)—reveal that 16% of whites, 45% of blacks, 34% of Hispanics, and 19% of

Asian Americans were in this economically marginal category in 1990 (U. S. Bureau of the Census, 1990).

These data also highlight that race and SES are related but nonequivalent concepts. For example, although the rate of poverty is three times higher for the black compared to the white elderly, two-thirds of the black elderly are not poor and two-thirds of all poor elderly are white. Recall that there are important variations within these categories. For example, although the overall rate of poverty among Hispanic elders was 22.5% in 1990, the rate for Puerto Ricans was 31.7% (Chen, 1995). Similarly, 1990 census data reveal dramatic variations in poverty among subgroups of the Asian category. For all age groups of the Asian population, the Cambodian (42.6 %), Hmong (63.6%), and Laotians (34.7%) had rates of poverty that were considerably higher than those of African Americans, whereas some other Asian groups, such as the Japanese (7%), Filipino (6.4%), and Asian Indians (9.7%), had levels of poverty that were lower than that of the white population (Waters & Eschbach, 1995). Presumably, similar patterns exist among elderly subgroups of the API population.

Relatedly, there are large racial differences in income across elderly groups. The 1998 median income for elderly whites ($22,442) was 1.6 times that of elderly blacks ($13,936) (U.S. Bureau of the Census, 1999). Given that blacks on average have larger households than whites, the income gap between these two racial groups increases when household size is taken into consideration. For example, the 1992 per capita household income for older blacks was $7,810, just about half that of their white counterparts. There are also large disparities in the sources of income. In 1998, income from Social Security provided at least 50% of the total income for 63% of the beneficiaries (Social Security Administration, 2000). For 18% of all beneficiaries,

the Social Security check was the only source of income, for 12%, it provided 90–99% of income, and for 33% it provided 50–89% of total income. There is a greater reliance on Social Security among minority elders than majority elders. For example, 33% of black and Hispanic and 30% of American Indian elders, compared to 16% of whites, depend on Social Security for all of their income. Similarly, 45% of blacks and 44% of Hispanics, compared to 29% of whites, relied on this source for 90% of their total income (Hendley & Bilimoria, 1999). There are also racial differences in the receipt of private pensions. One in every three whites was a beneficiary of income from this source compared to less than one in five blacks and about one in four Hispanics. In contrast, 1 in 20 white elderly receive income from public assistance, compared to one in every four black and Hispanic elderly (Grad, 1990; see also chapter 19 by Crown, this volume).

Income as a measure of financial status provides only a partial picture of the economic resources of the elderly and understates the magnitude of racial differences in SES. Income provides information on the flow of economic resources into the household, but it does not address the wealth or economic resources that households have to cushion a shortfall in income. Most of the elderly are retirees, and income decreases during the postretirement period. Wealth captures an important dimension of the economic standing of individuals age 65 and older, and racial differences in wealth are much larger than those for income. In the Asset and Health Dynamics Among the Oldest Old (AHEAD) study, Smith (1997) documented that the racial and ethnic differences in mean net worth are large, with black elderly households having 26 cents of wealth for every dollar in total net worth of white households. Similarly, Hispanic households over age 70 had 33 cents in wealth to every dollar owned by whites. Racial disparities in net worth were even larger for some subtypes of wealth. Financial assets of white households were eleven times that of blacks and eight times that of Hispanics. The smallest disparity among the racial groups was found in home equity, with whites aged 70 and over having about four times as much equity as their African American and Latino peers. Assets are important as economic reserves, but they are also a key source of supplemental income for the elderly. Seventy two percent of white elders received income from assets as compared to 27% of blacks and 37% of Hispanics (Grad, 1990).

Gender is another predictor of variations in economic circumstances among the elderly. Across all racial groups, women are more likely than men to be poor (U.S. Bureau of the Census, 1996). Older men are more likely to have pensions and less likely to live alone than older women. Thus, although women constitute 58% of the total elderly population, they are 74% of the elderly poor.

IV. Health and Well-Being of the Minority Elderly

A. Racial Differences in Health

Race differences in SES among the elderly are important because of the profound effect of SES on health. A substantial body of research indicates that SES is one of the most important determinants of health status (Adler et al., 1994; Williams & Collins, 1995). The finding of an inverse relationship between SES and ill health across most indicators of health status has persisted over time in both developed and developing countries. However, the role of SES in health appears to be weaker among the elderly than among younger persons. In a careful analysis of this issue using U.S. national data, House and his colleagues (1992) found that the

effect of SES on health is small in early adulthood, increases markedly in middle and early old age, and decreases in late old age. They suggest that the increase in the association between SES and health in middle and early old age is due to differential exposure to major risk factors for poor health. This effect is not evident in early adulthood because it takes time for those risk factors to significantly impact health outcomes. These differences are diminished in late old age because social policies and programs such as Social Security and Medicare have improved the circumstances of the elderly, reduced SES differentials in exposure to important psychosocial risk factors, and thus provided some protection from adverse health outcomes.

Given the strong relationship between race or ethnicity and SES, and the role of SES in health, it would be expected that the minority elderly have elevated rates of disease and death. Before we review health data on the minority elderly and explanations for the observed patterns, it is worth considering the magnitude of racial differences in survival to older ages. Table 9.2 presents racial differences in survival to age 65 and 85. Data were available only for blacks and whites. For both males and females, the data show that there are large racial differences in survival to age 65 and 85. For example, of every 100,000 black and white men born alive, 17,000 more white males survive to age 65 than do black males, and 10,400 more white males than black males survive to age 85. Similar patterns are evident among women, although the racial differences, while substantial, are smaller than those for men. From an initial 100,000 of each race, 10,100 fewer black females make it to age 65, and 11,600 fewer black females reach their 85th birthday, compared to white females. These are striking differences, and they reveal that the early onset of chronic disease and premature death substantially reduces the

Table 9.2
Survival to Age 65 and 85 by Race U.S. 1997[a]

	Male			Female		
Age	White	Black	Difference	White	Black	Difference
Age 65	78,788	61,787	17,001	87,106	77,014	10,092
Age 85	26,491	16,051	10,440	43,261	31,664	11,597

[a]From National Center for Health Statistics, 1999a. For 100,000 persons born alive, number surviving to ages 65 and 85.

number of black elderly who make it to age 65 and beyond. Similar patterns are likely to exist for American Indians given their higher age-specific death rates under age 65 (John, 1996). Thus, among whites, there is a larger representation of birth cohorts at older ages than for blacks and American Indians. Accordingly, any assessment of racial differences in health among the elderly must take into account this large effect due to differential survival.

Table 9.3 presents death rates for all causes for whites and minority–white ratios for three age groups for persons aged 65 and older. Mortality is often used as a general indicator of health status, but this measure is limited because it is a summary indicator of health and does not provide the same information as data on the incidence (or new cases) of disease and the prevalence of disease. For example, in

1996, the number of persons aged 65 years and older hospitalized for cancer was almost twice the number of persons who died from this disease; for diabetes, stroke, and heart disease the number of elderly hospitalized was at least four times the number of those who died (National Center for Health Statistics, 1998, 1999a). Death rates in a given year are a function not only of the number of persons with a specific illness but also of the severity and progression of that disease. Higher death rates for blacks than whites tend to reflect both higher levels of ill health and greater severity of disease. They can also reflect differences in access to medical care and racial disparities in the quality of medical treatment.

Table 9.3 reveals that, for the three age groups considered (65–74, 75–84, and 85 and older), APIs and Hispanics have markedly lower death rates than the

Table 9.3
Death Rates for All Causes for Whites (per 100,000) and Minority–White Ratios for Persons
Aged 65 and Older (1997)[a,b]

Age	W[b]	Black/W ratio	API/W[b] ratio	AI/W[c] ratio	Hispanic/W ratio
Males					
65–74	3,122.7	1.38	0.61	0.91	0.72
75–84	7,086.0	1.17	0.67	0.68	0.67
85 and older	17,767.1	0.91	0.66	0.44	0.59
Females					
65–74	1,900.5	1.44	0.59	1.01	0.73
75–84	4,786.3	1.18	0.64	0.74	0.67
85 and older	14,681.4	0.93	0.57	0.39	0.59

[a]From National Center for Health Statistics, 1999b.
[b]W, White; API, Asian and Pacific Islander; AI, American Indian.
[c]AI = American Indian.

white population, and blacks have a much higher death rate in the youngest age category, and a somewhat higher rate in the age 75–84 category. This is true for both males and females. For American Indians, the death rates for females in the 65–74 age group is virtually identical to those of whites and, for males in that age group, it is slightly lower than those of whites. At the older ages, American Indians also have markedly lower death rates than those of whites. Data quality problems affect the accuracy of mortality rates for American Indian, Hispanic, and API populations (Hahn, 1992; Williams, 1996). Data for the calculation of death rates come from death certificates. As race is reported on death certificates by funeral home directors and other officials, a relatively high proportion of American Indians and Asian Americans are misclassified as white. This undercount in the numerator suppresses the death rates for these groups and leads to officially reported mortality rates that are lower than they actually are. One study, for example, matched the race obtained during an interview in the Current Population Survey with the race for that individual recorded on the death certificate (Sorlie, Rogot, & Johnson, 1992). It found that the degree of agreement was very high for blacks and whites. However, 26% of persons who had self-identified in the survey as American Indian, 18% of APIs, and 10% of Hispanics were classified into a different racial category (mainly white) on the death certificate. It is also worth noting that the death rates reported by the Indian Health Service (IHS) for American Indians are higher than the nationally reported rates. The IHS is a federal program that provides health care to about 60% of the American Indian population that live on or near reservations. IHS data reveal that American Indians have higher death rates than whites up through age 65. Between ages 65 and 74, the rates between the two groups are comparable, and there

is evidence of mortality crossover beyond age 75, where the rates for American Indians are lower than those of whites (Indian Health Service, 1995).

In spite of these data quality problems, the evidence nonetheless suggests that both Hispanics and APIs have lower mortality rates than that of the white population (Markides, Rudkin, Angel, & Espino, 1997; Vega & Amaro, 1994). How do we make sense of these data? First, the earlier noted ethnic diversity within each of these large racial and ethnic categories captures important differences in socioeconomic circumstances and in health. For example, for the Hispanic population, Cuban Americans are higher in SES, on average, than Mexicans and Puerto Ricans. Sorlie, Backlund, Johnson, and Rogot (1993) report that elderly Cubans of both sexes have higher life expectancy than their Mexican and Puerto Rican counterparts. Second, the relatively good health profile of the Hispanic and Asian American populations importantly reflects the impact of immigration. On the surface, it is surprising that the health profile of Hispanics would be as good as or better than the white population given the high levels of exposure to adverse socioeconomic circumstances within this population. However, a large proportion of both the Hispanic and API population is foreign born. Research reveals that, across all racial and ethnic groups in the United States, immigrants tend to enjoy better health than the native born, even when those immigrants are lower in SES (Hummer, Rogers, Nam, & LeClere, 1999). Studies of Mexican Americans (Vega & Amaro, 1994) and the Japanese (Marmot & Syme, 1976) reveal that disease rates increase progressively with degree of acculturation to the United States. As length of stay in the United States increases, fiber consumption and breastfeeding decline, but the use of cigarettes, alcohol, and illicit drugs increases (Vega & Amaro, 1994). Thus, it is likely that increasing length of stay and greater acculturation of the Hispanic and Asian population will lead to trends of worsening health for the elderly in future years.

In contrast to the patterns for the non-black minorities, Table 9.3 shows that black males and females between the ages of 65 and 74 have a mortality rate that is 1.4 times higher than that of whites. In the 75 to 84 age group, the death rate across both genders is 1.2 times higher than that of their white peers. In contrast, black men and women aged 85 and above have lower rates of mortality than similarly aged whites. The pattern of black–white differences in mortality has generated considerable speculation and controversy.

B. Explanations of Racial Differences in Health

Competing hypotheses have been proposed to explain the differences in health between majority and minority elders (Dowd & Bengtson, 1978; Ferraro & Farmer, 1996). One such hypothesis is the *double jeopardy* perspective, which was originally intended to draw attention to the disadvantages of elderly blacks in areas of income, health, life satisfaction, and housing. It suggested that minority elders would experience greater negative consequences than their majority counterparts because they bear both the burdens of being minority and elderly, resulting in a double disadvantage to their health status (Wykle & Kaskel, 1995).

An alternative viewpoint is the *age-as-leveler* hypothesis, which posits that the differences between minorities and majorities may in fact decline over time (Dowd & Bengtson, 1978). Proponents of this hypothesis argue that minorities seem to do better in the later years of their lives because aging challenges health and functional abilities in unique ways that cut across racial categories. Additionally,

minorities are confronted with prejudice and discrimination over the life span for which they develop coping skills that may be transferred to their struggles with age discrimination. Empirical research has found little support for either perspective and uncovered instead, evidence of the persistence of inequalities between blacks and whites throughout the life span (Ferraro & Farmer, 1996).

The observation that black mortality rates exceed those of whites until, at some age later in life, deaths among blacks "crossover" and thereafter decline relative to whites has stirred considerable debate. This crossover in black mortality occurs between the ages of 85–89 for males and 90–94 for females (Elo & Preston, 1997). However, the age at which the white mortality rates exceed that of blacks has not been constant over time, although the general pattern of crossover at later years has been consistent (Jackson, 1988). The *selective survival* hypothesis has been proposed to explain this pattern. It argues that this phenomenon is a function of the "survival of the fittest" in which the higher mortality of blacks at younger ages reflects the deaths of persons who are subject to adverse conditions and leads to the survival of the most biologically robust individuals (Elo & Preston, 1997; Markides & Black, 1996). Others have suggested that the Vital Statistics and Census data, which are most often used in the computation of this crossover effect, are inadequate for testing this observed pattern (Zelnik, 1969). Specifically, they contend that the misreporting of age and other computational errors account for the lowering of black mortality rates in later years. It is known that older blacks, many of whom were born in the South where many states were excluded from the birth registration process before 1920, were not likely to be registered at birth (Shapiro, 1950). Accordingly, some have examined the error in date of birth as a means of shedding light on the mortality crossover between blacks and whites.

An early study comparing age in the 1960 Census to age reported on the death certificate (Kitagawa & Hauser, 1973) found that among non-whites (92% were black), ages from both sources matched for only 44.7% of males and 36.9% of females. Ages in the census data were consistently higher than those reported on the death certificates, a discrepancy that increased with age. For whites, ages from both sources matched for 74.5% of males and 67.9% of females. Other studies have found similar discrepancies (Elo & Preston, 1994; Rosenwaike & Logue, 1983).

A recent study analyzed a national probability sample of 4,216 death certificates for native-born African Americans aged 60 and older and found higher match rates than previously reported (Rosenwaike, Hill, Preston, & Elo, 1998). These results highlight the need to reassess conclusions about the extent of age misreporting among blacks. Some have argued that there is no evidence that unequivocally demonstrates such inconsistencies in age reporting or that other computational errors account for the black–white mortality crossover in older adults; in fact, they insist that findings from many different sources of data consistently support the black–white mortality crossover hypothesis (Manton & Stallard, 1997).

Thus, the evidence about age misreporting is not conclusive, and it remains plausible that the adaptation or selection process may predispose sturdy blacks to live longer lives (Wykle & Kaskel, 1991).

C. Race, Socioeconomic Status, and Health

Racial differences in SES play a large role in accounting for variations in health in general and black–white differences in health in particular. Table 9.4 illustrates the contribution of SES to racial differences in health by presenting variations in life expectancy at age 65 by race and income together. These data reveal that SES is a strong predictor of variations in life expectancy for both blacks and whites. High-income white males live three years longer than their low-income counterparts. Similarly, high-income blacks have a life expectancy that is 2.5 years longer than that of their low-income peers. These differences are larger than the overall racial difference in life expectancy at age 65. A similar pattern is evident for females, although the SES differences are somewhat smaller. Low-income white women have a life expectancy at age 65 that is one year shorter than their high-income counterparts. Similarly, low-income African American females have a life expectancy that is 1.3 years shorter than those in the highest

Table 9.4

United States Life Expectancy, at Age 65, by Family Income, Sex, and Race (1979–1989)[a]

Family income (1980 dollars)	Male			Female		
	White	Black	Difference	White	Black	Difference
1. Less than $10,000	14.0	14.3	(0.3)	19.7	18.6	1.1
2. $10,000–$14,999	15.5	14.4	1.1	20.4	18.0	2.4
3. $15,000–$24,999	16.3	16.3	0.0	20.5	19.4	1.1
4. $25,000 or more	17.1	16.8	0.3	20.7	19.9	0.8

[a]From National Center for Health Statistics, 1998.

income group. The power of SES to shape differences in health is readily evident if we compare low-income whites with high-income blacks. High-income black males have a life expectancy at age 65 that is almost 3 years longer than that of white men in the lowest income group. The differences are smaller for women.

For all of the comparisons for women in Table 9.4 and for two of the comparisons for males, whites have higher levels of life expectancy than blacks, even at comparable levels of income. This pattern exists for multiple indicators of health and is even larger at younger ages (Williams, 1999). The difference is larger for females than for males and is consistent with the role of selective survival, given that Table 9.2 shows that its impact is much larger among males than females. That is, differential mortality among African-American males before age 65 is most likely to occur among those who are most vulnerable (those who are sick and those who are lower in income). These data emphasize the importance of adjusting for SES in efforts to understand racial differences in health. They also highlight the nonequivalence of SES indicators across race. Compared to whites, blacks have lower earnings at equivalent levels of education, less wealth at the same levels of income, and less purchasing power due to racial differences in residential environments (Williams & Collins 1995). Moreover, some evidence suggests that exposure to noneconomic forms of discrimination may also adversely affect the health of the African American elderly.

Research suggests that acute and chronic experiences of unfair treatment or discrimination are a source of stress that is adversely related to physical and mental health. National data reveal that one-third of the population reports exposure to major acute experiences of bias, and 60% report that they have experienced chronic, everyday experiences of discrimination (Kessler, Mickelson, &

Williams, 1999). Everyday discrimination includes perceptions of being treated with less courtesy than others and receiving poorer service than others in restaurants and stores. Unfair treatment experiences based on race is the most common type of bias in society (Kessler et al., 1999), and African Americans and other minorities report much higher levels of racial and ethnic bias than whites (Williams, 2000). Such experiences have been linked to poorer physical and mental health for African Americans, Asians, and Hispanics (Noh et al., 1999; Williams, 2000; Krieger, 1990). Moreover, some research indicates that perceptions of discrimination make an incremental contribution to racial disparities in health over that of SES (Williams, Yu, Jackson, & Anderson, 1997).

D. Racial Differences in Access and Quality of Medical Care

Data on racial differences in access to and especially the quality of medical care illustrate another way in which racial bias can affect health. In 1965, the Medicare program was established to reduce financial barriers to access to hospital and physician services for persons aged 65 and older (see the chapter 21 by Feder, Komisar, & Niefeld, this volume). In fact, as a prerequisite for participation in this program, hospitals were mandated to be in compliance with the title VI of the Civil Rights Act of 1964, which requires that no one can be excluded from federal benefits based on race, color, or national origin. This requirement played a large role in desegregating hospitals in the United States (Quadagno, 2000). However, although there is no doubt that access has improved overall, there is evidence that racial differences have not disappeared (McBean & Gornick, 1994).

Medicare does not cover some medical needs such as prescription drugs, dental care and long-term care, and out-of-pocket medical expenses can be substantial. In addition, Medicare requires a co-payment of 20% of physician charges, a yearly deductible of $100 for Part A, and the cost of one day of inpatient care (calculated as $764 in 1998). These medical expenses may present additional burdens to the elderly and especially the minority elderly who are more likely to live in poverty. Many older adults minimize their out-of-pocket expenses by purchasing supplemental private insurance. However, black and Hispanic elders are a little more than twice as likely than whites to have no supplemental insurance (Wallace, Enriquez-Haass, & Markides, 1998).

Research reveals that there are systematic racial differences in the kind and quality of medical care received even among Medicare beneficiaries (Escarce, Epstein, Colby, & Schwartz, 1993; McBean & Gornick, 1994). In an analysis of racial differences and the rates of procedures performed by hospitals for Medicare beneficiaries in 1992, McBean and Gornick (1994) found that black Medicare beneficiaries were less likely than their white counterparts to receive all of the 16 most commonly performed procedures. The differences appeared to be largest for referral-sensitive procedures. These researchers further examined the Medicare files to ascertain if there were any procedures that black beneficiaries of Medicare received more frequently than their white counterparts. They found that this was true of four nonelective procedures. All of these procedures reflected delayed diagnosis for initial treatment or failure in the management of chronic disease. For example, African-American Medicare beneficiaries were 3.6 times more likely to have the amputation of a lower limb (usually as a consequence of diabetes) and 2.2 times more likely to have the removal of both testes (generally performed because of cancer in males) than their white counterparts.

These racial differences in the quality of medical care among Medicare beneficiaries are consistent with a much larger literature that finds consistent and systematic racial differences in the receipt of a broad range of medical procedures. Multiple explanations have been offered for these racial disparities in medical care. It has been argued that they could reflect the geographic mal-distribution of health resources, racial differences in patient preferences, physiology, economic status, insurance coverage, place of treatment, and trust, knowledge, and prior experience with medical procedures. However, all of the available evidence suggests that systematic discrimination, some of which may be unconscious, remains the central, plausible explanation of this striking pattern of racial disparities (Williams & Rucker, 2000).

V. Social Resources of the Minority Elderly: Family, Religious, and Informal Support

Loneliness and isolation are potential threats to the physical and emotional well-being of the elderly. However, the elderly are not isolated from kinship networks, and family members often serve as the primary source of both instrumental and affective support (Taylor, 1988). Both black and white elderly have been found to interact with their children and grandchildren on a regular basis (Mitchell & Register, 1984). Elderly whites and blacks are more likely to seek help from their adult children than from their siblings or other relatives (Smerglia, Deimling, & Barresi, 1988). However, black families are more likely than white families to be involved in exchanging help across generations, to provide assistance to children and grandchildren, and to receive more help from their offspring (Mutran, 1985). Additionally, Chatters and Taylor (1990) found that African American elderly are more likely than whites to reside in extended families, less likely to live alone, and more likely to live with their children and grandchildren.

Traditionally, Hispanics are known for their strong emphasis on respect for the elderly and their commitment to assist family members during their later years (Cuellar, 1990). Hispanic households are more likely than those of non-Hispanic whites to have large social networks, multiple family members, and intergenerational living arrangements (Bean & Tienda, 1986). This in part accounts for the finding that when compared to non-Hispanic whites, Hispanics are more likely to rely on family for support than on friends (Commonwealth Fund Commission, 1989). However, this minority group is culturally diverse with different groups sharing different customs, values, beliefs, immigration history, migration patterns, and SES. These differences are not fully understood, and it is unclear the extent to which the general patterns among Hispanic elders are a function of socioeconomic factors or cultural factors linked to ethnicity (Cantor & Little, 1985).

The API population, while also a highly diverse group, is viewed in the literature as very family oriented with values that emphasize the importance of supporting and caring for the elderly. However, there appears to be a weakening of these traditional cultural values, as adult children are tending to rely more on formal care than did their predecessors (Morioka-Douglas & Yeo, 1990). Nonetheless, Asian elders are less likely to live alone than the elderly population in general, although this tends to vary by acculturation, SES, and country of birth. American Indians are known for their traditions of social support and the importance of the extended family in meeting the needs of the elderly. Yet, little empirical evidence exists about the effects of migration from

the reservation, area of residence, and the acculturation of younger American Indians on these traditional values. Additionally, little is also known about the extent to which levels of care vary by different tribes of American Indians (McCabe & Cuellar, 1994).

Religious involvement and participation is another important source of support among the elderly. The elderly generally express a higher degree of religiosity than the younger population (Greeley, 1989). National data reveal that almost half of older Americans attend church each week, about one in every four reads the Bible on a daily basis, and one out of five participates in a prayer group (Princeton Religious Research Center, 1984). Religion is also a critical source of social support over the life course. Interaction with fellow church members provides material and emotional support, information, advice, and spiritual benefits for the elderly. Additionally, religious organizations play an important role in providing material and economic assistance to church members.

Moreover, religious participation appears to be more consequential for the quality of life and health of older persons compared to their younger counterparts. As physical functioning declines in age, congregation members often play a key role in providing emotional and instrumental support (Koenig et al., 1997). Religious beliefs can be an important source of hope and comfort and can provide systems of meaning that can facilitate coping with stress, disability, and the loss of loved ones (Koenig, George, & Siegler, 1998). In dealing with the prospect of death, religious belief systems can also provide reassurance and perspective that enable many older adults to manage the fear and anxiety that may be associated with impending death. Religion can serve these functions for the elderly of all races, but religion may be especially salient in the lives of the minority elderly. For example, research has consistently found that levels of public and private religiosity are higher for blacks than for whites (Levin, Taylor, & Chatters, 1994).

VI. Future Trends and Research Needs

A number of factors can be identified that are likely to be important influences on the minority elderly in the future. It is likely that increasing length of residence and greater acculturation of the Hispanic and Asian populations will lead to worsening health. Across a broad range of health status indicators, the research indicates that foreign-born Hispanics have a better health profile than their counterparts born in the United States. Rates of infant mortality, low birthweight, cancer, high blood pressure, adolescent pregnancy, and psychiatric disorders increase with residence in the United States (Vega & Amaro, 1994).

Another trend that may have implications for the SES and quality of life of the minority elderly is the widening income inequality in the United States. Since the mid-1970s there has been an increase in income inequality, a growing concentration of wealth among the highest income groups, and a worsening of the economic conditions for a substantial portion of the population (Danziger & Gottschalk, 1993). Research from both Western Europe and the United States suggest that widening health status disparities parallel widening economic disparities (Williams & Collins, 1995). Given that the minority elderly are overrepresented among lower income groups, worsening health status linked to economic inequalities is likely to disproportionately affect these populations.

A third factor that is likely to affect the health of the minority elderly in the future is the high rates of childhood poverty. National data suggest that rates of childhood poverty are disconcertingly high in the United States. One in five of all children in the United States and two out of every five black and Latino children under the age of 18 are living in poverty (National Center for Health Statistics, 1998). In fact, if we combine persons in poverty with the near poor, 43% of all children in the United States, 31% white, 41% API, 68% black, and 73% Hispanic are economically vulnerable. Health status of adults is affected not only by current SES but also by exposure to economic deprivation over the life course. Several studies reveal that early life economic and health conditions have long-term adverse consequences for adult health (Elo & Preston, 1992).

Finally, the persistence of racism suggests that the disparities in minority health may linger for some time in the future. National data reveal that whites are more opposed to racially targeted policies than to similar policies targeted to the poor (Bobo & Kluegel, 1993). Moreover, the challenges for the African American population may be distinctive and greater than those of other minority groups. Although many groups have suffered and continue to experience prejudice and discrimination in the United States, blacks have always been at the bottom of the racial hierarchy, and the social stigma associated with this group is probably greatest. For example, African Americans continue to be the most discriminated against group in terms of residential segregation (Massey & Denton, 1993) and historically have had the greatest difficulties with socioeconomic mobility (Lieberson, 1980).

Research is needed that would identify the mechanisms and processes that link location in social structure to health outcomes. Such research must also attend to the resources and adaptive coping strategies within minority populations. Research on minority aging has focused heavily on pathologies and deficits and given scant attention to the resources and cultural strengths within minority communities. We have noted the role that high levels of religious involvement and family and kin support systems can play in enhancing health. Research is needed that would identify how a broader range of social and psychological resources, such as racial identity and cultural belief systems and behavior, may also facilitate coping and adaptation within minority populations. Future research must give greater attention to comprehensively assessing racial minority status and including identifiers for ethnic variation within each of the major racial and ethnic categories.

Researchers also need to be more self-critical about the collection, analysis, and interpretation of racial data (Williams, 1997). Greater consideration must be given to why race and ethnicity data are being collected, the limitations of racial data, and how the findings should be interpreted. Whenever feasible, additional information that captures the characteristics presumably linked to race, such as SES, acculturation, and economic and noneconomic aspects of discrimination, should be collected.

In contemporary American society, race is often viewed as a master status—a key determinant of social identity and access to power, privilege, and resources in society. Many minority elderly have been exposed to adverse social circumstances throughout their life courses. Many experienced deficits in education and health care during childhood and have been more likely to experience poverty, discrimination, and other forms of exclusion during adulthood. A growing number of the minority elderly in the United States have also had to adjust to a new host society at some point in their lives. The research literature suggests that many of these challenges persist into old age and shape the opportunities and outcomes for minority elders. However, our understanding of the lives of the elderly, especially those who are Hispanic, API, and American Indian is importantly limited by the unavailability of data. More than just more data, we need better data that would identify the ways in which exposures linked to the social, economic, political, and cultural context of elderly Americans combine with racism and migration to influence their lives in ways that can enhance or impair their physical and mental health. This is especially important given that the minority elderly are a large and growing portion of our aging population.

Acknowledgments

Preparation of this chapter was supported by grants R01 MH57425 and T32 MH16806 from the National Institute of Mental Health and by the John D. and Catherine T. MacArthur Foundation Research Network on Socioeconomic Status and Health. We thank Kathleen Boyle for assistance with the preparation of the manuscript.

References

Adler, N. E., Boyce, T., Chesney, M. A., Cohen, S., Folkman, S., Kahn, R. L., & Syme, S. L. (1994). Socioeconomic status and health: The challenge of the gradient. *American Psychologist, 49*, 15–24.

Angel, J., & Hogan, D. P. (1991). The demography of the minority aging populations. *Minority elders: Longevity, economics, and health* (pp. 1–13). In Jackson, J. S., Albright, J., Miles, T.P., Miranda, M. R., Nunez, C., Stanford, E. P., Yee, B. W. K., Yee, D. L. & Yeo, G. (Eds.), Washington, DC: The Gerontological Society of America.

Bean, F. D., & Tienda, M. (1986). *The Hispanic population of the United States.* New York: Russell Sage.

Bobo, L., & Kluegel, J. R. (1993). Opposition to race-targeting: Self-interest, stratification ideology, or racial attitudes. *American Sociological Review, 58*, 443–464.

Cantor, M. H., & Little, V. (1985). Aging and social care. In R. H. Binstock & E. Shanas

(Eds.), *Handbook of aging and social sciences* (2nd ed.) (pp. 754–781). New York: Van Nostrand Reinhold.

Chatters, L. M., & Taylor, R. J. (1990). Social integration. In Z. Harel, E. A. McKinney, & M. Williams (Eds.), *Black aged: Understanding diversity and service needs* (pp. 205–220). Newbury Park, CA: Sage.

Chen, Y.-P. (1995). Improving the economic security of minority persons as they enter old age. In J.S. Jackson, J. Albright, T.P. Miles, M.R. Miranda, C. Nunez, E.P. Stanford, B.W.K. Yee, D.L. Yee, & G. Yeo (Eds.), *Minority elders* (pp. 22–31). Washington, DC: The Gerontological Society of America.

Commonwealth Fund Commission. (1989). *Poverty and poor health among elderly Hispanic Americans.* Baltimore, MD: Commonwealth Fund Commission on Elderly People Living Alone.

Cubillos, H. L., & Prieto, M. M. (1987). *The Hispanic elderly: A demographic profile.* Washington, DC: Policy Analysis Center, National Council of LaRaza.

Cuellar, J. (1990). *Aging and health: Hispanic American elders.* Stanford, CA: Stanford Geriatric Education Center.

Danziger, S., & Gottschalk, P. (Eds.). (1993). *Uneven tides: Rising inequality in America.* New York: Russell Sage.

Dowd, J. J., & Bengtson, V. L. (1978). Aging in minority populations: An examination of the double jeopardy hypothesis. *Journal of Gerontology: Social Sciences, 33,* 427–436.

Elo, I.T., & Preston, S. H. (1992). Effects of early-life conditions on adult mortality: A review. *Population Index, 58,* 186–212.

Elo, I.T., & Preston, S. H. (1994). Estimating African-American mortality from inaccurate data. *Demography, 31,* 427–458.

Elo, I.T., & Preston, S. H. (1997). Racial and ethnic differences in mortality at older ages. L. Martin & B.J. Soldo (Eds.), *Racial and ethnic differences in the health of older Americans.* Washington, DC: National Academy Press.

Escarce, J. J., Epstein, K. R., Colby, D. C., & Schwartz, J. S. (1993). Racial differences in the elderly's use of medical procedures and diagnostic tests [see comments]. *American Journal of Public Health, 83*(7), 948–954.

Ferraro, K. F., & Farmer, M. M. (1996). Double jeopardy, aging as leveler, or persistent health inequality? A longitudinal analysis of white and black Americans. *Journal of Gerontology: Social Sciences, 51B,* S319–S328.

Fischer, C. S., Hout, M., Jankowski, M. S., Lucas, S. R., Swidler, A., & Voss, K. (1996). *Inequality by design: Cracking the bell curve myth.* Princeton, NJ: Princeton University Press.

Grad, S. (1990). *Income of the population 55 or older, 1998.* Social Security Administration. SSA Publication No. 13–11871 (June). Tables 1 and 4, 1, 9–11. Washington, DC: U. S. Department of Health and Human Services, Social Security Administration.

Greeley, A. M. (1989). *Religious change in America.* Cambridge, MA: Harvard University Press.

Hahn, R. A. (1992). The state of federal health statistics on racial and ethnic groups. *Journal of the American Medical Association, 267,* 268–271.

Hendley, A. A., & Bilimoria, N. F. (1999). Minorities and Social Security: An analysis of racial and ethnic differences in the current program. *Social Security Bulletin, 62*(2), 59–64.

House, J. S., Kessler, R. C., Herzog, A. R., Mero, R. P., Kinney, A. M., & Breslow, M. J. (1992). Social stratification, age, and health. In K. W. Schaie, D. Blazer, & J. S. House (Eds.), *Aging, health behaviors, and health outcomes* (pp. 1–32). Hillsdale, NJ: Erlbaum.

Hummer, R. A., Rogers, R. G., Nam, C. B., & LeClere, F. B. (1999). Race/ethnicity, nativity, and U.S. adult mortality. *Social Science Quarterly, 80,* 136–153.

Indian Health Service. (1995). *Trends in Indian health.* Washington, DC: U. S Department of Health and Human Services, Public Health Service, Indian Health Service, Office of Planning, Evaluation and Legislation, Division of Program Statistics.

Jackson, J. S. (Ed.) (1988). *The black American elderly: Research on physical and psychosocial health.* New York: Springer Publishing Company.

John, R. (1996). Demography of American Indian elders: Social, economic, and health status. In G.D. Sandefur, R.R. Rindfuss, & B. Cohen (Eds.), *Changing numbers, changing needs: American Indian demography and public health* (pp. 218–231). Washington, DC: National Academy Press.

Kessler, R. C., Mickelson, K. D., & Williams, D. R. (1999). The prevalence, distribution, and mental health correlates of perceived discrimination in the United States. *Journal of Health and Social Behavior, 40,* 208–230.

Kitagawa, E. M., & Hauser, P. M. (1973). *Differential mortality in the United States: A study in socioeconomic Epidemiology.* Cambridge, MA: Harvard University Press.

Koenig, H. G., George, L. K., & Siegler, I. C. (1998). The use of religion and other emotion-related coping strategies among older adults. *The Gerontologist, 18,* 303–310.

Koenig, H. G., Hayes, J. C., George, L. K., Blazer, D. G., Larson, D., & Landerman, L. R. (1997). Modeling the cross-sectional relationships between religion, physical health, social support, and depressive symptoms. *The American Journal of Geriatric Psychiatry, 5,* 131–144.

Krieger, N. (1990). Racial and gender discrimination: Risk Factors for high blood pressure? *Social Science and Medicine, 30*(12), 1273–1281.

Levin, J.S., Taylor, R. J., & Chatters, L. M. (1994). Race and gender differences in religiosity among older adults: Findings from four national surveys. *Journal of Gerontology: Social Sciences, 49,* S137–S145.

Lieberson, S. (1980). *A piece of the pie: Black and white immigrants since 1880.* Berkeley, CA: University of California Press.

Manton, K. G., & Stallard, E. (1997). Nonwhite and white age trajectories of mortality. In K. S. Markides & M. R. Miranda (Eds.), *Minorities, aging, and health* (pp. 1–14). Thousand Oaks, CA: Sage Publications.

Markides, K. S., & Black, S. (1996). Race, ethnicity and aging: The impact of inequality. In R. H. Binstock & L.K. George (Eds.), *Handbook of Aging and the Social Sciences* (4th ed.) (pp. 153–170). San Diego: Academic Press.

Markides, K. S., & Miranda, M. R. (Eds.). (1997). *Minorities, aging and health.* Thousand Oaks, CA: Sage Publications.

Markides, K. S., Rudkin, L., Angel, R. J., & Espino, D. V. (1997). Health status of Hispanic elderly in the United States. In L. J. Martin, B. Soldo, & K. Foote (Eds.), *Racial and*

ethnic differences in health of older Americans (pp. 285–300). Washington, DC: National Academy Press.

Marmot, M. G., & Syme, S. L. (1976). Acculturation and coronary heart disease in Japanese-Americans. *American Journal of Epidemiology, 104,* 225–247.

Massey, D. S., & Denton, N. A. (1993). *American apartheid: Segregation and the making of the underclass.* Cambridge, MA: Harvard University Press.

McBean, A. M., & Gornick, M. (1994). Differences by race in the rates of procedures performed in hospitals for Medicare beneficiaries. *Health Care Financing Review, 15*(4), 77–90.

McCabe, M., & Cuellar, J. (1994). *Aging and health: American Indian/Alaska Native elders.* Stanford, CA: Stanford Geriatric Education Center.

Mitchell, J. S., & Register, J. C. (1984). An exploration of family interaction with the elderly by race, socioeconomic status, and residence. *The Gerontologist, 24,* 48–54.

Morioka-Douglas, N., & Yeo, G. (1990). Aging and health: Asian/Pacific Island elders. SGEC Working Papers Series #3, *Ethnogeriatric Reviews.* Stanford, CA: Stanford Geriatric Education Center.

Mutran E. (1985). Intergenerational family support among blacks and whites: Response to culture or to socioeconomic differences? *Journal of Gerontology, 40,* 382–389.

National Center for Health Statistics (1998). *Health, United States: Socioeconomic status and health chartbook.* Hyattsville, MD: U.S. Department of Health and Human Services.

National Center for Health Statistics (1999a). U.S. life tables. *National Vital Statistics Report,* Vol. 47, No. 28. Hyattsville, Maryland.

National Center for Health Statistics. (1999b). *Health, United States, 1999: With health and aging chartbook.* Hyattsville, MD: U.S. Department of Health and Human Services.

Noh, S., Beiser, M., Kaspar, V., Hou, F., & Rummens, J. (1999). Discrimination and emotional well-being: Perceived racial discrimination, depression, and coping: A study of Southeast Asian refugees in Canada. *Journal of Health and Social Behavior, 40,* 193–207.

Princeton Religious Research Center. (1984). *Religion in America*. Princeton, NJ: Gallop Poll.

Quadagno J. (2000). Promoting civil rights through the welfare state: How Medicare integrated southern hospitals. *Social Problems, 47*, 68–89.

Rosenwaike, I., Hill, M. E., Preston, S. H., & Elo, I. T. (1998). Linking death certificates to early census records: The African American matched records sample. *Historical Methods*. Washington, D.C.: U. S. Bureau of the Census.

Rosenwaike, I., & Logue, B. (1983). Accuracy of death certificate ages for the extreme aged. *Demography, 20*, 569–585.

Sanchez-Ayendez, M. (1988). Elderly Puerto Ricans in the United States. In S. R. Applewhite (Ed.), *Hispanic elderly in transition: Theory, research, policy, and practice* (pp. 17–31). New York: Greenwood Press.

Shapiro, S. (1950). Development of birth registration and birth statistics in the United States. *Population Studies, 4*, 86–111.

Smerglia, V. L., Deimling, G. T., & Barresi, C. M. (1988). Black/white family comparisons in helping and decision making networks of impaired elderly. *Family Relations, 37*, 305–309.

Smith, J. P. (1997). Wealth inequality among older Americans. *Journal of Gerontology: Social Sciences, 52*, 74–81.

Social Security Administration. (2000). *Income of the aged chartbook*. Social Security Administration, Office of Policy, Office of Research, Evaluation, and Statistics.

Sorlie, P. D., Backlund, E., Johnson, N. J., & Rogot, E. (1993). Mortality by Hispanic status in the United States. *Journal of American Medical Association, 270*, 2464–2468.

Sorlie, P., Rogor, E., & Johnson, N.J. (1992). Validity of demographic characteristics on the death certificate. *Epidemiology, 3*, 181–184.

Tanjasiri, S. P., Wallace, S. P., & Shibata, K. (1995). Picture imperfect: Hidden problems among Asian Pacific Islander elderly. *Gerontologist, 35*, 753–760.

Taylor, R. J. (1988). Aging and supportive relationships: Research on physical and psychological health. In J. S. Jackson (Ed.), *The Black American elderly* (pp. 259–281). New York: Springer.

Tucker, C., McKay, R., Kojetin, B., Harrison, R., Puente, M., Stinson, L., & Robison, E. (1996). *Testing methods of collecting racial and ethnic information: Results of the current population survey supplement on race and ethnicity*. Bureau of Labor Statistical Notes, 40. Washington, DC: U.S. Department of Labor.

U.S. Bureau of the Census. (1990). *Population estimates by age, sex, race, and Hispanic origin: 1980 to 1988*. Current population reports Series P-25, No. 1045. Washington, DC: U. S. Government Printing Office.

U.S. Bureau of the Census. (1993). *U.S. census of population 1990, social and economic characteristics*. Current Population Reports, Series 2–1. Washington, DC: U.S. Government Printing Office.

U.S. Bureau of the Census. (1996). *65+ in the United States*. Current Population Reports, Special Studies, P-23–190. Washington, DC: U.S. Government Printing Office.

U. S. Bureau of the Census. (1997). *Poverty in the United States*. Current Population Reports, P60–201. Washington, DC: U. S. Government Printing Office.

U. S. Bureau of the Census. (1999). *Poverty in the United States: 1998*. Current Population Reports, Series P60–207. Washington, DC: U. S. Government Printing Office.

U.S. Bureau of the Census. (2000a). *Resident population estimates of the United States by age and sex: April 1, 1990 to July 1, 1999, with short-term projection to July 1, 2000*. Washington, DC: U.S. Government Printing Office.

U.S. Bureau of the Census. (2000b). *Projection of the total resident population by 5–year age groups, and sex with special age categories: Middle series, 1999–2100*. Washington, DC: U.S. Government Printing Office.

Vega, W. A., & Amaro, H. (1994). Latino outlook: Good health, uncertain prognosis. *Annual Review of Public Health, 15*, 39–67.

Wallace, S. P., Enriquez-Haass, V., & Markides, K. (1998). The consequences of color-blinding health policy for older racial and ethnic minorities. *Stanford Law and Policy Review, 9*, 329–346.

Waters, M. C., & Eschbach, K. (1995). Immigration and ethnic and racial inequality in the United States. *Annual Review of Sociology, 21*, 419–446.

Williams, D. R. (1996). Race/ethnicity and socioeconomic status: Measurement and
methodological issues. *International Journal of Health Services, 26*, 483–505.

Williams, D. R. (1997). Race and health: Basic
questions, emerging directions. *Annals of
Epidemiology, 7*, 322–333.

Williams, D. R. (1999). Race, SES, and health:
The added effects of racism and discrimin-
ation. *Annals of the New York Academy of
Sciences, 896*, 173–188.

Williams, D. R. (2000). Race, stress, and men-
tal health. In C. Hogue, M. Hargraves, & K.
Scott-Collins (Eds.), *Minority health in
America* (pp. 209–243). Baltimore, MD:
Johns Hopkins University Press.

Williams, D. R., & Collins, C. (1995). U.S. Socioeconomic and racial differences in health.
Annual Review of Sociology, 21, 349–386.

Williams, D. R., & Rucker, T. D. (2000). Understanding and addressing racial and ethnic
disparities in healthcare. *Health Care Financing Review, 21*, 75–90.

Williams, D. R., Yu, Y., Jackson, J., & Anderson, N. (1997). Racial differences in physical

and mental health: socioeconomic status,
stress, and discrimination. *Journal of Health
Psychology, 2*(3), 335–351.

Wykle, M., & Kaskel, B. (1991). Increasing the
longevity of minority older adults through
improved health status. In J.S. Jackson, J.
Albright, T.P. Miles, M.R. Miranda, C.
Nunez, E.P. Stanford, B.W.K. Yee, D.L. Yee,
& G. Yeo (Eds.), *Minority elders: Longevity,
economics, and health* (pp. 24–32).
Washington, DC: The Gerontological
Society of America.

Wykle, M., & Kaskel, B. (1995). Increasing the
longevity of minority older adults through
improved health status. In J.S. Jackson, J.
Albright, T.P. Miles, M.R. Miranda, C.
Nunez, E.P. Stanford, B.W.K. Yee, D.L. Yee,
& G. Yeo (Eds.), *Minority elders: Five goals
toward building a public base* (2nd ed.) (pp.
32–39). Washington, DC: The Gerontological Society of America.

Zelnik, M. (1969). Age patterns of mortality of
American Negroes 1900–02 to 1959–61.
*Journal of the American Statistical Associ-
ation, 64*, 433–451.

Ten

The Gendered Life Course

Phyllis Moen

I. Introduction

A. Commonality and Variations in Circumstance

Although being male or female is grounded in biological differences, most gender distinctions are socially constructed (Bem, 1999). One way gender "matters" is in men's and women's different locations in the social fabric of roles and relationships at different life stages. For example, we know that marriage has salutary consequences for the well-being of both older men and older women, but women are progressively less likely to be married as they age (Easterlin, 1996; George, 1996). Men are both more likely to remain married and to remarry as they grow older. Women, on the other hand, are more likely to become widows, and, if divorced or widowed, less likely to remarry. Specifically, 46% of women 65 and older in 1995 were widowed, compared to only 16% of men (U.S. Census Bureau, 1997, p. 874). They also live longer than do men. In 1997, life expectancy at birth for men was 73.6 years; for women it was 79.2 years (U.S. Census Bureau, 1999). As a result of these trends,

women are more likely than men to (1) live to be old and (2) face old age living alone. Given that they are more apt to experience widowhood, they are also likely to see this as a triggering event for residential relocation (Chevan, 1995). And, given their greater longevity and the fact that they are less apt to have a spouse to care for them, women are more likely than men to spend their last years in nursing homes.

Although it is well established that gender shapes men's and women's lives and lifestyles in the early adult years, producing considerable differences in roles, relationships, and resources, gender continues to shape the biographical pacing of later adulthood as well (e.g., Moen, Fields, Quick, & Hofmeister, 2000; Moen & Wethington, 1999; O'Rand & Henretta, 1999; Settersten, 1997). For example, as discussed in this chapter, men are more likely to work for pay after retirement from their career jobs, and women are more likely to care for ailing or infirm spouses, other relatives, or friends. Clearly, gender has direct effects on the incidence, timing, and duration of roles, as well as on social relations.

Handbook of Aging and the Social Sciences, Fifth Edition
Copyright © 2001 by Academic Press
All rights of reproduction in any form reserved.

B. Gender as Context

A second way that gender matters is when men and women in the same types of roles and relationships experience distinct impacts. This *role context* approach (Moen, Dempster-McClain, & Williams, 1989; Musick, Herzog, & House, 1999) suggests that particular roles may have beneficial or detrimental effects depending on other circumstances (such as the gendered experiences men and women bring to them). For example, social isolation, although less common for men, appears to be more stressful for men than for women, with the greatest proportion of suicides occurring among men over age 65. Also, men are more likely to benefit psychologically from postretirement employment than are women (Kim & Moen, 2001; Moen, Fields, Quick & Hofmeister, 2000). A third example of the gendered context of roles is what happens when individuals take on the care of ailing or infirm relatives. Employed women who become caregivers in late midlife are more likely to retire from their jobs, whereas employed men who become caregivers are more apt to delay their retirement (Dentinger & Clarkberg, 1999; Pavalko & Artis, 1997).

C. Gender in Context: Race, Class, Culture, Cohort and Life Stage

Gender itself is embedded in the larger contexts of race, class, culture, cohort, and life stage. Other chapters in this volume capture the interplay between gender and age for particular subgroups of the population (see, e.g., chapter 11 by O'Rand, and chapter 9 by Williams and Wilson, this volume). They show that gender effects are grounded in both class and ethnic backgrounds and the interplay between the two. These other contextual impacts intersect as well with life-course themes of biography and history, trajectories and transitions, experi-

ences and perceptions. For example, although middle-class women moving to communal living arrangements may perceive their move as disadvantageous, women with less socioeconomic status (SES) welcome the services and security such communal housing provides (Redfoot, 1987).

The following sections highlight the importance of the gendered life course, building on and extending a previous review (Moen, 1996a). First, gendered processes are described and discussed in terms of biographical paths and pacing, social relations, turning points, and enduring inequality. Next, retirement is used as an example of a gendered life-course process. Health and psychological well-being in the later years are then examined from the lens of a gendered life course. The chapter concludes with implications for policy and research.

II. Gendered Processes: Life-Course Patterns

A life-course focus on gendered lives emphasizes the significance of *historical context* (Elder, 1996; Moen, 1998; Settersten & Mayer, 1997). This is known as the life stage principle: the timing of events—such as wartime experiences—in individual lives shapes their effects on subsequent life paths. Frequently, the effects of historical events are different for men and women (Elder, 1996, 1998; Giele & Elder, 1998). Another fundamental life-course principle concerns the ways *experiences at one point in life shape the subsequent life course*. Both these processes, along with changes in the opportunity structure, result in members of different cohorts (born at different points in time) having vastly different biographies as they age (see George, 1993; Moen, 1997; Pavalko, 1997).

A. Biographical Paths and Pacing

There are clear gendered cohort differences in normative expectations regarding the later life course (Kim & Moen, 2001). For example, contemporary women in late midlife and older may view these years as a time of opportunity, whereas their grandmothers may have seen them as a time of decline. Men, too, may see the postretirement years as a time of possibility. They are certainly more likely than their fathers to retire earlier and to work postretirement. Whether there are gender differences in contemporary cohorts' perspectives about timing and aging is currently a topic of investigation.

Though much has been written about social clocks and mental maps in the form of age-graded norms for life-course transitions and trajectories (e.g., Hagestad & Neugarten, 1985; Riley, 1987), the evidence suggests that expectations about family and occupational career timing are looser than in the past. For example, Settersten and Hagestad (1996a, 1996b) found in their 1989 random sample of adults a broad range of "deadlines" for both work and family transitions, with, for example, the deadline for reaching the peak of the work career (on average age 42 for men, age 40 for women) ranging 41 years, from 20 to 60. Retirement (on average 61 for men, 59 for women) spanned the years 48 to 75. Historically, the life course has been organized and regulated in terms of paid work (Kohli, 1986). Settersten and Hagestad (1996a, 1996b) point out that there are now few clear deadlines for family or occupational transitions.

Gendered differences across cohorts can be explained in part by differences in the economic and policy climate. But changes in fertility and longevity have also had enormous influence on the gendered life course. Thus, women (the traditional caretakers) are far more likely at the dawn of the 21st century to have an aging parent still alive as they enter their 60s than were women at the beginning of the 20th century (going from a 3% to an 80% probability—see Watkins, Menken, & Bongaarts, 1987).

Baby boomers, those born following World War II (from 1946 through 1964), will come to old age having had an average of about two children, compared to an average of three for their parents (Easterlin, 1996). They are also less likely to have married or to have remained married to one spouse, meaning that they are more apt to confront the later years of adulthood on their own. Women in particular, are more apt to face aging alone.

B. Relational Careers

Another key life-course theme is that of *linked lives*: individuals' life paths are played out in tandem with the life courses of parents, spouses, children, friends, and co-workers (Antonucci, 1994; Elder, 1996, 1998; Ryff & Seltzer, 1996). Scholars of later life transitions and trajectories are increasingly recognizing the importance of viewing the couple as the unit of analysis. In fact, some of the most innovative research on gender and the life course is investigating married couples' conjoint experiences, such as Henretta, O'Rand, and Chan's (1993a, 1993b; O'Rand, Henretta, & Krecker, 1992) studies documenting the linked, but also gendered, aspects of couples' retirement timing and decision making (See also Blau, 1998; Smith & Moen, 1998; Szinovacz, 1987).

The importance of viewing couples as a unit of analysis is underscored by Suitor and Pillemer's (1994) study of married women caregivers of parents and parents-in-law. Husbands' assessment of their wives' family role performance (whether the wives were neglecting their other traditional role obligations) predicted wives' marital satisfaction.

Scholars are studying the relational careers between parents and children as well

(Pillemer & Suitor, 2000). For example, parents who have provided economic support for their (adult) children in the past are more apt to be cared for by their children in their later years (Henretta, Hill, Li, Soldo, & Wolf, 1997). There may be other forms of informal exchange as well—such as babysitting—provided by older parents (typically women) living with their adult children.

Family members, friends, and co-workers have been described as a "convoy of social support" (Antonucci, 1994; Kahn & Antonucci, 1981), moving through life together. Moreover, children's lives and ongoing ties with children affect the social integration and identities of their parents (Pillemer & Suitor, 2000; Ryff & Seltzer, 1996; Umberson, 1992). But participation in this "convoy" differs by gender. Women are not only more likely than men to be doing care work as they age— for their husbands, their children, their own parents—they are also more likely than men to experience strain in doing so (Brody, 1990; Young & Kahana, 1989). Antonucci (1994) suggests that women both have more close ties and are more burdened by them than are men. Because women as wives, mothers, and daughters take time out of the workforce for family responsibilities, they are less advantaged than men in terms of pensions, Social Security, and other financial resources (Hardy & Shuey 2000; Meyer, Street, & Quadagno, 1994; Myles & Quadagno, 1991).

C. Turning Points and Counterpoints

Key turning points shaping the entire life course for men and women are marriage and parenthood. These family roles anchor men to their occupational careers while disrupting women's. Han and Moen (1999a, 1999b; see also Moen & Han, 2001a, 2001b) point to the distinctive biographical pacing of men's and women's occupational careers resulting from men's breadwinning and women's family roles. They found men's career paths are not influenced by those of their wives; however, women's employment paths are very much contingent on their husbands', with implications for women's retirement timing, status, and income.

Caregiving for older or infirm relatives is another key turning point, as is the onset of disability or poor health. Women in particular tend to be both more likely to become caregivers and to experience changes from it (Moen, Robison, & Dempster-McClain, 1995; Moen, Robison, & Fields, 1994; Pavalko & Artis, 1997; Pavalko & Smith, 1999; Robison, Moen, & Dempster-McClain, 1995). Two other gradual transitions, also gendered, include the loss of driving ability/privileges (e.g., Glasgow, 2000) and changes in sexuality (e.g., Campbell, 1995).

Life-course markers can be either objective changes in behavior and circumstance or subjective psychological turning points, defined by individuals as key changes in their lives, with the one related to the other (Clausen, 1998; Moen & Wethington, 1999). Wethington and colleagues (Wethington, Cooper, & Holmes, 1997) find that reports of psychological turning points are more frequent among women than men, but less frequent for both as they age.

Riley, Kahn, and Foner (1994) describe "counterpoints" that occur when changes in one person's life affects another—as when, for example, a husband retires or becomes disabled or a daughter has a child. One would assume that if older women are more responsive to their husbands' life changes, then they would experience more such counterpoints and undesirable life events (Gotlib & Wheaton, 1997; Kessler & McLeod, 1984).

Whether events are viewed positively or negatively depends on past experiences and current resources (Thoits, 1986; Wheaton, 1990; Wortman & Silver, 1990).

For example, a study of individuals moving into a continuing care retirement community (CCRC) in upstate New York found that although men and women reported similar levels of perceived social integration prior to their move (in 1995), women reported higher perceived integration following the move (in 1998), especially women without spouses. They appear to have more close friends at the CCRC than do married men and women (Erickson, Dempster-McClain, Whitlow, & Moen, 2000).

D. Enduring Inequality, Historical Convergence, and Structural Lag

One of the stories that will surely define the latter half of the 20th century and the beginning of the 21st is the story of women's changing experiences and options. As women's biographies have intersected with the historical events of the times (Mills, 1959), the two most fundamental societal institutions—work and family—are being transformed.

Mayer and Mueller (1986, p. 167) describe institutional careers as the orderly flow of persons through segmented institutions. Such a framework, based on the notion of (occupational) status sequence (Merton, 1968), is how sociologists and economists have usually characterized the typical (male) biography. But women's life paths are neither orderly nor neatly segmented, as they move in and out of education, employment, community, and family roles. When women are the subject matter, scholars find they must carefully unpack the meaning of careers for both women *and* men, in terms of biography, cultural norms, historical context, adaptive strategies, and the institutionalized opportunity structure (e.g., Moen & Wethington, 1992). The challenge to do so is all the more pressing given the changes that have occurred over the past 50 years.

The study of women's experiences has almost of necessity been framed by a life course orientation, given the historical shifts and temporal contingencies shaping the social patterning of women's lives (e.g., Gee, 1986; Hochschild, 1989; Krueger, 1996; Moen, 1996b, 1997). Sociological life course scholarship on women's life paths has contributed to our understanding of the utility of the life-course approach on four analytical levels. First, it has demonstrated how prior choices, institutional arrangements, and chance events so obviously shape life paths and possibilities (e.g., Burkhauser & Duncan, 1989; Esterberg, Moen, & Dempster-McClain, 1994; Flippen & Tienda, 2000; Forest, Moen, & Dempster-McClain, 1995; Hardy, Hazelrigg, & Quadagno, 1996; Hardy & Shuey, 2000; Pavalko & Smith, 1999). Second, it has contributed to our understanding of the links between macrolevel and microlevel events and processes. Historical forces have broadened women's options in unprecedented ways, while, at the same time, structural lag in policies and practices has persisted in constraining their choices (e.g., Blair-Loy, 1999; Blossfeld & Hakim, 1997; Bradburn, Moen, & Dempster-McClain, 1995; Riley & Riley, 1994). Third, the study of the relational aspects shaping women's choices has underscored how individual biographies and institutionalized roles and rules are clearly embedded in and mediated through the lives of others (e.g., Burton & Bengtson, 1985; Clausen, 1993; Cooney & Uhlenberg, 1992; Henretta, O'Rand, & Chan, 1993a, 1993b; Lüscher & Pillemer, 1998; Pavalko & Elder, 1993). This has pointed to the value of a growing body of work on social networks, while simultaneously moving the study of social relations into a more dynamic, temporal, and contextual orientation. Finally, women's experiences constitute fertile ground for the understanding of the intersecting nature of work and family roles, suggesting a broadening of the occupation career concept in ways that better reflects women's as well as men's life pathways, as they negotiate the status passages of work and family *in tandem* (e.g., Moen & Han, 2001a, 2001b).

It is important to examine cohort variations in aging and life-course progression as they interact with gender. For example, historical events, such as the women's movement and the shift towards a service economy, have transformed women's and men's education and employment experiences (Bradburn et al., 1995; Elman & O'Rand, 1998a, 1998b; Farkas & O'Rand, 1998; Moen, 1994), meaning that many aspects of women's and men's life patterns are becoming more similar. As a case in point, women are increasingly undergoing the retirement transition, and couples increasingly face the reality of conjoint retirement exits (Han & Moen, 1999a, 1999b). Still, given the structural lag in gender as well as in age stratification (Moen, 1994; Riley et al., 1994), there remain enduring inequalities by gender across the life course, producing for women what is often a cumulation of disadvantage.

III. Retirement as a Gendered Life-Course Process

Men and women frequently experience different transitions and trajectories in the later adult years, but even the *same* transition can be vastly different by gender. Consider a key late-midlife transition: retirement. Retirement can be conceptualized as a three-stage process involving preparation (planning), execution (actually exiting one's career job), and constructing a postretirement lifestyle.

A. Planning and Expectations

Most studies of retirement have focused on men, in part because until recently it represented what was the culmination of the typical male career path. Recent research reveals that the whole process of retirement planning and expectations is different for women than men, in part because of the historical difference in their attachment to the labor force. When men leave their jobs they are exiting from a role that has typically dominated their adult years (Han & Moen, 1999b; Weiss, 1997).

Women, on the other hand, commonly experience greater discontinuity, moving in and out of the labor force, in and out of part-time jobs in tandem with shifting family responsibilities (e.g., Han & Moen, 1999b; Moen, 1985; Rosenfeld, 1980; Sorensen, 1983). Consequently, they are less likely to have the same duration of employment or accumulation of work experience as men. Given occupational segregation by gender and their less stable employment histories, women are also less likely to be covered by pensions than are men, and those with pensions have incomes far lower than men's (Farkas & O'Rand, 1998; Hardy & Shuey, 2000). Quick and Moen (1998) found that the vast majority of men and women in their 50s and 60s engaged in at least some preretirement planning, but men were significantly more likely than women to have planned (93.5% compared to 84.8%).

The increasing numbers of women in the workforce is another trend changing retirement planning and timing. Not only are more women now confronting retirement, the majority of both men and women workers are having to take into account their spouses' career plans in the formulation of their own preferences and expectations (Henretta et al., 1993a; Smith & Moen, 1998; see review by Kim & Moen, 2001). Both the processes of planning for retirement in these times of uncertainty and the coordination of both spouses' retirement planning largely remain fruitful topics for future research.

Retirement planning is one way to maintain career continuity, with retirement representing the attainment of an earlier goal. The evidence suggests that retirement planning is positively related to retirement satisfaction and well-being. Dorfman (1989) showed that the amount of planning that men did to prepare for retirement was one of the most important predictors of their retirement satisfaction, whereas, for women, the impact of retirement planning on satisfaction was less pronounced. Quick and Moen (1998) found that men in their 50s, 60s, and early 70s who planned "a lot" were four times more likely to rate their retirement years as better than men who did not plan as much. Just over 4 out of 10 (44.7%) retirees who did not plan at all felt that their retirement years were better than the preretirement years, over half (56.6%) of those who planned "some" or "a little" felt this way, and 3 in 4 (75.9%) of those who planned "a lot" reported their retirement years to be better. This relationship between planning and retirement satisfaction was significant for men and women alike, but recall that Quick and Moen found women in their pre-baby boom sample were less apt to plan.

B. Retirement Timing and Transitions

An important proposition of life-course analysis is that an understanding of one life phase, such as retirement, requires it to be placed in the larger context of life pathways (Elder, 1998; Geile & Elder, 1998; Hayward, Friedman, & Chen, 1998; Moen & Han, 2000, 2001; Pavalko, 1997; Reitzes, Mutran, & Fernandez, 1998; Settersten, 1997). In other words, past experiences matter. Although family, educational, and other experiences all help to shape the retirement transition, employment history is paramount.

Earlier studies of men found that blue-collar workers were especially eager to retire early, whereas those in higher status jobs were more apt to want to keep their employment and retire later. In the 1980s and 1990s, scholars began to document differential experiences of men and women approaching retirement (Hayward & Liu, 1992; Henretta & O'Rand, 1980; Herzog, Kahn, Morgan, Jackson, & Antonucci, 1989; O'Rand et al., 1992; Pienta, Burr, & Mutchler, 1994). Older men who are well educated and in professional jobs are the most likely to continue working (Hayward et al., 1998; Hayward, Hardy, & Grady, 1990).

Control over the timing of retirement is important for subsequent well-being. For example, Szinovacz (1987) found that the preference for later retirement was negatively related to women's retirement satisfaction. Both men and women who retire at the age that they had expected are more likely to report that they are very satisfied with retirement (Quick & Moen, 1998). In their 1986 survey of individuals aged 50 to 70, Herzog, House, and Morgan (1991) documented that both men and women who stopped work and felt they had little or no choice (28% of those not working) reported lower levels of health and well-being compared both to the voluntarily retired and those working the amount they would like.

Both current and long-term work and family experiences can shape subsequent life-course passages. O'Rand and colleoques' (1992) analysis of dual-earner couples found that prior employment patterns of earlier life stages (such as whether the wife worked when there were preschoolers in the home) affected the couples' retirement timing.

Lee and Shehan (1989) drew on a 1980 sample of Washington state respondents (ages 55 and older) to examine the impacts of both spouses' employment and retirement status. They found no positive effect of retirement on men's marital satisfaction and in fact conclude that the husbands' retirement may be somewhat stressful for both spouses. The lowest marital satisfaction was reported by employed women whose husbands' were retired. By contrast, women in their sample were most satisfied with their marriages when *they* were retired and their *husbands* were employed. Lee and Shehan propose a household division of labor explanation. Since retired husbands spend little time on domestic chores (Rexroat & Shehan, 1987), when wives are employed outside the home the inequity in housework may be particularly stressful (see also Dorfman, 1992).

Szinovacz and Harpster (1994) actually investigated how the employment and retirement status of both spouses relates to the division of household labor (using the National Survey of Families and Households), finding that retired husbands whose wives are employed spend more time (than dual-earner couples) on traditionally "male" tasks (i.e., outdoor tasks, shopping, paying bills), whereas employed husbands whose wives are retired do fewer of these tasks. When their husbands are employed and the wives are either retired or are homemakers, wives do most of the male and female tasks around the home, but they continue to do most of the female tasks when both spouses are retired. This study points to the utility of looking at both spouses' circumstances as well as the gendered domains of housework in order to understand gender differences in domestic work over the life course.

An analysis by Blau (1998) of married couples (using data from the Retirement History Survey aged 55 and older interviewed biannually in the 1970s) showed the strong proclivity of couples to schedule joint retirement transitions. Moreover, having one spouse not employed reduces the likelihood that the other re-enters the labor force. Blau (1998) points out that this has major policy implications in that incentives affecting the retirement behavior of one spouse are likely to affect the behavior of the other spouse as well.

Caregiving relations also shape retirement timing. A study (using data from the 1987–1988 National Survey of Families and Households) found that women in their 50s and 60s were more apt to be caregivers of an ill or disabled household member if they were retired from the workforce rather than still employed (Hatch & Thompson, 1992).

Other scholars have captured the dynamics of the paid work–care work relationship in late midlife. O'Rand et al. (1992) found that having an older female relative living with them increased the likelihood of wives' (but not husbands') retirement. Pavalko and Artis (1997) examined two waves (1984 and 1987) of data from the National Longitudinal Survey of Mature Women (ages 47–61 in 1984) to find that short-term caregiving increases late midlife women's likelihood of either reducing their work hours or leaving the workforce. Dentinger and Clarkberg (1999), drawing on data from the Cornell Retirement and Well-Being Study, report similar findings, with short-term caregiving resulting in an early retirement exit (although long-term caregiving reduced the likelihood of an early exit). Carr and Sheridan (1999) (drawing on panel data from 1975 and 1992/3) from the Wisconsin Longitudinal Study found that men (ages 35–53) who were informal caregivers (providing instrumental assistance) were more apt than those not providing care to leave their career jobs (an exit but not necessarily retirement). They did not find this to be the case for women in their study.

C. Gendered Lives after Retirement

Gender remains a key factor in shaping the life course of older adults, even after they retire from their primary "career" jobs. Social integration continues to be shaped by gender in the second half of the life course (Pillemer, Moen, Glasgow, & Wethington, 2000). One important source of continuing integration is friends and neighbors, with older women having larger networks than men (Campbell & Lee, 1992; Wethington & Kavey, 2000). Two major forms of integration into the larger community are postretirement employment and unpaid community service.

1. Postretirement Employment

Employment provides a key source of generativity (Danigelis & McIntosh, 1993; MacDermid, Franz, & De Reus, 1998). Men are more likely than women to take on paid work after retirement from their primary "career" jobs (Han & Moen, 1999a, 1999b; Hardy, 1991; Herzog et al., 1989; Moen et al., 2000; Moen, Kim, & Hofmeister, 2001). In fact, the U.S. Census Bureau (1999) reports that 16.5% of men 65 and older are in the labor force, compared to only 8.6% of women. Occupational position and pathways shape individuals' positions in the broader opportunity structure, which in turn affect the range of strategies and options from which older persons can construct their retirement transitions.

2. Volunteer Community Service

Another key form of generativity is formal community participation. Although Herzog and colleagues (1989) found that older women were slightly more likely than older men to participate in volunteer work, other studies have reported little difference (e.g., Fischer, Mueller, & Cooper, 1991). A number of people are highlighting the value of unpaid community service for those in their retirement years (Freedman, 1999; Moen, 1998; Moen et al., 2000). A recent national survey found that 45% of retired women describe community service as playing an important role in retirement, compared to 35% of men (Peter D. Hart Research Associates, 1999).

IV. Health and Psychological Well-Being

A life-course perspective underscores the importance of gendered pathways to health and well-being in later adulthood (Moen, 1997; Moen, et al., 1992; Pavalko & Smith, 1999). Poor health is related to aging, but this varies across subgroups, including by gender (House, et al., 1994; Mirowsky & Ross, 1992). For example, Atchley (1998) followed adults over 50 for a 16-year period, finding that prior poor health predicts women's subsequent functional capacity better than men's.

Some research focuses on the "multiple jeopardy" of older women who have a combination of social disadvantages (Hammond, 1995). Other scholars examine gendered differences in behavior. For example, Vertinsky (1995) notes that older women tend to exercise less than do older men. The social construction of the roles and identities of older men is formed against a lifetime of paid employment as a principal source of identity. For some men, exit from their work role is linked to lower levels of health and well-being (Hearn, 1995). The social construction of women's lives gives primacy to their domestic roles, even as they are entering, reentering, or remaining in the workforce in unprecedented numbers.

The institution of gender can shape life chances, choices, and expectations—affecting health and well-being. A growing body of research points to the positive physical and psychological impacts, for women as well as men, of employment, especially under working conditions that promote a sense of control (e.g., Adelmann, Antonucci, Crohan, & Coleman, 1990; House, Stecher, Metzner, & Robbins, 1986; Lennon, 1994; Ross & Mirowsky, 1995). Unstable work conditions are related to poor health (Hibbard & Pope, 1993; Jahn, Becker, Jöckel, & Pohlabeln, 1995). On the other hand, although retirement from the paid labor force is often a consequence of poor health, retirement itself is not necessarily linked to subsequent poor physical or psychological health of men or women (Bosse, Aldwin, Levenson, & Ekerdt, 1987; Ekerdt, Baden, Bosse, & Dibbs, 1983; Moen et al., 2000).

Other investigators are documenting the health and well-being effects of unpaid community service. For example, Musick, Herzog, and House (1999) drew on a nationally representative sample to show the longevity effects of volunteering for both men and women (see also Moen et al., 1989).

Although men's effective adjustment has been tied to their occupational achievement or accepting their limited success (Drebing & Gooden, 1991), the implications of women's divergent life paths are only beginning to be investigated. One such study was conducted by Carr (1997) using panel data from the Wisconsin Longitudinal Study of 1957 high school graduates who were reinterviewed when they were in their 30s and 50s (1992–1993). She found that falling short of aspirations in one's 30s increased depression and reduced the sense of purpose in life for women in their 50s. However, surpassing earlier career goals had no positive mental health effects.

Gender differences in health and psychological well-being in later adulthood reflect both (a) women's and men's differential roles, relationships, and resources and (b) the gendered context in which they are experienced. For example, recall that women are more likely than men to serve as caregivers, including caring for one's spouse. Longitudinal analyses over a 20–year period (1974–1994) offer compelling evidence that providing care to spouses predicts lower psychological well-being (Strawbridge, Wallhagen, Sherma, & Kaplan, 1997). Employment combined with caregiving may either exacerbate or reduce psychological distress, depending on whether it offers an escape

or added role strain (Brody, 1990; Moen, Robison, & Fields, 1994). Suitor and Pillemer's (1994) study of caregiving daughters (or daughters-in-law) found that whether their husbands felt they (the daughters) were neglecting other roles affected the daughters' marital quality during the first year of caregiving. Caregiving can also produce a sense of entrapment, eliminating other possibilities (Marks, 1998). Investigators are continuing to document the complexity of the links between roles, relationships, and well-being.

V. Conclusions

Three of the trends that defined the gendered life course in the 20th century and continue to shape it in the 21st are increasing longevity and the concomitant aging of the population, women's changing experiences and options, and the institutionalization (and subsequent movement toward greater individuation) of retirement. As women's and men's biographies have intersected with the historical events of the times, the realities of both gender and growing older have been literally transformed. This chapter has proposed the value of a life-course approach for understanding women's and men's lives, leading both to (a) a fuller consideration of the gendered aspects of growing older, and (b) a deeper awareness of the historical, structural, and biographical forces shaping the later years of men and women. We next consider both the policy and research implications of gendered opportunity structures, networks, and identities.

A. Gendered Realities: Policy Implications

Despite the remarkable advances in longevity, in pensions, and in opportunities for women, the nation remains hampered by both cultural and structural lag, in that societal norms, institutions, and practices have not accommodated to the shifting realities of contemporary life for women or men (Riley & Riley, 1994). This results in the perpetuation of a complex web of gendered and age-related opportunity structures, networks and identities.

Women's and men's roles and resources are *socially constructed*, a consequence of the different life paths and stereotypes that exist in our society. These factors can contribute to a lifetime of cumulative advantage for men and a lifetime of cumulative disadvantage for women (e.g., Hardy & Shuey, 2000; Heath, Ciscel, & Sharp, 1998; Lopata, 1994; Moen, 1996b, 1998; O'Rand, 1996). A striking and blatant example is the differential health-care options that are available for men and women (Laurence & Weinhouoo, 1997). More subtle is the stereotypical nature and shape of "the expected life course," which begins with a period of education, followed by years of productive work, and then retirement (Kohli, 1986; Riley, 1987; Riley & Riley, 1989). This sequence is so embedded in our institutions and our ways of thinking that we fail to consider that this life-course sequence is a relatively recent, 20th century invention, and characterizes the experience of men, not women. As women have sought equality, they have tried to accommodate to this model of men's life course, while simultaneously pursuing the housework and care work traditionally allocated to them. This has resulted in women's restricted occupational participation, culminating in a later adulthood with fewer roles and resources available to them.

Sewell (1992) describes "structure" as one of most important and most elusive of social science terms. He makes the point that *structure*, the noun, always implies *structuring*, the verb. Thus employment, domestic and community work, and retirement serve "to structure" virtually all aspects of both men's and women's adult life course, directly and indirectly, but in different ways, at different times, and with different consequences. Women's lives are typically *contingent* lives, shaped around the experiences of others: their husbands, children, and parents. Although this is obvious in the early child-rearing years of adulthood, in this chapter we have pointed out that late midlife women continue to shape their choices (involving retirement, for instance) around those of their husbands and their caregiving of aging and infirm relatives.

In fact, it is the reality of women's lives, along with recent changes in retirement and career paths, that has rendered the lock-step sequence of education, employment, and retirement obsolete for both men and women, a cultural relic of a society that no longer exists. What is required is a thoughtful reappraisal of existing life patterns, taking into account the hidden domestic and care work that has been the province of women. This could lead to a reconfiguration of the life course in ways that create more options and more variety for both men and women in youth, early adulthood, midlife, and the later years.

We in the United States, individually and collectively, remain uncertain and often divided as to what men's and women's roles should be, and what it means to grow old in a society where increasing numbers of people are in and beyond their sixth decade. Prevailing attitudes about gender and age remain ambivalent and contradictory. This is a matter of pivotal importance in seeking to understand the absence of coherent political and private sector response to the demographic revolutions in this country. To deal with the new realities of increased longevity, women's changing experiences and options, and the institutionalization and individuation of retirement, powerful forces for change must be mustered, leading to new social inventions (structural "leads" rather than lags) in the policy arena that permit productive engagement for men and women at all stages of the life course (e.g., Freedman, 1999; Moen, 1994; Pampel, 1998).

B. Gendered Realities: Research Possibilities

Social science has fostered an unreal view of aging, segmenting this life stage from all others. Scholars either study older individuals as if they were independent of prior experiences or study the larger demographic, economic, social, political, and cultural environments. Moreover, particular areas of life are investigated in isolation. Not only is this true of the sociology of aging and the sociology of gender, it is the case as well for the sociology of work and occupations and sociology of the family. Researchers have also accepted the commonplace notion of individualism, too frequently ignoring the interdependence of husbands and wives, parents and children, and co-workers. A life-course approach puts together individual lives and institutions, gender and age. Just as the nature of aging, gender, retirement, and career paths are being transformed, so too should the nature of sociological inquiry into them. Sara Arber (1995) points to the value of considering both gender and age together, thereby contributing to the sociology of gender, the sociology of aging, and, indeed, sociology more generally. There is also value to studying gendered pathways to later adulthood, which can additionally inform occupational, family, and, life-course sociology (e.g., Han & Moen, 1999a, 1999b; Moen & Han, 2001a, 2001b; Palvako, 1999). Considering the interplay between gender, biographical pacing, aging, and the policy environment can serve to link individuals' choices (agency) with the constraints of their social environment, as well as the macro and micro aspects of the gendered life course (e.g., Bury, 1995; Moen, 1996a, 1998).

Acknowledgments

Support for the research reported here was provided by the National Institute on Aging (grant #P50 AG11711, Karl Pillemer and Phyllis Moen, Principal Investigators), by grants from the Alfred P. Sloan Foundation (#96-6-9 and #99-6-23, Phyllis Moen, Principal Investigator) and by support for the Pathways to Life Quality Project.

References

Adelmann, P. K., Antonucci, T., Crohan, S. E., & Coleman, L. M. (1990). A causal analysis of employment and health in midlife women. *Women and Health*, 16, 5–20.

Antonucci, T. C. (1994). A lifespan view of women's social relations. In B. F. Turner & L. E. Troll (Eds.), *Women growing older: psychological perspectives* (pp. 239–269). Thousand Oaks, CA: Sage.

Arber, S. (1995). Connecting gender and ageing: a new beginning? In S. Arber & J. Ginn (Eds.), *Connecting gender and ageing: A sociological approach* (pp. 173–178). Buckingham, UK: Open University Press.

Atchley, R. C. (1998). Long-range antecedents of functional capability in later life. *Journal of Aging and Health*, 10, 3–19.

Bem, S. (1999). Gender, sexuality, and inequality: When many become one, who is the one and what happens to the other? In P. Moen, D. Dempster-McClain, & H. A. Walker (Eds.), *A nation divided: Diversity, inequality, and community in American society* (pp. 70–86). Ithaca, NY: Cornell University Press.

Blair-Loy, M. F. (1999). Career patterns of executive women in finance: An optimal matching analysis. *American Journal of Sociology*, 104, 1346–1397.

Blau, D. M. (1998). Labor force dynamics of older married couples. *Journal of Labor Economics*, 16, 595–629.

Blossfeld, H-P., & Hakim, C. (Eds.) (1997). *Between equalization and marginalization: Women working part-time in Europe and the United States of America*. New York : Oxford University Press.

Bosse, R., Aldwin, C. M., Levenson, M. R., & Ekerdt, D. J. (1987). Mental health differences among retirees and workers: Findings from the Normative Aging Study. *Psychology and Aging, 2,* 383–389.

Bradburn, E. M., Moen, P., & Dempster-McClain, D. (1995). Women's return to school following the transition to motherhood. *Social Forces, 73,* 1517–1551.

Brody, E. M. (1990). *Women in the middle: Their parent-care years.* New York: Springer Publishing Company.

Burkhauser, R. V., & Duncan, G. J. (1989). Economic Risks of Gender Roles: Income Loss and Life Events Over the Life Course. *Social Science Quarterly, 70,* 2–23.

Burton, L. M., & Bengtson, V. L. (1985). Black grandmothers: Issues of timing and continuity of roles. In V. L. Bengtson & J. F. Robertson (Eds.), *Grandparenthood.* Beverly Hills, CA: Sage.

Bury, M. (1995). Ageing, gender and sociological theory. In S. Arber & J. Ginn (Eds.), *Connecting gender and ageing: A sociological approach* (pp. 15–19). Buckingham, UK: Open University Press.

Campbell, J. M. (1995). Sexuality in the older woman. *Gerontology & Geriatrics Education, 16,* 71–81.

Campbell, K. E., & Lee, B. A. (1992). Sources of personal neighbor networks: Social integration, need, or time? *Social Forces, 70,* 1077–1100.

Carr, D. (1997). The fulfillment of career dreams at midlife: Does it matter for women's mental health? *Journal of Health and Social Behavior, 38,* 331–344.

Carr, D., & Sheridan, J. (1999). "Family transitions at midlife: Do they trigger men's and women's career changes." Paper presented at Population Association of America Annual Meeting, (March 1999), New York.

Chevan, A. (1995). Holding on and letting go: Residential mobility during widowhood. *Research on Aging, 17,* 278–302.

Clausen, J. A. (1993). *American lives: Looking back at the children of the Great Depression.* New York: Free Press.

Clausen, J. A. (1998). Life reviews and life stories. In J. Z. Giele & G. H. Elder, Jr. (Eds.), *Methods of life course research: Qualitative and quantitative resources* (pp. 189–212). Thousand Oaks, CA: Sage Publications, Inc.

Cooney, T. M., & Uhlenberg, P. (1992). Support from parents over the life course: The adult child's perspective. *Social Forces, 71,* 63–84.

Danigelis, N. L., & McIntosh, B. R. (1993). Resources and the productive activity of elders: Race and gender as contexts. *Journal of Gerontology: Social Sciences, 48,* S192–S293.

Dentinger, E., & Clarkberg, M. (1999). *Informal caregiving effects on retirement timing: A life course approach.* BLCC Working Paper Series #99–14 (Cornell Employment and Family Careers Institute).

Drebing, C.E.L., & Gooden, W. E. (1991). The impact of the dream on mental health functioning in the male midlife transition. *International Journal of Aging and Human Development, 32,* 277–287.

Dorfman, L. T. (1989). Retirement preparation and retirement satisfaction in the rural elderly. *Journal of Applied Gerontology, 8,* 432–450.

Dorfman, L. T. (1992). Couples in retirement: Division of household work. In M. Szinovacz, D. Ekerdt, & B. Vinick (Eds.), *Families and retirement.* Newbury Park, CA: Sage.

Easterlin, R. A. (1996). *Growth triumphant: The twenty-first century in historical perspective.* Ann Arbor, MI: University of Michigan Press.

Ekerdt, D. J., Baden, L., Bosse, R., & Dibbs, E. (1983). The effect of retirement on physical health. *American Journal of Public Health, 73,* 779–783.

Elder, G. H., Jr. (1996). The life course paradigm: Social change and individual development. In P. Moen, G. H. Elder, Jr., & K. Lüscher (Eds.) *Examining lives in context: Perspectives on the ecology of human development* (pp. 101–139). Washington, DC: APA Press.

Elder, G. H., Jr. (1998). The life course as developmental theory. *Child Development, 69,* 1–12.

Elman, C., & O'Rand, A. M. (1998a). Midlife work pathways and educational entry. *Research on Aging, 20,* 475–505.

Elman, C., & O'Rand, A. M. (1998b). Midlife entry into vocational training: A mobility model. *Social Science Research, 27,* 128–158.

Erickson, M. A., Dempster-McClain, D., Whitlow, C., & Moen, P. (2000). Does moving to a continuing care retirement community reduce or enhance social integration? In K. Pillemer, P. Moen, E. Wethington, & N. Glasgow (Eds.), *Social integration in the second half of the life course*. Baltimore: Johns Hopkins University Press.

Esterberg, K. G., Moen, P., & Dempster-McClain, D. (1994). Transition to divorce: A life-course approach to women's marital duration and dissolution. *The Sociological Quarterly, 35*, 289–307.

Farkas, J. I., & O'Rand, A. M. (1998). The pension mix for women in middle and late life: More evidence of the changing employment relationship. *Social Forces, 76*, 1007–1032.

Fischer, L. R., Mueller, D. P., & Cooper, P. W. (1991). Older volunteers: A discussion of the Minnesota Senior Study. *The Gerontologist, 31*, 183–194.

Flippen, C., & Tienda, M. (2000). Pathways to retirement: Patterns of labor force participation and labor market exit among the pre-retirement population by race, Hispanic origin, and sex. *Journal of Gerontology: Social Sciences, 55B*, S14–S27.

Forest, K. B., Moen, P., & Dempster-McClain, D. (1995). Cohort differences in the transition to motherhood: The variable effects of education and employment before marriage. *The Sociological Quarterly, 36*, 315–336.

Freedman, M. (1999). *Prime time: How baby-boomers will revolutionize retirement and transform America*. New York: Public Affairs.

Gee, E. M. (1986). The life course of Canadian women: A historical and demographic analysis. *Social Indicators Research, 18*, 263–283.

George, L. K. (1993). Sociological perspectives on life transitions. *Annual Review of Sociology, 19*, 353–373.

George, L. K. (1996). Social factors and illness. In R. H. Binstock & L. K. George (Eds.), *Handbook of aging and the social sciences* (4th ed.) (pp. 229–252). San Diego, CA: Academic Press.

Glasgow, N. (2000). Transportation transitions and social integration of nonmetropolitan older persons. Forthcoming in K. Pillemer, P. Moen, N. Glasgow, & E. Wethington (Eds.), *Social integration in the second half of life*. Baltimore, MD: Johns Hopkins University Press.

Giele, J. Z., & Elder, G. H., Jr. (Eds.). (1998). *Methods of life course research: Qualitative and quantitative approaches*. Thousand Oaks, CA: Sage.

Gotlib, I. H., & Wheaton, B. (1997). *Stress and adversity over the life course: Trajectories and turning points*. New York: Cambridge University Press.

Hagestad, G. O., & Neugarten, B. L. (1985). Age and the life course. In R.H. Binstock & E. Shanas (Eds.), *Handbook of aging and the social sciences* (pp. 35–61). New York: Van Nostrand Reinhold.

Hammond, J. M. (1995). Multiple jeopardy or multiple resources? The intersection of age, race living arrangements, and education level and the health of older women. *Journal of Women and Aging, 7* (3), 5–24.

Han, S-K., & Moen, P. (1999a). Work and family over time: A life course approach. *The Annals of the American Academy of Political and Social Sciences, 562*, 98–110.

Han, S-K., & Moen, P. (1999b). Clocking out: Temporal patterning of retirement. *American Journal of Sociology, 105*, 191–236.

Hardy, M. A. (1991). Employment after retirement: Who gets back in? *Research on Aging, 13*, 267–288.

Hardy, M. A., Hazelrigg, L., & Quadagno, J. (1996). *Ending a career in the auto industry: 30 and out*. New York: Plenum Press.

Hardy, M. A., & Shuey, K. (2000). Pension decisions in a changing economy: Gender, structure and choice. *Journal of Gerontology: Social Sciences, 55B* (September).

Hatch, L. R., & Thompson, A. (1992). Family responsibilities and retirement. In M. Szinovacz, D. Ekerdt, & B. Vinick (Eds.), *Families and retirement*. Newbury Park, CA: Sage.

Hayward, M. D., Friedman, S., & Chen, H. (1998). Career trajectories and older men's retirement. *Journal of Gerontology: Social Sciences, 53B*, S91–S103.

Hayward, M. D., Hardy, M. A., & Grady, W. R. (1990). Work and retirement among a cohort of older men in the United States, 1966–83. *Demography, 27*, 337–356.

Hayward, M. D., & Lui, M-C. (1992). Men and women in their retirement years: A demographic profile. In M. Szinovacz, D. J. Ekerdt, & B. H. Vinick (Eds.). *Families and retirement*. Newbury Park, CA: Sage.

Hearn, J. (1995). Imaging the aging of men. In M. Featherstone & A. Wernick (Eds.), *Images of aging: Cultural representations of later life* (pp. 97–115). London: Routledge.

Heath, J., Ciscel, D., & Sharp, D. (1998). The work of families: The provision of market and household labor and the role of public policy. *Review of Social Economy, 56,* 501–21.

Henretta, J.C., Hill, M.S., Li,,W., Soldo, B.J., & Wolf, W. (1997). Selection of children to provide care: The effect of earlier parental transfers. *The Journal of Gerontology: Psychological Sciences and Social Sciences, 52B,* 110–119. (special issue).

Henretta, J. C., & O'Rand, A. M. (1980). Labor force participation of older married women. *Social Security Bulletin, 43,* 29–39.

Henretta, J. C., O'Rand, A. M., & Chan, C. G. (1993a). Gender differences in employment after spouse's retirement. *Research on Aging, 15 (2),* 148–169.

Henretta, J. C., O'Rand, A. M., & Chan, C. G. (1993b). Joint role investments and synchronization of retirement: A sequential approach to couples' retirement timing. *Social Forces, 71,* 981–1000.

Herzog, A. R., House, J. S., & Morgan, J. N. (1991). Relation of work and retirement to health and well-being in older age. *Psychology and Aging, 6,* 202–211.

Herzog, A. R., Kahn, R. L., Morgan, J. N., Jackson, J. S., & Antonucci., T. C (1989). Age differences in productive activities. *Journal of Gerontology: Social Sciences, 44,* S129–S138.

Hibbard, J. H., & Pope, C. R. (1993). Health effects of discontinuities in female employment and marital status. *Social Science and Medicine, 36,* 1099–1104.

Hochschild, A. (1989). *The second shift.* New York: Avon Books.

House, J. S., Stecher, V., Metzner, H. L., & Robbins, C. A. (1986). Occupational stress and health among men and women in the Tecumseh community health study. *Journal of Health and Social Behavior, 27,* 62–77.

House, J. S., Lepkowski, J. M., Kinney, A. M., Mero, R. P., Kessler, R. C, & Herzog, A. R., (1994). The social stratification of aging and health. *Journal of Health and Social Behavior, 5,* 213–234.

Jahn, I., Becker, U., Jöckel, K -H , & Pohlabeln, H. (1995). Occupational life course and lung cancer risk in men: Findings from a socio-epidemiological analysis of job-changing histories in a case-control study. *Social Science and Medicine, 40,* 961–975.

Kahn, R. L., & Antonucci, T. C. (1981). Convoys of social support: A life course approach. In S. B. Kiesler, J. N. Morgan, & V. K. Oppenheimer (Eds.), *Aging: Social change* (pp. 383–405). New York: Academic Press.

Kessler, R. C., & McLeod, J. D. (1984). Sex differences in vulnerability to undesirable life events. *American Sociological Review, 49,* 620–631.

Kim, J., & Moen, P. (2001). Late midlife work status and transitions. In M. Lachman (Ed.), *Handbook of midlife development.* New York: John Wiley & Sons. (In press).

Kohli, M. (1986). The world we forget: A historical review of the life course. In V. W. Marshall (Ed.), *Later life: The social psychology of aging* (pp. 271–303). Beverly Hills, CA: Sage.

Krueger, H. (1996). Normative interpretations of biographical processes. In A. Weymann & W. R. Heinz (Eds.), *Society and biography: Interrelationships between social structure, institutions and the life course* (pp. 129–146). Deutscher Studien Verlag: Weinheim.

Laurence, L., & Weinhouse, B. (1997). *Outrageous practices: How gender bias threatens women's health.* New Brunswick, NJ: Rutgers University Press.

Lee, G. R., & Shehan, C. L. (1989). Retirement and Marital Satisfaction. *Journal of Gerontology, 44,* S226–30.

Lennon, M. C. (1994). Women, work, and well-being: The importance of work conditions. *Journal of Health and Social Behavior, 35,* 235–247.

Lopata, H. Z. (1994). *Circles and settings: Role changes of American women.* Albany, NY: SUNY Press.

Lüscher, K., & Pillemer, K (1998). Intergenerational ambivalence: A new approach to the study of parent-child relations in later life. *Journal of Marriage and the Family, 60,* 413–425.

MacDermid, S. M., Franz, C. E, & De Reus, L. A. (1998). Generativity: At the crossroads of social roles and personality. In D. P. McAdams & E. de St. Aubin (Eds.), *Generativity and adult development: How and why we care for the next generation* (pp. 181–226). Washington, DC: American Psychological Association.

Marks, N. (1998). Does it hurt to care? Caregiving, work-family conflict, and midlife well-being. *Journal of Marriage and the Family, 60,* 951–966.

Mayer, K. U., & Mueller, W. (1986). The state and the structure of the life course. In A. B. Sorensen, F. E. Weinert, & L. R. Sherod (Eds.), *Human development and the life course: Multidisciplinary perspectives.* Hillsdale, NJ: Lawrence Erlbaum.

Merton, R. K. (1968). *Social theory and social structure.* New York: The Free Press.

Meyer, M. H., Street, D., & Quadagno, J. (1994). The impact of family status on income security and health care in old age: A comparison of western nations. *The International Journal of Sociology and Social Policy, 14,* 53–83.

Mills, C. W. (1959). *The sociological imagination.* New York: Oxford University Press.

Mirowsky, J., & Ross, C. E. (1992). Age and depression. *Journal of Health and Social Behavior, 33,* 187–205.

Moen, P. (1985). Continuities and discontinuities in women's labor force participation. In Glen H. Elder, Jr. (Ed.), *Life course dynamics* (pp. 113–155). Ithaca, NY: Cornell University Press.

Moen, P. (1994). Women, work and family: A sociological perspective on changing roles. In M. W. Riley, R. L. Kahn, & A. Foner (Eds.), *Age and structural lag: The mismatch between people's lives and opportunities in work, family, and leisure* (pp. 151–70). New York: John Wiley & Sons.

Moen, P. (1996a). Gender, age and the life course. In R.H. Binstock & L. K. George (Eds.), *Handbook of aging and the social sciences* (4th ed.) (pp. 171–187). San Diego, CA: Academic Press, Inc.

Moen, P. (1996b). A life course perspective on retirement, gender, and well-being. *Journal of Occupational Health Psychology, 1,* 131–144.

Moen, P. (1997). Women's roles and resilience: Trajectories of advantage or turning points? In I. H. Gotlib & B. Wheaton (Eds.), *Stress and adversity over the life course* (pp. 133–

156). New York: Cambridge University Press.

Moen, P. (1998). Recasting careers: Changing reference groups, risks, and realities. *Generations, 22,* 40–45.

Moen, P., Dempster-McClain, D., & Williams, R. M., Jr. (1989). Social integration and longevity: An event history analysis of women's roles and resilience. *American Sociological Review, 54,* 635–47.

Moen, P., Dempster-McClain, D., & Williams, R. M., Jr. (1992). Successful aging: A life-course perspective on women's roles and health. *American Journal of Sociology, 97,* 1612–1638.

Moen, P., Fields, V., Quick, H. E., & Hofmeister, H. (2000). A life course approach to retirement and social integration. In K. Pillemer, P. Moen, N. Glasgow, & E. Wethington (Eds.), *Social integration in the second half of life* (pp. 75–107). Baltimore, MD: Johns Hopkins University Press.

Moen, P., & Han, S-K. (2001a). Gendered careers: A life course perspective. In R. Hertz (Ed.), *Work and family: Today's realities and tomorrow's visions.* Berkeley, CA: University of California Press.

Moen, P., & Han, S-K. (2001b). Reframing careers: Work, family, and gender. Forthcoming in V. Marshall (Ed.), *Restructuring work and the life course.* Toronto: University of Toronto Press.

Moen, P., Kim, J., & Hofmeister, H. (2001). Couples' work status transitions and marriage quality in late midlife. *Social Psychology Quarterly, 64.*

Moen, P., Robison, J., & Fields, V. (1994). Women's work and caregiving roles: A life-course approach. *Journal of Gerontology: Social Sciences, 49,* S176–S186.

Moen, P., Robison, J., & Dempster-McClain, D. (1995). Caregiving and women's well-being: A life course approach. *The Journal of Health and Social Behavior, 36,* 259–273.

Moen, P., & Wethington, E. (1992). The concept of family adaptive strategies. *Annual Review of Sociology, 18,* 233–251.

Moen, P., & Wethington, E. (1999). Midlife development in a life course context. In S. L. Willis & J. D. Reid (Eds.), *Life in the middle* (pp. 3–23). San Diego, CA: Academic Press.

Musick, M. A., Herzog, A. R., & House, J. S. (1999). Volunteering and mortality among older adults: Findings from a national sample. *Journal of Gerontology, 54B*, S173–S180.

Myles, J., & Quadagno, J. (Eds.) (1991). *States, labor markets, and the future of old age policy.* Philadelphia: Temple University Press.

O'Rand, A.M. (1996). The precious and the precocious: Understanding cumulative disadvantage and cumulative advantage over the life course. *The Gerontologist, 36,* 230–238.

O'Rand, A. M., & Henretta, J. C. (1999). *Age and inequality: Diverse pathways through later life.* Boulder, CO: Westview Press.

O'Rand, A. M., Henretta, J. C., & Krecker, M. L. (1992). Family pathways to retirement. In M. Szinovacz, D. J. Ekerdt, & B. H. Vinick (Eds.), *Families and retirement* (pp. 81–98). Newbury Park, CA: Sage.

Pampel, F. C. (1998). *Aging, social inequality, and public policy.* Thousand Oaks, CA: Pine Forge.

Pavalko, E. K. (1997). Beyond trajectories: Multiple concepts for analyzing long-term process. In M. A. Hardy (Ed.), *Studying aging and social change: Conceptual and methodological issues* (pp. 129–147). Thousand Oaks, CA: Sage.

Pavalko, E. K., & Artis, J. E. (1997). Women's caregiving and paid work: Causal relationships in late mid-life. *Journal of Gerontology: Social Sciences, 52B,* S1–S10.

Pavalko, E. K., & Elder, G. H, Jr. (1993). Women behind the men: Variations in wives' support of husbands' careers. *Gender and Society, 7,* 548–567.

Pavalko, E.K., & Smith, B. (1999). The rhythm of work: Health effects on women's work dynamics. *Social Forces, 77,* 1141–1162.

Peter D. Hart Research Associates. (1999, May). Study #5486a, Milken Senior tack-on. [On-line] Available: http://www.mff.org/conf1999/newsroom/Seniors.pdf

Pienta, A. M., Burr, A. B., & Mutchler, J. E. (1994). Women's labor force participation in later life: The effects of early work and family experiences. *Journal of Gerontology: Social Sciences, 49,* S231–S239.

Pillemer, K., Moen, P., Glasgow, N., & Wethington, E. (Eds.) (2000). *Social integration in the second half of life.* Baltimore, MD: Johns Hopkins University Press.

Pillemer, K., Suitor, J. J., & Keeton, S. A. (2000). Intergenerational Relations. In E. Borgatta & R. J. V. Montgomery (Eds.), *Encyclopedia of sociology* (2nd ed.) (pp. 1386–1393). New York: Macmillan.

Quick, H., & Moen, P. (1998). Gender, employment, and retirement quality: A life-course approach to the differential experiences of men and women. *Journal of Occupational Health Psychology, 3,* 44–64.

Redfoot, D. L. (1987). On the separatin' place: Social class and relocation among older women. *Social Forces, 66,* 486–500.

Reitzes, D. C., Mutran, E. J., & Fernandez, M. E. (1998). The decision to retire: A career perspective. *Social Science Quarterly, 79,* 607–619.

Rexroat, C., & Shehan, C. (1987). The family life cycle and spouses' time in housework. *Journal of Marriage and the Family, 49,* 737–750.

Riley, M.W. (1987). On the significance of age in sociology. *American Sociological Review, 52,* 1–14.

Riley, M. W., & Riley, J. W. (1989). The lives of old people and changing social roles. *The Annals of the American Academy of Political and Social Science, 503,* 14–28.

Riley, M. W., & Riley, J. W. (1994). Structural lag: Past and future. In M. W. Riley, R. L. Kahn, & A. Foner (Eds.), *Age and structural lag* (pp. 15–36). New York: Wiley.

Riley, M. W., Kahn, R. L., & Foner, A. (1994). *Age and structural lag: The mismatch between people's lives and opportunities in work, family, and leisure.* New York: Wiley.

Robison, J., Moen, P., & Dempster-McClain, D. (1995). Women's caregiving: A life course perspective. *Journal of Gerontology: Social Sciences, 50B,* S362–S373.

Rosenfeld, R. A. (1980). Race and sex differences in career dynamics. *American Sociological Review, 42,* 210–217.

Ross, C. E., & Mirowsky, J. (1995). Does employment affect health? *Journal of Health and Social Behavior, 36,* 230–243.

Ryff, C. D., & Seltzer, M. M. (Eds.) (1996). *The parental experience in midlife.* Chicago: University of Chicago Press.

Settersten, R. A. Jr. (1997). The salience of age in the life course. *Human Development, 40,* 257–281.

Settersten, R. A., Jr., & Hagestad, G. O. (1996a). What's the latest? Cultural age deadlines for family transitions. *The Gerontologist, 36,* 178–188.

Settersten, R. A., Jr., & Hagestad, G. O. (1996b). What's the latest? II. Cultural age deadlines for educational and work transitions. *The Gerontologist, 36,* 602–613.

Settersten, R. A., Jr., & Mayer, K. U. (1997). The measurement of age, age structuring, and the life course. *Annual Review of Sociology, 23,* 233–261.

Sewell, W. H., Jr. (1992). A theory of structure: Duality, agency, and transformations. *American Journal of Sociology, 98,* 1–29.

Smith, D. B., & Moen, P. (1998). Spouse's influence on the retirement decision: His, her, and their perceptions. *Journal of Marriage and the Family, 60,* 734–744.

Sorensen, A. (1983). Women's employment patterns after marriage. *Journal of Marriage and the Family, 45,* 311–321.

Strawbridge, W. J., Wallhagen, M. I., Sherma, S. J., & Kaplan, G. A. (1997). New burdens or more of the same? Comparing grandparent, spouse, and adult-child caregivers. *The Gerontologist, 37,* 505–510.

Suitor, J. J., & Pillemer, K. (1994). Family caregiving and marital satisfaction: Findings from a one-year panel study of women caring for parents with dementia. *Journal of Marriage and the Family, 56,* 681–690.

Szinovacz, M. (1987). Preferred retirement timing and retirement satisfaction in women. *International Journal of Aging and Human Development, 24,* 301–317.

Szinovacz, M., & Harpster, P. (1994). Couples' employment/retirement status and the division of household tasks. *Journal of Gerontology: Social Sciences, 40,* S125–S136.

Thoits, P. A. (1986). Multiple identities: Examining gender and marital status differences in distress. *American Sociological Review, 51,* 143–159.

Umberson, D. (1992). Relationships between adult children and their parents. *Journal of Marriage and the Family, 54,* 664–674.

U.S. Census Bureau. (1997). Marital status and living arrangements: March 1997 (update). *Current Population Reports,* PPL-90.

U.S. Census Bureau. (1999). *Statistical Abstract of the United States, 1999.*

Vertinsky, P. A. (1995). Stereotypes of aging women and exercise: A historical perspective. *Journal of Aging and Physical Activity, 3,* 223–237.

Watkins, S. C., Menken, J. A., & Bongaarts, J. (1987). Demographic foundations of family change. *American Sociological Review, 52,* 346–358.

Weiss, R. (1997). Adaptation to retirement. In Ian H. Gotlib and Blair Wheaton *Stress and adversity across the life course* (pp. 232–248). New York: Cambridge University Press.

Wethington, E., & Kavey, A. (2000). Neighboring as a form of social integration and support. In K. Pillemer, P. Moen, N. Glasgow, & E. Wethington (Eds.), *Social integration in the second half of life* (pp. 190–210). Baltimore, MD: Johns Hopkins University Press.

Wethington, E., Cooper, H., & Holmes, C. (1997). Turning points in midlife. In H. Gotlib and B. Wheaton, *Stress and adversity across the life course* (pp. 215–231). New York: Cambridge University Press.

Wheaton, B. (1990). Life transitions, role histories, and mental health. *American Sociological Review, 55,* 209–223.

Wortman, C. B., & Silver, R. C. (1990). Successful mastery of bereavement and widowhood: A life course perspective. In P. B. Baltes & M. M. Baltes (Eds.), *Successful aging: Perspectives from the behaviorally sciences* (pp. 225–264). New York: Cambridge University Press.

Young, R., & Kahana, E. (1989). Specifying caregiver outcomes: Gender and relationship aspects of caregiving strain. *The Gerontologist, 29,* 660–666.

Eleven

Stratification and the Life Course

The Forms of Life-Course Capital and Their Interrelationships

Angela M. O'Rand

I. Introduction

Patterns of inequality within and between cohorts and their consequences for life-course outcomes, including mortality and health and well-being over the life span, have always been core concerns of research on aging. However, recent trends in societal inequality coupled with improved databases for studying inequality across time, societal level, and countries have pushed this topic of study to the forefront. Across industrialized societies, major structural and demographic changes have generated several trends, including increased earnings and income inequality in societies with diverse welfare systems (Gustafsson & Johansson, 1999; Gottschalk & Smeeding, 1997); persistent—if not widening—social inequalities in health in spite of advances in medical technology (Marmot, Bobak, & Smith, 1995; Wilkinson, 1986, 1996); and shifts away from social welfare policies towards market-centered strategies for income and health maintenance (Poland, Coburn, Robinson, & Eakin, 1998). Above and beyond the putatively positive effects of increased levels of national wealth and economic progress on general health and well-being (Pritchett & Summers, 1996), growing economic and social inequalities within populations yield negative outcomes in health and well-being. This puzzle of rising tides but uneven fortunes is now among the more widely studied and debated topics in our field.

The heart of the puzzle is the latent construct of stratification or inequality as a fundamental and pervasive, but complex, social condition that underlies the life course. It is multidimensional, consisting of economic, social, and psychosocial components. Moreover, it is multilevel, meaning it operates across societal planes extending from the economy and state through the community and household to the individual. Finally, it is not fixed, but dynamic in its effects on lives over time. Such complexity renders the construct as powerful but also as diffuse and often intractable.

This chapter offers a broad review of the relationship of stratification to the life course. The approach to this review hangs on the extension of the concept of

Handbook of Aging and the Social Sciences, Fifth Edition

"capital" as a means of simplifying the discussion of the multidimensionality and temporal complexity of this relationship. Although the logic of this approach is parsimony, it also has foundation in the extensive literatures on the effects of human capital and social capital on life-course outcomes such as health and wealth. And, I will argue, it is useful to consider other forms of capital as well, including psychophysical capital (mental and physical health), personal capital, institutional and community capital, and moral capital. The concept is heuristic to the extent that it permits the treatment of multiple dimensions of stratification using a common term that has quantitative and qualitative implications.

II. Capital over the Life Course: Evolutionary and Social Bases

Evolutionary anthropologists argue that the human life course (referred to as "human life history" in this literature) is a product of the coevolution of the human brain and its capacity for intelligence with four other distinctively human characteristics: a long life span; a relatively extended period of juvenile dependence on parents; the male role in the reproductive process that includes the provisioning of females and their offspring; and the support of reproduction by older postre-productive individuals (Kaplan, Hill, Lancaster, & Hurtado, 2000). They propose that this complement of traits is the evolutionary response to a dietary shift towards higher quality food sources that are harder to acquire. The shift required the acquisition of higher levels of knowledge, skills, and physical–mental co-ordination, which, in turn, required significant investments in development. Accordingly, the extended educational

phase of the human life course, longevity well past reproductive ages, and intergenerational flows of resources are founded on evolutionary processes centered around the accumulation, conservation, conversion, and transmission of resources or capital.

Human societies organized around advanced information technologies at the turn of the 21st century reflect extensions of the evolutionary processes summarized above. Ever-extending life expectancy accompanied by declines in morbidity (Manton, Stallard, & Corder, 1997; Manton, Corder & Stallard, 1997); the prolongation of the educational phase of the life course into adulthood (Elman & O'Rand, 1998); and the expansion of multigenerational caregiving and resource transfers over the entire life course and across three or more generations (Bengtson & Silverstein, 1993) are prominent features of human lives in advanced societies. However, these demographic trends interact with and are mediated by institutional arrangements that differentiate subpopulations and allocate resources unevenly to them. Some populations live longer healthier lives than others; some populations benefit from the advantage of longer periods of education; and multigenerational transfers assume different forms and configurations depending upon the relative fortunes of succeeding generations. As such, longevity, the transfer of resources between generations, and the quality and extent of the educational career continue to be significant features of the life course, but they are unequally distributed across and within societies.

Life expectancy increased rapidly in technologically advanced societies over the second half of the 20th century and is now spreading over the entire world. In advanced countries, "active life expectancy" or the extended period of the life span lived, on average, without significant health limitations or disabilities, continues to grow (Manton, Stallard, & Liu, 1993; Manton, Stallard, & Corder, 1997; Vaupel & Lundstrom, 1994). Forecasts of continued or even accelerated extensions of longevity and morbidity decline in the 21st century are sources of regular speculation (Fogel & Costa, 1997). But, in the United States, disadvantaged groups still live shorter lives with more years spent in poor health than their more advantaged counterparts. Hayward and Heron (1999) report that while Caucasian and Asian groups have longer lives with fewer years lived in poor health, African Americans and Native Americans suffer relatively more from extended periods with chronic illness. Mortality rates are highest among African Americans until the oldest ages.

Similarly, although women live longer than men across socioeconomic status (SES) and ethnic status groups, a socioeconomic gradient of morbidity and mortality differentiates them as well (McDonough, Williams, House, & Duncan, 1999; Ross & Bird, 1994). The correlations between SES and health among women match men's. In addition, women's longer lives are associated with extended suffering from often multiple chronic and acute disabilities (Verbrugge & Jette, 1994) that survival curves of active life expectancy can mask (Verbrugge, 1991).

Race and class stratification of the fortunes of the U.S. population across the life course end with the highest levels of inequality among the elderly (Smeeding, 1997) that are correlated with patterns of ill health (Smith & Kington, 1997a,b). Better than half of persons over age 65 rely heavily on Social Security (Clark & Quinn, 1999). Wealth inequality is also highest in the United States among young and old, and correlated with health. When home equity is excluded from calculations of household wealth holdings, financial wealth in the older population is modest. A recent study reports that after excluding home equity persons in their 50s had a median financial wealth of $16,000 in 1992, whereas those over age 70 had only $9,000 (Smith, 1997, using the Health and Retirement Study [HRS] and the Asset and Health Dynamics Among the Oldest Old [AHEAD] data. Median financial wealth, excluding home equity, was zero for African American Hispanic households in these age groups in 1992. And, persons aged 70 and over who report excellent health, are three times wealthier than those who report poor health (Smith, 1997).

Notwithstanding recent debates over whether the older population is relatively better off in meeting their daily needs than the younger (Hardy & Hazelrigg, 1999; Mirowsky & Ross, 1999a,b), the inequality *within* cohorts as they age exerts a unique and pervasive influence on the extension and quality of life. In the U.S. context, intergenerational transmission of wealth and health is stratified and is reproduced through the differential capacities of subpopulations to invest in education for themselves and their offspring. Education converts to skills, market advantage, healthier life spans, and economic and social well-being (House et al., 1990; House et al., 1994; Reynolds & Ross, 1998).

In advanced technological societies dominated by strong market institutions and weak welfare systems, the conversion of family capital into human capital and, in turn, of human capital into economic capital that can be exchanged for health maintenance and a better quality of life are the central tasks of the life course. These tasks are anchored to deep evolutionary processes that underlie the human life course, but they are also socially defined by institutional arrangements that produce inequalities within aging cohorts.

III. The Heuristic Value of the Concept of "Capital" for Life-Course Research

Unequal investment in the early life course contributes significantly to unequal fortunes at the end. The process by which this occurs is complex, but the application of a simplifying concept, such as "capital," has heuristic value for this purpose. The concept of capital, like some other concepts in the sciences (e.g., life cycle, evolution), has such linguistic economy in its representation of complex phenomena that it has been borrowed across disciplines, used metaphorically to advantage, and perhaps occasionally misapplied (see O'Rand & Krecker, 1990, for a similar treatment of the uses of the concept of "life cycle"). The history and uses of the concept of capital have been well summarized elsewhere. Rosen (1998), Coleman (1988, 1990), Portes (1998), Lin (1999a,b), and others have proposed the continued and expanded usefulness of the concept in studying different aspects of social behavior. Criticisms have also been presented warning of the limitations of some applications of the concept of capital (e.g., Foley & Edwards, 1999).

Modern uses of the concept originate in economics. For our purposes, the concept of human capital in economics is the starting point. *Human capital* (HC) refers to "the productive capacities of human beings as income producing agents in the economy...Human capital is the stock of skills and productive knowledge embodied in people" (Rosen, 1998, pp. 681–682). HC is usually measured as years of education or schooling and experience in the workforce. In a market-centered society, the value of an individual's labor measured in wages is a direct function of HC (Becker, 1964; Schulz, 1961). Over the life course, the accumulation of HC through extended acquisition of valued skills and knowledge and par-

ticipation in the paid labor force is *a* primary mechanism of social inequality within cohorts because it influences income streams and wealth accumulation, which, in turn, affect the ongoing well-being of individuals and their capacities to invest in their offspring and to support their families.

The key element of the HC concept that can be adapted to other social behaviors over the life course is the idea of "stock"—or the accumulation of resources as capital that can be divested or deployed to satisfy basic human needs and wants, including economic, social, and psychophysical well-being. Other forms of stock are distinguishable from, but interdependent with, economic capital. *Social capital* (SC) is the stock of direct and indirect social relationships ("strong ties and weak ties") that can be mobilized to advantage (or disadvantage) by individuals (Coleman, 1990; Lin, 1999a,b; Loury, 1977; Portes, 1998; Portes & Landolt, 1996). Whereas HC focuses on economic investment in the individual, SC focuses on the social integration of the individual in systems of social relationships, which themselves carry variable economic and social value. SC can be deployed to improve HC, as in the case of the use of sponsors or strategic third parties in getting a job (Lin, 1999a). SC is the noneconomic stock of social relationships that can substitute for HC and related resources that follow in meeting human needs, as in the case of family members' informal, unpaid caregiving of dependents such as children or the elderly (Lin & Peek, 1999; Elder, George, & Shanahan, 1996). SC can also constrain the attainment of value when it serves (a) to exclude nonmembers and thus hoard opportunities, as in the case of gender or racial discrimination in the labor market (Tilly, 1998) or (b) to isolate inwardly oriented, marginal subgroups from mainstream opportunity structures for achieving human capital, as in the case of some ethnic groups' social closure based on cultural patterns such as language use, a lower value placed on education, or traditional family systems in the division of labor (Portes & Landolt, 1996).

The stock of health, or psychophysical well-being, can be conceptualized as psychophysical capital (PPC). Here we can draw on stress and biological theories of aging and senescence as foundations for the PPC concept. The diversity of health and illness patterns long observed among the elderly has provoked extensive research since the 1950s on both the underlying biological bases of aging and the impact of the environment on health. Stress theories of aging are predicated on the argument that observed differences in the trajectories of aging stem from differential patterns of neuroendocrine response to environmentally produced (physical, social, and psychological) challenges (Finch & Seeman, 1999). Resiliency to stress over the life span is an ongoing homeostatic regulatory process in which the hypothalmic-pituitary-adrenal (HPA) axis and the sympathetic nervous system (SNS) respond to stressors in the environment to return the body to homeostasis. Dysregulation occurs with age as these systems increasingly fail to maintain or to regain homeostasis. In this instance, homeostatic resiliency is physiological stock, which the body acts to maintain; wear-and-tear over time can deplete this stock.

Biological theories of senescence are numerous, but Cristofalo, Tresino, Francis, and Voller (1999) suggest that they fall into two categories: stochastic and programmed. The former category postulates that senescence is a result of random damage, while the latter proposes that senescence results from developmental and genetic processes. Current thinking, which questions whether an absolute biological limit to the life span has been established (see Fogel & Costa, 1997; Vaupel & Lundstrom, 1994), assumes that both developmental and genetic processes and random damage interact over the life span to produce diverse trajectories of physical and mental health and senescence. Although it is not appropriate here to remark on these theories in detail, suffice it to say that the implicit notion of genetic or developmental "capital" or "stock" (PPC) can be applied to senescence processes. Initial stocks of genetically based information program (i.e., establish the potentials and capabilities for) biological development, resiliency, and longevity. Environmental factors, which can have both random and nonrandom origins, can serve to invest in or support PPC or, alternatively, to assault and deplete PPC. Such environmental factors range from physical conditions such as exposure to or protection from environmental pollution and infectious disease to social conditions such as socioeconomic circumstances and social welfare policies.

The disablement process, a sociomedical model of disability proposed by Verbrugge and Jette (1994), expresses the dynamics between biological and environmental capital as a "gap between personal capability and environmental demand" (p. 1). Chronic and acute conditions develop primarily in mid-to late life—although some persons suffer throughout their lives from them—but they lead less quickly to death than to prolonged suffering. These conditions often accumulate into patterns of comorbidity and levy heavy physical, economic, and social costs. Personal and environmental factors can exacerbate or ameliorate these conditions. Besides medical interventions, significant environmental factors that can abate or even fend off disablement include SES and its correlates (e.g., HC, relative access to health insurance and medical care), SC and its correlates (e.g., personal assistance, social support, social integration), and *personal capital* (PC) and its correlates (e.g., resiliency, positive affect, self-confidence, and locus of control). The disablement process imposes costs on all forms of capital and is accelerated or decelerated by relative access to different stocks of resources.

PC is a nontrivial component of stratification in the life course. The psychosocial dimension links the individual as perceiver and actor to his or her environment. Cumulative efficacy (Bandura, 1995) and competence (Clausen, 1993) in the performance of social roles and in the successful negotiation of stressful life events (Elder et al., 1996) over the life course build a stock of personal capital with implications for economic and health outcomes. Identity theory (e.g., Thoits, 1991) subsumes these elements of personal stock at its core, since it argues that the accumulation of role identities (self-evaluations of efficacy and competence relative to cultural expectations) is the foundation of self-esteem, which in turn is found repeatedly to be positively correlated with psychological and physical health.

IV. The Dynamic Interdependence of Forms of Capital Over the Life Course

All forms of capital discussed so far appear to be intertwined across the life course. HC, SC, PPC, and PC interact from the beginning of life. The timing of their impact on each other is often difficult to separate, but when it is possible to do so it has been demonstrated that any form of capital can influence the others, with deleterious or ameliorative effects. HC can influence physical health; SC and PC can influence PPC; PPC can constrain human capital and social capital; and so on. Ross and Wu's (1995) study of the links between education (HC) and health (PPC) offers one explanation of how these forms of capital are associated.

They use a cross-sectional and a longitudinal data set to estimate disparities in self-reported health and find that level of educational attainment operates to enhance (a) HC through employment, job satisfaction, and higher income; (b) SC through higher levels of social support, and (c) PC through a greater sense of personal control and healthier lifestyle.

Whatever the formative causal sequence in early life among forms of capital, the subsequent developmental course is one of interdependent exchange of capital. The complexity of these dynamic and contingent relationships warns against reductionist, single-level, and unidisciplinary approaches.

Recent research linking genetics, physiology, demography, and sociology with diverse historical, retrospective, and longitudinal databases further supports the argument of the interdependence of forms of life-course capital, although the problem of causal directionality remains a preoccupation. Several examples are presented here. First, an early marker of infant health is birthweight, which provides the strategic opportunity to explore the relationship between SES and health at a point in the life course when issues of causal directionality are seemingly less murky. Conley and Bennett (2000) use intergenerational data from the Panel Study of Income Dynamics between 1968 and 1992 to ask two questions: Does the SES of the mother during pregnancy affect her chances of having a low birth weight baby net of her own birth weight, the father's birth weight, and other unobserved, family-related factors? And does birth weight affect adult life chances, net of mother's SES at birth? Siblings are compared using family fixed-effects models. They find that maternal SES during pregnancy (measured as an income-to-needs ratio) is unrelated to infant birth weight, but that low birth weight predicts lower educational attainment of the child controlling for other factors, including gender, race, mother's education, and parents' birth weights. Excluded from these controls were subsequent, intervening indicators of forms of life-course capital such as family SES at adolescence, time-varying family social capital, and trajectories of PPC. Also, the fixed-effects design (comparing siblings) accounts for variations within families rather than between families, thus masking the potential influence of variations in parents' SES. Hence, the study does not sufficiently adjudicate the self-imposed problem of causal ordering, but it does find associations that support the argument of the interdependence of capital.

Second, childhood adversity related to poor nutrition or poverty has been found to have serious formative implications for subsequent acquisition of HC and maintenance of health. Lynch, Kaplan, and Salonen (1997) examine data from the Kuopio Ischaemic Heart Disease Risk Factor Study, a study of Finnish men with retrospective information on their family SES at age 10 and their own educational and occupational attainments. They find a high correlation between childhood and adult SES. Also, a number of detrimental health behaviors (smoking, poor diet, alcohol abuse), psychosocial characteristics such as depression, hostility and hopelessness, and heart disease in adulthood were positively associated with lower SES in childhood. Similar omissions of intervening life-course events and transitions in their models result again in a partial test of the causal ordering of SES and health, but the strong association over time among multiple forms of capital is upheld.

Alternatively, some studies demonstrate that childhood adversity can be ameliorated through investment of HC and SC. Furstenberg and Hughes (1995) report findings from the Baltimore longitudinal study of a sample of young mothers and their children. The study sampled approximately 400 pregnant teenagers in the mid-1960s and reinterviewed them 1, 3, and 5 years after their children were born and again in 1984 when the children were between the ages of 15 and 17 and in 1987 when they were between 18 and 21. By 1987 the majority of youth were high school graduates (63%), exhibited robust mental health (78%), had avoided pregnancy before age 19 (females only, 65%), or had avoided criminal activity (males only, 65%). But, a substantial minority was struggling through the transition to adulthood. A significant source of variation in the relative success of these youths to graduate from high school, to enroll in college, to remain in the labor force, to avoid early pregnancy, to avoid criminal activity, and to retain robust mental health was SC, measured as family cohesion (defined as extended involvement with extended family), support to and from own mother, father in home, mother's educational aspiration for and encouragement of child, family help network, and school quality, among other indicators.

Another area of study that is focused on the interrelationships among forms of life-course capital is found in the U.S. literature on the relationship between race and health. Race is a major parameter of economic inequality and health disparities (Smith & Kington, 1997b). The higher rate of essential hypertension among African Americans, in particular, is well established (Cooper & Rotimi, 1994). The bases of this disparity are not yet fully determined across relevant literatures in medicine, sociology, and psychology, but genetic and environmental (including social factors) risks are believed to interact to produce this outcome, following expectations from stress theory (Williams, Mourney, & Warren, 1994). Some research in this area suggests that after taking SES or HC into account, community relationships (SC) and personal identity (PC) have significant effects on health (e.g., see Dressler, 1996, who links social identity with arterial blood pressure among African Americans). In fact, the implication is that race (specifically white versus African American) and the extensity of community contacts interact in their effects on health. African Americans who are more extensively exposed to contacts in the wider community encounter more negative and stressful interactions that reduce PC or social identity. This is presumably a source of persistent, perhaps unrelenting, stress in some communities that influences hypertension directly or indirectly through health behaviors.

Following the argument so far in this chapter, the research on race and life-course capital probably reveals at least two patterns that capture the basic association between stratification and the life course. The first is a *cumulative advantage–cumulative hardship pattern* in which lower initial levels of most or all forms of life-course capital interact and are compounded over time to place minority groups, and especially African-Americans, at permanent and perhaps increasing disadvantage relative to others with age. The second is a *deflection pattern*, or a developmental sequence in which the significant infusion (or depletion) of some form of life-course capital redirects the economic, social, health, and/or personal trajectory away from initial circumstances. At the individual level, these patterns parallel cohort level trajectories (e.g., see O'Rand, 1995).

However, these findings suggest that another, more structural, argument is needed to embed the capital concept. The life-course literatures that link gender, class, and race to HC, SC, and health trajectories suggest further that capital should also be measured at higher levels of analysis. Individual capital is embedded in social structures and is largely derivative or epiphenomenal. In this regard, stratification is always better conceived as a structural phenomenon, not

merely a distribution that emerges from underlying individual attributes. And the linkage between structural and individual capital is the topic to which we now turn.

V. Macro–Micro Links of Capital: Community, Institutional, and Moral Capital

To this point, the emphasis has been on individual-level capital. Such an emphasis may imply that absolute levels of individual capital interact to produce diverse life-course outcomes without regard to context. Or, it may imply that only the absolute condition of poverty or deprivation matters. However, the cross-national comparisons of inequality and health disparities, with which we introduced this chapter, and studies of race and health point out very clearly that stratification is also a *relational* phenomenon. Countries with lower general levels of economic inequality appear to have smaller health disparities in their populations. The Black Report in the United Kingdom (UK), which unambiguously linked health disparities to social class, triggered the most recent international debates over this phenomenon. After all, on an absolute scale the UK is economically better off on average than most countries of the world. However, within the UK, class inequalities, usually measured as occupational status, have had a persistent impact on mortality rates and health (Townseal, Davidson & Whitehead, 1992).

Marmot, Bobak, and Smith (1995) review the history of class–health–mortality relationships in the UK and elsewhere and provide several explanations of social inequalities in health. Their original study in 1978 of British civil servants (called the Whitehall Study) revealed a striking inverse relationship between grade of employment in the system and mortality, with administrative and professional/executive groups demonstrating significantly lower mortality rates than clerical and other workers. When the Black Report was published 10 years later (Black et al., 1988), not much had changed in these relationships. Their fundamental argument hangs on two ideas. The first is *relative deprivation or susceptibility*—the idea that a social gradient in mortality and health is observable across advanced societies (i.e., those in the highest per capita gross national product [GNP] categories) within which unequal distributions of health risks and health resources produce differential selection into illness and death. Wilkinson (1996) has documented that the relationship between per capita GNP and life expectancy at birth is only significant in the poorest countries. Among other countries, the degree of income dispersion is more explanatory of health disparities. Marmot et al. (1995) cite some of Wilkinson's work with the Organization for Economic Development and Cooperation showing that when life expectancy at birth is plotted against the percent of disposable income below the 70th percentile of the income distribution, those countries with lower shares of disposable income among the less well-off 70% have lower life expectancies (West Germany, U.K., U.S.A), and those with higher shares of disposable income among the less well-off 70% have higher life expectancies at birth (Switzerland, Sweden and Norway). They suggest, following Wilkinson (1986), that factors operating early in life lead to "indirect selection," in which adult patterns of health and disease have childhood origins. Differential vulnerability and susceptibility based on relative deprivation are also associated with class-related health behaviors, such as smoking, that contribute to patterns of "indirect selection." In effect, they do not want to "explain away" structural class effects by introducing family background or lifestyle; instead, their argu-

ment is that class is the fundamental cause that induces experiences and behaviors that result in patterns of health and death.

The second idea is *equity*. By equity, they borrow economists' definition of the "fair allocation of resources" to those who will benefit from them. Where the idea of relative deprivation or susceptibility is taken from the vantage points of those arrayed in the social hierarchy that select them into specific pathways, equity is a redistributive or allocative notion. It presumes that economic inequality is a "social negative" (Marmot et al., 1995) because it comes at the expense of the disadvantaged or relatively deprived. Typically, we associate equity with welfare state structures, not markets. Income inequality is inversely associated with the strength of welfare institutions across advanced countries (O'Rand & Henretta, 1999; Smeeding, 1997). Poverty is highest in those advanced societies with weaker welfare mechanisms, such as those based on means tests, and it is lowest where entitlements on the basis of citizenship are stronger. Similarly, health disparities in advanced democratic societies with weaker welfare institutions are greater (Wilkinson, 1996).

Equity is a structural form of capital—*institutional capital*. Here stocks of public goods (government-provided resources) such as health-care support, pensions, child support, public education, and so on, are available collectively and allocated to those who will benefit by them. It is the social insurance by which individual capital in all forms discussed so far (HC, SC, PPC, PC) is reinforced and protected.

Within the United States context, where weaker national welfare institutions lead to variability across regions, states, and local communities in the provision for life-course risks in health and income maintenance (see O'Rand &

Henretta, 1999), the operation of institutional capital is more readily observed at these lower levels (the state, the community, the neighborhood). This produces a different conception of capital—*community capital*—which theoretically reflects the sum of market, state, and human resources available at that level to provide a collective stock of resources. Accordingly, diverse measures of aggregate income, poverty rates, employment rates, tax bases, and various community services can constitute community capital or a potentially mobilizable collective (as opposed to individual) stock of resources.

Several recent studies reveal a complex set of associations between institutional capital and individual capital that challenge the logic of the simple individual-level gradient, especially in the U.S. context. Most studies find positive correlations between SES and health, but the empirical generalization emanating from this literature is not that the relationship is monotonic or linear, but nonlinear: at the lower end of the distribution smaller increments in SES yield greater gains in health, whereas at the upper end of the distribution smaller health gains are accrued from increments in SES. Unobserved contextual effects that might amplify or attenuate this robust result have not been provided. However, more effort is being made to address this question, although findings across studies are inconsistent.

Daly, Duncan, Kaplan, and Lynch (1998) examine state-level mortality, income level, and income inequality. They link the National Center for Health Statistics Compressed Mortality File and the decennial censuses for 1980 and 1990 to the Panel Study of Income Dynamics (PSID) at two time points, 1978–1982 and 1988–1992, when the possible mortality of persons aged 25 and older is tracked. The mortality experiences of the two PSID subsamples are then matched

with the state-level data. Income inequality is measured in three ways: first, they measure the proportion of total household income in each state received by the bottom 50% of the population, which they name the Kaplan measure (after Kaplan, Pamuk, Lynch, Cohen, & Balfour, 1996); second, they measure the ratios of the 90th to the 10th and the 80th to the 20th deciles of the household income distribution; and third, they measure the decile ratios 90th/50th, 80th/50th and 50th/10th, 50th/20th, respectively, to capture the dispersion of income at the high end versus the low end of the income distribution (in an effort to determine symmetry).

Their results show increases in overall inequality between the two periods across all three measures. Second, inequality increased more at the top 90th/50th and 80th/50th than at the bottom 50th/10th and 50th/20th, suggesting that changes in the United States between 1980 and 1990 were more "affluence sensitive" than "poverty sensitive." When state-level associations are revealed on their own and in association with the individual data, a complex picture emerges. State-level mortality is more strongly associated with income dispersion at the bottom, and the deeper the poverty in a state the higher the rate of mortality. In the micro-macro-linked data, after controlling for age, race, sex, family size, and median state-of-residence income, the introduction of family income does not achieve significance in predicting mortality in the full sample. When the sample is broken out by age group and income level, only the middle income nonelderly (aged 25–64) exhibit a significant positive relationship between income inequality and mortality risk, and the strongest set of associations are poverty sensitive. In effect, the depth of poverty of the state's poor, rather than the height of wealth of the state's rich, influences mortality rates, and especially among the preretirement, middle-income portion of the distribution.

Although their analysis could not fully test the operation of community capital, Daly et al. (1998) suggest that objective or material inequality, in whatever form, may actually operate through persons' perceptions more than directly on its own. They also suggest that SC at the community level may condition the psychosocial response to absolute economic inequality via perceptions of societal fairness. Communities that invest and distribute resources and networks widely produce social cohesion and a sense of fairness or equity in spite of absolute inequalities. In many respects, this proposal comes close to the argument that aggregate economic capital influences aggregate SC, an idea without much support in the broader comparative welfare state literature.

The strong poverty sensitivity of the state-level results suggests alternative interpretations based on the interaction between SC and HC. Perhaps unmeasured characteristics of the states that are associated with greater deprivation (deeper poverty, more environmental pollution, the most unevenly distributed health services, etc.) actually operate directly on mortality rates, rather than indirectly through perceived fairness or relative deprivation. As such, absolute deprivation is less influenced by SC. Alternatively, among the least isolated (least deprived but less privileged) subgroups of the population, SC does interact with absolute deprivation; if the richest and the poorest can be deemed to be the most socially enclosed, then the middle-income, middle-aged category as the most socially integrated may also be at risk of negative health effects, without finding itself at the bottom. Greater social integration exposes individuals to both positive *and* negative social relationships, or to ties throughout the community that do not present unitary positive feedback and so-

cial support. As such, social integration is not always equivalent with social support.

In a review of a number of studies on community factors and health, Robert (1999) finds that the literature points to two possible pathways to individual health. The most commonly researched pathway she labels the *individual pathway*, whereby community and demographic factors have impact on individual health by way of individuals' socioeconomic positions. This is the underlying perspective of the Daly et al. (1998) study summarized above. The second pathway she defines as the *community pathway* and deems it "less intuitive." This pathway specifies direct effects of socioeconomic context on individual health. In some respects, this is more intuitive from a Durkheimian or "strong sociological" perspective. Independent of persons' individual perceptions and circumstances, larger social processes may be operating to effect negative outcomes. Indeed, Robert cites Wilson's (1987) theory of concentration and isolation of the urban poor as exemplary of the community pathway argument. However, she turns to SC theory (especially to Coleman, 1988) to suggest that typically unmeasured aspects of civic participation, reciprocity, and social networks may be operating through individuals' perceptions to produce health outcomes. Lower levels of cohesion or high levels of atomization may reduce trust and increase feelings of relative deprivation, leading to negative outcomes, but lower institutional and community capital have strong direct effects.

The community pathway suggests that relative deprivation at the individual level may not be pivotal for the flow of effects from community to health. Along these lines, the work in Chicago on neighborhood differences in levels of violent crime by Sampson and his colleagues (Sampson, Raudenbesh, & Earls, 1997)

rests its argument on the structural notion of "collective efficacy"—the idea
that the system of social relationships in
neighborhoods has direct effects in controlling violence net of their socioeconomic characteristics. So too, social and
community capital may operate to abate
health disparities otherwise produced by
individual-level inequality.

Robert (1999) cites work by Kawachi,
Kennedy, Lochner, and Prothrow-Smith
(1997) that bears directly on this issue.
This study uses the General Social
Surveys (GSS) to test correlations between SC and mortality rates. SC is
measured by responses to GSS questions
about degree of mistrust, perceived
reciprocity, and membership in voluntary associations aggregated to the state
level. After controlling for state income
and poverty characteristics, each SC
indicator was significantly and meaning-
fully correlated with mortality rates to
provide general support to the SC hypothesis.

The promise of the SC hypothesis at
the individual and community levels of
analysis is perhaps the major new impetus for sociologically motivated research in aging over the past decade and
a half (see, for example, Berkman, 1984;
Lin, 1999a,b; Lin & Peek, 1999). The principal obstacle for these studies is the limited availability of data on associational
patterns among individuals and within
communities. Moving to aggregate-level
data abstracted from national surveys (as
in the case of the GSS, PSID, or the decennial censuses) rather than from "real"
communities may not be the best solution for data scarcity. Nevertheless, the
theoretical motivations have spawned
creative efforts to approximate communities.

One approach in this direction is represented by Hayward, Pienta, and
McLaughlin's (1997) study of the relationships among men's mortality, SES, and
geographic context. They are specifically

motivated, though not in their own terminology, by the interaction between SES
and SC in disparities in mortality rates
across geographic contexts. Using the National Longitudinal Survey of Older Men
(1966–1990), they examine rural–urban
disparities in mortality related to health-
care service availability and residents'
socioeconomic resources. Contrary to
traditional expectations, they find rural
advantages in life expectancy. Rural communities offer greater social integration
and more equitable life chances (i.e.,
have lower social and economic inequality), while urban communities reflect less
social integration and higher levels of inequality in spite of a richer environment
of health resources. As such, lower inequality and higher levels of SC reflected
by more diffuse and extensive community relations in rural communities has
positive health outcomes. The web of social relationships in communities provides the infrastructure for trust and
common identity that have been identified in some studies cited earlier to be
associated with SC.

A final use of capital in life-course research might be referred to as *moral capital*. Moral capital refers to the stock of
aggregate or collective mutual sympathy
and identity. This idea stems from recent
applications of the concept of "moral
economy" in the aging literature (e.g.,
see Kohli, 1987) that has engaged the debate on intergenerational equity (see also
Hardy & Hazelrigg, 1999). Borrowed from
E. P. Thompson's (1964) classic studies of
premarket economies and the emergence
of the working class in Britain, the idea of
moral economy or moral capital depends,
in part, on the relational fabric of communities represented by the network-
oriented SC concept, but it goes beyond
to include two more ideas: (a) *social identity*, or the level of affinity of wider
groups in the society or community
within which limited social relations
may actually occur; and (b) *valence or*

attachment, which assumes the behavioral characteristic of caring.

The wider use of this idea in life-course research is most promising for the caregiving literature. Caregiving, as a concept, is now largely restricted to the study of women's lifetime unpaid roles in the family and kinship system (Sainsbury, 1996) and to the stress and social support literature (Elder, George, & Shanahan, 1996). Both literatures handle the concept similarly. Caregiving is costly to caregivers in human capital to the extent that it is informal and unpaid. It is costly in SC to the extent that it can isolate the caregiver from wider community participation. It is costly in PPC to the extent that the caregiver burden can produce sustained and disabling stress for the caregiver.

This orientation to the concept reflects wider social values regarding gender, unpaid work, and care receivers. Some societies reward caregivers with economic supports for childbearing and child care through child-centered welfare and through retirement policies that entitle all citizens to pension support in old age (Sainsbury, 1996). Sweden is the often-used case of a "caregiver friendly" society since it has historically been the most socially democratic welfare state in the West and has rewarded caregiving by supporting women and children and not penalizing part-time employment in the market. But it is also a society that exhibits higher levels of collective identity and attachment. Arguably, the extent to which caregiving is not stigmatized or penalized in a society is associated with moral capital (i.e., with shared values and identities that are resources over the life course).

A recent review by Glenn (2000) comes closest to delineating a concept of moral capital, although she does not adopt this terminology. Glenn addresses the contemporary problem of care in U.S. society—citing much of the gender and social support literature alluded to earlier. She argues that in a "caring society," caring is recognized as "real work" with the social recognition and entitlements that follow, and those who need care are empowered to influence the form and course of that care. Recognition and power are forms of capital that come from investments in caring. Thus, societies can be compared along this dimension. Glenn's (2000) agenda, of course, includes recommendations for social change that include rethinking social citizenship, "defamilizing" personal care by the reallocation of resources, and reorienting the workplace to be more responsive to caregiving activities. Some activity has occurred in the third area already with passage of family leave legislation and the spread of family policies across employing organizations. The extent to which all these changes occur in the near or distant future will have implications for the other forms of capital that have received attention in this chapter.

Current treatments of caregiving also reflect a highly individualistic and economistic bias in our research. With the development of the SC concept, there is hope for the life-course literature to move beyond exclusively individualistic research and to adapt economistic concepts like "capital" to sociological domains. Values are subjects of serious scientific concern for social scientists in general. Where do values come from? And how do they affect the quality of life?

VI. Conclusions

Social inequality has pervasive effects on individual lives because the construct is multidimensional and multilevel in major respects. At the core of the idea is the notion of capital, defined here as unevenly distributed stocks of diverse resources available to populations for meeting their needs and achieving their desires. HC, SC, PPC, and PC are typically studied at the individual level and found to be interdependent over the life course. Community capital, institutional capital, and moral capital refer to variations in the stocks of resources held collectively but with related outcomes for the life course. The interactions among these forms of life course capital have implications for outcomes in wealth, morbidity, and mortality, over the life span.

The human life history is distinguished by its longevity, prolonged childhood dependence, and extended intergenerational relationships. However, much variability in human life histories is observable within and between societies when comparing patterns of mortality, physical and mental health, social integration, and general economic inequality. This variability stems from the interaction over the life span between genetic, developmental, and environmental factors. Among the latter are the social conditions encountered over the life span stemming from market, familial, civic, and welfare institutions. The pervasive feature of these social conditions is stratification or inequality. They can be reduced to forms of capital that can, with relative success, be converted to positive outcomes in health and well-being.

The task of life-course research is to uncover the patterns of relationship among forms of capital and their effects. Much of this research is preoccupied with the determination of a single causal ordering. What comes first? Health or SES? At the most general level, the evidence is conflicting. Within the confines of specific studies usually focused on narrow phases of the life course, the answer is usually untenable, because of unobserved sources of variation resulting from observational and/or theoretical limitations. When this research is viewed as a whole, it becomes clear that a single causal ordering at one level of analysis should not be the only legitimate goal of this project.

SES refers to individuals' positions in a hierarchy, but social stratification is a complex underlying social condition founded on market, state, civic, and familial institutions that influence individual lives both directly and indirectly. The causal ordering of two individual-level variables does not represent the phenomenon. Individual and structural factors are both important, and they interact in complex ways over time that can produce cumulative patterns of well-being or hardship as well as reversals or deflections from prior trajectories of well-being or hardship.

Moreover, the practical implications of this strong correlation deserve equal attention. Ultimately, health and SES are two forms of capital involving both individual and collective investments in human and physical resources. And the recognition that the absolute wealth of nations or communities is accompanied by the relative wealth within them for predicting critical life-course outcomes makes clear that the symmetry of this strong association is as important as its sought-after asymmetry. Health and wealth are basic parameters of the life course that are inextricably intertwined across the life span and emanate from structural and individual sources.

References

Bandura, A. (1995). *Self-efficacy: The exercise of control*. New York: Freeman.

Becker, G. (1964). *Human capital* (2nd Edition). New York: Columbia University Press.

Bengtson, V. L., & Silverstein, M. (1993). Families, aging and social change: Seven agendas for 21st century researchers. In G. Maddox & M. P. Lawson (Eds.), Kinship, aging and social change, Vol. 13, *Annual Review of Gerontology and Geriatrics* (pp. 15–38). New York: Springer.

Berkman, L. F. (1984). Assessing the physical health effects of social networks and social support. *Annual Review of Public Health, 5*, 413–432.

Black, D., Morris, J. N., Smith, C., Townsend, P. & Whitehead, M. (1988). *Inequalities in health: The Black report: The health divide.* London: Penguin Group.

Clark, R. L., & Quinn, J. F. (1999). The economic status of the elderly. *Medicare Brief No. 4.* Washington, DC: National Academy of Social Insurance.

Clausen, J. A. (1993). *American lives: Looking back at the children of the Great Depression.* New York: Free Press.

Coleman, J. S. (1988). Social capital in the creation of human capital. *American Journal of Sociology, 94,* S95–S121.

Coleman, J. S. (1990). *Foundations of social theory.* Cambridge, MA: Harvard University Press.

Conley, D., & Bennett, N. G. (2000). Is biology destiny? Birth weight and life chances. *American Sociological Review, 65,* 458–467.

Cooper, R., & Rotimi, C. (1994). Hypertension in populations of West African origin: Is there a genetic predisposition? *Journal of Hypertension, 12,* 215–227.

Cristofalo, V. J., Tresini, M., Francis, M. K., & Volker, C. (1999). Biological theories of senescence. In V. L. Bengtson & K. W. Schaie (Eds.), *Handbook of theories on aging.* (pp. 98–112). New York: Springer.

Daly, M. C., Duncan, G. J., Kaplan, G. A., & Lynch, J. W. (1998). Macro-to-micro links in the relation between income inequality and mortality. *The Milbank Quarterly, 76,* 315–339.

Dressler, W. W. (1996). Social identity and arterial blood pressure in the African-American community. *Ethnicity & Disease, 6,* 176–189.

Elder, G. H., Jr., George, L. K., & Shanahan, M. J. (1996). Psychosocial stress over the life course. In H. B. Kaplan (Ed.), *Psychosocial stress: perspectives on structure, theory, life course, and methods* (pp. 247–292). Orlando, FL: Academic Press.

Elman, C., & O'Rand, A. M. (1998). Midlife entry into vocational training: A mobility model. *Social Science Research, 27,* 128–158.

Finch, C. E., & Seeman, T. E. (1999). Stress theories of aging. In V. Bengtson & K. W Schaie (Eds.), *Handbook of theories on aging* (pp. 81–97). New York: Springer Publishing Company.

Fogel, R. W., & Costa, D. L. (1997). A theory of technophysio evolution, with some implications for forecasting population, health care costs, and pension costs. *Demography, 34,* 49–66.

Foley, M. W., & Edwards, B. (1999). Is it time to disinvest in social capital? *Journal of Public Policy, 19,* 141–173.

Furstenberg, F., & Hughes, M. E. (1995). Social capital and successful development of at-risk youth. *Journal of Marriage and the Family, 57,* 580–592.

Glenn, E. N. (2000). Creating a caring society. *Contemporary Sociology, 29,* 84–94.

Gottschalk, P., & Smeeding, T. M. (1997). Cross national comparisons of earnings and income inequality. *Journal of Economic Literature, 35,* 633–687.

Gustafsson, B., & Johansson, M. (1999). What makes income inequality vary across countries? *American Sociological Review, 64,* 585–605.

Hardy, M. A., & Hazelrigg, L. (1999). Fueling the politics of age: On economic hardship across the life course. *American Sociological Review, 64,* 570–576.

Hayward, M. D., & Heron, M. (1999). Racial inequality in active life expectancy among adult Americans. *Demography, 36,* 77–91.

Hayward, M. D., Pienta, A. M., & McLaughlin, D. K. (1997). Inequality in men's mortality: The socioeconomic status gradient and geographic context. *Journal of Health and Social Behavior, 38,* 313–330.

House, J. S., Kessler, R. C., Herzog, A. R., Mero, R. P., Kinney, A. M., & Breslow, M. J. (1990). Age, socioeconomic status and health. *The Milbank Quarterly 68,* 383–411.

House, J. S., Lepkowski, J. M., Kinney, A. M., Mero, R. P., Kessler, R. C. & Herzog, A. R. (1994) The social stratification of aging and health. *Journal of Health and Social Behavior, 35,* 213–234.

Kaplan, G. A., Pamuk, E., Lynch, J. W., Cohen, R. D., & Balfour, J. L. (1996). Income inequality and mortality in the United States. *British Medical Journal, 312,* 999–1003.

Kaplan, H., Hill, K., Lancaster, J., & Hurtado, A. M. (2000). A theory of human life history evolution: Diet, intelligence and longevity. *Evolutionary Anthropology, 9,* 1–30.

Kawachi, I., Kennedy, B. P., Lochner, K., & Prothrow-Stith, D. (1997). Social capital, income inequality, and mortality. *American Journal of Public Health, 87,* 1491–1498.

Kohli, M. (1987). Retirement and the moral economy: An historical interpretation of the German case. *Journal of Aging Studies, 1,* 125–144.

Lin, N. (1999a). Social networks and status attainment. *Annual Review of Sociology, 25,* 467–487.

Lin, N. (1999b). Building a network theory of social capital. *Connections, 22,* 28–51.

Lin, N., & Peek, K. M. (1999). Social networks and social support. In A. Horwitz & L. T. Scheid (Eds.), *A handbook for the study of mental health* (pp. 241–258). New York: Cambridge.

Loury, G. (1977). A dynamic theory of racial income differences. In P. Wallace & A. La-Mond (Eds.), *Women, minorities and employment discrimination* (pp. 153–186). Lexington, MA: Lexington Books.

Lynch, J. W., Kaplan, G. A., & Salonen, J.T. (1997). Why do poor people behave poorly? Variation in adult health behaviors and psychosocial characteristics by stages of the socioeconomic lifecourse. *Social Science and Medicine, 44,* 809–819.

Manton, K. G., Corder, L. S., & Stallard, E. (1997). Chronic disability trends in elderly U.S. populations, 1982–1994. *Proceedings of the National Academy of Science, 94,* 2593–2598.

Manton, K. G., Stallard, E., & Corder, L. (1997). Changes in the age dependence of mortality and disability: Cohort and other determinants. *Demography, 34,* 135–157.

Manton, K. G., Stallard, E., & Liu, K. (1993). Forecasts of active life expectancy: Policy and fiscal implications. *Journals of Gerontology, 48* (Special Issue), 11–26.

Marmot, M., Bobak, M., & Smith, G. D. (1995). Explanations for social inequalities in health. In B. C. Amick, III, S. Levine, A. R. Tarlov, & D. C. Walsh (Eds.), *Society and health* (pp. 172–210). New York: Oxford University Press.

McDonough, P., Williams, D. R., House, J. S., & Duncan, G. J. (1999). Gender and the socioeconomic gradient in mortality. *Journal of Health and Social Behavior, 40,* 17–31.

Mirowsky, J., & Ross, C. E. (1999a). Economic hardship across the life course. *American Sociological Review, 64,* 548–569.

Mirowsky, J., & Ross, C.E. (1999b). Economic hardship declines with age: Reply to Hardy & Hazelrigg. *American Sociological Review, 64,* 577–584.

O'Rand, A. M. (1995). The cumulative stratification of the life course. In R. H. Binstock & L. K. George (Eds.), *Handbook of aging and the social science* (4th ed.) (pp. 188–207). San Diego: Academic Press.

O'Rand, A. M., & Henretta, J. C. (1999). *Age and inequality: Diverse pathways through later life.* Boulder, CO: Westview Press.

O'Rand, A. M., & Krecker, M. L. (1990). Concepts of the "life cycle": Their history, meanings, and uses in the social sciences. *Annual Review of Sociology, 16,* 241–263.

Poland, B., Coburn, D., Robertson, A., & Eakin, J. (1998). Wealth, equity and health care: A critique of a "population health" perspective on the determinants of health. *Social Science and Medicine, 46,* 785–798.

Portes, A. (1998). Social capital: Its origins and application in modern sociology. *Annual Review of Sociology, 24,* 1–14.

Portes, A., & Landolt, P. (1996). The downside of social capital. *The American Prospect, 26,* 18–22.

Pritchett, L. & Summers, L. H. (1996). Wealthier is healthier. *Journal of Human Resources, XXXI,* 841–867.

Reynolds, J. R., & Ross, C. E. (1998). Social stratification and health: Education's benefit beyond economic status and social origins. *Social Problems, 45,* 221–247.

Robert, S. A. (1999). Socioeconomic position and health: The independent contribution of community socioeconomic context. *Annual Review of Sociology, 25,* 489–516.

Rosen, S. (1998). Human capital. In P. Newman (Ed.), *The new palgrave dictionary of economics and the law, vol. 2* (pp. 681–690). London: Macmillan.

Ross, C. E., & Bird, C. (1994). Sex stratification and health lifestyle: Consequences for men's and women's perceived health. *Journal of Health and Social Behavior 35,* 161–178.

Ross, C. E., & Wu, C. (1995). The links between education and health. *American Sociological Review, 60,* 719–745.

Sainsbury, D. (1996). *Gender, equality and welfare states.* Cambridge, UK: Cambridge University Press.

Sampson, R., Raudenbesh, S., & Earls, F. (1997). Neighborhoods and violent crime: A multilevel study of collective efficacy. *Science, 277* (August 15), 918–924.

Schulz, T. W. (1961). Investment in human capital. *American Economic Review, LI*, 1–17.

Smeeding, T. (1997). Reshuffling responsibilities in old age: The United States in comparative perspective. In *Working Paper No. 153, Luxembourg Income Study*. Syracuse, NY: Syracuse University, Maxwell School of Citizenship and Public Affairs.

Smith, J. P. (1997). Wealth inequality among older Americans. *Journals of Gerontology, 52B, Special Issue*, 74–81.

Smith, J. P., & Kington, R. S. (1997a). Demographic and economic correlates of health in old age. *Demography, 34*, 159–170.

Smith, J. P., & Kington, R. S. (1997b). Race, socioeconomic status, and health late in life. In L. G. Martin & B. Soldo (Eds.), *Racial and ethnic difference in the health of older Americans* (pp. 105–162). Washington, DC: National Academy Press.

Tilly, C. (1998) *Durable inequality*. Berkeley: University of California Press.

Thoits, P.A. (1991). On merging identity theory and stress research. *Social Psychology Quarterly, 54*, 101–112.

Thompson, E. P. (1964). *The making of the English working class*. New York: Pantheon.

Townsend, P., Davidson, N., & Whitehead, M. (Eds.) (1992). *Inequalities in health: The Black report and the health divide*. New York: Penguin.

Vaupel, J. W., & Lundstrom, H. (1994). Prospects for a longer life expectancy. In D. Wise (Ed.) *Studies in the economics of aging* (pp. 79–94). Chicago: University of Chicago Press.

Verbrugge, L. M. (1991). Survival curves, prevalence rates, and dark matters therein. *Journal of Aging and Health, 3*, 217–236.

Verbrugge, L. M., & Jette, A. M. (1994). The disablement process. *Social Science and Medicine, 38*, 1–14.

Wilkinson, R. G. (Ed.) (1986). *Class and health: Research and longitudinal data*. London, UK: Tavistock.

Wilkinson, R. G. (1996). *Unhealthy societies—The afflictions of inequality*. London: Routledge.

Williams, D. R., Mourney, R. L., & Warren, R. C. (1994). The concept of race and health status in America. *Public Health Reports, 109*, 26–41.

Wilson, W. J. (1987). *The truly disadvantaged*. Chicago, IL: University of Chicago Press.

Part Three

Social Factors and Social Institutions

Twelve

The Social Psychology of Health

Linda K. George

It is, by now, widely recognized that health is the product of processes operating at many levels, including the biological, psychological, social, and cultural. Consequently, our understanding of health has been informed by the theories, concepts, and methods of multiple disciplines. The purpose of this chapter is to examine health in late life through the lens of social psychology. A central tenet of this examination is the proposition that the union of social psychology and health has been a productive one—that social psychology provides a useful armamentarium of theories and concepts for elucidating the dynamics of health and, in turn, that health provides an excellent strategic site for testing and refining concepts and theories that are central to social psychology.

The chapter begins with a brief overview of the major conceptual traditions that characterize social psychological theory and research. Most of the chapter is devoted to examination of four issues that illustrate key links between social psychological processes and health. These issues should be viewed as representatives of a broader and richer universe of connections between social psychology and health. The last section of the chapter addresses priority issues for further research.

I. Major Traditions of Social Psychological Theory and Research

Social psychology is a large field of inquiry, encompassing a myriad of theories and concepts. Numerous scholars have developed frameworks for summarizing the scope and nature of the field. The framework used in this chapter was originally proposed by House (1977) as the "three faces of social psychology"; it continues to guide much of the field, including the recent reference work sponsored by the Social Psychology Section of the American Sociological Association (Cook, Fine, & House, 1995). Defining characteristics of these three research traditions and their implications for research on health and illness will be briefly described.

A. Psychological Social Psychology

As the label implies, this branch of social psychology is closest to the parent

Handbook of Aging and the Social Sciences, Fifth Edition

discipline of psychology. The central focus of psychological social psychology is the relationship between mental or emotional processes and behavior. Key cognitive and emotional concepts explored in this tradition include attitudes, attributions, motivation, social cognition, and emotion. Behaviors that have received substantial attention in this tradition include conformity, compliance, obedience, provision of assistance to those in need, and aggression. The causal order of these factors varies across studies, with some investigators examining the impact of mental or emotional processes on behavior and others focusing on the ways that behavior affects mental and emotional processes. The "social" component of psychological social psychology is evidenced in a persistent focus on the ways in which the presence of other persons affects mental or emotional processing and/or behavior. Scholars in this tradition typically view their results in nomothetic terms, that is, they believe that the processes and relationships their research reveals are widely, indeed, perhaps universally applicable.

Most research in this tradition is based on experimental research designs, and the majority of experiments are conducted in laboratories. The strength of these methods is that, because of the high degree of experimenter control, they produce the best available evidence for making causal inferences. The major limitation of experimental studies, especially those conducted under laboratory conditions, is problems in generalizing findings to natural situations and settings. The fact that research participants may purposely or unconsciously alter usual behavior patterns while in laboratory settings is only one part of this concern. More broadly, there is strong evidence that behavior is, to a significant degree, contextually embedded. Consequently, social scientists require evidence of generalizability across multiple social and cultural contexts.

Very few studies of health and illness in later life have been based on experimental designs; even fewer are laboratory-based. Although the usual methods of psychological social psychology have had little spillover to research on health, many of the concepts that emerged from this research tradition have become important tools for understanding health and health behaviors in late life. Key among these concepts, to be explored in this chapter, include the role of attribution in defining health and its role in help seeking for medical problems, use of social comparisons in determinations of health and illness, and the effects of self-attributions on health.

B. Symbolic Interactionism

Symbolic interactionism (SI) is vastly different in focus and method from psychological social psychology. Scholars in the symbolic interaction tradition emphasize the critical role of interpretation and meaning in attitudes and behaviors. They are interested in the processes by which meaning is constructed via social interaction and how that meaning, in turn, generates action. From the SI perspective, the key element of social life is interaction; it is via interaction that we construct meaning and acquire social and cultural meanings. In addition, however, individuals interpret their experiences and have latitude in the meanings that they attach to situations, other persons, and themselves. Consequently, SI theorists view behavior as inherently less predictable (i.e., less subject to universal or nearly universal laws) than do psychological social psychology scholars. Compatible with a focus on interpretation and meaning, SI scholars rely on qualitative research methods, although multiple data collection strategies—ranging from observation, to content analysis, and, especially, semistructured interviews—are used.

Historically, SI was strongly linked to the investigation of the self in social interaction, that is, how we come to know and evaluate ourselves via interaction with others. But its use has broadened over subsequent years to encompass investigation of other forms of social and cultural meaning. At this point, few social psychologists label themselves as symbolic interactionists. With the increased popularity of general propositions concerning the social construction of reality, investigators are now more likely to label themselves as social constructionists or even, in line with their methodological allegiances, as simply qualitative researchers or ethnomethodologists.

Traditional SI has had little direct translation into research on health in later life beyond the fact that all research on the self owes much to early SI contributions. An emphasis on interpretation and meaning, however, is a consistent theme in health belief models as well as in some models of health-care utilization. Similarly, a relatively small but rich body of qualitative research has greatly broadened our understanding of how older persons define health, make decisions about help-seeking or self-care, and cope with the physical, psychological, and social consequences of chronic diseases.

C. Social Structure and Personality

This tradition in social psychology is closest to sociology. The key characteristic of this tradition is its focus on the ways in which broad social structures—not simply the immediate presence of others—affect individual attitudes and behavior. Examples of the kinds of social structures examined in this research tradition include social class, the organization of work environments, structural sources of stress, and family and other social networks. At its best, social structure and personality research traces the complex paths and mechanisms by which broad social arrangements come to affect the attitudes and behaviors of individuals. A key element in the link between this tradition and our understanding of health is that many health indicators are subjective assessments or rely on the self-reports of mental or emotional symptoms.

The primary methodology of social structure and personality investigators is the social survey, coupled with complex statistical models. Researchers in this tradition pay much greater attention to issues of sample size and representativeness than those in the other two branches of social psychology. In high-quality surveys, careful attention is paid to measurement; as a result, complex, multidimensional issues can be assessed using standardized surveys. Nonetheless, survey data have substantial limitations because they cannot provide the compelling evidence for causal inference provided by experiments and, at the same time, they lack the depth and richness of qualitative data.

In terms of sheer volume, social structure and personality has made more contributions to our understanding of health in late life than the other two branches of social psychology. Research on the stress process, on the effects of family and other social relationships on health, and on the links between socioeconomic status (SES) and health, for example, all fall under the conceptual umbrella of social structure and personality. Much of the research in this tradition was reviewed in the last edition of this handbook (George, 1996). Because of the considerable volume of such research, in this chapter only one component of social structure and personality research will be reviewed: models in which social psychological processes such as social comparisons, attributions, and self-evaluations are studied as potential mechanisms by which social structure affects health.

D. The Changing Landscape of Social Psychology

Any area of inquiry that engages the energies of numerous scholars over long periods of time undergoes changes. This is certainly true of social psychology. Over the last quarter century, the boundaries among psychological social psychology, symbolic interactionism, and social structure and personality have blurred considerably, especially at the conceptual, as compared to the methodologic, level. Concepts that emerged in psychological social psychology and SI are now routinely incorporated in survey-based social structure and personality research. For example, standardized measures now exist for concepts such as attributional style and various dimensions of the self. Similarly, social cognition has become the dominant conceptual foundation of psychological social psychology over the past two decades. As a result, psychological social psychology and symbolic interactionism now share concepts and research problems to a degree that previously would have been unthinkable. A few scholars argue against the merging of concepts across research traditions or claim that concepts can only be validly assessed using a specific methodology. The dominant trend, however, is one of increased awareness of the ability to investigate important issues using multiple methods, from varying conceptual frameworks. As a result, the research reviewed below does not always emerge distinctly from a single branch of social psychology.

II. Symptom Appraisal and Attribution

Both social and clinical scientists distinguish between disease and illness. Disease refers to biological pathology and is categorized using diagnostic standards; illness refers to the experience of poor health and is affected by social and cultural meanings as well as by physical or emotional discomfort (e.g., Barondess, 1979; Eisenberg & Kleinman, 1981). The focus here is on the illness experience. Early research on illness focused on differences across groups (e.g., racial/ethnic groups, religious groups, social classes) in the ways that symptoms are experienced and described (e.g., Zola, 1966).

An important concept for understanding illness experience is attribution. Attribution theory was originally developed to explain the cognitive processes by which individuals reach conclusions about the causes of others' behaviors (e.g., Kelley, 1973). It soon became clear that individuals come to know themselves, as well, using attributional processes (e.g., Steele, 1988), although attributions to both self and others involve specific and different biases (e.g., Gilbert, Pelham, & Krull, 1988). Attribution is now used more broadly to refer to the causal inferences that individuals reach about themselves and others.

With the advent of the Health Belief Model (HBM) in the mid 1970s, symptom attribution reached the forefront of social and behavioral research on health. HBM was developed to explain the process by which individuals decide whether or not to seek medical attention for their symptoms. In the original HBM model, medical help seeking was proposed to be a product of four kinds of beliefs: attributions of perceived susceptibility to disease, perceptions of symptom severity, the perceived benefits to be derived from treatment, and the perceived costs of obtaining treatment (Rosenstock & Kirscht, 1974). The model was subsequently enlarged to include self-efficacy as a fifth determinant of help seeking (Rosenstock, Strecher, & Becker, 1988). HBM has proven to be a broadly useful framework for understanding individuals' decisions to seek help for illness, attempts to change health behaviors, and success in changing health behaviors (e.g., Strecher, Champion, & Rosenstock, 1997). An important contribution of HBM was its focus on the variability of symptom attribution, that is, individuals and social groups differ in the extent to which bodily experiences are attributed to disease, the extent to which symptoms are perceived as severe, and the extent to which symptoms are viewed as responsive to treatment.

Symptom attribution is independent of medical professionals' definitions of disease. Indeed, physicians and their patients frequently disagree about the cause and severity of patients' symptoms. In the public health literature, health education is often justified as a way to increase the "accuracy" of symptom attribution by health-care consumers. From this perspective, there are two forms of "inaccurate" symptom attribution: (a) failure to recognize important symptoms, leading to delay in treatment, unnecessary suffering, and perhaps poorer prognosis; and (b) exaggerated attributions made to mild, transitory, or nonmedical symptoms, resulting in wasted health-care resources (e.g., Levkoff, Cleary, Wetle, & Besdine, 1989). The concept of "symptom attribution" was developed, however, for the purpose of understanding how individuals experience and reach conclusions about their symptoms. It was not developed for the purposes of determining the "accuracy" of individuals' perceptions, with physicians serving as a "gold standard." Although it is undoubtedly useful to educate people to be effective health-care consumers, scientific interest in symptom attribution is much broader and focuses primarily upon the meanings individuals attach to their experiences.

A. Age Differences in Symptom Attribution

Given higher rates of diagnosed illness in late life, questions arise as to whether older adults exhibit distinctive patterns of symptom attribution. Research to date suggests that adults of all ages share common understandings about the nature and characteristics of specific illnesses (e.g., Leventhal & Prohaska, 1986). In reports of how people interpret their symptoms, however, age differences are observed. Compared to young and middle-aged persons, older adults see themselves as more susceptible to disease, view their symptoms as more severe, and yet are less afraid of being ill (Leventhal, 1984; Leventhal & Prohaska, 1986; Prohaska, Leventhal, Leventhal, & Keller, 1985). Older persons are more likely than their younger peers, however, to discount or ignore mild symptoms (Prohaska et al., 1985).

Overall, these results suggest that what has variously been called "lay understanding of disease" and the "social construction of illness" is broadly shared among adults of all ages. Age differences concern the experience and perceived significance of symptoms.

B. Normal Aging or Illness: An Attributional Quandary

Symptom attribution acquires additional complexity during late life because individuals are confronted with the challenges of separating bodily changes that are part of the aging process from those that result from disease. There is substantial evidence that large proportions of older adults "normalize" at least some of their symptoms, attributing them to aging rather than illness. For example, Stoller (1993; Stoller & Forster, 1994), using data from health diaries, reports that 51% of the sample attributed at least one symptom to aging—and 5.5% attributed all of their symptoms to aging. Qualitative studies also reveal the difficulties older persons face in deciding whether symptoms are caused by aging or by disease (e.g., Abrums, 2000). An especially rich account of this quandary is presented by Siegel, Dean, and Schrimshaw (1999) in a qualitative study of middle-aged and older persons with HIV/AIDS.

Little is known about the conditions under which individuals attribute their symptoms to aging or disease. Stoller (1993) reports that number of symptoms reported and individuals' global health perceptions are related to symptom attribution. She found that older adults who reported a large number of symptoms and/or poor self-rated health were more likely to see their symptoms as resulting from disease, whereas participants with fewer symptoms were more likely to normalize them. Both social support and role involvement also were related to perceived severity of symptoms. High levels of social support were associated with perceptions of less severe symptoms; high numbers of formal social roles (e.g., in the family, labor force, and community), however, were associated with perceptions of more severe symptoms. Leventhal (1984) reports that symptoms perceived as mild are especially likely to be attributed to old age.

Based on research to date, the consequences of attributing symptoms to aging rather than disease are mixed. Van Doorn (1999) reports that attributing symptoms to age is associated with "health optimism"—a positive orientation towards one's present and future health, even in the face of current impairment. In contrast, Leventhal and Prohaska (1986) found that attributing symptoms to age was associated with passive coping, focused on restricting activities and failure to engage in self-care activities. Perhaps the most dramatic consequences of attributing symptoms to old age are reported by Rakowski and Hickey (1993), who found that controlling for demographic characteristics, self-rated health, participation in social activities, and chronic illness/disability, such attributions were associated with

significantly increased odds of near-term death.

III. Self-Rated Health

Symptom attribution refers to the interpretation of specific bodily experiences. In contrast, self-rated health refers to individuals' global assessments of their health and has a long history in the study of health in later life. Initial research efforts in this area focused on the validity of self-rated health as a proxy for more objective indicators of health status, including physician assessment and chronic illness. And, indeed, there are strong relationships between objective health measures and self-rated health (e.g., Fillenbaum, 1979; Tessler & Mechanic, 1978). More recent interest in self-rated health was triggered by evidence from numerous studies that self-rated health is a significant predictor of mortality (for intervals ranging from 2–28 years), even when the effects of physical health, chronic illnesses, and functional status are taken into account (e.g., Idler & Kasl, 1991; Strawbridge & Wallhagen, 1999).

A. The Meanings of Self-Rated Health

The robust relationships observed between self-rated health and a variety of health outcomes have triggered substantial attention to its meanings and antecedents. It is one of the most easily measured concepts in the social sciences; typically, individuals are asked to rate their overall health as poor, fair, good, or excellent (with some studies adding "very good" as a fifth option). Three research traditions have contributed to our understanding of self-rated health: quantitative studies in which survey data are used to identify the antecedents of self-rated health, studies of social comparison processes in late life, and qualitative studies that have explored the referents individuals use in assessing the quality of their health.

1. Quantitative Studies

Several quantitative studies, based on survey data, have examined the predictors of self-rated health in late life. The factors examined as potential predictors might be termed the "usual suspects" in studies of social factors and illness: basic demographic variables (age, sex, race), SES and its components, social activities and relationships, health behaviors (usually smoking, obesity, and heavy alcohol use), and, sometimes, life satisfaction. In all the studies cited here, the effects of these factors were examined with the effects of physical health and/or disability appropriately controlled.

The association between gender and self-rated health is inconsistent across studies—in some, older women report higher levels (e.g., Idler, 1993); in most, however, men report higher levels (e.g., Fillenbaum, 1979; Hansell & Mechanic, 1991). Overall, African Americans report lower levels of self-rated health than whites (e.g., Gibson, 1991), but Ferraro (1993) reports an interaction of gender and race, with older African American men reporting unusually high levels of self-rated health and older African American women reporting the lowest levels. There is substantial evidence that age is positively related to perceptions of health (e.g., Benyamini, Idler, Leventhal, & Leventhal, 2000; Idler, 1993), even when the comparison is between the "young-old" and the "old-old"—a counterintuitive pattern that, in part, results from selective mortality.

Both education and health behaviors (e.g., Hirdes & Forbes, 1993) are associated with higher levels of self-rated health (all studies cited in this section are of older people as indicated in the first sentence of the section). Somewhat surprisingly, however, social networks and social support are consistently unrelated to self-rated health (e.g., Benyamini et al., 2000; Hirdes & Forbes, 1993). Results concerning the relationship between life satisfaction and self-rated health are inconsistent, but Benyamini and colleagues (2000) recently reported that life satisfaction at baseline predicts changes in self-rated health over a 6-year interval, with high levels of satisfaction helping to sustain high and stable levels of self-rated health.

Three social psychological factors also have been demonstrated to predict self-rated health. First, psychological distress is strongly related to health appraisals (e.g., Okun & George, 1984; Tessler & Mechanic, 1978), although this has been largely ignored in recent studies. Second, Engle and Graney (1985) report that identification of oneself as old (a self-label to which very few older people subscribe) is associated with perceptions of poorer health. Third, Hansell and Mechanic (1991) found that older adults who scored higher on bodily awareness rated their health as poorer than those who scored low on this self-attribution.

With the possible exception of age identity and bodily awareness, the predictors of self-rated health identified in previous research are more useful for helping us to understand *who* appraises their health as good and bad than for understanding *why* and *how* individuals appraise their health as they do. Both social comparisons research and qualitative studies have made the major contributions to those issues.

2. Social Comparisons

Social comparison theory (Festinger, 1954) has a long and esteemed history in social psychology. Individuals find it difficult to evaluate many aspects of themselves because there is no "yardstick" for most of the characteristics about which they care (e.g., sense of humor, attractiveness).

Thus, people often compare themselves to others to learn about themselves. There are a variety of ways that social comparisons can be consciously or unconsciously manipulated so that one comes away with favorable conclusions about oneself. Indeed, most people use social comparisons not only to learn about themselves, but also to protect or enhance feelings of self-worth (e.g., Wood, 1989).

The vast majority of older adults describe their health as "good" or "excellent" (e.g., Ferraro, 1993; Hirdes & Forbes, 1993). And there is strong evidence that they frequently compare themselves to their age peers in making health appraisals (e.g., Jylha, 1994; Smith, Shelley, & Dennerstein, 1994). As is true for social comparisons more broadly, this does not mean that older adults accurately assess their status relative to others. Indeed, it appears that the accuracy of health-related social comparisons is quite low. Most older adults believe that they are exceptions to the usual patterns of aging and that their health is superior to that of most of their age peers (e.g., Smith et al., 1994). Similarly, Leventhal (1984) reports that older adults in her study believed that the future would bring declining health for their age peers, but that their own health would remain stable.

Older adults have two referents for social comparisons: comparing themselves to their age peers or comparing their present status to their past statuses. Psychologists have speculated that older adults might substitute temporal comparisons for social comparisons. Instead, like their younger peers, older adults show a strong preference for social rather than temporal comparisons (Robinson-Whelen & Kiecolt-Glaser, 1997). As one function of social comparisons is to protect feelings of self-worth, older adults' preferences for social comparisons are not surprising.

3. Qualitative Studies

Three qualitative studies have substantially furthered our understanding of the meanings of health and, hence, the basis for personal health appraisals in late life. All three studies relied on the concepts of "health optimists," "health pessimists," and "health realists." These distinctions are based on a comparison of participants' objective health status (e.g., chronic illness, functional disability) to their self-rated health. As the labels imply, health optimists report their health to be good or excellent despite evidence of poor physical health or functioning, and health pessimists describe their health as fair or poor although there is no evidence of illness or disability that interferes with daily life. Health realists are people whose self-rated health is congruent with their objective health status.

The most ambitious study to date collected qualitative data on older adults' explanations for their health appraisals and used content analysis to identify five attributional styles: appraisals based on purely physical health status; a "health-transcendent" style in which individuals recognize, yet discount health problems; appraisals based on behavioral and attitudinal criteria (e.g., staying active and alert); an attributional style that relied on the assessments of others (e.g., family members, physicians); and a nondirective style in which participants were unable to articulate a rationale for their health appraisals (Borawski, Kinney, & Kahana, 1996). Health optimists used primarily health-transcendent attributions and behavioral/ attitudinal criteria in explaining their health appraisals. Health pessimists relied primarily on purely physical attributions. In longitudinal analysis, attributional style predicted mortality over three years, with the effects of demographic variables, physical health status, and self-rated health statistically controlled. The nondirective attributional style was the strongest predictor of earlier mortality. Similarly, Chipperfield (1993a), using quantitative data from a representative community sample, found that health optimism was a significant predictor of longevity, with the effects of demographic variables, baseline health and functioning, and social factors statistically controlled. This is powerful evidence that illness cognitions have important consequences. In a study of more limited scope, Idler and colleagues (Idler, Hudson, & Leventhal, 1999) also found that health pessimists and realists tended to base their health appraisals on purely medical issues, whereas health optimists took a broader view that incorporated additional issues (e.g., social relationships, emotions, spiritual commitments).

In a somewhat different vein, Van Doorn (1999) found that health optimists and health pessimists differed in the use of social comparisons. Health optimists used social comparisons to justify their health appraisals more than health realists, and health pessimists avoided comparing themselves to others. The optimists also tended to normalize symptoms by attributing them to old age rather than illness.

IV. Self-Care, Lay Consultation, and Help Seeking

Symptom attribution and, to a lesser extent, global perceptions of health provide individuals with a day-to-day sense of their physical well-being. An obvious next question is to ask how individuals respond to their symptoms—whether or not they take action and, if so, the form of action taken—and the extent to which social psychological factors affect these decisions. In a study of older adults' responses to symptoms of illness, Verbrugge and Ascione (1987) observed a clear sequence of responses. The first reaction to symptoms was to use medica-

tions on hand, both prescription and over-the-counter medications. If medications did not alleviate the symptoms, the second step was to talk to significant others about the symptoms and solicit their advice. The third step was to restrict activities, presumably under the assumption that rest would allow the body to "heal itself." The final step, taken by very few of their study participants, was to seek for medical care from a physician. These steps correspond to three distinct, but related bodies of research on self-care, lay consultation, and formal help seeking, each of which is examined below. First, however, it is helpful to consider the size of the problem—that is, the prevalence of symptoms in later life.

Research evidence suggests that, at minimum, half of older adults living in the community frequently experience illness symptoms. Most studies rely on the use of diaries in which older persons record their symptoms (and, usually, how they responded to them) on a daily basis for periods of time ranging from a few days to a few weeks. Other studies elicit reports of all symptoms experienced during a specified time interval (e.g., the past month). Using a predetermined set of 20 symptoms, Brody and Kleban (1981) found that 50% of their sample reported experiencing one or more symptoms during the past month. The prevalence of symptoms is even higher, however, if respondents keep diaries of or are permitted to report all their symptoms, as compared to responding to a list such as that used by Brody and Kleban. For example, Stoller (1993) found that 83% of her sample reported one or more symptoms over a 3-week interval, and Edwardson, Dean, and Brauer (1995) report that 91% of their sample experienced one or more symptoms over a four-week interval. Clearly, older adults frequently face decisions about how to respond to health-related symptoms.

A. Self-Care

For our purposes, *self-care* is defined as a response in which individuals take sole responsibility for treating or not treating their symptoms. Major forms of self-care treatment include taking medicines (prescription drugs already available, or over-the counter medications, or both), restricting daily activities, making dietary changes in response to symptoms, and managing the emotional distress associated with symptoms (e.g., Clark et al., 1991; Haug, Wykle, & Namazi, 1989). As noted above, self-care is often a first step in a larger process of responding to symptoms. More often, however, self-care is the *only* response made to symptoms—indeed, only a small minority of symptoms (usually fewer than 5%) culminate in formal help seeking (e.g., Brody, Kleban, & Moles, 1983; Rakowski, Julius, Hickey, Verbrugge, & Halter, 1988; Stoller & Forster, 1994).

Social and personal characteristics are associated with differential use of self-care and the diversity of self-care practices employed. In these studies, comparisons are based on self-care versus taking no action—the two most common responses to symptoms. The strongest correlate of self-care is gender: older women use self-care more often than older men (compared to taking no action) and also use a wider range of self-care practices (e.g., Kart & Engler, 1995; Rakowski et al., 1988; Verbrugge, 1985). Other correlates of engaging in self-care, for which evidence is more limited, include education (Verbrugge, 1985), older age (Verbrugge, 1985), higher numbers of chronic illnesses (Kart & Engler, 1995), and poorer self-rated health (Kart & Engler, 1995).

Although there is considerable speculation that self-care is frequently effective in responding to symptoms, evidence supporting this conclusion is based almost exclusively on evaluations of health education programs that teach patients appropriate self-care responses for their symptoms (e.g., Lorig, Mazonson, & Holman, 1993; Lorig et al., 1999). It is doubtful that persons who have been trained in appropriate self-care techniques (and agreed to participate in self-care training programs) are comparable to the more common scenario in which older adults select their self-care strategies in the absence of targeted training. Edwardson and Dean (1999), however, examined factors associated with the use of *medically appropriate* self-care among community-dwelling older adults. Although a majority of older persons used appropriate self-care strategies, there were clear gender differences in the factors that affected appropriate versus inappropriate use. Social support was a more important determinant of appropriate self-care for men than for women; in contrast, women relied more on symptom characteristics in their choice of self-care strategies. Stoller, Pollow, and Forster (1994) took a slightly different approach—they interviewed older adults about how they would respond to 15 common symptoms. They found that although none of the self-care techniques was inherently harmful, two-thirds of them could be harmful under specific conditions. Clark et al. (1991) point out that, with the exception of prescribed drugs already at hand, there is little specificity in the self-care techniques used by older adults. That is, the typically reported techniques, such as restricting activities and altering food intake, tend to be used regardless of the nature of the symptom. Although such techniques may not be *inappropriate*, they also are not targeted to the specific characteristics of the symptom or illness.

B. Lay Consultation

Lay consultation refers to the situation in which individuals report their symptoms to family members or friends, seeking advice about how to best respond to the symptoms. As noted above, Verbrugge and Ascione (1987) found lay consultation to be a common step in the process toward formal medical care. Other scholars also report that large proportions of symptoms experienced by older adults are discussed with family and/or friends. In two samples, Brody and Kleban (1981; Brody et al., 1983) found that older adults had discussed more than 50% of their symptoms with significant others. Similarly, Edwardson et al. (1995) found that 55% of older adults' symptoms were discussed with friends and family.

Several studies have found that lay consultation is a significant predictor of subsequent help seeking from physicians (Cameron, Leventhal, & Leventhal, 1993; Edwardson et al., 1995; Hurwicz & Berkanovic, 1991; Verbrugge & Ascione, 1987). Beyond this, little is known about lay consultation or its effects on health outcomes. Edwardson et al. (1995) found that older adults were nearly twice as likely to discuss their symptoms with women than with men, regardless of the gender of the older adult. Sample members also reported the most common outcomes of lay consultation: no advice was offered (36%), recommendations to restrict activities (15%), recommendations to see a physician (14%), and expressions of sympathy or empathy (12%). Thus, although lay consultation increases the likelihood of seeking medical care, most of the time family members and friends do not recommend physician contact.

C. Seeking Medical Care

Two primary conceptual models have been used to understand the conditions under which individuals do and do not seek medical care: the illness behavior model and the behavioral model. Despite similarities in labels, these two models rest on very different views of help seeking. The illness behavior model is the one

covered here, it is a direct descendent of the HBM and focuses on the social psychological processes associated with symptom recognition, symptom attribution, and the responses made to symptoms. The behavioral model, developed by Andersen and Newman (1973), is presented as a model of health-care utilization rather than help seeking. Consequently, it is frequently used to examine volume of health care and source of health care (e.g., primary care versus specialty care), as well as help seeking (i.e., initiating care). In brief, the behavioral model conceptualizes health care as a function of three classes of variables: predisposing characteristics, enabling factors, and need factors. The only social psychological variable recommended by Andersen and Newman for the behavioral model was global attitudes toward the medical profession, and most studies based on this model have ignored this factor. Andersen and Newman's behavioral model of health service use will not be reviewed here because it is of tangential relevance to this chapter. It should be noted, however, that the behavioral model has been used extensively to determine the extent to which social and economic factors alter the probability that need for services will lead to utilization of them. Moreover, there is no inherent contradiction between the illness behavior model, reviewed here, and the behavioral model.

From the perspective of the illness behavior model, the central issue regarding help seeking is identification of the conditions under which the experience of symptoms does and does not lead to medical care. The major contribution of the model has been identification of the specific symptom characteristics, as perceived by the individual, that result in seeking physician care. An obvious predictor of seeking medical care is symptom duration and/or failure of self-care strategies to bring relief (e.g., Cameron et al.,

1993; Verbrugge, 1985). This finding highlights the fact that seeking medical care is seldom an initial response to symptoms. Evidence to date suggests that several symptom attributes are associated with seeking medical care: degree of pain or discomfort (e.g., Stoller, Forster, & Portugal, 1993), perceived severity of the symptom(s) (e.g., Cameron et al., 1993; Stoller et al., 1993), and symptom ambiguity (e.g., Cameron, Leventhal, & Leventhal, 1995). These are, of course, precisely the types of symptoms that the HBM predicted would result in formal help seeking.

Evidence is less consistent for other predictors of help seeking. For example, Cameron et al. (1995) report that the co-occurrence of life stressors and symptoms delays formal help seeking, which is the opposite of what they observed in an earlier study (Cameron et al., 1993). Verbrugge (1985) reports that malaise, depression, and distress are "triggers" that lead to medical care. In contrast, in a large-scale study of Medicare beneficiaries, Berkanovic and Hurwicz (1989) found that distress decreased the likelihood of seeking medical attention.

Issues of timing may account for these conflicting findings. Leventhal and colleagues (Leventhal, Easterling, Leventhal, & Cameron, 1995; Leventhal, Leventhal, Schaefer, & Easterling, 1993) demonstrated the importance of distinguishing between "ever sought care" and "time till sought care," noting that some of the most distinctive patterns of illness behavior concern how soon individuals present their symptoms to physicians. For purposes of understanding timing, the interval between symptom onset and formal help seeking is divided into two phases: the appraisal phase (from symptom onset to attribution as a health problem) and the illness phase (from attribution as a health problem to help seeking). Their results suggest that there are distinctive and fascinating differences in illness behavior that are observed in

timing issues. First, older adults move more quickly through both phases than their middle-aged and younger peers. As a consequence, older adults seek help for their symptoms more quickly. Second, women move through both phases more quickly than men do, a pattern also observed, using health diary data, by Verbrugge (1985).

The conflicting findings for stressors and psychological distress may result from differences between the appraisal and illness stages. It may be, for example, that stressors and/or the experience of psychological distress prolong the appraisal phase, but shorten the illness phase. That is, it may take longer to attribute a symptom to medical causes if one is simultaneously stressed or distressed. Once the attribution is made, however, these complicating factors may operate to speed up help seeking.

D. Symptom Reporting

Given that symptom characteristics are significant predictors of the decision to seek medical care, it may seem obvious that those symptoms are the focus of the medical encounter. Available evidence suggests, however, that this is not the case. A large literature reviews doctor–patient interaction and the fact that it is typically dissatisfying—at least to the patient (e.g., Stoeckle, 1987; West, 1984). At the most basic level, the communication gap between patients and physicians results from an incongruity between the diagnostic categories used by the latter and the illness experience of patients (e.g., Kleinman, 1988; Waitzkin, 1989). This underlying incongruity in perspectives can be further complicated by the social characteristics of patients. There is substantial evidence that communication problems are especially common between physicians and persons of lower SES (e.g., Pendleton & Bochner, 1980; Rost & Frankel, 1993), women (e.g.,

Meeuwesen, Schaap, & Van Der Staak, 1991), and older persons (e.g., Greene, Adelman, Charon, & Friedmann, 1989).

For our purposes, two studies are especially relevant because they carefully analyzed the congruence between the symptoms that triggered physician care and those addressed in the physician visit. Using health diaries and interviews, Stoller and Kart (1995) found that, on average, older persons reported only one-third of the symptoms that prompted help-seeking to their physicians—and, indeed, only about 8% of them reported all their symptoms. The symptoms reported were not random; they tended to occur in natural clusters, to be unusual, and/or to have remained despite self-care efforts to alleviate them. Interestingly, having sought lay consultation prior to the physician visit was associated with reporting a smaller proportion of symptoms. Similarly, Rost and Frankel (1993) interviewed older diabetes patients just prior to their physician appointments, eliciting information about their "agendas" for the visit (i.e., the symptoms and problems that they expected to tell the doctor). The subsequent physician visit was then audiotaped and patients' agendas were compared to the medical visit. Again, the results suggest that very little of the patients' agendas were addressed: 56% of the patients failed to report at least one symptom that concerned them and fully 25% were unable to report any of the problems that they had intended to raise with their physicians.

It is not possible to determine the extent to which patients simply failed to report their symptoms versus the extent to which physician dominance during the medical visits precluded symptom reports. Most observers (i.e., those who directly observe or tape physician–patient interaction), however, place the responsibility on the physician (e.g., Waitzkin, 1989; West, 1984). Whatever the reason, it is clear that most patients do not report all of their symptoms during physician visits, and this problem is particularly prevalent among older adults.

V. The Mediating Role of the Self

Although there is a much larger body of research on aging and health based on the social structure and personality perspective, the focus here is upon studies that examine the ways that various dimensions of the self mediate between social factors and health in late life. These studies suggest that social psychological processes are important *mechanisms* by which more objective and/or structural social phenomena influence health.

The stress paradigm is arguably the dominant framework guiding investigations of social factors and health (e.g., Kessler, House, Anspach, & Williams, 1995). Although early studies focused on the rather simple task of demonstrating that stress is robustly and prospectively associated with illness onset (see Rabkin & Struening, 1976, for a review of early studies), it soon became clear that a broader conceptual framework was needed to (a) explain individual differences in the health consequences of stress and (b) understand the social structural sources of stressors. In a now classic article, Pearlin and colleagues (Pearlin, Lieberman, Menaghan, & Mullin, 1981) articulated a theory of the stress process that became the organizing paradigm for stress research in the social sciences. In brief, Pearlin et al.'s theory posits that most stressors have their roots in the roles that tie individuals to social structure and that are allocated, in part, on the basis of social characteristics. Thus, most stressors are far from randomly distributed (c.f., Aneshensel, 1992). The impact of stressors on health and well-being is a function of the social and social psychological resources available. For our purposes, the most noteworthy aspect of this theory is that two components of the self are viewed as the most proximal determinants of the effects of stress on health: self-esteem, or feelings of self-worth, and mastery, or a sense of self-efficacy.

At the same time that the stress paradigm focused attention on self-esteem and self-efficacy, other social psychologists also came to the conclusion that these are two of the most consequential dimensions of the self. Research supporting this conclusion included work on the effects of social class, work environments, and social relationships on the self, as well as studies of the components of the self that individuals work hardest to protect or enhance (for a review, see Gecas & Burke, 1995). Yet another body of research highlighted the importance of self-efficacy. Scholars investigating the effects of interventions designed to promote changes in health behaviors (e.g., smoking, exercise) found self-efficacy to be a strong predictor of successful behavior change—and that interventions can enhance self-efficacy and, hence, behavior change (e.g., Strecher, DeVellis, Becker, & Rosenstock, 1986).

The concept of locus of control is relevant to the mediating role of the self as well. Initially, locus of control referred to basic attributional beliefs about the causes of life experience (Rotter, 1966), with attributions to oneself (internal locus of control) or external forces comprising the crucial distinction. Subsequently, investigators discovered that it is important to distinguish between two types of control beliefs: those concerning the *general* ability of individuals to control the events and experiences of their lives (contingency control) and those concerning one's *personal* ability to control the events and experiences of one's life (personal control or self-efficacy) (Bandura, 1986). Personal control is sometimes disaggregated further into control in specific domains such as health and

social relationships. Self-efficacy is the dimension of control that is most compatible with the hypothesis, explicit in the stress paradigm, that specific components of the self are among the mechanisms by which social factors affect health. The research base, however, includes studies that have examined the mediating roles of both self-efficacy (general and domain-specific) and contingency control.

A. The Mediating Role of the Self: Empirical Findings

A broad body of research examines self-esteem, self-efficacy, and sense of control as mediators of the effects of stress and other social factors on health among age-heterogeneous samples; investigations restricted to older adults are less plentiful. To date, there is no evidence that the mediating role of the self operates differently for older adults than for their younger peers. The following discussion reports results primarily from studies of older adults. Results from studies based on age-heterogeneous samples are included (and explicitly described as such) only when an important issue has not been addressed in samples of older adults.

There is impressive evidence that self-esteem, self-efficacy, and sense of control mediate the effects of a variety of social factors on health outcomes. These components of the self have been shown to mediate the effects of acute stress (e.g., Holahan & Holahan, 1987; Krause, 1992, 1994; Norris & Murrell, 1984), chronic stressors [e.g., widowhood (Johnson, Lund, & Dimond, 1986), chronic illness (Essex & Klein, 1989; Heidrich, 1996), and financial strain (Krause, 1987a) on depressive symptoms. Evidence for health outcomes other than depression or distress is very limited, although self-esteem is a predictor of self-rated health (Ferraro & Feller, 1996), and general control beliefs predict mortality 12 years later, statistically controlling for baseline demographics, health and functional status, and other social factors (e.g., SES) (Chipperfield, 1993b).

The relationships among social support, dimensions of the self, and health outcomes are less clear because investigators model them in different ways. In an important study based on an age-heterogeneous sample, Ross and Mirowsky (1989) identified two major pathways by which social support and feelings of control affect psychological distress. In one, feelings of control were shown to increase active coping, which, in turn, reduced distress. In the other, high levels of social support increased talking about one's problems with significant others, which, in turn, increased distress. An especially interesting finding was that the effects of social support differed, depending on whether participants reported talking about their problems. Social support decreased distress in the absence of talking about one's problems, but it also increased the likelihood of talking about one's problems, which increased distress. Other studies find support for alternate models of the relationships among social support, the self, and distress. Two studies support the hypothesis that one of the mechanisms by which social support protects health is by increasing feelings of control (Bisconti & Bergeman, 1999) or self-esteem (Krause, 1987b). Holahan and Holahan (1987) find support for yet another model: that high levels of self-efficacy lead to higher levels of social support which, in turn, reduce depression.

B. Identity and Meaning

Another way of examining the self is to examine components of identity. Identity generally refers to those aspects of the self that reflect significant investments of time, energy, and personal commitment. In general, the more important an element of the self is to one's identity, the greater the distress if it is threatened.

Using data from age-heterogeneous samples, Thoits (1983, 1992) and Simon (1997) found that stresses experienced in highly salient roles that are central to personal identity generated greater distress than stresses experienced in less identity-relevant roles. Moreover, role salience and the meaning attached to roles explained demographic differences in distress (e.g., gender, marital status).

The extent to which role salience and identity affects health in late life has received limited attention, but the results are promising. Krause (1994) found a strong association between role salience and distress; indeed, it was only stressors related to roles reported to be highly salient that were associated with distress. In a subsequent study, Krause (1999) hypothesized that when older adults experienced stress in highly salient roles, they would devalue (i.e., reduce their commitment to) those roles in order to alleviate distress. The results suggested just the opposite: when confronting stress in highly salient roles, older adults increased their commitments to them. These results suggest that role salience is one factor that helps to explain the conditions under which stressors do and do not lead to distress.

C. The Effects of Health on the Aging Self

Interestingly, although a broad body of research has examined the effects of the self on health, almost none has considered the opposite possibility: that health problems may affect the self. Many scholars interested in the extent to which components of the self change with age have speculated that the common vicissitudes of late life, including the onset of health problems, have the potential to threaten self-esteem, self-efficacy, or personal identity (e.g., Kuypers & Bengtson, 1973). But this discussion has stayed largely at the level of speculation and has received little empirical attention. It is especially surprising that the large survey databases so commonly used to estimate models of the effects of the self on health have not been used to examine the opposite alternative.

Two qualitative studies, however, explicitly address the effects of chronic illness on the self. Charmaz (1983, 1991) provides the most comprehensive work on this topic. Her focus is on the chronically ill rather than older adults *per se*, but, as age differences in the prevalence of chronic illness suggest, the majority of her sample were old. To briefly summarize this rich body of qualitative work, Charmaz finds that multiple aspects of the self are threatened and often changed by chronic illness. The most common identity losses were in the areas of lack of independence, the feeling of being devalued, and social isolation. In addition, the time and energy required for management of chronic illness are so great that identity as a person who is sick becomes a central component of the self-concept. Belgrave (1990) examined the role of chronic illness in the everyday lives of a small sample of older women. She found changes in the self, especially adoption of a central identity as a sick person, to be less common than reported by Charmaz. The older women in this sample reported that restrictions in their activities were the most difficult consequences of their illnesses, but these problems seemed to threaten the identity of only a minority. Although the effects of health on the aging self have been the focus of only a few qualitative studies, a number of other qualitative studies, focused more generally on the lives of older adults, suggest that health problems and fears are an important component of late life (e.g., Hochschild, 1973; Matthews, 1979).

Finally, one additional study examined the impact of health-care utilization on health-related locus of control (Goldsteen, Counte, & Goldsteen, 1994), arguing

against the view that dimensions of the self are stable traits, impervious to experience. As hypothesized, it found that high levels of health-care utilization were associated with increases by patients in external attributions about health and the ability to control it. This study lends further support to the potential importance of further research on the effects of health on the aging self.

VI. Final Thoughts and Future Directions

The purpose of this chapter has been to document the importance of basic social psychological concepts and processes for our understanding of health and illness in late life. At least two major themes emerge from this review. First, although symbolic interactionism *per se* has seldom been the explicit foundation of research in this area, the importance that tradition attaches to interpretation emerges as a central theme. This review cited numerous studies in which interpretation (e.g., of symptoms, of illness, of self as compared to others) plays a critical role in illness recognition and response. Especially important is the variability of interpretation and its consequences. Moreover, the consequences cannot be simply labeled as constructive or dysfunctional. For example, normalizing symptoms can simultaneously protect one's sense of competence and yet prolong one's suffering or delay needed medical treatment.

A second theme emerging from this review is the importance of the self. To the extent that nonexperimental data can demonstrate causality, it is clear that specific dimensions of the self are proximally implicated in the onset of psychological distress. Self-esteem, self-efficacy, and control expectancies are psychosocial resources that strongly determine whether stressors will harm health and help to explain patterns in the distribution of disease (e.g., gender differences in depression).

Despite their empirical potency, interpretation and the self are largely absent from most of the more epidemiologic research on health and illness in late life. Survey research has taught us a great deal about the distribution of illness and disability in late life, their correlates, and, increasingly, their long-term trajectories and outcomes. I work primarily in that tradition and am, thus, generally a supporter rather than critic of it. Nonetheless, survey research has neglected to take seriously the lessons that social psychology has to teach us. We rarely view self-reports as attributions rather than fact and we worry more about what variables predict than what they mean or the processes that generate them in the lives of older people. Many times, arguably most of the time, survey research cannot directly study interpretative processes and/or the dynamics of the self. The results of social psychological research can be used, however, to temper and inform how research results are interpreted. Thus, merging the concepts and insights of social psychological research with other forms of inquiry is a high priority for future scholarship.

A limitation of the kinds of research reviewed in this chapter is that a large proportion of it, especially in the social structure and personality tradition, focuses on depression or psychological distress. Social structure and personality is an important tradition in social psychology, it is the one that generates the most replicable and generalizable results. It is time for investigators in this tradition to better demonstrate that the stress paradigm, which is the foundation of their work, helps us to understand the social dynamics of physical illness and disability, as well as of depression.

Finally, investigators applying the basic and fundamental concepts of social psychology to health in late life need to continue and intensify their efforts. At its best, social psychology captures the basic processes by which persons understand, respond to, and influence their experiences and environments. Social psychology reveals the fundamental bases of human experience while devoting appropriate attention to both the needs and capacities of the individual and the ways social structures both constrain and enhance human lives. The ways in which these processes are woven into health and illness remains inadequately explored terrain.

References

Abrums, M. (2000). "Jesus will fix it after awhile": Meanings and health. *Social Science and Medicine, 50*, 89–105.

Andersen, R. M., & Newman, J. F. (1973). Societal and individual determinants of medical care utilization in the United States. *Milbank Memorial Fund Quarterly, 51*, 95–121.

Aneshensel, C. S. (1992). Social stress: Theory and research. *Annual Review of Sociology, 18*, 15–38.

Bandura, A. (1986). *Social foundations of thought and action: A social cognitive theory*. Englewood Cliffs, NJ: Prentice-Hall.

Barondess, J. A. (1979). Disease and illness: A crucial distinction. *American Journal of Medicine, 66*, 375–376.

Belgrave, L. L. (1990). The relevance of chronic illness in the everyday lives of elderly women. *Journal of Aging and Health, 2*, 475–500.

Benyamini, Y., Idler, E. L., Leventhal, H., & Leventhal, E. M. (2000). Positive affect and function as influences on self-assessments of health: Expanding our view beyond illness and disability. *Journal of Gerontology: Psychological Sciences, 55B*, P107–P116.

Berkanovic, E., & Hurwicz, M. L. (1989). Psychological distress and the decision to seek medical care among a Medicare population. *Medical Care, 27*, 1058–1075.

Bisconti, T. L., & Bergeman, C. S. (1999). Perceived social control as a mediator of the relationships among social support, psychological well-being, and perceived health. *The Gerontologist, 39,* 94–103.

Borawski, E. A., Kinney, J. M., & Kahana, E. (1996). The meaning of older adults' health appraisals: Congruence with health status and determinant of mortality. *Journal of Gerontology: Social Sciences, 51B,* S157–S170.

Brody, E. M., & Kleban, M. H. (1981). Physical and mental health symptoms of older people: Who do they tell? *Journal of the American Geriatrics Society, 29,* 442–449.

Brody, E. M., Kleban, M. H., & Moles, E. (1983). What do older people do about their day-to-day mental and physical health symptoms? *Journal of the American Geriatrics Society, 31,* 489–498.

Cameron, L., Leventhal, E. A., & Leventhal, H. (1993). Symptom representations and affect as determinants of care seeking in a community-dwelling adult sample population. *Health Psychology, 12,* 171–179.

Cameron, L., Leventhal, E. A., & Leventhal, H. (1995). Seeking medical care in response to symptoms and life stress. *Psychosomatic Medicine, 57,* 37–47.

Charmaz, K. C. (1983). Loss of self: A fundamental form of suffering in the chronically ill. *Sociology of Health and Illness, 5,* 168–195.

Charmaz, K. C. (1991). *Good days, bad days: The self in chronic illness.* New Brunswick, NJ: Rutgers University Press.

Chipperfield, J. G. (1993a). Incongruence between health perceptions and health problems: Implications for survival among seniors. *Journal of Aging and Health, 5,* 475–496.

Chipperfield, J. G. (1993b). Perceived barriers in coping with health problems: A twelve-year longitudinal study of survival among elderly individuals. *Journal of Aging and Health, 5,* 123–139.

Clark, N. M., Becker, M. H., Janz, N. K., Lorig, K., Rakowski, W., & Anderson, L. (1991). Self-management of chronic disease by older adults: A review and questions for research. *Journal of Aging and Health, 3,* 3–27.

Cook, K. S., Fine, G. A., & House, J. S. (Eds.) (1995). *Sociological perspectives on social psychology.* Boston: Allyn and Bacon.

Edwardson, S. R., & Dean, K. J. (1999). Appropriateness of self-care responses to symp-

toms among elders: Identifying pathways of influence. *Research in Nursing and Health, 22,* 329–339.

Edwardson, S. R., Dean, K. J., & Brauer, D. J. (1995). Symptom consultation in lay networks in an elderly population. *Journal of Aging and Health, 7,* 402–416.

Eisenberg, L., & Kleinman, A. (1981). *The relevance of social science for medicine.* Boston: Reidel.

Engle, V. F., & Graney, M. J. (1985). Self-assessed and functional health of older women. *International Journal of Aging and Human Development, 22,* 301–313.

Essex, M. J., & Klein, M. H. (1989). The importance of self-concept and coping responses in explaining physical health status and depression among older women. *Journal of Aging and Health, 1,* 327–348.

Ferraro, K. F. (1993). Are black older adults health-pessimistic? *Journal of Health and Social Behavior, 34,* 201–214.

Ferraro, K. F., & Feller, J. R. (1996). Self and age differences in defining health situations: A comparison of measurement strategies. *Research on Aging, 18,* 175–201.

Festinger, L. (1954). A theory of social comparison processes. *Human Relations, 7,* 117–140.

Fillenbaum, G. G. (1979). Social context and self-assessments of health among the elderly. *Journal of Health and Social Behavior, 20,* 45–51.

Gecas, V., & Burke, P. J. (1995). Self and identity. In K. S. Cook, G. A. Fine, & J. S. House (Eds.), *Sociological perspectives on social psychology* (pp. 41–67). Boston: Allyn and Bacon.

George, L. K. (1996). Social factors and illness. In R. H. Binstock & L. K. George (Eds.), *Handbook of aging and the social sciences* (4th ed.) (pp. 229–253). San Diego: Academic Press.

Gibson, R. C. (1991). Race and the self-reported health of elderly persons. *Journal of Gerontology: Social Sciences, 46,* S235–S242.

Gilbert, D. T., Pelham, B. W., & Krull, D. S. (1988). On cognitive business: When person perceivers meet persons perceived. *Journal of Personality and Social Psychology, 54,* 733–740.

Goldsteen, R. L., Counte, M. A., & Goldsteen, K. (1994). Examining the relationship between health locus of control and the use of medical care services. *Journal of Aging and Health, 6*, 314–335.

Greene, M. G., Adelman, R. D., Charon, R., & Friedmann, E. (1989). Concordance between physicians and their older and younger patients in the primary care medical encounter. *The Gerontologist, 29*, 808–813.

Hansell, S., & Mechanic, D. (1991). Body awareness and self-assessed health among older adults. *Journal of Aging and Health, 3*, 473–492.

Haug, M. R., Wykle, M. L., & Namazi, K. H. (1989). Self-care among older adults. *Social Science and Medicine, 29*, 171–183.

Heidrich, S. M. (1996). Mechanisms related to psychological well-being in older women with chronic illnesses: Age and disease comparisons. *Research in Nursing and Health, 19*, 225–235.

Hirdes, J. P., & Forbes, W. F. (1993). Factors associated with the maintenance of good self-rated health. *Journal of Aging and Health, 5*, 101–122.

Hochschild, A. R. (1973). *The unexpected community*. Berkeley: University of California Press.

Holahan, C. K., & Holahan, C. J. (1987). Self-efficacy, social support, and depression in aging: A longitudinal analysis. *Journal of Gerontology, 42*, 65–68.

House, J.S. (1977). The three faces of social psychology. *Sociometry, 40*, 161–177.

Hurwicz, M. L., & Berkanovic, E. (1991). Care seeking for musculoskeletal and respiratory episodes in a Medicare population. *Medical Care, 29*, 1130–1145.

Idler, E. L. (1993). Age differences in self-assessments of health: Age changes, cohort differences, or survivorship? *Journal of Gerontology: Social Sciences, 48*, S289–S300.

Idler, E. L., Hudson, S. V., & Leventhal, H. (1999). The meanings of self-ratings of health: A qualitative and quantitative approach. *Research on Aging, 21*, 458–276.

Idler, E. L., & Kasl, S. V. (1991). Health perceptions and survival: Do global evaluations of health status really predict mortality? *Journal of Gerontology: Social Sciences, 46*, S55–S65.

Johnson, R., Lund, D., & Dimond, M. (1986). Stress, self-esteem, and coping during bereavement among the elderly. *Social Psychology Quarterly, 49*, 273–279.

Jylha, M. (1994). Self-rated health revisited: Exploring survey interview episodes with elderly respondents. *Social Science and Medicine, 39*, 983–990.

Kart, C. S., & Engler, C. A. (1995). Self-health care among the elderly: A test of the health-behavior model. *Journal of Aging and Health, 17*, 434–458.

Kelley, H. H. (1973). The process of causal attribution. *American Psychologist, 28*, 107–128.

Kessler, R. C., House, J. S., Anspach, R. R., & Williams, D. R. (1995). Social psychology and health. In K. S. Cook, G. A. Fine, & J. S. House (Eds.), *Sociological perspectives on social psychology* (pp. 548–570). Boston: Allyn and Bacon.

Kleinman, A. (1988). *The illness narratives: Suffering, healing, and the human condition*. New York: Basic Books.

Krause, N. (1987a). Chronic strain, locus of control, and distress in older adults. *Psychology and Aging, 2*, 375–382.

Krause, N. (1987b). Life stress, social support, and self-esteem in an elderly population. *Psychology and Aging, 2*, 349–356.

Krause, N. (1992). Stress, religiosity, and psychological well-being among older blacks. *Journal of Aging and Health, 4*, 412–439.

Krause, N. (1994). Stressors in salient social roles and well-being in later life. *Journal of Gerontology: Psychological Sciences, 49*, P137–P148.

Krause, N. (1999). Stress and the devaluation of highly salient roles in late life. *Journal of Gerontology: Social Sciences, 54B*, S99–S108.

Kuypers, J. A., & Bengtson, V. L. (1973). Social breakdown and competence. *Human Development, 16*, 181–201.

Leventhal, E. A. (1984). Aging and the perception of illness. *Research on Aging, 6*, 119–135.

Leventhal, E. A., Easterling, D., Leventhal, H., & Cameron, L. (1995). Conservation of energy, uncertainty reduction, and swift utilization of medical care among the elderly: II. *Medical Care, 33*, 988–1000.

Leventhal, E. A., Leventhal, H., Schaefer, P., & Easterling, D. (1993). Conservation of energy, uncertainty reduction, and swift utilization of medical care among the elderly. *Journal of Gerontology: Psychological Sciences, 48*, P78–P86.

Leventhal, E. A., & Prohaska, T. B. (1986). Age, symptom interpretation, and health behavior. *Journal of the American Geriatrics Society, 34*, 185–191.

Levkoff, S. E., Cleary, P. D., Wetle, T., & Besdine, R. W. (1989). Illness behavior in the aged: Implications for clinicians. *Journal of the American Geriatrics Society, 36*, 622–629.

Lorig, K. R., Mazonson, P. D., & Holman, H. R. (1993). Evidence suggesting that health education for self-management in patients with chronic arthritis has sustained health benefits while reducing health care costs. *Arthritis and Rheumatism, 36*, 439–446.

Lorig, K. R., Sobel, D. S., Stewart, A. L., Brown, B. W., Jr., Bandura, A., Ritter, P., Gonzalez, V. M., Laurent, D. D., & Homan, H. R. (1999). Evidence suggesting that a chronic disease self-management program can improve health status while reducing hospitalization. *Medical Care, 37*, 5–14.

Matthews, S. H. (1979). *The social world of old women: Management of self-identity*. Beverly Hills, CA: Sage.

Meeuwesen, L., Schaap, C., & Van Der Staak, C. (1991). Verbal analysis of doctor-patient communication. *Social Science and Medicine, 32*, 1143–1150.

Okun, M. A., & George, L. K. (1984). Physician- and self-ratings of health, neuroticism, and subjective well-being among men and women. *Personality and Individual Differences, 5*, 533–540.

Norris, F. H., & Murrell, S. A. (1984). Protective function of resources related to life events, global stress, and depression in older adults. *Journal of Health and Social Behavior, 25*, 424–437.

Pearlin, L. I., Lieberman, M. A., Menaghan, E. G., & Mullin, J. T. (1981). The stress process. *Journal of Health and Social Behavior, 22*, 337–356.

Pendleton, D., & Bochner, S. (1980). The communication of medical information in general practice consultations as a function of patients' social class. *Social Science and Medicine, 14A*, 669–673.

Prohaska, T. B., Leventhal, E. A., Leventhal, H., & Keller, M. L. (1985). Health practices

and illness cognition in young, middle-aged, and elderly adults. *Journal of Gerontology: 40*, 569–578.

Rabkin, J. G., & Struening, E. L. (1976). Life events, stress, and illness. *Science, 194*, 1013–1020.

Rakowski, W., & Hickey, T. (1993). Mortality and the attribution of health problems to aging among older adults. *American Journal of Public Health, 82*, 1131–1141.

Rakowski, W., Julius, M., Hickey, T., Verbrugge, L. M., & Halter, J. B. (1988). Daily symptoms and behavioral responses: Results of a health diary with older adults. *Medical Care, 26*, 278–297.

Robinson-Whelen, S., & Kiecolt-Glaser, J. (1997). The importance of social versus temporal comparison appraisals among older adults. *Journal of Applied Social Psychology, 27*, 959–966.

Rosenstock, I. M., & Kirscht, J. P. (1974). The health belief model and personal health behavior. *Health Education Monographs, 2*, 470–473.

Rosenstock, I. M., Strecher, V. J., & Becker, M. H. (1988). Social learning theory and the health belief model. *Health Education Quarterly, 15*, 175–183.

Ross, C. E., & Mirowsky, J. (1989). Explaining the social patterns of depression: Control and problem-solving or support and talking? *Journal of Health and Social Behavior, 30*, 206–219.

Rost, K., & Frankel, R. (1993). The introduction of the older patient's problems in the medical visit. *Journal of Aging and Health, 5*, 387–401.

Rotter, J. B. (1966). Generalized expectancies for internal versus external control of reinforcement. *Psychological Monographs, 80*, 1–28.

Siegel, K., Dean, L., & Schrimshaw, E. W. (1999). Symptom ambiguity among late-middle-aged and older adults with HIV. *Research on Aging, 21*, 595–618.

Simon, R. W. (1997). The meanings individuals attach to role identities and their implications for mental health. *Journal of Health and Social Behavior, 38*, 256–274.

Smith, A. M. A., Shelley, J. M., & Dennerstein, L. (1994). Self-rated health: Biological continuum or social discontinuity? *Social Science and Medicine, 39*, 77–83.

Steele, C. M. (1988). The psychology of self-affirmation: Sustaining the integrity of the self. *Advances in Experimental Social Psychology, 21,* 261–302.

Stoeckle, J. (1987). *Encounters between patients and doctors.* Cambridge, MA: MIT Press.

Stoller, E. P. (1993). Interpretations of symptoms by older people: A health diary study of illness behavior. *Journal of Aging and Health, 5,* 58–81.

Stoller, E. P., & Forster, L. E. (1994). The impact of symptom interpretation on physician utilization. *Journal of Aging and Health, 6,* 507–534.

Stoller, E. P., Forster, L. E., & Portugal, S. (1993). Self-care responses to symptoms by older people: A health diary study of illness behavior. *Medical Care, 31,* 24–42.

Stoller, E. P., & Kart, C. S. (1995). Symptom reporting during physician consultation: Results of a health diary study. *Journal of Aging and Health, 7,* 200–232.

Stoller, E. P., Pollow, R., & Forster, L.E. (1994). Older people's recommendations for treating symptoms: Repertoires of lay knowledge and disease. *Medical Care, 32,* 847–862.

Strawbridge, W. J., & Wallhagen, M. I. (1999). Self-rated health and mortality over three decades: Results from a time-dependent covariate analysis. *Research on Aging, 21,* 402–416.

Strecher, V. J., Champion, V. L., & Rosenstock, I. M. (1997). The health belief model and health behavior. In D. S. Gochman (Ed.), *Handbook of health behavior research, vol. 1: Personal and social determinants* (pp. 71–91). New York: Plenum.

Strecher, V. J., DeVellis, B. M., Becker, M. H., & Rosenstock, I. M. (1986). The role of self-efficacy in achieving health behavior change. *Health Education Quarterly, 13,* 73–92.

Tessler, R., & Mechanic, D. (1978). Psychological distress and perceived health status. *Journal of Health and Social Behavior, 19,* 254–262.

Thoits, P. A. (1983). Multiple identities and psychological well-being. *American Sociological Review, 51,* 259–272.

Thoits, P. A. (1992). Identity structures and psychological well-being: Gender and marital status comparisons. *Social Psychology Quarterly, 55,* 236–256.

Van Doorn, C. (1999). A qualitative approach to studying health optimism, realism, and pessimism. *Research on Aging, 21,* 440–457.

Verbrugge, L. M. (1985). Triggers of symptoms and health care. *Social Science and Medicine, 20,* 855–876.

Verbrugge, L. M., & Ascione, F. J. (1987). Exploring the iceberg: Common symptoms and how people care for them. *Medical Care, 25,* 539–569.

Waitzkin, H. (1989). A critical theory of medical discourse: Ideology, social control, and the processing of social context in medical encounters. *Journal of Health and Social Behavior, 30,* 220–239.

West, C. (1984). *Routine complications: Troubles with talk between doctors and patients.* Bloomington: Indiana University Press.

Wood, J. V. (1989). Theory and research concerning social comparisons of personal attributes. *Psychological Bulletin, 106,* 231–248.

Zola, I. K. (1966). Culture and symptoms—An analysis of patients' presenting complaints. *American Sociological Review, 31,* 615–630.

Thirteen

Caregiving by Adult Children
Involvement, Role Disruption, and Health

Leonard I. Pearlin, Mark F. Pioli, and Amy E. McLaughlin

I. Introduction

Scholars engaged in life-course and aging research hardly need to be told that there is considerable interest in caregiving to impaired elders; even the most hasty perusal of appropriate journals is testimony to this interest. What may be less readily apparent than the sheer volume of writing in this area are the reasons for it. One explanation lies with the changing demography of societies brought on by extended longevity and the resultant increase in the proportion of older people in the population. Unfortunately, there is often a price elders must pay for their long lives; it comes in the form of a greater need to rely on others for things they could once do for themselves. The dependence on the assistance of others sharply escalates with age, since the health problems that limit functional autonomy also increase with age. Understandably, as the population of older people expands, so too does the population of caregivers, who are typically family members. In part, then, the attention being given by scholars to caregiving can be understood as a response to historical demographic shifts and the emerging social, familial,

and personal problems created by the burgeoning numbers of people entering late life. Kindred to these kinds of changes and also contributing to the heightened interest in caregiving is the intensified effort by professionals and service providers to construct interventions designed to prevent or alleviate the pain and suffering that is commonly experienced by both impaired people and their caregivers.

Although these changing conditions substantially fuel the attention currently given caregiving, they cannot fully account for the concentration of work in this area by researchers representing multiple disciplines and theoretical orientations. It is our contention that caregiving has drawn the attention of researchers because its study can be used to illuminate fundamental issues of social and psychological processes whose importance extends beyond caregiving itself. It is essentially a two-way street: whereas the theoretical orientations of social and behavioral science have guided much of the research into caregiving, studies of caregiving, in turn, have helped to refine our theoretical orientations.

Handbook of Aging and the Social Sciences, Fifth Edition

Some of the early studies of caregiving stand as examples of this view. To a considerable extent, these inquiries were as much aimed at the understanding of family structure and functioning as with the provision of care (Johnson & Catalano, 1981, 1983; Shanas, 1979; Shanas & Streib, 1968). This interest, in turn, grew in response to Talcott Parsons's (1949) theoretical perspectives on families. Aside from reproduction, he considered the family in industrialized societies to primarily function as a socializing agent for its young before they went off to establish their own families. What was missing from this important work of 40 and 50 years ago was recognition of the emotional bonds that are normatively developed among family members (Sussman, 1953) and the powerful and persistent reciprocities among them (George, 1986). Moreover, these ties and commitments are present in the extended family as well as in the nuclear household (Bengtson & Kuypers, 1985; Bengtson, Mangen, & Landry, 1984; Bengtson & Schrader, 1982; Sussman, 1959). Along with other research that was broadening the picture of family life, then, these early studies of caregiving were a departure from Parsonian theories of family structure and functioning and helped to correct the deficiencies of these theories. They did so by bringing into view the intense and enduring attachments among family members and the lasting devotion one comes to have to the well-being of others.

As indicated above, research into caregiving can also be understood within the context of the considerable scholarly work addressed to generational issues, a matter that has a prominent presence in the present chapter. The notion of generation has been placed in the service of at least two major analytic purposes. One is its use as a broad construct—generational succession—that is treated as a vehicle for societal continuities and change

through time (Mannheim, 1952). Second, and closer to caregiving, it has been employed as a basic component of family organization. In recent years, especially in the influential work of Bengtson and his colleagues (e.g., Bengtson, Burgess, & Parrott, 1997), the commitments and obligations that crisscross generational lines are taken as evidence of family solidarity. The attachments that cut across multiple generations are further testimony, of course, of the untenability of theories of family life that prevailed in earlier decades.

In caregiving research, generational issues have tended to acquire a highly specialized focus, graphically described as "the sandwich generation." This label calls attention to the conflicts and dilemmas that adult children or grandchildren experience in the course of providing assistance to an impaired relative while at the same time having obligations to other activities and relationships, especially their own children (e.g., Brody, 1990; Dobson & Dobson, 1985; Miller, 1981; Nichols & Junk, 1997; Raphael & Schlesinger, 1993). Although the construct of the sandwich generation has been useful in raising awareness of the very real problems that adult children confront when they become caregivers in the midst of being breadwinners and job holders, spouses, and parents, it may be misleading on two counts. First, we submit that it is more instructive to consider such problems in the general context of theory and research into multiple roles and their integration than as specifically being caught between obligations to multiple generations. Second, and related, when understood as a matter involving the reconciliation of multiple roles, it can be seen that the sandwiching of people is certainly not confined to the generation of adult children. Spousal caregivers, no less than their children, are also forced to restructure the array of their established roles and activities in order to accommodate the surfacing demands of caregiving. Anyone, regardless of generation, who takes on a long-term role as caregiver is likely to face conflicting obligations that are not easily reconciled.

What we wish to emphasize here is the fact that studies of caregiving, just as they contribute to other areas of inquiry, can inform the considerable interest in multiple roles and their consequences. Empirical evidence indicates that in general people are likely to be the beneficiaries of multiple roles (Moen, Robison, & Fields, 1994), especially, perhaps, when each role contributes in a positive way to self-identities (Thoits, 1983, 1986). These benefits may also depend on the particular mix of roles (Aneshensel, Rutler, & Lachenbruch, 1991; Jackson, 1997; Menaghan, 1989) and the meanings and importance attached to roles (Simon, 1995). Clearly, what is needed is a specification of the conditions that lead to one or the other of these effects. In this chapter, which examines the addition of caregiving to the prior organization of people's roles, we have the opportunity to specify further the conditions determining the effects of multiple roles on well-being. For many people, taking on this additional role reverberates unfavorably across the entire range of their other roles, creating a disruption of activities and obligations outside of caregiving. It is to be noted that caregiving to a parent with Alzheimer's disease (AD), which we observe here, is not transient or typically short-lived. Instead, it entails assistance over the lengthy course of a cognitive decline and necessitates more and more energy and attention.

Thus, whereas being an incumbent of multiple roles may in general have salubrious effects, this is not likely to be the case where a new and, in a sense, unexpected "career" (Pearlin & Aneshensel, 1994), having escalating demands, comes to encroach on the enactment and organ-

ization of other roles. Based on what can be deduced from caregiving research, we surmise that incumbency in multiple roles contributes to well-being when there is a stable and mutually supporting organization among multiple roles. When these conditions are not realized because of the competition and conflict among roles, as is often the case with caregivers to loved ones with AD, one's multiple roles become a detriment to well-being. Again, the matter of multiple roles represents still another instance in which the concepts and substance of one field can be brought to bear on an understanding of caregiving and its consequences; at the same time, the study of caregiving can bring greater specification and clarity to that area.

This brings us to what has probably been the most pronounced convergence of caregiving with a field of research that has different intellectual origins and is conceptually and substantively distinct. We refer, of course, to the study of stress and its health outcomes. Whereas earlier studies tended to ask who was doing what in caring for impaired elders, the question that gradually gained dominance during the 1980s asked what the consequences of caregiving are for caregivers. Probably beginning with the seminal work of Zarit and his colleagues (e.g., Zarit, Reeves, & Bach-Peterson, 1980), there was a heavy flow of research reports contributing to the rapid and irrefutable accumulation of evidence that caregiving can be tough on the well-being of caregivers. Indeed, the rapid piling up of literature attesting to the psychological burdens and strains of caregiving inspired discussions in a leading gerontological journal questioning the need for further research along these lines (George, 1990; Zarit, 1989).

The research has, in fact, continued up to the present, building upon but shifting from earlier inquiries in an important manner. Specifically, the more recent work has aimed not only at documenting that prolonged caregiving can tax the well-being of caregivers, but has also sought to specify the conditions and mechanisms accounting for these consequences. In so doing, these studies also help to explain why some people are relatively unaffected by the role, whereas the well-being of others is put at risk. This line of inquiry has been influenced by what has come to be referred to as the stress process framework (Pearlin, Lieberman, Menaghan, & Mullen, 1981). Since this is the framework that substantially guides the data presented in this chapter, it merits a brief and selective overview.

As indicated by the label, the stress process framework considers stress as an unfolding process involving changes among related components. The components include the *stressors* that potentially impinge on people (i.e., the hardships, demands, frustrations, threats or other conditions that challenge people's adaptive capacities) (Pearlin, 1989). Based on empirical findings from various studies indicating that exposure to one set of stressors often leads to other stressors (Pearlin & Johnson, 1977; Pearlin & Lieberman, 1979), we have distinguished *primary* from *secondary stressors* (Pearlin, Aneshensel, & LeBlanc, 1997). These terms are not meant to imply a difference in their importance. Instead, they are meant to reflect the tendency toward stress proliferation; this occurs when exposure to one stressor or set of stressors creates additional stressors in domains of life outside the boundaries within which the primary stressors arose. Both primary and secondary stressors may affect the second major component of the stress process, the *health outcomes*. Health outcomes are assessed by a variety of indicators of both psychological well-being and physical health. *Moderators*, the third component of the stress process, are comprised of personal and social resources, such as coping repertoires, social

supports, and certain self-concepts that function to regulate or govern the effects of stressors on outcomes. Moderators are among the constructs generally used to account for observed differences in the ways people's health is impacted despite their exposure to similar stressors. Such differences may also result from people being exposed to the same primary stressor but to different constellations of secondary stressors. Finally, and importantly, all of the components of the stress process should be viewed as being embedded in the context of people's social and economic characteristics. These characteristics can potentially influence the stressors to which people are exposed, the moderating resources they possess, and the outcomes they manifest.

Research into caregiving has arisen out of a rich and lively theoretical past and it is sustained by a similarly rich present. It is neither an accidentally discovered area of inquiry, nor does it continue simply on the strength of its acquired momentum. To some extent, the issues and questions that we explore here span the past and present. It is very much in the domain of the multigenerational family, since it concerns the care of impaired parents by adult children; it is also concerned with multiple roles, especially as the continuity of their enactment is disrupted by the emergence of caregiving; and it seeks to provide some coherent explanation for differences in health outcomes by placing its findings within a stress process framework. With regard to the stress process, it can be noted that AD provides an unusual, though poignant, opportunity to study a situation that often gives rise to a host of enduring stressors. The population of caregivers to family members impaired with this disease is especially appropriate for those of us who seek to understand the effects of chronic stressors that surface in the lives of ordinary people engaged in ordinary social relationships.

II. Background and Sample

The data presented here are drawn from interviews with 125 adults having a mother or father who is the principal caregiver to a husband or wife impaired by AD. The original sample of 200 spousal caregivers met two inclusion criteria: they were providing assistance to the person with AD in activities of daily living (ADLs) that the person could no longer perform by himself or herself and, second, this assistance was given in the home, not in an institutional setting. The spousal caregivers, who reside in Northern Virginia, the District of Columbia, and in a band of three Maryland counties, were recruited through a variety of channels, including newspaper and television advertisements, day care centers, notices in newsletters of local chapters of the Alzheimer's Association, and through the cooperation of a university diagnostic clinic. Special efforts were aimed at the enlistment of minority group members by posting notices in neighborhoods whose residents are predominantly African American or Hispanic.

At the time of the screening interview, spousal caregivers were told that the study was designed to include interviews with both themselves and, where possible, an adult child. Participants were then asked whether they had a child living within an hour's drive and, if so, if the child provided even minimal assistance, either directly to the impaired parent or indirectly to the parent who was the principal caregiver. In cases where multiple children fit this description, respondents were asked to name the child most active in providing help. Only 16 of the 200 spousal caregivers had no living children, and the children of another 13 lived beyond an hour's radius. Another 22 reported that their children, although living within an hour, provided no help, and still another 13 refused to give the names, telephone numbers, or addresses of their children, thus opting that their children not participate. Of the 136 children for whom we had contact information (and, at least, the tacit approval of their parent), 6 subsequently refused participation, 4 could not be located, and 1 lost eligibility because of the intervening death of the impaired parent. There was but a single interview with the 125 eligible adult children and, consequently, the data shown here are cross-sectional.

We focus on adult children in this analysis not because we believe that they are subjected to more severe stressors than those experienced by spousal caregivers, nor because their exposure to stressors has some unique consequences for their health and well-being. Indeed, we assume that caregiving parents, being on the front lines of providing assistance, are much more likely to bear the brunt of caring for their impaired spouse. It is precisely because they are in the second line of providers that the consequences of their caregiving commitments are instructive. To the extent that there are such consequences, they give some further indication that the effects of caregiving to a loved one can transcend generational divisions and affect the family as a whole.

Table 13.1 shows some of the key social and economic characteristics of the sample of children. The composition of a representative sample of adult children having a secondary part in the care of an impaired parent is unknown. However, given the methods by which the sample was assembled, no claim can be made for its representativeness. What is more crucial than representativeness to the following analysis is the diversity of the sample. Thus, differences in age, gender, marital, parental, and employment statuses, as well as in the extent of their involvement in caregiving activities are sufficiently great to allow the examination of their effects. It can be seen in Table 13.1 that on average, the sample

Table 13.1
Demographic and Socioeconomic Characteristics of Adult-Child Caregivers and Parents with Alzheimer's Disease[a]

	Adult children	Parents with Alzheimer's
Social characteristics		
Age (mean)[b]	44.2 (7.9)	75.3 (7.9)
Gender (% women)	60.0	39.2
Race (% white)	88.8	89.6
Marital status (% married)	66.4	100.0
Parental status (% with children)	72.0	100.0
Socioeconomic status		
Education (%)		
Less than high school	0.8	13.6
High school degree	11.2	31.2
Some post-high school	20.0	20.0
College degree	33.6	16.0
Some postgraduate	2.4	5.6
Postgraduate degree	32.0	13.6
Income (%)		
$0–19,999	7.3[c]	11.0
$20,000–39,999	17.1	40.0
$40,000–59,999	24.4	21.0
$60,000–79,999	16.3	18.5
$80,000 +	35.0	9.5
Employment status (%)		
Full time	65.6	N/A
Part time	24.0	N/A
Retired	3.2	N/A
Unemployed	7.2	N/A
Caregiver/Alzheimer's disease gender pairs (%)		
Daughter/mother	24.0	—
Daughter/father	36.0	—
Son/mother	15.2	—
Son/father	24.8	—

[a]$N = 125$.
[b]Ages range from 54.6–88.6 years for persons with Alzheimer's disease and 20–63 years for adult children.
[c]Adult-child incomes are based on 123 cases due to missing data.

enjoys a somewhat higher income and has a more advanced educational level than others within the same age distribution; it is evident, too, that the proportion of minority group members in the sample is less than in the general population. These tilts notwithstanding, there is sufficient differentiation of social and economic characteristics in the sample to explore their influences on the chain of consequences that result from efforts to accommodate a new role in the context of one's established multiple roles.

III. Key Concepts and Their Measures

Much of the following analysis rests on the premise that the constriction and disruption of established activities increase with involvement in caregiving and that these dislocations, in turn, have deleterious consequences for well-being. We shall first describe our assessment of involvement in caregiving and then turn to indicators of role disruption and to a description of measures of health and well-being.

A. Involvement in Caregiving

Understandably, there is considerable varation in the extent to which adult children are actively involved in caregiving activities. Providing assistance to a person with a progressive cognitive disease can absorb as much work and effort as one is willing or able to devote to it, and we find, in fact, that some children are quite fully involved. However, because of competing commitments and other inhibiting circumstances, other children may be only marginally engaged. To capture these kinds of differences, we rely on a series of two-part questions. First, respondents were asked the following questions about the assistance they provide in various aspects of ADLs and instrumental ADLs (IADLs): Do you *personally* (1) do things for your (impaired parent) such as feeding, bathing, or toileting; (2) help with activities such as shopping, transportation, or other household chores; (3) do things for your parents like handling money or arranging for programs and services; and (4) ever just stay with your (impaired parent) while your mother/father does things other than caregiving? The numbers saying "yes" to each of the four queries are, respectively, 49, 94, 43, and 93. In each case where the responses were in the affirmative, the adult children were then asked this question: On average, how many hours per week would you say you spend providing this care? The measure of caregiving involvement, then, is made up of the total number of hours people report devoting to the four types of assistance. Exploratory analysis revealed that the form of the ADL or IADL assistance people provide their relatives is less consequential than the amount of time devoted to these activities, a reflection of how engulfed their lives become in the course of providing the assistance.

B. Role Disruption

At the core of our inquiry is the question of how involvement in the emerging caregiving role impacts on other, established roles. A basic assumption, of course, is that the consequences of caregiving demands can be observed to disrupt the patterns of activities and relationships formerly entailed by these roles. The proliferation of adverse consequences is examined in three major roles: marital, parental, and occupational.

Married adult children were asked three questions that provide the measure of marital disruption: To what extent (very much, somewhat, not much, or not at all) has your parent's illness (1) interfered with the time that you and your (spouse) have just for yourselves; (2) led to disagreements between you and your (spouse); and (3) interfered with things you and your (spouse) used to do together? Principal component factor analysis yielded a single factor from these items and, when tested for internal reliability, they were found to have a Cronbach's alpha of .72.

Four items probe the disruption respondents experience in their parental role. As with the above, they were asked: To what extent (from very much to not at all) has your parent's illness (1) interfered with the time you have to spend with your child(ren); (2) affected your ability to get involved with the social activities of your child(ren); (3) led to disagreements between you and your child(ren); and (4) interfered with your knowing what's going on in the lives of your child(ren)? These items, too, form a single factor and have an alpha of .79.

A third measure is of the strains created at the intersection of caregiving and work among those who have employment outside the household. In particular, it taps the extent to which caregiving responsibilities encroach on the domain of work. To do this, the following three questions were directed to respondents: From your own personal experience, please tell me whether you strongly agree, agree, disagree, or strongly disagree with each of these statements: (1) In the last 2 months or so, I have had less energy for my work; (2) in the last 2 months or so, I have missed too many work days; and (3) in the last 2 months or so, I have been dissatisfied with the quality of my work. These three items form a single factor having an alpha of .72.

A final measure is of the constriction of social and leisure life. Although this aspect of people's lives does not concern an institutionalized role as do our preceding measures, we wished to see, first, if it varies with caregiving involvement and, second, whether it is associated with mental and physical health. Respondents were asked to what extent (from very much to not at all) their parent's illness has interfered with (1) the time you have for leisure activities; (2) the time you have for friends; and (3) the time you have just for yourself. The alpha for this scale is .88.

C. Indicators of Health and Well-Being

The ultimate analytic question that is of interest asks whether the disruption of roles affects the well-being of the adult child caregivers. Two indicators of such consequences are employed, one measuring depression and the other self-rated health. The measure of depression is an abridged version of the Hopkins Check List (Derogatis, Lipman, Covi, & Rickles, 1971) comprised of seven items. It asks, In the past week, on how many days (5 or more, 3 or 4, 1 or 2, or no days) did you (1) lack enthusiasm for doing anything; (2) feel bored or have little interest in anything; (3) cry easily or feel like crying; (4) feel downhearted or blue; (5) feel slowed down or low in energy; (6) blame yourself for everything; and (7) have your feelings hurt easily? This single-factor scale has an alpha of .81.

Self-rated health is assessed by one item: In general, would you describe your health as excellent, very good, good, fair, or poor? This item, or items similar to it, have repeatedly been found to be related to objective indicators of health and to the risk of mortality (e.g., Idler & Kasl, 1991). Although it is certainly not a substitute for objective assessments of acute or chronic ailments, these kinds of relationships stand as evidence that people are able with some sensitivity to monitor (albeit not diagnose) their inner states of physical health.

IV. Results

As indicated by our discussions above, the following analysis first considers the conditions associated with variations in the extent to which adult children are involved in caregiving activities. This is followed by an examination of how involvement and its demands may lead to exposure to stressors and problems in other major life domains and, third, whether such exposure has an adverse affect on well-being.

A. Conditions Influencing Involvement

From one perspective, it might seem hardly worthwhile to ask why family members, including adult children, provide assistance to an impaired relative. At first the answer might appear rather self-evident: they do it because that's what people do for loved ones. There is no doubt that powerful norms do operate within families that might make the probing of reasons for giving assistance seem an unnecessary exercise. Nevertheless, it is a question that needs to be asked because, from all indications, the explanations accounting for caregiving and the provision of assistance are somewhat more complex than might be expected. Indeed, even where there is a normative imperative for caregiving, there can be other conditions that either constrain or enable caregiving. As a consequence, people who share the same desire to assist their relatives may differ considerably in the extent to which they actually engage themselves in caregiving activities. This is reflected in the wide variations in caregiving involvement among adult children. In the course of examining the conditions associated with these variations we have also discovered a number of factors that we fully anticipated would appreciably regulate caregiving involvement but that, in fact, emerge as insignificant.

These "nonexplanations" deserve some discussion because their very elimination helps to illuminate and underscore the sources of caregiver involvement. Two related conditions were among those that we expected would contribute to the magnitude of adult children's involvement in caregiving activities. The first of these is the scope of the impaired parents' needs for assistance and, second, the presence of health problems among the primary caregivers (i.e., the spouses of the impaired person) that would limit the level of assistance they are able to provide their husbands or wives. However, after controlling for a number of background characteristics, which are presented in Table 13.2,

neither of these considerations plays a part in accounting for differences in the caregiving involvement of adult children. The needs of the impaired parent were assessed in multiple ways: the number and severity of ADL and IADL dependencies, their cognitive status, and behavioral problems. None of these is associated with the participation of children in the care of their parents. With regard to possible health limitations of the spousal caregivers, we found that their own symptoms of depression, self-rated health, illness symptoms, diagnosed physical ailments, and their sense of overload had no effect on their children's involvement. Moreover, children's subjective assessments of the physical and emotional health of their caregiving parents had no significant bearing on their involvement in providing help and assistance.

Another set of conditions that we had hypothesized would influence the involvement of adult children in the care of their parents concerned the *quality* of their past and present relationship with the caregiving parent. One multi-item measure essentially inquires into the solidarity of the relationship prior to the onset of AD in the family and another assesses the same dimension of the relationship but as it currently stands. A third

Table 13.2
Adult-Child's Time Involvement in Caregiving: Contributing Factors

Independent variables	I.	II.	III.	IV.
Socioeconomic characteristics				
Age	0.115	0.107	0.126	0.096
Race (white)	0.831	2.513	5.995	5.744
Gender (women)	−0.103	0.524	−1.990	−1.545
Income	−1.339**	−0.858	−0.744	−0.268
Education	0.195	−0.261	−0.429	−0.909
Constraining and enabling conditions				
Number of roles (0–3)		−3.224*	−3.090*	−4.023*
Reduction of job commitments			10.722***	10.126***
Financial insecurity				−3.084*
R^2	0.073	0.104	0.213	0.242

$*p \leq .05; ** p \leq .01; ***p \leq .001.$

and final scale taps the presence of disagreements and conflicts arising from the caregiving situation. Our general reasoning posited that the greater the harmony and solidarity of the relationship the more motivated the child would be to help the impaired parent and in this way, at least, lend indirect support to the caregiving parent. However plausible the reasoning, it is not supported by our empirical findings.

What is apparent from these unexpected findings, then, is that the level of involvement of children whose parent is severely impaired is not higher than those whose parent is less impaired, that the health and vigor of the caregiving parent has no appreciable influence on the caregiving of the adult child, and close family relationships are no more likely than distant and conflictory relationships to lead to involvement in caregiving activities. Stated simply, need and attachment do not significantly explain differences in the time that adult children devote to caregiving and supportive activities. As shown in Table 13.2, what appears to make a difference to their involvement are differences in their exposure to various structural constraints.

Three such constraints in particular have been identified: the number of major roles of which the adult children are incumbents; the reduction of commitments to employment outside the household; and concerns and insecurities about finances. The number of roles is determined by whether one is a parent, married, and has outside employment; thus the multiplicity of roles can range from zero to three. The reduction of job commitments is established by a question asking respondents whether they changed their work situation because of their (mother's/father's) illness. If they answered in the affirmative, they were then asked what changes they made. Virtually all change involved either a reduction from full to part time or to no time or from part time to no time. Financial in-

security, finally, is assessed by a scale based on answers to three questions: How concerned are you (from very to not) about (1) being deeply in debt; (2) meeting monthly payment on bills; and (3) having a lower standard of living than you would like?

The first model of Table 13.2, in which the measure of involvement is regressed on the social and economic characteristics of respondents, shows only income to be related to caregiving involvements. Specifically, the greater one's income, the less likely one is to be engaged in caregiving. The number of role incumbencies is added to the regression equation in the second model, revealing that the larger the number of roles, the lower is the level of caregiving involvement. However, occasionally people are able to manipulate their employment and their hours of work. Unlike parental and marital roles whose obligations are relatively inflexible, some people have it within their discretionary power to decrease their commitments to outside employment in order, apparently, to increase the time they are able to devote to caregiving activities. As can be seen in the third model, the exercise of this discretion is closely related to the level of caregiving involvement. We can report in passing that women more than men are likely to make these adjustments to their work life, but it can be noted that gender makes no significant independent contribution to involvement. Finally, and independently of the other constraints, the sheer precariousness of adult children's finances acts to inhibit their caregiving involvement. We speculate that caregiving, to the extent that it entails some out-of pocket expenses on the part on the child, might constitute an additional drain on what are already scarce resources. It would also seem that activities in general that intrude on paid work would be avoided by people harboring concerns about their financial situation.

There are clearly other factors that help to explain variations in caregiving involvements among adult children. What can be observed here is that the assumption of a new role and the commitments that can be made to it depend appreciably on the prior organization of people's lives around major roles. Nevertheless, it is evident that many people either do not face these constraints or they manage to find enough flexibility in their lives to enable them to take on substantial responsibilities for the care of their impaired parents. But in doing so, we shall see, they potentially expose themselves to consequences that are inimical to their health and well-being. We turn now from considering the factors influencing caregiver involvement to an examination of the possible consequences of involvement.

B. Caregiving Involvement and Role Disruption

The consequences we focus on concern the disruptions in the enactment of major social roles, primarily in the form of problems that arise within the roles and the interactions they entail. These disruptions, whose measurements were described above, entail difficulties that people may experience as parents, as marital partners, and as workers. Though not technically a role, we also examine the impact of caregiving involvement on the social and leisure activities of the adult children. Table 13.3 shows the relationships between the level of involvement in caregiving activities and the problems that can be detected in each of these four domains. It can be noted that the N for each of the columns differs, a reflection of variations in the numbers who are incumbents of the different roles under examination. It would be possible to score nonincumbents of a role as experiencing no disruptions in the role, a strategy that has the advantage of allowing the inclusion of the entire sample of adult children. The disadvantage of this strategy, underlying our decision not to employ it, is its questionable treatment of nonincumbents as identical with those who are incumbents but who are free of disruptive experiences. Because each role includes a somewhat different subgroup of the sample, we also include as controls for each group their social and economic characteristics.

It is amply evident from the results that the disruption of people's lives increases significantly with their involvements in the care of an impaired parent. For example, when the measure of marital strains

Table 13.3
The Level of Caregiving Involvement and the Disruption of Roles

Independent Variables	Disruption of marital role ($N = 84$)	Disruption of parenting role ($N = 88$)	Work–caregiving conflict ($N = 109$)	Constriction of social life ($N = 123$)
Socioeconomic characteristics				
Age	0.024**	0.005	−0.005	−0.005
Race (white)	0.198	0.209	−0.236	0.115
Gender (women)	0.194	0.196	0.454***	0.522***
Income	−0.033	−0.036	0.026	−0.038
Education	0.120	0.084	0.029	0.170***
Level of caregiving involvement	0.024***	0.021***	0.010*	0.025***
R^2	0.352	0.321	0.141	0.353

*$p \leq .05$; ** $p \leq .01$; ***$p \leq .001$.

is regressed on the level of involvement, we find that the likelihood that people will experience such strains increases with the effort they devote to caregiving. This link, furthermore, is independent of the tendency for marital strain to be positively associated with age. Parallel results are found in the other domains as well. In the case of conflicts between work and caregiving, it is apparent that women more than men are likely to be exposed to this strain; once again, however, involvement still has an independent part in the generation of this strain. In the case of the constriction of social and leisure activities, involvement has a similar function, independent of the significant contributions of gender and income to this life strain.

These findings clearly point to the conclusion that the demands of caregiving on time and energy have effects that reach into multiple corners of people's lives, even among family members who are not the principal caregivers. We have here evidence in support of observations that stressors in one domain tend to beget stressors in other domains, a process referred to as stress proliferation (Pearlin, 1989). This process helps to account for the fact that those who at first experience one hardship are likely to come to be surrounded by a varied constellation of secondary hardships. Indeed, it will be seen that these secondary hardships may constitute a more direct threat to well-being than the condition from which they stemmed.

C. The Health Consequences of Caregiving Involvement and Role Disruption

The test to determine if circumstances thought to be stressful actually are stressful has traditionally relied on establishing their associations with a wide variety of indicators of health and well-being, which in this analysis are symptoms of depression and self-rated health. In Table 13.4 we focus on the possible effects on depression of both the extent of people's caregiving involvements and the disruptive impact they were shown to have on

Table 13.4
Role Disruption and Depression

Independent variables	I. $(N = 124)$	II. $(N = 124)$	III. $(N = 84)$	IV. $(N = 88)$	V. $(N = 109)$	VI. $(N = 123)$
Socioeconomic characteristics						
Age	0.008	0.007	0.001	0.005	0.007	0.006
Race (white)	0.039	0.030	0.003	−0.082	0.116	0.023
Gender (women)	0.218*	0.219*	0.135	0.095	0.097	0.178
Income	−0.029	−0.016	−0.014	−0.012	−0.020	−0.012
Education	−0.055	−0.057	−0.087	−0.099	−0.070	−0.072
Extent of caregiving involvement		0.010**	0.003	0.007	0.005	0.008
Disruption of marital role			0.275*			
Disruption of parenting role				0.248*		
Work–caregiving conflict					0.331***	
Constriction of social life						0.093
R^2	0.108	0.165	0.209	0.258	0.276	0.176

$^*p \leq .05$; $^{**}p \leq .01$; $^{***}p \leq .001$.

the various domains of activity. As in the preceding table, we regress depression separately on the different roles because of the variations in role incumbency among the respondents. This is reflected in the different Ns in models III, IV, and V of the table.

The first model shows that women more than men tend to express depressive affect, a finding certainly consistent with research literature (e.g., Aneshensel et al., 1991). As expected, the extent of caregiver involvement, entered in the second model, is also significantly related to depression. What can be noted in the following three models is that sheer involvement in caregiving no longer matters to depression once role disruptions are taken into account. Whether we consider marital, parental, or work–caregiver strains, it is seen in each instance that it is the disruptions that may occur in these important life domains that contribute to depression. These findings should not be interpreted to mean that the extent of involvement in caregiving activities is of no consequence to depression; to the contrary, it is very important. Its importance,

however, is indirect, exercised through its impact on the three roles that were observed in Table 13.3. Indeed, this can be viewed as an excellent example of an initial set of demands and hardships resulting in secondary stressors that now stand as a greater risk than the primary stressors to well-being. It can further be noted that the constriction of social and leisure life is different in this respect from role disruptions. That is, although constriction increases with involvement, it is apparent that it does not contribute to depression.

Table 13.5 substitutes self-rated health for depression as an indicator of well-being but in other respects follows the same analytic lines as the preceding table. As in the case of depression, those most engaged in caregiving activities also tend to rate their health more negatively, with the relevance of gender and education varying across the models. What can be underscored once again is that the statistical significance of the relationship between the level of involvement and this indicator of health is erased when the degree of disruption in the marital and par-

Table 13.5
Role Disruption and Self-Rated Physical Health

Independent variables	I. ($N = 124$)	II. ($N = 124$)	III. ($N = 84$)	IV. ($N = 88$)	V. ($N = 109$)	VI. ($N = 123$)
Socioeconomic characteristics						
Age	−0.009	−0.007	−0.002	−0.008	−0.001	−0.008
Race (white)	0.420	0.434	0.322	0.526	0.053	0.454
Gender (women)	0.088	0.086	0.389	0.472*	0.097	0.171
Income	0.006	−0.018	0.000	−0.001	−0.026	−0.024
Education	0.017	0.176*	0.174	0.274**	0.110	0.203*
Extent of caregiving involvement		−0.018**	−0.003	−0.008	−0.027***	−0.014*
Disruption of marital role			−0.497**			
Disruption of parenting role				−0.409*		
Work–caregiving conflict					−0.317*	
Constriction of social life						−0.157
R^2	0.065	0.125	0.173	0.224	0.211	0.137

*$p \leq .05$; **$p \leq .01$; ***$p \leq .001$.

ental roles is brought into the equation. In the case of work–caregiving conflict, the extent of caregiving involvement remains independently significant. In each instance, the greater the role disruption, the lower the health rating. The effect of caregiving on self-rated health, therefore, is channeled largely through the problems and stressors it creates in the enactment of established roles. In this regard, the constriction of social and leisure life again plays no appreciable part.

V. Implications

One of the features of the sample from which this analysis is drawn has important implications for the intergenerational reach and power of family caregiving. Although all of the adult children in the sample have a parent with AD, and most give at least some assistance to that parent, none is a primary caregiver. As described earlier, each has a parent who is taking major responsibility for the care of the other, impaired, parent. Despite having a principal caregiver standing between them and their impaired parent, many adults still face conditions that place their well-being at risk. Even being at some distance from the moment-to-moment care that may be required by a loved one with a progressive dementia, as most of them are, they may nevertheless be drawn into a process that leads to a build-up of stressors. Observing this process in a group of secondary caregivers helps us to appreciate even more the health-threatening hardships experienced by principal caregivers, usually older spousal caregivers.

However, to some extent, our sample must be considered as highly selective. Because the adult children were named by the parental caregiver as most involved in sharing the care of the impaired member, we are unable to consider other children who may also be in the family but who do less or no caregiving. The selectivity of the sample is most easily seen in the fact that fully 60% of the designated children are women, although there is no reason to suppose that this represents the gender distribution of adult children in the families recruited to the study. It must be assumed that those who were named also are different from those who were not in other characteristics and dispositions. There are probably other, less discernible selective factors also at work. Whatever additional selective factors may be at work, it needs to be recognized that our findings cannot be generalized to all children but only to those who are identified as the most actively involved. Though there are differences in caregiving involvement among the adult children identified by their caregiving parent, there are probably greater differences in this regard between those so identified and those not.

Our analysis was designed both to explore the penetration across generational lines of the effects of AD and especially to identify the pathways through which this penetration takes place. At the outset of the analysis it was assumed that people are not uniformly affected by having a parent with AD. One of the keys to this difference is the extent to which children are involved in providing assistance to their impaired parent. The kind of assistance that children give is a less important element of involvement than the sheer amount of time they devote to the assistance. Whether it is direct hands-on care or simply watching over the parent, for example, is of less relevance than the extent to which they may become embedded in the role at the expense of other roles and interests, what Skaff and Pearlin (1992) have described as role engulfment.

Among the factors that constrain the extent of caregiving involvement is the sheer number of other roles of which one is an incumbent, with fewer commitments to major social roles enabling greater involvement in caregiving. Being a parent, a spouse, or being employed can impose limitations on the time one is able to give to the welfare of an impaired parent, quite aside from one's motivation to be helpful. Of the roles we examined, the most discretionary is that of work—one does not as easily reduce commitments to being a parent or a spouse—and we saw that those who left or reduced employment are more involved than others. A final constraining condition pertains to the concerns that adult children have about their own economic status and their financial needs. We assume that people's concerns about their ability to satisfy these needs functions to divert time and energy from caregiving activities.

However, many people do take on caregiving activities, even in the face of these constraining factors. Where a loved one needs the help of family members, one may very well feel there is no choice. But regardless of the motivation, the assumption of caregiving activities is likely to disrupt established roles and interests and the time and effort that had been allocated to them. As people become more engulfed, there is a commensurate need for them to restructure their lives. If one's life is already full, as it is for many, taking on an additional role is apt to have deleterious repercussions across the entire organization of one's life.

Such restructuring can be painful for people when it entails separation from strong commitments that are part of self-identity. To reduce or erase these commitments can engender feelings of loss and conflict. Yet, if caregivers attempt to maintain their ordinary activities, they are left vulnerable to a sense of having let down a loved one. Whichever way they turn, caregivers run the risk of abandoning internalized commitments to salient activities and identities. One can find one's self in a situation from

which it is difficult to emerge unscathed. Given the social and cultural salience of the roles we have examined here, it would be surprising, indeed, if their disruption had no adverse effects on well-being. In fact, with the exception of the constriction of social and leisure life, they do. In each instance, the disruption that the adult children experience is directly related to both their symptoms of depression and their self-rated health.

Research into caregiving is important for its own sake. As is widely recognized, the population of both impaired elders and those providing care for them is likely to grow steeply in coming decades. The identification of the exigencies that confront both the donors and recipients of care should prepare the society for dealing more effectively with what can be anticipated in the future.

Yet, the importance of research into caregiving stems from other sources as well. We refer particularly to its standing at the intersection of a number of basic social and behavioral issues lying outside of an immediate concern with caregiving and its usefulness in illuminating these issues. It informs us about the powerful bonds that exist among family members, the extension of those bonds across generational lines, and the sustained solidarity in the absence of manifest reciprocity (George, 1986). It also provides a view of the integration of multiple roles located in different institutional domains, such as family and occupation, and the conditions under which the possession of multiple roles becomes a health liability rather than a benefit.

Perhaps most of all, the population of long-term caregivers stands in some respects as a general model for a variety of situations giving rise to chronic demands and hardships. Research into this population, therefore, can help to inform us of the health consequences of life experiences that are enduringly difficult and to reveal the mechanisms contributing to these consequences. Although AD and the demands it imposes on caregivers are in some respects distinctively different from those found in other situations, much of what we are able to learn from studies of this population is relevant to different circumstances and different populations. Especially salient in this regard is the tendency for problems in one life domain to proliferate in the form of conflicts and losses to other domains. Some people obviously are in situations or have the resources that enable them to restructure their lives in ways that minimize or block this process. But for others, there may be a clustering of stressors that develops beyond the arena of caregiving. Under these conditions, their health and well-being come under even greater risk. We agree with Moen et al. (1994) that caregiving is not a discrete and contained set of activities. Like other situations with which people must often deal, caregiving is more accurately appreciated as the beginning of a process that encompasses many components capable of affecting people across a substantial arc of their life course.

Acknowledgments

This work was supported by Merit Award MH 42122 and AG 1746 (Leonard I. Pearlin, P.I.).

References

Aneshensel, C. S., Rutter, C. M., & Lachenbruch, P. A. (1991). Social structure, stress, and mental health: Competing conceptual and analytic models. *American Sociological Review*, 56, 166–178.

Bengtson, V. L., Burgess, E. O., & Parrott, T. M. (1997). Theory, explanation, and a third generation of theoretical development in social gerontology. *Journals of Gerontology: Social Sciences, 52B*, S72–S88.

Bengtson, V. L., & Kuypers, J. A. (1985). The family support cycle: Psychosocial issues in the aging family. In J. M. A. Munnichs, P. Mussen, & E. Olbrich (Eds.), *Life span and change in a gerontological perspective* (pp. 61–77). New York: Academic Press.

Bengtson, V. L., Mangen, D. J., & Landry, P. J. (1984). The multi-generational family: Concepts and findings. In V. Garms Homolova, E. M. Hoerning, & D. Schaeffer (Eds.), *Intergenerational relationships* (pp. 63–80). Lewiston, NY: C. J. Hogrefe.

Bengtson, V. L., & Schrader, S. S. (1982). Parent-child relations. In D. Mangen & W. Peterson (Eds.), *Handbook of research instruments in social gerontology* (Vol. 2, pp. 115–185). Minneapolis: University of Minnesota Press.

Brody, E. (1990). *Women in the middle: Their parent-care years.* New York: Springer Publishing Company.

Derogatis, L. R., Lipman, R. S., Covi, L., & Rickles, K. (1971). Neurotic symptom dimensions. *Archives of General Psychiatry, 24*, 454–464.

Dobson, J. E., & Dobson, R. L. (1985). The sandwich generation: Dealing with aging parents. *Journal of Counseling and Development, 63*, 572–574.

George, L. (1986). Caregiver burden: Conflict between norms of reciprocity and solidarity. In K. A. Pillemer & R. S. Wolf (Eds.), *Elder abuse: Conflict in the family* (pp. 67–92). Dover, MA: Auburn House.

George, L. (1990). Caregiver stress studies – There really is more to learn. *The Gerontologist, 30*, 580–581.

Idler, E., & Kasl, S. (1991). Health perceptions and survival: Do global evaluations of health status really predict mortality? *Journal of Gerontology: Social Sciences, 46*, S55–S65.

Jackson, P. B. (1997). Role occupancy and minority mental health. *Journal of Health and Social Behavior, 38*, 237–255.

Johnson, C. L., & Catalano, D. J. (1981). The childless elderly and their family supports. *The Gerontologist, 21*, 610–618.

Johnson, C. L., & Catalano, D. J. (1983). A longitudinal study on family supports to impaired elderly. *The Gerontologist, 23*, 612–618.

Mannheim, K. (1952). The problem of generations. In D. Kecskemeti (Ed.), *Essays on the sociology of knowledge* (pp. 276–322). London: Routledge & Kegan Paul.

Menaghan, E. (1989). Role changes and psychological well-being: Variations in effects by gender and role repertoire. *Social Forces*, 67, 693–714.

Miller, D. A. (1981). The "sandwich" generation: Adult children of the aging ["sandwiched" between their aging parents and their own maturing children]. *Social Work*, 26, 419–423.

Moen, P., Robison, J., & Fields, V. (1994). Women's work and caregiving roles: A life course approach. *Journal of Gerontology: Social Sciences*, 49, S176–S186.

Nichols, L. S., & Junk, V. (1997). The sandwich generation: Dependency, proximity, and task assistance needs of parents. *Journal of Family and Economic Issues*, 18, 299–326.

Parsons, T. (1949). The kinship system of the contemporary United States. In T. Parsons (Ed.), *Essays in sociological theory, pure and applied* (pp. 233–250). Glencoe, IL: Free Press.

Pearlin, L. I. (1989). The sociological study of stress. *Journal of Health and Social Behavior*, 30, 241–156.

Pearlin, L. I., & Aneshensel, C. S. (1994). Caregiving: The unexpected career. *Social Justice Research*, 7, 373–390.

Pearlin, L. I., Aneshensel, C. S., & LeBlanc, A. J. (1997). The forms and mechanisms of stress proliferation: The case of AIDS caregivers. *Journal of Health and Social Behavior*, 38, 223–236.

Pearlin, L. I., & Johnson, J. S. (1977). Marital status, life strains, and depression. *American Sociological Review*, 42, 704–715.

Pearlin, L. I., & Lieberman, M. A. (1979). Social sources of emotional distress. *Research in Community and Mental Health*, 1, 217–248.

Pearlin, L. I., Lieberman, M., Menaghan, E., & Mullen, J. T. (1981). The stress process. *Journal of Health and Social Behavior*, 22, 337–356.

Raphael, D., & Schlesinger, B. (1993). Caring for elderly parents and adult children living at home: Interactions of a sandwich generation family. *Social Work Research & Abstracts*, 29, 3–8.

Shanas, E. (1979). The family as a support system in old age. *The Gerontologist*, 19, 169–174.

Shanas, E., & Streib, G. F. (1968). *Old people in three industrialized societies*. New York: Atherton.

Simon, R. (1995). Gender, multiple roles, role meaning, and mental health. *Journal of Health and Social Behavior*, 36, 182–194.

Skaff, M. M., & Pearlin, L. I. (1992). Caregiving: Role engulfment and the loss of self. *The Gerontologist*, 32, 656–664.

Sussman, M.B. (1953). The help pattern in the middle classs family. *American Sociological Review*, 18, 22–28.

Sussman, M.B. (1959). The isolated nuclear family: Fact or fiction? *Social Problems*, 6, 333–340.

Thoits, P. (1983). Multiple identities and psychological well-being: A reformulation and test of the social isolation hypothesis. *American Sociological Review*, 48, 174–187.

Thoits, P. (1986). Multiple identities: Examining gender and marital status differences in distress. *American Sociological Review*, 51, 258–272.

Zarit, S. (1989). Do we need another "stress and caregiving" study? *The Gerontologist*, 29, 147–148.

Zarit, S., Reeves, K., & Bach-Peterson, J. (1980). Relatives of impaired elderly: Correlates of feelings of burden. *The Gerontologist*, 20, 649–655.

Fourteen

Work and Retirement

John C. Henretta

I. Introduction

The work and retirement patterns of the older population have become a topic of intense policy concern in most industrialized nations in recent years, partly motivated by the trends of earlier labor force exit and population aging (e.g., Bosworth & Burtless, 1998; Gruber & Wise, 1997). In the United States, much of this attention has focused on the looming retirement of the large post-war birth cohorts beginning in the second decade of this century. Yet the current emphasis on the imminent retirement of the baby boom is at least partly misplaced. The postwar baby boom is conventionally defined as the 1946 to 1964 birth cohorts, and those born at its peak in the late 1950s (Easterlin, 1978; Easterlin, Schaeffer, & Macunovich 1993) are just now entering their early forties. Before these large cohorts retire, they will be older workers and will be a numerically important component of the labor force for many years—even ignoring the possible rise in the average age at which workers retire that many observers speculate will occur. Hence the second half of the work career will have a numerical importance that equals the significance of this career segment for affecting older workers' security, the timing of their retirement, and their financial status in retirement.

The growing importance of the second half of the work career coincides with other trends that affect the late career. There has been extensive scholarly interest during the last decade in the general hypothesis of increasing heterogeneity in the pattern of individual work careers and retirement pathways. There is also continuing public policy interest in extending the working lives of the baby boom to reduce the publicly borne cost of their retirement. Both interests are relevant to the latter part of the work career as well as to the retirement transition. Although workplace and career changes may have supported earlier and more variable retirement, the concern for extending working lives has gone beyond discussion, as illustrated by the gradual rise in Social Security "normal" retirement age for cohorts born in 1938 and later that was legislated in 1983. What will be the result of the seeming conflict between workplace trends that have favored earlier retirement and current public policy initiatives designed to delay it?

As in any period of extensive change, there is only partial agreement on the description and amount of recent change and much less on its significance. Yet, despite the hyperbole often attached to demographic, workplace, and public policy trends, there is little doubt that the combination of large cohorts of midlife workers, changing institutional patterns of employment, and public policy initiatives designed to delay retirement create compelling research issues.

Retirement is notoriously difficult to define, and analysts have adopted a number of different approaches (see O'Rand & Henretta, 1999). This chapter will use a simple conceptual definition: retirement is used as a shorthand term to refer to a labor force exit that is not reversed for a substantial period of time. This definition will be familiar to most analysts, though some will find it unsatisfactory for a variety of reasons.

This chapter focuses on research addressing the changing environment faced by successive cohorts as they pursue employment past midlife and enter retirement in the early part of the 21 century. This focus complements rather than replaces the chapters on work and retirement in the two editions of this handbook published in the 1990s. These two previous chapters gave extensive attention to the individual retirement decision (Quinn & Burkhauser, 1990) and the historical development and social context of public and private pension systems (Quadagno & Hardy, 1996). These topics are not considered in any detail here, and interested readers should consult the earlier editions.

After discussing changing patterns of labor force participation in the next section, this chapter examines individuation of the life course and changes in employment. Next, it analyzes evidence for the changing institutional structure of employment and late career employment changes. The final sections of the chapter

discuss the possibility of increased later-life employment in the future and possible research directions for the coming decade.

II. Trends in Labor Force Participation

The level of labor force participation—the proportion of the population either working or actively looking for work—provides one standard measure of work and retirement patterns. Table 14.1 illustrates the main trends for men and women in prime age categories for retirement: ages 60–64 and 65–69. It shows the well-known decline in men's labor force participation before 1985, in both age categories, and relative stability since then. These pre-1985 declines were particularly large for men aged 60 and older, but they extended to younger ages as well. In recent years, however, there has been a change in this trend. Since the mid-1980s, labor force participation rates for older men have stabilized at their new, lower level. There has even been a slight but noticeable increase, particularly among men aged 65 and older. Women's patterns show a small upward trend in both age categories, particularly between 1985 and 1995. The 1994 redesign of the Current Population Survey (the source of these data) may have contributed to the increase in the measured labor force participation after age 65 (Fullerton, 1995; Gendell, 1998; Polivka, 1994), suggesting the need for caution in interpretation of the increases in the older age group shown in the Table.

A. Labor Force Participation and Individual Careers

There are a number of very good reasons that labor force participation measures play a central role in discussions of work and retirement. Generally comparable

Table 14.1
Percent of Men and Women in the Labor Force by
Age, 1975–1999[a]

Year	Men		Women	
	Age 60–64	Age 65–69	Age 60–64	Age 65–69
1975	65.5	31.7	33.2	14.5
1985	55.6	24.5	33.4	13.5
1995	53.2	27.0	38.0	17.5
1999	54.8	28.5	38.8	18.4

[a]Source: U.S. Bureau of Labor Statistics, (1988; 1996; 2000)

data are available over many years in the United States, and similar time-series measures are available for other countries. Moreover, labor force participation is an important indicator of aggregate trends and can tell us a great deal about the status of the population at one time or change over time.

It is particularly important, however, to distinguish labor force participation rates and trends from the individual work and retirement careers that underlie them. Some reasons for the difference in concepts are obvious and well appreciated. For example, being out of the labor force does not necessarily conform to an analyst's or an older person's concept of retirement. More basic, however, are the individual career events that produce labor force participation. Three individual-level processes—mortality, labor force exit, and reentry—affect labor force participation rates, but the aggregate measure does not identify their relative contributions (Gendell & Siegel, 1992; Hayward, Crimmins, & Wray, 1994). For example, declines in mortality may increase the proportion who ever retire and raise the mean age of exit from the labor force to retirement (Reimers, 1976) while not affecting age-specific labor force participation. In addition, labor force participation is a static measure of status, although the individual may occupy different states over time. Labor

force participation at any one point in time results from flows out of the labor force as well as flows into it. The reentry issue is the topic of a significant debate because higher levels of reentry would have substantial effects on the typical individual late career but would not necessarily be revealed by labor force participation rates. Although it is clear that returns to the labor force decline with age and are fairly rare after age 65, there is disagreement over the substantive significance of reentry. Some analysts attach relatively little substantive significance to reentry (Hurd, 1990; Rust, 1990), while others accord it a more important position (Hayward, Crimmins, & Wray, 1994).

B. Explanations for Labor Force Participation Change

There is general agreement that the rising level of income and wealth (Costa, 1998), the level of pensions and Social Security (Ippolito, 1990, 1997), and disability benefits (Henretta & Lee, 1996) play a role in the long-term decline in U.S. men's labor force participation. It is particularly important to allow that different factors may be responsible for declines at different ages (Casey, 1989; Henretta, 1992). For example, Anderson, Gustman, and Steinmeier (1997) find that pension and Social Security changes in the 1970s and 1980s account for about one-quarter of the change in labor force participation for men in their early 60s but none of the change for those over 65.

The significance of the recent stability in men's labor force participation is uncertain. Labor force participation has declined considerably over the long run, and it is unrealistic to extrapolate past declines indefinitely into the future. For example, in a heterogeneous working population, some workers will be less affected by further change in the push-and-pull factors that have led to past declines;

this process will produce a floor effect at some point, making further reductions more difficult. On the other hand, some analysts point to changes in the environment surrounding work and retirement that could have the effect of stemming or reversing the decline in labor force participation. These include the desire of workers to retain employer-provided health insurance, the growth of defined contribution pensions, reduction in Social Security work disincentives at later ages, the federal law abolishing mandatory retirement in 1986, and the low unemployment environment of the 1990s (Ruhm, 1996; Quinn, 1997, 1998).

Women's labor force participation trends are more complex to interpret. The increase in participation at later ages is strongly influenced by cohort trends, as higher midlife levels of labor force participation by more recent cohorts produce higher participation at later ages. Although this cohort change hides a trend toward earlier net withdrawal, women's trend toward earlier exit also appears to have halted (Gendell & Siegel, 1992; O'Rand & Henretta, 1999).

As noted earlier, aggregate labor force participation levels do not necessarily provide insight into the process of work exit and reentry. Hence, stability in labor force participation does not necessarily indicate a lack of change in late career and retirement patterns. The next section examines these employment pathways.

III. Individuation of the Life Course and Changing Employment

The modern tripartite division of the life course into education, employment, and retirement segments (Kohli, 1987; Kohli & Meyer, 1986) is produced by the institutions surrounding employment and the welfare state that produce regular, age-related transitions from one segment to another. According to the sociological "institutionalization of the life course" hypothesis, the long-term trend has been for individual lives to have become more organized along the lines of this tripartite division as individuals have become increasingly subject to relatively uniform age-based rules found in the institutions of the workplace and the state (Anderson, 1985; Kohli, 1987; Mayer & Schoepflin, 1989). The clustering of retirement ages around the Social Security retirement age is one illustration of the effect of age-based rules. However, a number of analysts argue that recent change in employment and retirement institutions has eroded the institutionalized life course, producing a trend toward greater individuation—that is, an increase in within-cohort heterogeneity in the pattern of the late work career and transition to retirement. This account was originally developed in the context of Germany and France, where the strong and uniform influence of state pension systems on labor force exit has been supplanted by the more variable effects of unemployment and disability mechanisms (Guillemard, 1991; Jacobs, Kohli, & Rein, 1991). The argument has been applied to the United States and Britain, as well (Anderson, 1985; Henretta, 1992; Guillemard & Rein, 1993), though it applies in a weaker form. In these latter two countries, the uniform public pension system does not dominate labor force exit as it once did in continental Europe (Kohli, 1994).

There is considerable evidence for variability in retirement pathways. The traditionally strong role played by employment-based institutions in U.S. retirement timing (Casey, 1989) is an important factor producing this individuation. For example, some defined benefit pension plans provide strong incentives to leave the firm before age 62 and even as early as age 55 (Wise, 1997), but such eligibility is highly variable depending on the firm and the individual's tenure. Although the more uniform rules governing Social Security retirement benefit eligibility could affect labor force behavior before age 62, there is some evidence in the economic literature that workers are liquidity constrained (Hurd, 1996)—that is, it is difficult for them to borrow against future benefits—and therefore the effect of future benefits is reduced. Highly variable workplace institutions and processes are likely responsible for the long slow decline in labor force participation before age 62, whereas the uniform age-based rules of Social Security (plus workplace rules coordinated with Social Security) contribute to faster exit after this age (Henretta, 1992).

Support for the hypothesis of *increasing* individuation, however, is more limited. Available evidence, which is discussed below, includes the changing nature and uses of pension plans, higher job loss rates among older than younger workers, declining older men's job tenure, use of short-term bridge jobs, returns to work after exit, and general blurring of the work-to-retirement transition. These changes provide some indication that late career patterns are more variable than in the past along a number of dimensions.

IV. Changing Pension Types and Uses

The changing structure of pensions provides one piece of evidence that age structuring of employment is eroding, though the reasons leading to pension change are diverse (Clark & McDermed, 1990). Pension plans in the United States can be divided into two types: defined benefit and defined contribution plans. There is extensive variation within each type of plan (Mitchell, 1999). Defined benefit plans are ones in which the pension plan rules specify a formula, using some combination of years of service, final salary, and age, to determine a promised benefit. Individual workers accrue a right to receive the formula amount at the age specified in the plan. Almost all defined benefit plans are solely employer funded (Mitchell, 1999), so that the employer bears full responsibility for paying the promised amount. These pensions discourage employers from hiring older workers because of the age-related pension costs, while the greater benefit accrual at later ages could discourage workers from leaving the job. To deal with this latter issue, the benefit formulas in defined benefit pensions often include strong incentives to exit relatively early (Wise, 1997). Use of defined benefit pensions in this way allows employers one way to end seniority-protected employment (Brown, 1997; Hurd, 1997). Defined benefit pensions induce early exit from the job among a segment of the work force and introduce heterogeneity into the late career.

Defined contribution plans are ones in which employees usually contribute, have some control over investments, and bear investment risk. In these plans, individual workers accrue money in an individual, separate account, with the amount dependent on the contribution level and the individual's own investment returns. Employees may have the option of participating and employers may match a contribution (Mitchell, 1999). Because of this structure, defined contribution plans do not contain age-specific retirement incentives, though increasing pension wealth will tend to encourage retirement (Gustman, Mitchell, & Steinmeier, 1995). Although there are several types of defined contribution plans (Mitchell, 1999), 401k plans that require a voluntary employee contribution now predominate (Clark & Schieber, 1998).

In the last quarter-century, the number of defined benefit plans has declined among employers with fewer than 100 employees, while the number of defined contribution plans has risen. Larger employers have maintained defined benefit plans but have also added defined contribution plans, often as a supplement. Among smaller employers, the defined contribution plan is typically the only pension plan (Mitchell & Schieber, 1998). The overall effect has been a rise in the relative prevalence of defined contribution plans; by the early 1990s, equal numbers of workers participated in defined benefit and defined contribution pensions (Ippolito, 1997; Mitchell, Gordon, & Twinney, 1997).

Pension plans have a range of implications for workers during their careers. They may affect decisions about changing jobs, with the effect varying by age. Defined benefit plans are part of an employer policy that has the effect of encouraging long tenure. Gustman and Steinmeier (1995) show that the structure of defined benefit plans typically discourage leaving the employer before eligibility for retirement, and the incentive may be very large in the years approaching the early retirement age; however they find that this disincentive is not responsible for the lower turnover among young and midcareer workers in firms with defined benefit plans. Defined contribution plans do not contain specific age-structured incentives to remain or leave an employer, though they may serve to retain good employees (Ippolito, 1997).

The growth of defined contribution plans is part of the individuation of the life course. Their lack of specific seniority-based incentives means that institutional structures play a smaller part in determining age at retirement. A second factor is the greater variation in accruals likely to arise in defined contribution plans. Of course, incentives in defined benefit plans are also highly variable dependent on coverage, the specifics of the plan, and the individual's lifetime employment career pattern. The difference arises in that defined contribution plans tend to give workers more direct control over retirement accumulations so that workers with the same tenure in a particular plan may have different outcomes. Concern for the increased heterogeneity induced by the switch to defined contribution pensions has led to investigation of a variety of issues. The results of this research provide some insight into the process of individuation. Higher income workers are more likely to participate in 401k plans (Clark & Schieber, 1998), and two aspects of employer behavior—providing education programs about investment and providing an employer match—increase participation rates (Bernheim, 1998). Lower income workers (Goodfellow & Schieber, 1997) and women (Hinz, McCarthy, & Turner, 1997) make more conservative investment decisions, a factor that may reduce their potential final account balances. However, Poterba, Venti, and Wise (1999) find that preretirement withdrawals will have little effect on final accumulations.

One way that employers produce additional heterogeneity in exit timing while still maintaining traditional seniority-based incentives, such as defined benefit plans, is through the use of special early-retirement incentives. These offers are sometimes called early retirement "windows" because they are typically offered for a limited period of time in order to reduce the number of higher wage workers in certain job categories. Early retirement incentives may take the form of one-time cash payments, increases in lifetime pension payments, or supplements lasting until the employee reaches Social Security retirement age (Brown, 1997; Mutschler, 1996). Many large firms used such plans in the 1980s and early 1990s (LaRock, 1992; Meier, 1986; U.S. General Accounting Office, 1990), and Brown (1997) presents evidence that the proportion of workers offered such incentives increased over the 1989–1994 period.

Although most data on incentive plans focus on the firms that offer them, some very useful data on their impact on decisions to exit from a specific job come from an analysis of the Health and Retirement Study (HRS) data by Charles Brown (1997). Nearly 9% of male and female workers aged 51–61 in 1992 reported having received at least one early retirement incentive offer. Slightly more than half of those who had received an offer had accepted one. Between 1992 and 1994, such offers accounted for 10% of all job departures, indicating they are an important component of labor turnover. Brown also finds that those who receive such offers are more likely to be in high-wage industries, be in managerial or professional occupations (see, also, Mutschler, 1996), average over 20 years tenure, be covered by union contracts, and participate in a defined benefit pension.

The acceptance of an early retirement incentive does not necessarily indicate retirement. Brown (1997) found that 45% of those who had accepted an offer anytime in the past were employed in 1994 (when they were ages 53 to 63), and an additional 13% were self-employed. However, they worked fewer hours and at lower wages than they had on their pre-incentive job. In a similar vein, Herz (1995) finds increasing rates of employment among pension recipients under age 65 between 1984 and 1993, much of it part-time. Although her data are not limited to those receiving an early retirement incentive, they do indicate that early pension receipt does not necessarily mean permanent labor force withdrawal. These patterns of early pension receipt and later employment certainly have contributed to the number of workers who end their careers in "bridge jobs" that span the time between exit from a long-term job and final retirement and may contribute to the rate of reentry into the labor force. The lower wages typically provided by bridge jobs suggest an undesirable shift from a "good" to a "bad" job. However, early retirement incentive programs may carry a very different connotation. Those who accept retirement window offers are likely to see their future prospects for increased earnings with the firm more pessimistically than those who reject offers, and about half of workers reject offers (Brown, 1997). Continuation of long-term employment with one firm is not a "good" job if the prospects for earnings growth and security are poor. Early pension window acceptance combined with later work may offer an overall better opportunity.

V. Late Career Employment Changes

A. Age Discrimination in Employment

Since the removal of an upper age limit from the 1967 Age Discrimination in Employment Act (ADEA) in 1986 (Hood, 1998), employees over age 40 have had legal protection against discrimination in hiring, firing, promotion, and wages. The 1990 Older Workers Benefit Protection Act (OWBPA) extended these protections to the provision of employee benefits, but also allowed early retirement incentive programs that are "voluntary" and "consistent" with the ADEA (Ventrell-Monsees, 1999). Other legislation also protectively governs treatment of older workers (Mitchell, 1999). Although some legal analysts view the overall effect of these laws as excessively advantaging older workers who have already benefited from increasing seniority protection (Issacharoff & Harris, 1997), others argue that the conservative trend in the judiciary and the techniques used by employers to reduce parts of their workforce mean that current protection is inadequate to ensure that older workers receive the expected benefits of an implicit long-term employment contract in which rewards are concentrated at career end (Minda, 1997).

Age discrimination may occur in hiring decisions and in treatment of current, often long-term, employees. Citing a number of sources from the 1980s, Issacharoff and Harris (1997) argue that most ADEA cases arise from termination of employment, whereas much smaller numbers arise from other claims by current employees. A very small proportion of cases—under 10%—arise from failure to hire. They argue that the disparity in cases is related to the characteristics of discharge cases and the legal process, not an absence of discrimination in hiring. Terminated workers may be more motivated to pursue a lawsuit because of the difficulty they are likely to experience in finding new employment and the resentment caused by termination from long-term employment. In addition, finding a lawyer may be easier because termination cases are more lucrative and easier to prove than failure to hire cases. Because of the disparity in cases, they argue that the law has primarily affected long-term employees, not job seekers.

B. Job Loss and Finding New Employment

Under current judicial interpretation, age discrimination law does not prohibit some behaviors that have differential effects on older workers—for example, decisions made on the basis of health, seniority, or other factors that are conceptually separate from age (Hood, 1998; Issacharoff & Harris, 1997; Minda, 1997; Ventrell-Monsees, 1999). The finding of discrimination is a conclusion that is distinct from the fact of differential treatment or outcomes for older workers. Hence, in the following discussion focusing on the social scientific literature, the focus is on outcomes and possible explanations, not on whether such differences constitute discrimination.

Worker displacement—losing a job through a plant closing, a lack of work, or abolition of a position—is particularly consequential for older workers because of their limited possibilities of finding new employment at comparable wages. Data from the HRS indicate that involuntary job separation is more common among minorities and women (Flippen & Tienda, 2000). In the strong economy of the latter half of the 1990s, the 1998 Displaced Worker Supplement to the Current Population Survey indicated that older workers (those over age 55) were very slightly more likely to be displaced than younger workers. For example, although 2.9% of workers aged 20 and older with 3 years or more tenure were displaced in 1995 and 1996, 3.3% of workers aged 55–64 were displaced (Hipple, 1999). More telling is the outcome of job displacement. By early 1998, over 85% of displaced workers under age 55 were reemployed, compared to 64% of those aged 55–64. Among the older group, 28% had left the labor force, and unemployment rates were also higher than among younger workers. Given the selection involved in older workers who took new jobs, it is not particularly surprising that their median weeks without work were not much different than younger workers. However, among reemployed workers aged 45–54—most of whom are not yet eligible for pension payments and therefore were more likely to remain in the labor force—the median number of weeks without work were particularly high. Moreover, workers over aged 45 showed a decline in wages on their new job that was larger than those of younger age groups (Hipple, 1999); other research yields similar findings (Couch, 1998; Quinn, Burkhauser, & Myers, 1990).

These recent findings indicate a new trend because in the previous decade, the

1980s, older workers were less likely than younger workers to be displaced (Gardner, 1995). Hence the protection of older workers from job loss through seniority and other mechanisms appears to be less effective than in the past. However, it is difficult to interpret the significance of labor force exit after losing a job because some older workers are already eligible for Social Security or pension benefits (Osterman, 1988; Sheppard, 1991).

Hutchens (1988) finds that older workers take new jobs in a more limited set of industries and occupations than younger workers do. This outcome might result from older workers' being hired in jobs in which there is not a large investment in training because fixed costs of training can be spread over fewer years for older workers (see also Hurd, 1996). In addition, there is some evidence that employers who provide defined benefit pensions are less likely to hire older workers for entry-level positions because of the greater costs of pensions (Garen, Berger, & Scott, 1996). The wages available to older workers in new jobs may be lower than on the previous job because the previous wage reflected firm-specific experience (Hurd, 1996) or a long-term implicit contract that provides higher wages at career end (Straka, 1992). Neither of these seniority effects transfers to the new employer.

C. Changing Job Tenure and Bridge Jobs

Another indicator of individuation of late careers is recent data on job tenure of older workers. Over the 1983 to 1998 period, the proportion of men aged 40–65 who had worked 10 or more years with their current employer generally declined. That decline has continued in the most recent comparison between 1996 and 1998 except for men aged 55–64. Over the same period, the proportion of women with long tenure has been stable

or increased slightly (U.S. Bureau of Labor Statistics, 1998). The long-term decline in the proportion of men with long tenure and increasing proportions of women with more long-term jobs has produced a reduction in the gap between men and women in job tenure. This reduction is consistent with the observation that changes in the structure of employment have affected jobs typically held by men more than those typically held by women (Wilson, 1996).

Today slightly more than half of workers in their 50s have more than 10 years tenure with their current employer compared to about two thirds of men and slightly more than half of women in the 1980s. This finding suggests that final retirement for men will occur from a more short-term job than in the past. Shorter job tenure is not necessarily undesirable. For example, voluntary job changes will also produce shorter tenure, and, as noted, some early pension recipients return to the labor force. However, the difficulties that older workers experience in finding new employment with similar wages after they lose a job militates against a simple, benign view of declining job tenure.

Declining tenure among older male workers fits very well with the "bridge job" literature that began developing in the late 1980s and 1990s (Doeringer, 1990; Quinn et al., 1990; Ruhm, 1990). In contrast to the model of near-lifetime attachment to one employer—called the "career job"—the bridge job model argues that many workers hold jobs after the career job that span the time between career job exit and final retirement. Considerable research using data from the 1970s to the 1990s indicates that a substantial proportion of workers exit from jobs held for 10 or fewer years (Quinn, 1999; Quinn & Kozy, 1996; Ruhm, 1990).

There are a number of unsettled issues concerning the bridge job concept and research. First, it is not certain whether use of bridge jobs is increasing, and an increase would seem to be required if use of bridge jobs is to be evidence for changing late career patterns. The bridge job is certainly not a new pattern. Much of the early research indicating its existence utilized the Social Security Administration Longitudinal Retirement History Study, which collected data between 1969 and 1979 (e.g., Quinn et al., 1990; Ruhm, 1990). Research using more recent data (e.g., Quinn, 1999; Quinn & Kozy, 1996) confirms that the pattern continues. Four pieces of evidence, discussed earlier, suggest the possibility of an increase in bridge job incidence: the use of early pension incentives; the increase in the labor force participation of early pension recipients; the higher rate of job displacement among older compared to younger workers; and evidence of declining older men's tenure. A second issue is that it is not clear how existing data should be interpreted. Definitions of career and bridge jobs are arbitrary (Hurd, 1996; Quinn, 1999). Results can differ depending on the tenure chosen for the bridge job definition as well as a number of other analytic decisions each researcher must make. Hence it is difficult to say whether the phenomenon is "common." In addition, bridge jobs have widely different meanings to workers. For some they are a continuation of a work career characterized by short-term jobs. For others, they may reflect a desire to continue work even if it is not necessary. For still others, the bridge job reflects economic necessity (Quinn, 1999).

D. Blurred Exits and Labor Force Reentry

Mutchler, Burr, Pienta, and Massagli (1997) used Survey of Income and Program Participation (SIPP) data from the mid-1980s to estimate the incidence of "blurred" and "crisp" labor force patterns

over 28 months. Although most respondents experienced no change (remaining employed or out of the labor force continuously over the observation period), one-quarter of their respondents between ages 55 and 74 experienced some change, and more than half experienced a "blurred" exit. These authors defined a blurred exit as one in which a respondent had two changes in labor force status over the eight interviews, for example, an exit and reentry. The blurred pattern was particularly common before age 64.

Other studies provide some evidence of increasing incidence of blurred exits. Elder and Pavalko (1993) use the Terman data, a selected sample of high measured IQ children born in California between 1900 and 1920. They divide their sample into two 10-year birth cohorts that attained age 65 around 1970 and 1980, respectively. They find that one-step retirements decline and sporadic patterns increase. Sporadic patterns were ones in which work effort substantially declined and then increased and therefore included both exit and reentry patterns as well as an interval of part-time employment. Hayward, Crimmins, and Wray (1994) use January-to-January Current Population Survey data from 1972 and 1980 to show increasing rates of reentry over 1 year. As with Mutchler et al. (1997), reentry rates were higher before age 65.

An exit and reentry is likely to be reentry to a bridge job, and these patterns in the years before Social Security eligibility may also reflect job loss or early pension receipt. Hence the various indicators of heterogeneity are not independent of each other. Moreover, as is the case with bridge jobs, differences in definition may lead to different results. For example, Sum and Fogg (1990) find that reentry rates among men who had been out of the labor force during the previous year declined between 1974 and 1988. This finding is consistent with the generalization that reentry occurs quickly or not at all (Quinn, et al., 1990).

E. An Overall Evaluation

There is considerable evidence that the simple, uniform model of abrupt retirement from a long-term job is not an accurate description of the late career patterns of a substantial minority of older workers. Although, the data are not fully adequate for a comprehensive evaluation of change, there is some evidence of increasing late career heterogeneity: the growing prevalence of defined contribution pensions, higher rates of job loss among older compared to younger workers, some evidence that early retirement pension offers are becoming more common, increasing rates of employment among pension recipients, the decline in men's job tenure, and some evidence for increasing reentry rates. These trends suggest that the stability or slight increase in labor force participation in recent years should not be mistaken for a lack of change in the pattern of individual careers. Stable aggregate labor force participation is the sum of a number of increasingly diverse career and retirement pathways.

Does this evidence, together, mount a credible challenge to the idea of the highly institutionalized age-based life course? An affirmative answer is probably justified, but caution is in order because a number of factors qualify the results presented (O'Rand & Henretta, 1999). Most workers retire in one step (Rust, 1990), leaving the labor force from full-time work (Hurd, 1996). Further, estimates of bridge jobs are highly dependent on the definition of such jobs that researchers employ (Hurd, 1996), suggesting a great deal of subjectivity in the concept. Finally, the short intervals generally observed between exit and reentry (Quinn, et al., 1990) suggest that returns to the labor force are a short-term interruption that may not indicate a substantial blurring of work exit.

VI. Will Older Workers Remain in the Labor Force Longer?

Whether the future holds the prospect of older workers remaining in the labor force longer is a topic of great speculation. There are a number of demographic factors and cohort differences that may produce an increase in the demand for older workers (Besi & Kale, 1996; Henretta, 2000). By the second decade of the 21st century, the number of persons aged 60–64 will be larger, relative to numbers of younger persons than is true today. Hence employers will face a loss of trained workers larger relative to their work force than today and, given a particular level of demand for experienced workers, may be more anxious to retain them. In addition, cohort educational changes mean that older workers in their early 60s in the 1990s had noticeably lower levels of schooling than younger workers. That will no longer be true in 20 years because the high levels of schooling attained by the baby boom have not been surpassed by more recent cohorts.

In addition, the trend in public policy, both in the U.S. and Europe has been to encourage later retirement through changes in public retirement systems (O'Rand & Henretta, 1999). There are three U.S. changes that should have this effect: the increase in the Social Security full benefit eligibility age for cohorts born in 1938 and later, changes in the earnings test that allow Social Security recipients to earn more before losing benefits or without losing them at all, and greater increases in benefits for each year retirement is delayed after the normal retirement age—age 65 for cohorts born before 1938 (Quinn, 1999). The earlier discussed change in pension types from defined benefit to defined contribution pensions should also remove some of the incentive for early retirement. In addition, there is considerable evidence that some older workers would like to continue employment (Henretta, 2000). However, the design of most career jobs makes it difficult to take advantage of accumulated experience on a job but work fewer hours. Job changing, which is usually required to reduce work hours, normally involves a lower wage (Hurd, 1996).

Despite the likely convergence of factors favoring later retirement, it is probably wise to retain skepticism about the trend. It is important not to engage in crude demographic determinism in projecting increases in the demand for older workers because numbers are only one of many factors. Demographic trends will have the qualitative effect of increasing employers' desire to retain experienced workers, but it is not possible to say whether the quantitative effect will be trivial or significant. Even though older workers will have schooling levels equal to those of younger workers, employers may see the current training of older workers as outmoded. They may not wish to invest in new training because of the relatively short expected tenure of older workers. Moreover, employers have a number of options to deal with the retirement of experienced workers. They may invest in physical capital to use available labor more efficiently, depend on immigrant labor, or focus on drawing more women into the labor force (Schulz, 1995). Finally, public policy changes are likely to fall with very uneven effect. Examining wealth of households in the HRS, Moore and Mitchell (1997) found that Social Security wealth constitutes over three-fifths of the wealth in the bottom 30% of the wealth distribution and less than one-quarter for those in the top 30%. Greater pension wealth and financial assets at the higher end of the wealth distribution produce a smaller role for Social Security wealth—making it likely that changes in public policy will have highly variable effects. For example, Wise (1997) shows that the legislated

changes in Social Security would have very small effects on a worker covered by a typical defined benefit pension plan but would have very large effects on a worker without pension coverage. Hence, it is likely that changes in Social Security will have noticeable effects, but (unless there is widespread change in pension structures to harmonize them with Social Security changes) the effects will be highly variable and fall primarily on those without pensions or other significant financial assets.

There is also reason to maintain some skepticism that higher retirement ages in public policy will be maintained when they begin to bite. Although it is politically popular to reduce current disincentives to work at older ages, the legislation that reduces lifetime Social Security benefits through later retirement ages applies to the future. The U.S.-legislated change in Social Security has just begun to take effect—those reaching age 62 in 2000 (the 1938 birth cohort) will see their Social Security retirement age increased by one month (U.S. Social Security Administration, 1994). These provisions are likely to become less popular as they affect older workers—particularly less economically advantaged workers—in a substantially meaningful way. This point is pure speculation but is worth keeping in mind. (For a discussion of this issue with particular reference to Europe, see Guillemard & Rein, 1993; Kohli, 1992, 1994).

VII. Research and Data Issues for the Next Decade

There has always been extensive intra-cohort heterogeneity in work careers and retirement, but a number of trends have increased interest in these variable late-career trajectories. Relatively low labor force participation rates at ages before Social Security retirement eligibility indicates the important role of workplace institutions in structuring late-career and retirement patterns. The diversity of these institutions across employers is a force for variability in work and retirement. On balance, there is some evidence for increasing variability in work and retirement patterns that is consistent with a more variable institutional structure. Tracing these patterns of heterogeneity across successive cohorts and carefully linking them to changes in the workplace institutions has not been done, and this task constitutes an important research agenda for the next several years.

Public policy has traditionally been a force favoring more homogeneous retirement because of its relatively uniform rule structure. Yet, legislated changes in Social Security retirement ages are likely to create greater variability in retirement ages, dividing the working population along lines of pension coverage. Changes in firm pension policy or laws governing firm pensions could change this picture, but in their absence, the changing Social Security retirement age will favor increased intracohort variability in retirement. In examining the effects of public policy, it will be critical that analysts pay attention to the segmentation of older workers.

The final element in the mix is a changing age structure, which is now reflected in a large cohort of older workers—over age 40—that in future years will produce a larger retirement age cohort. This large cohort has the potential for major societal transformation in attitudes and opportunities. Will the large cohort of older workers lead to the design of attractive opportunities for continued work in career jobs, gradual retirement, or new part-time opportunities? Or will employers focus on one of the alternative sources of labor?

Until recently, researchers were limited in their analysis of these issues because available data reflected an earlier historical period. For example, much of our knowledge of bridge jobs is based on the Retirement History Study, data that reflect the environment of the 1970s. Awareness of the changing historical context of retirement (including the demographic, public policy, and social environments) led to funding of the HRS with its first data collection in 1992 (Juster & Suzman, 1995). There are several characteristics of the HRS that make it particularly useful to study retirement. The original data collection in 1992 included the 1931–1941 birth cohorts at ages 51–61 (and their spouses or partners, regardless of birth cohort), and the 1942–1947 birth cohorts were added in 1998 as they were entering their fifties. The 1948–1953 birth cohorts are tentatively scheduled to enter the sample in 2004 (Health and Retirement Study, 2000). The usefulness of this design is that it allows comparisons across cohorts as new developments rapidly change the environment faced by older workers.

Trends in the workplace, public policy, and age structure suggest that late career and retirement patterns will continue to change over the next two decades, perhaps at an accelerated pace. These issues are particularly compelling and exciting because they are integrally related to some of the major trends of the current era—population aging, increasing inequality and heterogeneity, and a changing work environment. Tracing the highly diverse outcomes of these processes presents an intriguing agenda for social scientists.

References

Anderson, M. (1985). The emergence of the modern life cycle in Britain. *Social History*, 10, 69–87.

Anderson, P. M., Gustman, A. L., & Steinmeier, T. L. (1997). *Trends in male labor force participation and retirement: Some evidence on the role of pensions and social security in the 1970s and 1980s* (Working

Paper 6208). Cambridge, MA: National Bureau of Economic Research.

Bernheim, B. D. (1998). Financial illiteracy, education, and retirement saving. In O.S. Mitchell & S. J. Schieber (Eds.), *Living with defined contribution pensions: Remaking responsibility for retirement* (pp. 38–68). Philadelphia, PA: University of Pennsylvania Press.

Besi, J. R., & Kale, B. D. (1996). Older workers in the 21st century: Active and educated, a case study. *Monthly Labor Review, 119*(6), 18–28.

Bosworth, B., & Burtless, G. (Eds.). (1998). *Aging societies: The global dimension*. Washington, DC: Brookings Institution Press.

Brown, C. (1997). *Early retirement windows: Evidence from the Health and Retirement Study*. Unpublished paper, University of Michigan, Ann Arbor.

Casey, B. (1989). Early retirement: The problems of "instrument substitution" and "cost shifting" and their implications for restructuring the process of retirement. In W. Schmähl (Ed.), *Redefining the process of retirement* (pp. 133–150). Berlin: Springer-Verlag.

Clark, R. L., & McDermed. A. A. (1990). *The choice of pension plans in a changing regulatory environment*. Washington, OC: American Enterprise Institute.

Clark, R. L., & Schieber, S. J. (1998). Factors affecting participation rates and contribution levels in 401k plans. In O. S. Mitchell & S. J. Schieber (Eds.), *Living with defined contribution pensions: Remaking responsibility for retirement* (pp. 69–97). Philadelphia, PA: University of Pennsylvania.

Costa, D. L. (1998). *The evolution of retirement: An American economic history, 1880–1990*. Chicago: The University of Chicago Press.

Couch, K. A. (1998). Late life job displacement. *The Gerontologist, 38*, 7–17.

Doeringer, P. B. (1990). Economic security, labor market flexibility, and bridges to retirement. In P. B. Doeringer (Ed.), *Bridges to retirement: Older workers in a changing labor market* (pp. 3–23). Ithaca, NY: ILR Press.

Easterlin, R. A. (1978). What will 1984 be like? Socioeconomic implications of recent twists in age structure. *Demography, 15*, 397–432.

Easterlin, R. A., Schaeffer, C. M., & Macunovich, D. J. (1993). Will the baby boomers be less well off than their parents? Income, wealth, and family circumstances over the life course in the United States. *Population and Development Review, 19*, 497–522.

Elder, G. H., Jr., & Pavalko, E. K. (1993). Work careers in men's later years: transitions, trajectories, and historical change. *Journal of Gerontology: Social Sciences, 48*, S180–191.

Flippen, C., & Tienda, M. (2000). Pathways to retirement: Patterns of labor force participation and labor market exit among the preretirement population by race, Hispanic origin, and sex. *Journal of Gerontology: Social Sciences, 55B*, S14–S27.

Fullerton, H. N. (1995). The 2005 labor force: Growing, but slowly. *Monthly Labor Review, 118*(11), 25–44.

Gardner, J. M. (1995). Worker displacement: A decade of change. *Monthly Labor Review, 118*(4), 45–57.

Garen, J., Berger, M., & Scott, F. (1996). Pensions, non-discrimination policies, and the employment of older workers. *Quarterly Review of Economics and Finance, 36*, 417–429.

Gendell, M. (1998). Trends in retirement age in four countries, 1965–95. *Monthly Labor Review, 121*(8), 20–30.

Gendell, M., & Siegel, J. S. (1992). Trends in retirement age by sex, 1950–2005. *Monthly Labor Review, 115*(7), 22–29.

Goodfellow, G. P., & Schieber, S. J. (1997). Investment of assets in self-directed retirement plans. In M. S. Gordon, O. S. Mitchell, & M. M. Twinney (Eds.), *Positioning pensions for the twenty-first century* (pp. 67–90). Philadelphia, PA: University of Pennsylvania.

Gruber, J., & Wise, D. A. (1997). Social security programs and retirement around the world. (Working Paper 6134). Cambridge, MA: National Bureau of Economic Research.

Guillemard, A.-M. (1991). France: Massive exit through unemployment compensation. In M. Kohli, M. Rein, A.-M. Guillemard, & H. van Gunsteren (Eds.), *Time for retirement: Comparative studies of early exit from the labor force* (pp. 127–180). New York: Cambridge University Press.

Guillemard, A.-M., & Rein, M. (1993). Comparative patterns in retirement. *Annual Review of Sociology, 19*, 469–503.

Gustman, A. L., Mitchell, O. S., & Steinmeier, T. L. (1995). Retirement measures in the health and retirement study. *The Journal of Human Resources, 30*, S57–S83.

Gustman, A. L., & Steinmeier, T. L. (1995). *Pension incentives and job mobility.* Kalamazoo, MI: W.E. Upjohn Institute for Employment Research.

Hayward, M. D., Crimmins, E. M., & Wray, L.A. (1994). The relationship between retirement life cycle changes and older men's labor force participation rates. *Journal of Gerontology: Social Sciences, 49*, S219–230.

Health and Retirement Study. (2000). Added cohorts and movement to steady state. HRS/AHEAD web page. ([On-line] Available: http://www.umich.edu/~hrswww/studydet/develop/steady.htm)

Henretta, J. C. (1992). Uniformity and diversity: Life course institutionalization and late-life work exit. *The Sociological Quarterly, 33*, 265–279.

Henretta, J. C. (2000). The future of age integration in employment. *The Gerontologist, 40*, 286–292.

Henretta, J. C., & Lee, H. (1996). Cohort differences in men's late-life labor force participation. *Work and Occupations, 23*, 214–235.

Herz, D. E. (1995). Work after early retirement: An increasing trend among men. *Monthly Labor Review, 118*(4), 13–20.

Hinz, R. P., McCarthy, D. D., & Turner, J. A. (1997). Are women conservative investors? Gender differences in participant-directed pension investments. In M. S. Gordon, O. S. Mitchell, & M. M. Twinney (Eds.), *Positioning pensions for the twenty-first century* (pp. 91–106). Philadelphia, PA: University of Pennsylvania.

Hipple, S. (1999). Worker displacement in the mid-1990s. *Monthly Labor Review, 122*(7), 15–32.

Hood, C. K. (1998). Age discrimination in employment and the Americans with Disabilities Act: "A second bite of the apple." *The Elder Law Journal, 6*, 1–30.

Hurd, M. D. (1990). Research on the elderly: Economic status, retirement, and consumption and saving. *Journal of Economic Literature, 28*, 565–637.

Hurd, M. D. (1996). The effect of labor market rigidities on the labor force behavior of older workers. In D. A. Wise (Ed.), *Advances in the economics of aging* (pp. 11–60). Chicago: University of Chicago.

Hutchens, R. M. (1988). Do job opportunities decline with age? *Industrial and Labor Relations Review, 42*, 89–99.

Ippolito, R. A. (1990). Toward explaining earlier retirement after 1970. *Industrial and Labor Relations Review, 43*, 556–569.

Ippolito, R. A. (1997). *Pension plans and employee performance.* Chicago: University of Chicago Press.

Issacharoff, S., & Harris, E. W. (1997). Is age discrimination really age discrimination? The ADEA's unnatural solution. *New York University Law Review, 72*, 780–840.

Jacobs, K., Kohli, M., & Rein, M. (1991). Germany: The diversity of pathways. In M. Kohli, M. Rein, A.-M. Guillemard, & H. van Gunsteren (Eds.), *Time for retirement: Comparative studies of early exit from the labor force* (pp. 181–221). New York: Cambridge University Press.

Juster, F. T., & Suzman, R. (1995). An overview of the Health and Retirement Study. *Journal of Human Resources, 30*, S7–S56.

Kohli, M. (1987). Retirement and the moral economy: An historical interpretation of the German case. *Journal of Aging Studies, 1*, 125–144.

Kohli, M. (1992). Labour market perspectives and activity patterns of the elderly in an ageing society. In W. van den Heuvel, R. Illsley, A. Jamieson, & C. Knipscheer (Eds.), *Opportunities and challenges in an ageing society* (pp. 90–105). Amsterdam: North Holland.

Kohli, M. (1994). Work and retirement: A comparative perspective. In M.W. Riley, R.L. Kahn, & A. Foner (Eds.), *Age and structural lag* (pp. 80–106). New York: Wiley-Interscience.

Kohli, M., & Meyer, J. W. (1986). Social structure and social construction of life stages. *Human Development, 29*, 145–149.

LaRock, S. (1992). Both private and public sector employers use early retirement sweeteners. *Employee Benefit Plan Review,* August, 14–20.

Mayer, K. U., & Schoepflin, U. (1989). The state and the life course. *Annual Review of Sociology, 15*, 187–209.

Meier, E. L. (1986). Early retirement incentive programs: Trends and implications (Research

Paper 8604). Washington, DC: Public Policy Institute, American Association for Retired Persons.

Minda, G. (1997). Opportunistic downsizing of aging workers: The 1990s version of age and pension discrimination in employment. *Hastings Law Journal, 48*, 511–576.

Mitchell, O. S. (1999). New trends in pension benefit and retirement provisions (Working Paper 7381). Cambridge, MA: National Bureau of Economic Research.

Mitchell, O. S., Gordon, M. S., & Twinney, M. M. (1997). Introduction: Assessing the challenges to the pension system. In M. S. Gordon, O. S. Mitchell, & M. M. Twinney (Eds.), *Positioning pensions for the twenty-first century* (pp. 1–11). Philadelphia, PA: University of Pennsylvania.

Mitchell, O. S., & Schieber, S. J. (1998). Defined contribution pensions: New opportunities, new risks. In O. S. Mitchell and S. J. Schieber (Eds). *Living with defined contribution pensions: Remaking responsibility for retirement* (pp. 1–14). Philadelphia, PA: Univeristy of Pennsylvania Press.

Moore, J. F., & Mitchell, O. S. (1997). Projected retirement wealth and savings adequacy in the Health and Retirement Study (Working Paper 6240). Cambridge, MA: National Bureau of Economic Research.

Mutchler, J. E., Burr, J. A., Pienta, A. M., & Massagli, M. P. (1997). Pathways to labor force exit: Work transitions and work instability. *Journal of Gerontology: Social Sciences, 52B*, S4–S12.

Mutschler, P. H. (1996). Early retirement incentive programs (ERIPS): Mechanisms for encouraging early retirement. In W. H. Crown (Ed.), *Handbook on employment and the elderly* (pp. 182–193). Westport, CT: Greenwood Press.

O'Rand, A. M., & Henretta, J. C. (1999). *Age and inequality: Diverse pathways through later life*. Boulder, CO: Westview Press.

Osterman, P. (1988). *Employment futures*. New York: Oxford University Press.

Polivka, A. E. (1994). Comparisons of labor force estimates from the parallel survey and the CPS during 1993: Major labor force estimates (CPS Overlap Analysis Team Technical Report 1). Washington, DC: Bureau of Labor Statistics. http://www.bls.gov.

Poterba, J. M., Venti, S. F., & Wise, D. A. (1999). Pre-retirement cashouts and foregone retirement saving: Implications for 401 (k) asset accumulation (Working Paper 7314). Cambridge, MA: National Bureau of Economic Research.

Quadagno, J., & Hardy, M. (1996). Work and retirement. In R. H. Binstock & L. K. George (Eds.), *Handbook of aging and the social sciences* (4th ed.) (pp. 325–345). San Diego, CA: Academic Press.

Quinn, J. F. (1997). Retirement trends and patterns in the 1990s: The end of an era? *Public Policy and Aging Report, 8*, 10–15.

Quinn, J. F. (1998). Employment and the elderly. *Gerontologist, 38*, 254–259.

Quinn, J. F. (1999). Retirement patterns and bridge jobs in the 1990s (Issue Brief 206). Washington, D.C.: Employee Benefit Research Institute.

Quinn, J. F., & Burkhauser, R. V. (1990). Work and retirement. In R. H. Binstock & L. K. George (Eds.) *Handbook of aging and the social sciences, third edition* (pp. 308–327). San Diego, CA: Academic Press.

Quinn, J. F., Burkhauser, R. V., & Myers, D. A. (1990). *Passing the torch: The influence of economic incentives on work and retirement*. Kalamazoo, MI: W. E. Upjohn Institute for Employment Research.

Quinn, J. F., & Kozy, M. (1996). The role of bridge jobs in the retirement transition: Gender, race, ethnicity. *Gerontologist, 36*, 363–372.

Reimers, C. (1976). Is the average age at retirement changing? *Journal of the American Statistical Association, 71*, 552–558.

Ruhm, C. J. (1990). Career jobs, bridge employment, and retirement. In P. B. Doeringer (Ed.), *Bridges to retirement: Older workers in a changing labor market* (pp. 92–110). Ithaca, NY: ILR Press.

Ruhm, C. J. (1996). Historical trends in the employment and labor force participation of older Americans. In W. H. Crown (Ed.), *Handbook on employment and the elderly* (pp. 81–102). Westport, Ct.: Greenwood Press.

Rust, J. (1990). Behavior of male workers at the end of the life cycle: An empirical analysis of states and controls. In D. A. Wise (Ed.), *Issues in the economics of aging* (pp. 317–379). Chicago: University of Chicago.

Schulz, J. H. (1995). *The economics of aging, sixth edition.* Westport, CT: Auburn House.

Sheppard, H. L. (1991). The United States: The privatization of exit. In M. Kohli, M. Rein, A.-M. Guillemard, & H. van Gunsteren (Eds.), *Time for retirement: Comparative studies of early exit from the labor force* (pp. 252–283). Cambridge, UK: Cambridge University.

Straka, J. W. (1992). *The demand for older workers: The neglected side of a labor market.* Studies in Income Distribution, No. 15. (SSA Publication No. 13–11776 (15)). Washington, DC: Social Security Administration.

Sum, A. M., & Fogg, W. N. (1990). Profile of the labor market for older workers. In P. B. Doeringer (Ed.), *Bridges to retirement: Older workers in a changing labor market* (pp. 33–63). Ithaca, NY: ILR Press.

U.S. Bureau of Labor Statistics. (1988). *Labor force statistics derived from the current population survey, 1948–87,* Bulletin 2307. Washington, DC: Government Printing Office.

U.S. Bureau of Labor Statistics. (1991). Employment status of the civilian noninstitutional population by age, sex, and race. *Employment and Earnings,* 38(1), 164.

U.S. Bureau of Labor Statistics. (1996). Employment status of the civilian noninstitutional population by age, sex, and race. *Employment and Earnings,* 43(1), 160.

U.S. Bureau of Labor Statistics. (1998). Employee tenure in 1998. News release 98–387. [On-line] Available: http://stats.bls.gov/newsrels.htm.

U.S. Bureau of Labor Statistics. (2000). Employment status of the civilian noninstitutional population by age, sex, and race. *Employment and Earnings,* 47(1), 168.

U.S. General Accounting Office. (1990). *Age discrimination: Use of age-specific provisions in company exit incentive plans.* Washington, DC: General Accounting Office. HRD-90–87BR.

U.S. Social Security Administration. (1994). Worldwide trend towards raising the retirement age. *Social Security Bulletin,* 57 (2), 83–84.

Ventrell-Monsees, C. (1999). 'Take the money and run or it's too late baby'': Early retirement incentives and the Age Discrimination in Employment Act. *University of Memphis Law Review,* 29, 783– 822.

Wilson, W. J. (1996). *When work disappears: The world of the new urban poor.* New York: Random House.

Wise, D. A. (1997). Retirement against the demographic trend: More older people living longer, working less, and saving less. *Demography,* 34, 83–95.

Fifteen

Social Support

Neal Krause

A convincing body of research indicates that social support is a key determinant of successful aging (Rowe & Kahn, 1998). More specifically, these studies suggest that older adults who are embedded in supportive social networks tend to enjoy better physical (Bosworth & Schaie, 1997) and mental health (Krause, 1997a) than elderly people who do not maintain meaningful ties with others. Studies on mortality provide especially compelling findings in this respect. This literature reveals that social support significantly increases the odds of living longer (Liang et al., 1999; Seeman et al., 1993).

Due in part to the impressive findings from research on social support, health, and well-being, a number of investigators have devised interventions that are designed to bolster the social ties of at-risk elders (Berkman, Heinik, Rosenthal, & Burke, 1999; Harris, Brown, & Robinson, 1999; Strawn, Hester, & Brown, 1998). Unfortunately, these interventions have not always been successful (Heller, Thompson, Trueba, Hogg, & Vlachos-Weber, 1991). Although the failure of these interventions is undoubtedly due to a number of factors, at least part of

the problem may be attributed to gaps in the knowledge base regarding the nature and function of social support (Gottlieb, 1992).

A necessary first step toward addressing the problems identified by Gottlieb (1992) involves developing well-articulated conceptual frameworks that more fully illuminate the ways in which supportive relationships affect the lives of older adults. This requires depth, not breadth, of thought. Consequently, the purpose of this chapter is to selectively review the literature with an eye toward crafting new ways of explaining the relationship between a few key dimensions of social support and health in late life. Toward this end, the discussion that follows is divided into four main sections. First, the definition of social support is considered briefly. Second, current thinking on the interface between social support, health, and well-being is extended and elaborated. Section three focuses on social support in religious settings. Section four focuses on socioeconomic status (SES) variations in the social support process. Throughout, the intent is to view social support in an increasingly wider social context.

Handbook of Aging and the Social Sciences, Fifth Edition

I. What Is Social Support?

As Babbie (1983) points out, there are at least two ways to define a construct—real definitions and operational definitions. Real definitions are statements that attempt to describe the essential nature or core attributes of a construct, whereas operational definitions are concerned with how constructs are measured. When research on social support first emerged, a number of attempts were made to provide real definitions of social support. Unfortunately, these efforts met with little success. Instead, many definitions were either circular or simply too narrow. Evidence of circularity may be found in the work of Kaplan, Cassel, and Gore (1977). They define social support as the "gratification of a person's basic social needs (approval, esteem, succorance, etc.), through environmental supplies of social support" (Kaplan et al., 1977, p. 50). Problems with definitions of support that are too narrow can be seen in research by Cobb (1976). He proposed that social support comprises three components: "(1) information leading the subject to believe that he is cared for and loved; (2) information leading the subject to believe that he is esteemed and valued; and (3) information leading the subject to believe that he belongs to a network of communication and mutual obligations" (Cobb, 1976, p. 300). This definition falls short because it deals primarily with emotional support. But as the discussion provided below will reveal, there is far more to social support than this.

More recently, it appears that few researchers even try to provide real definitions of social support. This is understandable given the broad purview of this unwieldy conceptual domain. Instead, the focus now is primarily on operational definitions of this illusive construct. Unfortunately, this has led to a plethora of options because social support may be measured in many ways. Even so, Barrera's (1986) straightforward classification scheme provides a useful way of getting a handle on this literature. He proposes that there are three kinds of informal social support measures: measures of social embeddedness (e.g., indicators assessing the frequency of contact with others), received support (e.g., measures of the amount of tangible help actually provided by social network members), and perceived support (subjective evaluations of supportive exchanges, such as satisfaction with social support). This classification scheme has proven to be quite helpful because research consistently shows that measures of perceived support exert the strongest and most consistent effects on health and well-being in late life (Norris & Kaniasty, 1996). Given these findings, it appears that efforts to better understand the social support process will be more profitably directed toward the study of perceived support. It is for this reason that the main thrust of the discussion that follows is concerned primarily with subjective evaluations of supportive social ties.

II. How Does Social Support Affect Health and Well-Being?

If the goal is to develop more explicit theories of how social support operates in late life, then it is important to accomplish two tasks. First, researchers must determine which dimensions or types of support play an especially important role in shaping health and well-being. Second, investigators must pinpoint the precise social mechanisms responsible for these salubrious effects. Although several support constructs could be selected for this purpose, two appear to be especially promising: anticipated support and negative interaction. Anticipated support is defined as the belief that significant others will provide assistance in the future should the need arise (Wethington & Kessler, 1986). In contrast, negative interaction refers to unpleasant social encounters that are characterized by criticism, rejection, competition, the violation of privacy, and the lack or reciprocity (Rook, 1984). In addition, ineffective assistance or excessive helping are subsumed under the broad rubric of this construct as well (Coyne, Wortman, & Lehman, 1988). An emphasis is placed on these particular constructs because research consistently shows that anticipated support (Krause, 1997a; Krause, Liang, & Gu, 1998) and negative interaction (Finch, Okun, Barrera et al., 1989; Okun & Keith, 1998) exert a greater effect on health and well-being than measures of received support or indicators of social embeddedness.

A. Anticipated Support

The discussion of anticipated support begins with a quick overview of the theoretical rationale linking this type of support with health and well-being. Then, this conceptual framework is elaborated and extended by turning to Schulz and Heckhausen's (1996) life span model of successful aging. Finally, the genesis of anticipated support is explored by highlighting the social factors that shape this key dimension of social relationships in late life.

1. Anticipated Support and Well-Being

The study of anticipated support and well-being is intimately related to the stress process. More specifically, research indicates that anticipated support may offset the noxious effects of stress, and that it may be a more effective coping resource than the assistance that is actually provided by social network members (Krause, 1997a, 1997b). In order to see why this may be the case, it is helpful to

first consider how people typically attempt to cope with stress.

Although the selection of a particular coping response is undoubtedly shaped by many factors (Aldwin, 1994), research reviewed by Eckenrode and Wethington (1990) indicates that instead of immediately turning to social network members for assistance, individuals often try to resolve their problems on their own. After this, they may seek help from others, but only if their own personal resources are ineffective (Wethington & Kessler, 1986). It is for this reason that some investigators view received support as a marker of failed individual coping efforts (Eckenrode & Wethington, 1990).

There are three reasons why anticipated support may be an especially efficacious coping resource. The first has to do with the promotion of individual coping responses, the second involves the enhancement of smooth network functioning, and the third is concerned with the maintenance of hope.

As Wethington and Kessler (1986) point out, the realization that others stand ready to help if the need arises constitutes a social safety net that promotes risk taking, and encourages individuals to resolve problems on their own. The experience of successfully confronting a stressor without the direct intervention of others may be an especially effective way to promote feelings of well-being because self-directed action is likely to enhance feelings of self-worth and personal control (Rodin, 1990).

In addition to this more overt function, anticipated support may benefit support providers as well as elderly help recipients in ways that are less evident. Social relations are fragile phenomena that can easily go awry (Rook, 1984). For example, support providers may feel overburdened or put upon when they face repeated requests for assistance (La Gaipa, 1990). In fact, there is ample evidence that too much assistance may not be beneficial for, or even preferred by, older adults (Lee, 1985). By encouraging elders to take care of their own needs, anticipated support may reduce feelings of burden among support providers and enhance feelings of independence on the part of older support recipients. Averting social network conflict in this way may, in turn, promote feelings of well-being among elderly people.

Finally, the belief that significant others are ready to assist may foster the perception that even though a stressor may be present, there is a chance it will ultimately subside. Stated simply, the social safety net afforded by anticipated support may promote a sense of hope. This is important because research indicates that individuals can endure tremendous adversity as long as they have hope and believe that a difficult situation will eventually be resolved (Nunn, 1996). Viewed the other way around, the loss of hope is a critical factor that plays a central role in the etiology of depressive disorders (Nunn, 1996).

2. Elaborations and Extensions

Schulz and Heckhausen's (1996) life span model of successful aging provides a useful point of departure for flushing out a more well-developed theoretical explanation for the beneficial effects of anticipated support. This work is helpful because it focuses on one of the purported benefits of anticipated support—the enhancement of personal control. However, by making a distinction between primary and secondary control, Schulz and Heckhausen (1996) provide a way to think about anticipated support that has not appeared before in the literature.

Viewed in general terms, Schulz and Heckhausen (1996) argue that primary control refers to efforts aimed at changing the external environment, whereas secondary control is concerned with changing internal cognitions (e.g., one's

attitudes, attributions, or perceptions) rather than trying to alter or master the external world. Although Schulz and Heckhausen (1996) have been criticized for the way they conceptualize secondary control (Skinner, 1996), the broader process they identify is initially of greater interest.

In particular, Schulz and Heckhausen (1996) maintain that as people get older, resources dwindle and the ratio of gains to losses becomes less favorable. Following the theory of optimization with compensation (Baltes, 1991), they argue that elders cope with this situation by relinquishing primary control in some areas of life so that available resources may be devoted to maintaining primary control in other life domains.

Unfortunately, Schulz and Heckhausen (1996) do not examine the potentially important role played by social support in this process. The main thrust of the argument provided below is to highlight the social foundation of this process by showing that feelings of primary control are enhanced by anticipated support, whereas secondary control is more likely to be bolstered by received support. In order to see why this is the case, it is important to reexamine the way Schulz and Heckhausen (1996) conceptualize secondary control.

As noted earlier, Schulz and Heckhausen (1996) view secondary control solely in terms of internal cognitions. Included among these cognitions are things like downplaying the importance of previously valued goals. But if this is all there is to it, then important role commitments may simply be left unattended. This is hardly a form of control per se, and instead reflects what are largely ineffective forms of denial (see Aldwin, 1994, for a discussion of denial).

Perhaps more importantly, the exclusive focus on internal cognitions falls short because it overlooks numerous discussions in the literature that show

how significant others can help a focal person maintain a sense of control. This can be seen, for example, in the early work by Fromm (1941). He identified the tendency of people to align themselves with influential individuals and groups in order to enhance their own sense of power (Fromm, 1941). More recently, Rothbaum, Weisz, and Snyder (1982) discuss how people identify with powerful others in an effort to promote what they call "vicarious secondary control." But the social essence of secondary control is perhaps best captured in Antonovsky's (1979) work on the sense of coherence. According to this perspective, control may be relinquished to a significant other who subsequently acts in the best interest of the focal person. This means, for example, that an elderly widow may be able to maintain a sense of control over her financial situation by having her son manage her fiscal affairs. In this way, she is able to feel as though, "... things are under control," even though she is not directly in charge of the situation herself (Antonovsky, 1979, p. 155). Viewed in this way, it is possible to provide a plausible mechanism for the central process described by Schulz and Heckhausen (1996). In particular, elderly people may relinquish control in a select life domain by turning responsibility over to a trusted significant other who operates with the best interests of the focal elderly person in mind. Stated simply, this theoretical rationale suggests that secondary control is determined by received or enacted support.

But the crux of the process outlined by Schulz and Heckhausen (1996) is that the purpose of secondary control strategies is to facilitate the development and maintenance of primary control. In order to further develop the social foundations of this process, it is important to show how social support plays a central role in enhancing this type of control as well. This can be accomplished by taking a closer look at how anticipated support affects well-being.

Earlier it was argued that knowing others are available if needed serves as a social safety net that promotes risk taking and encourages individuals to resolve problems on their own. Doing so should facilitate the acquisition of new coping responses and strengthen or reinforce existing ones. The enrichment of one's coping repertoire should bolster self-confidence, and ultimately enhance feelings of primary control. After all, it not clear why an older adult would feel they were personally in control of a situation if someone else was taking care of everything for them (as in secondary control). But this does not mean that feelings of primary control arise in a social vacuum. Instead, it is important not to lose sight of the fact that elderly people will be more likely to engage in self-directed coping efforts if they believe that benevolent others are ready to help if needed. Stated more generally, this rationale suggests that anticipated support determines feelings of primary control.

3. The Social Roots of Anticipated Support

An emphasis has been placed throughout the discussion in this section on illuminating the social foundations of primary and secondary control. Anticipated support has figured prominently in this respect. Ironically, some psychologists maintain that anticipated support is little more than an underlying personality trait (Sarason, Sarason, & Pierce, 1994). Unfortunately, this orientation overlooks the possibility that anticipated support may be influenced by wider social factors as well. There are at least four ways this can happen.

First, perceptions of support availability in the future are likely to be based on the amount of assistance that has actually been provided in the past. Empirical evidence of this may be found in research by Krause (1997a), who reports that the more assistance elders have received from others in the past, the more likely they are to believe that social network members will be willing to help in the future ($\beta = .310; p < .005$).

Second, instead of providing support directly, social network members may merely let an elderly person know they are willing to help out should the need ever arise. This can happen in a number of ways. For example, significant others may offer assistance, but older adults may elect not to avail themselves of the opportunity. In this instance, the offer in and of itself creates a reasonable expectation that assistance will be available in the future, even though support was never actually provided.

Third, elderly people may develop a sense of anticipated support by observing social exchanges among other people in their social network. In this instance, however, support is not provided (or even offered directly) to the focal elder. Instead, the roots of anticipated support may lie in vicariously taking part in the exchange process by observing social network members help each other.

Finally, older adults may expect others to help in the future because of prevailing social norms. Evidence of this may be found in Antonucci's (1985) work with the support bank. According to this perspective, elderly people expect to receive help from grown offspring because they provided assistance to their children when they were young.

Care must be taken to place the conceptual framework devised in this section in a proper perspective. In particular, the discussion provided above deals with ideal types (Weber, 1925). This means that in reality, primary control is probably not determined solely by anticipated support, nor is secondary control a simple function of received support. Instead, both types of control likely reflect the influence of anticipated as well as received support, but differ only in the relative influence of these social support measures. More specifically, anticipated support may play a larger role in shaping primary control, whereas received support figures more prominently in the genesis of secondary control. Even so, the conceptual scheme developed here helps to clarify the complex processes that are at work, thereby allowing the predominant forces shaping primary and secondary control to be grasped more easily.

B. Negative Interaction

Interpersonal conflict seems to arise even in the closest relationships (Rook, 1984). Consequently, a more complete understanding of social support in late life requires a thorough examination of the negative as well as the positive aspects of interpersonal ties. Three issues are explored below in an effort to round out our understanding of the social support process. Current explanations for the deleterious effects of negative interaction are examined first. Following this, recent empirical work is reviewed briefly in an effort to extend the conceptual underpinnings of how unpleasant social encounters affect health and well-being in late life. Finally, research on the relationship between positive and negative interaction is explored. Here, the intent is to weave what we know about these facets of social ties into a more coherent whole by reflecting on how both can be present without destroying a relationship.

1. Negative Interaction and Well-Being

In their thought-provoking paper on negative interaction, Rook and Pietromonaco (1987) provide three explanations for the adverse effects of unpleasant social interaction. First, these investigators suggest that negative interaction is a rare event that stands in sharp contrast to the normal smooth functioning of social networks. Consequently, it catches people by surprise and shatters expectations that pleasant encounters in the past will continue unabated into the future.

The second explanation for the deleterious effects of negative interaction has to do with causal attributions (i.e., explanations derived by older adults for the behavior of others). In particular, Rook and Pietromonaco (1987) maintain that it is difficult to make unambiguous attributions for the prosocial behavior of another because it is hard to know whether the support they provide is genuine, or whether it merely arose from a sense of obligation. In contrast, negative behavior is starkly counter-normative and unambiguously violates social norms that promote the proper conduct of social interaction. As a result, an elderly person is likely to quickly conclude that bad behavior reflects malicious intent or insufficient caring. According to Rook and Pietromonaco (1987), the painful attributions associated with negative interaction outweigh or offset the uncertain attributions associated with beneficial behavior, resulting in greater distress.

Finally, Rook and Pietromonaco (1987) suggest that the deleterious effects of negative interaction may be explained by focusing on their adaptive significance. Due in part to our ancestral past, these investigators suggest that people have an innate tendency to be especially vigilant against threats. As a result, far greater attention is given to negative than positive interaction. Presumably, the drain on psychic resources (e.g., energy and effort) engendered by this heightened sensitivity ensures that the impact of negative interaction will be greater than the corresponding effects of the positive things that people do.

2. Elaborations and Extensions

The rationale devised by Rook and Pietromonaco (1987) has yet to be evaluated empirically. Doing so should be a high priority. However, it is important to keep in mind that there are other ways to explain the noxious effects of negative interaction that are not considered by these investigators. The purpose of this section is to explore some additional possibilities that arise from recent empirical work on negative interaction in late life.

Based on data provided by a nationally representative sample of older people, Krause and Rook (2000) explored a straightforward issue that has been largely overlooked in the literature on negative interaction. In particular, they assessed the stability of unpleasant social interaction over time. The findings suggest that negative interaction is quite stable over a 6-year period ($\beta = .569$; $p < .001$). This simple observation points to two possible explanations for the pernicious effects of unpleasant social encounters.

First, the fact that negative interaction is stable over time suggests that at least some older people may become ensnared in unhealthy relationships that are difficult to terminate. Carstensen's (1992) theory of socioemotional selectivity shows how this can happen. She argues that as people grow older, they tend to extricate themselves from peripheral social relationships, resulting in social networks that are comprised of a smaller number of core ties. These core network members are often kin, not friends. The fact that family becomes increasingly important with age is noteworthy because family ties are involuntary and based primarily on a sense of obligation (Litwak, 1981). In contrast, friendship ties are dissolved with greater ease because they are entered into voluntarily. Because ties with family members cannot be dissolved easily, conflict with kin may have an especially pronounced effect on health and well-being in late life. Evidence of this may be found in the literature on psychotherapy. In particular, Hargrave and Anderson (1992) devote an entire volume to the treatment of intergenerational conflict. It is especially important to note that the family conflicts they discuss often linger for decades.

Viewing negative interaction as a stable or ongoing problem makes it possible to take advantage of the vast literature on chronic strains (Gottlieb, 1997). In essence, this research indicates that it is the very persistence of some stressors that makes them so pernicious. More specifically, as Gottlieb (1997) points out, ongoing problems may create the impression they will continue unabated into the future. Believing there is no end in sight to a problem may erode feelings of hope and optimism. These constructs are important because research indicates that hope and optimism are important for the maintenance of health and well-being (Nunn, 1996; Peterson, Seligman, & Vaillant, 1988). In addition to this mechanism, Gottlieb (1997) suggests that the intense watchfulness and vigilance associated with ongoing strains may eventually wear down the physical reserves of those confronted by chronic strain. The similarity between this observation and the views developed by Rook and Pietromonaco (1987) is striking.

The empirical findings reported by Krause and Rook (2000) suggest a second explanation for the deleterious effects of negative interaction. When reading research in this field, one is often left with the impression that unpleasant social encounters are initiated solely by others. In contrast, there is relatively little discussion of how the locus or impetus for negative interaction may reside within the focal person. There are a number of ways that individuals may create the interpersonal problems they have with others. For example, some older people may not get along with others because they have poor interpersonal skills (Hansson & Carpenter, 1990).

A preliminary test of this perspective can be performed by assessing negative interaction within specific relationships (e.g., a spouse and a child), and then evaluating the extent to which these measures are correlated. If the lack of social skills is a factor, then elderly people who have interpersonal problems in one relationship should encounter them in others as well. Okun and Keith (1998) conducted one of the few studies that evaluates this issue empirically. Based on data provided by older adults, they report the following intercorrelations among relationship-specific measures of negative interaction: negative interaction with a spouse and negative interaction with children $(r = .40)$; negative interaction with children and negative interaction with other relatives and friends $(r = .29)$, and negative interaction with a spouse and negative interaction with other relative and friends $(r = .38)$. Unfortunately, these investigators do not provide significance tests for these estimates, nor do they discuss the theoretical implications of these results. Nevertheless, the findings suggest that it is important to consider the role played by the focal person in the genesis of unpleasant social interaction.

3. The Relationship between Positive and Negative Interaction

At first glance, it would appear that older adults should have a natural proclivity to avoid relationships that are aversive and cultivate those that are rewarding. To the extent this is true, there should be a strong negative correlation between unpleasant interaction and positive support. However, it is somewhat surprising to find that empirical work on the relationship between positive and negative interaction reveals that the correlation between these constructs is modest at best (Barrera, Chassin, & Rogosch, 1993; Okun & Keith, 1998; Rook, 1990). This is true even when researchers focus on positive and negative exchanges within specific dyadic relationships (Schuster, Kessler, & Aseltine, 1990). Viewed more generally, these findings point to a gap in our knowledge of the social support process and challenge investigators to develop theoretical explanations that are capable of reconciling the dual nature of interpersonal ties. The discussion that follows takes a modest step in this direction by exploring two explanations for the low correlation between positive and negative social encounters.

First, most investigators approach the study of negative interaction as if it produces only undesirable outcomes. However, a small but intriguing cluster of studies suggest this may not always be the case. Instead, negative interaction may take the form of social sanctions that are intended to get older adults to engage in behavior that is in their own best interests. More specifically, social network members may become critical and demanding of an elderly person because they want him or her to engage in beneficial health behaviors (Lewis & Rook, 1999). So, for example, a wife may be critical of her diabetic husband for not following an appropriate diet.

But it is unlikely that most negative interaction is initiated with the best interests of a focal elder in mind. Instead, even casual observation suggests that, either deliberately or inadvertently, everyone at some time hurts those who are closest to them. Yet it is not entirely clear how social relationships persevere in the face of these difficulties. A central premise in this section is that the study of forgiveness can provide valuable insight into this issue. Forgiveness is defined as the process of "overcoming negative affect and judgment toward the offender, not by denying ourselves the right to such affect and judgment, but by endeavoring to view the offender with compassion, benevolence, and love while recognizing that he or she has abandoned

the right to them" (Enright, Gassin, & Wu, 1992, p. 101). It is important to emphasize that forgiveness can be religiously motivated (Krause & Ingersoll-Dayton, 2000) or entirely secular in nature (Enright & North, 1998).

Although there has been fairly extensive work on forgiveness (Enright & North, 1998; Scobie & Scobie, 1998), it is surprising to find that it is rarely considered in mainstream research on social support. This is especially true in social gerontology. Even so, there is reason to believe that the process of forgiving others may become more important as people grow older. Evidence of this may be found in Butler's research on the life review (Butler & Lewis, 1982). He argues that as people enter late life, they invest a significant amount of time reviewing experiences they've had in an effort toward weaving their lives into a more coherent whole. Themes of forgiveness figure prominently in this respect. In particular, Butler argues that one of the developmental tasks of the life review process is the, "expiation of guilt, the resolution of conflicts, and the reconciliation of family relationships" (Butler & Lewis, 1982, p. 236). Consistent with the views of Butler and Lewis (1982), there is some evidence that people tend to be more forgiving with age. More specifically, Girard and Mullet (1997) studied 236 people at different points in the life cycle ranging from adolescence to old age. Their data suggest that as people grow older, there is a linear increase in the tendency to forgive others.

In order to understand how forgiveness operates, it is useful to first think more deeply about the deleterious effects of negative interaction. When someone is hurt by a significant other, the immediate reaction is often to return the hurt. Moreover, it is often difficult to let go of the feelings of anger and resentment arising from the bad behavior of another. Left unattended, a person may fixate or ruminate on these negative emotions. Eventually, these undesirable cognitions may be manifest behaviorally in an endless cycle of recrimination and revenge that further erodes the integrity of a relationship. Perhaps forgiveness functions by providing an expeditious way of letting go of these negative emotions, thereby assuaging the hurt associated with interpersonal transgressions. Ultimately, this may help mend damaged interpersonal ties. In fact, some clinicians have built entire therapeutic programs that focus explicitly on the use of forgiveness to heal relationships that are riddled with conflict (Hargrave, 1994). Stated simply, forgiveness may be viewed as an essential social lubricant that keeps support systems running smoothly in the face of interpersonal problems that inevitably arise within them.

So far there has been relatively little empirical research on the relationship between negative interaction, forgiveness, and social support. Nevertheless, it may be helpful to speculate on how forgiveness may operate in this context. Casting the discussion in terms of statistical interaction effects provides a helpful point of departure. If the rationale developed in this section is valid, there should be a statistical interaction effect between negative interaction and forgiveness on positive social support. This means that when negative interaction is present in a relationship, but older adults are unwilling to forgive, there should be a strong inverse relationship between unpleasant social encounters and positive support. But when negative interaction is encountered and elderly people are more forgiving, the correlation between unpleasant social encounters and positive support should be reduced significantly.

III. Social Support in Religious Settings

An impressive number of studies suggest that religion may be related to health and well-being in late life (Koenig, 1999). Taken as a whole, this literature indicates that elderly people who are more involved in, and committed to, their faith tend to enjoy better physical and mental health then older adults who are not as religious. Subsequent efforts to explain the connection between religion and health reveal that at least part of the reason for these findings may be attributed to the social ties that seem to flourish in religious settings (Ellison & Levin, 1998). Because there is some evidence that religion becomes increasingly salient with age (Beit-Hallahmi & Argyle, 1998), the support received in a religious setting may be especially beneficial for older adults.

The purpose of this section is to review research on social support and religion. The discussion that follows is divided into three sections. Select dimensions or types of religious support are reviewed first. Then, potentially unique ways in which religious support may affect health and well-being are examined in section II. B. Finally, recent research on negative aspects of social ties in the church are explored and extended.

A. Social Support in Religious Organizations

The literature on social support in religious settings is not well developed. Rather than assessing the full range of dimensions discussed by Barrera (1986), most investigators focus on measures of enacted or received support. More specifically, this research indicates that people who are members of formal religious organizations receive a good deal of emotional (Krause, Ellison, & Wulff, 1998) and tangible assistance (Taylor & Chatters, 1988) from their fellow parishioners.

But coreligionists may do far more than merely exchange emotional and tangible support. In particular, they help each other in ways that are more explicitly religious in nature. Unfortunately, this issue is rarely addressed in the literature. Even so, it is important to begin to delineate the specific forms that overtly religious assistance may take. Three are discussed here in an effort to promote further work in this area. First, coreligionists may encourage each other to devote more time to the practice of their faith, including more frequent prayer or church attendance, as well as more frequent reading of sacred texts. Second, fellow parishioners may help each other better understand their faith by discussing religious texts or sharing personal religious experiences. Third, people who worship together may encourage each other to use religious coping responses in times of stress (Pargament, 1997).

B. Unique Aspects of Support in Religious Settings

If support that people get in religious organizations exerts a beneficial effect on their health, then it is important to know whether there is something unique about it, or whether we are merely observing a largely secular process that happens to be taking place in the context of a particular organization. Taken at face value, there does not appear to be anything unique about enacted support that is exchanged in religious settings. This can be illustrated by examining the following indicator that was taken from the work of Krause et al. (1998): "During the past year, how often have the people in your congregation made you feel loved and cared for?" Even a moment's reflection reveals that many people who are not religious readily exchange this type of assistance as well.

But this initial impression may be deceiving because the religious context in which enacted support is exchanged may subtly influence its quality and effectiveness. This may be seen by returning to Rook and Pietromonaco's (1987) discus-

sion of negative interaction. Based on the attribution literature, they argue that support is likely to be more effective when the recipient feels the provider was motivated by genuine care and concern. Support recipients in religious settings may be especially inclined to feel this way, because helping those confronted by adversity is a central tenet in virtually every religion in the world (Coward, 1986). For example, the Christian faith eschews negative judgments of those in distress and extols the virtues of altruistic or selfless helping behaviors. Because these values and beliefs are likely to be shared by those who worship together, secular types of help that are exchanged in religious settings may prove to be especially efficacious (Ellison & Levin, 1998).

But the empirical evaluation of secular support in religious settings is fraught with difficulty. Initially, it would appear that the following two-step strategy would be sufficient. First, investigators would obtain separate measures of secular support in religious settings and secular support obtained outside of religious organizations (e.g., from friends or neighbors). Second, some form of multivariate analysis would then be used to see which support measure exerts the most salubrious effect on health or well-being. However, informal social networks outside religious settings may not be purely secular in nature. For example, an older adult who is a Methodist may get emotional support from a neighbor who happens to be a devout Presbyterian. Although they don't worship in the same church, their common Christian heritage may, nevertheless, ensure that they share similar values about the helping process. Moreover, some deeply religious elders may feel that the proper exercise of their faith requires helping people who do not worship with them and who may not be religious at all. In fact, this is one reason why many churches have community outreach programs that focus explicitly on those who are not coreligionists.

In addition to secular support in religious settings, assistance that is explicitly religious may also affect health and well-being in relatively unique ways. These potential advantages are highlighted below by focusing on the connection between religious support and religious coping. This is an especially important issue to examine because a well-developed literature suggests that religious coping responses are associated with better physical and mental health in late life (Krause, 1998).

Researchers who study secular coping responses rarely consider the influence significant others may exert on the way people respond to stressful life events (Aldwin, 1994). This is true with respect to religious coping as well. Nevertheless, evidence of the important role played by significant others in secular settings is highlighted in Caplan's (1981) seminal research. He argues that social network members help define the problem situation, develop a plan of action, assist in implementing the plan, and provide feedback and guidance as the plan is being executed.

There are at least two ways that the connection between social support and coping may be unique in religious settings. First, the relationship between religious support and coping may be much stronger than the relationship between support in secular settings and coping responses. Second, religious coping may, in turn, lead to forms of secondary control that have not been discussed up to this point.

1. Religious Support and Religious Coping

There are a number of reasons why co-religionists may be especially likely to encourage each other to use explicitly religious coping responses. To begin with, religious texts are replete with guidance on how to deal with stressful situations, and the common value placed by coreligionists on these documents should increase the likelihood that they are shared and adopted. In addition, religious organizations often provide formal mechanisms for the transmission and adoption of religious coping responses,-including prayer groups and bible study groups. Finally, the typically warm atmosphere in religious organizations may promote a sense of bonding, cohesiveness, and solidarity. This becomes fertile ground for the adoption of religious values and practices because people are more willing to listen to, learn from, and emulate individuals who are close to them. Religious coping responses are likely to be among the practices that are adopted in this context.

2. Religious Support and Secondary Control

The main thrust of Caplan's (1981) discussion of social support and coping was to show how significant others ultimately help support recipients to develop and maintain a sense of mastery or personal control. There is some evidence that this may happen in religious settings as well. As the discussion provided below will reveal, exploring this issue in greater detail may provide valuable insight into the secondary control process.

Earlier, secondary control was defined as turning the resolution of a problem over to a benevolent other who operates with the best interests of the focal person in mind. There is some evidence that this may occur in relatively unique ways in religious settings. This is captured in the work of Pargament (1997), who has devised the most well-developed measures of religious coping in the literature. In particular, one coping response involves turning problems over to God. This is reflected in the following item taken from Pargament's religious coping scale: "In carrying out solutions to my problems, I wait for God to take control and know somehow He'll work it out" (Pargament, 1997, p. 181).

Taken at face value, the item devised by Pargament (1997) suggests that once people turn their difficulties over to God, their own coping efforts cease and they merely wait for God to resolve problem situations. In fact, a careful reading of secular discussions of secondary control conveys the same impression. However, a recent qualitative study by Krause, Morgan, Chatters, and Meltzer (2000) indicates that this process may not be as straightforward as it seems.

Krause et al. (2000) conducted eight focus groups with older adults in order to learn more about how they practice religion. During the course of the group discussions, numerous references were made to "turning it all over to God" and "letting God have it." These investigators were intrigued by this issue, so more detailed follow-up questions were devised to learn more about it. In particular, these researchers wanted to know if turning over a problem to God meant that a person no longer did anything to resolve difficulties on his or her own. Subsequent discussion revealed that this was not the case. Instead, the older adults in this study indicated that turning problems over to God involved a three-step process: (a) differentiating between things that can and cannot be changed; (b) focusing one's own efforts on the facets of a problem that can be altered; and (c) emotionally disengaging from those aspects of a problem that are outside one's own control by focusing on the reassurance that God will ultimately ensure the best possible outcome.

Although the findings provided by Krause et al. (2000) deal solely with religious secondary control, they nevertheless speak to the wider literature in this area as well. In particular, it may be best to view secondary control as an ideal type

(Weber, 1925) because older adults may not relinquish primary control entirely. Instead, they may strive to resolve their problems by relying on a mix of self-initiated action and direct involvement of others.

C. Negative Interaction in Religious Institutions

Religious organizations are largely a human endeavor, and as a result they are not perfect. Consequently, unpleasant interaction may arise in places of worship, just as it does in the secular world. The purpose of the discussion in this section is to suggest that even though the study of negative interaction in religious settings is underdeveloped, further work in this field may help shed light on wider secular studies of unpleasant social encounters as well.

One of the few studies on negative interaction in sacred settings was conducted by Krause, Ellison, and Wulff (1998). The data for this study come from a nationwide survey of Presbyterians. Data on negative interaction in the church were obtained from clergy, elders (i.e., lay leaders of the church), and rank-and-file members. The findings indicate that negative interaction with coreligionists exerts a deleterious effect on psychological well-being. However, the results further reveal that members of the clergy were most vulnerable, followed by elders and regular members, respectively.

There are at least two ways to explain these findings. The first involves expectancy theory and shows why negative interaction may be problematic for anyone who is involved in religion (Olson, Roese, & Zanna, 1996). The second is concerned with why these effects may be especially pronounced for those who are more deeply committed to their faith.

Expressed in general terms, expectancies are beliefs about how things will turn out in the future (Olson et al., 1996). These beliefs are essential because social behavior would not be possible unless people feel they can predict what others will do. However, Olson et al. (1996) point out that expectancies may not always be accurate, and the disconfirmation of these beliefs may create psychological distress. Because respect and concern for others figures prominently in many religious teachings, co-religionists are likely to believe that social ties in religious organizations will be particularly close. Consequently, negative interaction may be especially pernicious if it arises in religious settings because it shatters previously held expectations about the benevolence and good intentions of others.

Recent extensions of identity theory help to show why negative interaction should be especially pernicious for the very religious (Thoits, 1991). According to this view, the impact of a stressor on well-being depends upon the salience of the life domain in which it emerged. Within the context of the present discussion, this means that the impact of negative interaction with coreligionists will be more pronounced for individuals who place a high value on a religious life. Although there are exceptions, members of the clergy tend to be more deeply committed to religion than elders or members. Perhaps this is why Krause, Ellison, and Wulff (1998) found that unpleasant interaction exerted an especially deleterious effect on clergy.

But the findings in the study by Krause, Ellison, and Wulff (1998) have potentially important implications for those studying negative interaction in secular settings as well. In particular, investigators may learn more about the noxious effects of negative interaction by assessing whether they are more pronounced in roles or life domains that are valued highly by elderly people.

IV. Socioeconomic Status and Social Support

There is considerable evidence that physical as well as mental health problems are more prevalent in lower socioeconomic status (SES) groups (Adler et al., 1994; Kessler et al., 1994). If social support plays a role in the etiology of physical and mental disorders, then turning to the study of interpersonal relationships may help explain why SES variations in health outcomes exist. Unfortunately, the literature on SES and social support in social gerontology is underdeveloped. Most studies are concerned with either dyadic relationships or immediate social networks. In fact, this emphasis has become so pronounced that some researchers claim the study of social support has become "overly psychologized" (Lieberman, 1986). The purpose of this section is to redress this imbalance in the literature by highlighting ways in which SES may shape interpersonal exchanges during late life.

There are at least two ways in which SES variations in social support may be manifest. First, there may be SES differences in the amount of social support. Second, there may be SES differences in the impact of social support on health and well-being. After examining these issues below, the distinction between primary and secondary control is revisited in an effort to show how this process is influenced by the interplay between social support and SES factors.

A. SES Variations in the Amount of Social Support

One way to approach the study of SES and social support is to see whether there are mean differences in the level or amount of assistance that is exchanged in different SES groups. This research would help investigators determine whether lower

SES elders are at risk because they do not get enough assistance from the people who are close to them. However, as noted earlier, the social support construct encompasses a wide range of dimensions that have been evaluated with a plethora of scales (Barrera, 1986). Consequently, the study of SES and support requires that researchers explore a full complement of social support measures or dimensions.

Krause and Borawski-Clark (1995) conducted one of the few studies that examines SES variations in social support with a range of support indices. Using education and income as key markers of SES, these investigators evaluated whether there are mean SES differences in six types of social support: contact with friends, contact with family, support received from others, support provided by older adults to their social network members, negative interaction, and satisfaction with support received from family and friends. When income served as the measure of SES, the data reveal that higher SES elders report having greater contact with family as well as more contact with friends. In addition, older adults who are more well-to-do indicate they give more support to social network members and they are more satisfied with the help they get than their lower SES counterparts. Similar findings emerged when SES was assessed with education. There was, however, one exception. Differences in contact with family members failed to emerge in the data even though this appeared to be the case when SES was measured with income.

Although the work of Krause and Borawski-Clark (1995) is helpful, there is much that remains to be done. In particular, we need to know whether SES variations arise in dimensions of support that are not examined by these investigators. This is especially true of anticipated support. In addition, researchers need to explain *why* SES differences emerge in some

types of assistance (e.g., support provided by older adults to social network members) but not others (e.g., negative interaction).

One way to begin devising explanations for SES variations in mean levels of support is to start with the premise that there are potentially important causal relationships among the different dimensions of social support (Krause, 1995). This means, for example, that negative interaction is determined, at least in part, by the amount of support that is received from and provided to significant others. In particular, social exchange theory would predict that conflict will arise when older adults either give more support than they receive, or get more from others than they give in return (Dowd, 1975). Even so, the data provided by Krause and Borawski-Clark (1995) hint at a potentially important deviation from this proposition. In particular, although there are no SES differences in the amount of support received from others, lower SES elders report giving less in return. Exchange theory would predict that this imbalance should promote more negative interaction in lower SES networks, but the findings provided by Krause and Borawski-Clark (1995) indicate this may not be the case. Although care must be taken when examining data at the aggregate level, this pattern of findings suggests that some social mechanism may permit the accommodation of unbalanced exchanges in lower SES social networks. One possibility may be found by returning to the study of religion.

Although elderly people appear to be more religious than those who are younger, research further indicates that those who are disenfranchised (e.g., minority group members and those in the lower SES groups) are especially likely to be involved in religion (Pargament, 1997). One of the fundamental tenets of Christianity is that, "It is more blessed to give than to receive" (Acts 20: 35, King James

Version of the Bible). Perhaps religious norms and values like this help to allay negative feelings that would otherwise arise in lower SES groups when the social exchange process is unbalanced.

B. SES Differences in the Impact of Support on Health

Although there may be mean SES differences in the amount of support that is exchanged in late life, it is also possible that the impact of support on health and well-being may vary across SES groups as well. Cast in more statistical terms, the differential impact of support on health and well-being would be assessed with regression coefficients, not means (Kessler, 1979). This suggests that at the same mean level of assistance, the impact of support on health would not be the same for lower and upper SES older adults.

Unfortunately, few investigators have examined SES differences in the impact of social support on health and well-being in social gerontology. Nevertheless, there are at least two reasons why such SES variations may arise. The first has to do with SES variations in the quality of assistance received from others, whereas the second is concerned with SES differences in the impact of support provided by older adults to their social network members.

1. SES Variations in the Quality of Received Support

Research indicates that social networks are typically composed of people with a similar socioeconomic background (Lin, 1982). It is for this reason that a number of investigators propose that the general lack of resources in lower SES groups tends to insure that stressors confronting one social network member will affect others as well (Hobfoll, 1998). This problem is perhaps best illustrated by focusing on economic stressors. When older adults are confronted with a financial crisis, there is a good chance their significant others will be grappling with economic problems of their own. This may affect the helping process in two ways. First, having to provide support when one lacks the very resources that are required by another may diminish the quality of assistance that is provided (Belle, 1990). For example, significant others may make older support recipients feel they are burdensome. Second, the financial problems facing lower SES elders are often continuous and ongoing (i.e., they are a form of chronic strain—see Pearlin, 1999). As Coyne et al. (1988) describe in detail, problems that are intractable gradually wear down or burn out support providers, resulting in assistance that is ineffective at best, and openly hostile at its worst.

2. SES Variations in the Quality of Support Provided to Others

By far, most studies of the social support process focus solely on assistance that is received by older adults. However, elderly people are often support providers themselves. Assessing SES variations in this process serves as a useful forum for exploring support provided by older adults to their social network members. Two issues are discussed below. First, general benefits associated with assisting others are outlined briefly. Following this, factors that may erode the benefits derived from helping others in lower SES groups are explored.

Mental health professionals have argued for decades that people are especially likely to profit when they help others. Evidence for this may be found, for example, in Reissman's (1965) classic paper on the helper principle. Based on his research with self-help groups, Reissman (1965) found that doing something worthwhile for a person in need is a fulfilling and self-validating experience that bolsters the self-esteem of support providers. The emphasis in Reissman's (1965) theory on self-esteem is noteworthy because research consistently shows that feelings of self-worth are an important precursor of well-being in late life (e.g., Krause, 1987).

In order to understand why there may be SES variations in the relationship between providing support to others and well-being, it is important to pinpoint the precise mechanisms responsible for these salubrious effects. In a recent paper, Krause and Shaw (2000) argue that at least part of the answer may be found by focusing on the outcome of the helping process. In particular, these investigators propose that older adults will be more likely to benefit from helping others if the support recipient's situation improves because of the help they have been given. Viewed the other way around, if elders provide assistance to others, but the support recipient's circumstances do not improve, then it is not clear why help providers should feel they have done something worthwhile. By assisting others, older adults are, in effect, investing part of themselves in the helping process. This means their abilities, skills, and resources are placed in a social arena where they are subject to evaluation by the provider, the recipient, and other social network members. If the recipient fails to improve when help is given, it may reflect poorly on the support provider. More specifically, help givers may feel the assistance they provided was inadequate, and they lack the skill or resources needed to make a difference. As a result, the support provider may assume part of the blame when a positive outcome is not forthcoming (Coyne et al., 1988). Assuming the blame for a failed helping outcome should diminish, rather than bolster, the self-esteem of older support providers.

As noted earlier, the problems faced by lower SES support recipients are likely to be chronic and, therefore, difficult to eradicate (Pearlin, 1999). If problems linger after assistance is given, lower SES support providers may not reap the benefits associated with helping others. The paper by Krause and Shaw (2000) provides some preliminary support for this theoretical rationale. In particular, their longitudinal analyses suggest that helping others initially enhances the self-esteem of support providers regardless of their SES. But these salutary effects slowly dissipate over time for lower SES elders only.

C. SES, Primary Control, and Secondary Control

Research consistently shows that SES is inversely related to feelings of personal control: compared to upper SES elders, older adults in lower SES groups are less likely to feel they can influence the course of events in their lives (Argyle, 1994). The purpose of this section is to extend thinking in this area by assessing potentially important linkages between SES and primary, as well as secondary, feelings of control. Throughout, an emphasis will be placed on the social basis of this process by showing how the interplay between SES and social support shapes these key dimensions of control in late life.

So far, the theoretical rationale devised by Schulz and Heckhausen (1996) holds that elderly people relinquish primary control in some life domains in order to maintain a sense of primary control in other domains. However, two key issues remain unexamined. First, we need to know how many domains are targeted for the exercise of primary control. Second, we need to know more about the ways in which SES and social support may influence this decision.

For decades, sociologists and psychologists have argued that people who occupy more roles tend to have better mental health than those who have fewer roles

(Barnett, 1993). But the theoretical rationale for this relationship is not fully developed. Viewing this research in terms of primary and secondary control may provide some useful insight. In particular, the key issue may not be the sheer number of roles per se that are occupied; instead, the critical factor may be the number of roles in which a person is able to exercise primary control. This may be important for the following reason. As noted earlier, the coping repertoire of older adults is likely to be strengthened or enhanced by self-directed efforts aimed at achieving primary control. Attempting to exercise primary control in a larger number of roles or life domains should, therefore, lead to a more diverse coping repertoire. Finally, having a wider range of coping responses may, in turn, promote better physical and mental health (Mattlin, Wethington, & Kessler, 1990).

But SES and social support may influence the number of roles or domains in which primary control is exercised. In particular, the number of domains reserved for primary control and the number that are delegated to the control of significant others are likely to be determined by the resources available to older adults and their social network members. Included among these resources are the very cornerstones of SES: education and income. When older adults possess adequate resources, it follows that they will strive to maintain primary control in relatively more domains than elderly people who have fewer resources at their disposal. Similarly, the resources available to social network members are likely to affect their willingness and ability to assume control of a life domain on behalf of a focal elder. Viewed in this way, it is possible to see that lower SES elders are placed in a doubly difficult situation. Lacking adequate resources of their own, they may strive to relinquish primary control in relatively more life domains

than their upper SES counterparts. But the transfer of control may not proceed smoothly for lower SES elders because their social network members are not likely to have adequate resources of their own.

Once again, the process may not be as straightforward as it appears initially. Significant others of lower SES elders obviously care very deeply for them and make every effort to do what they can, even if it entails some sacrifice. This means that the critical issue is not whether primary control is transferred to a trusted other in lower SES groups; instead, it is more likely to involve the effectiveness of social network members in managing the affairs of a focal elder. More specifically, it is important to think carefully about what happens when a trusted other attempts to assume control on behalf of a lower SES elder, but is unable to successfully execute these responsibilities. Some mechanisms have been identified in the previous sections (e.g., social network strain arising from overly burdening help providers), but it is important to consider other factors that have not been discussed up to this point.

Brown and his colleagues provide dramatic evidence of what can happen when significant others fail to deliver assistance that a focal person is counting on receiving (Brown, Andrews, Harris, Adler, & Bridge, 1986). The purpose of this longitudinal study was to evaluate the consequences of being let down by social network members. In particular, Brown and his associates assessed how much support respondents thought they would receive at the baseline survey, and then followed these subjects over time to see if significant others subsequently helped out when needed. Brown et al. (1986) found that the risk of becoming clinically depressed increased 20-fold when initial anticipated support failed to subsequently materialize. These findings are important for the following reason. Lower SES elders may be at risk if they turn over control in a life domain to a significant other, but lower SES support providers are unable to follow through.

V. Conclusions

A recent check of a computerized database maintained by the American Psychological Association (PsychINFO) reveals there are approximately 2,500 citations for studies on social support and aging. Yet, despite this flurry of activity, we know remarkably little about how the potential benefits of social support arise. The purpose of this chapter was to take a modest step in this direction by elaborating and extending promising leads in the literature. This was accomplished by focusing on the factors that shape social ties in late life (i.e., religion and SES) as well as assessing the immediate sequelae of the social support process (i.e., primary and secondary control). But this exercise was, of necessity, restricted to a few key issues. A great deal was left on the cutting room floor, including a discussion of formal and informal social support (and the interface between them) as well as changes in social support over the life course. Moreover, a number of critical methodological issues were not examined even though theory and methods are inextricably linked. For example, researchers have yet to reach a consensus on how to score or code responses to closed-ended questions about received support. Instead, some focus on the amount of support that has been received; others are concerned with how often help has been provided; and yet other investigators gauge the number of social network members who give a certain type of assistance. In addition, we know little about the comparability of social support measures in different SES and ethnic groups. For example, we don't know if existing questions on emotional support received from others measure the same thing or are interpreted in different ways by lower and upper SES elders.

Despite the importance of methodological issues, the thrust of the discussion provided above was decidedly theoretical or conceptual in nature. The rationale for this was best expressed over half a century ago by Kurt Lewin. In particular, he maintained that, "There is nothing as practical as a good theory" (Lewin, 1943). But developing good theory is far from a simple matter. As Maxim (1999) points out, the term *theory* is used in a number of ways, ranging from the grand theory of our sociological past (e.g., Parsons, 1951) to more specific theoretical specifications embedded in contemporary latent variable models. Perhaps the best way to proceed is to follow the advice of Merton (1967), who argued persuasively for the development of midrange theories that are firmly anchored in specific substantive domains.

We don't have good midrange theories about the social support process. Developing them should be a high priority. The task that lies before us involves thinking more deeply about the work that has been done, and logically extending this research to elucidate wider principles and processes. Hopefully, the thoughts sketched out in this chapter take a modest first step in this direction.

References

Adler, N. E., Boyce, T., Chesney, M. A., Cohen, S., Folkman, S., Kahn, R. L., & Syme, S. L. (1994). Socioeconomic status and health. *American Psychologist, 49,* 15–24.

Aldwin, C. M. (1994). *Stress, coping, and development.* New York: Guilford.

Antonucci, T. C. (1985). Personality characteristics, social support and social behavior. In R. H. Binstock & L. K. George (Eds.), *Handbook of aging and the social sciences* (pp. 94–128). New York: Van Nostrand-Reinhold.

Antonovsky, A. (1979). *Health, stress, and coping.* San Francisco: Jossey-Bass.

Argyle, M. (1994). *The psychology of social class.* London: Routledge.

Babbie, R. (1983). *The practice of social research.* Belmont, CA: Wadsworth.

Baltes, P. B. (1991). The many faces of human aging: Toward a psychological culture of old age. *Psychological Medicine, 21,* 837–854.

Barnett, R. C. (1993). Multiple roles, gender, and psychological distress. In L. Goldberer & S. Breznitz (Eds.), *Handbook of stress: Theoretical and clinical aspects* (pp. 427–445). New York: Free Press.

Barrera, M. (1986). Distinctions between social support concepts, measures, and models. *American Journal of Community Psychology, 14,* 413–445.

Barrera, M., Chassin, L., & Rogosch, F. (1993). Effects of social support and conflict on adolescent children of alcoholic and nonalcoholic fathers. *Journal of Personality and Social Psychology, 64,* 602–612.

Belle, D. (1990). Poverty and women's mental health. *American Psychologist, 45,* 385–389.

Beit-Hallahmi, B., & Argyle, M. (1998). *The psychology of religious behavior and experience.* London: Routledge.

Berkman, P., Heinik, J., Rosenthal, M., & Burke, M. (1999). Supportive telephone outreach as an intervention strategy for elderly patients in a period of crisis. *Social Work in Health Care, 28,* 63–76.

Bosworth, H. B., & Schaie, K. W. (1997). The relationship of social environment, social networks, and health outcomes in the Seattle Longitudinal Study: Two analytic approaches. *Journal of Gerontology: Psychological Sciences, 52B,* P197–P205.

Brown, G. W., Andrews, B., Harris, T., Adler, Z., & Bridge, L. (1986). Social support, self-esteem, and depression. *Psychological Medicine, 16,* 813–831.

Butler, R. N., & Lewis, M. I. (1982). *Aging and mental health.* Saint Louis: Mosby.

Caplan, G. (1981). Mastery of stress: Psychosocial aspects. *American Journal of Psychiatry, 138,* 413–420.

Carstensen, L. L. (1992). Social and emotional patterns in adulthood: Support for socioemotional selectivity theory. *Psychology and Aging, 7,* 331–338.

Cobb, S. (1976). Social support as a moderator of stress. *Psychosomatic Medicine, 38,* 300–314.

Coward, H. (1986). Intolerance in the world's religions. *Studies in Religion, 15,* 419–431.

Coyne, J. C., Wortman, C. B., & Lehman, D. R. (1988). The other side of support: Emotional overinvolvement and miscarried helping. In B. H. Gottlieb (Ed.), *Marshaling social support: Formats, processes, and effects* (pp. 305–330). Newbury Park, CA: Sage.

Dowd, J. J. (1975). Aging as exchange: A preface to a theory. *Journal of Gerontology, 30,* 584–594.

Eckenrode, J., & Wethington, E. (1990). The process and outcome of mobilizing social support. In S. Duck (Ed.), *Personal relationships and social support* (pp. 83–103). Newbury Park, CA: Sage.

Ellison, C. G., & Levin, J. S. (1998). The religion-health connection: Evidence, theory, and future directions. *Health Education & Behavior, 25,* 700–720.

Enright, R. D., & North, J. (1998). *Exploring forgiveness.* Madison, WI: University of Wisconsin Press.

Enright, R. D., Gassin, E. A., & Wu, C. (1992). Forgiveness: A developmental view. *Journal of Moral Education, 21,* 99–114.

Finch, J. F., Okun, M. A., Barrera, M., Zautra, A. J., & Reich, J. W. (1989). Positive and negative social ties among older adults: Measurement models and the prediction of psychological distress and well-being. *American Journal of Community Psychology, 17,* 585–605.

Fromm, E. (1941). *Escape from freedom.* New York: Reinhart.

Girard, M., & Mullet, E. (1997). Forgiveness in adolescents, young, middle-aged, and older adults. *Journal of Adult Development, 4,* 209–220.

Gottlieb, B. H. (1992). Quandaries in translating support concepts to intervention. In H. O. Viel & U. Baumann (Eds.), *The meaning and measurement of social support* (pp. 293–309). New York: Hemisphere Publishing Corp.

Gottlieb, B. H. (1997). *Coping with chronic stress.* New York: Plenum.

Hansson, R. O., & Carpenter, B. N. (1990). Relational competence and adjustment in older adults: Implications for the demands of aging. In M. A. Stephens, J. H. Crowther, S. E. Hobfoll, & D. L. Tennenbaum (Eds.), *Stress and coping in later-life families* (pp. 131–152). New York: Hemisphere Publishing Corp.

Hargrave, T. D. (1994). *Families and forgiveness: Healing wounds in the intergenerational family.* New York: Brunner/Mazel.

Hargrave, T. D., & Anderson, W. T. (1992). *Finishing well: Aging and reparation in the intergenerational family.* New York: Brunner/Mazel.

Harris, T., Brown, G. W., & Robinson, R. (1999). Befriending as an intervention for chronic depression among women in an inner city: Randomised control trial. *British Journal of Psychiatry, 174,* 219–224.

Heller, K., Thompson, M. G., Trueba, P. E., Hogg, J. R., & Vlachos-Weber, I. (1991). Peer support telephone dyads for elderly women: Was this the wrong intervention? *American Journal of Community Psychology, 19,* 53–74.

Hobfoll, S. E. (1998). *Stress, culture, and community.* New York: Plenum.

Kaplan, B. H., Cassel, J. C., & Gore, S. (1977). Social support and health. *Medical Care, 15,* 47–62.

Kessler, R. C. (1979). A strategy for studying differential vulnerability to the psychological consequences of stress. *Journal of Health and Social Behavior, 20,* 100–108.

Kessler, R. C., McGonagle, K. A., Zhao, S., Nelson, C. B., Hughes, M., Eshleman, S., Wittchen, H., & Kendler, K. S. (1994). Lifetime and 12-month prevalence of DSM-III-R psychiatric disorders in the United States: Results from a national comorbidity survey. *Archives of General Psychiatry, 51,* 8–19.

Koenig, H. G. (1999). *The healing power of faith: Science explores medicine's last great frontier.* New York: Simon & Schuster.

Krause, N. (1987). Life stress, social support, and self-esteem in an elderly population. *Psychology and Aging, 2,* 349–356.

Krause, N. (1995). Negative interaction and satisfaction with social support among older adults. *Journal of Gerontology: Psychological Sciences, 50B,* P59–P73.

Krause, N. (1997a). Anticipated support, received support, and economic stress among older adults. *Journal of Gerontology: Psychological Sciences, 52B,* P284–P293.

Krause, N. (1997b). Received support, anticipated support, and mortality. *Research on Aging, 19,* 387–422.

Krause, N. (1998). Neighborhood deterioration, religious coping, and changes in health during late life. *The Gerontologist, 38,* 653–664.

Krause, N., & Borawski-Clark, E. (1995). Social class differences in social support among older adults. *The Gerontologist, 35,* 498–508.

Krause, N., Ellison, C. G., & Wulff, K. M. (1998). Church-based support, negative interaction, and well-being. *Journal for the Scientific Study of Religion, 37,* 725–741.

Krause, N., & Ingersoll-Dayton, B. (in press). Religion and the process of forgiveness in late life. *Review of Religious Research.*

Krause, N., Liang, J., & Gu, S. (1998). Financial strain, received support, and anticipated support in the P.R.C. *Psychology and Aging, 13,* 58–68.

Krause, N., Morgan, D., Chatters, L., & Meltzer, T. (2000). Using focus groups to explore the nature of prayer in late life. *Journal of Aging Studies 14,* 191–212.

Krause, N., & Rook, K. S. (2000). *Negative interaction in late life.* Unpublished manuscript.

Krause, N., & Shaw, B. (2000). Giving social support to others, socioeconomic status, and changes in self-esteem in late life. Under review at the *Journal of Gerontology: Social Sciences.*

La Gaipa, J. J. (1990). The negative effects of informal support systems. In S. Duck (Ed.), *Personal relationships and social support* (pp. 122–139). Newbury Park, CA: Sage.

Lee, G. (1985). Kinship and social support of the elderly: The case of the United States. *Ageing and Society, 5,* 19–38.

Lewin, K. (1943). Psychology and the process of group living. *Journal of Social Psychology, 17,* 113–131.

Lewis, M. A., & Rook, K. S. (1999). Social control in personal relationships: Impact on health behaviors and psychological distress. *Health Psychology, 18,* 63–71.

Liang, J., Bennett, J. M., Krause, N. M., Chang, M., Lin. S., Chuang, Y. L., & Wo, S. (1999). Stress, social relationships, and old age mortality in Taiwan. *Journal of Clinical Epidemiology, 52,* 983–995.

Lieberman, M. A. (1986). Social supports—The consequences of psychologizing: A commentary. *Journal of Consulting and Clinical Psychology, 54,* 461–465.

Lin, N. (1982). Social resources and instrumental action. In P. V. Marsden & N. Lin (Eds.), *Social structure and network analysis* (pp. 131–145). Beverly Hills, CA: Sage.

Litwak, E. (1981). *The modified extended family, social networks, and research continuities in aging.* New York: Columbia University Center for Social Sciences.

Mattlin, J. A., Wethington, E., & Kessler, R. C. (1990). Situational determinants of coping and coping effectiveness. *Journal of Health and Social Behavior, 31,* 103–122.

Maxim, P. S. (1999). *Quantitative research methods in the social sciences.* New York: Oxford University Press.

Merton, R. K. (1967). *On theoretical sociology.* New York: Free Press.

Norris, F. H., & Kaniasty, K. (1996). Received and perceived social support in times of stress: A test of the social support deterioration deterrence model. *Journal of Personality and Social Psychology, 71,* 498–511.

Nunn, K. P. (1996). Personal hopefulness: A conceptual review of the relevance of the perceived future to psychiatry. *British Journal of Medical Psychology, 69,* 227–245.

Okun, M. A., & Keith, V. M. (1998). Effects of positive and negative social exchanges with various sources of depressive in younger and older adults. *Journal of Gerontology: Psychological Sciences, 53B,* P4–P20.

Olson, J. M., Roese, N. J., & Zanna, M. P. (1996). Expectancies. In E. T. Higgins & A. W. Kruglanski (Eds.), *Social psychology: Handbook of basic principles* (pp. 211–238). New York: Guilford.

Pargament, K. I. (1997). *The psychology of religion and coping: Theory, research, and practice.* New York: Guilford.

Parsons, T. (1951). *The social system.* Glencoe, IL: Free Press.

Pearlin, L. I. (1999). The stress process revisited: Reflections on concepts and their interrelationships. In C. S. Aneshensel & J. C. Phelan (Eds.), *Handbook of the sociology of mental health* (pp. 395–415). New York: Plenum.

Peterson, C., Seligman, M., & Vaillant, G. (1988). Pessimistic explanatory style is a risk factor for physical illness: A thirty-five year longitudinal survey. *Journal of Personality and Social Psychology, 55,* 23–37.

Reissman, F. (1965). The "helper" therapy principle. *Social Work, 10,* 27–32.

Rodin, J. (1990). Control by any other name: Definitions, concepts, and processes. In J. Rodin, C. Schooler, & K. W. Schaie (Eds.), *Self-directedness: Cause and effects through the life course* (pp. 1–18). Hillsdale, NJ: Erlbaum.

Rook, K. S. (1984). The negative side of social interaction: Impact on psychological well-being. *Journal of Personality and Social Psychology, 46,* 1097–1108.

Rook, K. S. (1990). Parallels in the study of social support and social strain. *Journal of Social and Clinical Psychology, 9,* 118–132.

Rook, K. S., & Pietromonaco, P. (1987). Close relationships: Ties that heal or ties that bind? In W. H. Jones & D. Perlman (Eds.), *Advances in Personal Relationships, Volume 1* (pp. 1–35). Greenwich, CT: JAI Press.

Rothbaum, F., Weisz, J. R., & Snyder, S. S. (1982). Changing the world and changing the self: A two-process model of perceived control. *Journal of Personality and Social Psychology, 42,* 5–37.

Rowe, J. W., & Kahn, R. L. (1998). *Successful aging.* New York: Pantheon.

Sarason, I. G., Sarason, B. R., & Pierce G. R. (1994). Relationship-specific social support: Toward a model for the analysis of supportive interactions. In B. R. Burleson, T. L. Albrecht, & I. G. Sarason (Eds.), *Communication of social support: Messages, interactions, relationships, and community* (pp. 91–112). Thousand Oaks, CA: Sage.

Scobie, E. D., & Scobie, G. E. (1998). Damaging events: The perceived need for forgiveness. *Journal for the Theory of Social Behavior, 28,* 373–401.

Schulz, R., & Heckhausen, J. (1996). A life span model of successful aging. *American Psychologist, 51,* 702–714.

Schuster, T. L., Kessler, R. C., & Aseltine, R. H. (1990). Supportive interactions, negative interactions, and depressed mood. *American Journal of Community Psychology, 18,* 423–438.

Seeman, T. E., Berkman, L. F., Kohout, F., Lacroix, A., Glynn, R., & Blazer, D. (1993). Intercommunity variations in the association between social ties and mortality in the elderly. *Annals of Epidemiology, 3,* 325–335.

Skinner, E. A. (1996). A guide to the construct of control. *Journal of Personality and Social Psychology, 71,* 549–570.

Strawn, B. D., Hester, S., & Brown, W. S. (1998). Telecare: A social support intervention for family caregivers of dementia victims. *Clinical Geronotologist, 18,* 66–69.

Taylor, R. J., & Chatters, L. M. (1988). Church members as a source of informal social support. *Review of Religious Research, 30,* 193–202.

Thoits, P. A. (1991). On merging identity theory with stress research. *Social Psychology Quarterly, 54,* 101–112.

Weber, M. (1925). *From Max Weber: Essays in sociology,* H. Gerth & S. Wright Mills (Eds.). New York: Oxford University Press.

Wethington, E., & Kessler, R. C. (1986). Perceived support, received support, and adjustment to stressful life events. *Journal of Health and Social Behavior, 27,* 78–89.

Sixteen

The Aging Self in Social Contexts

Roseann Giarrusso, J. Beth Mabry, and Vern L. Bengtson

William James (1910) aptly portrayed the dual nature of the self by differentiating between the "I" (the self as subject) and the "me" (the self as object). Similarly, George Herbert Mead (1934) also referred to the "I" as the initiator of action and the "me" as an object to itself. Thus, the self is simultaneously both subject and object. The focus of this chapter is on the self as object. The goal of this chapter is to examine how the self as object changes or remains stable over time as a result of continuity and change in the social contexts in which it is embedded.

I. Cross-Fertilization of Life-Course and Social Psychological Perspectives

Although a subjective state such as the self is clearly a social psychological construct, we approach the definition of social context from both a life-course and social psychological perspective. We borrow from the life-course perspective its emphasis on historical and biographical dimensions of time and culture; we borrow from social psychology its emphasis

on culture and social structure. This "cross-fertilization" of life-course and social psychological perspectives, as suggested by George (1996), makes it possible to gain greater insights about the reciprocal influence of the self, aging, and social contexts.

The purpose of this chapter is to describe theories and empirical evidence on continuity and change in the self across three major social contexts: (a) time, (b) culture, and (c) social structure. We address several questions: Does the self change across social contexts? More specifically, are individuals' *descriptions*, and/or *evaluations*, of self influenced by biographical and historical time? By culture and social structural position? By the interaction of these social contexts? If so, what is the pattern of that change? In answering these questions we draw from theories and research in sociology, gerontology, and psychology.

The self is an important topic of study because various aspects of the self have been linked to individual and social outcomes. On an individual level, self-perceptions are related to individuals' well-being, coping abilities, achievements and failures, relationships with

Handbook of Aging and the Social Sciences, Fifth Edition

others, health, and even mortality. On a social level, historical and cultural trends influence individuals' self-concepts and collectively alter society. For example, the women's movement of the 1960s and 1970s presented women with alternative possibilities which in turn likely contributed to changes in women's self-perceptions and self-motivated actions. These changes had profound consequences for family life (Rosenberg, 1981). The way people view themselves in later life plays an important role in health and well-being and in social trends, such as the varied and changing meanings and nature of retirement.

We begin the chapter with a description of the self and social contexts. Second, we describe theories that deal with continuity and change in the self. Third, we present results showing the influence of social contexts on the self. Fourth, we discuss ways in which the self, in turn, influences the social context. Finally, we draw conclusions about the state of theory and research on the aging self in social context and discuss directions for future research.

A. What Is the Self?

The self is made up of three basic components: the *cognitive*—the content of who we think we are; the *affective*—our feelings about who we are; and the *conative*—our actions on the basis of our self-perceptions.

First, in terms of cognitions, our self-concepts reflect the content of the self: our social roles and identities, our characteristics and traits. These are the aspects of the self that we typically use to describe ourselves. Our *roles* come from our relationships with other people, such as daughter or son, parent, grandparent, student, spouse, friend, co-worker. Each role has a counterpart and each role comes with certain social rights and expectations according to the norms of our culture. Our identities also come from the social categories to which we belong such as our gender, ethnicity, occupation, religion, social class, nationality, and other group memberships. A person's identity might include being a man, an Hispanic, a graphic designer, a golfer, an American, a Harvard alumna, and a member of the Jones family. We also define ourselves according to our perceptions of our traits, such as extroversion, openness, and agreeableness, as well as characteristics such as being honest, caring, outspoken, and analytical. These are things we tend to think of as "facts about ourselves" (Bengtson, Reedy, & Gordon, 1985).

Second, the affective component of the self is composed of our evaluations of ourselves. We may see ourselves as good or bad, strong or weak, in control of our lives or subject to the whims of fate. Self-esteem refers to our sense of worth, how positively or negatively we feel about ourselves. Self-efficacy refers to our sense of control, how much or how little effect we feel we have on our own outcomes. We have both general feelings about our self-worth ("global self-esteem") and our effectiveness in the world, as well as domain-specific feelings about ourselves. An individual might feel generally good about herself as a person (high global self-esteem) but not about herself as an athlete (low domain-specific self-esteem).

The third or conative dimension of the self encompasses actions motivated by our self-conceptions (Bengtson et al., 1985). Most people strive to maintain positive, consistent views of themselves. Accordingly, we tend to pay more attention to feedback we receive from others that reinforces our self-perceptions, especially those aspects of ourselves that are particularly important to us, while ignoring information that is inconsistent with our views of ourselves. We also are inclined to avoid people and situations that contradict our self-conceptions. And, when we do not like something about ourselves, we may be motivated to change in order to achieve a more ideal self.

When we interact with others, we continually pick up cues and feedback about ourselves from others and from our observations of ourselves. We interpret this information and integrate it into our self-concepts—who we think we are, how we feel about ourselves, and how we act. Thus, there are three basic ways we get information about ourselves: reflected appraisals, social comparisons, and self-evaluations. These processes inform the content of our self-perceptions.

Reflected appraisals are the way we think others see us. It is the view of the self that we get when we look at ourselves through the eyes of others, our "looking glass self" (Cooley, 1968). *Social comparisons* tell us how we measure up on a particular aspect of ourselves compared with similar people (Festinger, 1954). For instance, a person might evaluate her swimming performance by comparing herself with her friend, but not to an Olympic swimmer. *Self-evaluations* are our own assessments of ourselves based on criteria we set for ourselves. A high school sophomore, for example, strives for a grade of B in a course because he has received a B in similar courses in the past. Even though grades are a form of feedback about a person's academic performance as well as a mechanism for ranking students in comparison to one another, in this case, the student is setting his own criteria for self-evaluation. Another aspect of our self-evaluations are *self-attributions*. We tend to attribute our outcomes, whether they are successes or failures, either to internal or external causes. Our self-attributions typically serve to enhance our self-perceptions as people often assign successes to internal causes and failures to external causes (Greenwald, 1980).

Because the process of observing, interpreting, and evaluating ourselves is ongoing, it might be justified to assume that the self is ever changing. Indeed, our views of ourselves do vary to some extent from moment to moment (Demo, 1992). Much research suggests that our overall self-conceptions—our sense of who we are and our global perceptions of how good or bad, potent or weak—remain fairly stable over time. Based on short-term longitudinal research, it appears that individuals work very hard to maintain consistent views of themselves, even if those views are negative (Swann, 1987). However, the degree to which there is stability or change in the self over the life course remains an empirical question, as is discussed in more detail below, because there have been only a few long-term longitudinal studies that have examined this issue.

The majority of empirical work is on the affective component of the self; the least amount is on the conative component. In keeping with the dominant body of literature, the remainder of this chapter is limited to theories and research on the affective and cognitive components of the self. We examine how these components are influenced by three major social contexts.

B. What are the Social Contexts?

In determining the social contexts in which the self is embedded, we turn to life-course and social psychology perspectives. By cross-fertilizing these two paradigms, we hope to bring greater insight to the study of the self. As George (1996) described, life-course researchers need to acknowledge that there is a reciprocal relationship between life-course experiences and subjective states. For example, life-course experiences shape the content of the self, and the content of the self also influences life-course experiences. On the other hand, George points out that social psychologists need to understand that subjective states are influenced not only by the contemporaneous environment but also by early life-course experiences, as would be suggested by the life course perspective.

Although social psychologists tend to limit their research to short time intervals, life-course researchers take a broader view of time. Furthermore, life-course researchers recognize that individual lives are influenced by multiple dimensions of time—biographical, social, and historical—that result in aging, cohort, and period effects.

Aging effects refer to biographical time (i.e., the influence of maturation or biological aging). For example, for decades research findings suggested that declines in intelligence were an aging effect. Conclusions about age and intelligence were based on cross-sectional data that scholars used to compare intelligence between age groups (Elder & O'Rand, 1995). However, cross-sectional studies cannot tell us whether differences between younger individuals and older individuals are due to aging or cohort effects. People in different age groups (cohorts) experienced differences in education that might account for age differences in intelligence reflected by cross-sectional studies.

Cohort effects refer to social time (i.e., groups born during a particular period of history who share common events). For example, the cohort that came of age during the Great Depression experienced historically different social and economic circumstances than prior or successive cohorts, and these different circumstances resulted in different life-course patterns (Elder, 1974). However, birth cohorts are not necessarily uniform in their experience of historical events. That is, within cohorts there is substantial variation that cohort comparisons may not capture, such as those resulting from differences in ethnicity, gender, and social class. For instance, the Great Depression affected middle-class and working class families differently, and Word War II affected young adult men and women differently (Elder & O'Rand, 1995).

Period effects refer to historical influences of social change that affect members of all cohorts. Changes in family life during the second half of the 20th century had an impact on individuals across age groups. Women's increasing workforce participation, the rise in divorce, and delayed marriage and childbearing affected children, parents, and grandparents, although the effects were different for each cohort.

The social psychological perspective complements the life-course perspective by showing that there are other social contexts besides time that must be considered. The self is also influenced by culture and social structure. Social psychologists' often show how social structure and culture influence individuals' attitudes and behaviors by employing the concept of roles. Roles allow social psychologists to bridge the micro- and macrolevels of analyses. Culture refers to the perspective one gains from shared experiences in a particular group or nation. Social structural positions, such as those based on gender, race/ethnicity, and social class, afford individuals different opportunities and barriers in society, and consequently another context for the self.

In the next two sections we review the theories and research that show how the affective and cognitive components of the self are influenced by changes in these major social contexts: biographical time, historical time, culture, and social structure.

II. How Social Contexts Influence Self-Esteem—The Affective Component of the Self

A. Biographical Time

Does self-esteem change with age? If so, does the aging process have a negative or a positive impact on self-esteem? Does the change form a linear or curvilinear pattern? The answers to these questions depend on the theoretical approach taken. Both sociological and gerontological theories make use of role-related concepts and principles, whereas psychological theory does not.

According to structural role theory, individuals are engaged in the process of role acquisition, role transition, and role loss throughout life (Rosow, 1974, 1985). Involvement in multiple roles links the individual to society and provides the individual with many opportunities for social rewards and feelings of competence and achievement (Adelmann,1994; Reitzes & Mutran, 1994; Reitzes, Mutran, & Fernandez, 1994, 1996; Reitzes, Mutran, & Verrill, 1995; Thoits, 1983, 1986). During early and middle adulthood, individuals acquire and transition into many new roles such as occupational, marital, and parental roles, typically resulting in high levels of self-esteem during these two stages in the life cycle. However, during late adulthood individuals experience role loss such as retirement, widowhood, the empty nest, and declining health. Consequently, individuals are less integrated with society and have fewer opportunities for social rewards and feelings of competence and achievement. Structural role theorists would predict that the lack of involvement in social roles would lead to low self-esteem in the later stages of life (Adelmann, 1994).

Another sociological theory—identity theory—has its roots in structural symbolic interactionism (Stryker, 1980). Predictions from identity theory are less clear because they depend on individuals' interpretations of the meaning of their roles. Whether self-esteem would increase or decrease with age would depend on whether individuals perceived their roles and identities to be salient to their sense of self and whether they perceived the quality of their performance in those

salient roles to be competent (as judged by themselves and significant others) (Nuttbrock & Freudiger, 1991; Stryker, 1968, 1980). Thus, according to identity theory, self-esteem would have the potential to increase with age as long as individuals perceived an improvement in role performance and in reflected appraisals over time.

Gerontological theories would make predictions similar to structural role theory. Activity theory is the application of structural role theory to the elderly. According to activity theory, social interaction is important for the maintenance of self-esteem (Reitzes et al., 1995). Since the elderly lack formal roles and statuses within the main institutions of society, it may be difficult for them to maintain positive self-evaluations. Continuity theory, another off-shoot of role theory used in gerontology, makes a slightly different prediction. It suggests that a reduction in role activity does not lead to a decrease in self-esteem as long as the individual maintains some continuity between past roles and current interests and behaviors (Atchley, 1999).

Life-span developmental psychology grows out of the work of Buhler (1935) and Erikson (1963, 1968, 1982). According to life-span developmental psychology, there is a biological basis to development; hence, development is universal and occurs in a sequence of stages closely corresponding to age (Baltes, Dittman-Kohli, & Dixon, 1984; Schaie, 1977–78). The self develops through the resolution of a series of "crises" of two conflicting, "age-appropriate" concerns, such as when autonomy outweighs shame during early childhood. "Normal" development progresses from high levels of ego involvement and self-serving activities in early and middle stages of life to high levels of integrity and altruism in late life (Erikson, 1959/1980, 1968). These types of developmental changes lead to a less critical evaluation of self. Thus, the life-span developmental perspective implies that normal aging, rather than being problematic, is a positive process. Life-span developmental theorists would predict that self-esteem would progressively increase over the life course.

According to personality theorists (Field, 1991), individuals' personalities continue to change until young adulthood and then remain relatively stable. Based on data from multiple longitudinal studies using different methods, personality theorists (McCrae & Costa, 1988) argue that there is little evidence of age-related changes in personality during the adult years. The pattern of continuity found suggests a five-factor model of personality known as the "Big Five" which includes neuroticism, extraversion, openness to experience, agreeableness, and conscientiousness (NEO-AC). Thus, since personality traits are assumed to be relatively stable once the individual reaches adulthood, personality or trait theorists would predict that self-esteem would remain stable across the life course.

Researchers studying the affective or evaluative component of the self often use long-standing attitude scales to measure self-esteem. Several standard scales are available to measure self-esteem. Some of the most popular include the Total Positive Scale from the Tennessee Self-Concept Scales, the Rosenberg Self-Esteem Scale, and the Monge Semantic Differential scales (Bengtson et al., 1985; Breytspraak & George, 1982).

Despite the voluminous research literature on self-esteem, over the last 50 years a relatively small number of studies have investigated the effect of age on self-esteem (Dietz, 1996; Elliott, 1996; Gove, Ortega, & Style, 1989; McCrae & Costa, 1988; Oates, 1997; for earlier reviews see Bengtson et al., 1985, and Kogan, 1990). Some studies found a decrease in self-esteem with age, while others have found an increase with age. A few studies indicated a curvilinear relationship between age and self-esteem. Although these studies have produced somewhat contradictory findings as to whether self-esteem changes or remains the same across age groups, taken as a whole they suggest that self-esteem increases slightly from early adolescence through the remainder of the life course.

However, since the majority of the studies used a cross-sectional design in which age and cohort effects were confounded, no definitive conclusions can be drawn. Thus, it is not possible to determine if age differences in self-esteem actually represent changes in self-esteem over time or whether they represent cohort differences. Further, among the studies that do examine self-esteem over time, there are no longitudinal studies of stability or change in self-esteem *across the adult life course* (Demo, 1992). The few longitudinal studies that have been conducted have focused on younger age groups to the exclusion of older age groups and have followed their respondents for relatively short periods of time (e.g., Elliott, 1996; Oates, 1997). There are two exceptions. One study followed adolescents over a span of 20 years and found a moderate level of stability in self-esteem for individuals aging across the early stage of the life course (Roberts & Bengtson, 1996). Another study followed grandparents, parents, and adult children over 20 years and found a low to moderate level of stability in self-esteem, as well as a low to moderate increase in self-esteem across time, for all three age groups (Giarrusso, Feng, Silverstein, & Bengston, 2000).

To adequately study the effects of aging on self-esteem, it is necessary to follow adults across several stages of the life course. Without the inclusion of respondents from all age groups and an examination of the same individuals across a large number of life stages, studies can lead to incomplete findings regarding the pattern and determinants of change in self-esteem across the life course. Future research is needed to address these methodological challenges.

B. Historical Time

Social gerontologists seeking to determine whether self-esteem changes with aging cannot address the question without taking into account the historical context in which the individuals live. Macrosocial events such as the Great Depression, major wars, and various social and political movements are experienced differently by individuals from different birth cohorts (Elder, 1974). For example, individuals of draft age during the Vietnam War may have experienced this event differently than individuals who were a decade younger. Both birth cohorts lived during the same historical period yet the effect of the historical period on members of each cohort was very different. The level of self-esteem for individuals from a particular birth cohort may, due to historical events, start out lower or higher than other birth cohorts. In order to determine how historical events might influence the affective component of the self, researchers must compare different birth cohorts across long periods of time in order to separate the age, period, and cohort effects. The direction of change on self-esteem, either positive or negative, would depend on how historical events were experienced.

To test such a model requires a cohort sequential design. Until recently no data set with this design had data on self-esteem. However, Bengtson, Biblarz, and Roberts (in press) were able to assess whether there were historical differences in individuals' evaluations of self by using a generational sequential design. That is, two generations (parents and adult children) from the same families were examined over a period of 26 years. This length of time allowed the self-esteem of parents and children to be compared when the parents and children were at the same approximate age but during different historical periods. The results revealed that gender interacted with historical period. That is, there were no differences by historical period in the level of self-esteem for mothers and daughters, but there were differences between fathers and sons. When daughters were an average age of 20 in 1997, their self-esteem was comparable to that of their mothers when their mothers were an average age of 20 back in 1971. However, the self-esteem of sons when they were an average age of 20 in 1997 was significantly higher than that of their fathers when their fathers were 20 in 1971. These findings suggest historical effects on self-esteem, at least for men. It appears that historical events, most probably the Vietnam War, had a negative influence on the self-confidence of draft-eligible men in the older cohort.

C. Culture

Cross-cultural research has been increasing in recent years. However, there are still few studies that have examined whether there are cultural differences in levels of self-esteem. Yet comparative research allows researchers to explore how social and historical conditions affect individuals from very different cultures.

For example, Markus and Kitayama (1991) examined sources of self-esteem among Japanese and American samples. They found that self-esteem among Japanese depends largely on fitting in and accommodating others as a result of the Eastern cultural emphasis on interdependence and harmony. In contrast, self-esteem among Americans relies on a sense of individuality and standing out, consistent with the Western cultural values of independence and individualism.

Much more research is needed to examine the nature and extent of the similarities and differences in the self among people of different cultures. Furthermore, the impact of expansive modernization and globalization on the self is not known. For instance, does the "Westernization" of Eastern cultures mean changes in sources of self-esteem based less on interdependence and more on individualism? What effect might these culture shifts have on the aging selves of older individuals in Eastern societies?

D. Social Structure

Does self-esteem differ by social structural position? That is, are there differences in self-esteem by gender, race and ethnicity, or social class? These questions have received considerable attention in the literature over the years (Porter & Washington, 1993; Wells & Marwell, 1986; Wylie, 1979). Surprisingly, few differences have been found in self-esteem by gender (Schwalbe & Staples, 1991), race and ethnicity (Hughes & Demo, 1989), or social class (Demo & Savin-Williams, 1983). A crucial distinction in interpreting these findings has to do with whether a status position is ascribed or achieved (Gecas & Burke, 1995). Achieved statuses appear to influence self-esteem while ascribed statuses do not. Because gender and race and ethnicity are ascribed characteristics they have little affect on self-esteem. Social class has no affect on the self-esteem of children (Wiltfang & Scarbecz, 1990), for whom social class is an ascribed status (based on their parents' rather than their own achievements). However, once individuals reach adulthood, social class has some influence on self-esteem (Schwalbe, 1985). Individuals who achieve a high social class enjoy higher levels of self-esteem than their lower social class counterparts.

III. How Social Contexts Influence Self-Descriptions of Who You Are—The Cognitive Component of the Self

Researchers interested in the cognitive component of the self want to know the beliefs individuals have about who they are. For instance, they are interested in whether individuals think of themselves primarily in terms of role identities or dispositional identities. Role identities refer to beliefs about the self related to social roles (teacher, spouse, friend), social categories (age, race/ethnicity, gender), and group membership (religious denomination, political party, family). Dispositional identities refer to beliefs about the self that are related to character traits (such as honest, kind, strong) and behavioral tendencies (such as politically active, financially conservative, hard working).

Following a by now classic tradition, the majority of researchers studying this component of the self have done so by asking individuals to provide twenty answers to the question "Who Am I?" Hence, the name of this technique: the Twenty Statements Test or TST (Kuhn & McPartland, 1954). Although many schemas have been developed to code individual's answers to the TST, a common one involves counting the number of role versus dispositional identities cited by an individual (e.g., Leary, Wheeler, & Jenkins, 1986; Snow & Phillips, 1982; Zurcher, 1977).

Research has shown that individuals who cite more role identities than dispositional identities differ from individuals who show the reverse pattern of citations in the behaviors they prefer to engage in. For example, individuals who primarily cite role identities tend to prefer occupations offering social rewards such as status and friendship, whereas individuals who primarily cite dispositional identities prefer occupations offering rewards like personal growth and self-expression (Leary et al., 1986). Thus, knowing about the cognitive component of the self is also useful in predicting some future behaviors of individuals.

A. Biographical Time

Social gerontologists are interested in whether individuals change the way they describe themselves as they age over biographical time. Several theories suggest that individuals would answer the question, Who am I? differently as they age across the life course. Sociological, gerontological, and psychological theories make different predictions about continuity and change in self-descriptions across the life course.

Sociological theories employ the concept of roles. Structural role theory suggests that early and late in life people have fewer roles (Rosow, 1985). This may result in younger and older people answering with fewer role statements and with more statements of psychological characteristics than middle-age people. Identity theory (Stryker, 1980) would suggest that individuals would respond to the TST with the roles that are most salient to their sense of identity at each stage of life.

Gerontological theories such as Activity Theory (Lemon, Bengtson, & Peterson, 1972; Longino & Kart, 1982; Reitzes, Mutran, & Verril, 1995) and Continuity Theory (Atchley, 1999) would make predictions similar to role theory about how individuals would respond to the question, Who am I? That is, older adults who were still actively engaged in numerous activities and social roles would be more likely to answer the question with role identities than older adults who are no longer actively engaged.

Psychological theories of maturation or development (such as Erikson, 1982) would predict that individuals would respond to the TST with dispositional characteristics central to the issues they were trying to resolve at that particular stage of development. Personality theory would suggest that individuals would respond predominantly with dispositional characteristics or statements about personality traits that would remain stable over time.

Some research using the TST compares the responses of different age groups of older persons. For example, Freund and Smith (1999) examined individuals between 70 and 103 years of age. The results revealed that the ratio of positive to negative statements was less favorable for individuals 85 years of age and older compared to those under 85. Farnsworth, Pett, & Lund (1989) found that although age was a significant predictor of statements indicating psychological strength and coping, it only had a weak effect. However, since these studies are cross-sectional, it is not clear whether aging or historical change contributes to age differences in responses to the TST.

As yet we have no long-term longitudinal studies using the TST in which statements of the same individuals are examined across time as they age. Therefore, no definitive statements can be made as to how biographical time influences the cognitive component of the self. This is an area that needs to be addressed in future research.

B. Historical Time

Although no gerontological and psychological theories make predictions about how historical time would influence how individuals would respond to the TST, one sociological theory does. According to Zurcher's (1977) theory of the Mutuable Self, historical events shape individuals' conceptions of themselves. For example, rapid social change that began in the mid-1960s made it untenable for individuals to continue to base their sense of self on social institutions. Historical events like the Vietnam War and the Watergate scandal resulted in a loss of faith in the political institution, while recessions led to a growing distrust of the economic institution. In order for people to achieve a greater sense of control during these turbulent times, individuals should have begun to identify themselves more in terms of their own personal qualities rather than in terms of institutional affiliations. Thus, Zurcher predicted that a shift would occur in the content of the self from role identities to dispositional identities as a result of these historical trends.

A series of cross-sectional studies (Snow & Philips, 1982; Trafimow, Triandis, & Goto, 1991; Zurcher, 1977), conducted on young adults every decade over the last 50 years, allows us to see whether young adults living during different historical periods differentially describe the cognitive component of the self. Consistent with Zurcher's theory, this body of research has found that young adults in the 1950s and 1960s were more likely to describe themselves in terms of social roles, whereas young adults in the 1970s, 1980s, and 1990s were more likely to identify themselves in terms of dispositional and psychological characteristics.

It is unclear whether historical events have the same influence on older cohorts. It is possible that older cohorts remain more connected to social institutions than younger cohorts. This is a topic that needs to be addressed in future research.

C. Culture

Researchers interested in whether culture influences individuals' sense of self have conducted cross-cultural comparisons of individuals' responses to the TST. This research shows that differing cultural perspectives influence the degree to which individuals identify with groups in their society, and this identification process is reflected in the way individuals conceive of their sense of self. That is, individuals in Western cultures are

socialized to think of themselves as separate and independent of others. Furthermore, they learn to value this independence and uniqueness. In contrast, individuals in Eastern cultures are socialized to think of themselves in terms of their relationships with other people and to value interdependence and group cohesion.

This differing cultural emphasis on independence and interdependence is reflected in how individuals answer the TST. Cousins (1989) found that Japanese individuals listed a greater number of social identities and fewer dispositional identities than their American counterparts. Trafimow et al. (1991) found the same pattern when comparing Chinese and Americans. Rhee, Uleman, Lee, and Roman (1995) extended this finding to Koreans. Furthermore, they found that a emphasis on collectivism in Eastern cultures leads to self-definitions that are not only social but concrete. Conversely, the emphasis on individualism in Western cultures leads to self-definitions that are abstract as well as psychological.

Thus, research suggests that the differing cultural perspectives of individualism and collectivism influence the nature of the self. In Western cultures, individuals have an independent view of the self, defining themselves in terms of abstract thoughts, feelings, and behaviors, without reference to others. In contrast, in many Asian and other non-Western cultures, individuals have an interdependent view of the self, defining themselves in concrete ways and in terms of their relationships to other people (Bochner, 1994). However, because researchers have limited their samples to young adults, it is unclear whether these findings would hold true for older adults.

D. Social Structure

Researchers interested in the influence of social structure on the cognitive component of the self examine the influence of such characteristics as gender, race/ethnicity, and social class. For example, research comparing men and women generally has found that women are more likely to have an interdependent view of themselves, whereas men are more likely to have an independent view of themselves (Cross & Madson, 1997). That is, women tend to define themselves in relation to other people. MacRae (1995) found that, among women homemakers aged 65–98, self-identity was organized around social relationships rather than around formal roles.

However, whether women hold an interdependent view of self may be partially dependent on their participation in the workforce, and this, in turn, may have implications for the ease with which they make later life transitions, such as retirement. For example, Erdner and Guy (1990) found that women teachers who listed "teacher" as one of their 20 identities had significantly more negative attitudes toward retirement than those who did not list their occupation. They argue that women whose sense of self is organized around formal roles (such as work roles) rather than around social relationships will be more likely to experience retirement problems similar to those of men. Thus, women and men who work outside the home may need alternative means of meeting their needs for prestige and achievement after retirement.

Research on the influence of race and ethnicity on the cognitive component of the self is sparse. Despite research demonstrating that American culture promotes independence (and hence responses to the TST that are psychological and abstract), there should be variability among Americans based on race and ethnicity. That is, even though American Indians, African Americans, Mexican Americans, and Asian Americans live in a culture that promotes individualism, their cultural heritage promotes collectivism. Although survey research (Oyserman, 1993) reveals that ethnic Americans show both individualist and collectivist tendencies, there has been little research using the TST to study this biculturalism. One exception is the study by Rhee et al. (1995) who found differences among Asian Americans on the TST. Asian Americans who did not list their race/ethnicity on the TST had a response pattern similar to their Euro-American counterparts when describing themselves. On the other hand, Asian Americans who listed their race/ethnicity once or twice on the TST had a response pattern more like individuals from Eastern cultures when describing themselves.

Despite the fact that social class is one of the most widely used independent variables in survey research, surprisingly, we were unable to find any published research on the influence of social class on the cognitive component of the self. Like race and ethnicity, the influence of social class on self-descriptions should be examined in future research.

However, there are other societal influences on the self beyond those that occur as a result of the individuals' gender and race and ethnicity. Although social institutions such as the family, economy, and educational and political systems also serve as important contexts that must be considered, these social contexts are beyond the scope of this discussion. For coverage of the ways in which contexts such as the family, occupation, the health-care system, and social policy influence the self see Shaie and Hendricks (2000) and Ryff and Marshall (1999).

IV. How Social Contexts Are Influenced by the Self

Social contexts are also influenced by the self. Social psychological perspectives stress the "agentic" aspects of the self (i.e., the self is an agent that acts upon the social context as well as a product of it). Self-efficacy is the concept used to refer to the volitional nature of the self.

Even though social psychologists study self-efficacy, their generally short-term methodology can make it difficult to see the long-term effect of individuals' earlier volitional behavior. Thus, the cross-ferti-lization of the social psychological and life-course perspectives can bring greater meaning to the concept of self-efficacy by casting it in a broader time frame. By studying historical events that are beyond the control of individuals, life-course pro-ponents often failed to consider the pro-active nature of individuals. However, more recent developments in life-course theorizing have acknowledged the initia-tive of the individual actor. Agency is a crucial concept in Elder's (1999) recent discussions of the life-course perspective. He argues that despite social and histori-cal forces, individuals are still active agents in charting the courses of their lives. Individuals self-select themselves into environments that influence later life-course outcomes. The broader tem-porality of the life-course perspective makes this insight more apparent than the narrow time frame of most social psy-chological research.

Self-efficacy is important because it serves as a resource that affects people's ability to cope with problems and, conse-quently, influences well-being (Gecas, 1989; Mirowsky & Ross, 1989). Self-efficacy denotes a personal belief about one's own control over his or her out-comes, synonymous with instrumental-ism, mastery, and internal locus of control, and in contrast to fatalism, help-lessness, or powerlessness (Aneshensel, 1992; Mirowsky, Ross, & Van Willi-gen,1996). Although not precisely the same, these concepts are generally inter-changeable in a wide variety of circum-stances (Gecas, 1989; Mirowsky & Ross,1989).

Self-efficacy has both a motivation component, encouraging action that al-lows one to experience oneself as effec-tive, and a cognitive component, the expectancy of control (Gecas, 1989; Gecas & Burke, 1995). High self-efficacy predicts more positive outcomes, such as greater satisfaction and well-being, whereas fatalism and powerlessness con-tribute to more negative outcomes, in-cluding distress and depression (Gecas, 1989; Gecas & Burke, 1995; Mirowsky & Ross,1989). Sociological perspectives on self-efficacy can be traced back to Karl Marx's work on alienation and the theme of self-creation through efficacious action, particularly at work (Gecas, 1989). "Self-efficacy may be the most direct ex-pression of the self-concept as a social force" (Gecas & Burke, 1995, p. 47).

This broad view of self-efficacy does not differentiate between self-judgments of general competency and more action-spe-cific expectations about success. Bandura (1977) further specifies self-efficacy theory to account for efficacy expectations, a per-son's beliefs about successfully perform-ing particular actions. Bandura also differentiates efficacy expectations from outcome expectations, more contextual-ized estimates of whether certain actions will result in particular outcomes in given circumstances (Gecas, 1989). For example, according to Bandura's distinctions, indi-viduals may have generally high self-effi-cacy, but low efficacy expectations about their success in exercising regularly, or low outcome expectations that asking an employer for a salary raise will result in receiving a raise. In the later case, the out-come expectation points to the indivi-dual's belief about the responsiveness of an external factor (the employer's willing-ness to give a raise) to a given action (the request for a raise). Thus, Bandura distin-guishes self-appraisals from estimations of the responsiveness of the system or en-vironment (Gecas, 1989). Although these refinements of self-efficacy theory offer greater specificity, most research focuses on global self-efficacy.

Self-efficacy also seems to affect self-esteem. High self-esteem may result, at least in part, from efficacious activity. For example, school performance has a greater effect on self-esteem than self-esteem has on school performance (Gecas & Burke, 1995). Self-efficacy also is greatly influenced by one's social status, whereas self-esteem depends more on proximal influences, such as social niches, and interpersonal contexts (Aneshensel, 1992; Gecas, 1989; Gecas & Burke, 1995; Hughes & Demo, 1989). Stress research shows that self-esteem is less important than self-efficacy in coping with stressful circumstances and events (Pearlin & Schooler, 1978), although self-esteem's effect on stress has been less frequently investigated (Thoits, 1995).

The conditions of individuals' structural locations largely determine their chances to develop a sense of self-efficacy (Gecas, 1989). Self-efficacy depends upon the experience of efficacious activity. Opportunity to be efficacious is affected by dimensions of institutional inequality, such as occupational prestige, education and income, and by practices associated with cultural beliefs that result in discrimination (Hughes & Demo, 1989). Logically, performing effectively contributes to high self-efficacy. However, because "social contexts that are particularly conducive to efficacious activity are institutional in nature—part of the macrostructure of society—indicators of a individual's location in the macrostructure (specifically, social class and work) should be strong predictors of personal efficacy" (Hughes & Demo, 1989, p.138). Thus, relatively disadvantaged groups such as the poor, minorities, and women should have lower self-efficacy. Indeed, whites, men, and people with higher income, education, and occupational prestige have relatively higher levels of self-efficacy than minorities, women, and people of lower socioeconomic status (Gecas, 1989; Thoits, 1995).

Self-efficacy influences people's well-being through coping behavior (Aneshensel, 1992) because "what people do or fail to do in dealing with their problems can make a difference to their well-being" (Pearlin & Schooler, 1978, p.18). In coping with difficulty, self-efficacy makes instrumental, problem-solving behavior more likely than passive or avoidant behavior (Aneshensel, 1992; Chwalisz, Altmaier, & Russell, 1992; Thoits, 1995). Problem-focused coping that changes the situation or its meaning appears to be more beneficial for well-being than passive coping that merely manages distressing feelings but does not change the situation or its meaning (Pearlin & Schooler, 1978; Thoits, 1995).

Does self-efficacy change over biographical time, particularly in later life? Using a cross-sectional design, Dietz (1996) found that adult respondents 65 years of age and older had higher levels of self-efficacy than younger respondents. However, Mirowsky and Ross (1989) found that a sense of control diminished with age. Furthermore, it is possible that age interacts with other status characteristics, such as gender and ethnicity, which may further influence age-related changes in self-efficacy (Gecas, 1989). For instance, we might expect older ethnic minority women to have substantially lower levels of self-efficacy than young white men. Additional research is needed to untangle these more complex issues of age and other social characteristics.

Does self-efficacy change with historical time? This is another important question that should be investigated in future research using longitudinal data.

V. Directions for Future Research

In this chapter we argued that the cross-fertilization of social psychological and life-course perspectives would allow us to advance the study of the self by allowing us to define three important social contexts in which the self is embedded: time, culture, and social structure. First, we described the components of the self and the major social contexts in which the self is embedded. Next, we discussed sociological, gerontological, and psychological theories and research on the self. Finally, we showed how the self is both a product and an agent of social context.

Our review of the literature shows that the self is a crucial construct in 21st century research on aging. Over the last decade the self has been investigated as an independent variable, a mediating variable, and a dependent variable. Yet gaps remain. Research tends to be clustered in certain areas while other areas remain fallow. Furthermore, the cross-fertilization of life-course and social psychological perspectives suggests additional fruitful areas of investigation.

The first area suggested by the synthesis of these two paradigms is the persisting effect of early life experiences on the self. Some important studies of this nature have already begun to be conducted in the area of the family. For example, research by Roberts and Bengtson (1993, 1996) revealed that the positive effect of parents's affection on children's self-esteem persists over several decades after their children have become adults. Similarly, Yabiku, Axinn, and Thornton (1999) found that family integration of parents early in a child's life is positively related to the child's self-esteem 23 years later. Related questions still in need of investigation include, How do early, compared to contemporaneous, family experiences influence the self? Can positive contemporaneous family experiences compensate for early negative experiences? Can positive early family experiences buffer the self from negative contemporaneous family experiences? These same types of questions can be asked about other social institutions in which the self is embedded.

A second area of future research suggested by the merger of social psychological and life-course perspectives is how the self influences the selection of roles for entry, their timing, duration, and trajectory—all issues related to temporality. According to George (1996, p. 253) "the single greatest weakness of social psychological research" is its neglect of temporality. Therefore, the greatest contribution of the life-course perspective to the social psychological study of the self is an emphasis on biographical and historical time. Another benefit of the merger of the two perspectives is an increased emphasis on agency. What aspects of the self lead individuals to select certain roles at certain stages of the life course? What aspects of the self influence the duration and trajectory of those transitions? And, related to the discussion above, how do these early role choices influence later opportunities and subsequent choices?

This line of research may help to explain how entry into certain roles in early adulthood does not lead to an increase in self-esteem in later adulthood, although entry into other roles does. Again, using the institution of the family as an example, research has shown that entry into the spouse role as a result of marriage contributes to an increase in self-esteem up to 20 years later (Elliott, 1996; Giarrusso et al., 2000, Horwitz, White, & Howell-White, 1996). Conversely, entry into the parent role as a result of the birth of a child does not influence self-esteem either contemporaneously or 20 years later (Elliott, 1996; Giarrusso et al., 2000 Oates, 1997). Why is this? These divergent findings may have to do with the agency of individuals in self-selecting themselves into these roles. Generally, individuals assume the spouse role voluntarily. This is not always true for the parent role; some individuals enter parent role "accidentally." The heterogeneity among parents in the degree to which they were proactive in their selection of roles may be responsible for the lack of a relationship between parenthood and self-esteem.

This leads to a related question: How do historical events, culture, and social structure facilitate or impede self-selection into roles at different points in the life course? For the cross-fertilization of social psychology and life-course perspectives to be complete, researchers must do more than examine the influence of social contexts in isolation. To advance knowledge on the self, researchers must investigate how social contexts interact with one another in their influence on the self. For example, we need to know how the *intersection* of biological time, historical time, culture, and social structure influences the self. For example, 50 years ago individuals had much less choice as to whether they would or would not enter the parent role. How did this influence the cultural meaning of the role of parent and how did this contribute to individuals' sense of self? Was the contribution of the parent role to the sense of self different for men and women? These kinds of questions will require new types of data and methods of analysis.

However, the future of research on the self is promising. Although past research on the self was limited by the data and methods available, great methodological strides are being made today. Longitudinal data are being collected over longer time periods and on broader samples of individuals, [e.g., Asset and Health Dynamics Among the Oldest Old (AHEAD) and National Study of Families and Households (NSFH)] and advanced statistical capabilities are making it possible to analyze increasingly more complicated models. Furthermore, current researchers have access to more creative ways of measuring aspects of the self. New technologies such as pagers, wireless phones, videoconferencing, and e-mail will enable researchers to measure aspects of the self in ways, and at time intervals, never before possible.

References

Adelmann, P. K. (1994). Multiple roles and psychological well-being in a national sample of older adults. *Journal of Gerontology: Social Sciences, 49,* S277–S285.

Aneshensel, C. S. (1992). Social stress: Theory and research. *Annual Review of Sociology, 18,* 15–38.

Atchley, R. C. (1999). Continuity theory, self, and social structure. In C. D. Ryff & V. W. Marshall (Eds.), *The self and society in aging processes* (pp. 94–122). New York: Springer Publishing.

Baltes, P., Dittman-Kohli, F., & Dixon, R. (1984). New perspectives in the development of intelligence in adulthood: Toward a dual-process concept and a model of selective optimization with compensation. In P. Baltes & O. Brim (Eds.), *Life span development and behavior* (pp. 33–76). New York: Academic Press.

Bandura, A. (1977). Self-efficacy: Toward a unifying theory of behavioral change. *Psychological Review, 84,* 191–215.

Bengtson, V. L., Biblarz, T. J., & Roberts, R. E. L. (in press). *Do families still matter? Baby boomers, Generation Xers, and the transmission of achievement orientations.* New York: Cambridge University Press.

Bengtson, V. L., Reedy, M., & Gordon, C. (1985). Aging and self-concept: Personality processes and social contexts. In J. E. Birren & K. W. Schaie (Eds.), *Handbook of the psychology of aging* (2nd ed., pp. 544–593). New York: Van Nostrand Reinhold.

Bochner, S. (1994). Cross-cultural differences in the self concept: A test of Hofstede's individualism/collectivism distinction. *Journal of Cross-Cultural Psychology, 25,* 273–283.

Breytspraak, L. M., & George, L. K. (1982). Self-concept and self-esteem. In D. J. Mangen & W. A. Peterson (Eds.), *Clinical and social psychology* (pp. 241–302). Minneapolis: University of Minnesota Press.

Buhler, C. (1935). The curve of life as studied in biographies. *Journal of Applied Psychology, 19,* 405–409.

Chwalisz, K., Altmaier, E. M., & Russell, D. W. (1992). Causal attributions, self-efficacy cognitions, and coping with stress. *Journal of Social and Clinical Psychology, 11,* 377–400.

Cooley, C. H. (1968). The social self: On the meanings of "I." In C. Gordon & K. Gergen (Eds.), *The self in social interaction* (pp. 87–92). New York: Wiley.

Cousins, S. D. (1989). Culture and self-perception in Japan and the United States. *Journal of Personality and Social Psychology, 56,* 124–131.

Cross, S. E., & Madson, L. (1997). Models of the self: Self-construals and gender. *Psychological Bulletin, 122,* 5–37.

Cousins, S.D. (1989). Culture and selfhood in Japan and the U.S. *Journal of Personality and Social Psychology, 56,* 124–131.

Demo, D. H. (1992). The self-concept over time: Research issues and directions. *Annual Review of Sociology, 18,* 303–326.

Demo, D. H., & Savin-Williams, R.C. (1983). Early adolescent self-esteem as a function of social class: Rosenberg and Pearlin revisited. *American Journal of Sociology, 88,* 763–774.

Dietz, B. E. (1996). Relationship of aging to self-esteem: The relative effects of maturation and role accumulation. *International Journal of Aging and Human Development, 43,* 249–266.

Elder, G. H., Jr. (1974). *Children of the great depression: Social change in life experience.* Chicago: University of Chicago Press.

Elder, G. H., Jr. (1999, August). *The life course and aging: Some reflections.* Distinguished scholar lecture, Section on Aging, meeting of the American Sociological Association, Chicago.

Elder, G. H., Jr., & O'Rand, A. M. (1995). Adult lives in a changing society. In K. S. Cook, G. A. Fine, & J. S. House (Eds.), *Sociological perspectives on social psychology* (pp.451–475). Boston: Allyn and Bacon.

Elliott, M. (1996). Impact of work, family, and welfare receipt on women's self-esteem in young adulthood. *Social Psychology Quarterly, 59,* 80–95.

Erdner, R. A., & Guy, R. F. (1990). Career identification and women's attitudes toward retirement. *International Journal of Aging and Human Development, 30,* 129–139.

Erikson, E. (1959/1980). *Identity and the life cycle.* New York: Norton.

Erikson, E. (1963). *Childhood and society.* New York: Norton.

Erikson, E. (1968). Generativity and ego integrity. In B. Neugarten (Ed.), *Middle age and aging* (pp. 75–87). Chicago: University of Chicago Press.

Erikson, E. (1982). *The life cycle completed.* New York: Norton.

Farnsworth, J., Pett, M. A., & Lund, D. A. (1989). Predictors of loss management and well-being in later life widowhood and divorce. *Journal of Family Issues, 10,* 101–121.

Festinger, L. (1954). A theory of social comparison processes. *Human Relations, 7,* 117–140.

Field, D. (1991). Continuity and change in personality in old age–evidence from five longitudinal studies: Introduction to a special issue. *Journal of Gerontology, 46,* 271–274.

Freund, A. M., & Smith, J. (1999). Content and function of the self-definition in old and very old age. *Journals of Gerontology, 54,* P55–P67.

Gecas, V. (1989). The social psychology of self-efficacy. *Annual Review of Sociology 15,* 291–316.

Gecas, V., & Burke, P. J. (1995). Self and identity. In K. S. Cook, J. S. House, & G. A. Fine (Eds.), *Sociological perspectives on social psychology* (pp. 41–67). Boston, MA: Allyn and Bacon.

George, L. K. (1996). Missing Links: The case for a social psychology of the life course. *The Gerontologist, 36,* 248–255.

Giarrusso, R., Feng, D., Silverstein, M., & Bengtson, V. L. (2000). Self in the context of the family. In K.W. Schaie & J. Hendricks (Eds.), *The Evolution of the aging self: The societal impact on the aging process* (pp. 63–98). New York: Springer. Publishing Company.

Gove, W. R., Ortega, S. T., & Style, C. B. (1989). The maturational and role perspectives on aging and self through the adult years: An empirical evaluation. *American Journal of Sociology, 94,* 1117–1145.

Greenwald, A.G. (1980). The totalitarian ego: Fabrication and revision of personal history. *American Psychologist, 35,* 603–618.

Horwitz, A. V., White, H. R., & Howell-White, S. (1996). Becoming married and mental health: A longitudinal study of a cohort of young adults. *Journal of Marriage and the Family, 58,* 895–907.

Hughes, M. D., & Demo, D. H.. (1989). Self-perceptions of black Americans: Self-esteem and personal efficacy. *American Journal of Sociology, 95,* 132–159.

James, W. (1910). *The principles of psychology.* London: Macmillan.

Kogan, N. (1990). Personality and aging. In J. E. Birren & K. W. Schaie (Eds.), *Handbook of the psychology of aging* (3rd ed.) (pp. 330–346). San Diego, CA: Academic Press.

Kuhn, M. H., & McParland, T. S. (1954). An empirical investigation of self-attitudes. *American Sociological Review, 19,* 68–76.

Labouvie-Vief, G., Diehl, M., Tarnowski, A., & Shen, J. (2000). Age differences in adult personality: Findings from the United States and China. *Journal of Gerontology, 55B,* 4–17.

Leary, M. R., Wheeler, D. S., & Jenkins, T. B. (1986). Aspects of identity and behavioral preference: Studies of occupational and recreational choice. *Social Psychology Quarterly, 49,* 11–18.

Lemon, B. W., Bengtson, V. L., & Peterson, J. A. (1972). An exploration of the activity theory of aging: Activity types and life satisfaction among in-movers to a retirement community. *Journal of Gerontology, 27,* 511–523.

Longino, C. F., & Kart, C. S. (1982). Explicating activity theory: A formal replication. *Journal of Gerontology, 37,* 713–722.

Markus, H. R., & Kitayama, S. (1991). Culture and the self: Implications for cognition, emotion, and motivation. *Psychological Review, 98,* 224–253.

MacRae, H. M. (1995). Women and caring: Constructing self through others. *Journal of Women and Aging, 7,* 145–167.

McCrae, R. R., & Costa, P. T., Jr. (1988). Age, personality, and the spontaneous self-concept. *Journal of Gerontology: Social Sciences, 43,* 177–185.

Mead, G. H. (1934). *Mind, self, and society.* Chicago: University of Chicago Press.

Mirowsky, J., & Ross, C. E. (1989). *Social causes of psychological distress.* New York: Aldine de Gruyter.

Mirowsky, J., Ross, C. E., & Van Willigen, M. (1996). Instrumentalism in the land of opportunity: Socioeconomic causes and emotional consequences. *Social Psychology Quarterly, 59,* 322–337.

Nuttbrock, L., & Freudiger, P. (1991). Identity salience and motherhood: A test of Stryker's theory. *Social Psychology Quarterly, 54,* 146–157.

Oates, G. L. (1997). Self-esteem enhancement through fertility? Socioeconomic prospects, gender, and mutual influence. *American Sociological Review, 62,* 965–973.

Oyserman, D. (1993). The lens of personhood: Viewing the self and others in a multicultural society. *Journal of Personality and Social Psychology, 65,* 993–1009.

Pearlin, L. I., & Schooler, C. (1978). The structure of coping. *Journal of Health and Social Behavior, 19,* 2–21.

Porter, J. R., & Washington, R. E. (1993). Minority identity and self-esteem. *Annual Review of Sociology, 19,* 139–161.

Reitzes, D. C., & Mutran, E. J. (1994). Multiple roles and identities: Factors influencing self-esteem among middle-aged working men and women. *Social Psychology Quarterly, 57,* 313–325).

Reitzes, D. C., Mutran, E. J., & Fernandez, M. E. (1994). Middle-aged working men and women. *Research on Aging, 16,* 355–374.

Reitzes, D. C., Mutran, E. J., & Fernandez, M. E. (1996). Preretirement influences on postretirement self-esteem. *Journal of Gerontology, 51,* 242–249.

Reitzes, D. C., Mutran, E. J., & Verrill, L. A. (1995). Activities and self-esteem: Continuing the development of activity theory. *Research on Aging, 17,* 260–277.

Rhee, E., Uleman, J. S., Lee, H. K., & Roman, R. J. (1995). Spontaneous self-descriptions and ethnic identities in individualistic and collectivistic cultures. *Journal of Personality and Social Psychology, 69,* 142–152.

Roberts, R. E. L., & Bengtson, V. L. (1993). Relationships with parents, self-esteem, and psychological well-being in young adulthood. *Social Psychology Quarterly, 56,* 263–277.

Roberts, R. E. L., & Bengtson, V. L. (1996). Affective ties to parents in early adulthood and self-esteem across 20 years. *Social Psychology Quarterly, 59,* 96–106.

Rosenberg, M. (1981). The self: Social product and social force. In M. Rosenberg & R. H. Turner (Eds.), *Social psychology: Sociological perspectives* (pp. 593–624). New York: Basic Books

Rosow, I. (1974). *Socialization to old age.* Berkeley, CA: University of California Press.

Rosow, I. (1985). Status and role change through the life cycle. In R. H. Binstock & E. Shanas (Eds.), *Handbook of aging and the social sciences* (2nd ed.), (pp. 62–93). New York: Van Nostrand-Reinhold.

Ryff, C. D., & Marshall, V. W. (Eds.). (1999). *The self and society in aging processes*. New York: Springer Publishing Company.

Schaie, K. W. (1977–78). Toward a stage theory of cognitive development. *Journal of Aging and Human Development, 8*, 129–138.

Schaie, K. W., & Hendricks, J. (Eds.) (2000). *Evolution of the aging self*. New York: Springer Publishing Company.

Schwalbe, M. L. (1985). Autonomy in work and self-esteem. *The Sociological Quarterly, 26*, 519–535.

Schwalbe M. L., & Staples, C. L. (1991). Gender differences in sources of self-esteem. *Social Psychological Quarterly, 54*, 158–168.

Snow, D. A., & Philips, C. L. (1982). The changing self-orientations of college students: From institution to impulse. *Social Science Quarterly, 63*, 462–476.

Stryker, S. (1968). Identity salience and role performance: The relevance of symbolic interaction theory for family research. *Journal of Marriage and the Family, 30*, 558–564.

Stryker, S. (1980). *Symbolic interactionism: A social structural version*. Menlo Park, CA: The Benjamin/Cummings Publishing Co.

Swann, W. B. (1987). Identity negotiation: Where two roads meet. *Journal of Personality and Social Psychology, 53*, 1038–1051.

Thoits, P. A. (1983). Multiple identities and psychological well-being: A reformulation and test of the social isolation hypothesis. *American Sociological Review, 48*, 174–178.

Thoits, P. A. (1986). Multiple identities: Examining gender and marital status differences in distress. *American Sociological Review, 51*, 259–272.

Thoits, P. A. (1995). Stress, coping, and social support processes: Where are we? What next? *Journal of Health and Social Behavior (Extra Issue)*, 53–79.

Trafimow, D., Triandis, H. C., & Goto, S. G. (1991). Some tests of the distinction between the private and the collective self. *Journal of Personality and Social Psychology, 60*, 649–655.

Wells, L. E., & Marwell, G. (1986). *Self-esteem: Its conceptualization and measurement*. Beverly Hills, CA: Sage.

Wiltfang, G.L., & Scarbecz, M. (1990). Social class and adolescents' self esteem: Another look. *Social Psychological Quarterly, 53*, 174–183.

Wylie, R. (1979). *The self-concept*. Lincoln: University of Nebraska Press.

Yabiku, S. T., Axinn, W. G., & Thornton, A. (1999). Family integration and children's self-esteem. *American Journal of Sociology, 104*, 1494–1524.

Yang, J., McCrae, R. R., & Costa, P. T. (1998). Adult age differences in personality traits in the United States and the People's Republic of China. *Journal of Gerontology, 53*, 375–383.

Zurcher, L. A. (1977). *The mutable self*. Beverly Hills, CA: Sage.

Seventeen

Aging and Role Transitions

Kenneth F. Ferraro

Social scientists have long considered the study of roles and role transitions pivotal to understanding the aging process. Riley, Johnson, and Foner (1972) defined aging as involving "the accumulation of experience through participation in a *succession of social roles*" [italics added] (p. 10). Roles help define the aging process and one's sense of passage through the life course. They provide normative guidance to a person occupying a given social status and therefore help shape expectations of the life course as roles are added and relinquished.

Although several role transitions are considered separately in other chapters of this volume, the purpose of this chapter is to systematically examine the constellation of role transitions to better understand the dialectic between aging and role transitions; aging influences role transitions, and role transitions, in turn, influence the aging process. This chapter discusses the way in which research on the impact of role transitions has changed over the past 50 years, systematically reviews the literature on such transitions, and considers models that help explain findings from the literature.

I. Fifty Years of Research on Role Transitions

Social scientific approaches to the study of role transitions have changed considerably over time. Before examining the impact of role transitions, it may be useful to briefly consider some of the basic changes in the theories and methods used to study role transitions. An overview of the basic approaches is designed to provide a background for how and why the literature has developed the way it has. Scientific knowledge is socially constructed, and briefly reviewing the paradigmatic approaches to the study of role transitions may help us understand why the literature emphasizes certain findings and events.

A. The "Problem" of Role Transitions

It is probably not an oversimplification to say that the earliest studies of role transitions viewed them as part of the "problem" of aging. Anchored in the Chicago school of symbolic interactionism, many of the earliest studies of role transitions were designed to understand personal adjustment in the face of role transitions presumed to cause personal problems. The publication of Personal Adjustment in Old Age by Cavan, Burgess, Havighurst, and Goldhamer (1949) was one of the defining works of the time. Cavan and colleagues set the stage for decades of systematic investigation into the "big two": widowhood and retirement. Each, as a form of role loss, was viewed as creating challenges to personal adjustment. Their findings and conclusions for optimal adjustment led to the formation of the activity theory of aging. In its simplest form, the theory posited that the more active older adults were also more satisfied with life. The loss of roles in work and family (e.g., retirement and widowhood) meant that older adults needed to find satisfaction in other, often newly substituted, roles if they desired to maintain a positive sense of self (Havighurst & Albrecht, 1953).

This problem orientation continued through much of the 1960s and early 1970s. The provocative disengagement theory that emerged in the early 1960s was an explicit attempt to understand interaction and life satisfaction across the life course (Cumming, Dean, Newell, & McCaffrey, 1960; Cumming & Henry, 1961). The theory was vigorously attacked for its unilateral emphasis on the voluntariness and inevitability of social withdrawal (Achenbaum & Bengtson, 1994). Scholars also criticized it for the assertion that the expectation of death and the perception of a decreasing life space were the cause of decreased social activity. Despite this resounding attack on the reasons for social withdrawal, many scholars of the day accepted the general thesis of a reduction in social activity associated with aging. Role transitions were seen as the prime triggers of the reduced social activity, not the expectation of death or the perception of a decreasing life space.

Part of this emphasis on loss is probably due to behavioral and social science inter-

est at the time in the stress process and the identification of life events requiring readjustment. Holmes and Rahe's (1967) creation of the social readjustment rating scale listed death of spouse as the event requiring the most readjustment, followed closely by other role transitions (losses) such as divorce, marital separation, and retirement.

Role loss was typically seen as creating social isolation and decrements in morale and even physical health. Rosow (1973) summarized the social dimension of this view:

The most crucial single rule by far involves the progressive loss of roles and functions of the aged, for this change represents a critical introduction of stress. Role loss generates the pressures and sets the conditions for the emerging crisis, and taken together, these delineate the social context of the aging self. What does this involve? First, the loss of roles *excludes the aged from significant social participation and devalues them.* [italics added]. (p. 82)

In short, most role transitions were considered role losses and viewed as life crises accompanied by decrements in individual and social functioning.

B. Varied Responses to Role Transitions

The late 1970s and 1980s led to more of a "contingency perspective" on the consequences of role transitions. Although previous research had focused on social withdrawal and decrements in functioning, research during the 1980s showed that these were actually among a wider range of outcomes. Decrements in social and health status were likely outcomes under certain circumstances, but not under others. Whether it was Lopata's (1973) study of widowhood or Streib and Schneider's (1971) study of retirement, role transitions were seen as leading to a much wider range of outcomes. Rather than omnibus declines in social activity and physical health, the research began to paint a much more complicated picture of personal adjustment due to role transitions. Some transitions were very deleterious to some persons, but not to others. Some transitions actually increased social participation or improved health.

Probably the single most important reason for the shift in perspective on role transitions was due to more rigorous research designs. First and foremost, longitudinal investigations of role transitions showed that there are important continuities in social and physical health status that were not as easily discerned from cross-sectional studies. In addition, longitudinal studies paved the way for the analysis of change. In many studies, the role transition could be studied prospectively—a type of quasi-experiment was possible if role transitions were experienced after baseline measurement in a panel study. Second, probability sampling became much more widespread in the 1970s and 1980s and even implemented for national samples. Instead of the earlier reliance on studies of only those who experienced the event, more investigations were based on community samples comparing those who had and had not experienced the event (Ferraro, 1989). As one might expect, longitudinal investigations of this type greatly enhanced the stock of knowledge on the subject and highlighted the need for an approach to the study of role transitions that could accommodate a wider range of outcomes.

The study of role transitions during this period led to an appreciation for the diversity of the aging experience and the complexity of personal adjustment. Role transitions could be life crises for some people, but others might handle them with considerable resiliency (George, 1980). This variability emerged as yet another instance where the diversity of the older adult population was evident (Dannefer, 1988). Models and theories of the diverse outcomes tended to emphasize the consequences of multiple roles (Thoits, 1983), compensatory mechanisms (Bäckman & Dixon, 1992; Baltes &

Carstensen, 1996), or the role of social resources (George, 1980). In addition, models of life transitions gave greater attention to the *negotiation* of roles in varied social contexts (Marshall, 1995)

C. Role Transitions and Life Trajectories

During the 1990s, a slightly different approach to the study of role transitions developed, which incorporated the contingent perspective common in the 1980s, but placed greater emphasis upon understanding how role transitions are both influenced by earlier life experiences and shape subsequent paths of personal adjustment. The development of the life-course perspective greatly aided the literature (Elder, 1994), but investigators also built upon life-span developmental psychology (Baltes, Reese, & Lipsitt, 1980) and the age-stratification perspective (Riley, 1987) to take "the long way" of studying role transitions.

The object of this approach is to view the experience of role transitions as related to earlier life circumstances and transitions (George, 1993). It is not simply a matter of continuity in personality or behavior, but uncovering the relatedness of earlier indicators of personality or behavior to later ones and assessing the influence of the role transitions. Many models of the "life cycle" were viewed as too predictable, but the research on role transitions and life trajectories encompassed the rich diversity of possible outcomes and sought to identify antecedents of them in the biography, historical time, and social resources of the individual.

One of the most important features of this approach has been to consider the endogeneity of role transitions. Some roles are experienced by only a select set of adults. Thus, rather than just studying the "effect" of the role transition, researchers are increasingly interested in coupling analysis of the selection process that led to the role transition with analysis of the effects due to it. This is quite obvious with some role transitions, such as retirement, grandparenthood, or caregiver. Yet, it is appropriate to consider endogeneity even with role transitions that are typically seen as exogenous. Even widowhood has different consequences depending upon when and how the spouse dies. By considering the occurrence of role transitions along with their consequences, investigators believe that they have the best chance of uncovering the *process* of personal adjustment. Accelerating the trend observed earlier, the interest in role transitions and life trajectories now relies heavily on the use of longitudinal data to study the process of adjustment. We shall elaborate our discussion of this approach at the conclusion of this chapter while discussing future directions for research.

II. The Impact of Role Transitions

With this brief overview of the major orientations for studying role transitions, it is clear that social scientists have moved from a "life problem" to a "life trajectory" or life-course orientation. It may now be useful to review the literature on some of the major role transitions, emphasizing those works that help us to understand this more dynamic view of role transitions. Although widowhood and retirement started out as the two most important events to study, the avalanche of research on caregiving leads to an obvious "big three." This review will consider these three in some detail, but earlier chapters in this volume provide systematic consideration of caregiving (chapter 13 by Pearlin et al.) and retirement (chapter 14 by Henretta). In addition, other chapters of Part III provide excellent reviews of the consequences of role transition on health (chapter 12 by George) and the self (chapter 16 by Giarruso et al.) as

well as the role that social support plays in the adjustment process (chapter 15 by Krause).

It may be helpful to consider role transitions that are related to major social institutions so that the relatedness of various transitions may be more apparent. Hence, we begin with a consideration of role transitions in the family.

A. Family Role Transitions

When one thinks of family role transitions in later life, death of a spouse easily emerges as the most salient. Over half of all persons 65 years of age or older have lost a spouse, compared to less than 10% of those under 65 years of age (Kinsella & Taeuber, 1993). Widowhood is typically seen as involuntary, although long-term care, advance directives, and caregiving roles may actually influence the timing of death of a spouse. In another vein, marital quality may be associated with longevity, thus influencing the timing of the death of a spouse (Zick & Smith, 1991). Nonetheless, for most persons, death of spouse is experienced as an "involuntary" event over which one has little or no control. Indeed, social scientists and psychiatrists have long recognized that the perceived involuntariness of any transition is associated with greater existential impact and is more deleterious to health and well-being (Ferraro, 1981; Holmes & Rahe, 1967; Hyman, 1983).

Death of one's spouse, like several of the other family transitions, is much more likely to be experienced by women than by men. Despite the low likelihood of widowhood among men—or perhaps because of it—studies show that mortality risk is greater for men than women experiencing death of a spouse (Helsing & Szklo, 1981; Hyman, 1983). Owing to the availability of partners, men are also much more likely to "cope" with widowhood through remarriage.

There is considerable evidence showing that widowhood leads to decrements in physical and mental health, at least for the time immediately following the event (Feld & George, 1994; Ferraro, Mutran, & Barresi, 1984). Yet the bulk of the research shows that most widows recover emotionally from the event after about a 1-year period of intense grieving (Arbuckle & de Vries, 1995). Even more revealing is that social participation does not generally decline—at least not over the long term. Contrary to the decremental models of role loss, death of one's spouse does not necessarily generate social isolation. Instead, it appears from longitudinal research that widows, even in advanced old age, are fairly active in social life relative to their level of activity before the event. It has also been shown that some types of social participation actually *increase* 2 or 3 years after the death of a spouse, indicating a compensatory effect (Ferraro et al., 1984). Widowhood spurs a realignment in social life, often fostering high levels of activity with friends who have also experienced the event (Ferraro, 1989; S. Gallagher & Gerstel, 1993; Waite & Harrison, 1992). A "society of widows" often offers more time and practical help than is the case for kin relations; engagement in them is, therefore, highly predictive of widows' morale (S. Gallagher & Gerstel, 1993; Kohen, 1983).

Lopata's (1973) research on "compensations in widowhood" opened a new vista of research on the subject. She pointed out that the quality of married life was critical to the adjustment process (Lopata, 1979). Lopata noted that many widows, despite intense feelings of grief, found some benefits such as free time or perhaps seeing their spouse relieved of suffering (see also Bass & Bowman, 1990; Bass, Bowman, & Noelker, 1991; Mullan, 1992; Wortman & Silver, 1989). This should not be interpreted as minimizing the trauma of death of one's spouse. It

should, however, point out that there is a wide range of outcomes from the death of one's spouse.

A life-trajectory approach to widowhood recognizes that the timing of the event is also critical to understanding how one experiences the role transition. The bulk of the research shows that death of a spouse is actually more detrimental to the health and well-being of the survivor when experienced early in life (D. Gallagher, Thompson, & Peterson, 1982). Older couples have had more years to enjoy—and the loss is often acute—but the loss is typically anticipated and, sometimes, a relief from the spouse's suffering. A life-trajectory approach to the role transition of death of spouse is contingent on many factors. Investigators need to be attentive to the quality of the marital relationship, the health status of the survivor prior to the death of spouse, the type of death to which the partner succumbs, and the personal and social resources available to the survivor.

Research on adaptation to widowhood shows that the role of spousal caregiver frequently precedes the role of widow. In addition, the caregiver role may shape the way that the death of spouse is experienced. Just as the quality of the marital relationship is important for adjustment to the death of a spouse, it is also important to the entrance into the role of caregiver. In a study of men and women receiving treatment for cancer, Allen, Goldscheider, and Ciambrone (1999) found that marital intimacy was important to being considered as the caregiver of choice should the need arise. More generally, Lieberman and Fisher (1999) found that resolution of family conflict was key to the quantity of support provided to elders with Alzheimer's disease; endemic conflict reduces the likelihood of caregiving to dependent family members. Past social relationships help determine whether the role of caregiver will be activated. In actuality, two roles are being activated. First, the caregiver is absorbing additional responsibilities in the care of the family member. Second, the other person is assuming the role of care recipient, one that contains considerable dependency.

Previous research on caregivers shows that it is a challenging role, replete with the burdens associated with daily care, emotional support, and loss of independence (Aneshensel, Pearlin, & Schuler, 1993; Bass, McClendon, Deimling, & Mukherjee, 1994; Hughes et al. 1999; Miller & McFall, 1991). Caregiver burden appears to be greater in situations with low family income, probably reflecting a lack of access to resources for help with care. It is clear that adult day care and respite care can reduce the burden experienced by caregivers (Zarit, Stephens, Townsend, & Greene, 1998), yet these resources are not available to all. While the bulk of the literature focuses on the burdens accompanying caregiving, it should also be pointed out that caregivers occasionally express some satisfaction in fulfilling family responsibilities (Albert, 1991). Caregiving is a taxing social engagement, but the transition into this role is experienced in varied ways depending upon the characteristics of the care receiver, the caregiver's relationship to him or her, the resources available for assistance, and the timing of the experience.

Other family role transitions that have not garnered nearly as much attention concern relationships with or care for children or grandchildren. Although parenthood is not typically initiated in later life, the changing character of the parent–child relationship is meaningful for understanding role transitions during the later years. There are elements of solidarity across the generations in most families after child launching, but this is coupled with significant levels of conflict as well—some fairly innocuous, some fairly serious (Clarke, Preston, Raksin, &

Bengtson, 1999). Children remain a potential resource for older parents, and the quality of their relationship is an important determinant of both seeking and receiving social support. Adult children can be an important resource for overcoming loneliness and detachment as well as providing tangible assistance with tasks formerly performed by a spouse (Brody, 1990; Lopata, 1979). In response to death of one's spouse or growing functional impairment, some adults may even choose to relocate closer to one of their adult children. When return migration is contemplated in these situations, parents apparently assess the resourcefulness of their adult children in terms of relational quality, financial status, target amenities, and gender (Silverstein & Angelelli, 1998). Daughters are more likely to be the target child of choice, especially when the parent is functionally impaired. Although parenthood is rarely initiated in the later years, the role of parent may change dramatically, either due to needs on the part of the parent, or, in some cases, the needs of descendants.

Grandparenthood is an important role for many older people, and the needs of descendants often shape the role performance in substantial ways. The onset of grandparenthood typically occurs during middle age, and a growing percentage of grandparents survive beyond their grandchildren's adolescence (Szinovacz, 1998). There are varied levels of involvement in the grandparent role, but it is clear that those with greater perceived self- efficacy are more involved in the role (King & Elder, 1998). If they are in physical proximity, grandparents often provide a significant amount of child care, or for those in sound financial condition, they often contribute to the expenses of child rearing (education, housing, and/or orthodontic care). Most grandparents, especially grandmothers, find the role satisfying, but disagreements over child-rearing practices may temper the satisfaction

(Somary & Stricker, 1998; Thompson & Walker, 1987).

Grandparents are often substantially involved in the care of their grandchildren, but there has been a recent increase in another, more involving, role transition: custodial grandparenting, sometimes referred to as surrogate parenting. Although African-American households have long been more likely to be engaged in custodial grandparenting, there has been an increase in this form of grandparenting among both White and African-American households in recent decades (Pruchno, 1999). Black women are more likely to have lived in multigenerational households and apparently accommodate custodial grandparenting with less psychological burden than their White counterparts. Among both Black and White households, the role transition of becoming a custodial grandparent increases depressive symptoms among grandmothers but not grandfathers (Szinovacz, DeViney, & Atkinson, 1999). Custodial grandparenting is more likely for grandsons than granddaughters, leading some researchers to suggest that boys, especially boys with behavioral problems, are more difficult for parents or grandparents to raise (Hayslip, Shore, Henderson, & Lambert, 1998). Indeed, custodial grandparenting reflects the endogeneity of role transitions mentioned earlier. Not all grandparents have an equal probability of raising their grandchildren. Characteristics of the grandparent, adult children, and grandchildren convene to shape the likelihood of custodial grandparenting (Hayslip et al. 1998; Pruchno, 1999). More and more grandparents are involved in the custodial role, and they report that it is taxing on their time, finances, and health.

B. Occupational Role Transitions

Concurrent to many of the role transitions in the family is a set of transitions associated with occupation or work roles. There are many such role transitions, and the timing of them is increasingly diverse in Western societies (Henretta, 1992). These role transitions might include entry or reentry into the labor force, seeking or accepting a promotion at one's place of employment, or modifying domestic occupation because of child launching, remarriage, or custodial grandparenting.

Although the types of role transitions are varied, most of the research interest has focused on departures from work. One type of departure is job displacement—when a job held for at least 3 years is lost due to plant closure, downsizing, or layoff. Although the rate of job displacement has been fairly stable over the past two decades, the incidence of it among older workers (55+) has increased in the past decade (Carrington, 1993; Couch, 1998). The earnings of displaced workers are reduced nearly 40%, and these lost earnings are not typically replaced through pension income (Fallick, 1996). Job displacement also often entails a loss of health insurance, which may be a serious concern among older workers. African and Hispanic Americans are more prone to late life job displacement and the economic vulnerability of it. Relatively little is known about the health consequences of job displacement in the later years, but job-displaced men in poor health are much less likely to reenter the labor force (Mutchler, Burr, Massagli, & Pienta, 1999).

Although job displacement in the later years could be described as an understudied subject, retirement, as one of the "big two" role transitions, has a long history of systematic investigation. Much of the early research during the 1950s and 1960s characterized retirement as a "crisis"—the roleless role—often leading to an atrophy of social relations and a decline in health. More recent research shows that the decision to retire is a complex one shaped by work history (Hayward, Friedman, & Chen, 1998), spousal work status and intentions (Henkens, 1999), family history and economic status (Szinovac & DeViney, 1999), and health status (Mutchler et al. 1999). Given the reduction in the average age of retirement in the United States, sometimes seen as "early retirement," and the availability of pension security for many retirees, it is clear that the retirement experience is not nearly as pejorative as depicted by the problem orientation of many early gerontological studies.

One area where this has become clear is in the relationship between retirement and health. Many early studies pointed to the adverse consequences of retirement on health. Although many people may still consider retirement hazardous to health, the evidence has become quite compelling that this is not true (Ekerdt, 1987; Ekerdt, Baden, Bosse, & Dibbs, 1983; Mutchler et al., 1999). When people die shortly after retirement, it is almost always their failing health *before* retirement that both prompted the retirement and led to death. There is even evidence that retirement may *improve* health in some cases (Ekerdt, Bosse, & LoCastro, 1983; Midanik, Soghikian, Ransom, & Tekawa, 1995).

There is no sound empirical evidence that retirement leads to social isolation and depression, either. Although this may occur for some people, the majority of retirees find new avenues for social life and seem to adjust fairly well (Sterns, Matheson, & Park, 1997). Findings from the longitudinal Normative Aging Study in Boston generally show that retirement does not significantly affect quantitative or qualitative measures of social support (Bosse, Aldwin, Levenson, Spiro, & Mroczek, 1993). Although social ties and activities change with retirement, overall social engagement does not. Most people compensate for the reduced interaction

with co-workers by strengthening existing relations with other people or adding social ties with "retired people" (Atchley, 1971; Mutran & Reitzes, 1981; Streib & Schneider, 1971).

These findings are consistent with the "convoy model" of social adjustment that specifies that the inner circle of intimates remains quite stable, but that the intermediate and outer circles are often replaced by interactions with nonwork-related associates (Antonucci, 1990; Kahn & Antonucci, 1980). In short, retirement involves a realignment of role relationships, rather than sheer loss, and the outcomes of the adjustment are contingent on several characteristics, most notably social class standing (Hayward, Friedman, & Chen, 1998; Mutran & Reitzes, 1981). Persons of higher social class typically engage in more long-term planning and have more financial resources to enhance retirement well-being.

C. Role Transitions in Community Networks

Community networks provide additional opportunities for role transitions. A common theme of much of the research reviewed thus far is that many role transitions involve a realignment of role relationships. It is not so much a matter of reduced social interaction as many of the early works on role transitions depicted, but a shifting of social interaction as selected roles are exited and new roles are adopted. Although mean levels of interaction may decline somewhat, failure to consider the shifting of personal and social involvement leads to a fairly pedestrian understanding of aging and role transitions. Moreover, it leads to an underestimation of the social engagement of older people.

Research by Herzog and Morgan (1992) examined the personal "productivity" of Americans based on paid and unpaid work. Using several approaches to estimating productivity—both economic and noneconomic—the authors found widespread evidence of older adults' engagement in productive activities (see also Herzog, Kahn, Morgan, Jackson, & Antonucci, 1989). Such activities included, but were not limited to, child care, housework, volunteer roles, and informal help. Herzog and Morgan (1992) concluded from their research that "many older people contribute to society by helping each other as well as by helping members of younger generations" (p. 197). Indeed, the literature on intergenerational helping also indicates that older adults make use of free time to aid the well-being of younger persons in a variety of ways.

Certain types of people are more apt to assume the volunteer role, and older people are among those adopting higher levels of voluntary association participation. This is especially the case if they have been active in volunteer roles earlier in life (e.g., a long-term commitment to altruistic roles). From a life-trajectory approach, many people shift from work roles to volunteer roles in middle and especially later life. Whether it is working the polls during elections or carrying flowers to hospital patients, older adults are actively engaged in voluntarism. Ekerdt (1986) argued that there is a "busy ethic" that leads retirees to voluntarism. He sees that the busy ethic is "at once a statement of value as well as an expectation of retired people—shared by retirees and nonretirees alike—that their lives should be active and earnest" (p. 240). Middle-aged and older adults often play important roles in voluntary fraternal organizations (e.g., Shriners, Daughters of the American Revolution) or organizations devoted to the arts, collections, or the preservation of skills (e.g., gemology, historical societies). Although these roles may be harder to define and not be as enduring as others, they nonetheless represent an important social engagement for millions of older people, especially those who have left the labor force.

Although voluntary action may seem useful only as a mechanism for the consumption of free time, research indicates that there are other benefits. Assuming the role of volunteer has been shown to have important benefits on physical and mental health and to even reduce the risk of mortality (Moen, Dempster- McClain, & Williams, 1989; Musick, Herzog, & House, 1999). The benefits of voluntarism appear to be stronger for those focusing their efforts on one organization or reporting low levels of informal social interaction.

Another type of participation in community networks may involve religious roles. Numerous studies show that older adults generally have higher levels of participation in religious activities than is the case for younger adults (Ainlay & Smith, 1984; Moberg, 1997). This participation may entail the adoption of volunteer (lay) roles in religious organizations (e.g., church elder) or it could be routine assistance with religious education or benevolent care. There are also volunteer roles that integrate religious and helping organizational interests (Filinson, 1988).

Black churches and religious organizations seem particularly active in recruiting volunteers to help others groups (Chaves & Higgins, 1992; Taylor & Chatters, 1988; Walls & Zarit, 1991). Taylor and Chatters (1988) show that Black churches not only provide information and advice to their members, but also "are extremely involved in the provision of...material, emotional, and spiritual assistance" (p. 194). Thus, it should be recognized that some religious groups, especially Black churches, are more oriented toward coupling religious and voluntary activity roles. Consistent with the literature on voluntarism, there appear to be positive outcomes on health and longevity for those who adopt such religious roles (Ferraro & Koch, 1994;

Strawbridge, Cohen, Shema, & Kaplan, 1997).

III. Contemporary Models for Role Transitions

Although many different role transitions were considered in this review, there are certain generalizations that issue forth from the literature and point the way to more useful models and methods for studying aging and life transitions. It may be useful to begin by summarizing some of the major sociological contributions from the review of the research findings on role transitions, and then turn to a consideration of the models and methods that will help to advance the literature in meaningful ways.

First, many of the role losses such as death of a spouse and custodial grandparenting may indeed involve considerable stress for the individual, but most older adults cope fairly effectively with these transitions. In this sense, most adults 50 years of age and older are more resilient than the early "life crisis" or decremental models implied. Second, rather than unilateral declines in health and effective functioning, role transitions spur a process in which older adults may realign their lives or compensate for the loss in new ways (Bäckman & Dixon, 1992; Elder, 1994). There is a much wider range of outcomes to these experiences than was often believed (Dannefer, 1987). Third, in the studies of virtually all role transitions, it was apparent that a number of social resources, often operating as modifying factors, are involved in shaping the outcomes of role transitions. As such, models of role transitions need to incorporate basic variables such as social class, ethnicity, and gender that differentiate people in a system of social stratification (George, 1980; O'Rand, 1990). In addition, many studies have found that social support, even having

just one confidant, is an important resource for individuals moving into or out of roles.

Finally, the study of role transitions needs to consider related transitions in a dynamic perspective from birth to death. Many of the early studies focused on the consequences of one role transition on health or social functioning, but the evidence points increasingly to the relatedness of earlier life experiences and adjustments to the outcomes in later life. A welcome development is the attention given to studying multiple roles simultaneously (Cochran, Brown, & McGregor, 1999; Reid & Hardy, 1999), but the literature would benefit from dynamic analyses of the accumulation of roles and their effects on physical and mental health.

To reflect on this more dynamic and interactive view of role transitions, it may be useful to consider the analogy of a vortex of aging and role transitions. Figure 17.1 depicts a simplified version of the vortex for heuristic purposes. The idea is to see the relatedness of role transitions across the life course due to the interaction of social structure and human agency. The vortex may be seen as one's life course from birth to death being infused with jets of influence from family, occupation, and community networks. Social resources condition the influence, and the individual helps shape the trajectory of his or her life while attempting to accommodate the forces exerted by the structure of social institutions. The key to the application of the vortex analogy is that role transitions in family, occupation, and community networks are related to one another along the individual's life course. Thus, role transitions are endogenous, but consequential to subsequent transitions. Role transitions need to be viewed as influenced by historical processes and as part of the individual's biography. Gerontologists need to consider how role transitions

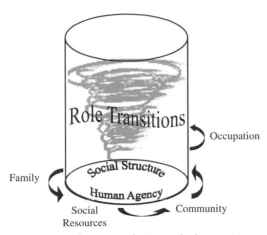

Figure 17.1   The vortex of aging and role transitions.

experienced later in life are related to earlier transitions in the life course.

If the goal of research on role transitions is to better understand both the endogeneity of role transitions and their consequences on personal adjustment over the life course, then it is clear that certain theoretical perspectives and models may be more useful in this endeavor. We conclude this chapter by identifying three such perspectives and suggesting the types of research that will lead to more substantial contributions in the understanding of aging and role transitions.

A. Life Course

Given the excellent reviews of the life-course perspective offered in chapters 10 (Moen) and 11 (O'Rand) of this volume, it is necessary only to briefly describe the perspective and identify its unique potential for the study of role transitions.

Elder and Johnson (in press) recently identified five principles of the life-course perspective. For the study of role transitions, these principles may be adapted and summarized as follows: (a) human development and aging are life-long processes; (b) the antecedents and consequences of role transitions vary according to their timing in a person's life; (c) a net-

work of shared relationships influences life-course adjustment; (d) role transitions are embedded in and shaped by history and culture; and (e) human agency operates despite the constraints of social forces—individuals construct their own life course.

In the vortex of aging and role transitions, the life-course perspective helps investigators systematically examine the interplay of history and biography to understand the process of role succession. For example, does the timing of child bearing, especially first child bearing, influence work history and retirement decisions? Might it influence the experience of grandparenting or even the likelihood of custodial grandparenting? The timing of other family role transitions such as marital dissolution and remarriage may shape not only family role transitions such as grandparenting and caregiving, but occupational and/or community role transitions (Clausen, 1993; Elder & Johnson, in press). The life-course perspective helps us to use the "long way" of studying role transitions to uncover such interdependencies.

B. Cumulative Disadvantage

A second theoretical perspective that holds considerable promise for the study of aging and role transitions is cumulative disadvantage theory. Drawn principally from the age-stratification (Riley, 1987), life-course (Elder, 1985), and life-span developmental perspectives (Baltes et al., 1980), cumulative disadvantage theory asserts that the effects of risk factors accumulate over the life course, thereby increasing heterogeneity in later life (Dannefer, 1987, 1988; O'Rand, 1996; Ross & Wu, 1996). Personal change (or adjustment) is seen as closely related to traits or characteristics displayed earlier in the life course. Change is anticipated, but the nature of the change is conceptually linked with earlier experiences, abilities, and resources. Thus, cumulative disadvantage theory stresses the way in which personal or social trajectories are formed from the interplay of biological, behavioral, and social-structural forces.

Inasmuch as role transitions are considered endogenous in the vortex, it is important to realize that some people are at greater risk of experiencing selected role transitions, such as divorce or custodial grandparenting. Even for those transitions experienced by the vast majority of the population, the timing of the role transitions may be nonnormative. Is it possible that early life experiences such as childhood disease or victimization or adverse conditions in middle age increase the risk of failure in some roles and early exit from others? Emerging evidence from a wide range of studies suggests that this may be so (Crystal & Shea, 1990; Kerckhoff, 1993; O'Rand, 1996; Rosenbaum, 1984; Ross & Wu, 1996; Wadsworth, 1997).

It is clear that some persons are advantaged in the early years, and this advantage may compound over time. Others are disadvantaged due to genetic or environmental factors, and these disadvantages also accumulate. The phenomenon may be seen as one of accentuation. Some people are launched on promising trajectories: the early advantages and successes likely lead to further advantage. Others are launched with disadvantage and have to work harder or endure more in order to attain the same social or health status. Of course, many do not overcome the early disadvantage and, thus, face additional risks to the effective performance of roles and this, in turn, influences health, wealth, and well-being.

Cumulative disadvantage theory stresses the possibility of feedback mechanisms and cyclical change over the life course. The growing use of longitudinal data in research is pointing to precisely such mechanisms of spiral decline (Bruce, Seeman, Merrill, & Blazer, 1994; Farmer & Ferraro, 1997; Ferraro, Farmer, & Wybraniec, 1997; Verbrugge, Reoma, & Gruber-Baldini, 1994). For those beginning with a serious health disadvantage, Verbrugge and Jette (1994) describe the cumulative disadvantage as involving "pernicious loops of dysfunction" (p. 1). To elucidate the vortex of role transitions, we need research that tracks how role transitions and events accumulate over the life course. With that type of research, we will be in a better position to describe the dialectic between social structure and human agency for persons on various life trajectories and to intervene most effectively for the most disadvantaged. If cumulative disadvantage theory is supported through role transition research, it would lead to a powerful call for an "ounce of prevention."

C. Compensation

Another theoretical perspective that has garnered considerable support in the study of role transitions is compensation. Increasing evidence shows that adults adjust to role transitions with a variety of coping methods, and one widely used adaptive response is compensation (Bäckman & Dixon, 1992). The idea of compensation is implicit in most classical sociological theories of action. Whether it is structural-functionalism, symbolic interactionism, or exchange theory, actors are viewed as continually involved in evaluating lines of action and attempting to adjust their behavior to reach desired goals. When loss is experienced or inequity perceived, actors often attempt to make up for or counterbalance such an experience. In short, actors compensate.

The compensation model of role transitions bears considerable resemblance to Atchley's continuity perspective. Atchley (1989) states that a central premise of "continuity theory is that, in making adaptive choices, middle-aged and older adults attempt to preserve and maintain existing internal and external structures and that they prefer to accomplish this objective by using continuity" (p. 183). Although the preservation and maintenance of internal and external structures may not always be a plausible objective in confronting some changes—such as loss of spouse—continuity in strategies and values seem endemic to adaptation. The point is that personal change is continuous and that there is an overall persistence of lifestyle in social activities and attitudes. If health status and/or social involvement are lost through role transitions, people may try to compensate to bring them back to their former levels.

The idea of compensating for either loss or certain disadvantages is not new to the social sciences but can be seen to exist in the writings of researchers interested in a variety of topics (Ellison & London, 1992; Ferraro & Farmer, 1995). Moreover, the theme of compensation in social activity has arisen in the writings of many theories of aging. For instance, activity theory anticipates compensation after role loss; it is the vehicle to restore life satisfaction. Exchange theories of aging also permit the possibility of compensation as a normal adaptive response, although the contingencies of reinforcement for compensation are unlikely for many older adults. Models and theories that account for compensatory mechanisms provide investigators with a wider array of outcomes of role transitions.

Compensation theory has been integrated in the metamodel of selective optimization with compensation, developed by Baltes and Baltes (1990). This model "takes gains and losses jointly into account, pays attention to the great heterogeneity in ageing and successful ageing, and views successful mastery of goals in the face of losses endemic to advanced age" (Baltes & Carstensen, 1996, p. 397). In this framework, compensatory action may be indicative of successful aging if

the individual selects the behavioral arena as important to the maintenance of well-being. This approach also appears to handle the vortex of aging and role transitions and shows just how far the science of aging has come in the past 50 years.

IV. Future Research Directions

Although several research directions have been noted throughout the chapter, it might be valuable to mention or highlight a few that could substantially aid further research on aging and role transitions. To begin, research on aging and role transitions across the life course will benefit greatly from incorporating advances in sociometry and the study of social support and social networks. As reviewed in chapter 15 (Krause) of this volume, numerous studies over the past two decades have advanced our conceptualization and measurement of social support and structure. It is clear that role transitions do not occur in a social vacuum. Thus, we need to know more about how social structures and processes shape the experience of role transitions.

It is also quite clear that future research on aging and role transitions needs to implement a life-course or life-trajectory approach that will enable us to study *transitions*. There may be important insights that will come from either cross-sectional or retrospective studies of aging and role transitions. However, long-term longitudinal research, especially on probability samples of communities, is needed to identify personal patterns of oscillation, social interaction, and health. We are only beginning to understand the dynamics of role transitions over the life course. Better specification is needed for the consequences—or lack thereof—due to nonnormative or "off-time" transitions to physical and mental health. Both quantitative and qualitative studies are needed.

Research on role embracement and role salience represents another important consideration for social gerontology. Research by Krause (1999) shows that older adults do not devalue salient roles during times of stress, but actually become more committed to them at such times. Research on caregiving and custodial grandparenting are prime targets for considerations of this type. There has been so much research over the years on the decrements and losses that older people experience during role transitions. It could be argued that it is time to study the other side of aging and role transitions involving concepts such as personal hardiness, resoluteness of purpose, and resiliency. In some ways, this may be seen as the province of human agency, but researchers need to be careful to avoid blaming the victim when studying the endogeneity of events experienced and whether psychosocial factors mediate the personal adjustment.

It is clear that personal characteristics and abilities shape adjustment to role transitions. At the same time, we need to know more about how disadvantage or limited resources lead to the experience of events and how those experiences eventually may act back on psychological resourcefulness. Do adverse circumstances and events decrease the likelihood of persons developing resiliency and resoluteness of purpose? Some important panel studies of related subjects indicate that this may be so (e.g., Johnson, Cohen, Dohrenwend, Link, & Brook, 1999). Nevertheless, there are plenty of examples of persons who have experienced very dire circumstances during the life course and emerge in later life with a sense of coherence and generativity (Antonovsky, 1987; Baltes & Baltes, 1990; Rowe & Kahn, 1998). Longitudinal research examining the interplay of such resiliency and role transitions would greatly enhance our understanding of life-course transitions into and out of social roles.

References

Achenbaum, W. A., & Bengtson, V. L. (1994). Re-engaging the disengagement theory of aging: On the history and assessment of theory development in gerontology. *The Gerontologist 34*, 756–763.

Ainlay, S. C., & Smith, R. (1984). Aging and religious participation. *Journal of Gerontology, 39*, 357–363.

Albert, S. M. (1991). Cognition of caregiving tasks: Multidimensional scaling of caregiver task domain. *The Gerontologist, 31*, 726–734.

Allen, S. M., Goldscheider, F., & Ciambrone, D. A. (1999). Gender roles, marital intimacy, and nomination of spouse as primary caregiver. *The Gerontologist, 39*, 150–158.

Aneshensel, C. S., Pearlin, L. I., & Schuler, R. H. (1993). Stress, role captivity, and cessation of caregiving. *Journal of Health and Social Behavior, 34*, 54–70.

Antonovsky, A. (1987). *Unraveling the mystery of health: How people manage stress and stay well.* San Francisco: Jossey- Bass.

Antonucci, T. C. (1990). Social support and social relationships. In R. H. Binstock & L. K. George (Eds.), *Handbook of aging and the social sciences* (3rd ed.) (pp. 205–226). San Diego, CA: Academic Press, Inc.

Arbuckle, N. W., & de Vries, B. (1995). The long-term effects of later life spousal and parental bereavement on personal functioning. *The Gerontologist, 35*, 637–647.

Atchley, R. C. (1971). Retirement and leisure participation: Continuity or crisis? *The Gerontologist, 11*, 13–17.

Atchley, R. C. (1989). A continuity theory of normal aging. *The Gerontologist, 29*, 183–190.

Bäckman, L., & Dixon, R. A. (1992). Psychological compensation: A theoretical framework. *Psychological Bulletin, 112*, 259–283.

Baltes, P. B., & Baltes, M. M. (1990). Psychological perspectives on successful aging: The model of selective optimization with compensation. In P. B. Baltes & M. M. Baltes (Eds.), *Successful aging: Perspectives from the behavioral sciences* (pp. 1–34). Cambridge, UK: Cambridge University Press.

Baltes, M. M., & Carstensen, L. L. (1996). The process of successful ageing. *Ageing and Society, 16*, 397–422.

Baltes, P. B., Reese, H. W., & Lipsitt, L. P. (1980). Life-span developmental psychology. *Annual Review of Psychology, 31,* 65–110.

Bass, D. M., & Bowman, K. (1990). The transition from caregiving to bereavement: The relationship of care-related strain and adjustment to death. *The Gerontologist, 30,* 35–44.

Bass, D. M., Bowman, K., & Noelker, L. S. (1991). The influence of caregiving and bereavement support on adjusting to an older relative's death. *The Gerontologist, 31,* 32–42.

Bass, D. M., McClendon, M. J., Deimling, G. T., & Mukherjee, S. (1994). The influence of a diagnosed mental impairment on family caregiver strain. *Journal of Gerontology: Social Sciences, 49,* S146–S155.

Bosse, R., Aldwin, C. M., Levenson, M. R., Spiro III, A., & Mroczek, D. K. (1993). Change in social support after retirement: Longitudinal findings from the normative aging study. *Journal of Gerontology: Psychological Sciences, 48,* P210–P217.

Brody, E. M. (1990). *Women in the middle: Their parent-care years.* New York: Springer Publishing Company.

Bruce, M. L., Seeman, T. E., Merrill, S. S., & Blazer, D. G. (1994). The impact of depressive symptomatology on physical disability: MacArthur studies of successful aging. *American Journal of Public Health, 84,* 1796–9.

Carrington, W. (1993). Wage losses for displaced workers: Is it really the firm that matters? *Journal of Human Resources, 28,* 435–462.

Cavan, R. S., Burgess, E. W., Havighurst, R. J., & Goldhamer, H. (1949). *Personal adjustment in old age.* Chicago: University of Chicago Press.

Chaves, M., & Higgins, L. M. (1992). Comparing the community involvement of black and white congregations. *Journal for the Scientific Study of Religion, 31,* 425–440.

Clarke, E. J., Preston, M., Raskin, J., & Bengtson, V. L. (1999). Types of conflicts and tensions between older parents and adult children. *The Gerontologist, 39,* 261–270.

Clausen, J. A. (1993). *American lives: Looking back at the children of the Great Depression.* New York: Free Press.

Cochran, D. L., Brown, D. R., & McGregor, K. C. (1999). Racial differences in the multiple social roles of older women: Implications for depressive symptoms. *The Gerontologist, 39,* 465–472.

Couch, K. A. (1998). Late life job displacement. *The Gerontologist, 38,* 7–17.

Crystal, S., & Shea, D. (1990). Cumulative advantage, cumulative disadvantage, and inequality among elderly people. *The Gerontologist, 30,* 437–443.

Cumming, E., Dean, L., Newell, D., & McCaffrey, I. (1960). Disengagement—a tentative theory of aging. *Sociometry, 73,* 23–35.

Cumming, E., & Henry, W. E. (1961). *Growing old: The process of disengagement.* New York: Basic Books.

Dannefer, D. (1987). Aging as intracohort differentiation: Accentuation, the Matthew effect, and the life course. *Sociological Forum, 2,* 211–236.

Dannefer, D. (1988). What's in a name? An account of the neglect of variability in the study of aging. In J. E. Birren & V. L. Bengtson (Eds.), *Emergent theories of aging* (pp. 356–384). New York: Springer Publishing Company.

Ekerdt, D. J. (1986). The busy ethic: Moral continuity between work and retirement. *The Gerontologist, 26,* 239–244.

Ekerdt, D. J. (1987). Why the notion persists that retirement harms health. *The Gerontologist, 77,* 454–457.

Ekerdt, D. J., Baden, L., Bosse, R., & Dibbs, E. (1983). The effect of retirement on physical health. *American Journal of Public Health, 73,* 779–783.

Ekerdt, D. J., Bosse, R., & LoCastro, J. S. (1983). Claims that retirement improves health. *Journal of Gerontology, 38,* 231–236.

Elder, G. H., Jr. (1985). *Life-course dynamics.* Ithaca, NY: Cornell University Press.

Elder, G. H., Jr. (1994). Time, human agency, and social change: Perspectives on the life course. *Social Psychology Quarterly, 57,* 4–15.

Elder, G. H., Jr., & Johnson, M. K. (in press). The life course and aging: Challenges, lessons and new directions. In R. A. Settersten, Jr. (Ed.), *Invitation to the life course: Toward new understandings of later life.* Amityville, NY: Baywood Publishing Company.

Ellison, C. G., & London, B. (1992). The social and political participation of black Americans: Compensatory and ethnic community theories revisited. *Social Forces, 70,* 681–701.

Fallick, B. C. (1996). A review of the recent literature on displaced workers. *Industrial and Labor Relations Review, 50,* 5–16.

Farmer, M. M., & Ferraro, K. F. (1997). Distress and perceived health: Mechanisms of health decline. *Journal of Health and Social Behavior, 38,* 298–311.

Feld, S., & George, L. K. (1994). Moderating effects of prior social resources on the hospitalizations of elders who become widowed. *Journal of Aging and Health, 6,* 275–295.

Ferraro, K. F. (1981). Relocation desires and outcomes among the elderly: A longitudinal analysis. *Research on Aging, 3,* 166–181.

Ferraro, K. F. (1989). Widowhood and health. In K. Markides & C. L. Cooper (Eds.), *Aging, stress, social support and health* (pp. 69–89). New York: John Wiley.

Ferraro, K. F., & Farmer, M. M. (1995). Social compensation in adulthood and later life. In R. A. Dixon & L. Bäckman (Eds.), *Compensating for psychological deficits and declines: Managing losses and promoting gains* (pp. 127–145). Mahwah, NJ: Lawrence Erlbaum.

Ferraro, K. F., Farmer, M. M., & Wybraniec, J. A. (1997). Health trajectories: Long-term dynamics among black and white adults. *Journal of Health and Social Behavior, 38,* 38–54.

Ferraro, K. F., & Koch, J. R. (1994). Religion and health among black and white adults: Examining social support and consolation. *Journal for the Scientific Study of Religion, 33,* 362–375.

Ferraro, K. F., Mutran, E., & Barresi, C. M. (1984). Widowhood, health, and friendship support in later life. *Journal of Health and Social Behavior, 25,* 245–259.

Filinson, R. (1988). A model for church-based services for frail elderly persons and their families. *The Gerontologist, 28,* 483–485.

Gallagher, D. E., Thompson, L. W., & Peterson, J. A. (1982). Psycho-social factors affecting adaptation to bereavement in the elderly. *International Journal of Aging and Human Development, 14,* 79–95.

Gallagher, S. K., & Gerstel, N. (1993). Kinkeeping and friend keeping among older women: The effect of marriage. *The Gerontologist, 33,* 675–681.

George, L. K. (1980). *Role transitions in later life.* Monterey, CA: Brooks\Cole.

George, L. K. (1993). Sociological perspectives on life transitions. *Annual Review of Sociology, 19,* 353–373.

Havighurst, R. J., & Albrecht, R. (1953). *Older people.* New York: Longmans, Green.

Hayslip, B., Jr., Shore, R. J., Henderson, C. E., & Lambert P. L. (1998). Custodial grandparenting and the impact of grandchildren with problems on role satisfaction and role meaning. *Journal of Gerontology: Social Sciences, 53B,* S164–S173.

Hayward, M. D., Friedman, S., & Chen H. (1998). Career trajectories and older men's retirement. *Journal of Gerontology: Social Sciences, 53B,* S91–S103.

Helsing, K. J., & Szklo, M. (1981). Mortality after bereavement. *American Journal of Epidemiology, 114,* 41–52.

Henkens, K. (1999). Retirement intentions and spousal support: A multi-actor approach. *Journal of Gerontology: Social Sciences, 54B,* S63–S73.

Henretta, J. C. (1992). Uniformity and diversity: Life course institutionalization and late-life work exit. *Sociological Quarterly, 33,* 265–279.

Herzog, A. R., Kahn, R. L., Morgan, J. N., Jackson, J. S., & Antonucci, T. C. (1989). Age differences in productive activities. *Journal of Gerontology, 44,* S129–138.

Herzog, A. R., & Morgan, J. N. (1992). Age and gender differences in the value of productive activities. *Research on Aging, 14,* 169–198.

Holmes, T. H., & Rahe, R. H. (1967). The social readjustment rating scale. *Journal of Psychosomatic Research, 11,* 213–218.

Hughes, S. L., Giobbie-Hurder, A., Weaver, F. M., Kubal, J. D., & Henderson, W. (1999). Relationship between caregiver burden and health-related quality of life. *The Gerontologist, 39,* 534–545.

Hyman, H. H. (1983). *Of time and widowhood.* Durham, NC: Duke University Press.

Johnson, J. G., Cohen, P., Dohrenwend, B. P., Link, B. G., & Brook, J. S. (1999). A longitudinal investigation of social causation and social selection processes involved in the association between socioeconomic status and psychiatric disorders. *Journal of Abnormal Psychology, 108,* 490–499.

Kahn, R. L., & Antonucci, T. C. (1980). Convoys over the life course: Attachment, roles, and social support. In P. B. Baltes & O. G. Brim, Jr. (Eds.), *Life-span development and behavior* (pp. 253–286). New York: Academic Press.

Kerckhoff, A. C. (1993). *Diverging pathways: Social structure and career deflections.* New York: Cambridge University Press.

King, V., & Elder, G. H., Jr. (1998). Perceived self-efficacy and grandparenting. *Journal of Gerontology: Social Sciences, 53B,* S249–S257.

Kinsella, K., & Taeuber, C. M. (1993). *An aging world II.* Washington, DC: U.S. Bureau of the Census.

Kohen, J. A. (1983). Old but not alone: Informal social supports among the elderly by marital status and sex. *The Gerontologist, 23,* 57–63.

Krause, N. (1999). Stress and the devaluation of highly salient roles in later life. *Journal of Gerontology: Social Sciences, 54B,* S99–S108.

Lieberman, M. A., & Fisher, L. (1999). The effects of family conflict resolution and decision making on the provision of help for an elder with Alzheimer's disease. *The Gerontologist, 39,* 159–166.

Lopata, H. Z. (1973). *Widowhood in an American city.* Cambridge, MA: Schenkman.

Lopata, H. Z. (1979). *Women as widows.* New York: Elsevier.

Marshall, V. W. (1995). Social models of aging. *Canadian Journal of Aging, 14,* 12–34.

Midanik, L. T., Soghikian, K., Ransom, L. J., & Tekawa, I. S. (1995). The effect of retirement on mental health and health behaviors: The Kaiser Permanente retirement study. *Journal of Gerontology: Social Sciences, 50B,* S59–S61.

Miller, B., & McFall, S. (1991). Stability and change in the informal task support network of frail older persons. *The Gerontologist, 31,* 735–745.

Moberg, D. O. (1997). Religion and aging. In K. F. Ferraro (Ed.), *Gerontology: Perspectives and issues* (pp. 193–220). New York: Springer Publishing Company.

Moen, P., Dempster McClain, D., & Williams, R. M. (1989). Social integration and longev-

ity: An event history analysis of women's roles and resilience. *American Sociological Review, 54,* 635–647.

Mullan, J. T. (1992). The bereaved caregiver: A prospective study of changes in well-being. *The Gerontologist, 32,* 673–683.

Musick, M. A., Herzog, A. R., & House, J. S. (1999). Volunteering and mortality among older adults: Findings from a national sample. *Journal of Gerontology: Social Sciences, 54B,* S173–S180.

Mutchler, J. E., Burr, J. A., Massagli, M. P., & Pienta, A. (1999). Work transitions and health in later life. *Journal of Gerontology: Social Sciences, 54B,* S252–S261.

Mutran, E., & Reitzes, D. C. (1981). Retirement, identity, and well-being: Realignment of role relationships. *Journal of Gerontology, 36,* 733–740.

O'Rand, A. M. (1990). Stratification and the life course. In R. H. Binstock & L. K. George (Eds.), *Handbook of aging and the social sciences* (3rd ed.) (pp. 130–148). San Diego: Academic Press.

O'Rand, A. M. (1996). The precious and the precocious: Understanding cumulative disadvantage and cumulative advantage over the life course. *The Gerontologist, 36,* 230–238.

Pruchno, R. (1999). Raising grandchildren: The experiences of black and white grandmothers. *The Gerontologist, 39,* 209–221.

Reid, J., & Hardy, M. (1999). Multiple roles and well-being among midlife women: Testing role strain and role enhancement theories. *Journal of Gerontology: Social Sciences, 54B,* S329–S338.

Riley, M. W. (1987). On the significance of age in sociology. *American Sociological Review, 52,* 1–14.

Riley, M. W., Johnson, M., & Foner, A. (1972). *Aging and society: Vol. 3. A sociology of age stratification.* New York: Russell Sage Foundation.

Rosenbaum, J. E. (1984). *Career mobility in a corporate hierarchy.* New York: Academic Press.

Rosow, I. (1973). The social context of the aging self. *The Gerontologist, 13,* 82–87.

Ross, C. E., & Wu, C. E. (1996). Education, age, and the cumulative advantage in health. *Journal of Health and Social Behavior, 37,* 104–120.

Rowe, J. W., & Kahn, R. L. (1998). *Successful aging*. New York: Pantheon.

Silverstein, M., & Angelelli, J. J. (1998). Older parents' expectations of moving closer to their children. *Journal of Gerontology: Social Sciences, 53B*, S153–S163.

Somary, K., & Stricker, G. (1998). Becoming a grandparent: A longitudinal study of expectations and early experiences as a function of sex and lineage. *The Gerontologist, 38*, 53–61.

Sterns, H. L., Matheson, N. K., & Park, L. S. (1997). Work and retirement. In K. F. Ferraro (Ed.), *Gerontology: Perspectives and issues* (pp. 171–192). New York: Springer Publishing Company.

Strawbridge, W. J., Cohen, R. D., Shema, S. J., & Kaplan, G. A. (1997). Frequent attendance at religious services and mortality over 28 years. *American Journal of Public Health, 87*, 957–961.

Streib, G. F., & Schneider, C. J. (1971). *Retirement in American society*. Ithaca, NY: Cornell University Press.

Szinovacz, M. E. (1998). Grandparents today: A demographic profile. *The Gerontologist, 38*, 37–52.

Szinovacz, M. E., & DeViney, S. (1999). The retiree identity: Gender race differences. *Journal of Gerontology: Social Sciences, 54B*, S207–S218.

Szinovacz, M. E., DeViney, S., & Atkinson, M. P. (1999). Effects of surrogate parenting on grandparents' well-being. *Journal of Gerontology: Social Sciences, 54B*, S376–S388.

Taylor, R. J., & Chatters, L. M. (1988). Church members as a source of informal social support. *Review of Religious Research, 30*, 93–203.

Thoits, P. (1983). Multiple identities and psychological well- being: A test of the social isolation hypothesis. *American Sociological Review, 48*, 174–187.

Thompson, L., & Walker, A. (1987). Mothers as mediators of intimacy between grandmothers and their young adult granddaughters. *Family Relations, 36*, 72–77.

Verbrugge, L. M., & Jette, A. M. (1994). The disablement process. *Social Science and Medicine, 38*, 1–14.

Verbrugge, L. M., Reoma, J.M., & Gruber-Baldini, A. L. (1994). Short-term dynamics of disability and well-being. *Journal of Health and Social Behavior, 35*, 97–117.

Wadsworth, M. E. J. (1997). Health inequalities in the life course perspective. *Social Science and Medicine, 44*, 859–869.

Waite, L. J., & Harrison, S. C. (1992). Keeping in touch: How women in mid-life allocate social contacts among kith and kin. *Social Forces, 70*, 637–655.

Walls, C. T., & Zarit, S. H. (1991). Informal support from Black churches and the well-being of elderly Blacks. *The Gerontologist, 31*, 490–495.

Wortman, C. B., & Silver, R. C. (1989). The myths of coping with loss. *Journal of Consulting and Clinical Psychology, 57*, 349–357.

Zarit, S. H., Stephens, M. A. P., Townsend, A., & Greene, R. (1998). Stress reduction for family caregivers: Effects of adult day care use. *Journal of Gerontology: Social Sciences, 53B*, S267–S277.

Zick, C. D., & Smith, K. R. (1991). Marital transitions, poverty, and gender differences in mortality. *Journal of Marriage and the Family, 53*, 327–337.

Part Four

Aging and Social Intervention

Eighteen

Aging and Politics

Robert H. Binstock and Jill Quadagno

I. Introduction

The subject of aging and politics encompasses a number of areas of inquiry ranging from the level of individuals to the level of nations. It includes the political orientations, attitudes, and behavior of people as they age and are elderly; organized old-age-based political action; and the politics of government action to establish and revise policies toward older people. Also relevant are the broader societal forces that shape the status of older persons and generate and suppress issues regarding whether and how they should be objects of government intervention.

Some scholars in the field of gerontology (e.g., Estes, Linkins, & Binney, 1996) have examined the larger social context that shapes the status of older persons through an approach termed *political economy*, referring to the interplay of the public and private sectors—the state and the market. The objective of this approach, which is less a formal theory of aging than it is a framework, is to explain age-related patterned inequality with particular emphasis on inequality based on class, gender, and race (Bengtson, Parrot,

& Burgess, 1997). This framework seeks to identify the characteristics of societal organization that create differential opportunities over the life course and across generations, and is also concerned with the role of ideology in creating and sustaining systems of domination (Marshall, 1996). Ideology is a crucial component in defining the social construction of the "problem" to be solved and in circumscribing the remedies that are invoked at the policy level (Estes et al., 1996). Inherent in this political economy argument is the assumption that the power to construct the definition of the problem is unequally distributed and that some groups shape public opinion far more readily than others. Whether or not one accepts the notion that ideology creates and sustains systems of *domination*, it is clear that ideology and political culture shape the ways in which societies view their collective responsibilities for their citizens (see, e.g., Berezin, 1997; Binstock, 2001; Esping-Andersen, 1999).

In the late 19th and 20th centuries, the welfare state became a major civil function of government, and the aged became the primary beneficiaries of the programs

Handbook of Aging and the Social Sciences, Fifth Edition

of the welfare state. Accordingly, conflicts surrounding the distributional issues associated with the welfare state invariably involve conflicts about the aged. These conflicts partially concern the amount of resources distributed across age groups and social classes. They also involve struggles over the amount of resources that will be distributed through the public sector as opposed to the private sector. Although resources that remain within the private sector are distributed primarily on the basis of market criteria, resources distributed through the public sector are subject to democratic processes of decision making.

Thus, even though the larger social contexts of ideology and unequal distribution of status and power may define the agenda of public sector issues and shape the broad outlines of their resolution, the processes of democratic decision making are of substantial consequence. This chapter focuses on those processes as they involve older individuals, collective old-age-based political activities, and the agenda of public-sector issues affecting older people. Space limitations make it impossible to treat with sufficient depth every subject relevant to aging and politics in one chapter. We have given priority to those topics that are most directly salient to the political controversies regarding public policies and aging that are currently prominent in developed nations. Accordingly, we do not include full reviews of the literature on the political orientations and attitudes of older people, and on their involvement in political activities other than voting and old-age political organizations; readers interested in fuller treatments of these particular topics are referred to the chapter on aging and politics in the fourth edition of this handbook (Binstock & Day, 1996). We do discuss these phenomena, however, where they are directly relevant to voting behavior and organized old-age-based political activity.

II. Voting Behavior

The theory of selective withdrawal and augmentation suggests that as individuals age they reduce some forms of political participation while expanding others or substituting new activities for previous ones (Jennings & Markus, 1988). Compared to younger people, the elderly tend to engage in fewer of the more demanding and energetic forms of participation, such as demonstrations or working in electoral campaigns, but participate more heavily in relatively low-intensity political activities, especially voting, (Delli Carpini, 1986; Jennings & Markus, 1988; MacManus, 1996; Milbrath & Goel, 1977; Verba & Nie, 1972).

Studies of voting participation over several decades have shown that voter turnout is lowest among young adults, increases rapidly up to ages 35–45, and then continues to increase (more slowly), declining only slightly after the age of 70 or 80 in the United States, and at somewhat younger ages in Sweden and Germany (Delli Carpini, 1986; Glenn & Grimes, 1968; Hout & Knoke, 1975; Miller & Shanks, 1996; Myers & Agree, 1993; Wolfinger & Rosenstone, 1980). Consequently, the percentage of the total vote cast by older people in elections is greater than their proportion of the voting-age population. In the 1996 U.S. presidential election, for example, people aged 65 and older were 16.5% of the voting age population, but cast 20.3% of the vote; the turnout rates were 32% among those aged 18–24, 49% among those aged 25–44, 64% among those aged 45–64, and 68% among those 65 years and older (Binstock, 2000a).

Why do older people turn out to vote at higher rates than middle-aged and younger people? Although the connection between age and voting participation has been investigated a great deal, overall the reasons for this relationship remain a source of controversy. Various explanations for age-group differences in turnout have helped to define the issues, but they have not resolved them.

Miller and Shanks (Miller, 1992; Miller & Shanks, 1996) are among those who hypothesize that the relatively high voting rate of older Americans during the past several decades can be attributed to birth cohort replacement. They focus on the contrasting participation rates of the New Deal cohort and subsequent cohorts whose political attitudes and behavior have been shaped by the effects of historical periods and specific political events that they have lived through (e.g., Vietnam and Watergate) at different ages in the life cycle. Supporting this view is the fact that during these decades the rates of age-group participation have been dynamic, not static, as the various cohorts have entered different stages of the life cycle. From the 1972 election through the 1996 election, the participation rate of persons aged 65 and older increased by 6.5%, whereas the rates for all other age groups declined—by 9% in the 45–64-year-old category, 21.5% in the 25–44-year-old category, and 34.7% in the 18–24-year-old category (Binstock, 2000a). But other analyses (e.g., Rosenstone & Hansen, 1993; Teixera, 1992) suggest that the contribution of cohort replacement to voting turnout rates may be overestimated. Moreover, a study by Myers and Agree (1993) found age-group differences in voting turnout in Sweden and Germany over four decades to be similar to those in the United States, despite the fact that cohorts in these three nations experienced different political events distinctive to their respective countries. This suggests that life cycle factors may be at work.

A contributing factor to the higher voting rate of older persons is age-group differences in voting registration, an essential precursor to voting. A two-stage study of voter registration and turnout in U.S. national elections (Timpone, 1998) found that increased age (from age 18 to 88) is monotonically related to being registered and that another aging-related factor, length of residence in one's own home, also has a substantial influence. Another contributing factor is that persons who are comparatively well informed about politics and public affairs are more likely to register and vote (Flanigan & Zingale, 1998; Palfrey & Poole, 1987); older people are more likely than younger people to pay attention to the news (MacManus, 1996), are more generally knowledgeable about politics (Delli Carpini & Keeter, 1993; Luskin, 1987), and report the highest level of interest in political campaigns and public affairs, generally (Jennings & Markus, 1988). Indeed, interest in and knowledge about politics increases with age and declines only slightly at advanced old ages (Strate, Parrish, Elder, & Ford, 1989). Still another contributing factor is the well-established connection between the strength of political party identification and higher rates of voting (see, e.g., Caldeira, Patterson, & Markko, 1985; Flanigan & Zingale, 1998; Rosenstone & Hansen, 1993). Older people identify with the major political parties more strongly than younger persons (MacManus, 1996; MacManus & Tenpas, 1998). Indeed, a long-standing hypothesis is that the longer individuals identify with a party, the stronger their partisanship (Converse, 1976). Yet, the relative strength of partisan attachment observed among older persons in recent decades may be due to cohort effects rather than a life cycle phenomenon. The baby boom cohort in the United States is less identified with the major political parties than preceding cohorts, and this is even more the case among post-baby boom cohorts (Alwin, 1998).

Although older people vote at a high rate, they are as diverse in their voting decisions as any other age group; their votes divide along the same partisan, economic, social, gender, and other lines as those of the electorate at large. Accordingly, the various cohorts of older Americans during the past 50 years, for example, have tended to distribute their votes among presidential candidates in roughly the same proportions as other age groups do; exit polls show sharp divisions within each age group, and very small differences between age groups (see Binstock, 1997a; Campbell & Strate, 1981). A great deal of empirical evidence indicates that the situation is similar throughout Europe (Naegele & Walker, 1999). One exception to this general pattern in the United States is that older partisans are less likely to abandon their political party to vote for an independent candidate (Flanigan & Zingale, 1998), most likely because, as indicated above, the elderly are more strongly attached to their parties than younger age groups. This tendency was clear in the 1980, 1992, and 1996 presidential elections in which the older the age group, the less heavily it voted for the Independent candidate (Binstock, 1997a).

Journalists and other political commentators conventionally assume that old-age policy issues play a major role in influencing the electoral choices of older voters because the elderly have a self-interested stake in government policies that provide old-age benefits. This assumption has its roots in neoclassical economics and statistical decision theory, which predict that each voter's decision among candidates is rationally calculated on the basis of complete and accurate information to optimize her or his self-interest. But there are intellectual flaws in this model of electoral behavior (see, e.g., Downs, 1957; Flanigan & Zingale, 1998; Simon, 1985), and substantial empirical evidence that policy issues have low levels of impact on voters of all ages (e.g., Abramson, Aldrich, & Rohde, 1999; Gelman & King, 1992; Miller & Shanks, 1996). Moreover, the self-interests of older people in relation to old-age policy issues, and the intensity of their interests may vary substantially. Consider, for example, the relative importance of Social Security as a source of income for U.S. aged persons who are in the lowest and highest income quintiles. Social Security provides about 82% of income for those in the lowest quintile, but only about 18% for those in the highest (Radner, 1995). Some older persons have much more at stake than others do in policy proposals that would reduce, maintain, or enhance Social Security benefit payments.

There is no evidence from exit polls that old-age policy issues critically influence older persons' votes for candidates, and there are many reasons to expect that they would not be so influenced. Old age is only one of many personal characteristics of aged people, and only one with which they may identify themselves and their self-interests. Even if some older voters primarily identify themselves in terms of their age status, this does not mean that their self-interests in old-age policies are the most important factors in their electoral decisions. Other policy issues, strong and long-standing partisan attachments, and many other electoral stimuli in an electoral campaign can be of equal or greater importance. Even in local referenda, when issues (rather than candidates) are presented on the ballot, there is little evidence that older people are more likely than other voters to oppose taxes for services that do not directly benefit them (Button & Rosenbaum, 1989; Chomitz, 1987). Button's (1992) precinct-level examination of school and tax referenda in Florida during the late 1980s did indicate that older voters were more likely than other age groups to oppose school bond issues, but not other tax issues. Voting against school bond issues, however, is not necessarily in the self-interest of older homeowners because a common assumption is that greater expenditures on schools improves their quality and, thereby, enhances the market value of residential property in a school district. Overall, the weight of the evidence indicates that older people's electoral choices are rarely, if ever, based on age-group interests. Simon's (1985) discussion of the inappropriateness of applying economic theory regarding self-interest to voting behavior, as compared with the appropriateness of applying psychological theory, helps to explain these research findings.

III. Organized Political Action

By the end of the first half of the 20th century most western European nations and the United States had instituted national welfare states by enacting programs for old-age pensions, unemployment insurance, workmen's compensation and, in most of these countries, health insurance (Orloff, 1993). These programs were designed as systems of social insurance, organized around the principles of sharing the collective risks of market failure and promoting social solidarity (see chapter 20 by Kingson & Williamson, this volume). Preceding their establishment, collective political action focused on income protection for older people emerged in some countries.

The United States, for example, was a distinct "welfare state laggard," not establishing a national old-age pension until it enacted Social Security in 1935 (Amenta, 1998; Quadagno, 1988). Prior to this New Deal legislation, the lack of adequate income protection for the elderly triggered some grassroots political efforts to obtain governmental assistance. Following the Civil War, for instance, hundreds of thousands of former soldiers from the Union army organized veterans' associations to pressure Congress to provide better benefits for veterans. The largest and most successful of these interest groups was the Grand Army of the Republic (GAR), which built its membership

base by lobbying to extend eligibility for Civil War pensions to aging veterans. As a result of GAR activities, Civil War pensions became *de facto* old-age pensions, deflecting political momentum for a national old-age pension (Skocpol, 1992). Another example is the Fraternal Order of Eagles, which launched a drive in 1910 for old-age pensions to be enacted by state governments. The Eagles succeeded in getting states to enact pension legislation; however, by 1929 only six states had programs that were actually operating, and even then, not in all counties (Quadagno, 1988). The Railroad Employees National Pension Association was vigorous from its founding in 1930 to 1934 when the Railroad Retirement Act, its sole objective, was enacted by Congress (Polner, 1962).

The Townsend Movement, founded in 1933 by a retired physician, Dr. Francis Townsend, proposed that the federal government give all people aged 60 and older a monthly pension of $200. At its peak in 1936 it may have had as many as 1.5 million members in a nationwide network of Townsend Clubs that maintained a dense communication network, mobilized resources, and recruited members in blocs (Amenta & Zylon, 1991; Holtzman, 1963). This organization, and a later and much smaller "Ham and Eggs" organization active in California politics (Pinner, Jacobs, & Selznick, 1959), may be better understood as social movements than as interest groups in that they were expressions of broad-based and time-bound discontent rather than enduring interests and concerns associated with old age (Carlie, 1969), and sometimes blended protests and other forms of extrainstitutional actions with traditional lobbying of governmental officials (see McAdam & Snow, 1997). Some scholars credit the Townsend Movement with hastening the establishment of Social Security Act in 1935 (Amenta & Zylon, 1991; Holtzman, 1963), but a number of scholars, as well as participants in the enactment of Social Security, have tended to dismiss the movement's role (e.g., Altmeyer, 1968; Schlesinger, 1958; Witte, 1962). In any event, the Townsend Movement died out following the passage of Social Security (Messinger, 1955), and political action focused on the needs of seniors entered a "coalescent phase" for nearly 30 years (Powell, Branco, & Williamson, 1996).

In the second half of the 20th century developed nations throughout the world witnessed a tremendous expansion in the number of old-age political organizations, the size of their memberships, and their visibility. In contrast to the earlier groups and movements in the United States, these have been stable and enduring organizations, and some of them have substantial bureaucracies (e.g., see Day, 1998; Morris, 1996; Pratt, 1976, 1993; A. Walker & Naegele, 1999; Wallace & Williamson, 1992). In the United States alone there are over 100 national organizations focused on aging policies and concerns, with thousands of local chapters. These include mass membership groups representing older people in general or subgroups of the elderly, single-issue advocacy groups, and organizations of professionals and service providers (Binstock, 1997b; Day, 1998; Van Tassel & Meyer, 1992). Although the United States has probably seen the largest number of older people organized into the most numerous and diverse array of such groups, aging-based political organizations have also emerged in Australia (Kendig & McCallum, 1990), Canada (Gifford, 1990), Japan (Campbell, 1992), and throughout Europe (A. Walker & Naegele, 1999). Among such organizations in Europe, for example, are the Senior Protection Association in Germany, the Italian pensioner party, the National Pensioners Convention in the United Kingdom, the Party of National Solidarity in Poland, and the C Team in Denmark, which has the characteristics of a social movement in that it

arranges mass demonstrations and other extrainstitutional political actions (A. Walker, 1999).

The proliferation of stable old-age political organizations can be traced to several factors. First, the existence of policies on aging, in itself, tends to create old-age-based political organizations and action (Hudson, 1999). The expansion of old-age benefits that took place following World War II gave the elderly and those who serve them a substantial stake in protecting what they had gained. In the United States, for instance, perceptions that old-age benefit programs were in financial and political jeopardy in the late 1970s and early 1980s led directly to the formation of the National Committee to Preserve Social Security and Medicare (NCPSSM) and a broad coalition of organizations, Save Our Security (Pratt, 1993). Second, grants and contracts from government agencies, as well as foundations, have propelled the growth of existing interest groups and the emergence of new ones (Pratt, 1993; J. L. Walker, 1983). And third, in keeping with Salisbury's (1969) exchange theory of interest groups, the stability and growth of old-age organizations have been effectively promoted by a variety of incentives that attract members and maintain political legitimacy.

Clark and Wilson's (1961) incentive systems theory of organizations—distinguishing among material, associational or solidary, and purposive incentives (which may overlap within a given organization)—provides a useful framework for distinguishing among types of old-age organizations. Among U.S. organizations that are primarily characterized by purposive incentives are NCPSSM and the United Seniors Association; a number of organizations focused on improving the status of elderly minority group members (e.g., the National Hispanic Council on Aging); trade associations of service providers to older people (e.g., the National Association of Nutrition and Aging

Services Providers); and the National Council for Senior Citizens, the Older Women's League, and the National Association of Retired Federal Employees (although these latter three also have solidary incentives in the form of local chapters).

The archetype of an old-age interest group that has been maintained and has grown primarily through material incentives that attract mass memberships is AARP (formerly the American Association of Retired Persons). For a $10 enrollment fee it provides publications, drug and travel discounts, assistance in filing taxes, and driver training programs, and offers its members insurance programs, investment funds, and a variety of other "affinity" products (see Morris, 1996). With these incentives it achieved a membership of about 36 million and total revenues of $485 million in 1999 (AARP, 2000), and it is currently promoting membership enrollment internationally. AARP also provides solidary incentives in the form of local chapters, but only 3% of the membership is involved in them (Day, 1998). In addition, it expends about 11% of its revenue on lobbying and public policy research (AARP, 2000). But the staff and volunteer leaders have long recognized that the organization's large membership is inherently diverse in political views, and they try to avoid taking stands on what they regard as "hopelessly divisive issues" (Rother, 1995). Nonetheless, on several occasions in recent years the leadership's issues positions have generated angry dissent from members and substantial resignations (Binstock, 1997b).

Even as no one organization can fully represent the diversity of the elderly, the groups themselves are diverse in terms of constituencies, tactics, decision-making procedures, and are often divided on old-age policy issues (Day, 1990; Pratt, 1983; A. Walker & Naegele, 1999). Coalition building has been a political strategy for these organizations to help them cope, somewhat, with the problems of diversity. One contemporary type of coalition, as exemplified by the 40–organization Leadership Council of Aging Organizations in the United States, unites old-age groups in defense of current benefit levels in old-age programs. Another type, such as Generations United, combines elderly and nonelderly groups to defend and support the expansion of various social welfare programs, generally (Torres-Gil, 1992). Yet, the effectiveness of these coalitions tends to be limited because they often have internal divisions on a number of important issues (Day, 1998).

IV. Power and Impact on Policy

As suggested by the political economy framework, any assessment of the political power of older persons and old-age political organizations should begin with the recognition that the very presence (and absence) of issues on the public policy agenda is shaped fundamentally by larger societal forces such as political ideology and culture, the distribution of economic and social power, and the interplay of the public and private sectors. Within this context, what can be said about the impact of older people and old-age interest groups and movements in bringing issues to the agenda and influencing their outcomes?

Summarizing an overview of political participation and representation of older people in Europe, Walker noted, "[old] age per se is not a sound basis for political mobilization" (A. Walker, 1999, p. 7). Similarly, regarding U.S. politics, Heclo concluded, "The elderly is really a category created by policy analysts, pension officials, and mechanical models of interest group politics" (1988, p. 393). These are sound global generalizations, but older people and their organizations are not wholly without influence. In the

Netherlands, for instance, controversial national policies relevant to older people led to the establishment of two national parties, the General Senior Citizens' Union and Union 55+ which, together, won 7 of the 150 seats in parliament in 1994 (Schuyt, García, & Knipscheer, 1999). And in recent decades, older people and old-age organizations have been perceived as an important force in U.S. policy processes by journalists, some scholars, and members of Congress and their staffs (e.g., Cook & Barrett, 1992; Day, 1998; Feldmann, 1999; Pratt, 1997; Thurow, 1999).

Although there is no credible evidence of old-age voting blocs or voting cohesion in the United States (Street, 1999), mass membership old-age interest groups, casting themselves as "representatives" of older voters, do have some forms of political influence. Although they have not demonstrated a capacity to swing the votes of older persons, they do play a role in the policy process. In the classic pattern of U.S. interest group politics (Lowi, 1969), public officials find it both useful and incumbent upon them to invite such organizations to participate in policy activities. In this way public officials are provided with a ready means of having been "in touch" symbolically with tens of millions of older persons, thereby legitimizing subsequent policy actions and inactions. A brief meeting with the leaders of major old-age organizations can enable an official to claim that he or she has obtained duly the represented views of a mass constituency.

The symbolic legitimacy that old-age organizations have for participating in interest group politics gives them several types of power. First, they have easy informal access to public officials: members of Congress and their staffs; career bureaucrats; appointed officials; and occasionally to the White House. Second, their legitimacy enables them to obtain public platforms in the national media,

congressional hearings, and in national conferences and commissions dealing with old age, health, and a variety of subjects relevant to policies affecting aging. Third, mass membership groups can mobilize their members in large numbers to contact policymakers and register displeasure when changes are being contemplated in old-age programs.

Perhaps the most important form of power available to the old-age interest groups might be termed "the electoral bluff." Although these organizations have not demonstrated a capacity to swing a decisive bloc of older voters, the perception of being powerful is, in itself, a source of political influence (see Banfield, 1961). Incumbent members of Congress are hardly inclined to risk upsetting the existing distribution of votes that puts them and keeps them in office. Few politicians, of course, want to call the bluff of the aged or any other latent mass constituency if it is possible to avoid doing so. Hence, when congressional offices are flooded with letters, faxes, e-mail messages, and phone calls expressing the (not necessarily representative) views of older persons, members of Congress take heed (Day, 1998).

Nonetheless, these forms of power have been quite limited in their impact. The old-age interest groups have had little to do with the enactment and amendment of major old-age policies such as Social Security and Medicare. Rather, such actions have been largely attributable to the initiatives of public officials in the White House, Congress, and the bureaucracy who were focused on their own agendas for social and economic policy (e.g., on Social Security, see Derthick, 1979, and Light, 1985; on Medicare, see Ball, 1995, Cohen, 1985, and Iglehart, 1989; cf. Pratt, 1976 and Pratt, 1993). Support for old-age benefits in Congress has been linked more to perceptions of need and deservingness than to group or constituency pressures (Cook & Barrett, 1992; Lubomudrov, 1987). The impact of old-age interest groups in policy innovation has been largely confined to the successful efforts of relatively small purposive organizations that have been successful in lobbying for relatively minor policies that have distributed benefits to professionals and practitioners in the field of aging rather than directly to older persons themselves (e.g., see Estes, 1979; Fox, 1989; Lockett, 1983).

The power of old-age interest groups has been largely defensive, aimed at protecting existing programs and fighting the imposition of new taxes on older people such as the income surtax levied in the Medicare Catastrophic Coverage Act of 1988 (see Day, 1993; Himmelfarb, 1995). But these organizations have not been able to prevent significant (though not radical) policy reforms that have been perceived to be adverse to the interests of an artificially homogenized constituency of "the elderly" (see Binstock, 1994a; Day, 1998). Moreover, the mass membership groups have been largely inattentive to the needs of the poorest and most disadvantaged elderly (see chapters 9 and 19, this volume); even if they became more concerned in this respect, they would probably be unable to influence the sweeping redistributive changes that would be required to make a difference.

The political legitimacy of old-age interest groups in the United States has been eroding over the past 10 years (see Binstock, 1997b; Day, 1998; Street, 1999). To some extent this erosion can be traced to the ineffective roles they played in specific political episodes such as the enactment of the Medicare Catastrophic in 1988 and its partial repeal in 1989 (Himmelfarb, 1995) and the saga of health-care reform efforts in 1993 and 1994 (Binstock, 1994b). Following these events, the most powerful of the old-age organizations, AARP, came under attack at two U.S. Senate hearings in which various witnesses criticized its organizational practices and tax-exempt status (see Binstock, 1997b). One senator even questioned whether AARP represented its own constituency, charging that the organization "imposes a policy agenda on an unwilling membership" (Pear, 1995). Symbolic of this decline in the political legitimacy of old-age interest groups, perhaps, is that none of President Clinton's 1997 appointments to the National Bipartisan Commission on the Future of Medicare was a representative of organized old-age interests (New York Times, 1997).

But the erosion in the legitimacy of old-age interest groups is not simply due to their own political behavior. It is also due to broader changes in the political context of policies on aging.

V. The Changing Political Context of Old-Age Policies

Since the 1980s, constraints associated with globalization and international competition, rising public budgets, and population aging have generated issues about the social programs that were constructed when developed nations had a very different demographic structure, so that they are now perceived as "social problems" (see, e.g., Kendig & McCallum, 1990; Nielsen, 1991; Schulz, Borowski, & Crown, 1991; A. Walker, 1991, 1993). Most European countries have begun a process of restructuring their public programs of income security and health care (A. Walker & Naegele, 1999). Some have reduced social expenditures, like Sweden, for example, which recently cut benefits for unemployment and reduced its pension promises to retirees (Myles & Pierson, in press). A few, however, have added new programs, like Germany and Austria, which both established national long-term care programs in the 1990s (Cuellar & Wiener, 2000; Smeeding, 1998), as did Japan (Campbell & Ikegami, 2000).

The task of restructuring programs is fundamentally different from adding new programs. As large social programs become a part of the political landscape, they mobilize public support and create entrenched interest group constituencies. Myles and Pierson (in press) have examined the transformation of public pension programs and conclude that the structure of the existing system has enormous influence on the direction of policy change. Nations with mature social insurance systems have been unable to make radical changes because existing programs create constituencies that oppose program change. By contrast, countries that lacked mature social insurance systems have been able to reduce public expenditures more readily. Reforms in Great Britain, for example, have allowed workers to contract out of a public pension system that was introduced as recently as 1978 and did not have the same degree of popular support as more mature programs in other nations.

The outcomes of policy struggles over old-age and other programs depend not only on the alignment of power, but also on who frames the issues for debate and who determines which interpretations are appropriate to place on the national agenda (e.g., see Williamson, Watts-Roy, & Kingson, 1999). Broad cultural themes are mobilized in the service of politics (Berezin, 1997), and are wielded as tools in social and political struggles (Williams, 1995). In any emergent national "crisis," "scandal," or "social problem," there exist competing definitions and a variety of solutions (Edelman, 1995), which attempt to rationalize and institutionalize the relative advantages of counterpoised groups and classes through policies enacted to solve the problem or crisis as defined. Indeed, "the very description of the axis upon which equity is to be judged tends to circumscribe the major options available for rendering justice" (Binstock, 1994c, p. 162).

In the United States, the competitive party system and the lack of a corporatist negotiating structure have meant that any politician who openly proposes cuts in benefits risks alienating the public (Pierson, 1994). Consequently, a strategy often adopted by politicians seeking to cut benefits is to alter public discourse by redefining the issues. A change in how issues are defined can dramatically alter policy outcomes by activating new groups to take an interest in the policy, by splintering the existing configuration of support, and by limiting the parameters of potential options for change. Struggles over social policy thus often become struggles over information (Weir, 1998).

During the 1980s and 1990s the theme of "crisis" has been prominent in defining old-age policy issues (Estes, Linkins, & Binney 1996). The crisis has centered around two themes, that of generational equity (Kingson & Williamson, 1993; Thurow, 1996; Williamson et al., 1999) and that of an entitlement crisis (Quadagno, 1989, 1996). These themes are not exclusive to the United States. In New Zealand and Great Britain, for example, similar issues of equity across generations have been raised (Thomson, 1996; A. Walker, 1996). Although the concept of generational equity has also appeared in Canada in the context of public policy discussions, it rarely appears in the media and is not really a factor in public policy debates (Cook, Marshall, Marshall, & Kaufman, 1994). In U.S. policy debates, by contrast, these issues have played a far more prominent role (Marmor, Cook, & Scher, 1997).

A. Generational Equity

The term *generational equity* refers to the argument that the elderly have been the recipients of an unfair distribution of public resources for income, health care, and social services, and that the large share of national resources granted to older people is no longer justified, because the elderly as a group are financially better off than the non-aged population (e.g., see Lamm, 1999; Peterson, 1993). Because the flow of resources to the elderly seems "intergenerationally inequitable," this definition of a problem sets the stage for intergenerational conflict (Kingson, Hirshorn, & Cornman, 1986).

The argument that there is a political trade-off between meeting the needs of the young and the old first gained credence when the distinguished demographer, Samuel Preston (1984), published an article noting that public expenditures on children had been declining even as expenditures on older people rose. This argument was then repeated in more sensational terms by generational equity proponents like Phillip Longman, who argued that we should not be "squandering the nation's limited wealth on an unproductive segment of the population" (Longman, 1982, p. 24). Factors that contributed to the portrayal of the aged as a burdensome responsibility included the tremendous growth of federal dollars expended on aging people and notable improvements in the status of the aged (Binstock, 1994c; Hudson, 1978).

Social scientists who have critically evaluated the merits of the generational equity argument have responded that in American politics, claims of crisis are frequently made to attract attention. There are always competing illustrations to demonstrate the nature of the problem and the course of potential solution (Marmor, Cook, & Scher, 1997). Complex statistics are often presented to justify a single policy response to a complex social problem. As Munnell (1999) points out, the costs of Social Security and Medicare are often lumped together and treated as a single "crisis" when in fact, these are separate programs that are financed separately and face different problems. Further, public opinion polls show that the public supports spending on Social Security and

that fewer than 6% of U.S. citizens favor reducing Social Security benefits (Cook & Barrett, 1992; Pampel, 1998).

The central issue in the generational equity debate, whether there is a trade-off between spending on the elderly and spending on children, is an empirical question that has been analyzed by Pampel (1994), who examined international trends in social spending in 18 Western nations. He found no association between high spending for the elderly and low spending for children. Rather his research indicated that nations with high levels of spending on the elderly also spent more on children.

B. The Entitlement Crisis

As it became clear that the notion of generational conflict did not resonate with the public, the ideological debate shifted to an "entitlement crisis" (Peterson, 1996, 1999). In the federal budget there are more than 100 programs defined as entitlements, that is "mandatory spending" programs that are governed by formulas set in law and not subject to annual appropriations by Congress. Entitlements stand in distinction to two other federal budget categories, discretionary spending, which includes domestic and defense spending, and net interest on the debt. The three largest entitlement programs are Social Security, Medicare, and Medicaid; well over one-third of the federal budget is spent on benefits to older persons, largely due to these particular programs (Binstock, 2000b).

The core thesis of the "entitlement crisis" is that entitlement spending is consuming a disproportionate share of the federal budget and crowding out funds for other social needs (Penny & Schier, 1996; Quadagno, 1996, 1998). In this scenario spending on entitlements is not sustainable at current levels, and the "graying of the welfare state is likely to have catastrophic consequences for the after-tax living standards of most work-ing-age Americans" (Howe, 1997, p. 36). As Thurow argues, "Already the needs and demands of the elderly have shaken the social welfare state to its foundations, causing it for all practical purposes to go broke.... interest plus entitlements are swallowing government budgets" (1999, p. 59).

This framing of the issue was made credible by a rising budget deficit, which roughly doubled between 1981 and 1985. By the late 1990s, however, the budget deficit had disappeared, and politicians instead were debating how best to spend the unanticipated budget surplus. Although the problem had became moot, the concept of an "entitlement crisis" has had an impact on policy debates, and the charts and measures used to define the "crisis" have become an accepted way for framing the problem and for defining possible solutions. Social insurance bene-ficiaries have become "unfunded liabil-ities," the grand distributional issues of the day have become budget dilemmas, and the objective of social welfare expend-itures has become that of increasing sav-ings and investments (Quadagno, 1999). The changing political culture has trans-formed public debate about Social Secur-ity reform so as to legitimate proposals for privatizing the program (see chapter 20 by Kingson & Williamson, this volume).

C. The Era of Capital Investment

The current political culture surrounding the welfare state, and by implication its largest program, Social Security, centers upon the claim that social benefits are crippling rigidities that increase the costs of labor, undermine productivity, and drain the public budget (Antonio & Bonnano, 1996). This represents a distinct shift from the view that the welfare state consists of programs of social insurance organized around the principles of sharing the collective risks of market failure and promoting social solidarity. The objective of social insurance is to insure those who contributed to the system against various life course risks. The main beneficiaries are workers, benefits are based on work history, and the programs include an ele-ment of income redistribution. These fea-tures stand in sharp contrast to a "capital investment welfare state," where the ob-jectives are to increase savings and invest-ment, the primary beneficiaries are investors, levels of benefits are deter-mined by an individual's investment portfolio, and benefits are skewed to the more prosperous (Quadagno, 1998, 1999). The transition to the capital investment paradigm is visible in efforts to restructure public benefits to coincide with trends in the private sector, and in proposals to transform public welfare programs from cash benefits and direct services into incentives for saving and investing (Schie-ber, 1997). On a larger scale the debate really is about reducing public-sector re-sponsibility for the health and income security of the older population and trans-ferring this responsibility to the private sector, along with substantial funds to carry it out.

In an earlier era, the politics of aging was predominantly shaped by compassion-ate concerns about the status of older people (e.g., see Binstock, 1983). Today, in the United States and in most of the developed nations, policy issues affecting older persons are much more framed by larger concerns about the balance of pri-vate- and public-sector resources, as well as trade-offs between the status of older persons and other citizens, and the costs of the welfare state—particularly as the large post-World War II birth cohorts are about to enter the ranks of old age. In this context, advocacy for the needs of older persons by old-age interest groups has become less salient in the policy arena than in the past. The central issues have become framed in a fashion that gives powerful private-sector economic interests—far more powerful than old-age political organizations—a considerable stake in the future of old-age policies.

VI. Issues for Further Research

Findings from research on the aspects of aging and politics discussed in this chapter have been generally consistent for several decades. Nonetheless, ongoing research is needed in several areas.

One topic that requires greater attention is cross-national comparisons of the voting behavior of older persons. There is increasing evidence, for example, of a growing political mobilization of the aged in European nations (Naegele & Walker, 1999). If patterns of voting participation and electoral choice are found to be significantly different among industrialized nations, one would then want to explore how the politics of older people may be shaped by, and shape, various types of political cultures and institutions.

A related cross-national issue is how the political context in which debates about cutting social expenditures occur varies across nations. To what extent are these debates being framed around issues of generational conflict, fiscal responsibility, or the "threat" of population aging?

Another topic that merits investigation is whether the new and relatively large post-World War II cohorts in developed nations, soon to enter the ranks of old age, exhibit voting participation patterns different from those of their predecessors (see Alwin, 1998). Research of this kind would help to clarify whether age-related participation patterns are due more to cohort or life cycle effects. Moreover, radical policy proposals regarding old-age benefit policies might engender greater age-group consciousness and voting cohesion among the elderly than has been manifest so far, as older voters find that old-age policy issues transcend other considerations in the context of election campaigns (see Binstock, 2000a).

Research on the nature and extent of the power of contemporary old-age organizations, their true impact on specific policy decisions, and their overall role in various national political systems has been relatively sparse. Although many (but not all) scholarly and journalistic treatments of these organizations describe them as "powerful," such characterizations are largely based on reputational data rather than systematic empirical investigations. This area of inquiry would benefit substantially from more thorough, detailed analyses of the actual processes of policy decision making, framed by theory on the bases and dynamics of political influence (e.g., Banfield, 1961). An excellent opportunity for such research is likely to occur, for example, in the United States, where proposals to raise the age of eligibility for old-age benefits are beginning to emerge on the policy agenda as measures to control expenditures on Social Security and Medicare when the Baby Boom becomes eligible for these programs. When such a 2-year age increase in eligibility for full Social Security benefits was enacted in 1983, there was little opposition from old-age organizations because relatively few older persons were likely to be affected. That increase was scheduled to begin, gradually, starting 20 years in the future (2003), and take another 24 years (until 2027) to be fully implemented. But if proposals to raise the age for benefit eligibility within a relatively short time frame are placed on the legislative agenda (which it appears they will be), they may well evoke strong opposition from old-age interest groups, and provide an excellent opportunity to examine the sources, nature, and limits of power exercised by those groups.

More broadly, contemporary efforts to restructure the welfare state in many developed nations may give rise to a macropolitics of aging that is very different than what has been experienced in the past. Shifts from a social insurance model to a capital investment model—reallocating resources from the public to the private sector—may undermine the longstanding political legitimacy that has enabled the welfare of all older persons to be viewed as a collective responsibility. In addition, attempts to substantially cut back public benefits for growing elderly populations may set older voters at odds with their fellow citizens in shaping the future of the welfare state. Economist Lester Thurow (1996) prophesizes that, "Universal suffrage...is going to meet the ultimate test in the elderly.... In the years ahead,, class warfare is apt to be redefined as the young against the old, rather than the poor against the rich" (p. 47). Whether or not Thurow's apocalyptic vision comes to pass, many changes in the politics of aging and the welfare state will take place in the coming decades, presenting interesting and societally important issues for research.

References

AARP. (2000). *AARP annual report*. [On-line] Available: http://www.aarp.org [August, 23, 2000].

Abramson, P. R., Aldrich, J. H., & Rohde, D. W. (1999). *Change and continuity in the 1996 and 1998 elections*. Washington, DC: CQ Press.

Altmeyer, A. J. (1968). *The formative years of Social Security*. Madison, WI: University of Wisconsin Press.

Alwin, D. F. (1998). The political impact of the baby boom: Are there persistent generational differences in political beliefs and behavior? *Generations, 22(1)*, 46–54.

Amenta, E. (1998). *Bold relief: Institutional politics and the origins of modern American social policy*. Princeton, NJ: University Press.

Amenta, E., & Zylon, Y. (1991). It happened here: Political opportunity, the new institu-

tionalism, and the Townsend Movement. *American Sociological Review, 56*, 262–272.

Antonio, R., & Bonnano, A. (1996). Post-Fordism in the United States: The poverty of market-centered democracy. *Current Perspectives in Social Theory, 16*, 3–32.

Ball, R. M. (1995). What Medicare's architects had in mind. *Health Affairs, 14(4)*, 62–72.

Banfield, E. C. (1961). *Political influence: A new theory of urban politics*. New York: The Free Press.

Bengtson, V., Parrott, T., & Burgess, E. (1997). Theory, explanation, and a third generation of theoretical developments in social gerontology. *Journal of Gerontology: Social Sciences, 52B*, S72–88.

Berezin, M. (1997). Politics and culture: A less fissured terrain. *Annual Review of Sociology, 23*, 361–83.

Binstock, R. H. (1983). The aged as scapegoat. *Gerontologist, 23*, 136–143.

Binstock, R. H. (1994a). Changing criteria in old-age programs: The introduction of economic status and need for services. *Gerontologist, 34*, 726–730.

Binstock, R. H. (1994b). Older Americans and health care reform in the nineties. In P. V. Rosenau (Ed.), *Health care reform in the nineties* (pp. 213–235). Thousand Oaks, CA: Sage Publications.

Binstock, R. H. (1994c). Transcending intergenerational equity. In T. R. Marmor, T. M. Smeeding, & V. L. Greene (Eds.), *Economic security and intergenerational justice: A look at North America* (pp.155–185). Washington, DC: The Urban Institute Press.

Binstock, R. H. (1997a). The 1996 election: Older voters and implications for policies on aging. *Gerontologist, 37*, 15–19.

Binstock, R. H. (1997b). The old-age lobby in a new political era. In R.B. Hudson (Ed.), *The future of age-based public policy* (pp. 56–74). Baltimore, MD: Johns Hopkins University Press.

Binstock, R. H. (2000a). Older people and voting participation: Past and future. *Gerontologist, 40*, 18–31.

Binstock, R. H. (2000b). The politics of near-term action to deal with the aging of the baby boom. *Journal of Aging and Social Policy, 11 (2/3)*, 19–29.

Binstock, R. H. (2001). The politics of caring. In L. E. Cluff & R. H. Binstock (Eds.), *The* lost art of caring: A challenge to health professionals, families, communities, and society (pp. 219–242). Baltimore, MD: Johns Hopkins University Press.

Binstock, R. H., & Day, C. L. (1996). Aging and politics. In R. H. Binstock & L. K. George (Eds.), Handbook of aging and the social sciences (4th ed.) (pp. 362–387). San Diego, CA: Academic Press.

Button, J. W. (1992). A sign of generational conflict: The impact of Florida's aging voters on local school and tax referenda. Social Science Quarterly, 73, 786–797.

Button, J. W., & Rosenbaum, W. A. (1989). Seeing gray: School bond issues and the aging in Florida. Research on Aging, 11, 158–173.

Caldeira, G. A., Patterson, S. C., & Markko, G. A. (1985). The mobilization of voters in congressional elections. Journal of Politics, 47, 490–509.

Campbell, J. C. (1992). How policies change: The Japanese government and the aging society. Princeton, NJ: Princeton University Press.

Campbell, J. C., & Ikegami, N. (2000). Long-term care insurance comes to Japan. Health Affairs, 9(3), 26–39.

Campbell, J. C., & Strate, J. (1981). Are older people conservative? Gerontologist, 21, 580–591.

Carlie, M. K. (1969). The politics of age: Interest group or social movement. Gerontologist, 9, 259–263.

Chomitz, K. M. (1987). Demographic influences on local public education expenditures: A review of econometric evidence. In Committee on Population, Commission on Behavioral and Social Sciences and Education, National Research Council (Ed.), Demographic change and the well-being of children and the elderly (pp. 45–53). Washington, D.C.: National Academy Press.

Clark, P. B., & Wilson, J. Q. (1961). Incentive systems: A theory of organizations. Administrative Science Quarterly, 6, 219–266.

Cohen, W. J. (1985). Reflections on the enactment of Medicare and Medicaid. Health Care Financing Review, Annual Supplement, 3–11.

Converse, P. E. (1976). The dynamics of party support: Cohort-analyzing party identification. Beverly Hills, CA: Sage Publications.

Cook, F. L., & Barrett, E. J. (1992). Support for the American welfare state. New York: Columbia University Press.

Cook, F. L., Marshall, V. W., Marshall, J. G., & Kaufman, J. (1994). Public opinion and the elderly in Canada and the United States. In T. R. Marmor, T. M. Smeeding, & V. L. Greene (Eds.), Economic security and intergenerational justice: A look at North America (pp. 91–129). Washington, D.C.: Urban Institute Press.

Cuellar, A. E., & Wiener, J. M. (2000). Can social insurance for long-term care work? The experience of Germany. Health Affairs, 19(3), 8–25.

Day, C. L. (1990). What older Americans think: Interest groups and aging policy. Princeton, NJ: Princeton University Press.

Day, C. L. (1993). Older Americans' attitudes toward the Medicare Catastrophic Coverage Act of 1988. Journal of Politics, 55, 167–177.

Day, C. L. (1998). Old-age interest groups in the 1990s: Coalition, competition, strategy. In J. S. Steckenrider & T. M. Parrott (Eds.) New directions in old-age policies (pp. 131–150). Albany, NY: State University of New York Press.

Delli Carpini, M. X. (1986). Stability and change in American politics: The coming of age of the generation of the 1960s. New York: New York University Press.

Delli Carpini, M. X., & Keeter, S. (1993). Measuring political knowledge: Putting first things first. American Journal of Political Science, 37, 1179–1206.

Derthick, M. (1979). Policymaking for Social Security. Washington, DC: Brookings Institution.

Downs, A. (1957). An economic theory of democracy. New York: Harper and Brothers.

Edelman, M. (1995). Constructing the political spectacle. Chicago: University of Chicago Press.

Esping Andersen, G. (1999). Social foundations of postindustrial economics. New York: Oxford University Press.

Estes, C. L. (1979). The aging enterprise. San Francisco: Jossey-Bass.

Estes, C. L., Linkins, K. W., & Binney, E. A. (1996). The political economy of aging. In R. H. Binstock & L. K. George (Eds.), Handbook of aging and the social sciences (4th ed.) (pp. 346–359). San Diego: Academic Press.

Feldmann, L. (1999). Control of Congress in seniors' hands. *Christian Science Monitor*, June 21, p. 1.

Flanigan, W. H., & Zingale, N. H. (1998). *Political behavior of the American electorate, ninth edition*. Washington, DC: CQ Press.

Fox, P. (1989). From senility to Alzheimer's disease: The rise of the Alzheimer's disease movement. *The Milbank Quarterly, 67*, 58–102.

Gelman, A., & King, G. (1992). *Why do presidential election campaign polls vary so much when the vote is so predictable?* Cambridge, MA: Littauer Center, Harvard University.

Gifford, C. G. (1990). *Canada's fighting seniors*. Toronto: James Lorimer & Co.

Glenn, N. D., & Grimes, M. (1968). Aging, voting, and political interest. *American Sociological Review, 33*, 563–575.

Heclo, H. (1988). Generational politics. In J. L. Palmer, T. Smeeding, & B. Boyle Torrey (Eds.), *The vulnerable* (pp. 381–411). Washington, DC: Urban Institute Press.

Himmelfarb, R. (1995). *Catastrophic politics: The rise and fall of the Medicare Catastrophic Coverage Act of 1988*. University Park, PA: Pennsylvania State University Press.

Holtzman, A. (1963). *The Townsend Movement: A political study*. New York: Bookman Associates.

Hout, M., & Knoke, D. (1975). Change in voting turnout, 1952–1972. *Public Opinion Quarterly, 39*, 52–68.

Howe, N. (1997). Why the graying of the welfare state threatens to flatten the American dream—or worse. In R. B. Hudson (Ed.), *The future of age-based policy* (pp. 35–45). Baltimore, MD: Johns Hopkins University Press.

Hudson, R. B. (1978). The "graying" of the federal budget and its consequences for old age policy. *Gerontologist, 18*, 428–440.

Hudson, R. B. (1999). Conflict in today's aging politics: New population encounters old ideology. *Social Service Review, 73*, 358–379.

Iglehart, J. K. (1989). Medicare's new benefits: Catastrophic health insurance. *New England Journal of Medicine, 320*, 329–336.

Jennings, M. K., & Markus, G. B. (1988). Political involvement in the later years: A longitudinal survey. *American Journal of Political Science, 32*, 302–316.

Kendig, H. L., & McCallum, J. (Eds.) (1990). *Grey policy: Australian policies for an ageing society*. Sydney, Australia: Allen & Unwin.

Kingson, E. R., Hirshorn, B. A., & Cornman, J. M. (1986). *Ties that bind: The interdependence of generations*. Washington, DC: Seven Locks Press.

Kingson, E. R., & Williamson, J. B. (1993). The generational equity debate: A progressive framing of a conservative debate. *Journal of Aging and Social Policy, 5*, 31–53.

Lamm, R. (1999). Care for the elderly: What about our children? In J. B. Williamson, D. M. Watts-Roy, & E. R. Kingson (Eds.), *The generational equity debate* (pp. 87–100). New York: Columbia University Press.

Light, P. (1985). *Artful work: The politics of Social Security reform*. New York: Random House.

Lockett, B. A. (1983). *Aging, politics, and research: Setting the federal agenda for research on aging*. New York: Springer Publishing Company.

Longman, P. (1982). Justice between generations. *Atlantic Monthly, 9*, 73–81.

Lowi, T. J. (1969). *The end of liberalism*. New York: W. W. Norton.

Lubomudrov, S. (1987). Congressional perceptions of the elderly: The use of stereotypes in the legislative process. *Gerontologist, 27*, 77–81.

Luskin, R. C. (1987). Measuring political sophistication. *American Journal of Political Science, 31*, 856–899.

MacManus, S. A. (1996). *Young v. old: Generational combat in the 21st century*. Boulder, CO: Westview Press.

MacManus, S. A., & Tenpas, K. D. (1998). The changing political activism patterns of older Americans: "Don't throw dirt over us yet." In J. S. Steckenrider & T. M. Parrott (Eds.), *New directions in old-age policies* (pp. 111–130). Albany, NY: State University of New York Press.

Marmor, T. R., Cook, F. L., & Scher, S. (1997). Social Security politics and the conflict between generations: Are we asking the right questions? In E. R. Kingson & J. H. Schulz

(Eds.), *Social Security in the twenty-first century* (pp. 195–207). New York: Oxford University Press.

Marshall, V. (1996). The state of theory in aging and the social sciences. In R. H. Binstock & L. K. George (Eds.), *Handbook of aging and the social sciences* (4th ed.) (pp. 12–20). San Diego: Academic Press.

McAdam, D., & Snow, D. (1997). *Social movements*. Los Angeles, CA: Roxbury.

Messinger, S. L. (1955). Organizational transformation: A case study of a declining social movement. *American Sociological Review*, 20, 3–10.

Milbrath, L. W., & Goel, M. L. (1977). *Political participation*. Chicago: Rand McNally.

Miller, W. E. (1992.) The puzzle transformed: Explaining declining turnout. *Political Behavior, 14*(1), 1–43.

Miller, W. E., & Shanks, J. M. (1996). *The new American voter*. Cambridge, MA: Harvard University Press.

Morris, C. R. (1996). *The AARP: America's most powerful lobby and the clash of generations*. New York: Times Books.

Munnell, A. H. (1999). America can afford to grow old. In J. B. Williamson, D. M. Watts-Roy, & E. R. Kingson (Eds.), *The generational equity debate* (pp. 117–139). New York: Columbia University Press.

Myers, G. C., & Agree, E. M. (1993). Social and political implications of population aging: Aging of the electorate. In *Proceedings of the International Population Conference, Montreal 1993, Volume 3* (pp. 37–49). Liege, Belgium: International Union for the Scientific Study of Population.

Myles, J., & Pierson, P. (in press.) The comparative political economy of pension reform. In P. Pierson (Ed.), *The new politics of the welfare state*. New York: Oxford University Press.

Naegele, G., & Walker, A. (1999). Conclusion. In A. Walker & G. Naegele (Eds.), *The politics of old age in Europe* (pp. 197–209). Buckingham, PA: Open University Press.

New York Times. (1997). Members of the panel on Medicare. December 6, A16.

Nielsen, F. v. N. (1991). The politics of aging in Scandinavian countries. In J. Myles & J. Quadagno (Eds.), *States, labor markets, and the future of old-age policy* (pp. 127–174). Philadelphia: Temple University Press.

Orloff, A. S. (1993). *The politics of pensions*. Madison, WI: University of Wisconsin Press.

Palfrey, T. R., & Poole, K. T. (1987). The relationship between information, ideology, and voting behavior. *American Journal of Political Science, 31*, 511–530.

Pampel, F. C. (1994). Population aging, class context, and age inequality in public spending. *American Journal of Sociology, 100*, 153–95.

Pampel, F. C. (1998). *Aging, social inequality and public policy*. Thousand Oaks, CA: Pine Forge Press.

Pear, R. (1995). Senator challenges the practices of a retirees association. *New York Times*, June 14, A14.

Penny, T., & Schier, S. (1996). *Payment due: A nation in debt, a generation in trouble*. Boulder, CO: Westview Press.

Peterson, P. G. (1993). *Facing up: How to rescue the economy from crushing debt & restore the American dream*. New York: Simon & Schuster.

Peterson, P. (1996). *Will America grow up before it grows old?* New York: Random House.

Peterson, P. G. (1999). *Gray dawn: How the age wave will transform America—and the world*. New York: Times Books.

Pierson, P. (1994). *Dismantling the welfare state*. Cambridge, UK: Cambridge University Press.

Pinner, F. A., Jacobs, P., & Selznick, P. (1959). *Old age and political behavior*. Berkeley, CA: University of California Press.

Polner, W. (1962). The aged in politics: A successful example, the NPA and the Passage of the Railroad Retirement Act. *Gerontologist, 2*, 207–215.

Powell, L. A., Branco, K. J., & Williamson, J. B. (1996). *The senior rights movement: Framing the policy debate in America*. New York: Twayne Publishers.

Pratt, H. J. (1976). *The gray lobby*. Chicago: University of Chicago Press.

Pratt, H. J. (1983). National interest groups among the elderly: Consolidation and constraint. In W. P. Browne & L. K. Olson (Eds.), *Aging and public policy: The politics of growing old in America* (pp. 145–179). Westport, CT: Greenwood.

Pratt, H. J. (1993). *Gray agendas: Interest groups and public pensions in Canada,*

Britain, and the United States. Ann Arbor: University of Michigan Press.

Pratt, H. J. (1997). Do the elderly really have political clout? In A. E. Scharlach & L W. Kaye (Eds.), *Controversial issues in aging* (pp. 82–85). Boston, MA: Allyn and Bacon.

Preston, S. H. (1984). Children and the elderly in the U.S. *Scientific American, 251(6)*, 44–49.

Quadagno, J. (1988). *The transformation of old age security*. Chicago, IL: University of Chicago Press.

Quadagno, J. (1989). Generational equity and the politics of the welfare state. *Politics and Society, 17*, 353–376.

Quadagno, J. (1996). Social Security and the myth of the entitlement crisis. *Gerontologist, 36*, 391–399.

Quadagno, J. (1998). Social Security and the entitlement debate in the Clinton administration: The new American exceptionalism. In M. Schwartz & C. Lo (Eds.), *Clinton and the conservative political agenda* (pp. 95–117). London: Blackwell Publishers.

Quadagno, J. (1999). Creating the capital investment welfare state: The new American exceptionalism. *American Sociological Review, 64*, 1–11.

Radner, D. R. (1995). Income of the elderly and nonelderly, 1967–1992. *Social Security Bulletin, 58(4)*, 82–97.

Rother, J. (1995). Letter to Robert H. Binstock, February 7.

Rosenstone, S. J., & Hansen, J. M. (1993). *Mobilization, participation, and democracy*. New York: Macmillan.

Salisbury, R. H. (1969). An exchange theory of interest groups. *Midwest Journal of Political Science, 8*, 1–32.

Schieber, S. J. (1997). A new vision for Social Security. In R. B. Hudson (Ed.), *The future of age-based policy* (pp. 134–143). Baltimore, MD: Johns Hopkins University Press.

Schlesinger, A. (1958). *The politics of upheaval*. Boston, MA: Houghton Mifflin.

Schulz, J. H., Borowski, A., & Crown, W. H. (1991). *Economics of population aging: The "graying" of Australia, Japan, and the United States*. New York: Auburn House.

Schuyt, T., García, L. L., & Knipscheer, K. (1999). The politics of old age in the Netherlands. In A. Walker & G. Naegele (Eds.), *The

politics of old age in Europe* (pp. 123–134). Buckingham, PA: Open University Press.

Simon, H. A. (1985). Human nature in politics: The dialogue of psychology with political science. *American Political Science Review, 79*, 293–304.

Skocpol, T. (1992). *Protecting soldiers and mothers*. Cambridge, MA: Harvard University Press.

Smeeding, T. M. (1998). Reshuffling responsibility in old age: The United States in comparative perspective. In J. Gonyea (Ed.), *Resecuring Social Security and Medicare: Understanding privatization and risk* (pp. pp. 24–36). Washington, D.C.: Gerontological Society of America.

Strate, J. M., Parrish, C. J., Elder, C. D., & Ford, C., III (1989). Life span civic development and voting participation. *American Political Science Review, 83*, 443–464.

Street, D. (1999). Special interests or citizens' rights? "Senior power," Social Security, and Medicare. In M. Minkler & C. L. Estes (Eds.), *Critical gerontology: Perspectives from political and moral economy* (pp. 109–130). Amityville, NY: Baywood Publishing Company, Inc.

Teixera, R. A. (1992). *The disappearing American voter*. Washington, DC: The Brookings Institution.

Thomson, D. (1996.) *Selfish generations? How welfare states grow old*. Wellington, New Zealand: White Horse Press.

Thurow, L. C. (1996). The birth of a revolutionary class. *New York Times Magazine, May 19*, 46–47.

Thurow, L. C. (1999). Generational equity and the birth of a revolutionary class. In J. B. Williamson, Watts-Roy, D. M., & Kingson, E. R. (Eds.), *The generational equity debate* (pp. 58–74). New York: Columbia University Press.

Timpone, R. J. (1998). Structure, behavior, and voter turnout in the United States. *American Political Science Review, 92*, 145–158.

Torres-Gil, F. M. (1992). *The new aging: Politics and change in America*. New York: Auburn House.

Van Tassel, D. D., & Meyer, J. E. W. (1992). *U.S. aging policy interest groups: Institutional profiles*. New York: Greenwood.

Verba, S., & Nie, N. H. (1972). *Participation in America*. New York: Harper & Row.

Walker, A. (1991). Thatcherism and the new politics of old age. In J. Myles & J. Quadagno (Eds.), *States, labor markets, and the future of old-age policy* (pp. 19–35). Philadelphia: Temple University Press.

Walker, A. (1993). Intergenerational relations and welfare restructuring: The social construction of an intergenerational problem. In V. L. Bengtson & W. A. Achenbaum (Eds.), *The changing contract across generations* (pp. 141–165). New York: Aldine De Gruyter.

Walker. A. (1996). *The new generational contract: Intergenerational relations, old age and welfare.* London, UK: Taylor and Francis.

Walker, A. (1999). Political participation and representation of older people. In A. Walker & G. Naegele (Eds.), *The politics of old age in Europe* (pp. 7–24). Philadelphia, PA: Open University Press.

Walker, A., & Naegele, G. (Eds.) (1999). *The politics of old age in Europe.* Philadelphia, PA: Open University Press.

Walker, J. L. (1983). The origins and maintenance of interest groups in America. *American Political Science Review, 77,* 390–406.

Wallace, S. P., & Williamson, J. B. (1992). *The senior movement: References and resources.* New York: G. K. Hall.

Weir, M. (1998). Political parties and social policymaking. In M. Weir (Ed.), *The social divide* (pp. 1–47). Washington, DC: The Brookings Institution Press.

Williams, R. H. (1995.) Constructing the public good: Social movements and cultural resources. *Social Problems, 42,* 124–144.

Williamson, J. B., Watts-Roy, D. M., & Kingson, E. R. (Eds.) (1999). *The generational equity debate.* New York: Columbia University Press.

Witte, E. (1962). *The development of the Social Security Act.* Madison, WI: University of Wisconsin Press.

Wolfinger, R. E., & Rosenstone, S. J. (1980) *Who votes?* New Haven: Yale University Press.

Nineteen

Economic Status of the Elderly

William Crown

I. Introduction

How well off are the elderly? Finding the answer to this simple question is remarkably difficult. Our perceptions of the economic status of any group are a function of how we think they are doing relative to other groups, how the relative economic status of different groups has changed over time, what income sources and assets we count when making comparisons of economic status and the economic needs of the different groups.

In the mid-20th century, Duesenberry (1949) argued that people judge their economic status by where they are in the income distribution relative to the rest of the population—the notion of "keeping up with the Joneses." When one thinks about it, all measures of income adequacy are relative measures of some sort. Basic measures of income adequacy such as poverty status involve the comparison of one's income to a threshold value that varies by age and household size. Similarly, an assessment of what constitutes an adequate retirement income "replacement rate" involves comparison of an individual's pre- and postretirement incomes. And, of course, any measure of the relative economic status of different population groups involves the comparison of their incomes.

Typically, retirement income systems begin by emphasizing minimum standards (e.g., keeping older people out of poverty). In most industrialized countries, for instance, Social Security was originally intended to be one leg of a three-legged stool—Social Security benefits, personal savings, and income from employer-sponsored pensions. The income-adequacy goals of Social Security were thus initially modest and were designed to provide only one segment of retirement income—what Schulz and Myles (1990) characterize as the "social assistance welfare state." Over time, however, the income goals of Social Security, starting in Europe and later in the United States, moved in the direction of maintaining preretirement standards of living (President's Commission on Pension Policy, 1981; Schulz et al., 1974).

In addition to income adequacy, retirement income polices must be concerned with the closely related issue of equity. Three definitions of equity are commonly used in designing and evaluating retirement income systems (Jackson, 1982;

Lampman, 1975). The criterion of *horizontal equity* stipulates that individuals in similar situations should be treated in the same way (Plotnick, 1985). Under horizontal equity, families with a given set of characteristics such as a particular family size or earnings history should receive the same retirement benefits. *Vertical equity* stipulates that individuals or families in different situations be treated differently. Under vertical equity, one might argue for a weighted benefit formula to give lower income workers a retirement benefit that replaces a higher percentage of their pre-retirement earnings than workers with higher earnings. Note that it is possible for horizontal and vertical equity measures to overlap. For example, all individuals with a particular earnings history and marital status will receive the same retirement benefits under Social Security. This meets the horizontal equity criteria; it also meets the vertical equity criteria because individuals with different earnings histories and marital status will receive different benefits under Social Security. Finally, there is the objective of *individual equity*. Individual equity objectives tie retirement benefits to an individual's contribution to the system.

For the first four decades of Social Security's operation, there was a widespread public misconception that workers' contributions were saved for them in earmarked accounts. Policy makers did little to educate the public about this misconception, and it really didn't matter since, on average, retirees received many times their contributions in the form of benefits (Achenbaum, 1986; Derthick, 1979). As the Social Security system matured, however, the ratio of lifetime Social Security benefits to contributions steadily declined, and the situation regarding individual equity changed. Some groups of workers (single, low earners) can still expect to receive more in lifetime benefits than they pay into the system; others (such as certain white, unmarried males) can expect to receive less in benefits than their lifetime contributions (Myers & Schobel, 1992).

II. Poverty among the Elderly—A Subsistence Adequacy Measure

Given the significant improvements that have occurred over recent years, it is easy to forget that in the early 1970s, there was great concern about the economic status of the elderly. In 1970, 25% of the older population was in poverty. (The limitations of the official poverty statistics published by the U.S. Bureau of the Census are widely recognized and will not be repeated here; see, e.g., Ruggles, 1990; Schulz, 2000; Smeeding, 1984). The risk for certain subgroups of the older population was considerably higher in 1970—37% for black older Americans, 47% for unrelated individuals, and 78% for black women living alone (Crown, 1989).

In the three ensuing decades, great progress has been made in reducing the rate of poverty among the elderly. In 1998, the poverty rate of 11% for the population age 65 and over was comparable to that of the population under age 65. Yet, despite these improvements, significant pockets of poverty remain among elderly subpopulations (U.S. Bureau of the Census, 1999a). In addition to the 11% of the older population in poverty, another 6% of the older population have incomes between the poverty level and 125% of the poverty line. The risk of poverty also differs markedly by race, gender, and living arrangements. Only 9% of white older Americans are in poverty compared to 26% of African Americans, and 21% of Hispanics. The poverty rate among older women is 13% compared to 7% for older men. It is 20% for older persons living alone, but only 6% for older persons living in families. African-American women living alone are at greatest risk of poverty; their poverty rate is 49%.

A large literature has examined the higher risk of poverty among older women and minorities (e.g., Holden, Burkhauser, & Myers, 1986; Jackson, 1970) and of the effects of life-course events on female labor-force participation (O'Grady-LeShane, 1996). Although numerous studies have examined the magnitude of, and reasons for, pay differentials by gender and race (e.g., Blau, Ferber, & Winkler, 1998; Gunderson, 1989), very few have examined the implications of such differentials for retirement income. Mitchell, Levine, and Phillips (1999), however, have recently examined the effects of occupational segregation and pay differentials by gender and race on income in retirement, using the Health and Retirement Study (HRS) linked to the Pension Provider File (PPF) to calculate Social Security and private pension wealth measures. They find that two-thirds of the difference in retirement incomes of nonmarried older women and older men (nearly $8,000) could be attributed to occupational segregation and pay differentials by gender after controlling for such factors as education level and years worked. Comparisons of expected retirement incomes stratifying by gender, marital status, and race/ethnicity (Black, Hispanic, and White) indicate that Black and Hispanic groups have lower expected incomes than their White counterparts in each of the gender and marital status strata. The biggest gaps in income tend to occur in income from sources other than Social Security and pensions. For example, Black nonmarried women had expected income from nonpension sources (including Social Security) that was $7,577 less than their White counterparts. The gap for Hispanic nonmarried women was even larger—$11,512. Comparable figures for Black and Hispanic men relative to their White counterparts were $25,168 and $14,959, respectively. Similar patterns in sources of income other than Social Security, by gender and race,

were found for married men and women. In contrast, the gaps in Social Security within race/ethnicity, gender, and marital status strata were comparatively small. The higher replacement rates generated by Social Security for low-wage earners help to counter the impacts of occupational segregation and pay differentials by gender and race.

III. Trends in Income Levels and Composition

Table 19.1 reports the trends in median incomes of older persons by marital status and race, from 1967 to 1996. Real median income increased substantially for all groups over the period—by 76% for married couples, 84% for nonmarried persons, 90% for whites, and 53% for blacks.

For the older population as a whole, these income changes were accompanied by substantial changes in the composition of income over the same period. As shown in Figure 19.1, in 1967 the aged received 34% of their income from Social Security, 15% from assets, 12% from pensions, 29% from earnings, and 10% from other sources. By 1996, the share of income received from Social Security had risen to 40%, asset income increased to 18%, pension income increased to 19%, earnings decreased to 20%, and about 3% of income came from other sources. These changes in income composition of older persons can be traced to the legislative history of Social Security over this period, factors affecting asset accumulation and pensions, and trends in retirement.

A. Social Security

Although Congress increased Social Security benefits several times during the 1950s and 1960s, it was not until the early 1970s that strong support coalesced for a more stable mechanism to protect

Table 19.1
Median Income of Persons Aged 65 and Older, in 1996 Dollars, by Marital
Status and Race, Selected Years[a]

Year	Marital status		Race	
	Married Couples	Nonmarried Persons	White	Black
1967	15,845	6,135	8,935	6,314
1971	20,757	7,938	12,575	7,334
1976	21,756	9,265	13,622	8,245
1978	22,765	9,409	14,342	7,821
1980	22,888	9,102	14,129	7,731
1982	24,600	9,560	15,365	7,772
1984	26,049	10,103	16,551	8,260
1986	27,042	10,279	16,864	8,518
1988	26,930	10,515	17,397	8,360
1990	28,033	10,981	17,457	8,388
1992	26,635	10,684	16,802	8,346
1994	26,515	11,016	16,887	9,288
1996	27,944	11,302	16,954	9,649

[a]From Social Security Administration (1998).

the purchasing power of benefits from inflation. Partly in response to this growing support, Congress passed legislation in 1972 to substantially increase benefit levels and then automatically adjust benefits *during* retirement for annual increases in the Consumer Price Index (CPI). In addition, benefit levels produced by the

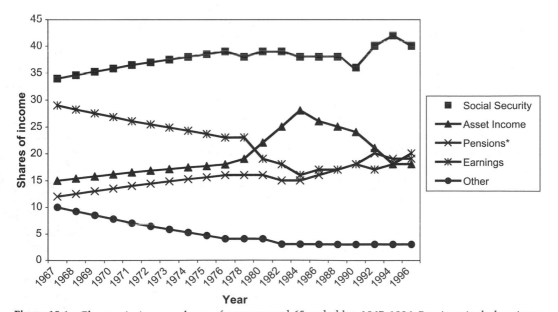

Figure 19.1 Changes in income shares of persons aged 65 and older, 1967–1996. Pensions include private pensions and annuities, government employee pensions, Railroad Retirement, and IRA, Keogh, and 401 (k) payments. (From: Social Security Administration, 1998.)

program formulas at the time of retirement were tied to increases in earnings over time. These changes, which became operational in 1974, were motivated by two horizontal equity considerations: (a) to stabilize Social Security replacement rates across beneficiary cohorts and (b) to maintain the economic status of retirees relative to those still in the labor force.

It quickly became apparent, however, that adjusting benefits for both wage and price increases was a technical error because it overcompensated retirees for the erosion of benefits due to inflation and for their inability to share in the benefits of economic growth. The benefit liberalizations and double indexing of benefits created by the 1972 amendments caused the real value of benefits to increase rapidly between 1972 and 1977. Although Congress amended the benefit formula to correct the overindexing problem in 1977, sustained price increases between 1977 and 1982 continued to inflate the absolute magnitude of Social Security benefits. Since 1982, the share of Social Security in the income composition has fluctuated somewhat but was just slightly higher in 1996 than in 1982. The 1972 Social Security Amendments, which significantly increased real benefit levels, had the rather immediate effect of lowering poverty among the elderly from 25% in 1970 to about 15% in 1974. By 1989, the percentage of the older population falling below the minimum adequacy (poverty) level had declined to 11%; it has remained at roughly this level ever since. The substantial real growth in the average economic status of older persons, however, resulted in attention to issues of horizontal equity between older and younger age groups in the population. In contrast to the 41% increase in real median income of older households over 1970–1989, the real median income of younger households increased by less than 4 percent over the same period. Even more alarming was the very high rate of poverty among children. In 1989, 20 percent of the population under age 18 lived in poverty; in 1998 the figure was 19 percent.

This led some to argue that the improving economic status of the elderly has come at the expense of children (Longman, 1985; Preston, 1984). Others dispute this viewpoint, arguing that the trends in relative economic status of younger and older persons are largely unrelated (Hurd, 1990; Ryscavage, 1987; Scholl & Moon, 1988; Smolensky, Danziger, & Gottschalk, 1988).

B. Assets

One of the more interesting trends in Figure 19.1 is the growth in the importance of asset income between the late 1970s and mid-1980s, and the subsequent decline in the importance of asset income since then. The period of rising asset income share was characterized by double-digit inflation. In response, the Federal Reserve raised interest rates (also to double-digit levels). Those fortunate enough to have substantial financial assets benefited from these high interest rates—although it is less clear if they experienced substantial real gains. The declines in asset income among the elderly beginning in the mid-1980s appear to mirror the declines in mean net worth of older households over this period. Using data from the 1983, 1989, 1992, and 1995 Surveys of Consumer Finances, Wolff (1998) found that the real mean net worth of older households declined by a little less than 2% between 1983 and 1995. Changes in mean net worth among older households varied widely by income level, however. Households with incomes under $15,000 experienced increases in mean net worth of 34%; those with incomes of $15,000 to $24,999 experienced declines in net worth of 10%; those with incomes of $25,000–$49,999 experienced declines of 2%, those with incomes of

50,000–74,999 experienced increases of 7%; and those with incomes of $75,000 or higher experienced declines of 7%.

The magnitude of the net worth changes of households in different net worth brackets is probably a function of the net worth composition in each of the brackets. Wolff (1998) found that in the highest 1% of the household wealth distribution, 30% of wealth was held in corporate stock, financial securities, mutual funds, and personal trusts. Another 37% was held in unincorporated business equity, and only 6% of wealth was held in the principal residence. In the bottom 80% of the wealth distribution, however, unincorporated business equity contributed 3% to wealth, corporate stock, financial securities, mutual funds, and personal trusts contributed 4%, and 66% of wealth was held in the principal residence.

On a technical note, Wolff points out that the major advantage of using the Survey of Consumer Finances for wealth studies is the inclusion of a sample of persons with very high incomes. This leads to wealth estimates that are several times greater, at the highest income levels, than those obtained from the Survey of Income and Program Participation or the Panel Survey of Income Dynamics, two other surveys that are widely used for wealth estimates (Curtin, Juster, & Morgan, 1989; McNeil & Lamas, 1989).

C. Pensions

The number of workers participating in private employer-sponsored pensions increased by about 12% per year in the 1940s, 7% per year in the 1950s, and 3% per year in the 1960s and 1970s. As a consequence of expanded pension coverage, the percent of income that older households received from pensions rose from 12 to 16% between 1967 and the mid-1970s. The pension share remained at this level throughout most of the

1980s. Then, in the late 1980s, it began to increase again, reaching 20% in 1992. It has remained at about 19% since then.

Although pension coverage has remained fairly constant in recent years, the composition of pension coverage has changed substantially since the mid-1980s. Turner and Doescher (1996) report that the number of defined benefit plans fell from 175,000 in 1983 to 113,000 in 1990. During the same period, however, many employers began offering 401K plans to employees. Leavitt (1996) notes that in 1983, 7% of full-time wage and salary employees aged 55–59 were offered 401K plans; by 1993 this had risen to 35%. For workers aged 65 and older, the percentage offered 401K plans increased from 6 to 28% over the same period. (See chapter 14 by Henretta and chapter 20 by Kingson and Williamson this volume.)

D. Earnings

Between 1967 and 1980 the percentage contribution of earnings to the aggregate income of the elderly dropped from 29% to 19%. The primary reason for this decline is, of course, the well-known decline in the labor-force participation rates of older men. Rhum (1996) reports that the labor-force participation rate of men aged 55–64 declined from 90% to 67% between 1948 and 1982; that of men aged 65 and over declined from 47% to 16%, where it has remained since (see chapter 14 by Henretta, this volume). Despite an increase in the labor-force participation rate of women aged 45–64, the decline in the labor-force participation rate of older men resulted in an overall decline in the labor-force participation rate for the older population as a whole. The trends in elderly labor-force participation rates appear to correlate closely with the trends in aggregate income share from earnings over the same period. Of course, even without declines in the labor-force participation rates of older persons, relative increases in Social Security, asset income, and pension income would have caused the earnings income share to decline over time.

IV. Income Distribution of Families and Persons

Figure 19.2 shows the distribution of income for families headed by a person age 65 or older in 1998. Thirty-seven percent of older families had incomes of less than $25,000, another 37% had incomes of $25,000 to $49,000, and the remaining 26% had incomes of $50,000 or higher. Median family income was $31,368. Figure 19.3 shows the comparable income distribution for older persons—irrespective of living arrangements. Comparing the shape of the income distributions for older persons and older families clearly indicates that the former is more concen-

trated at lower income ranges. Fifty-seven percent of older persons had incomes less than $15,000 in 1998, 21% had incomes of $15,000 to $24,999, and 22% had incomes of $25,000 or higher. Median personal income was $13,768.

The differences in the shapes of the personal and family income distributions can be understood by thinking about the relative numbers of older persons who live alone versus those who live with a spouse, and the per capita incomes within these two groups. If all older persons lived with a spouse and household income was equally divided among the members, the shape of the family and personal income distributions would be exactly the same, but the personal income levels would be exactly one-half of those of the household income levels. But it is clear that twice the median personal income of $13,768 is less than the median household income of $31,368. This reflects the fact that sin-

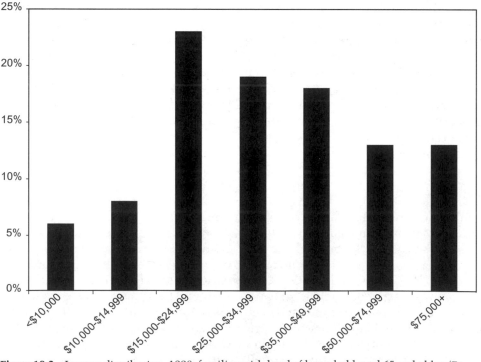

Figure 19.2 Income distribution, 1998, families with head of household aged 65 and older. (From U.S. Bureau of the Census 1999b.)

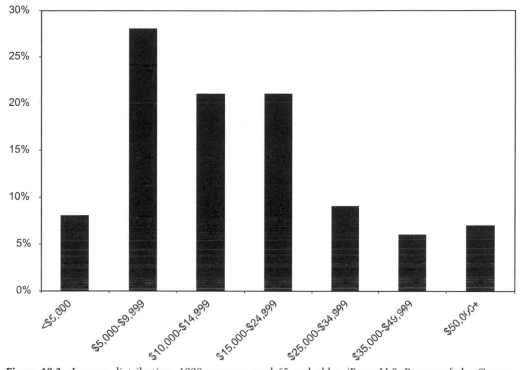

Figure 19.3 Income distribution, 1998, persons aged 65 and older. (From U.S. Bureau of the Census, 1999b.)

gle older persons tend to have lower incomes than married couples on a per capita basis. Moreover, because of household economies of scale, married couples probably do not need twice the income of a single person to maintain the same standard of living—further widening the gap between the economic status of single and married older persons (Crystal, 1996; Smeeding, 1990).

V. Composition of Income by Age Cohort

Table 19.2 reports differences in the composition of income by age cohort. As one would expect, household income is highest for the "preretirement" cohort age 55–61. Earnings decline from 80% of household income for those age 55–61 to 62% for those age 62–64, 35% for those age 65–

69, and decline further with each successive age cohort. The large drops in the earnings shares at ages 62–64 and 65–69 clearly indicate the effects of the availability of reduced and full Social Security benefits on labor-force participation decisions of older persons, as well as other factors that lead workers to retire at these ages. Nevertheless, earnings comprise 20% of household income for those aged 65 and older.

Conversely, the importance of Social Security income increases with early eligibility for benefits at ages 62–64 (12% of aggregate income) and grows steadily in older age brackets, from 29% of income for those aged 65–69 to 54% for those aged 85 and older.

As with Social Security, private pension income also increases by age cohort—up to ages 70–74. The falloff in the share of income contributed by private

Table 19.2

Household Units Headed by Persons Aged 55 and Older, by Age Groups, 1996: Percentage Distribution of Money Income from Particular Sources[a]

Unit source of income	Age 55–61	Age 62–64	Aged 65 and older					
			Total	65–69	70–74	75–79	80–84	85 and older
Number (in thousands)	10,821	3,951	24,553	6,681	6,286	5,317	3,555	2,713
Median income	$33,372	$24,947	$16,099	$20,893	$17,922	$14,985	13503.0	$11,251
Social Security	2.3	12.2	40.3	28.7	40.8	47.0	53.5	53.6
Railroad retirement	—	0.2	0.5	0.5	0.6	0.6	0.3	0.6
Government employee pensions	3.0	6.5	8.1	7.8	8.8	8.7	7.4	6.1
Private pensions or annuities	3.3	6.8	9.9	10.1	11.4	9.4	7.8	8.1
Earnings	80.3	61.6	20.0	34.6	17.9	11.3	5.6	6.0
Income from assets	8.2	9.7	18.0	15.2	17.7	19.5	22.2	22.0
Public assistance	0.7	0.8	0.8	0.7	0.7	0.9	0.9	1.7
Other	2.1	2.2	2.3	2.4	2.0	2.6	2.2	1.8

[a]From Social Security Administration (1998).

pensions in the older age cohorts could be due to several factors including lower rates of pension coverage among the very old, and the fact that private pension plans, in contrast to Social Security, seldom adjust benefits automatically for inflation, thereby losing income share to Social Security over time. Similarly, state and local government pensions often provide automatic cost-of-living adjustments that are capped at 2 or 3%. Of course, the limited automatic cost-of-living adjustments in most public and private pension plans also implies that retirees in these plans can experience substantial declines in the real purchasing power of their pension benefits over time (Crown & Mutschler, 1993).

In general, the share of income from assets rises with each successive age cohort—from 8% for those ages 55–61 to about 22% for those ages 80 and older. Everything else equal, one would expect that as the share from earnings declines at older ages the proportion of income attributable to assets and other sources would rise. In addition, asset income, like Social Security, will tend to increase over time and, consequently, the income share contributed to assets will tend to grow as well.

The second row in Table 19.2 reports the median income of household units headed by persons aged 55 or older by age group. It is well known that central tendency indicators for income and wealth variables, particularly means, can be misleading indicators because they tend to be "pulled up" by members at the upper end of the income and wealth distributions. By definition, the median represents the midpoint of such distributions. Of course, regardless of whether one uses the mean or median, it is not completely valid to compare family incomes across the different age groups because average household size and consumption needs differ by stage in the life cycle. An obvious correction for differences in household size is to calculate per capita incomes. However, per capita income is an overcorrection because it fails to account for economies of scale in larger household units. Several studies based upon household equivalence scales find that the incomes of older and younger households are roughly equivalent (Hurd, 1990). However, these studies are based upon a variety of assumptions and methodological techniques. A more conservative conclusion is that the economic status of the elderly is now a lot like that of the younger population—some poor, some wealthy, and most people in between (Schulz, 2000).

VI. Effects of Taxes and Transfers on Income

It is useful to examine the effects of government policies on the incomes of older and younger households, as well as income inequalities among households. Table 19.3 shows how 1998 median incomes for all households, households with a related child under 18, and households with members aged 65 and older differ, depending upon the income definition used. Table 19.3 also reports the Gini coefficient for each group. Gini coefficients are measures of income inequality based on the cumulative proportions of income received by cumulative proportions of the population. A value of 0 for a Gini coefficient indicates perfect income equality; a value of 1 indicates perfect income inequality.

The definition of income used in the first column of Table 19.3, pretax money income, is the same as used in Tables 19.1 and 19.2. The first column of Table 19.3 shows that the median income for younger households with children is higher than that for older households alone. The Gini Coefficients in Table 19.3, however, indicate that the inequality of money income is higher among aged households than among the general population. This conclusion is similar to that of several earlier studies (e.g., Hurd, 1990, although Fuchs, 1998, using a methodology that is less sensitive than the Gini Coefficient to mismeasurement of income at the extremes of the income distribution, concludes that income inequality is higher among the nonelderly population).

How is income inequality influenced by government policies? To answer this question, we need to recognize that governments can affect income inequality

Table 19.3
Median Household Income and Income Inequality, by Income Definition, 1998[a]

Household type	Pretax money income (1)	Adjusted pre-tax money income[b] (2)	Adjusted After-tax income[c] (3)	Adjusted after-tax income & transfers (4)	Adjusted after-tax income & transfers plus returns from home equity
All households					
Median Income	$38,885	$37,673	$31,816	$37,673	$39,308
Gini coefficient	0.446	0.509	0.484	0.405	0.399
Households with related child under 18					
Median income	$46,562	$48,765	$41,613	$44,028	$45,086
Gini coefficient	0.416	0.441	0.407	0.371	0.372
Households with members Age 65+					
Median income	$23,369	$10,337	$9,890	$30,314	$33,261
Gini coefficient	0.483	0.675	0.644	0.426	0.411

[a]From: U.S. Bureau of the Census (1999b).
[b]Money income less government transfers plus capital gains and employee health benefits.
[c]Adjusted pretax money income less Social Security taxes, federal taxes, state taxes, plus income tax credit.

through two income redistribution mechanisms—taxes and government transfers. The pretax money income figures in column 1 include the value of cash transfers from the government. To assess the effects of government transfers on income inequality, we need to construct an income figure net of these transfers. Moreover, to reflect the full value of pretax money income net of government transfers, it is necessary to add in the value of capital gains and employee health benefits that are not reflected in money income.

The resulting adjusted pretax money income is shown in the second column of Table 19.3. The median incomes of households in general decrease slightly after this adjustment. This indicates that the value of capital gains and employee health insurance is slightly less than the value of government transfers for the population as a whole. Income inequality increases slightly but not dramatically.

The effect of government transfers is very different for the younger and older populations, however. Among households with young children, government transfers have the effect of increasing median income and income inequality slightly. In contrast, median income for older households experiences a major decline when the value of government transfers is subtracted from pretax money income. Moreover, the Gini Coefficient measuring income inequality increases from 0.483 for unadjusted money income to 0.675 for the income figure net of government transfers. This, of course, largely reflects the importance of Social Security as an income source for older households.

Columns 3 and 4 of the table show the effects of taxation and government transfers, respectively, on household incomes. Government taxation (at all levels) reduces median incomes of the general population and younger households with children more than those of older households. These effects reflect the progressive nature of income taxation. The Gini

coefficients, however, indicate that taxation does not have a major influence in reducing income inequality, although its effects seem to be more pronounced for younger households than for older households.

In contrast, government transfers appear to have a major effect in reducing income inequality among older households. The after-tax Gini coefficient for older households declines from 0.644 for pretransfer income to 0.426 after government transfers have been added in. Similarly, Fuchs (1998) reports that Social Security plays a major role in reducing income inequality among older persons. On the other hand, income transfers have less effect in reducing income inequality in households in general—implying that income inequality in the general population is not influenced as strongly by government transfers. Again, however, such conclusions are sensitive to measurement issues. For example, recent studies that have measured the redistributional aspects of Social Security using lifetime income (rather than annual income) and other assumptions have reached dramatically different conclusions (Coronado, Fullerton, & Glass, 2000; Gustman & Steinmeier, 2000).

Gist (1992) points out that the federal income tax code has gradually become less favorable to the elderly over the past two decades. For example, 1983 legislation initiated the taxation of Social Security benefits for couples with incomes of $32,000 or higher, and individuals with incomes of $25,000 or higher. The 1993 Omnibus Budget Reconciliation Act further increased the taxation of Social Security benefits for higher income beneficiaries. Eighty-five percent of Social Security benefits are now taxable for couples with incomes of $44,000 or higher, or individuals with incomes of $34,000 or higher. Fifty percent of benefits are taxable for couples with incomes between $32,000 and $44,000, and individuals with incomes between $25,000 and $34,000 (Crown, 1996).

Similarly, the Tax Reform Act of 1986 changed several provisions of the tax code, raising federal tax payments for most of the older population (Zedlewski, 1988). Following passage of the Tax Reform Act, however, many states passed legislation designed to partially offset the increases in federal taxes for older persons. Gist (1992) found that, after taking account of such state legislation, there was a slight shift in tax burden from the nonelderly population to the elderly population. The increased tax burden was concentrated among the elderly in the top income decile.

VII. The Savings–Consumption Life Cycle, Wealth, and Retirement Income

In considering the economic status of the current and future elderly, few would argue that money income alone is the best measure. Another approach is to use *household wealth* as a measure of economic status, where wealth is defined as the total market value of such items as home equity, stocks and bonds, and savings accounts. Wealth is a conceptually important variable because it reflects the ability to have met consumption needs in the past (wealth will be positive if income has been higher than expenditures up to that point in one's life), as well as the capacity to finance future consumption by drawing upon wealth. A theoretical explanation of the relationships among income, consumption, and savings is provided by the Life Cycle Hypothesis (Ando & Modigliani, 1963; Modigliani & Ando, 1957; Modigliani & Brumberg, 1954). The Life Cycle Hypothesis begins with the assumption that consumption needs and income are unequal at various points in the life cycle. Younger people tend to have consumption needs that exceed

their income (housing and education). In middle age, earnings rise, enabling debts accumulated earlier in the life cycle to be paid off and savings to be accumulated. Finally, in retirement, incomes decline and individuals consume out of previously accumulated savings.

The empirical literature concerning the Life Cycle Hypothesis, however, has been inconclusive with regard to the savings behavior of older persons. A number of studies have found, seemingly in conflict with the Life Cycle Hypothesis, that the elderly continue to save in retirement (Danziger, van der Gaag, Smolensky, & Taussig, 1982; Juster, 1981; Menchik & David, 1983; Mirer, 1980; Torrey & Tauber, 1986). In contrast, however, Radner (1989) *did* find evidence of dissaving among the elderly. Similarly, Wolff (1998) reports age–wealth profiles that are consistent with the Life Cycle Hypothesis. It is reasonable to hypothesize that dissaving among the old-old may be related to rising medical and long-term care expenditures occurring at a point in the life cycle where, for many, the real value of their pension income has eroded over time.

Actually, both results are consistent with the Life Cycle Hypothesis. King (1985) notes that saving in retirement is not necessarily inconsistent with the Life Cycle Hypothesis if one accounts for the aversion of individuals to uncertainty about the future (e.g., how long they will live and future inflation). In addition, it is likely that dissaving in retirement would be much more evident if savings were defined more broadly to include the decumulation of claims on pension wealth.

Hurd (1990) provides an overview of the different ways in which researchers have used current income and wealth to measure economic status. A widely used approach is to convert wealth into an equivalent income stream (based on life expectancy and interest rate assumptions) and add this income stream to current income, excluding the income already being received from assets. Such studies consistently show that the income stream generated from assets is modest for most elderly—especially those who have low incomes to begin with. Consequently, annuitizing assets has limited promise as a mechanism for increasing the incomes of elderly with inadequate incomes.

If the Life Cycle Hypothesis is correct, one would expect the elderly (at least at the beginning of retirement) to have higher wealth holdings than younger households. Consistent with this expectation, Wolff (1998) found that mean household net worth was $173,700 for households under age 65 and $314,500 for households age 65 and older. Growing recognition of the greater wealth of older households relative to younger households has led to increased interest in the potential role of asset holdings for meeting public policy objectives (e.g., Merrill, 1984). An important example of this growing interest is the concern that elderly households with low money incomes but large amounts of home equity may be receiving public income transfers from younger households that have higher money incomes but who would not be as well-off as older households if one took account of wealth (Venti & Wise, 1990).

Studies have repeatedly found that, except for the most affluent of older households, the majority of net worth is held in the form of home equity. Eller (1994) found that, in 1991, the median net worth of older households was $88,192 but was only $26,442 with home equity excluded. The final column of Table 19.3 indicates that the effects of annuitizing household wealth are fairly similar across age groups, and that such a policy would have almost no effect on reducing household income inequality.

Although converting assets into an income stream is appealing because it en- ables current income and wealth variables to be combined into a single measure, there are some problems with using it to compare households in different age cohorts. First, there is the problem of choosing an appropriate discount rate for valuing the income stream produced by an asset. The discount rate can greatly influence the size of the income stream generated by an asset. In addition to the choice of an appropriate discount rate, there is the problem of changes in the size of income streams produced by assets at different stages in the life cycle. For a given amount of wealth, income streams will be larger for those with shorter life expectancies, making older households appear to be more affluent than younger households with the same amount of income and wealth. In addition, comparisons between older and younger households based on the income value of their assets will be influenced by the generally higher stock of durable goods held by older households.

VIII. Policy Implications and Directions for Future Research

There were substantial improvements in the economic status of the older population during the 1970s, primarily as a result of Social Security benefit liberalizations, rising private pension coverage, and rising asset income due to the high interest rates during this period. However, it is important to interpret aggregate metrics of improvements in the economic status of the elderly carefully, because not all subgroups within the older population have benefited equally.

The formulation of retirement income policy requires many assumptions—especially with respect to future economic growth and the characteristics of future retirees. The group of future retirees that most concerns policy makers is the enormous 1946–1964 baby boom cohort.

Members of the baby boom are just now entering middle age. The characteristics of today's middle-aged population will therefore have far-reaching implications for public policy and the future economic status of older persons.

Many commentators believe that members of the baby boom generation are headed for tough economic times in retirement because of possible future financing difficulties associated with the Social Security system (see the chapter 20 by Kingson & Williamson, this volume), and because of the competition that members of the baby boom generation have faced in the labor market, which has kept real wage growth low (Bernheim & Scholz, 1993; Welch, 1979). Others dispute this pessimistic outlook (Gale, 1998; Gist, Wu, & Ford, 1999). Easterlin, MacDonald, and Macunovich (1990) predict that members of the baby boom will enter retirement in an even better economic position than their pre-boom cohorts due to economic and demographic adjustments made by the middle aged, including deferred marriages, reduced child rearing, and increased labor-force participation of women.

Regardless of whether one thinks that future generations of older persons will be better or worse off than current generations, it is clear that an assessment of the evidence will involve much more than simple comparisons of retirement incomes. With the availability of several rich data sets—the Survey of Income and Program Participation, the Survey of Consumer Finances, and the Asset and Health Dynamics study, among others—researchers have begun to focus increasingly on questions involving savings behavior, household wealth and liabilities, and pension wealth. This is appropriate because the economic status of the elderly is influenced more strongly by a lifetime of choices and events than it is by those that occur in the retirement years alone. For example, decisions about marriage, family size and timing, and how much education to attain all influence work history, as well as consumption and savings decisions. In turn, this affects the savings that one enters retirement with, including access to and adequacy of pension benefits.

Given the prominence of the Life Cycle Model of Work, Savings, and Consumption among economists, it is interesting that so little work has been conducted on life cycle consumption behavior and the economic status of the elderly. An adequate assessment of the economic status of the elderly requires not only an understanding of economic resources, but also consumption needs. Surprisingly little has been written on the latter. The recent debates about the out-of-pocket health-care costs of older persons are a reflection of the intersection between economic resources, consumption needs, and public policy (Fuchs, 1998). The formulation of public policy for the elderly needs to recognize this intersection and to be informed by careful research that explicitly accounts for the effects of life cycle events on economic status in old age.

References

Achenbaum, W. A. (1986). *Social Security: Visions and revisions*. New York: Cambridge University Press.

Ando, A., & Modigliani, F. (1963). The life-cycle hypothesis of saving: Aggregate implications and tests. *American Economic Review, 53* (March), 55–84.

Blau, F., Ferber, M., & Winkler, A. (1998). *The economics of women, men, and work*. Englewood Cliffs, NJ: Prentice Hall.

Coronado, J., Fullerton, D., & Glass, T. (2000). *The progressivity of Social Security*. NBER Working Paper No. W7520. Cambridge, MA: National Bureau of Economic Research.

Crown, W. (1989). Trends in the economic status of the aged and the implications for state policy. *Journal of Aging and Social Policy, 1*(3/4), 89–128.

Crown, W. (1996). Policy implications of elderly income and wealth taxation. *Generations. 20*(3), 42–45.

Crown, W., & Mutschler, P. (1993). Pension benefits for state, local, and teacher retirees: Coping with inflation, 1982–1987. *Research on Aging, 15* (1), 33–49.

Crystal, S. (1996). Economic status of the elderly. In R.H. Binstock & L.K. George (Eds.), *Handbook of aging and the social sciences* (4th ed. pp. 388–409). San Diego, CA: Academic Press.

Curtin, R., Juster, T., & Morgan, J. (1989). Survey estimates of wealth: An assessment of quality. In R. Lipsey & H.S. Tice (Eds.), *The measurement of saving, investment, and wealth* (pp. 473–551). Chicago: University of Chicago Press.

Danziger, S., van der Gaag, J., Smolensky, E., & Taussig, M. (1982). The life-cycle hypothesis and the consumption behavior of the elderly. *Journal of Post-Keynesian Economics, 5*, 208–227.

Derthick, M. (1979). *Policymaking for Social Security.* Washington, DC: The Brookings Institution.

Duesenberry, J.S. (1949). *Income, saving, and the theory of consumer behavior.* Cambridge, MA: Harvard University Press.

Easterlin, R., MacDonald, C., & Macunovich, D. (1990). Retirement prospects of the baby boom generation: A different perspective. *The Gerontologist, 30*, 776–783.

Eller, T. J. (1994). *Household wealth and asset ownership: 1991.* Current Population Reports, P70–34. Washington, DC: U.S. Government Printing Office.

Fuchs, V. (1998). *Provide, provide: The economics of aging.* NBER Working Paper 6642. Cambridge, MA: National Bureau of Economic Research.

Gale, W. (1998). Will the baby boom be ready for retirement? *The Brookings Review, 16*(3), 5–9.

Gist, J. (1992). Did tax reform hurt the elderly? *Gerontologist, 32*, 472–477.

Gist, J., Wu, K., & Ford, C. (1999). *Do baby boomers save and, if so, what for?* Washington, DC: American Association of Retired Persons.

Gunderson, M. (1989). Male–female wage differentials and policy responses. *Journal of Economic Literature, 27*(1), 46–72.

Gustman, A., & Steinmeier, T. (2000). *How effective is redistribution under the Social Security benefit formula?* NBER Working Paper No. W7597. Cambridge, MA: National Bureau of Economic Research.

Holden, K., Burkhauser, R., & Myers, D. (1986). Income transitions of older stages of life: The dynamics of poverty. *Gerontologist, 26*, 292–297.

Hurd, M. (1990). Research on the aged: Economic status, retirement and consumption and saving. *Journal of Economic Literature, 28*, 565–637.

Jackson, J.J. (1970). Aged Negroes: Their cultural departures from statistical stereotypes of rural-urban Differences. *Gerontologist, 10*, 140–145.

Jackson, W. (1982). Universal and selective income support: Some equity and efficiency considerations. *Social Security Journal,* (June), 14–31.

Juster, F. T. (1981). Current and prospective financial status of the elderly population. In P. Cagan (Ed.), *Saving for retirement* (pp. 24–66). Washington, DC: American Council of Life Insurance.

King, M. (1985). The Economics of saving: A survey of recent contributions. In K. Arrow & S. Houkapohja (Eds.), *Frontiers of economics* (pp. 227–294). New York: Basil Blackwell, Inc.

Lampman, R. J. (1975). *Concepts of equity in the design of schemes for income redistribution.* Madison, WI: Institute for Research on Poverty, University of Wisconsin.

Leavitt, T. (1996). Labor force characteristics of older Americans. In W. Crown (Ed.), *Handbook on employment and the elderly (pp. 15–56).* Westport, CT: Greenwood Press.

Longman, P. (1985). Justice between generations. *Atlantic Monthly,* (June), 73–81.

McNeil, J., & Lamas, E. (1989). Year-apart estimates of household net-worth from the Survey of Income and Program Participation. In R. Lipsey & H.S. Tice (Eds.), *The measurement of saving, investment, and wealth* (pp. 431–471). Chicago: University of Chicago Press.

Menchik, P., & David, M. (1983). Income distribution, lifetime savings, and bequests. *American Economic Review, 73*, 672–690.

Merrill, S. (1984). Home equity and the elderly. In H. Aaron & G. Burtless (Eds.),

Retirement and economic behavior (pp. 197–227). Washington, DC: The Brookings Institution.

Mitchell, O., Levine, P., & Phillips, J. (1999). *The impact of pay inequality, occupational segregation, and lifetime work experience on the retirement income of women and minorities.* Washington, DC: AARP Public Policy Institute.

Mirer, T. (1980). The dissaving behavior of the retired aged. *Southern Economic Journal, 46,* 1197–1205.

Modigliani, F., & Ando, A. (1957). Tests of the life-cycle hypothesis of savings. *Bulletin of the Oxford University Insitute of Economics and Statistics, 19,* 99–124.

Modigliani, F., & Brumberg, R. (1954). Utility analysis and the consumption function. In K. Kurihara (Ed.), *Post-Keynesian economics* (pp. 338–436). New Brunswick, NJ: Rutgers University Press.

Myers, R., & Schobel, B. (1992). An updated money's worth analysis of Social Security retirement benefits. *Transactions of the Society of Actuaries, 44,* 247–287.

O'Grady-LeShane, R. (1996). Older women workers. In W. Crown (Ed.), *Handbook on employment and the elderly (pp. 103–109).* Westport, CT: Greenwood Press.

Plotnick, R. (1985). A comparison of measures of horizontal equity. In M. David & T. Smeeding (Eds.), *Horizontal equity, uncertainty, and economic well-being* (pp. 239–268). Chicago: University of Chicago Press.

President's Commission on Pension Policy. (1981). *Coming of age: Toward a national retirement income policy.* Report of the Commission. Washington, DC: The Commission.

Preston, S. (1984). Children and the elderly in the U.S. *Scientific American, 251*(6), 44–49.

Radner, D. (1989). The wealth of the aged and nonaged, 1984. In R. Lipsey & H. Tice (Eds.), *The measurement of saving, investment, and wealth* (pp. 645–689). Chicago, IL: The University of Chicago Press.

Rhum, C. (1996). Historical trends in the employment and labor force participation of older Americans. In W. Crown (Ed.), *Handbook on employment and the elderly (pp. 81–102).* Westport, CT: Greenwood Press.

Ruggles, P. (1990). *Drawing the line: Alternative poverty measures and their implica-*

tions for public policy. Washington, DC: Urban Institute Press.

Ryscavage, P. (1987). Income trends of the young and the elderly. *Family Economic Review, 2,* 1–8.

Scholl, K., & Moon, M. (1988). *Dispelling the myth of the undeserving rich.* Washington, DC: The Public Policy Institute, American Association for Retired Persons.

Schulz, J. (2000). *The economics of aging* (7th ed.). Westport, CT: Auburn House.

Schulz, J., & Myles (1990). Old age pensions: A comparative perspective. In R. H. Binstock & L. K. George (Eds.), *Handbook of aging and the social sciences* (3rd ed.) (pp. 398–414). San Diego, CA: Academic Press.

Schulz, J., Carrin, G., Krupp, H., Peschke, M., Sclar, E., & Van Steenberge, J. (1974). *Providing adequate retirement income—Pension reform in the United States and abroad.* Hanover, NH: New England Press for Brandeis University Press.

Smeeding, T. (1984). Approaches to measuring and valuing in-kind subsidies and the distribution of their benefits. In M. Moon (Ed.), *Economic transfers in the United States* (pp. 139–176). Chicago, IL: University of Chicago Press.

Smeeding, T. (1990). The economic status of the elderly. In R.H. Binstock & L.K. George (Eds.), *Handbook of aging and the social sciences* (3rd ed.) (pp. 362–382). San Diego, CA: Academic Press.

Smolensky, E., Danziger, S., & Gottschalk, P. (1988). The declining significance of age in the United States: Trends in the well-being of children and the elderly since 1939. In J. Palmer, T. Smeeding, & B. Torrey (Eds.), *The vulnerable: America's young and old in the industrial world* (pp. 29–54). Washington, DC: The Urban Institute Press.

Social Security Administration. (1998). *The income of the aged chartbook, 1996.* Washington, DC: The Social Security Administration.

Torrey, B., & Tauber, C. (1986). The importance of asset income among the elderly. *Review of Income and Wealth, 32,* 443–449.

Turner, J., & Doescher, T. (1996). Pensions and retirement. In W. Crown (Ed.), *Handbook on employment and the elderly* (pp. 165–181). Westport, CT: Greenwood Press.

U.S. Bureau of the Census. (1999a). *Poverty in the United States: 1998*. Current Population Reports, Series P60–207. Washington, DC: U.S. Government Printing Office.

U.S. Bureau of the Census. (1999b). *Consumer income: 1998*. Current Population Reports, Series P60–206. Washington, DC: U.S. Government Printing Office.

Venti, S., & Wise, D. (1990). *Aging and the income value of housing wealth*. NBER Working Paper No. 3547. Cambridge, MA: National Bureau of Economic Research.

Welch, F. (1979). Effects of cohort size on earnings: The baby boom babies' financial bust. *Journal of Political Economy, 87*, 565–596.

Wolff, E. (1998). Recent trends in the size distribution of household wealth. *Journal of Economic Perspectives, 12*(3), 131–150.

Zedlewski, S. (1988). The fiscal burden on the elderly. In J. Gist (Ed.), *Social Security and economic well-being across generations* (pp. 137–166). Washington, DC: American Association of Retired Persons.

Twenty

Economic Security Policies

Eric R. Kingson and John B. Williamson

I. Introduction

Improved economic security for older persons, an achievement of the 20th century, presents challenges for the next. These challenges include providing basic protections against losses of income for a growing elderly population, assuring the financial stability of private and public retirement income systems, and maintaining a fair and politically acceptable balance of costs and benefits across income classes, gender, and age cohorts.

This chapter examines the evolution of the old-age income security system in the United States and explores the financing, adequacy, and distributional implications of major policy options. It begins with a discussion of forces shaping the nation's retirement income system. Next, the public and private choices available to nations when structuring their systems are discussed, and the U.S. system is described. (The other major component of old-age security, health security, is addressed in chapter 21 by Feder et al., this volume). Major issues in various approaches to addressing the Social Security financing problem are reviewed. Important distributive issues, especially those

concerned with the economic security of older women, are identified. The chapter concludes by suggesting that retirement income policy making will benefit from research into the experience of other nations, including the distributive implications of various approaches to pension reform.

II. Why Economic Security for the Old?

The institution of retirement and related approaches to old-age income security emerged in the context of century-spanning economic transformations of the United States, taking shape in response to the needs of individuals and families to assure an adequate stream of income during their retirement years. It reflects social and political decisions with regard to the development of public and private forms of retirement income savings as well as understandings about the capacity and ethical obligations of working persons to prepare for their retirements while also providing some measure of support for nonworking older populations.

Handbook of Aging and the Social Sciences, Fifth Edition

A. Demographic and Economic Influences

At the turn of the 20th century, a rapidly industrializing and modernizing society created both need and opportunity for public and private income supports. Improvements in public health, nutrition, sanitation, and health care led to increases in life expectancies and in the size of the elderly population. A wage-dependent labor force became more subject to cyclical downturns of a market economy. The growing emphasis on speed and efficiency in production devalued the skills of older workers, further elevating employer and employee interest in pensions as vehicles for promoting the orderly exit of older workers, thereby hoping to assure greater opportunity for younger ones (see Achenbaum, 1986; Berkowitz, 1997; Graebner, 1980; Kingson & Berkowitz, 1993; Lubove, 1968; Schulz, 2000a; Schulz & Myles,1990).

The long-term growth of the economy in the 20th century translated into increased opportunities for improving living standards, increasing leisure, and addressing the material needs of persons who were not in the labor force. The increased productivity of the workforce created retirement, a new and today commonly welcomed period of leisure at the end of the life course. This productivity also made it possible to devote larger shares of national product towards the support of those older persons who, by virtue of health problems or dated employment skills, were marginal to the labor force.

B. Retirement Risks for the Individual

For the individual, the goal of retirement income planning is to assure a stream of income that maintains, no matter how long one lives, one's standard of living. Economist James Schulz notes that retirement planning takes place in the face of much uncertainty. Individuals do not know how long they will be able to work or how much they will earn. They do not know how child rearing, parental care, or disability may affect their earnings capacity. They do not know when they will retire or whether they will have employment options in old age. They do not know how many years they (and their spouse) will live, once retired. They do not know what the rate of inflation will be or how it may erode the value of their retirement assets. Neither do they know what their health-care costs will be (Schulz, 2000a).

Individuals and society do know that a need exists to prepare for an extended period of little or no income from employment in old age. To maintain existing standards of living during retirement, retirement income planners generally estimate that income from all sources (e.g., Old-Age, Survivors and Disability Insurance [OASDI], occupational pensions, assets) should replace between 65 and 85% of preretirement income (Schulz, 2000a).

C. Influence of Values and Contending Visions

Pensions and related retirement savings mechanisms provide a rational means for individuals to make modest contributions over a long period of time in exchange for protections against the financial losses that would otherwise accompany leaving work in old age. The nation's retirement income system—especially its commitment to the OASDI program—is, in part, an outgrowth of political decisions directed at institutionalizing a stable source of basic income support for the old, the severely disabled, and selected survivors and dependents. Politics, often reflecting compromises between contending values, gives shape to this system. It also structures the extent to which the nation relies on public versus employer-based retirement pensions and the extent to which responsibility is placed on the individuals as opposed to the collectivity.

Shared responsibility and securing protection against what President Franklin D. Roosevelt termed the "hazards and vicissitudes of life" inform the traditional view of the Social Security program (Heclo, 1998). A governmental Social Security program arises from a deeply embedded sense of mutual responsibility and the responsibility of those who can work to "provide for those who cannot . . . . The implied covenant is not a legal entity but it has a subtle and powerful force in a democracy, in which government must reflect a general consensus of its citizens" (Brown, 1972, pp. 31–32).

Policy debates concerning the retirement income system reflect value preferences with regard to the primacy of achieving retirement income security versus other important goals, such as increasing national savings and rewarding work effort. These approaches may reflect deep divisions in the philosophy of the extent to which the individual versus the national community should bear risks. Nowhere is this seen better than in the differing views of those who have supported compulsory social insurance approaches—to be supplemented by personal savings and other pensions—as the foundation of the retirement income system, as opposed to those who have favored relying more heavily on private and voluntary approaches to be supplemented when necessary by means-tested government programs.

From the perspective of those favoring the social insurance approach, the promotion of widespread financial security— with associated values of maintaining dignity and strengthening families and community—should have primacy over other policy goals. Stabilizing financing and assuring benefits that are adequate and can be counted upon regardless of inflation, business cycles, and market fluctuations are central objectives. Strong commitment typically exists for moderate redistribution that seeks to provide a minimally adequate floor of protection for those who have worked for many years at relatively low wages. "Bad" risks (e.g., people who are potentially expensive to the system) are not excluded. Because stable financing requires maintaining a balance between "good" and "bad" risks, participation must be compulsory (Thompson & Upp, 1997).

In contrast, strong belief in the primacy of individual responsibility and freedom of choice as the preeminent organizing values of society underlie the views of those who favor relying on voluntary, private savings approaches and limited means-tested public approaches. Their emphasis is on limiting the role of government in a market economy. Although safeguards may be built in for the most disadvantaged, by design this approach provides substantially greater reward to those with higher earnings. At heart, there is a belief that the market is an efficient and fair way of distributing goods and services and that social insurance programs are undermining free markets (see Marmor, Mashaw, & Harvey, 1990). Thus, it is not surprising that the shift from a largely private approach to retirement income security to one based on the social insurance model took place in the midst of the nation's greatest economic crisis, when public faith in the private sector was greatly diminished.

III. Approaches to Old-Age Income Security

A limited range of private, quasi-governmental and governmental mechanisms is available for underwriting retirement income security. Although the structure and mix of mechanisms used to promote retirement income security vary greatly among nations, most draw on many of these vehicles to build their old-age income security systems.

A. Addressing Retirement Risks: Choices

No matter how societies choose to approach retirement income security, at root, resources must be transferred from working persons to nonworking older persons. Retirement income "transfers," as used here, include the numerous private and public, cash and in-kind, vehicles that individuals, families, employers, and government use to shift resources from working to retired persons.

Although not commonly acknowledged, as such, private transfers within the family—including cash support to family members, housing, and time spent in caregiving—are arguably the nation's most significant transfer and therefore deserve mention. Caregiving alone has been estimated to be the equivalent of a yearly 30% of GDP (Morgan, 1983). In the absence of significant public or private employer retirement transfers, families would likely be relied upon far more heavily as a safety net for the old, both in terms of cash and in-kind support. In short, one choice in establishing a national old-age income security system is to emphasize reliance on the family.

A second choice is to promote individual savings for retirement and related risks. Although viewed as a private approach, government plays a major role in structuring and encouraging these transfers. In the United States, for example, government regulates the banking industry and insures savings deposits. It also uses tax policy and tax expenditures—an arrangement that reduces tax liabilities of individuals (or sometimes employers)—as a way of encouraging individual retirement savings through such mechanisms as Individual Retirement Accounts (Kingson & Berkowitz, 1993).

Another option involves government mandating individuals or employers to save for their own or their employees' retirements (Thompson & Upp, 1997). Chile mandates its workers to contribute 10% of their earnings into government approved privately administered pension funds and another 3% to pay for related disability and life insurance. Seeking to reduce reliance on its old-age benefits financed by the federal government using general revenues, Australia established in 1992 a mandatory employer contribution into a private pension fund—3% in 1992, rising to 9% in 2002. Even so, today, about 84% of all age-eligible Australians qualify for a full or partial government pension, which is means-tested (Congressional Budget Office, 1999).

Occupational pensions (i.e., employer or union sponsored plans) provide yet another retirement income transfer choice. As with mandates, this approach is not properly classified as an exclusively private transfer. Indeed, the tax exclusion of employer contributions to private pensions and pension fund earnings represents the largest federal tax expenditure, about $65 billion in fiscal year 1995 (Thompson & Upp, 1997).

Means-tested programs provide financial assistance to low-income persons whose incomes and or assets fall below a prescribed level. Such welfare transfers can be used, as is currently the case in Australia, as the foundation of a retirement income system. Alternatively, they can be used, as in the United States, as a safety net.

In contrast to welfare, the social insurance approach seeks to prevent economic insecurity primarily by taxing the wages of employees and employers, thereby establishing protections against identifiable risks such as loss of income in retirement, disability, or survivorship. Through the use of insurance principles, program costs are estimated and premiums set, thereby enabling the risks facing individuals and their families to be spread across the entire insurance pool. To finance social insurance programs, working persons generally make direct contributions—usually through a highly visible payroll tax—and indirectly through employer contributions. This strengthens the basis for viewing social insurance as an earned right, arguably enhancing the dignity of beneficiaries. Additionally, in the United States, a visible payroll tax is viewed by many as imposing fiscal discipline, because benefit amounts are linked directly to a tax on wages (see Ball, 1978; Myers, 1993; Thompson & Upp, 1997).

Providing widespread protection against income declines associated with retirement, especially for low- and moderate-income persons, is a—arguably "the"—driving goal of social insurance. Social Security gives expression to this concern through a weighted benefit formula that provides benefits that replace much more of preretirement earnings for low- and moderate-income workers. Simultaneously, the program's benefit structure is designed to be wage related, assuring that higher paid persons receive larger benefit amounts, therefore enabling Social Security to serve as a floor of protection for them as well.

Other non-means-tested universal approaches may be drawn upon to shape a nation's old-age income security system. For example, whether retired or not, at age 65, persons who have lived in Canada for 10 or more years past age 18 are eligible to receive a basic Old Age Security Benefit funded out of general revenues. The benefit amounts are conditioned only on the number of years of residence in Canada. Other components of the Canadian retirement income system utilize other approaches for protecting against risk. Many countries—including the United Kingdom and Sweden—only use age as a basis for eligibility for a flat-benefits tier of their pensions.

B. Assessing the Approaches

Each of the above approaches to economic security is associated with certain advantages and disadvantages. Hence, it is not surprising that nations always rely on several approaches to structuring their old-age income security system. Private savings vehicles and occupational pensions help middle income and higher income persons to achieve their economic security goals, but necessarily fall short in terms of achieving universal coverage and meeting adequacy goals. Welfare approaches target benefits to the poor, but such programs often lack the political base to sustain adequate benefits. Social insurance incorporates modest redistribution, but provides relatively smaller rates of returns to well-off individuals and is less efficient than welfare in terms of targeting to the poor (see Thompson & Upp, 1997; for further discussion see Ball, 1997; Kingson & Berkowitz, 1993; Steuerle & Bakija, 1994).

IV. The Old-Age Income Security System in the United States

A. Evolution

The social insurance approach to retirement was introduced in the United States early in the 20th century. The period prior to 1935 was characterized by minimal public assistance mechanisms and a struggle to gain legitimacy for the social insurance concept. The crisis precipitated by the Depression of the 1930s encouraged the passage of the Social Security Act of 1935. The act established two basic income maintenance programs—means-tested benefits for the poor and earnings-related benefits for certain workers. Until passage of the 1950 Amendments to the Social Security Act, with its substantial benefit increase and expansion of coverage, it was unclear whether a welfare or social insurance approach would drive the nation's retirement income system (see Berkowitz, 1991, 1997).

The growing economy of the post-World War II period contributed to the incremental expansion of coverage and benefits in Social Security and the nation's evolving occupation pension systems through the early 1970s. But as population aging accelerated and as the expansive growth of this period turned into the stagflation of the 1970s and 1980s, the financial picture changed, and the Social Security and occupational pension policy agendas shifted from concern for adequacy of benefits and coverage to concern for system financing (see Berkowitz, 1991; Kingson, 1984). This period has fostered a more contentious discussion of the future of the nation's retirement income system.

B. The Contemporary Old-Age Income Security System

The major components of the Old-Age Income Security System, as it has evolved, are now described.

1. Social Security

Social Security coverage is virtually universal, with over 95% of the U.S. workforce—151 million persons—contributing to the program in 2000. In January, 2000, nearly 45 million persons received benefits, including 27.7 million retired workers, 4.7 million surviving aged widow(er)s, 400,000 surviving mothers and fathers, 4.9 million disabled workers, and 3.8 million children. At age 62 nearly all covered workers are eligible to accept actuarially reduced early retirement benefits. At normal retirement age—age 65 and 2 months in 2000 and scheduled to gradually increase to age 67 by 2027—covered workers are eligible to receive full retired worker benefits. In January 2000, the average monthly benefit for retired workers was $804; the maximum benefit for a worker first retiring at age 65 was

$1,433. Those postponing acceptance of benefits past normal retirement age (and until age 70) receive credits that permanently increase the value of their monthly benefits, once received. Widows and widowers of retired workers may receive reduced survivor benefits at age 60 (or age 50 if severely disabled) based on the earnings history of their spouses or may be eligible to receive full benefits at age 65 or later. Other dependents of retired and deceased workers may also be eligible for monthly benefits.

Even with Social Security as a floor of protection, many older populations remain exposed to significant financial risks. Unmarried older women experience very high rates of poverty and near poverty, especially very old and minority women (see Holden, 1997; Moon, 1997; Smeeding, 1999). Divorce, death of a spouse, and increased longevity continue to pose significant risks. Intermittent work histories, lower wages, and costs incurred in giving care to family members (e.g., lost wages or lost promotions) also expose women to greater risk of economic insufficiency in old age. The differential treatment of one-earner versus two-earner couples remains an often discussed equity concern (see Holden, 1997). As groups overrepresented among low-wage workers, minority workers benefit disproportionately from Social Security because of the program's weighted benefit formula. Hence, benefit reductions—including increases in the age of eligibility for full benefits, across-the-board benefit reductions or reductions in annual cost-of-living adjustments (COLAs) to benefits—would have a disproportionately negative effect on minorities. (See chapter 19 by Crown, this volume, for more on the economic status of older persons.)

2. Occupational Pensions

There are basically two types of pension plans sponsored by private and governmental employers. Defined benefit plans utilize formulas that guarantee a benefit based on years of service times either a flat sum for each year or some measure of a worker's highest or average highest earnings. Defined contribution plans—including money purchase plans with 401(k) and profit-sharing plans—enable employers and employees to make direct contributions into employee retirement accounts. Retirement benefits are not guaranteed; rather, they reflect contributions and investment outcomes. Many variations exist in plan design, and hybrids exist combining elements of both the defined benefit and defined contribution approaches (Employee Benefit Research Institute, 2000; National Research Council, 1997). In recent years, there has been a proliferation of defined contribution plans.

Pension coverage varies among different segments of the population:

- Private-sector employees covered and accruing rights to a pension plan benefit increased from 12% in 1940 to 43% of all private-sector wage and salary workers in 1993 (about 50% of full-time workers).
- Pension coverage for workers under age 18 decreased from 29% in 1979 to 24% in 1993.
- Twenty-four percent of workers earning under $20,000 participated in a private pension plan compared to 68% of those earning $30,000 or more (Kramerich, 1999).
- Ninety-six percent of full-time state and local government employees participated in a pension plan in 1994. (Employee Benefit Research Institute, 2000). Participation of federal employees is nearly universal.
- In 1998, 31% of households with at least one member over age 65 reported receipt of private pension income (median benefit of $5,803); 7% of public employee pension income (median

benefit of $13,132) (U.S. Department of Health and Human Services, 2000).

Although occupational pensions provide important supplements to the retirement incomes of many employees, the system of occupational pensions is not without its problems. As Schulz (1996) discusses in the previous edition of this handbook, (a) the occupational pensions system fails to cover a large portion of the workforce, including a disproportionate number of the economically vulnerable workers; (b) vesting rules work to the disadvantage of job changers and short-term employees; (c) there is much risk, especially for the long-lived, that inflation will erode the value of occupational pension benefits; (d) employers may use pensions to encourage early retirement, even if it is not in the long-term interest of employees; (e) participants in defined benefit plans have been harmed, sometimes losing their pensions, by inadequate funding or the poor investment decisions of plan managers (see Schulz, 1996; also see National Research Council, 1997). Efforts to strengthen the occupational pension system, although often successful, have imposed significant regulatory requirements. This has resulted in higher administrative costs and a reluctance on the part of employers to start new plans, especially defined benefit plans.

3. Personal Savings Mechanisms

In addition to providing incentives for employees to make tax-deferred contributions to 401(k) and for the self-employed to make similar contributions to Keogh plans, tax laws encourage individuals and their spouses to contribute to Individual Retirement Accounts (IRAs). Established in 1974 for employed persons who were not covered by pension plans, participation increased when, in 1982, eligibility was expanded to include all employees and later declined in 1987 when restrictions were placed in the deductibility of the contributions of higher income persons. The restrictions on higher income employees were reduced in 1998, and a new after-tax IRA (Roth IRA) was established. The Roth IRA exempts investment earnings from being subject to taxation at retirement. The new provisions also exempt early IRA distributions from the tax penalty if used for certain educational expenses or buying a first home. In 1995, 4.3 million taxpayers made a total of $8.3 billion in deductible IRA contributions.

The deductibility of yearly contributions and deferred taxation on IRA earnings reduced the federal income tax base by an estimated $63 billion in 2000 ($22 billion for Keogh plans) (U.S. House of Representatives, 1998). Questions have been raised about the equity of IRAs and other plans that use the tax system to encourage personal savings since these tax breaks are of disproportionate benefit to persons with higher incomes (Burnes & Schulz, 2000.) Questions have also been raised about provisions allowing these funds to be used for purposes other than that initially intended since doing so undermines the goal of retirement income savings.

4. Public Assistance

Supplemental Security Income (SSI) is a federally administered welfare program that provided monthly benefits to 6.6 million aged, blind, or severely disabled persons in January 2000, including 2.0 million aged 65 and older, 3.7 million aged 18 to 64, and 0.9 million under age 18. The basic monthly benefit guarantee in 2000 was $512 ($769 for a couple), a federally funded benefit that many states supplement. SSI beneficiaries are generally eligible to receive food stamps and Medicaid as well as state-funded payment of their Medicare premiums. Even with state supplements, SSI benefits total less

than the poverty line. Moreover, many potentially eligible people do not apply for benefits.

To be eligible, countable income usually needs to be below $512 a month ($769 for a couple) and assets—excluding home, car, $1500 in burial funds, $1500 face value of life insurance—may not exceed $2000 ($3000 for a couple). Because SSI is an efficient means of targeting benefit, reforms in the program could be used as a vehicle to further improve the income positions of some of the most vulnerable elderly persons (see Smeeding, 1994; SSI Modernization Project Experts, 1992).

V. Proposals for Reforming Social Security in the United States

A. The Projected Shortfall

Under intermediate assumptions as presented in the 2001 report of the Social Security trustees, the combined OASDI trust fund is estimated to be able to meet its commitments until 2038. After that date there would be a shortfall of approximately 27 cents for every dollar promised under current legislation. Tax revenues (payroll tax receipts and receipts from taxation of benefits) will be exceeded by outlays in 2016. However, income from all sources, including interest on trust fund investment in U.S. Government bonds, is projected to exceed expenditures through about 2025 and the combined OASDI trust fund is projected to meet its commitments until 2038 (Board of Trustees, 2001). The current debate over the proposed privatization of Social Security is closely linked to this projected shortfall, which analysts have been aware of for many years, but it is also linked to the funding problems of the late 1970s and early 1980s.

B. Considerations When Assessing Financing Issues

When assessing the implications of financing reform options, careful consideration needs to be given to identifying various trade-offs and distributive implications. It is also important to acknowledge that the population-aging challenges faced by the United States are generally not as great as those of other industrial nations.

Reforms to address financing through benefit reductions would exacerbate some of the previously discussed adequacy shortcomings in the current retirement income system. Movement toward a more privatized approach would likely benefit long-term, high-income workers; those with intermittent work histories would be less protected. Tax increases, too, carry distributive implications. Increasing the amount of earnings subject to the payroll tax would fall most heavily on well-off individuals, but the burden from an increase in the payroll tax rate would arguably fall most heavily on low-income workers.

Although the United States must confront the shortfall problem in one way or another, it is not, as compared with other industrialized nations, in a very difficult position in trying to meet the problems of population aging. The United States per capita income is among the highest, $27,821 in 1996 U.S. dollars, as compared to the equivalent of $20,533 in France, $21,200 in Germany, and $18,636 in the United Kingdom. U.S. federal expenditures, as a percent of gross (GDP), are generally much lower than in other industrial democracies—21.6% in the United States in 1996, compared to 44.7% in France, 32.1% in Germany, 47.9% in Italy, 45.2% in Sweden, and 39.9% in the United Kingdom. The demography of population aging is also more manageable. There are approximately 19 persons aged 65 and over in the United States per hundred persons of working ages, compared to 18 in Canada, 24 in Germany, 24 in France, 26 in Italy, 24 in Japan, and 24 in the United Kingdom. By 2030, the elderly dependency ratio will grow to 37 in the United States, 39 in Canada, 39 in France, 49 in Germany, 48 in Japan, and 39 in the United Kingdom (Kalish & Tetsuya, 1999). Also, the overall dependency burden for U.S. workers—the ratio of the population aged 0–14 and 65 and older to so-called working aged persons—is projected to increase between 2000 and 2030 at a slower rate than that of the major industrial nations.

C. Proposals for Privatization

1. The Origins of the Debate

In 1972, Congress passed legislation that not only approved a large increase in benefit levels, but also introduced indexing to adjust for inflation and changes in productivity. These changes made the system more dependent than it had previously been on unemployment rates and inflation rates. Stagflation (high inflation together with high unemployment rates) caused in part by the dramatic increase in the price of oil, was one of several factors contributing to the short-term Social Security financing problem by the late 1970s (Williamson & Pampel, 1993). Modest policy changes enacted in 1977 dealt with the problem, but for only a few years. By the early 1980s the financing problem was back and new legislation was needed. The 1983 Social Security legislation made a number of policy changes that added up to tax increases and benefit cuts (Kingson, 1984).

During the early 1980s an interest in the partial privatization of Social Security began to emerge, stimulated in part by the crisis framing of the Social Security financing problem by conservative commentators, particularly those linked to the Cato Institute, a libertarian think tank (Williamson & Watts-Roy, 1999). Also contributing was the poor performance of the economy and warnings from Social Security's Board of Trustees about the future burden on OASDI when the boomers retired. Partial privatization was viewed by many advocates as a way to reduce the future Social Security burden and thus the need for substantial payroll tax increases (Ferrara, 1985). During the 1980s the views of those advocating the privatization of Social Security were not taken very seriously, but this changed during the 1990s. By 1997, with the publication of a major report prepared by the Advisory Council on Social Security (1997), the call for the partial privatization of Social Security had moved into the political mainstream.

Today, most advocates of privatizing Social Security have in mind the introduction of mandatory individual retirement savings accounts to be integrated with a somewhat scaled-down version of the current Social Security program. Although many mainstream policy analysts are discussing the pros and cons of the proposed partial privatization of Social Security, relatively few are calling for full privatization. However, some do argue that the full privatization of Social Security should be the eventual goal (Feldstein & Samwick, 1998; Peterson, 1999).

2. Various Privatization Proposals

One proposed approach to partial privatization is to increase the payroll tax by something between 1.5 and 2.0% with the additional money invested in individual accounts (with some choice of asset category) managed by the federal government. At retirement, workers would be required to use the assets in these "add-on" individual accounts to purchase an annuity (Advisory Council on Social Security, 1997).

A second approach calls for the diversion of a substantial proportion (e.g., 5.0

out of the current 6.2 percentage points) of the employee's share of the payroll tax into individual accounts. The "carve-out" individual accounts associated with this approach would be much larger than the add-on accounts just described and would allow workers to invest the money with a wide range of alternative private-sector money managers. These accounts would divert a substantial portion of a worker's Social Security contribution into a private-sector alternative (Advisory Council on Social Security, 1997).

A third approach to partial privatization calls for the creation of individual accounts with tax credits paid for by using the federal budget surplus projected for the next several years. At retirement the worker would be required to purchase an annuity with part of the annuity income being used to offset a portion of the Social Security defined benefit pension (Feldstein, 1998).

A fourth approach calls for voluntary individual accounts. One proposal would cut the Social Security payroll tax over the next several years (which would eventually be followed by a substantial payroll tax increase as the boomers retire) with tax incentives to encourage workers to take the money saved by the payroll tax cut and put it into a voluntary retirement savings account (Moynihan, 1998).

3. Trust Fund Investment in Private Equity Markets

Another approach that bears resemblance to privatization proposals calls for investing a substantial fraction of trust fund assets in private-sector equity markets. However, this approach does not call for the creation of individual accounts. Instead, the idea here is for the government to passively invest something like 40% of trust fund assets in a very broad equity index in an effort to obtain the higher long-term returns associated with equity investments. The rest of the trust fund assets would remain invested in the generally lower yielding treasury bonds currently used. Note that although this option does involve investing some of the trust fund in the private sector, it would leave the defined benefit structure of Social Security as it is today. Also, it would improve the long-term fiscal outlook of Social Security (Aaron & Reischauer, 1998; Advisory Council on Social Security, 1997).

D. Other Reform Options

In recent debates about the proposed partial privatization of Social Security, reform proposals have generally been presented as a package, one component of which is the call for individual retirement savings accounts. The reason is that few, if any, analysts believe that the partial privatization of Social Security would by itself bring projected revenues into line with projected benefits over the 75–year period used by the Social Security Administration's actuaries to decide whether or not the system is in balance. Estimates of the impact that each of the reform options that follow would have on the projected Social Security deficit can be found in a set of tables prepared by Fontenot (1999).

- **Means-test benefits:** Proposals to means-test Social Security benefits differ from the means-testing procedures currently used to determine eligibility for SSI or other welfare programs. Traditionally, means testing has been used to limit benefits to the poor and near poor. In contrast, this new form of means testing would exclude only those with high incomes and would be administered through the tax system. Some analysts use the term *affluence testing* to refer to this means testing approach. Means testing has a number of proponents who consider it an equitable way to address financing problems (Bipartisan Commission on Entitlement and Tax Reform, 1995; Peterson, 1994) and a number of critics who view it as inequitable, potentially undermining political support for the program, and a major disincentive to save for retirement (Burtless, 1996; Kingson & Schulz, 1997).

- **Increase the number of years used to compute the benefit:** Many reform proposals call for gradually increasing the number of years used to compute the Social Security benefit from the current 35 to 38 or 40 years. Although this approach has its advocates, a number of analysts argue that such a change would have an adverse impact on women and other low-wage workers (Iams & Sandell, 1998).

- **Increase the retirement age:** As noted above, the normal retirement age (NRA)—the age at which a worker becomes eligible for the full as opposed to actuarially reduced retirement pension—is scheduled to increase from 65 to 67 essentially between 2000 and 2027. In recent years there have been proposals to further increase the NRA to 68 or 70. Some have also suggested that it be increased to age 70 and then automatically increased in subsequent years to reflect any further increase in life expectancy (Advisory Council on Social Security, 1997; Moynihan, 1998). As the NRA increases, the age of early retirement will remain the same at 62, but the actuarial reduction for taking the pension early will increase. Moreover, as the NRA increases there will be modest incentives for workers to remain in the labor force longer, and those who do take early retirement will get lower pensions than at present. Both factors would reduce the projected increase in Social Security spending in the decades ahead. These changes may be particularly problematic for low-wage, marginally employed older workers.

- **Adjust the COLA downward:** A number of proposals have been made that call for shifting to a less generous COLA formula, one that adjusts for a specified amount (e.g., one percentage point) below the actual increase in the cost of living for the prior year (Moynihan, 1998; Center for Strategic and International Studies, 1999). Calls for a cut in the COLA of as much as 1.1% have been justified on the grounds that the current COLA overstates the true inflation rate. As it turns out there is much controversy about how to best measure changes in the cost of living (Duff, 1997). There is also some evidence suggesting that for the elderly the current Consumer Price Index may understate the true cost of living rather than overstate it (Stewart & Pavalone, 1996). COLA reductions would have their greatest effect on retirees who receive a larger proportion of their retirement income from Social Security, that is, low- and moderate-income elderly households.

- **Increase the payroll tax rate:** A very direct way to close the projected gap between revenues and expenditures when the boomers retire would be to increase the payroll tax. Proposals have been made to increase the tax between 1.0 and 1.2 percentage points on both the employer and the employee. Such proposals are regressive in that they would tax a greater share of the income of low-wage workers than of high-wage workers because income above the cap for OASDI payroll tax purposes ($76,200 in 2000) is not taxed. As women are disproportionately represented among low-wage workers, such a policy would also have adverse distributional consequences for them (Smeeding, Estes, & Glasse, 1999).

- **Make across-the-board reductions in Social Security pension benefits:** A substantial fraction of the projected long-term Social Security deficit could be resolved by reducing Social Security benefits by 3–5%. This approach would be a regressive policy alternative as it would put the burden primarily on women, African-Americans, and those toward the lower end of the income distribution. These groups depend upon Social Security for a much greater share of their retirement income (Smeeding et al., 1999; Williamson & Rix, 2000).

- **Increase the earnings cap for payroll tax purposes:** Raising the cap on the amount of wages and salaries subject to the OASDI payroll tax is another way to deal with the projected trust fund deficit. This is one of the few progressive reform options that have been proposed. One proposal for doing this is to eliminate the cap on the employer only, estimated to address more than one-half of the projected financing problem. Another is to increase the amount of income subject to the OASDI tax from the current level ($76,200 in 2000), which subjects about 86% of earned income to the Social Security tax, to a higher level at which 90% of earned income would be taxed (Moynihan, 1998). This proposal would place the burden of closing the Social Security funding gap on high-wage earners; it would have no impact on those with incomes below the current cap (Fontenot, 1999).

E. Distributional Issues

When major changes are made in a program that touches the lives of as many people as does Social Security, there are inevitably going to be questions as to who stands to benefit and who may be harmed. For this reason an important aspect of assessing any proposed change is a close look at the potential distributional implications of that reform, particularly those linked to race, class, and gender.

During the early decades, Social Security was a very good deal for both low-wage and high-wage workers; all income groups got out a lot more than they paid in. This is a structural characteristic of pay-as-you-go pension schemes during their first few decades; there are generally so many contributors and so few eligible retirees during the early years that the program can easily provide generous pensions. But as the system matures the ratio of retirees to contributing workers increases. If this trend is combined with population aging, the burden on contributing workers and employers increases substantially. As the payroll tax is increased and benefits are cut in an effort to keep the system in balance, some workers, particularly the affluent, can be expected to object to the low imputed rate of return on their contributions, to question the fairness of the scheme, and to push for changes that make the program less redistributive. Recent calls for the introduction of privatized individual accounts illustrate this (Cordes & Steuerle, 1999; Stephenson, Horlacher, & Colander, 1995).

One (often unstated) goal of privatization is to improve the "return" on Social Security contributions for high-wage workers. However, it is hard to come up with ways to improve the imputed return on contributions for high-wage workers that do not at the same time decrease the return on contributions for other groups, such as low-wage workers, women (particularly nonmarried women), African-Americans, and Hispanic-Americans. Efforts to boost returns for affluent workers typically call for cuts in the redistributive defined benefit component of Social Security. These cuts are designed to help finance the introduction of the individual defined contribution accounts. In short, the efforts to increase the imputed return for affluent Americans are likely to decrease the return for others and increase income inequality among Social Security

pensioners (Quinn & Mitchell, 1996; Williamson, 1997a).

Due to the association between race and income, there tends to be a close correspondence between the class (or income) implications of a proposed reform and the race implications of that same reform. Some proposed reforms, such as increasing the earnings cap for payroll tax purposes, would favor low-wage workers, African Americans, and Hispanics. But most of the reforms we have considered would impact low-wage workers and minority workers more adversely than high-wage workers (Fontenot, 1999).

Although Social Security reform is a class and a race issue, it is even more a gender issue. Women are more likely than men to be low-wage workers, and for this reason they are particularly vulnerable to the adverse distributional consequences of most privatization proposals. But they are also at risk in a number of other ways due to their status as wives, divorcees, and widows (Rix & Williamson, 1998). Many of the reforms being debated would reduce some of the protection for women implicit in Social Security as it is currently structured (Williamson & Rix, 2000). For example, the partial privatization and the creation of IRAs would over time lead to the erosion of benefits in the defined benefit component of Social Security (Jones, 1996). As women tend to earn less and to be out of the labor force more, they can be expected to on average have substantially less accumulated in these IRAs at the time of retirement (Williamson, 1997b).

VI. Challenges for Researchers

Central to the debate over the proposed partial privatization of Social Security is speculation as to what would happen to the economy and to various categories of workers if such a shift in policy were made. One way to obtain information about what might happen in the United States is to undertake research on what has happened in other countries that have privatized or partially privatized their Social Security systems.

One of the most important issues that can be explored based on evidence from other countries is the distributional impact of models emphasizing individual defined contribution accounts. When a shift is made from a public pay-as-you go (PAYG) defined benefit scheme to a fully or partially privatized alternative based on defined contribution accounts, it is inevitable that some people will get more than a proportionate share of the benefits, and others will absorb more than a proportionate share of the costs of the transition.

There are many ways to structure a privatized scheme. Chile (Kritzer, 1996), the United Kingdom (Liu, 1999; Schulz, 2000b), and Sweden (Sundén, 2000) offer dramatically different models. Even within Latin America there are many very different models (Huber & Stephens, 2000; Mesa-Lago, 1997). Over time these models will provide evidence as to the pros and cons of different ways of structuring privatized schemes.

- There is some preliminary evidence from Chile (Arenas de Mesa & Montecinos, 1999) and the United Kingdom (Schulz, 2000c) suggesting that the shift to individual accounts has had adverse consequences for women. Research is needed to assess the extent to which this is the case in other countries and the degree to which the adverse impact varies as a function of how the scheme is structured.
- There is also preliminary evidence from both Chile (Kritzer, 1996) and the United Kingdom (Liu, 1999) suggesting that low-wage workers do not fare as well in connection with privatized schemes as do high-wage workers. There is a need to explore how preva-

lent this effect is and how it varies from one country to another. Also relevant here is analysis of how well low-wage workers do relative to how they would have done in connection with the prior PAYG defined benefit scheme.

- Much attention has been given to the economic impact of privatizing public pension schemes. The economic impact of privatization in Chile and in the United Kingdom is still being hotly debated among experts. There are some analysts who argue that in these countries privatization has already had or in the future will have positive economic effects, such as contributing to an increase in the savings rate, an increase in the pool of investment capital, an increase in the rate of economic growth, a reduction in the size of the public pension burden, and a reduction in the size of the national debt (James, 1998; Queisser, 1999). There are also some who question claims with respect to the positive long-term economic consequences of privatization, particularly the claim that it contributes to economic growth (Schulz, 1999).
- A major issue with respect to the proposed partial privatization of Social Security in the United States is how to pay the transition costs of shifting from the current defined benefit PAYG scheme to an alternative based in part or in full on defined contribution individual accounts. Some countries such as Argentina seemed to have allowed pensions under the prior scheme to erode due to the influence of inflation (Williamson & Pampel, 1998). Sweden has introduced a PAYG defined contribution individual "notional" account scheme. There are many models to analyze; some put the burden on the currently retired; others shift much of the burden on future generations of retirees.
- What happens to the political support for privatized schemes when a country

experiences a period of prolonged economic contraction? The economic collapse in many Asian nations in 1997 had a major impact on financial markets in Chile and other Latin American countries. We can say something about short-term impacts based on that experience, but we still have no experience with what happens to the level of political support for such schemes during periods of prolonged economic contraction.

- Administrative costs tend to be high with privatized schemes, but there is also evidence suggesting that over time some countries have been able to reduce those costs (Huber & Stephens, 2000; James, 1998). If the United States were to partially privatize, administrative costs would go up; the experience in other nations may help us estimate how much.

As in Latin America and elsewhere, reform of the U.S. retirement income system will reflect the productivity of the economy, demographic change, work–leisure preferences, societal expectations, and competing views about the relative merits of various approaches to retirement income security. In seeking a balanced mix between these approaches, the policy-making process will benefit from research-based assessments of the experiences of other nations and the distributional implications of various approaches and policy options. The process will also benefit from a better and more explicit discussion of the values driving policy discussion and policy reforms.

Acknowledgments

Work on this paper was partially supported pursuant to a grant from the U.S. Social Security Administration (SSA) funded as part of the Retirement Research Consortium. The opinions and conclusions are solely those of the authors and should not be construed as representing the opinions or policy of SSA or any agency of the federal government or the Center for Retirement Research at Boston College.

References

Aaron, H. J., & Reischauer, R. D. (1998). *Countdown to reform: The great social security debate.* New York: The Century Foundation Press.

Achenbaum, W. A. (1986). *Social Security: Visions and revisions.* New York: Cambridge University Press.

Advisory Council on Social Security. (1997). *Report of the 1994 1996 Advisory Council on Social Security. Volume I: Findings and recommendations.* Washington, DC: U. S. Government Printing Office.

Arenas de Mesa, A., & Montecinos, V. (1999). The privatization of social security and women's welfare: Gender effects of the Chilean reform. *Latin American Research Review, 34*(3), 7–37.

Ball, R. M. (1978). *Social Security: Today and tomorrow.* New York: Columbia University Press.

Ball, R. M. (1997). Bridging the centuries: The case for traditional Social Security. In E. R. Kingson & J. H. Schulz (Eds.), *Social Security in the 21st century* (pp. 259–294). New York: Oxford University Press.

Berkowitz, E. D. (1991). *America's welfare state: From Roosevelt to Reagan.* Baltimore, MD: Johns Hopkins Press.

Berkowitz, E. D. (1997). The historical development of Social Security in the United States. In E. R. Kingson & J. H. Schulz (Eds.), *Social Security in the 21st century* (pp. 22–38). New York: Oxford University Press.

Bipartisan Commission on Entitlement and Tax Reform. (1995). *Final report to the President.* Washington, DC: U. S. Government Printing Office.

Board of Trustees of the Trustees of the Federal Old-Age and Survivors Insurance and Disability Insurance trust funds (2001). *2001 annual report of the trustees of the federal Old-Age and Survivors Insurance and Disability Insurance trust funds.* Washington, DC: U.S. Government Printing Office.

Brown, J. D. (1972). *An American philosophy of Social Security*. Princeton, NJ: Princeton University Press.

Burnes, J., & J. H. Schulz (2000). *Older women and private pensions in the United States*. Waltham, MA: National Center in Women and Aging.

Burtless G. (1996). The folly of means-testing Social Security. In P. A. Diamond, D. C. Lindeman, & H. Young (Eds.), *Social Security: What role for the future?* (pp. 172–180) Washington, DC: National Academy of Social Insurance.

Center for Strategic and International Studies, National Commission on Retirement Policy. (1999, March). *The 21st century retirement security plan*. Washington, DC: CSIS.

Congressional Budget Office. (1999, January). *Social Security privatization: experiences abroad*. Washington, DC: U.S. Government Printing Office.

Cordes, J. J., & Steuerle, E. (1999). *A primer on privatization*. Retirement Project (Occasional Paper No. 3). Washington, DC: Urban Institute.

Duff, C. (1997). Eyes on the price: Is the CPI accurate? *Wall Street Journal*, January 16, p.A1.

Employee Benefit Research Institute. (2000). Fact sheets. [On-line] Available: *http://www.ebri.org/facts*

Feldstein, M. (1998). A new plan to rescue Social Security: Savings grace. *The New Republic*, *218*(14), 14–16.

Feldstein, M., & Samwick, A. (1998). The transition path in privatizing Social Security. In M. Feldstein (Ed.), *Privatizing Social Security* (pp. 215–264). Chicago: University of Chicago Press.

Ferrara, P. J. (1985). Social Security and the super IRA: A populist proposal. In P. J. Ferrara (Ed.), *Social Security: Prospects for real reform* (pp. 193–220). Washington, DC: Cato Institute.

Fontenot, K. (1999). *Information on the distributional effects of various Social Security solvency options by gender and income*. Washington, DC: U.S. Social Security Administration. [On-line] Available: http://www.ssa.gov/policy/pubs/memDistImp.htm [accessed January 5, 2000].

Graebner, W. (1980). *A history of retirement: The meaning and function of an American institution, 1885–1978*. New Haven, CT: Yale University Press.

Heclo, H. (1998). Political risk and Social Security reform. *Social Security Brief*. September. Washington, DC: National Academy of Social Insurance.

Holden, K. C. (1997). Social Security and the economic security of women: Is it fair? In E. R. Kingson & J. H. Schulz (Eds.), *Social Security in the 21st century* (pp. 91–104). New York: Oxford University Press.

Huber, E., & Stephens, J. D. (2000, May). *The political economy of pension reform: Latin America in comparative perspective* (Occasional Paper No. 7). Geneva: United Nations Research Institute for Social Development.

Iams, H. M., & Sandell, S. H. (1998). Cost neutral policies to increase Social Security benefits for widows: A simulation for 1992. *Social Security Bulletin*, *61*(1), 34–43.

James, E. (1998). New models for old-age security: Experiments, evidence, and unanswered questions. *World Bank Research Observer*, *13*, 271–301.

Jones, T. W. (1996). Strengthening the current Social Security system. *The Public Policy and Aging Report*, *7*(3), 1, 3–6.

Kalisch, D. W., & Kalisch, T. A. (1999 off website). Retirement income systems: The reform process across OECD countries, OECD.

Kingson, E. R. (1984, September). Financing Social Security: Agenda-setting and the enactment of 1983 amendments to the Social Security Act. *Policy Studies Journal 11*(3), 131–155.

Kingson, E. R., & Berkowitz, E. D. (1993). *Social Security and Medicare: A policy primer*. Westport, CT: Auburn House Publishers.

Kingson, E. R., & Schulz, J. H. (1997). Should Social Security be means-tested?. In E. R. Kingson & J. H. Schulz (Eds.), *Social Security in the 21st century* (pp. 22–38). New York: Oxford University Press.

Kramerich, L. (1999). *Testimony before the Subcommittee on Oversight of the House Committee on Ways and Means*. Oversight Hearing on Pension Issues. Washington, D.C. (March 23).

Kritzer, B. E. (1996). Privatizing social security: The Chilean experience. *Social Security Bulletin*, *59*(3), 44–55.

Liu, L. (1999). Retirement income security in the United Kingdom. *Social Security Bulletin, 62*(1), 23–46.

Lubove, R. (1968). *The struggle for Social Security: 1900–1935.* Cambridge, MA: Harvard University Press.

Marmor, T. R., Mashaw, J. L., & Harvey, P. L. (1990). *The misunderstood welfare state: Persistent myths, enduring realities.* New York: Basic Books.

Mesa-Lago, C. (1997). Comparative analysis of structural pension reforms in eight Latin American countries: Description, evaluation, and lessons. In M. H. Pearce (Ed.), *Capitalization: A Bolivian model of social and economic reform* (pp. 381–461). Miami, FL: University of Miami Press.

Moon, M. (1997). Are Social Security benefits too high or too low? In E. R. Kingson & J. H. Schulz (Eds.), *Social Security in the 21st century* (pp. 62–75). New York: Oxford University Press.

Morgan, J. N. (1983). The redistribution of income by families and institutions and emergency help patterns. In G. J. Duncan & J. N. Morgan (Eds.), *Five thousand American families: Patterns of economic progress: Analysis of the first thirteen years of the Panel Study of Income Dynamics.* Ann Arbor, MI: University of Michigan Press.

Moynihan, D. P. (1998, March 18). A bill to reduce Social Security payroll taxes, and for other purposes, S. 1792, 105th Congress, 2nd session.

National Research Council. (1997). *Assessing policies for retirement income: Needs for data, research, and models.* Washington, DC: National Academy Press.

Myers, R. J. (1993). *Social Security.* Homewood, Ill: Richard D. Irwin.

Peterson, P. G. (1994, April 7). Entitlement reform: The way to eliminate the deficit. *New York Review of Books,* 3–19.

Peterson, P. G. (1999). How will America pay for the retirement of the baby boom generation? In J. B. Williamson, D. M. Watts-Roy, & E. R. Kingson (Eds.), *The generational equity debate* (pp. 41–57). New York: Columbia University.

Queisser, M. (1999). *Pension reform: Lessons from Latin America.* (Policy Brief No. 15). Paris: OECD Development Center.

Quinn, J. F., & Mitchell, O. S. (1996, May/June). Social Security on the table. *American Prospect, 7*(26), 76–81.

Rix, S. E., & Williamson, J. B. (1998). *Social Security reform: How might women fare?* (Issue Brief No. 31). Washington, DC: Public Policy Institute, AARP.

Schulz, J. H. (1996). Economic security policies. In R. H. Binstock & L. K. George (Eds.), *Handbook of aging and the social sciences* (4th ed.) (pp. 410–426). San Diego, CA: Academic Press.

Schulz, J. H. (1999). Saving, growth, and Social Security: Fighting our children over shares of the future economic pie? In R. N. Butler, L. K. Grossman, & M. R. Oberlink (Eds.), *Life in an older America.* New York: Century Foundation Press.

Schulz, J.H. (2000a). *The economics of aging* (7th ed.). Westport, CT: Auburn House.

Schulz, J.H. (2000b). The risk of pension privatization in Britain. *Challenge 43*(3), 93–104.

Schulz, J. H. (2000c). *Older women and private pensions in the United Kingdom.* Waltham, MA: National Center on Women and Aging, Heller School, Brandeis University.

Schulz, J. H., & Myles, J. (1990). Old age pensions: A comparative perspective. In R.H. Binstock & L.K. George (Eds.), *Handbook of aging and the social sciences* (3rd ed.) (pp. 398–411). San Diego: Academic Press.

Smeeding, T.M. (1994). Improving Supplemental Security Income. In R. B. Friedland, L. M. Etheredge, & B. C. Vladeck (Eds.), *Social welfare policy at the crossroads: Rethinking the roles of social insurance, tax expenditures, mandates, and means-testing* (pp. 97–108). Washington, DC: National Academy of Social Insurance.

Smeeding, T. (1999). Social Security reform: Improving benefit adequacy and economic security for women. *Aging Studies Program Policy Brief.* Syracuse, NY: Syracuse University, Maxwell School of Citizenship and Public Affairs, Center for Policy Research.

Smeeding, T. M., Estes, C. L., & Glasse, L. (1999). *Social Security reform and older women: improving the system.* Washington, DC: Gerontological Society of America.

SSI Modernization Project Experts. (1992, August). *Supplemental Security Income Modernization Project: Final report of the experts*. Baltimore, MD: Social Security Administration.

Stephenson, K., Horlacher, D., & Colander, D. (1995). An overview of the U. S. Social Security system: Problems and options. In K. Stephenson (Ed.), *Social Security: Time for a change* (pp. 3–23). Greenwich, CT: JAI Press.

Steuerle, C. E., & Bakija, J. M. (1994). *Retooling Social Security for the 21st century: Right & wrong approaches to reform*. Washington, DC: Urban Institute Press.

Stewart, K. J., & Pavalone, J. (1996, April). *Experimental consumer price index for Americans 62 years of age and older*. (CPI Detailed Report, pp. 4–7). Washington, DC: Bureau of Labor Statistics.

Sundén, A. (2000, March). *How will Sweden's new pension system work?* (Issue Brief No. 3). Chestnut Hill, MA: Center for Retirement Research, Boston College.

Thompson, L. H., & Upp, M. M. (1997). The social insurance approach and Social Security. In E. R. Kingson & J. H. Schulz (Eds.), *Social Security in the 21st century* (pp. 3–21). New York: Oxford University Press.

U.S. Department of Health and Human Services. (2000). *Income of the population 55 and over*. Washington, DC: Social Security Administration, Office of Research and Statistics. [On-line]. Available: *http://www.ssa.gov/statistics/incpop55/1998*

U.S. House of Representatives, Committee on Ways and Means. (1998). *Background material and data on programs within the jurisdiction of the Committee on Ways and Means*. Washington, DC: U.S. Government Printing Office.

Williamson, J. B. (1997a). A critique of the case for privatizing Social Security. *The Gerontologist, 37*, 561–571.

Williamson, J. B. (1997b). Should women support the privatization of Social Security? *Challenge, 40*(4), 97–108

Williamson, J. B., & Pampel, F. C. (1993). *Old-age security in comparative perspective*. New York: Oxford University Press.

Williamson, J. B., & Pampel, F. C. (1998). Does the privatization of social security make sense for developing nations? *International Social Security Review, 51* (4), 3–31.

Williamson, J. B., & Rix, S. E. (2000). Social Security reform: Implications for women. *Journal of Aging and Social Policy 11*(4), 41–68.

Williamson, J. B., & Watts-Roy, D. M. (1999). Framing the generational equity debate. In J. B. Williamson, D. M. Watts-Roy, & E. R. Kingson (Eds.), *The generational equity debate* (3–37). New York: Columbia University Press.

Twenty-One

The Financing and Organization of Health Care

Judith Feder, Harriet L. Komisar, and Marlene Niefeld

I. Introduction

The focus of this chapter is the nature of medical and long-term care financing and organization for the elderly population of the United States—its strengths, its limitations, and the policy and political issues it raises, particularly as a growing proportion of Americans become seniors. In contrast to all other age groups, almost all Americans age 65 and over are guaranteed health insurance by the federal government, regardless of their incomes or health status. Since 1965, this entitlement has contributed significantly to the health and financial security of elderly people (Moon, 1996). Today, however, the guarantee falls well short of care needs, most notably for prescription drugs and long-term care.

Before engaging in an analysis of this situation, it is worth considering how the United States came to single out older people for guaranteed health insurance, in comparison with most other industrialized nations in which government assures protection to people of all ages (Anderson & Poullier, 1999). The answer reflects a combination of political and economic conditions emerging in the

United States after World War II. At about the same time Great Britain was adopting national health insurance, the American Congress rejected it—one of several occasions over the 20th century when proponents failed to make government responsibility for health care politically palatable (Le Grand, 1999; Starr, 1982). However, this failure to enact public insurance protection was followed by the emergence of private health insurance protection through employment as the prime source of health insurance for most Americans. The next attempt to enact public health insurance—in the 1960s—was successful (though not easy) but focused on the retirees that employment coverage was unlikely to reach. Proponents of national health insurance saw targeting as a tactic, that is, a first step toward universal coverage (Ball, 1995). But it remained the only step.

In essence, over the latter half of the 20th century, employer-sponsored private health insurance—encouraged by tax subsidies—"crowded out" the potential for government-sponsored health insurance for all Americans. Today, about three-fourths of workers are offered health insurance through the workplace (O'Brien

Handbook of Aging and the Social Sciences, Fifth Edition

& Feder, 1999). However, experts agree that employer coverage will never reach everyone. Indeed, in 1999, 42 million Americans—disproportionately low-wage workers and their families—were without any health insurance protection at all (Fronstin, 2001).

Efforts to establish a government guarantee for health insurance have not disappeared. The most recent effort and, perhaps, most dramatic failure, occurred in 1994 (see Johnson & Broder, 1997). Furthermore, since that time, skepticism about government's role in insurance protection has extended beyond initiatives to expand insurance coverage to reconsideration of the coverage already in place through the Medicare program. The following analysis of coverage and gaps in coverage among the elderly— and the future of that coverage— can therefore be read as part of the broader tension in American health policy between social and individual responsibility.

II. Financing and Organization of Medical and Long-Term Care

Medical care and long-term care differ vastly in their delivery systems and financing. Medical care consists of services and products for preventing, diagnosing, and treating health conditions, usually delivered by or under the direction of physicians, in their offices, or at hospitals, clinics, or other facilities. Long-term care, in contrast, consists predominantly of assistance in basic activities—such as bathing, using the toilet, getting around the house, preparing meals, or shopping for necessities—for people who need this help because of a physical or mental condition or disability. Most elderly people with long-term care needs receive this type of care at home from relatives and friends, but nearly half use formal, paid

long-term care services—provided at home or in nursing homes (Komisar & Niefeld, 2000; Krauss & Altman, 1998). Long-term care, unlike medical care, is not widely insured. Medicare provides only limited coverage of nursing home and home health services. The federal and state Medicaid program—which finances about 40% of national spending for long-term care—only covers elderly people who are poor or who become poor after exhausting their resources on health and long-term care needs (Feder, Komisar, & Niefeld, 2000).

A. Medical Care

Nearly all Americans age 65 and older (as well as some younger disabled people and those with end-stage renal disease) have insurance for medical care from Medicare, a public insurance system managed by the federal government. Since its enactment, Medicare has dramatically improved the access of seniors to medical care and contributed to their financial security (Moon, 1996). But Medicare has substantial gaps in benefits and financing. As a result, other sources of financing play important roles for seniors. In 1996, Medicare financed over half (56%) of the medical care spending (including spending for home health care) of the non-institutionalized elderly population (Cohen, Machlin, Zuvekas, Stagnitti, & Thorpe, 2000). Private insurance was the next greatest source of financing, paying for nearly one-fifth (19%), followed by direct out-of-pocket spending, which accounted for 15%. The remainder was paid for by Medicaid (4%), and other private and public sources (5%).

1. Medicare

Medicare benefits are organized into two parts, financed through distinct mechanisms, each covering a specified set of benefits. Part A covers inpatient hospital services, short-term care in skilled nursing facilities, hospice care, and some home health care. Part B covers physician services, outpatient hospital services, diagnostic laboratory services, ambulatory surgical services, some home health care, and some preventive health services. Most covered services require significant beneficiary cost sharing and, unlike most private insurance, there is no cap on out-of-pocket spending (Health Care Financing Administration, 2001). Furthermore, some vital services are not covered—most importantly, outpatient prescription drugs and most long-term care. Part A—which accounted for 61% of Medicare expenditures in 1999—is financed almost entirely by a payroll tax paid by current employers and employees (Board of Trustees, Federal Hospital Insurance Trust Fund, 2000). In contrast, Part B is partially financed by beneficiary premiums ($50 per month in 2001), which in total pay for about one-fourth of Part B spending, and by general federal government revenue (Board of Trustees, Federal Supplementary Medical Insurance Trust Fund, 2000).

For the vast majority of beneficiaries, Medicare pays for medical care in the fee-for-service system. But Medicare managed care plans (such as health maintenance organizations) offered under the Medicare+Choice program (also called Part C) are an option for beneficiaries in some locations. Currently, about 14% of beneficiaries are enrolled in these private health plans (Health Care Financing Administration, January 2001). Plans contract with Medicare to provide all of the Part A and Part B benefits to enrollees, for which the plan receives a fixed, per person ("capitated") payment rate, which is adjusted for geographical location and selected beneficiary characteristics such as age and gender (Dubow, 2000). Plans have attracted enrollees by offering low cost sharing and, often, additional benefits such as prescription drug coverage,

although recently these benefits have been eroding (Health Care Financing Administration, September 1999). In exchange, enrollees typically must use only the plan's set of providers.

2. Medicaid

For older persons with low income and assets, and for many other elderly people who need extensive long-term care, Medicaid plays a crucial role. In 1996, about 11% of elderly Medicare beneficiaries were also enrolled in Medicaid (Moon, in press). Compared with other elderly Medicare beneficiaries, these "dual eligibles" are more likely to be in poor health and to be age 85 or older. An analysis of elderly dual eligibles in four states found that, in 1995, nearly half used Medicaid or Medicare long-term care services, primarily in nursing homes, and—reflecting their poorer health status—they used more hospital and physician services, on average, than other Medicare beneficiaries (Komisar, Feder, & Gilden, 2000).

About 9 in 10 dual eligibles qualify for the full array of Medicaid benefits available under their state's program, which fill most of Medicare's gaps (Alliance for Health Reform, 1997). Although the scope of benefits varies from state to state, for these dual eligibles Medicaid typically pays for prescription drugs and nursing home care, and often for eyeglasses, hearing aids, dental care, and transportation for medical care. In addition, Medicaid pays the Medicare premium for dual eligibles and may pay their Medicare cost-sharing amounts. About one-tenth of dual eligibles, however, qualify only for more limited help from Medicare. For some, Medicaid pays for Medicare's premiums and may pay Medicare's cost-sharing requirements; for others, Medicaid only pays, or pays in part, Medicare's Part B premium (Komisar, Feder, & Gilden, 2000).

3. Private Supplemental Insurance

Mainly because of Medicare's gaps, the majority of elderly Medicare beneficiaries also have private insurance coverage. In 1996, 27% had individual "Medigap" policies and 36% had plans sponsored by a former or current employer (Moon, in press). (For most of the elderly, such private coverage is a secondary payer after Medicare, but for people age 65 to 69 who are working, Medicare is a secondary payer after employer-sponsored coverage.) Individual Medigap policies are paid for in full by subscribers. Although most employer-sponsored plans are subsidized by the employer, about 40% of employers who offer retiree plans require Medicare-eligible retirees to pay the full cost of the plan (U.S. Department of Health and Human Services, 2000).

Despite improvements during the past decade, the Medigap market continues to be plagued by problems, which have recently led to deteriorating coverage. To reduce confusion about coverage and difficulty in comparing policies, the Omnibus Budget Reconciliation Act of 1990 restricts insurers to selling only policies that conform to 10 standardized benefit packages, though previously purchased, nonconforming policies can be renewed (Fox, Rice, & Alecxih, 1995). It also prohibits insurers from denying a policy to elderly Medicare beneficiaries during their first 6 months of Part B enrollment. Nonetheless, remaining problems in the Medigap market are currently eroding the availability and affordability of coverage: individuals with certain health conditions face a limited choice of policies (because of medical underwriting); most premiums increase automatically as subscribers age, making them less affordable, and overall premium rates are rising (Alecxih, Lutzky, Sevek, & Claxton, 1997). Rising premiums probably reflect not only increasing health-care costs, but also declining purchase of these policies by relatively

healthy elderly people. As premiums rise, relatively healthier people drop out, worsening the affordability problems for the purchasers who remain. At the same time, employer-sponsored coverage of retirees is also declining as some employers drop retiree coverage altogether and others raise premiums (U.S. Department of Health and Human Services, 2000).

Although Medicare+Choice managed care plans can serve as an alternative to Medigap insurance—typically at lower cost—recent trends indicate that this option, too, is eroding. Recent constraints on Medicare payments have made plans' participation in Medicare less profitable. Fewer plans are participating in Medicare +Choice, their benefits are shrinking, and premiums are rising. Between December 1998 and January 2001, the number of Medicare+Choice plans participating in Medicare fell by nearly half, from 346 to 174, reducing choice among plans and the range of geographic areas in which plans are available (Health Care Financing Administration, September 1999; Health Care Financing Administration, January 2001). Although enrollment has not dropped as steeply—in part because some enrollees shifted to other Medicare+Choice plans—participation in these plans dropped by 12% between December 1999 and January 2001 (Health Care Financing Administration, December 1999; Health Care Financing Administration, January 2001). Furthermore, recent trends indicate that even though premiums are rising, the benefits offered by Medicare+Choice plans are declining —specifically, many plans have adopted more restrictive dollar caps, as well as greater copayment rates for prescription drugs (Health Care Financing Administration, September 1999).

4. Out-of-Pocket Spending

The gaps in Medicare's benefits, the incomplete coverage of supplemental insurance, and the premiums for both Medicare and private supplemental coverage lead to substantial out-of-pocket medical care costs for the elderly. Lack of supplemental coverage and high costs of medical care present barriers to obtaining care for many seniors who have low incomes, but are not sufficiently poor to qualify for Medicaid.

Prescription drugs are a prominent and growing source of out-of-pocket expenses, reflecting both the lack of or limited drug coverage in many supplemental plans, and the high cost sharing that beneficiaries incur even when they do have supplemental coverage. In December 1996, 39% of community-based Medicare beneficiaries (of all ages) had no drug coverage (Stuart, Shea, & Briesacher, 2000). Drug coverage is much more common in employer-based plans and Medicare managed care plans than in individual Medigap policies—about 84% of community-based Medicare beneficiaries with employer-based supplemental coverage had drug coverage in December 1996, compared with only 35% of those with Medigap policies. But as drug expenditures continue to grow more rapidly than other health expenses, drug coverage has been eroding. Not only have Medicare managed care plans cut back coverage, but employers also report that they are considering cutting back drug coverage in their retiree plans (Health Care Financing Administration, September 1999; U.S. Department of Health and Human Services, 2000).

Overall, the elderly spend a substantial share of income on health care. In 1999, community-based elderly beneficiaries spent an estimated average of $2,430, or 19% of income, out-of-pocket for health services and insurance premiums, excluding spending on home care (Gross & Brangan, 1999). Insurance premiums account for nearly half (46%) of out-of-pocket spending: Medicare Part B premiums are 19%, and private insurance premiums (including any Medicare+Choice premiums) are 27%. Prescription drugs account for nearly one-fifth (17%) of out-of-pocket spending. The other 37% is for Medicare cost sharing and services Medicare does not cover, such as dental care. Among community-based seniors with income below the poverty threshold (see chapter 19 by Crown, this volume), out-of-pocket expenses consumed one-third of income, on average.

B. Long-Term Care

In contrast to medical care, for which Medicare provides protection regardless of an elderly person's income, long-term care services are largely financed by the means-tested Medicaid program. Medicare only finances long-term care tangentially, through its skilled nursing facility and home health care benefits. These benefits consist primarily of short-term rehabilitative care, typically following medical treatment, although people eligible for this care may also receive personal care services along with it. Overall, Medicare financed about one-fifth of national spending for nursing home and home-based care in 1998 (Feder et al., 2000). (Because the available data include rehabilitative, medically related care along with personal care services, they probably indicate a somewhat larger role for Medicare than they otherwise would.) Medicaid is the largest source of financing for long-term care services, accounting for two-fifths of national nursing home and home-care spending. Because few people have private insurance coverage for long-term care services, this source accounted for less than one-tenth of financing. People with long-term care needs and their families paid directly out-of-pocket for over one-quarter of long-term care services (Feder, et al., 2000).

One in five elderly people need long-term care. Just over three-quarters of this population live in the community, and just under a quarter reside in nursing homes (Komisar & Niefeld, 2000; Krauss & Altman, 1998). About two-thirds of home-dwelling elderly people who receive help with long-term care needs rely on help solely from family and friends (Liu, Manton, & Aragon, 2000). Given the high costs of long-term care—averaging approximately $56,000 annually for nursing home care in 1998 (Health Care Financing Administration, 2000) and more than $15,000 annually for substantially impaired people receiving five weekly visits at home (Stucki & Mulvey, 2000), individuals needing to purchase this care face a substantial financial burden.

1. Medicare

Medicare has always provided some benefits for skilled nursing facility and home health services. But these benefits were originally designed to mainly substitute for hospital care, and therefore were limited to medically related and rehabilitation services. Litigation and regulatory changes in the late 1980s broadened the interpretation of Medicare's coverage of home health care (U.S. General Accounting Office, 1996). The revisions effectively made a wider range of beneficiaries eligible for home health and allowed them to receive more visits than under prior practices (Komisar & Feder, 1998). Even near the height of Medicare's home health expansion in the mid-1990s, however, only 10% of disabled elderly beneficiaries who received assistance at home reported receiving Medicare-financed home care during the prior week (Liu, Manton, & Aragon, 2000). Recent policy changes enacted in the Balanced Budget Act of 1997 created incentives for home health agencies to limit the volume of care—especially for the patients needing the most care (Komisar & Feder, 1998). Spending growth has dropped sharply, a number of home health agencies have

closed or reduced capacity, and some beneficiaries—particularly, those with chronic and intensive needs—are facing greater difficulty in obtaining home health services (Levit et al., 2000; Medicare Payment Advisory Commission, 2000).

2. Medicaid

The federal and state Medicaid program is explicitly responsible for financing long-term care for older people who are poor or who have little income and assets left after paying for medical or long-term care expenses. There are a number of ways elderly people qualify for Medicaid. The primary ones are (a) as recipients of Supplemental Security Income (SSI); (b) as "medically needy" under state-specific rules; or (c) as nursing home residents with income and assets below a state-designated cap. Federal rules entitle elderly and disabled individuals to Medicaid benefits if their incomes and assets are sufficiently low to qualify them for the SSI cash assistance program—in 2000, income below $550 per month, and non-housing assets of not more than $2,000, for an individual (Social Security Administration, 2001). About two-thirds of states permit people to become eligible for Medicaid under "medically needy" programs, which allow people to exclude their medical and long-term care expenses from income in determining whether they meet specified income limits (Schneider, Fennel, & Keenan, 1999). States also have the option of covering nursing home residents with incomes below a state set cap of up to three times the SSI level. Furthermore, in states without medically needy coverage for nursing home residents, these residents may be able to use income trusts (known as Miller trusts) that are similar in effect to medically needy programs in allowing nursing home residents with incomes above the state cap to qualify for Medicaid (Nemore, April 1999). Nursing home residents covered by Medicaid must contribute all their income except a small personal needs allowance toward the cost of care (Merlis, 1999). In the case of one spouse living in the community while the other is institutionalized, the community spouse is allowed higher income and asset levels, which vary by state. Even with Medicaid's restrictions on eligibility, about two-thirds of nursing home residents are covered by the program (Krauss & Altman, 1998).

Medicaid's long-term-care spending is dominated by nursing home expenses, which account for about three-quarters of such expenditures (Burwell, 2000). Despite significant improvements following legislative efforts in the 1980s, concerns about nursing home quality persist (U.S. General Accounting Office, 1999). A further concern is that older people with long-term care needs do not have access to adequate support at home. Although the share of Medicaid's long-term care spending going to home-based care has increased during the past decade—rising from 13% in federal fiscal year 1989 to 26% in fiscal year 1999—eligibility and benefits for home care are limited and differ among geographic areas (Burwell, 2000). States restrict eligibility criteria for home- and community-based services, establish limits on the total number of people enrolled (regardless of eligibility), and target programs to selected areas or population groups within the state to control costs. Such restrictions by states reflect their concern that expanding home- and community-based services for the elderly will increase their total long-term-care budget because many people who would not seek care in a nursing facility would welcome assistance at home.

Because Medicaid is a state-administered program, spending on services varies considerably from state to state. In federal fiscal year 1999, Medicaid spending on long-term care (for persons of all ages) ranged from less than $120 per state resident in five states to more than three times that level in the top four states and the District of Columbia (Burwell, 2000).

3. Private Sources

Private insurance plays only a small part in financing long-term care. Like Medicare, most private health-care insurance provides little coverage of long-term care. Private long-term-care insurance is expensive, and the number of people eligible may be limited by underwriting criteria. A policy with inflation protection and nonforfeiture benefits bought at age 65 cost an average of $2,432 annually in 1996. This level of expense is often not affordable for the elderly, and younger people—for whom private long-term care insurance costs less—rarely buy it (Merlis, 1999). Although the number of people buying private long-term care insurance is growing, as of the end of 1996, fewer than five million policies had ever been sold (Coronel, 1998).

The sizable share of long-term-care costs paid directly out-of-pocket reflects the financing structure described above: the absence of an insurance system, public or private, that spreads the financial risk of needing long-term care and, in its place, reliance on a system that protects people only if they are, or become, impoverished. Limited financing for long-term care leaves many elderly people without needed help. Results from a national survey indicate that in 1995 nearly one-fifth of community-based elderly adults with long-term care needs reported an unmet need for help with basic activities (Komisar & Niefeld, 2000). Some respondents attribute these unmet needs to finding services too expensive, having difficulty finding help, or being ineligible for help from an agency because of income or medical eligibility criteria.

III. Issues for the Future

Current public policy mechanisms for financing medical and long-term care for the elderly have significant strengths and weaknesses. The strengths are the protection against the financial risks of illness and the access to care that Medicare and Medicaid provide. The weaknesses are the risks that elderly people continue to face (most particularly for the costs of prescription drugs and long-term care), while policymakers face the challenges of managing costs and assuring the quality of insurance protection. This mix of strengths and weaknesses reflects a tension in our political and policy processes between commitment to government's role in spreading risk, on the one hand, and concern about "excessive" taxes and government intervention on the other.

As we begin the 21st century, the tension between commitment and concern is rising, in part because the aging of the baby-boom cohort will increase the demands on government programs and public resources, and in part because of political trends that challenge the appropriateness and efficiency of reliance on government to meet even current demands. The future of financing and organization of medical and long-term care for the elderly will be determined by the resolution of this tension, particularly in three areas: the perpetuation or modification of Medicare's role for all the elderly, the nature of extra protections for low-income elderly beneficiaries, and the extension of insurance protection for long-term care.

A. The Future of Medicare

Since the mid-1990s, Medicare—its financing, its structure, and its benefits—has been at the center of debate about the size of the federal budget and the role of the federal government. Key policy issues have been the adequacy of Medicare's ex-

isting revenue sources (with heavy reliance on the payroll tax) to support health-care spending for a growing elderly population; the appropriate role of private insurers and a competitive market in offering Medicare benefits; and the failure of Medicare's benefits to reflect changes in medical treatment, most notably, with respect to prescription drugs (see chapter 22 by Kane & Kane, this volume). Underlying each of these issues, however, are some fundamental value questions about society's willingness to devote an increasing share of resources to the growing proportion of elderly citizens; diminished confidence in government and increasing pursuit of privatization; and whether commitment to social insurance or means testing should be the basis for distributing benefits to the elderly.

1. Adequacy of Medicare's Financing

Medicare's financing problem is relatively straightforward. At some point in the foreseeable future, the revenues Medicare relies upon will become insufficient to cover its expenses. Specifically, the payroll tax that funds Part A will fall short of Medicare expenses. The shortfall reflects two factors. First, health-care costs (not just for Medicare but for the system as a whole) rise faster than payroll (National Academy of Social Insurance, 1999). Second, as members of the baby boom turn age 65 and become eligible for Medicare, the number of people who depend upon the payroll tax will grow much faster than the number of workers who pay it. In 1970, there were 3.7 workers for each beneficiary; in 2015, there will be fewer than 3 workers per beneficiary and by 2030, about 2 (Board of Trustees, Federal Hospital Insurance Trust Fund, 2000). Even for Part B of Medicare—for which spending is not financed by revenue from a dedicated tax—growth in health-care costs per capita and in the number of beneficiaries implies that

Medicare will absorb a greater share of general tax revenues than it does today.

Recent policy actions have substantially slowed growth in Medicare spending and, in combination with the revenues generated by economic growth, delayed the time when resources are projected to be exhausted under the current program. Today, estimates are that the Part A Hospital Insurance Trust Fund runs out in 2025 (Board of Trustees, Federal Hospital Insurance Trust Fund, 2000); as recently as 1997, the estimated date was 2001 (Board of Trustees, Federal Hospital Insurance Trust Fund, 1997). On the expenditure side, this experience shows that even a one-time reduction in spending dramatically reduces cost projections for the future.

The lesson from recent experience is not that Medicare has no long term financing problem; it does. Rather, the lesson is that balancing revenues and expenditures is a problem, not a crisis, and that the problem is both less predictable and more manageable than has previously been assumed.

What, then, is the appropriate policy response? The answer depends upon whether the focus is solely on reducing program costs or, instead, on assuring affordable health insurance to the growing elderly population. The political debate has focused more on reducing costs—primarily through "restructuring"—than on raising revenues. Yet the evidence shows that even in light of the projections of the most recent trustees' report, assuring the adequacy of Medicare's financing to support, at a minimum, the protection that Medicare now provides, requires some additional revenue (National Academy of Social Insurance, 1999).

Medicare's (and the economy's) recent positive performance suggests that a combination of Medicare's traditional cost-containment tools and modest revenue increases would be adequate to address Medicare's financial needs. To illustrate

the size of the future revenue gap, the Trustees of the Hospital Insurance trust fund projected, in 2000, that a .605 percentage point increase in the 1.45% payroll tax on both employers and employees would make the trust fund solvent for 75 years (Board of Trustees, Federal Hospital Insurance trust fund, 2000). However, calls for "restructuring" Medicare continue to dominate, and the political process has produced few advocates of new revenues to secure Medicare's future. Because financing for the Medicare program is now expected to be sufficient until 2025 the sense of urgency to completely reform the system has dissipated.

2. Changes in Medicare's Structure[1]

Initiated by fiscal concerns and fueled by the "managed care revolution" outside the Medicare system, policy proposals to modernize and "restructure" Medicare have taken center stage. "Restructuring" has become a catchall word that, for the most part, means remodeling Medicare's single insurance system into a competitive market. To that end, proposals for Medicare's restructuring would shift Medicare's structure from a government-run "defined benefit" program—that is, a program entitling beneficiaries to a defined set of benefits or medical services, purchased directly, as well as paid for, by the government—to a "defined contribution" program entitling beneficiaries to a voucher usable for the purchase of insurance from private insurers as well as the government-run program. The terms that define the voucher and its use vary across proposals, most importantly in the degree to which they separate the value of the voucher from the price of the health insurance to which it applies. At one end of the spectrum fall proposals that would

[1] Section III. A. 2 is adapted from J. Feder and M. Moon, "Can Medicare survive its saviors?" *American Prospect* May–June, pp. 56–60. © 1999 American Prospect.

define the voucher as a fixed dollar amount, prescribed in law. At the other end fall proposals—called "premium support" proposals—that would tie the value of the voucher to the costs of health insurance plans from which beneficiaries could choose—for example, by setting it equal to the average cost of available plans.

The approaches are similar in promoting competition by making beneficiaries sensitive to the price of the insurance plan they choose. In theory, a market of health insurance plans competing for the vouchers of price-sensitive beneficiaries will promote efficient purchase and delivery of health-care services, thereby containing Medicare's costs.

However, approaches promoting competition differ in the degree to which they limit government or taxpayer liabilities. With fixed dollar vouchers, government liabilities are predetermined and can be set consistent with available revenues. If health-care costs exceed the value of the vouchers—as would be likely if, for example, they were set to increase at the rate of general inflation—beneficiaries, not taxpayers, would bear the risks. By contrast, with vouchers tied to the cost of plans, the program continues to share the risk with beneficiaries.

Regardless of approach, the shift away from a government-run defined benefit program to a defined contribution program challenges some fundamental principles underlying the Medicare program. As enacted in 1965, Medicare's structure reflected commitment to three fundamental principles regarding health care for the elderly: that insurance is the right way to spread the risk of sizable health-care costs; that redistributing income through the tax system is necessary to make that insurance affordable and universal; and that the insurance and taxes are best administered by the federal government if the system is to serve all elderly people, regardless of their income or health status.

Whatever its form, competition among private insurance plans for beneficiaries' vouchers runs counter to these principles of risk-spreading, redistribution, and government management. First, competition among health plans creates incentives for insurers and consumers that fragment the risk pool, separating the healthy from the sick. Second, vouchers threaten universal affordability, regardless of income. Even with vouchers tied to the costs of competing health plans, access to particular plans will vary with beneficiaries' ability to pay. Third, reliance on a private market threatens public accountability for health insurance protection. Academic advocates of competition recognize that if competition is to promote efficient service delivery rather than avoidance of risk and denial of care, government oversight is essential. However, whether the necessary rules and resources to enforce them will be forthcoming is subject to question.

Additionally, and perhaps most interesting about the restructuring debate, is that only in its extreme form—fixed dollar vouchers—does it address the financing problem that it is ostensibly trying to solve. Analysis shows that this competition would do little more to reduce Medicare's per capita costs than Medicare can already achieve using traditional cost controls. The recent slowdown in Medicare spending illustrates Medicare's longstanding ability to obtain the discounts in purchasing that private managed care plans discovered only in the 1990s. Medicare's costs have historically grown more slowly than the private sector—primarily because Medicare already takes advantage of the discounting strategy that the private sector has only recently employed (Moon, 1999). The only way to substantially exceed Medicare's performance is to constrain vouchers to growth rates well below the growth in health-care costs—shifting financial burdens to the beneficiaries rather than eliminating them through efficiencies.

Reflecting a change in values, the political process has, however, produced a marked acceptance of the need to restructure. Debate focuses less on the desirability of competition than on its form. So far, significant differences in reform proposals and a variety of external elements have prevented agreement. Medicare's and the economy's outstanding recent performance have eliminated a sense of urgency. The backlash against managed care among the working-age population promotes skepticism about competition. And electoral politics opens aggressive reformers to charges that they are 'destroying' Medicare. However, prosperity is unlikely to last forever; health-care costs will likely take off again, and political winds can shift. Whether and in what form Medicare will sustain its fundamental features of universality and redistribution remain to be seen.

3. Changes in Medicare's Benefits

Fiscal and budgetary issues put Medicare's future on the political agenda in the 1990s. But, once there, the inadequacies in its benefits also attracted considerable attention. As described above, Medicare's benefit package leaves beneficiaries with considerable out-of-pocket costs for premiums and cost sharing for services Medicare covers and the full costs of services that Medicare does not cover. Most notable among the latter are outpatient prescription drugs and long-term care.

Expansion of Medicare to cover either prescription drugs or long-term care would represent a major new role—and a sizable fiscal commitment—for the federal government. As described below, long-term care would likely be a bigger stretch in this regard; the appropriateness and willingness to finance public insurance for long-term care are subject to considerable question. Furthermore, although long-term care can represent a catastrophic cost for elderly (and younger) people who need it, this group is a minority of the elderly population. Prescription drug expenses, on the other hand, affect a substantial portion of the elderly.

Moreover, changes in standard medical care—and in the benefits of private, employer-sponsored insurance—call the continued absence of prescription drug coverage in Medicare into question. When Medicare was enacted, prescription drugs played a minor role in medical treatment and were not included in standard employer-based insurance. Today, prescription drugs have become a critical element of medical care and spending. Accordingly, for most of the working-age population, insurance plans have expanded to cover them. Because Medicare's benefits have not similarly adapted, they now fall far short of providing what is generally regarded as standard insurance protection.

Stimulated by the attractiveness of expansions rather than contractions in an election year, interest in a new drug benefit actually eclipsed Medicare restructuring as a political issue in 2000. The availability of affordable supplemental coverage had declined. Increasing prescription drug costs led employers to cut back benefits for retirees and raised premiums for Medigap policies. Managed care plans, which had initially used low-premium or even no-premium drug benefits to attract enrollees, cut back benefits in response to cutbacks in Medicare payment levels. As a result, the absence of drug coverage in Medicare became a bigger problem than was true a few years earlier.

Although there is a growing political consensus on the need to include drug coverage, there is considerable political debate on how to do it. Policy and political problems abound—including the high and rising cost of drugs, the pharmaceutical industry's fears of cost containment, and easily generated hostility to policies construed as "big government." Consistent with broader questions about

Medicare's future, two distinct approaches have emerged. One is to incorporate a new, but limited, prescription drug benefit in Medicare, for which premiums and cost sharing would be substantial. As with current Medicare benefits, protection against premium and cost-sharing costs for low-income beneficiaries would be provided through Medicaid. The second approach would, instead, target a new government drug benefit to low-income seniors; that is, it would take a means-tested rather than a universal approach. In some versions, it would also subsidize the purchase of private insurance through Medigap insurers and managed care plans for higher income seniors.

Both approaches have strengths and weaknesses in the adequacy of their protection. But the debate surrounding them is perhaps even more interesting for the values and philosophies it reveals. Neither proposal entails the social insurance approach of Medicare's hospital benefit; that is, they do not involve a mandatory contribution or dedicated tax establishing entitlement to benefits. The first approach, nevertheless, would build on Medicare's universality, while the second rejects it. The first approach would strengthen public insurance; the second would promote private insurance.

Interestingly, today's debate bears a marked resemblance to the debate that preceded Medicare's enactment. At that time, universality and means testing were also juxtaposed. Also similar are the issues of government "control" over industry (in this case, the pharmaceutical industry) raised by a new public benefit. It remains unclear how this debate will be resolved, but its resolution will likely reflect more skepticism about both government and industry, and less commitment to community and public spending, than were present in the 1960s when Medicare was created.

B. Insurance Protection for Low-Income Elderly

Designed to provide equal benefits to all eligible people regardless of income, Medicare has always posed financial barriers and burdens for low-income elderly. Helping low-income people with those barriers and burdens has always been the responsibility of Medicaid, an explicitly means-tested and totally separate program. This combination of a social insurance with a means-tested program serves both a policy and a political purpose: it provides the extra support that is essential for adequate protection for low-income people, while protecting the core program against the political risk of redistributing taxpayer dollars from better off individuals to the poor.

Reliance on states to decide how and how much to supplement Medicare poses significant issues in the adequacy and nature of health insurance for low-income people. First, it leads to considerable variation and, in many places, inadequacies in the support low- and modest-income people receive. Second, it creates what might be described as a fiscal tug-of-war between the federal and state governments, with the potential to undermine the Medicare entitlement for low-income people.

Federal law provides a mix of federal requirements and state discretion regarding Medicaid's role in supplementing Medicare. In general, states must provide full Medicaid benefits to all Supplemental Security Income (SSI) recipients and may assure their Medicare participation by paying the premiums on their behalf—that is, "buying them in." For Medicare beneficiaries with incomes above the SSI level, however, how much states can do and must do has varied over time. In the mid-1980s, federal law gave states the option to use Medicaid funds to pay Medicare cost sharing and premiums for Medicare beneficiaries with incomes above SSI but not greater than the poverty level and to pay premiums for beneficiaries with incomes up to 20% above the poverty level. The option became a mandate in 1989, creating a sore point in federal and state relations that lasted for many years. In 1997—at the same time that federal law extended Medicaid support for premiums to beneficiaries with incomes up to 135% of the poverty level—flexibility was explicitly given to states to reduce their contributions to Medicare cost sharing for beneficiaries with incomes below poverty.

In practice, the protections are problematic for low-income people in many parts of the country, with respect to support for both premiums and cost sharing. Recent estimates are that among noninstitutionalized Medicare beneficiaries with income below poverty, only about 55% participate. Participation rates fall even lower for eligible beneficiaries with slightly higher incomes, a result that analysts and advocates attribute to many states' reluctance to use recognized tools to make the program more accessible (Barents Group, 1999). Furthermore, many states have taken advantage of new flexibility to limit cost sharing support. Even before the legislative change, only 31 states reported paying Medicare cost sharing in full. Two years later (in 1999), only 16 states followed that policy (Nemore, 1999). Federal law prohibits providers from charging beneficiaries for amounts that Medicaid does not pay. But the resulting lower fees are likely to limit low-income beneficiaries' access to care.

The tension between the federal and state governments is not limited to Medicare supplementation; it has also begun to affect the nature of service delivery. In the 1990s, state Medicaid programs, like private employers, aggressively moved away from fee-for-service and into managed care. However, federal law prohibits states from requiring Medicare beneficiaries to participate in managed care plans. Although states share federal policy makers' concern about the inexperience of managed care plans dealing with a chronically ill rather than a predominantly healthy population (Retchin, Brown, Yeh, Chu, & Moreno, 1997; Shaughnessy, Schlenker, & Hittle, 1994; Ware, Bayliss, Rogers, Kosinski, & Tarlov, 1996; Schnelle et al., 1999), states nevertheless find the concept of capitation for Medicare and Medicaid services in combination to be highly attractive from a fiscal perspective (Friedland & Feder, 1998). Currently, states have little ability to control service use by Medicare beneficiaries and, as a result, the scope of their cost-sharing obligations. Furthermore, if they do control service use, it is Medicare and the federal treasury that reap the primary fiscal rewards. Capitation that combines Medicare and Medicaid funds would give states control over both programs, allowing states to capture savings in Medicaid expenditures that many assert would come from integrating acute and long-term-care services.

What is fiscally advantageous to states, however, is questionable from the perspectives of the federal government and beneficiaries. In essence, this combined capitated approach transforms Medicare from a benefit program for individuals to a block grant to states. As such, it abdicates federal control over federal dollars. For beneficiaries, it represents the loss of the Medicare entitlement and puts the most vulnerable beneficiaries—poor elderly people who need considerable medical and long-term care—at considerable risk.

As long as financing of extra support for low-income seniors is shared with the states, fiscal, policy, and political tension will persist. Clearly, states prefer to make their own fiscal choices, rather than simply accept the fiscal consequences of federal rules. Furthermore, from an equity perspective, they can object to rules requiring them to spend more on elderly than on other low-income Medicaid beneficiaries. With the federal–state partnership, then, comes the inevitable risk that the elderly poor will be treated more like other poor people, regardless of age, than like other seniors, regardless of income. Deciding how to manage that risk is necessary not only with respect to existing Medicare benefits but to the structure of any new benefits, for example, prescription drugs.

Two solutions to this federal–state structure are available: federalize the financing of means-tested health insurance for low-income elderly, as income support for the poor elderly was federalized with the establishment of SSI; or federalize health insurance for all low-income people, regardless of age, with protection on a par with Medicare benefits. Though the first option has received more attention than the second, neither has been adopted. The split in financial responsibility between the federal and state governments is likely to remain a political issue with significant consequences for beneficiaries for a long time to come.

C. Financing Long-Term Care

Medicare was explicitly designed to exclude protection for long-term care, and Medicaid has partially filled the breach. As a result, people are not insured against the financial catastrophe associated with the need for extensive long-term care services; rather, they get support for services only after financial catastrophe strikes. The burdens this situation poses for individuals—and the variation in protection for them across states—are not yet visible on the policy or political agenda. As described above, social insurance is under siege even for benefits Medicare already covers; and prescription drugs are ahead of long-term care on the policy agenda, if an expansion is to occur.

A variety of factors explain the political reluctance to address long-term care concerns (Feder, 1999). First, politicians perceive long-term care differently from medical care. Unlike medical care, most long-term care is not a very sophisticated or technical service; it is assumed to be a burden with which people can cope. Furthermore, it is a burden that is mistakenly presumed to be an inevitable consequence of aging, one for which people should themselves plan in advance by accumulating sufficient wealth to finance it. Finally, because people who need long-term care are perceived as about to die, governmental financial support for it is perceived as "bequest preservation"— enabling assets to be passed along through inheritance rather than spent on long-term care—a questionable role for scarce public resources. All these views can be challenged. Needs exceed families' extraordinary efforts to cope; insurance is clearly appropriate for the unpredictable, catastrophic burdens associated with long-term-care; not all long-term care users are close to death; and, if estates are preserved for people who die after heart surgery and other acute illnesses, why is it unacceptable for people unlucky enough to need long-term care?

Moreover, politicians are fearful of the expense associated with public insurance protection for long-term-care costs. People may too readily welcome government support for personal care and household needs. Furthermore, critics fear that public support would replace family support. Again evidence should somewhat mitigate these fears. States, and even private insurers, exercise control over service use, and help from family and friends continues when people get paid help (Hanley, Wiener, & Harris, 1991; Liu, Manton, & Aragon, 1999). However, given underfunding in the current long-term-care system and the difficulty of effectively designing and managing a public program, costs of a new public program insuring long-term care are likely to be substantial—currently in excess of political willingness to pay.

To the extent that long-term care financing is on the political agenda, commitments are constrained. The Clinton administration proposed the provision of modest tax credits to people with substantial long-term care needs. The proposal did not purport to address long-term care financing; rather, it proposed to provide limited financial assistance to people with substantial financial burdens for medical as well as long-term-care needs. On the insurance front, the focus is on support for private insurance, on grounds that, with a little help, the private market could spread the risk of long-term-care costs, reach a much larger (and a significant) portion of the population, and even reduce burdens on the public sector. Recent estimates by the American Council of Life Insurance (based on relatively generous assumptions about the likelihood that people will purchase private long-term-care insurance) are that private insurance could grow to finance 29% of nursing home costs in 2030, 10 times their estimate of 3% today (Merlis, 1999).

However, reliance on private insurance for future long-term-care needs raises critical policy questions. The first question is the adequacy of the protection private insurance is likely to provide. Observed inadequacies are numerous: market practices that make policies unavailable to people most likely to need long-term care; benefits that cover only a portion of the costs of care and are not guaranteed to keep pace with rising cost or changing practices of care; and the possibility of unanticipated premium increases (even with policies that promise the same premium for the life of the policy). These features of private insurance, which reflect insurers' incentives to limit the risks they face, create a barrier to risk spreading also apparent in the private market for individual health insurance policies. The nation's continued dissatisfaction with the individual health insurance market, which leaves many people most in need of insurance protection unable to afford it, should generate skepticism about following a similar path for long-term care.

A second question is whether tax support for private long-term-care insurance represents an equitable targeting of public resources. Subsidies through the tax system are far more likely to reach the higher than the lower end of the income spectrum—people already able to purchase long-term-care insurance, rather than those who cannot afford it. The Congressional Budget Office (CBO) estimates that even with a significant expansion of long-term-care insurance, a substantial increase in Medicaid spending—from $43 billion estimated in 2000 to $75 billion in 2020 (in year 2000 dollars)—will be necessary in order to assure even current levels of service to low and modest income people (Congressional Budget Office, 1999). Proponents of tax subsidies for private insurance argue that the need for public investment would be even greater in the absence of support for private insurance. CBO estimates that without any private long-term-care insurance, Medicaid long-term-care spending would rise to $88 billion in 2020 (in year 2000 dollars). However, to accept that argument is to assume that investment in public and private support will go hand in hand. In practice, advocacy of subsidies for private insurance is more likely to obscure the need to strengthen direct public support. The end result would be to target resources to the economically advantaged while leaving the disadvantaged at risk.

Expanded social insurance is an alternative to support for private insurance. For example, Medicare could be expanded to include long-term care, entitling all Americans, regardless of income, some insurance protection should they become significantly impaired. However, investment of resources to sustain the social insurance we have (Medicare and Social Security), let alone additional social insurance we might have (for long-term care) is currently subject to considerable debate. Despite the nation's current prosperity and underlying wealth, our willingness to redistribute resources to reflect the aging of the population seems to be in question (Friedland & Summer, 1999).

In these circumstances, better support for the economically disadvantaged—a more adequate means-tested safety net—should be a higher priority. Currently, we expect people to impoverish themselves completely before providing them assistance with long-term care. That system seems excessively harsh. It is also geographically inequitable (because of variation in state practices) and will become more so as the population ages. Analysis of future population growth and resources reveals that growth in the demand for long-term care and the ability to finance it will vary substantially across states as the population ages (Merlis, 1999). To create a stronger and fairer safety net for modest and low-income people will therefore require not just more dollars but more federal dollars to be fully effective.

D. Concluding Thoughts

Underneath the disparate and complicated issues surrounding Medicare's future, protections for low-income seniors, and financing for long-term care lies a clear philosophical and political choice. Will the nation's policy toward medical and long-term care for the elderly build upon and strengthen its commitment to government-guaranteed, universal protection? Or will it contain or scale back government's role, promoting individual responsibility and confidence in the private marketplace? In the political environment of the early 2000s, this choice is by no means limited to the policies that

are the focus of this chapter or even to policy focused on the elderly. It is at the core of virtually every social policy debate—on Social Security, welfare, health insurance coverage, and so on—in which the nation is currently engaged. But given the aging of the baby boom generation and the scope and costs of medical and long-term-care needs it will bring, this philosophical choice will have enormous consequences.

Between the years 2000 and 2030 the number of elderly Americans is expected to double. By 2030, one in five Americans (in contrast to today's one in eight) will be over the age of 65 (U.S. Census Bureau, 2000a, 2000b). Uncertainties abound as to the health, wealth, and technologies available to support this elderly population (Friedland & Summer, 1999). But there is little doubt that more of the nation's resources will be required to sustain even current levels of support for the significantly larger share of its people who will be elderly.

Proponents of individual responsibility and confidence in the marketplace regard current governmental commitments as "unsustainable" for this larger population. Not only do they challenge existing government programs as inefficient, relative to the private sector, they also challenge Americans' willingness to devote any more of their resources to the taxes that support government programs. From this perspective, a shift away from government guarantees becomes inevitable. The shift need not entail a dramatic withdrawal of current programs and benefits. Rather, a gradual replacement of government with market activity may chart a different course for the nation's future than has guided its past.

Proponents of community responsibility and confidence in government, by contrast, emphasize that the nation's resources are growing, not fixed. A richer nation faces choices about how to distribute new wealth, rather than the necessity of depriving one generation to support another. The inevitability, then, lies not in the limits to resources but in the care needs that elderly people and their families will face. From this perspective, it is political choices and fundamental values that will determine future quality of life for elderly people and their families.

Acknowledgments

The preparation of this paper was supported by The Commonwealth Fund. The views presented are those of the authors and should not be attributed to The Commonwealth Fund, or its directors, officers, or staff. The authors are grateful to Donald Jones for outstanding research support. In addition, the manuscript benefited from reviews by the editors and by Marilyn Moon. Section III.A.2 of this chapter draws extensively on Feder, J., & Moon, M. (1999). Can Medicare survive its saviors? *American Prospect*, *May-June*, 56–60.

References

Alliance for Health Reform. (1997). *Managed care and vulnerable Americans: Medicare and Medicaid dual eligibles.* Washington, DC.: Author.

Alecxih, L. M. B., Lutzky, S., Sevek, P., & Claxton, G. (1997). *Key issues affecting accessibility to Medigap insurance.* New York: The Commonwealth Fund.

Anderson, G. F., & Poullier, J. P. (1999). Health spending, access, and outcomes: Trends in industrialized countries. *Health Affairs*, *18*(3), 178–192.

Ball, R. M. (1995). What Medicare's architects had in mind. *Health Affairs*, *14*(4), 62–72.

Barents Group LLC. (1999). *A profile of QMB-eligible and SLMB-eligible Medicare beneficiaries.* Washington, DC: Author.

Board of Trustees, Federal Hospital Insurance Trust Fund. (1997). *1997 annual report of the Federal Hospital Insurance Trust Fund.* Washington, DC: U.S. Government Printing Office.

Board of Trustees, Federal Hospital Insurance Trust Fund. (2000). *2000 annual report of the Federal Hospital Insurance Trust Fund.* Washington, DC: U.S. Government Printing Office.

Board of Trustees, Federal Supplementary Medical Insurance Trust Fund. (2000). *2000 annual report of the Federal Supplementary Medical Insurance Trust Fund.* Washington, DC: U.S. Government Printing Office.

Burwell, B. (2000, April). *Medicaid long-term care expenditures in FY 1999, memorandum.* Cambridge, MA: The MEDSTAT Group.

Cohen, J. W., Machlin, S. R., Zuvekas, S. H., Stagnitti, M. N., & Thorpe, J. M. (2000). Health care expenses in the United States, 1996. *MEPS Research Findings No. 12.* Rockville, MD: Agency for Healthcare Research and Quality.

Congressional Budget Office. (1999). *Projections of expenditures for long-term care services for the elderly.* Washington, DC: Author.

Coronel, S. (1998). *Long-term care insurance in 1996.* Washington, DC: Health Insurance Association of America.

Dubow, J. (2000). *Payment to Medicare +Choice organizations.* Washington, DC: AARP, Public Policy Institute.

Feder, J. (1999). Improving public financing for long-term care: The political challenge. *Journal of Aging and Social Policy*, *10* (3), 1–6.

Feder, J., Komisar, H. L., & Niefeld, M. R. (2000). Long-term care in the United States: An overview. *Health Affairs*, *19*(3), 40–56.

Fox, P. D., Rice T., & Alecxih, L. (1995). Medigap regulation: Lessons for health care reform. *Journal of Health Politics, Policy and Law*, *20*, 31–48.

Friedland, R. B., & Feder, J. (1998). Managed care for elderly people with disabilities and chronic conditions. *Generations*, *XXII*(2), 51–57.

Friedland, R. B., & Summer, L. (1999). *Demography is not destiny.* Washington, DC: National Academy on an Aging Society.

Fronstin, P. (2000). *Sources of health insurance and characteristics of the uninsured: Analysis of the March 2000 Current Population Survey.* (EBRI Issue Brief Number 228.) Washington, DC: Employee Benefit Research Institute.

Gross, D., & Brangan, N. (1999). *Out-of-pocket spending on health are by Medicare beneficiaries age 65 and older: 1999 projections.* Washington, DC: AARP, Public Policy Institute.

Hanley, R. J., Wiener, J. M., & Harris, K. M. (1991). Will paid home care erode informal support? *Journal of Health Politics, Policy and Law, 16,* 507–521.

Health Care Financing Administration. (1999, September). *Medicare+Choice: Changes for the year 2000.* [On-line] Available: http://www.gov/medicare/mc00rept.htm [July 14, 2000].

Health Care Financing Administration. (1999, December). *Medicare managed care contract monthly summary report.* [On-line] Available: http://www.hcfa.gov/stats/mmcc1299.txt [July 17, 2000].

Health Care Financing Administration. (2000). Unpublished data. Office of National Statistics, Office of the Actuary.

Health Care Financing Administration. (2001). *Medicare and you 2001.* (Publication no. HCFA-10050). Baltimore, MD: U.S. Department of Health and Human Services.

Health Care Financing Administration. (2001, January). *Medicare managed care contract monthly summary report.* [On-line] Available: *http://www.hcfa.gov/stats/mmcc0101 .txt* [January 24, 2001].

Johnson, H., & Broder, D. S. (1997). *The System: The American way of politics at the breaking point.* Boston, MA: Little, Brown and Company.

Komisar, H. L., & Feder, J. (1998). *The Balanced Budget Act of 1997: Effects on Medicare's home health benefit and beneficiaries who need long-term care.* New York: The Commonwealth Fund.

Komisar, H. L., Feder, J., & Gilden, D. (2000). *The roles of Medicare and Medicaid in financing health and long-term care for low-income seniors: A chart book on Medicare-Medicaid enrollees in four states.* New York: The Commonwealth Fund.

Komisar, H. L., & Niefeld, M. R. (2000). *Long-term care needs, care arrangements, and unmet needs among community adults: Findings from the National Health Interview Survey on Disability.* (Working Paper no. IWP-00–102). Washington, DC: George-

town University, Institute for Health Care Research and Policy.

Krauss, N. A., & Altman, B. M. (1998). Characteristics of nursing home residents—1996. *MEPS Research Findings No. 5.* Rockville, MD: Agency for Health Care Policy and Research.

Le Grand, J. (1999). Competition, cooperation, or control? Tales from the British National Health Service. *Health Affairs, 18*(3), 27–39.

Levit, K., Cowan, C., Lazenby, H., Sensenig, A., McDonnell, P., Stiller, J., & Martin, A. (2000). Health Spending in 1998: Signals of Change. *Health Affairs, 19*(1), 124–132.

Liu, K., Manton, K. G., & Aragon, C. (2000). *Changes in home care use by older people with disabilities.* Washington, DC: AARP, Public Policy Institute.

Medicare Payment Advisory Commission. (2000, March). *Report to the Congress: Medicare payment policy.* Washington, DC: Author.

Merlis, M. (1999). *Financing long-term care in the twenty-first century: The public and private roles.* New York: The Commonwealth Fund.

Moon, M. (1996). What Medicare has meant to older Americans. *Health Care Financing Review, 18*(2), 49–59.

Moon, M. (1999). *Medicare matters: The value of social insurance.* Washington, DC: Testimony before the Committee on Finance, U.S. Senate, May 27, 1999.

Moon, M. & Storeygard, M. (in press). *Medicare spending by beneficiaries with health problems.* New York: The Commonwealth Fund.

National Academy of Social Insurance, Study Panel on Medicare Financing. (1999). *The financing needs of a restructured Medicare program.* (Medicare Brief). Washington, DC: National Academy of Social Insurance.

Nemore, P. (1999, April). *Income eligibility for Medicaid long-term care services in income cap states.* Washington, DC: National Senior Citizens Law Center.

Nemore, P. (1999). *Variations in state Medicaid buy-in practices, for low-income beneficiaries: A 1999 update.* National Senior Citizens Law Center. Washington, DC: The Henry J. Kaiser Family Foundation.

O'Brien, E., & Feder, J. (1999). *Employment-based health insurance coverage and its de-*

cline: *The growing plight of low-wage workers.* Washington, DC: The Henry J. Kaiser Family Foundation.

Retchin, S. M., Brown, R. S., Yeh, S. J., Chu, D., & Moreno, L. (1997). Outcomes of stroke patients in Medicare fee-for-service and managed care. *Journal of the American Medical Association, 278,* 119–124.

Schneider, A., Fennel, K., & Keenan, P. (1999). Medicaid eligibility for the elderly. Kaiser Commission on the Future of Medicaid. Washington, DC: The Henry J. Kaiser Family Foundation.

Schnelle, J. F., Ouslander, J. G., Buchanan, J., Zellman, G., Farley, D., Hirsch, S. H., & Reuben, D. B. (1999). Objective and subjective measure of the quality of managed care in nursing homes. *Medical Care, 37,* 375–383.

Shaughnessy, P., Schlenker, R. E., & Hittle, D. F. (1994). Home health care outcomes under capitated and fee-for-service payment. *Health Care Financing Review, 16*(1), 187–222.

Social Security Administration. (2001). *A desktop guide to SSI eligibility requirements.* (SSA publication no. 05–11001). Washington, DC: U.S. Government Printing Office.

Starr, P. (1982). *The social transformation of American medicine.* New York: Basic Books.

Stuart, B., Shea, D., & Briesacher, B. (2000). *Prescription drug costs for Medicare beneficiaries: Coverage and health status matter.* Issue Brief. New York: The Commonwealth Fund.

Stucki, B. R., & Mulvey, J. (2000). *Can aging baby boomers avoid the nursing home?*

Long-term care insurance for "aging in place". Washington, DC: American Council of Life Insurers.

U.S. Census Bureau. (2000a). *Projections of the total resident population by 5-year age groups, and sex with special age categories: middle series, 1999 to 2000.* NP-T3–A. [Online]. Available: http://www.census.gov/population/projections/nation/ summary/np-t3–a.txt [August 4, 2000].

U.S. Census Bureau. (2000b). *Projections of the total resident population by 5–year age groups, and sex with special age categories: middle series, 2025 to 2045.* NP-T3–F. [Online]. Available: http://www.census.gov/population/projections/nation/summary/np-t3–f.txt [August 4, 2000].

U.S. Department of Health and Human Services. (2000). *Prescription drug coverage, spending, utilization, and prices. Report to the President.* Washington, DC: Author.

U.S. General Accounting Office. (1996). *Medicare home health utilization expands while program controls deteriorate.* (GAO/HEHS-96–16). Washington, DC: Author.

U.S. General Accounting Office. (1999). *Nursing homes: Additional steps needed to strengthen enforcement of federal quality standards.* (GAO/HEHS-99–46). Washington, DC: Author.

Ware, J. F., Bayliss, M. S., Rogers, W. H., Kosinski, M., & Tarlov, A. R. (1996). Differences in 4-year health outcomes for elderly and poor, chronically ill patients treated in HMO and fee-for-service systems: Results from the Medical Outcomes Study. *Journal of the American Medical Association, 276,* 1039–1104.

Twenty-Two

Emerging Issues in Chronic Care

Robert L. Kane and Rosalie A. Kane

I. Chronic Care Paradigm

This chapter examines the failure of the medical care system to respond adequately to the reality of a dominant model of chronic disease. Older people are particularly affected by this oversight because they suffer from chronic diseases to an even larger extent than younger persons. We suggest appropriate steps to be taken to address the inadequate response of the medical care system.

A. The Paradox

Epidemiological data indicate that today (and indeed for some decades past) the most prevalent health problems for persons of all ages, but especially elders, are those associated with chronic illnesses (Hoffman, Rice, & Sung, 1996). The major killers among them include heart disease, cancer, stroke, and kidney disease. The most prevalent conditions (beyond hearing and vision problems) are arthritis and hypertension. Yet, medical care is still delivered in virtually the same fashion it was when infectious diseases prevailed. In effect, as we enter the 21st century, medicine is still practiced

along 19th-century lines (albeit with sophisticated technology and dramatically new scientific insights). This reluctance to acknowledge the practice implications of living in a world permeated by chronic disease has impeded the integration of medical and social services. This is true even though much of long-term-care service is directed toward addressing the impacts of chronic illness and its resulting disabilities.

In the acute-care model, practitioners become aware of patients only when they appear for care. There is an intense interaction, which is expected to produce beneficial results. (The interaction could be an office visit or a hospital stay.) The patients then disappear again until they make a new demand on the system (with some provision allowed for subsequent check-ups to assure that all has turned out well).

In contrast, a chronic-care model requires ongoing observation. It is based on a continuing episode rather than a single event. No single contact is meant to be definitive. It represents the equivalent of a movie as opposed to a series of snapshots. It implies some continuity of contact between health-care providers and

Handbook of Aging and the Social Sciences, Fifth Edition

patients, and some responsibility on the part of the health-care system for maintaining that contact and taking a long-range approach to disease prevention and management.

B. Implications of the Paradox

Converting to chronic-care practice means rethinking some of the fundamental components and relationships in the caring paradigm. Central among them are the role of patients, the meaning of time, and what constitutes reasonable goals for care. Table 22.1 summarizes some of the distinctions implicit in these two approaches.

1. Role of Patients

Medicine has drawn power and prestige from using its expertise to distance the practitioner from the patient, making pronouncements and conferring judgments, instructing and prognosticating. But in the context of chronic care, the patient assumes more expertise and authority. Precisely because formal contacts with health-care providers are brief and infre-

quent, much of the responsibility for management must rest with the patient. Ceding responsibility to the patient implies that the physician yields control as well. Client preferences and beliefs about what goals are most important must be respected.

Patients who are going to care for themselves must understand their diseases and their manifestations. They must be able to recognize early signs of problems. They must appreciate the rationale for treatment as well as its details, and they must believe in its efficacy. Consequently, traditional patient education strategies based on telling patients what to do need to be revisited (Lorig et al., 1999). The goal is no longer compliance; it is active participation. Patients need both motivation and skills. They need to learn how to measure clinical parameters and to track them to detect early signs of change. Historically, the best precedent for such behavior probably lies within diabetes care, where patients have been taught to measure their glucose levels in various body fluids and to record the findings systematically, often adjusting their insulin dosage on the basis of the patterns

Table 22.1
Comparison of Elements in Acute and Chronic Care

Elements	Acute care	Chronic care
Role of patients	Passive, compliance valued Decision-making role is to agree or disagree with recommendations Self-care not emphasized	Active involvement Patient makes decisions after receiving information on risks and benefits Self-care valued
Time horizon	Rapid response to specific event	Continuing observation Tracking conditions
Expectations and goals	Definitive action Cure	Management and control of condition or symptoms Prevention of exacerbations
Information	Therapeutic regimens	Therapeutic regimens Nature of disease Signs and symptoms Indications of change in status Side effects

detected. A similar strategy can be used with a variety of chronic diseases, such as congestive heart failure.

Activated patients will also be in a position to participate more fully in clinical decisions. Theoretically, patients have been the key decision makers for some time. Professionals provide them with information about the risks and benefits of various interventions, and they opt for the alternative that best suits them. The reality, however, is quite different. Rarely are patients given complete information. Often the source of information is prejudiced (by virtue of the physician's own specialty) toward one alternative. For example, surgeons, however hard they try to be objective, are likely to advocate for a surgical approach over medical management in most instances.

Too often the circumstances in which patients make key decisions are poor. For example, they are told about the risks of surgery just prior to the operation, or are asked to make major decisions about posthospital care under a time pressure for discharge from the hospital. Frail older persons are called upon to make decisions that will affect the rest of their lives under stressful circumstances Good decision making requires a suitable unhurried environment and a supportive structure. The optimal setting may include a facilitator who helps patients (and often their families) sort out what outcomes they want to maximize, who can provide them with unbiased information about the risks, costs, and benefits of available alternatives, and can help them through the steps of decision making, separating the choice of modalities (or care venues) from the subsequent choice of vendors for the venue selected. For example, a decision to get care in a nursing home, an assisted living setting, or to arrange it in one's own home is a choice of modality, and the decision about which facility to enter or home-care provider to use is a choice of vendor.

2. Time

The very term *chronic* implies a different role for time than in typical acute care. Changes often are expected to occur more slowly, and a more long-range view is needed. Care providers can make investments in care that are expected to yield dividends (in terms of better outcomes or less cost) in the future. For example, the value of comprehensive geriatric assessments (and even more the process of geriatric evaluation and management, where the care of frail older patients may be temporarily taken over until a more appropriate treatment regimen can be developed) in reducing mortality, improving function, and lowering institutional care use has been well documented (Stuck, Siu, Wieland, Adams, & Rubenstein, 1993).

3. Information

Making good decisions requires having good information. The current system of care relies heavily on imperfect information and hence places added weight on professional judgments. But the tide is turning. Increasingly, one hears a call for more evidence-based medicine (Sackett, 1997). As such information is developed, organized, and disseminated (through activities like the Cochrane Centers, which sponsor systematic assessments of the medical literature to provide the basis for evidence-based practice), that data will become more widely available. It can be made available in forms that are accessible and understood by lay audiences. Examples of such a presentation are the videotapes produced by the Shared Decision-Making (SDM) project developed at Dartmouth. Under SDM, persons who are contemplating a major procedure are exposed to videotaped material that shows the full range of treatment options. They provide both statistical information and interviews with patients who have experienced different types of treatment for the problem under discussion. The risks and benefits of each option are explained and interviews with persons who had each option indicate the range of consequences. Patients faced with a treatment decision can watch these videos as often as needed to understand the implications of the alternatives and make a decision that best fits their lifestyle goals. When patients going through this process have an opportunity to consider their options thoughtfully, many opt against invasive actions (Barry, Mulley, Fowler, & Wennberg, 1988; Kasper, Mulley, & Wennberg, 1992).

4. Expectations

Under chronic care, the expectations, or goals, of care are usually cast in terms of improvement or maintenance of a clinical state rather than cure. Good chronic care can be that which reduces the likelihood of exacerbations that will necessitate institutional care or crisis management (e.g., in an emergency room). In many cases, the effects of good chronic care can be seen only as a slowing in the rate of decline. In order to appreciate the benefits, one must have a point of comparison by which to see the difference in the slope between the actual and expected results. The latter data must come from large statistical databases that have not yet been developed.

II. Philosophies of Care

A. Compensatory versus Therapeutic

For some time, the coordination of health and social care has been handicapped by an insistence that compensatory and therapeutic approaches represented incompatible philosophies with different overall expectations regarding good care and outcomes. The compensatory approach is usually associated with care rendered under social services auspices, although it also encompasses the design and provision of special equipment to enhance functioning, ranging from wheelchairs to hearing aids. Under this rubric, clients are evaluated to ascertain their care needs, and a plan of care is developed to meet the deficiencies uncovered. A good care plan is defined as one that compensates for the client's weaknesses by providing care to address these needs. A good outcome under this model consists of meeting the need profile without incurring any untoward effects (e.g., pressure sores, falls) and freeing the individual to lead as meaningful a life as his or her condition permits. The alternative model, therapeutic care, is expected to make a difference in the client's clinical course. That is, receiving care should lead to outcomes that are different from those that would have occurred without it. These outcomes could be an improvement in the client's status or a slowing of decline that would otherwise occur. The outcomes addressed in the therapeutic model could be strictly clinical, but they could just as readily be expressed in terms of quality of life.

Although these two philosophies appear at first blush to be competitive, they are actually compatible (R. A. Kane, 1999). Artificial distinctions between the two approaches have led to fragmented systems of care where, for example, an older person is either deemed a candidate for rehabilitation and receives intensive interventions or is deemed unlikely to benefit and receives nothing. Or, in another example, the older person nearing the end of life opts for curative treatment and receives every intervention or opts for hospice and receives no life-prolonging treatments but attention to his or her quality of life.

In fact, older people and their families value *both* rehabilitative efforts and compensatory efforts. Physical therapy, occupational therapy, and speech therapy can be extremely helpful to achieve measurable goals for long-term nursing home residents and others not usually deemed "rehabilitatable" (Brzybylski, See, & Watkins, 1993). On the other hand, turning everyday life for older people with chronic illness and disabilities into a therapy (e.g., dance therapy, music therapy, pet therapy, garden therapy, reminiscence therapy) reflects an overenthusiastic embrace of the therapeutic approach. Similarly a compensatory model can go way beyond conventional provisions so as to maximize quality of life. For example, a home-care model that provides personal assistance for the homebound who meet strict disability criteria is less likely to promote normal lives for older people who need help than a personal assistant or attendant service that enables the older person to leave home and pursue his or her life in the community.

Reconciling the therapeutic and compensatory approaches would encourage an active approach to treating disease and dysfunction whenever possible, while simultaneously providing service that assists older people in living their preferred lives. Both approaches can enhance quality of life.

B. Outcome versus Process

The helping professions are not always willing to take responsibility for achieving outcomes, preferring instead to take solace in providing care according to correct processes. This distinction encourages chicken- and-egg arguments, with proponents of outcome approaches stating that providers should not be responsible for any processes unless they are unequivocally linked to outcomes, and proponents of process approaches saying that providers should not be held accountable for outcomes unless they can be shown a process by which the outcomes can be achieved. Thus far, few pro-

viders are willing to be judged largely on the outcomes they achieve, even when allowances are to be made for the status of the individual at the beginning of their care with that provider. Traditionally, most medical care has emphasized process measures as a basis for determining quality. Health-care professionals are reluctant to accept responsibility for results that may depend on differences in case mix or on factors they perceive are beyond their control (Jencks et al., 1988; Greenfield, Aronow, Elashoff, & Watanabe, 1988). (It is not a coincidence that physicians talk about poor patient compliance as if it were a phenomenon alien from their efforts.) But the tide is turning; the pressures from many quarters have pushed for more attention to outcomes as part of the emphasis on empirical practice (i.e., based on scientific evidence of effectiveness) and continuous quality improvement.

Social services providers have been about as willing (or more correctly unwilling) as medical ones to be judged on the basis of the results they achieve, although it is often harder to get social care providers to even define the specific outcomes they are pursuing. Notable exceptions would be the Long-term Care Channeling project (Kemper, 1988) and other similar efforts to test the effects of case management on a range of outcomes for frail older people.

III. Elements of Care

A. Health Professionals

Health care in the United States is organized differently from that in most other countries. The internationally predominant model features some provision for primary care, usually through a general practitioner who provides first-contact care and provides continuity over time. When problems become too complex for general practitioners, they refer their patients to specialists for advice and assistance in managing the case. In many countries, specialists are based in hospitals and exclusively manage all those admitted to hospitals as well as seeing patients on referral in outpatient clinics. American medicine is much more eclectic (Stephen, 1979). Specialists provide a substantial amount of primary care in the sense that patients may seek out medical specialists directly and return to them for regular care (Aiken et al., 1979), (Mottur-Pilson, 1995) and general practitioners (called family practitioners in the United States) often continue to care for their patients while they are hospitalized. Although managed care seems to provide a demand for more primary care and fewer specialists, it is not clear how this division of labor will evolve.

The question of the best blend of generalists and specialists in health care, especially for those with chronic illnesses, has not been satisfactorily resolved. There has never been a direct clinical trial where patients were randomly assigned to one type of care or the other. Studies based on less stringent designs show mixed results. Primary-care providers can be more attractive to payers than specialists because they use fewer services and hence may be less expensive (Carey et al., 1995; Greenfield, Rogers, Mangoitch, Carney, & Tarlov, 1995). But, for at least a selected subset of patients, care from specialists may ultimately be more cost-effective. Some patients with complex specific illnesses may be too complicated to be managed by the average generalist, who has rarely, if ever, confronted such a case. For example, a patient with unstable congestive heart failure may be better managed by a cardiologist who has the expertise in the dominant disease and its complications.

The evidence in support of greater use of specialists for delivering primary care is mixed (Gabriel, 1996). The results of the Medical Outcomes Study show little difference in the outcomes of care for hypertension and noninsulin-dependent diabetes given by specialists or generalists (Greenfield et al., 1995). In contrast, an earlier British study had found better outcomes associated with specialist care for type II diabetes (Hayes, 1984). Subspecialist care (by rheumatologists) was also associated with better outcomes in treating rheumatoid arthritis (Ward, Leigh, & Fries, 1993), and allergists were more effective than generalists in reducing the complications of at-risk asthmatics (Zeiger et al., 1991). Cardiologists had better results with acute myocardial infarction (i.e., heart attacks) than did generalists (Jollis et al., 1996). Neurologists caring for stroke patients in hospitals achieved lower mortality rates, although the care was more expensive (Mitchell et al., 1996).

Specialists assuming a primary-care role for those with chronic problems will need to change their modus operandi. They will have to address the needs of the whole person, paying closer attention to the functional aspects of care rather than addressing only the clinical parameters. Not all specialists will be comfortable with this broadened mandate (Speight & Blixt, 1995).

Beyond the general question about the role of specialists, the role of geriatric medicine is particularly complicated. Originally, geriatricians were envisioned as specialists, who would see patients on referral (R. L. Kane, Solomon, Beck, Keeler, & Kane, 1980). Their basic technology was the comprehensive geriatric assessment, which has been repeatedly shown to both improve outcomes and save money (Stuck et al., 1993). However, several factors make it difficult for geriatrics to succeed as a specialty: (a) Medicare payment rates did not cover the costs of the time involved in a comprehensive assessment, around which the identity of geriatricians is built; unlike most technologies, assessment takes a lot of time and hence does not provide great revenue per hour of effort; (b) patients receiving such assessments often found that this was the most careful attention they had received, and those without a strong attachment to a primary care physician sought to make the geriatricians their primary care providers; (c) the influence of managed care raised the status of primary care and suggested that the United States has an excess of specialists. As a result of all these forces, geriatrics redefined itself oxymoronically as a *primary-care specialty* (Burton & Solomon, 1993). Even now, the numbers of geriatricians being produced is far too small to make even a dent in the need for chronic care (Reuben & Beck, 1994). Were geriatricians more numerous, one might envision that the care of older persons be divided so that geriatricians would manage the complex cases of multiple interacting diseases while geriatric nurse practitioners would provide the basic primary care.

A case can be made for dramatic downward substitution, for example, using nurse practitioners in lieu of physicians to deliver much of the care given to older people with chronic diseases (Mundinger, 1994; Mundinger et al., 2000). This type of delegation is most feasible in the context of managed care, where each activity is not separately billed. Primary care providers' roles, like general practitioners working with chronically ill persons, can thus be seen as being squeezed from both the top (by specialists) and the bottom (by nurse practitioners).

B. Teamwork

Discussions about chronic care inevitably raise the issue of the role of teams. Much has been written extolling the virtue of interdisciplinary teamwork in the care of older complex patients, but such care is hard to accomplish (R. A. Kane, 1975; Siegler, Hyer, Fulmer, & Mezey, 1998).

Few organizations are willing to invest the time and effort required to develop and maintain truly collaborative teams. Even fewer are convinced that the benefits of such effort are repaid by savings through more effective or efficient care. Team meetings require substantial aggregate time. Their results must yield substantial savings to offset such an investment. Most health-care organizations acknowledge the value of using multiple disciplines and the importance of effective communication. They tend to rely on informal teamwork rather than supporting full-blown interdisciplinary teams. There are some strong examples of organizations committed to teamwork with elderly patients. Perhaps the best example is On Lok and its national replications through PACE (Program for All-inclusive Care of the Elderly). These programs use a multidisciplinary team mechanism to serve frail older persons who are deemed eligible for nursing home coverage under both Medicare and Medicaid. They have been successful at reducing the use of institutions including both hospitals and nursing homes (Chatterji, Burstein, Kidder, & White, 1998; Eng, Pedulla, Eleazer, McCann, & Fox, 1997).

C. Care Management

Another way to coordinate care provided by multiple disciplines over time is through care managers and care management systems. Sometimes also called case management, care management is often seen as the essential ingredient to make health care work on behalf of individual patients, to assist patients with decision making, and to minimize harmful or wasteful care in the system. Managed care programs, whereby one organization receives a fixed capitated payment and is at financial risk for providing a comprehensive set of services, has the notion of care management right in its name. However, as has been shown, most case management done under these auspices is really utilization management (Pacala et al., 1995). Less is done to address the fragmentation that can readily exist between the various providers within a managed care organization (Friedman & Kane, 1993). Whether care is capitated or fee-for-service, coordination is needed for individuals. Many of the programs discussed in the rest of this chapter attempt to improve coordination through care management.

Several issues are of note regarding care management. First, a tension exists because care managers typically have the dual role of advocate for high-quality care and gatekeeper and cost controller. Second, long-term care programs derived from a social model—many of which also fund health-related services—have evolved case-management systems of their own. Case management in a socially oriented long-term-care program and care coordination in a health program may simultaneously operate on the same individual, yet the two systems of coordination may run in parallel without communication (Finch, Shanahan, Mortimer, & Ryu, 1991; R. A. Kane, 2000).

IV. Lessons for Care

Care can be provided in a wide variety of settings. The most common location for health care is the physician's office. The most expensive is the hospital. Hospitals have become centers of technology. As the sophistication of their care has increased, so too have the associated costs. The pressures from these costs have, in turn, led to efforts to reduce hospital costs, and indirectly hospital use. In 1984 Medicare changed the way it paid hospitals. Instead of paying them on the basis of costs incurred, Medicare paid a fixed amount based on the expected length of stay for each of a cluster of diagnoses, called diagnosis-related groups

(DRGs). The hospitals responded by dramatically shortening lengths of stay or seeking other venues for providing care. This response has primarily involved transferring the locus of care to other venues either by shifting the site of care for the entire episode or shortening the hospital portion through early discharge. An example of the former would be outpatient surgery. Procedures that used to require a hospital stay of several days are now performed on outpatients thanks to improvements in technology (e.g., laparoscopic techniques for gall bladder removal).

Earlier hospital discharge has changed the nature of posthospital care and raised concerns about "quicker and sicker" discharges, despite any evidence that outcomes became worse after the transition (Kahn, Keeler, et al., 1990; Kahn, Rubinstein, et al., 1990). Patients who would have formerly recuperated in hospitals are now being sent to nursing homes or home with home health care. Needless to say, postacute care (the term applied to this posthospital care) became a major growth industry.

This shift changed the nature of nursing home care. What had been basically a repository for society's most frail people was now also challenged to care for patients who in previous years would have been in a hospital. Although many nursing homes have declared themselves (or portions of them) as subacute care units in light of higher payments provided under Medicare for patients needing more services, they were not always up to the task (R. L. Kane, Chen, Blewett, & Sangl, 1996; Kramer et al., 1997). Pressures had already been strong to increase the regulation of nursing homes in the wake of scandals (Institute of Medicine, 1986). As the acuity of residents increased, the pressure for better quality intensified. Then, too, as nursing homes became capable of caring for medically unstable and acutely ill Medicare beneficiaries in the immediate aftermath of their hospitalizations, a concept has emerged that nursing homes could care for some of their long-term residents during acute exacerbations that would have previously required them to be hospitalized.

At the same time, home health care began to change. Whereas Medicaid is the major public payer for nursing home care, Medicare is the predominant payer for home health care. Medicare was intended primarily to cover acute-care costs, but the definition of covered home health care gradually expanded until a substantial proportion of Medicare payments were going to persons who had received home health care for over 120 days (Vladeck & Miller, 1994). The fiscal response to this revelation was a change in the Medicare payment approach to introduce prospective payment.

Meanwhile the long-term care of older persons who required ongoing support was paid either privately or through Medicaid and state-funded programs, largely for low-income people. Most of the Medicaid money went to nursing homes, but there was growing interest in moving the venue for such care into the community, partly because most older people preferred to receive such care and partially because it was believed to be cheaper.

The debate about whether community-based long-term care is actually cheaper than nursing homes has raged for some time. Various arguments have been made in support of this proposition. Community care is often cheaper on a per unit basis, but the costs of nursing home care include room and board. As the intensity of care increases, however, the break-even point shifts. Also, because community care is less aversive for the consumer than nursing home care, it attracts clientele who would not enter a nursing home at all or so soon. This phenomenon of creating a new population for more attractive nursing home substitutes has been called the *woodwork effect* because clients are said to come out of the woodwork to use the service. On the other hand, community care was believed to have a protective effect. Care provided in the early stages of a chronic disability was expected to prevent later institutionalization, though most studies have not confirmed this belief (Carcagno & Kemper, 1988; Weissert & Hedrick, 1994).

Despite the lack of confirmatory findings that home care is cheaper, the Medicaid program allowed waivers under which states could establish community-based programs, with the requirement that they should be budget neutral (i.e., the state had to show commensurate savings in nursing home care to offset the projected community expenses). The use of these waivers has varied considerably from state to state, as does the proportion of a state's dollars (through Medicaid, Medicaid waivers, and all-state discretionary spending) that it expends on home- and community-based care as opposed to nursing home care (R. L. Kane, Kane, Ladd, & Nielsen, 1998). Some states have made remarkable strides in reducing nursing home expenditures and use while making a wide array of home and community-based services available (Alecxih, Lutzky, Corea, & Coleman, 1996; U.S. General Accounting Office, 1994). Such states typically have developed statewide, case-managed programs targeted to people with disabilities and have forged models of home care to meet extensive chronic-care needs.

A. Emergence of Alternative Settings

Another development that accelerated in the 1990s was the establishment of housing-and-services settings where older persons with disabilities can live in typical but disability-friendly homes and apartments with services tailored to their needs. These are variously licensed by states, for example, as assisted living, residential care facilities, personal care homes, rest homes, or (especially, if small and contained in private homes) adult foster homes or small group homes. In this chapter, we use the generic term *assisted living* for most group residential settings not licensed as a nursing home that provide or arrange for personal care and routine nursing services for people with disabilities (R. A. Kane & Wilson, 1993).

Such settings may be boarding homes with shared rooms and baths or be composed of self-contained, largely private-occupancy apartments with interior full bathrooms and kitchenettes. Mollica (1998) documented the wide range of state rules, which prohibit, permit, or require facilities to retain residents with specific types and levels of needs.

Assisted living recognizes the central role of housing and adaptive environments in improving long-term care. At its best, it aspires to provide each person with a living environment that permits considerable independence, control, choice, dignity, and privacy while offering meals in a congregate dining room and providing a wide range of services. Although a large national probability sample of assisted living residences found only 11% combined high privacy and autonomy with high service (Hawes, Rose, & Phillips, 1999), some states have configured their regulations to assure that any provider using the term is committed to autonomy- and privacy-enhancing features in their designs, high service levels, and aging in place. One such state is Oregon, where a recent evaluation showed no negative effects on functional status, mental well-being, pain and discomfort, or survival for residents who chose assisted living rather than nursing homes, controlling for differences in disability levels in the two settings (Frytak, Kane, Finch, Kane, & Maude-Griffin, in press).

Assisted-living facilities have proven attractive to consumers, and hence their rapid expansion. Care in these settings present many challenges, however. If assisted living is to serve a population comparable in health status to a group in nursing homes, some mechanism needs to be developed for better health-care provision. Closer links to primary care and more intensive health status monitoring need to be established without destroying the residential quality of the setting.

For a long time it was believed that the demand for nursing home care seemed virtually insatiable. Just as had been the case earlier with hospitals, the prevailing dogma suggested that any available nursing home bed would be filled. Efforts to divert potential users to other venues would only aggregate the situation by creating two users, one for the nursing home and another for the alternative site. Each year the number of nursing home residents rose. However, just as it had earlier with hospitals, the tide began to turn (Bishop, 1999). For the past several years, nursing home occupancy, which had historically run at greater than 90%, began to fall. Empty nursing home beds became more common.

The reason for this change is not immediately clear. Several factors seem to have coalesced. Alternative sources of care, especially assisted living, grew very quickly, filling a void by offering more attractive housing options, often at lower prices. Assisted living arose as an option primarily in the private sector. Home care also became more available. As Medicare-covered home health care expanded its coverage to longer periods, it provided at least something of a real insured alternative to the nursing home. At the same time, the nature of nursing home care changed dramatically. What had formerly been almost exclusively a long-term care vehicle, now became an active purveyor of subacute care, with much shorter lengths of stay. This higher turnover was inevitably associated with lower occupancy.

As alternatives to nursing home care seem to be becoming a reality, the dominance of the nursing home in the long-term-care sector may be waning. One strategy to open up the field of long-term care would be to end the current distinction between institutional and community-based care. The easiest way to accomplish this shift would be to separate clearly the payment for services from that for room and board (R. L. Kane & Kane, 1991). The merger that has been taken for granted for nursing homes (presumably as an extension of the hospital model) would be dismantled. Under the new mandate, persons would receive the services they needed regardless of their domicile. As a result, there would be an incentive to save for long-term care, because more financial resources would permit a better living situation. In effect, all long-term care would become community-based. Some people would live in their own homes; others would require new housing solutions; but housing circumstances would determine the services, not vice versa.

B. Linking Acute and Long-Term Care

The separation of medical and long-term care has been reenforced by differences in the primary funding source for each. As noted earlier, acute care is largely covered by Medicare, whereas long-term care is a Medicaid responsibility. Nonetheless, these two components of care are closely linked in practice. Persons receiving long-term care usually need more than average amounts of medical care, if only because the problems that produced their dependency are largely medical. Ironically, some of these people often receive little or no medical care and rarely are treated aggressively.

There are some indications that the situation may be improving. One encouraging model is that practiced by EverCare, a Medicare HMO that caters specifically to long-stay (i.e., not subacute) residents in nursing homes. EverCare receives a higher than average capitation rate from Medicare, which pays for all Medicare-covered services for this population. The higher rate reflects a statistical observation that nursing home residents incur higher fee-for-service Medicare expenditures than the older population, generally. This higher rate allows EverCare to invest in more primary care than the typical HMO, supporting nurse practitioners to pay close heed to the health status of their nursing home resident enrollees. The underlying principle for EverCare is that active primary care will pay for itself through earlier recognition of problems and interventions in time to avoid a costly hospitalization. Moreover, the availability of more primary care should permit more care to be given in the nursing home, thereby eliminating or reducing the need for hospital care (Kane & Huck, 2000).

Another positive sign is the growing number of geriatricians who are taking on the post of medical director in nursing homes. The staffing of these positions by geriatricians suggests that more will be done to provide appropriate medical care and develop methods of assuring more attentive caregiving.

As already noted, the coordination of care is often poor between Medicare and Medicaid, the two major public funding programs. For those persons eligible for services under both programs, it has been suggested that pooling funding into a single program might improve this coordination. Several pilot projects have been established to test the effects of such a pooling, but it is still too early to tell if the expected benefits have been realized. Although comingling of funds can promote collaboration, it can also lead to siphoning money away from the less powerful programs to support the more powerful. In this case, medical care can easily out-trump long-term care.

One area where health policy seems especially out of sync is the lack of Medicare coverage for prescription drugs. Medications have become important in treating illness, especially chronic illness. But they have become increasingly expensive as they have become more sophisticated. Lack of coverage for drugs leaves many older Americans unprotected for a major medical cost, particularly poor older persons who may be choosing between food and medications. Covering medical care without covering the medications needed to implement that care seems short sighted. Thus, pressure is growing for the Medicare program to include outpatient drug coverage, but in the face of strong pressure to contain the overall growth of the program. (See chapter 21 by Feder et al., this volume.)

C. Quality of Care

As government has become involved in health-care financing, it has assumed a responsibility for assuring that the quality of the services purchased is adequate. The introduction of Medicare and Medicaid has transformed the nature of quality assurance (Institute of Medicine, 1990). What had previously been left to professional associations to monitor has now become increasingly regulated. The history of regulation differs with the sector of care.

Nursing homes have been the most heavily regulated health industry. Emerging from a cloud of scandal for both poor care and misuse of money (Mendelson, 1974; Moss & Halamandaris, 1977; Vladeck, 1980), the nursing home industry has been viewed as one that must be closely overseen. A 1986 Institute of Medicine report proposed a major overhaul of the regulatory structure (Institute of Medicine, 1986), most of which was implemented through legislation the following year. The 1987 legislation called for the creation of a uniform assessment system, which was to form the basis for both care planning and oversight, the Minimum Data System (MDS) (Hawes et al., 1995; Morris et al., 1997). The MDS was nationally mandated in 1990. Although there is undoubtedly some variation in the quality of the data generated across the country, it stands as a major administrative feat. Other countries have adopted it on both a voluntary and a mandatory basis (Fries et al., 1997; Phillips, Zimmerman, Bernabei, & Jonsson, 1997). Items from the MDS have been used to construct quality indicators (QIs), measures that reflect potential quality problems (e.g., rate of pressure sores, evidence of malnutrition) (Zimmerman et al., 1995).

The initial attention was directed at measures of physical function. Less effort was spent trying to address less easily measured areas like quality of life. Indeed, the whole structure of the MDS lends itself to observation and reporting rather than to lending voice to the nursing home residents (and their families in the case of those who are cognitively impaired), who are the only legitimate source of information on the quality of their own lives. New efforts are underway to address this deficiency.

The press for regulation of nursing homes has created its own dilemma as new forms of long-term care emerge. On the one hand, these new forms are welcomed as new opportunities to create better approaches to care. At the same time, critics call for a level playing field, wherein all long-term care is subject to the same rules. However, this uniformity of regulation threatens the innovation being sought.

D. Prevention

Much has been said about the inherent desirability of preventing disease. It is proverbially rated 16 times better than cure. Efforts to calculate its actual cost-effectiveness demonstrate that the cost of life saved varies greatly. Most immunizations are quite cost-effective. Many screening programs are not.

Prevention is typically classified into three types:

1. *Primary*: addressing and eliminating the risks associated with disease, either by removing the threat (e.g., stopping cigarette smoking) or changing the host (e.g., immunization)
2. *Secondary*: detecting the presence of the disease before it manifests clinically
3. *Tertiary*: more active treatment can prevent the development of complications.

(Some also include a fourth level, which addresses rehabilitative efforts to prevent the development of disability from disease.)

In the case of older people, all three levels of prevention pertain. The most common form of primary prevention is immunizations, especially against influenza and pneumonia. Smoking cessation has been shown to have positive health effects even among men in their 80s (Jaijich, Ostfeld, & Freeman, 1984). Practicing good health habits, such as exercise, can have a variety of positive benefits from reducing osteoporosis to improving one's sense of well-being (Larson, 1991). Certain dietary and biological supplements have been recommended, but the evidence for their benefit is mixed. Replacement estrogens seem to have a number of benefits beyond controlling symptoms of menopause. They can delay bone loss (for as long as they are taken) and seem to offer cardiovascular protection. There is some suggestion they may have a positive effect on delaying dementia. However, they increase the risk of breast and ovarian cancer. Much has been written about antioxidants as protecting against a variety of insults associated with aging, but the evidence is still unclear.

Recommendations around screening for many diseases recognize the biological differences, especially in cancer, associated with aging. Less frequent screening for various cancers (e.g., breast and cervix) is usually favored because the tumors seem to grow less rapidly or other threats of death make treatment less desirable (U.S. Preventive Services Task Force, 1996). On the other hand, screening for other conditions, such as depression, vision, and hearing, take on more salience. Much has been demonstrated about the value of comprehensive geriatric assessments (Rubenstein, Wieland, & Bernabei, 1995; Stuck et al., 1993). Even a home visit by a nurse practitioner has been shown to have beneficial effects (Stuck et al., 1995).

Much of the efforts with regard to preventive care of older persons are directed toward the prevention of disability. Close monitoring of chronic illnesses can often delay these sequelae.

E. Managed Care

Policy makers for Medicare and even Medicaid have pinned their hopes on managed care as a way to save costs and improve quality. The success in both arenas is mixed at best. Although some argue that Medicare's form of managed care is overpriced, it would save money for the Medicare program if it cost less to purchase. Instead, there is evidence that payments are too large, because Medicare HMOs tend to enroll healthier persons whose costs of care are below average, yet they collect average payments for them (Brown, Clement, Hill, Retchin, & Bergeron, 1993). (See also chapter 21 by Feder et al., this volume)

In theory, managed care offers a fertile setting for developing just the models of good chronic care we need. It can afford to think in terms of investing in patient care, and thus can support comprehensive geriatric assessments, for example, in the expectation of subsequent savings. It can create an infrastructure with geriatric expertise to develop and oversee better "gerontologized" primary care. It can establish a management information system (MIS) that can screen for persons at risk, refer them for more comprehensive assessments and case management, and track the patterns of referrals to assure that there is active follow-up. The same MIS can track individual patients' clinical courses to identify when their status changes and they need more active intervention. All of this is feasible, but little of this is occurring (R. L. Kane, 1998).

V. Conclusions

Our medical system is out of touch with the demographic realities. Ironically, we know much more about how to deliver good chronic care for older persons than we are willing to put into practice. Table 22.2 summarizes the results of a number of randomized clinical trials and quasi-experimental evaluations that demonstrate the effectiveness, and even the cost-effectiveness of delivering care in new ways. However, few of these have been put into active practice.

The barriers to such implementation are several. As already noted, managed care has not proven to be the vehicle that some had hoped for. It will never achieve this end until a better system for case-mix adjustment is implemented to make chronic cases appropriately more lucrative. Consumers may prove to be a strong lever for change. They need to be educated to expect more and different care. Medical education (and education in all of the health professions) needs to champion a new style of practice.

Policy makers need to confront the realities of health care for older persons in this country. We will not have a medical care system or a long-term care system capable of addressing the needs of chronic illness until we are prepared to address the fundamental reforms needed in the infrastructure of care. We know much about how to provide better care, but we lack the will to implement that knowledge.

Table 22.2
Summary of Chronic Care Demonstration Studies[a]

Intervention	Study design	Findings[b]
ACE unit Landefeld et al., 1995 Covinsky et al., 1997	Randomized clinical trial	⇑ Satisfaction ⇑ Function = Costs ⇑ LOS
Home hospital Stressman et al., 1996	Quasi-experimental study	⇑ Hospital use ⇑ Costs
Nursing home dyad (NP/MD) Joseph & Boult, 1998 Reuben et al., 1999	Quasi-experimental study	⇑ Return to home = Visits to residents ⇑ LOS
PACE Eng et al., 1997 Chatterji et al., 1998	Quasi-experimental study	⇑ Use of hospitals ⇑ Nursing home use = Total costs = Health = Functional ability

(continues)

Table 22.2 *(Cont.)*

Intervention	Study design	Findings[b]
Interdisciplinary home care Zimmer, Groth-Juncker, & McCusker, 1985 Cummings et al., 1990 Melin, Hakansson, & Bygren, 1993	Randomized clinical trials	⇑ Satisfaction ⇑ Function ⇑ Hospital days ⇓ Nursing home use ⇑ Costs
Comprehensive geriatric Assessment by NP in Patients' Homes Stuck et al., 1995	Randomized clinical trials	⇑ Function ⇑ Nursing home use More MD visits
Outpatient GEM Williams et al., 1987 Engelhardt et al., 1996 Burns et al., 2000	Randomized clinical trials	⇑ Satisfaction ⇑ Function ⇑ Cognition ⇑ Depression ⇑ Health perception ⇑ Social activity = Mortality = Cost ⇑ Caregiver burden
Disease management (CHF) Rich et al., 1995	Randomized clinical trial	⇑ Quality of life ⇑ Hospital admissions for CHF ⇑ Costs
Group care Beck et al., 1997	Randomized clinical trial	⇑ Satisfaction ⇑ Health maintenance, advance directives ⇑ Urgent calls, visits to MDs ⇑ Visits to specialists, ERs ⇑ Costs
Self-management Lorig et al., 1999	Randomized clinical trial	⇑ Function ⇑ General health, energy ⇑ Hospital days ⇑ Costs
Case Management Gagnon, Schein, Mercy, & Bergman, 1999	Randomized clinical trial	= Costs = Health = Functional ability = Mortality
Hospital discharge planning Naylor et al., 1994	Randomized clinical trial	⇑ Readmissions for medical pts = Readmissions for surgical pts
Patient involvement in decision making Greenfield et al., 1988b Wagner et al., 1994		⇑ Physiological control ⇑ Disability ⇑ Surgery

[a]Adapted from Boult, Boult, & Pacala, 1998.
[b]⇑ = improved; LOS = length of stay; MD = physician; ⇓ = worsened; pts = patients; ER = emergency room; == no difference; CHF = congestive heart failure. NP = nurse practitioner GEM = geriatic evaluation and management

References

Aiken, L. H., Lewis, C. E., Craig, J., Mendenhall, R. C., Blendon, R. J., & Rogers, D. E. (1979). The contribution of specialists to the delivery of primary care. *New England Journal of Medicine, 300*(24), 1363–1370.

Alecxih, L. M. B., Lutzky, S., Corea, J., & Coleman, B. (1996). *Estimated costs savings from the use of home and community-based alternatives to nursing facility care in three states.* Washington, DC: Public Policy Institute–AARP.

Barry, M. J., Mulley, A. G. J., Fowler, F. J., & Wennberg, J. W. (1988). Watchful waiting vs. immediate transurethral resection for symptomatic prostatism: The importance of patients' preferences. *Journal of the American Medical Association, 259,* 3010–3017.

Beck, A., Scott, J., Williams, P., Robertson, B., Jackson, D., Gade, G., & Cowan, P. (1997). A randomized trial of group outpatient visits for chronically ill older HMO members: The cooperative health care clinic. *Journal of the American Geriatrics Society, 45,* 543–549.

Bishop, C. E. (1999). Where are the missing elders? The decline in nursing home use, 1985 and 1995. *Health Affairs, 18*(4), 146–155.

Boult, C., Boult, L., & Pacala, J. T. (1998). Systems of care for older populations of the future. *Journal of the American Geriatrics Society, 46,* 499–505.

Brown, R. S., Clement, D. G., Hill, J. W., Retchin, S. M., & Bergeron, J. W. (1993). Do health maintenance organizations work for Medicare? *Health Care Financing Review, 15*(1), 7–23.

Brzybylski, B., See, D., & Watkins, M. (1993). *A study of the outcomes of enhanced physical and occupational therapy hours offered to long-term care residents in a nursing home. Report to the Alberta Long-Term Care Branch, LeDuc.* Alberta: Salem Manor Nursing Home.

Burns, R., Nichols, L. O., Martindale-Adams, J., & Graney, M. J. (2000). Interdisciplinary geriatric primary care evaluation and management: Two-year outcomes. *Journal of the American Geriatrics Society, 48*(1), 8–13.

Burton, J., & Solomon, D. (1993). Geriatric medicine: a true primary care discipline. *Journal of the American Geriatrics Society, 41*(4), 459–461.

Carcagno, G. J., & Kemper, P. (1988). The evaluation of the national long term care demonstration: An overview of the channeling demonstration and its evaluation. *Health Services Research, 23*(1), 1–22.

Carey, T. S., Garrett, J., Jackman, A., McLaughlin, D. B. A., Fryer, J., Smucker, D. R., & North Carolina Back Pain Project. (1995). The outcomes and costs of care for acute low back pain among patients seen by primary care practitioners, chiropractors, and orthopedic surgeons. *New England Journal of Medicine, 333*(14), 913–917.

Chatterji, P., Burstein, N. R., Kidder, D., & White, A. J. (1998). *Evaluation of the Program of All-Inclusive Care for the Elderly (PACE).* Cambridge, MA: Abt Associates Inc.

Covinsky, K., King, J. J., Quinn, L., Siddique, R., Palmer, R., Kresevic, D., Fortinsky, R., Kowal, J., & Landefeld, C. (1997). Do acute care for elders units increase hospital costs? A cost analysis using the hospital perspective. *Journal of the American Geriatrics Society, 45*(6), 729–734.

Cummings, J. E., Hughes, S. L., Weaver, F. M., et al. (1990). Cost-effectiveness of Veterans Administration hospital-based home care: A randomized clinical trial. *Archives of Internal Medicine, 150*(6), 1274–1280.

Eng, C., Pedulla, J., Eleazer, G. P., McCann, R., & Fox, N. (1997). Program of All-inclusive Care for the Elderly (PACE): An innovative model of integrated geriatric care and financing. *Journal of the American Geriatrics Society, 45,* 223–232.

Engelhardt, J. B., Toseland, R. W., O'Donnell, J. C., Richie, J. T., Jue, D., & Banks, S. (1996). The effectiveness and efficiency of outpatient geriatric evaluation and management. *Journal of the American Geriatrics Society, 44,* 847–856.

Finch, M. D., Shanahan, J., Mortimer, T., & Ryu, S. (1991). Work experience and control orientation in adolescence. *Social Psychology Quarterly, 54,* 299–317.

Friedman, B., & Kane, R. L. (1993). HMO medical directors' perceptions of geriatric practice in Medicare HMOs. *Journal of the American Geriatrics Society, 41,* 1144–1149.

Fries, B. E., Schroll, M., Hawes, C., Gilgen, R., Jonsson, P. V., & Park, P. (1997). Approaching cross-national comparisons of nursing home residents. *Age and Ageing, 26*(S2), 13–18.

Frytak, J., Kane, R. A., Finch, M., Kane, R. L., & Maude-Griffin, R. (2001). Outcome trajectories for assisted living and nursing facility residents in Oregon. *Health Services Research, 36*(PT.1), 91–111.

Gabriel, S. E. (1996). Primary care: Specialists or generalists. *Mayo Clinic Proceedings, 71*, 415–419.

Gagnon, A., Schein, C., McVey, L., & Bergman, H. (1999). Randomized controlled trial of nurse case management of frail older people. *Journal of the American Geriatrics Society, 49*(9), 1118–1124.

Greenfield, S., Aronow, H. U., Elashoff, R. M., & Watanabe, D. (1988). Flaws in mortality data: The hazards of ignoring comorbid disease. *Journal of the American Medical Association, 260*, 2253–56.

Greenfield, S., Kaplan, S., Jr, J. W., Yano, E., & Frank, H. (1988). Patients' participation in medical care: effects on blood sugar control and quality of life in diabetes. *Journal of General Internal Medicine, 3*(5), 448–457.

Greenfield, S., Rogers, W., Mangoitch, M., Carney, M. F., & Tarlov, A. R. (1995). Outcomes of patients with hypertension and non-insulin-dependent diabetes mellitus treated by different systems and specialties: Results from the medical outcomes study. *Journal of the American Medical Association, 274*(18), 1436–1444.

Hawes, C., Morris, J. N., Phillips, C. D., Mor, V., Fries, B. E., & Nonemaker, S. (1995). Reliability estimates for the Minimum Data Set for Nursing Home Resident Assessment and care screening (MDS). *Gerontologist, 35*(2), 172–178.

Hawes, C., Rose, M., & Phillips, C. D. (1999). *A national study of assisted living for the frail elderly: Results of a national survey of facilities.* Beachwood, OH: Myers Research Institute, Menorah Park Center for Senior Living.

Hayes, T. M. (1984). Randomised controlled trial of routine hospital clinic care versus routine general practice care for type II diabetics. *British Medical Journal, 289*, 728–730.

Hoffman, C., Rice, D., & Sung, H. -Y. (1996). Persons with chronic conditions: Their prevalence and costs. *Journal of the American Medical Association, 276*(18), 1473–1479.

Institute of Medicine. (1986). *Improving the quality of care in nursing homes.* Washington, DC: National Academy Press.

Institute of Medicine. (1990). *Medicare: A strategy for quality assurance.* (Vol. I). Washington, DC: National Academy Press.

Jaijich, C. L., Ostfeld, A. M., & Freeman, D. H. (1984). Smoking and coronary heart disease mortality in the elderly. *Journal of the American Medical Association, 252*, 2831–2834.

Jencks, S. F., Daley, J., Draper, D., Thomas, N., Lenhart, G., & Walker, J. (1988). Interpreting hospital mortality data: The role of clinical risk adjustment. *Journal of the American Medical Association, 260*, 3611–3616.

Jollis, J. G., DeLong, E. R., Peterson, E. D., Muhlbaier, L. H., Fortin, D. F., Califf, R. M., & Mark, D. B. (1996). Outcome of acute myocardial infarction according to the specialty of the admitting physician. *New England Journal of Medicine, 335*(25), 1880–1887.

Joseph, A., & Boult, C. (1998). Managed primary care of nursing home residents. *Journal of the American Geriatrics Society, 46*(9), 1152–1156.

Kahn, K. L., Keeler, E. B., Sherwood, M. J., Rogers, W. H., Draper, D., Bentow, S. S., Reinisch, E. J., Rubenstein, L. V., Kosecoff, J., & Brook, R. H. (1990). Comparing outcomes of care before and after implementation of the DRG-based prospective payment system. *Journal of the American Medical Association, 264*(15), 1984–1988.

Kahn, K. L., Rubenstein, L. V., Draper, D., Kosecoff, J., Rogers, W. H., Keeler, E. B., & Brook, R. H. (1990). The effects of the DRG-based prospective payment system on quality of care for hospitalized Medicare patients: An introduction to the series. *Journal of the American Medical Association, 264*, 1953–1955.

Kane, R. A. (1975). *Interprofessional teamwork.* (Vol. 8). Syracuse, NY: Syracuse University School of Social Work.

Kane, R. A. (1999). Goals of home care: Therapeutic, compensatory, either, or both? *Journal of Aging and Health, 11*(3), 299–321.

Kane, R. A. (2000). Long-term case management for older adults. In R. L. Kane & R. A. Kane (Eds.), *Assessing older people: Measures, meaning, and practical applications*. New York: Oxford University Press.

Kane, R. A., & Wilson, K. B. (1993). *Assisted living in the United States: A new paradigm for residential care for frail older persons?* Washington, DC: American Association of Retired Persons.

Kane, R. L. (1998). Managed care as a vehicle for delivering more effective chronic care for older persons. *Journal of the American Geriatrics Society, 46*, 1034–1039.

Kane, R. L., Chen, Q., Blewett, L. A., & Sangl, J. (1996). Do rehabilitative nursing homes improve the outcomes of care? *Journal of the American Geriatrics Society, 44*, 545–554.

Kane, R. L., & Huck, S. (2000). The implementation of the EverCare demonstration project. *Journal of the American Geriatrics Society, 44*, 218–228.

Kane, R. L., & Kane, R. A. (1991). A nursing home in your future? *New England Journal of Medicine, 324*(9), 627–629.

Kane, R. L., Kane, R. A., Ladd, R. C., & Nielsen, W. (1998). Variation in state spending for long-term care: Factors associated with more balanced systems. *Journal of Health Politics, Policy and Law, 23*(2), 363–390.

Kane, R. L., Solomon, D., Beck, J., Keeler, E., & Kane, R.A (1980). The future need for geriatric manpower in the United States. *New England Journal of Medicine, 302*, 1327–1332.

Kasper, J. F., Mulley, A. G., & Wennberg, J. E. (1992). Developing shared decision-making programs to improve the quality of health care. *Quality Review Bulletin, 18*(6), 183–190.

Kemper, P. (1988). Evaluation of the National Channeling Demonstration: Overview of the findings. *Health Services Research, 23*(1), 161–174.

Kramer, A. M., Steiner, J. F., Schlenker, R. E., Eilertsen, T. B., Hrincevich, C. A., Tropea, D. A., Ahmad, L. A., & Eckhoff, D. G. (1997). Outcomes and costs after hip fracture and stroke: A comparison of rehabilitation settings. *Journal of the American Medical Association, 277*(5), 396–404.

Landefeld, C. S., Palmer, R M., Kresevic, D. M., Fortinsky, R. H., & Kowal, J. (1995). A randomized trial of care in a hospital medical unit especially designed to improve the functional outcomes of acutely ill older patients. *The New England Journal of Medicine, 332*(20), 1338–1344.

Larson, E. B. (1991). Exercise, functional decline, and frailty. *Journal of the American Geriatrics Society, 39*(6), 635–636.

Lorig, K. R., Sobel, D. S., Stewart, A. L., Brown, J., B. W., Bandura, A., Ritter, P., Gonzalez, V. M., Laurent, D. D., & Holman, H. R. (1999). Evidence suggesting that a chronic disease self-management program can improve health status while reducing hospitalization: A randomized trial. *Medical Care, 37*(1), 5–14.

Melin, A. L., Hakansson, S., & Bygren, L. O. (1993). The cost-effectiveness of rehabilitation in the home: A study of Swedish elderly. *American Journal of Public Health, 83*(3), 356–362.

Mendelson, M. A. (1974) *Tender loving greed.* New York: Alfred A. Knopf.

Mitchell, J. B., Ballard, D. J., Whisnant, J. P., Ammering, C. J., Samsa, G. P., & Matchar, D. B. (1996). What role do neurologists play in determining the costs and outcomes of stroke patients? *Stroke, 27*(11), 1937–1943.

Mollica, R. L. (1998). *State assisted living policy.* Portland, ME: National Academy for State Health Policy.

Morris, J. N., Fries, B. E., Steel, K., Ikegami, N., Bernabei, R., Carpenter, G. I., Gilgen, R., Hirdes, J. P., & Topinkova, E. (1997). Comprehensive clinical assessment in community setting: Applicability of the MDS-HC. *Journal of the American Geriatrics Society, 45*(8), 1017–1024.

Moss, F. E., & Halamandaris, V. J. (1977). *Too old, too sick, too bad: Nursing homes in America.* Germantown, MD: Aspen Systems Corp.

Mottur-Pilson, C. (1995). Primary care as form or content? *American Journal of Medical Quality, 10*(4), 177–182.

Mundinger, M. O. (1994). Advanced-practice nursing—Good medicine for physicians? *New England Journal of Medicine, 330*(3), 211–214.

Mundinger, M., Kane, R. L., Lenz, E., Totten, A., Tsai, W. -Y., Cleary, P., Friedewald, W., Siu, A., & Shelanski, M. L. (2000). Primary care outcomes in patients treated by nurse practitioners or physicians: A randomized trial. *Journal of the American Medical Association, 283*(1), 59–68.

Naylor, M., Brooten, D., Jones, R., Lavizzo-Mourey, R., Mezey, M., & Pauly, M. (1994). Comprehensive discharge planning for the hospitalized elderly: A randomized clinical trial. *Annals of Internal Medicine, 120*(12), 999–1006.

Pacala, J. T., Boult, C., Hepburn, K. W., Kane, R. A., Kane, R. L., Malone, J. K., Morishita, L., & Reed, R. L. (1995). Case management of older adults in health maintenance organizations. *Journal of the American Geriatrics Society, 43*(5), 538–542.

Phillips, C. D., Zimmerman, D., Bernabei, R., & Jonsson, P. V. (1997). Using the Resident Assessment Instrument for quality enhancement in nursing homes. *Age and Ageing, 26*(S2), 77–81.

Reuben, D. B., & Beck, J. C. (1994). *Training physicians to care for older Americans: Progress, obstacles, and future directions*: A background paper prepared for the Committee on Strengthening the Geriatric Content of Medical Education, Division of Health Care Services, Institute of Medicine, National Academy Press, Washington, DC.

Reuben, D. B., Schnelle, J. F., Buchanan, J. L., Kington, R., Zellman, G., Farley, D., Hirsch, S., & Ouslander, J. (1999). Primary care of long-stay nursing home residents: Approaches of three health maintenance organizations. *Journal of the American Geriatrics Society, 47*(2), 131–138.

Rich, M. W., Beckham, V., Wittenberg, C., Leven, C. L., Freedland, K. E., & Carney, R. M. (1995). A multidisciplinary intervention to prevent the readmission of elderly patients with congestive heart failure. *New England Journal of Medicine, 333*(18), 1190–1195.

Rubenstein, L., Wieland, D., & Bernabei, R. (1995). *Geriatric assessment technology: the state of the art*. Milan, Italy: Eidtrice Kurtis.

Sackett, D. L. (1997). *Evidence-based medicine: How to practice and teach EBM*. New York: Churchill Livingstone.

Siegler, E. L., Hyer, K., Fulmer, T., & Mezey, M. (Eds.). (1998). *Geriatric interdisciplinary team training*. New York: Springer Publishing Company.

Speight, J. D., & Blixt, S. L. (1995). Heart specialists' art of care. *Social Science and Medicine, 40*(4), 451–457.

Stephen, W. J. (1979). *An analysis of primary medical care: An international study*. Cambridge: Cambridge University Press.

Stressman, J., Ginsberg, G., Rozenberg-Hammerman, R., Friedman, R., Ronnen, D., Israel, A., & Cohen, A. (1996). Decreased hospital utilization by older adults attributable to a home hospital program. *Journal of the American Geriatrics Society, 44*, 591–598.

Stuck, A. E., Aronow, H. U., Steiner, A., Alessi, C. A., Bula, C. J., Gold, M. N., Yuhas, K. E., Nisenbaum, R., Rubenstein, L. Z., & Beck, J. C. (1995). A trial of annual in-home comprehensive geriatric assessments for elderly people living in the community. *New England Journal of Medicine, 333*(18), 1184–1189.

Stuck, A. E., Siu, A. L., Wieland, G. D., Adams, J., & Rubenstein, L. Z. (1993). Comprehensive geriatric assessment: a meta-analysis of controlled trials. *The Lancet, 342*, 1032–1036.

U.S. General Accounting Office (1994). *Medicaid Long-term care: Successful state efforts to expand home services while limiting costs* (GAO/HEHS-94-167). Washington, DC: U.S. Government Printing Office.

U.S. Preventive Services Task Force. (1996). *Guide to clinical preventive services: Report of the U.S. preventive services task force, second edition*. Baltimore, MD: Williams and Wilkins.

Vladeck, B. G. (1980). *Unloving care: The nursing home tragedy*. New York: Basic Books.

Vladeck, B. C., & Miller, N. A. (1994). The Medicare home health initiative. *Health Care Financing Review, 16*(1), 17–33.

Wagner, E. H., LaCroix, A. Z., Grothaus, L., Leveille, S. G., Hecht, J. A., Artz, K., Odle, K., & Buchner, D. M. (1994). Preventing disability and falls in older adults: A population-based randomized trial. *American Journal of Public Health, 84*(11), 1800–1806.

Ward, M. M., Leigh, J. P., & Fries, J. P. (1993). Progression of functional disability in patients with rheumatoid arthritis: Associations with rheumatology subspecialty care. *Archives of Internal Medicine, 153*, 2229–2237.

Weissert, W. G., & Hedrick, S. C. (1994). Lessons learned from research on effects of community-based long-term care. *Journal of the American Geriatrics Society, 42,* 348–353.

Williams, M. E., Williams, T. F., Zimmer, J. G., Jackson, Hall, W., & Podgorski, C. A. (1987). How does the team approach to outpatient geriatric evaluation compare with traditional care: A report of a randomized controlled trial. *Journal of the American Geriatrics Society, 35,* 1071–1078.

Williams, M. E., Williams, T. F., Zimmer, J. G., Jackson, Hall, W., & Podgorski, C. A. (1987). How does the team approach to outpatient geriatric evaluation compare with traditional care?: A report of a randomized controlled trial. *Journal of the American Geriatrics Society, 35,* 1071–1078.

Zeiger, R. S., Heller, S., Mellon, M. H., Wald, J., Falkoff, R., & Schatz, M. (1991). Facilitated referral to asthma specialist reduced relapses in asthma emergency room visits. *Journal of Allergy and Clinical Immunology, 87*(6), 1160–1168.

Zimmer, J. G., Groth-Juncker, A., & McCusker, J. (1985). A randomized controlled trial of a home health care team. *American Journal of Public Health, 75,* 134–141.

Zimmerman, D. R., Karon, S. L., Arling, G., Clark, B. R., Collins, T., Ross, R., & Sainfort, F. (1995). Development and testing of nursing home quality indicators. *Health Care Financing Review, 16*(4), 107–127.

Twenty-Three

Housing and Living Arrangements
A Transactional Perspective

George L. Maddox

I. Introduction

In the first four editions of this series of handbooks, housing and living arrangements diminished noticeably as topics of interest in gerontological theory. In the *Handbook of the Psychology of Aging*, housing was initially approached as a distinctive milieu for exploring ecological psychology theory. But by the third edition, housing waned as a focus and disappeared in the fourth edition entirely. In the *Handbook of Aging and the Social Sciences*, housing and living arrangements were also treated initially in terms of ecological theory but subsequently descriptive accounts dominated and interest in theory waned. Frances Carp, a pioneer in housing research and in the application of ecological theory in such research (see, e.g., Carp, 1976 and 1987), wrote the chapter on housing for the first edition of the *Handbook of Aging and the Social Sciences*. In subsequent editions, interest in gerontological theory diminished in social scientific accounts of housing. This diminution provides a pertinent illustration of why a concerned George Myers (1996) emphasized in the fourth edition of this *handbook* the im-

portance of theory both to interpret evidence and to lay the foundation for developing interventions to explore the beneficial modifiability of aging processes and the experience of aging. This chapter on housing and living arrangements responds to these challenges. Housing and living arrangements are proposed here as strategic sites for a new theory-driven research agenda.

In a recent monograph on theory in gerontology, O'Rand and Campbell (1999), in a chapter intended to revitalize interest in gerontological theory, review the argument of sociologist Robert Merton regarding the risk of losing a sense of purpose and direction in research not guided by theory. Two important points emerged. First, afloat in a sea of data without a compass, an investigator may need to "reestablish the phenomena" periodically by asking anew why one is interested in inquiring, for example, about housing and living arrangements. Does gerontological theory suggest salient issues to be explored when one consults data tables from the Census of Housing or the periodic American Housing Survey (AHS)? Second, having established the possible theoretical significance of an area of inquiry, can an

Handbook of Aging and the Social Sciences, Fifth Edition

investigator "specify the ignorance" one is attempting to dispel with questions derived from theory, for example, about how different housing and living arrangements affect aging processes and the experience of aging? What beneficial interventions might theory suggest?

The second section of this chapter will review and summarize, succinctly, standard descriptive accounts of housing and living arrangements from the Census of Housing in the United States and from the more frequent AHS. A major national survey of housing occurs once at the beginning of each decade. The profile of data from the 1990 Census of Housing used in the fourth edition of this handbook (e.g., supplemented by the periodic American Housing Survey), however, will be used here and can be expected to approximate evidence likely to be reported in the Year 2000 Census of Housing. Although there are no theoretically focused international comparative studies of housing and living arrangements of older adults, a few descriptive accounts, largely from Western industrial societies, are available (Heumann & Boldy, 1993; Folts & Yeats, 1994; Maddox & Lawton, 1993; Regnier, Hamilton & Yatabe, 1995). These primarily descriptive cross-national comparative studies document observed differences within and between societies in housing and living arrangements for older adults without exploring systematically their theoretical importance for understanding aging processes and outcomes.

The third section of the chapter will review some theoretical traditions useful for "reestablishing the phenomena" of housing and living arrangements as a significant opportunity for renewing interest in theory-based questions about social transactions in later life, drawing on theories suggested from the traditions of human development and social ecology. Particular attention will be paid to the theoretical perspectives of Bronfenbrenner, Antonovsky, Baltes, Bandura, and Kohn on the significance of social and spatial location for understanding social transactions and human resourcefulness. The complementary perspectives of Carp, Lawton, and Moos on the measurement and meaning of milieus in general, and of housing and living arrangements in particular, in relation to the health and well-being of older adults, we conclude, will focus our attention on assisted living housing (ALH) as a prime site for developing a new research agenda with potential for theory-building.

A final section develops a rationale for using ALH as a distinctive site for research and theory building in gerontology. ALH is a relatively recent type of residential care with a distinctive philosophy designed for older adults who are unable to live without compensatory supportive care. This distinctive type of housing, about which we will say more later, is not synonymous with residential care in earlier manifestations but is distinguished by a philosophy of caring (see, e.g., Kane & Wilson, 1993; Regnier et al, 1995; Stone, 2001). ALH constitutes an experiment in living arrangements with potential for testing an ecological theory of successful adaptation for elderly individuals at high risk for disability in later life. In particular, this model of housing with services provides a context for testing the theory of Baltes and Baltes regarding successful aging among older frail adults characterized as selective optimization with compensation. Furthermore, this model provides a context for exploring how disabled elderly who age successfully illustrate Albert Bandura's social learning theory, a theory that focuses on how a sense of self-efficacy can be developed in individuals and how a complementary sense of collective efficacy can be developed in social groups and communities.

In a society with a large and diverse older population, a wide range of housing options will surely be demanded and, therefore, will be of interest to gerontologists investigating the theoretical and practical implications of alternative housing options for older adults. AHL is not recommended here as an exclusive focus for theoretically driven research on housing in gerontology. Rather, the special attention to ALH is justified, we will argue, by its theoretical as well as practical importance for understanding successful aging among elderly individuals at risk for disability. Ecological and developmental theory both suggest how the model of ALH is designed to maximize a sense of self-efficacy while promising the reliable availability of compensatory care as required. As noted above, the theoretical significance of ALH as a distinctive research site is suggested by the work of a broad range of theorists in research on human development who highlight the transactions that occur continuously between individuals and the everyday milieus in which they function. The practical significance of ALH is suggested by the promised personal and societal benefits of identifying a type of housing and living arrangement based on principles which, if implemented, have the potential to stabilize and enhance the functional capacity of the growing number of very old adults at high risk for dependence. Not only does theory suggest ALH as a design of choice for many individuals in an aging society, but ALH is also a design of choice for potentially maximizing individual well-being of persons who are disabled or at high risk for disability at an economically and politically bearable price. These promised theoretical and practical benefits are not assured. But they are reasons enough for believing that AHL is a prime site for developing a new agenda for research and theory building in gerontology.

Special emphasis will be placed in this final section on the convergence of theories of social structure, ecological psychology, and adult development to re-establish the importance of housing and living arrangements in gerontological theory and practice. Emphasis will also be placed on outlining in broad terms a research agenda specifying questions which, if answered, promise to increase understanding of how model ALH facilities can help sustain both functional capacity and sense of well-being for older adults at high risk for dependence.

II. Housing and Living Arrangements: A Census Perspective

The typical descriptive profile of housing and living arrangements in the United States is adequately illustrated by the relevant chapter in the fourth edition of this handbook (Pynoos & Golant, 1996). From the perspective of "specifying ignorance," one would say that the chapter focuses primarily on describing what is known about estimates of the availability, affordability, and quality of housing for older adults. These estimates are based on the evidence available in 1995, but are supplemented here by more recent survey data on the situation of older adults (U.S. Department of Housing and Human Development [HUD], 1999). Available data provide descriptions that remain useful currently because such data change slowly. New evidence from the Year 2000 Census of Housing will be unlikely to present a substantially different picture.

The United States Census Bureau supplements its decennial census of housing with periodic applications of the AHS, which uses a basic probability sample of about 56,000 households. AHS is accessible on the Internet (*www.census.gov*) and covers a variety of housing topics, including an array of administrative and policy-relevant reports through 1997 on, for example, housing quality, recent moves, vacancy rates, and conditions of neighborhoods. Although a variety of topics can be explored with AHS data, controlling for chronological age of residents, multivariate analysis proves to be complex and time consuming. As an indication of this complexity, the listed publications on the Internet analyzing AHS data through 1999 include only one article in an academic journal using these data to assess the housing needs of elders (Geldersbloom & Mullins, 1995). That article described specifically the relatively higher housing cost of elderly renters compared with elderly homeowners.

Given the challenge of multivariate analysis of AHS data on housing and living arrangements, investigators will find useful the recent report from the U.S. Department of HUD (1999), *Housing Our Elders*. This report organizes AHS data through 1997 in terms of specific policy and administrative issues such as *adequacy*, *accessibility*, and *affordability*. Then the report moves to discuss, although with minimum references to data analysis, a significant new issue, *appropriateness*. Appropriateness refers to the matching of the types and levels of needs among older adults to a consideration of types and levels of service and aids available in a housing environment. The question of appropriateness is posed for housing occupied by older adults in the United States without, however, providing an answer. Later in the chapter the importance of this concept for theory building about housing and living arrangements will become evident.

In all available presentations of HUD data on housing, univariate analysis is the rule and multivariate analyses of data germane to testing hypotheses about adequacy, accessibility, and affordability for elderly persons are the exception. In the questions and answers that follow, therefore, there is minimal interest in theory and no specification of ignorance to be overcome beyond noting an opportunity to explore the issue of appropriateness of housing in relation to levels of disability. Generalizations about housing and living arrangements in the paragraphs below are drawn from available census data supplemented by evidence from HUD's *Housing Our Elders* (1999). For continually updated statistics on housing and living arrangements see www.aoa.dhhs.gov/stat/statpage.html. The reader is reminded that the data below are estimates that may be modified when data from the Year 2000 Census of Housing are available.

Question: What are the characteristics of housing occupied by elderly households?

Answer: About 95% of older adults live in their own homes and 77% of them are homeowners. Home ownership is characteristic even of the oldest old, those 85 years of age and older. Reflecting differences in availability of resources and possibly preferences across the life course, younger cohorts of older adults are less likely to own their homes than those who are currently old. And socioeconomic diversity is evident in lower rates of home ownership among African Americans (64%), Hispanics (55%), and lower income elderly (61%).

Question: What are the living arrangements of noninstitutionalized elderly?

Answer: Fifty-four percent of older adults live with a spouse; 31% live alone; 13% live with a related person, and 2% live with an unrelated person. Older women are more likely than men to live alone or with a related person.

Question: How many older adults do not live in the community?

Answer: For quite some time the estimated proportion of older adults living in institutional settings, typically in nursing homes, at any given time remained about 4 or 5% among persons 65 years of age and older. Residence in institutions is age-related, increasing from about 1.4% for those aged 65–74 to 22% of those 85 and older. By 1996, however, nursing home occupancy rates had decreased overall to

4.2%, with the rate of those 85 years and older decreasing to 19.8%. This trend probably reflects increased availability of home- and community-based services, and a new real estate market featuring special residential housing with services to be purchased as needed. It also may reflect new evidence that onset of disability is occurring at later ages and levels of disability prior to death in old age are declining. (See, e.g., Manton, Corder, & Stallard, 1997, for a review of recent epidemiological evidence).

Question: What is the condition of available housing?

Answer: An estimated 3–5% of housing in the United States is described as physically decrepit and overcrowded. In contrast, many older adults appear to be and consider themselves to be "overhoused" as a consequence of continuing to age in place in houses built initially for a family with children. The mismatch of need for and availability of appropriate residential space is especially a problem for older adults living alone. Overall, older adults in the United States are characterized as well housed.

Question: Have significant shifts in public policy and the market for housing occurred in the United States in recent decades?

Answer: Awareness has increased that the elderly as a category for public policy and programming comprises a diverse population with diverse needs. In the public sector, a significant facet of that awareness is growing recognition that age without reference to need is an inadequate basis for accessing special governmentally sponsored services or housing arrangements. And, in the private sector, real estate interests in the 1990s invested heavily in the marketing of ALH that promises to provide both housing and service needs in a residential environment. Although this development has been described as possibly providing affordable housing with services for low-income

elderly, ALH has more obviously been designed to attract middle and higher income older adults capable of out-of-pocket payment. Assessing strategies to achieve the eventual affordability of ALH for lower income elderly is an important challenge for the future.

The AHS, as a supplement to the decennial census, has continued to take note of administrative and public-policy-relevant questions. The survey recognizes, for example, the personal importance of housing as a costly item in individual budgets, and the public importance of knowing whether housing has adequate heating or why people move. No explicit theory of housing, or more broadly of habitat, is perceived to be necessary or useful for answering such questions. Hence the continuing relevance of Myers' complaint about lack of interest in theory in areas (e.g., such as housing and living arrangements). Although the "specification of ignorance" about housing for elderly persons, as noted, reasonably features administrative and public policy questions, these specifications are at some distance from an earlier broad theoretical focus of developmentalists and gerontologists on housing and living arrangements. Locating human beings as active agents, transacting with one another in defined milieus, and exploring the outcomes of those transactions were central issues in earlier research. Important aspects of this research are recalled in the next section, and a renewal of interest in a theoretical understanding of person–milieu transactions is recommended.

III. Housing and Living Arrangements: A Transactional Perspective

When a major handbook of environmental psychology appeared over a decade ago, Frances Carp (1987; see also 1976) declared *environment* to be a well-established domain in research on aging. Her own earlier research on the successful adaptation of older residents to a new planned housing site, Victoria Plaza, had demonstrated that voluntary movement of older adults to a new residence typically increased a sense of satisfaction and well-being. And by the mid-1980s she could reference research by Lawton and others in volumes of the *Handbook of the Psychology of Aging*, documenting the impact of milieus not only on well-being but also on sensory and perceptual mediation and on the interpersonal interaction of older adults. Assessment of the outcomes of transactions in living environments tended to focus particularly on the variable of *fit* between personal needs and capability of individuals and the resource availability in and demands of defined milieus. *Fit* is a construct whose explanatory potential in the study of person–milieu transactions was explored in a classic article in gerontological literature by Lawton and Nahemow (1973).

By the third edition of the *Handbook of the Psychology of Aging*, Parmalee and Lawton (1990) noted in their chapter on the design of special environments for the aged a lull in empirical research on environmental issues. They attributed this lull in part to diminished federal funding of research on housing and a shift in interest in housing issues away from ecological psychology toward the more practical interests of designers and architects. In spite of the perceived shift away from theory toward practical concerns, these authors reaffirmed the importance for older adults of balancing needs for both autonomy and security. And they anticipated correctly the emergence of new configurations of housing design to facilitate the negotiations of persons in their living environments to achieve both independence and security living environments such as the then-emerging

continuing care retirement communities and assisted living residential facilities.

In the fourth edition of the *Handbook of the Psychology of Aging*, no chapter updating the environmental psychological issues of person–milieu fit appeared. In that edition discussion focused on how biological and social influences affect behavior, and particular attention was given to genetics and the central nervous system rather than to an ecological analysis of transactions to achieve person–milieu fit.

The progressive diminution of interest in ecological psychology in gerontology generally, and in housing and living arrangements particularly, was matched in more recent volumes of the *Handbook of Aging and the Social Sciences* by a routine focus in social scientific gerontology on managerial and descriptive accounts of these topics. The opportunity, if not the necessity, of "reestablishing the phenomenon" (housing and living arrangements) as a theoretical interest in gerontology and "respecifying ignorance" regarding the questions gerontologists might benefit from exploring in their research were not obvious concerns.

This particular diminution of interest in theory is in sharp contrast to the chapter in the first edition authored by Frances Carp (1976), whose contribution to the environmental psychology of housing has already been noted. Carp's "Housing and Living Environments of Older People" displays an elegant interest in theoretical issues, (e.g., in her discussion of Irving Rosow's [1967] then controversial hypothesis on the beneficial effects on older adults of age segregation and age density of living environments). Carp was explicit in her interest in exploring the implications for gerontological theory and practice of research evidence from studies of housing and living arrangements. That evidence, as she interpreted it, made clear the necessity of longitudinal research for explaining the differential behavioral effects of various living arrangements; the important consequences of congruence (fit) between personal capacity and milieu resources, expectations and opportunities; and the availability of effective strategies for beneficial interventions, such as moving older adults into living environments designed to balance needs for security and autonomy. Carp drew another particularly important conclusion from her review of research on housing: A variety of housing and living arrangements, she anticipated, will be required to incorporate the various needs for prosthetic and therapeutic as well as for everyday living requirements of a very diverse older population. Carp's emphasis on a theory of person–environment transactions was unfortunately not sustained as social scientific gerontology progressively accumulated data on housing and living arrangements primarily to answer administrative and questions.

Interest in the theoretical implications of housing and living arrangements, more broadly of transactions between persons and milieus, now resides at the margins of gerontology. The work of Powell Lawton (2000) remains a notable exception. Fortunately, the research and scholarship of a number of theorists who have focused on the dynamics and outcomes of person–milieu transactions have compensated for the changing interests of gerontologists. Cumulatively their focus on person–milieu transactions and the consequences of milieu design intersect with developmental theory in gerontology and anticipate the model of milieu design for the special type of housing with services discussed in the last section of this chapter. Urie Bronfenbrenner's (1979) work provides an excellent point of departure for revitalizing the interest of gerontologists in housing as a research site.

Although Bronfenbrenner's (1979) distinctive trademark is captured in his *The Ecology of Human Development*, the full sweep and influence of his intellectual

career as reflected in his publications, his colleagues, and his students are conveniently summarized in a more recent testamentary volume in his honor (Moen, Elder, & Lüscher, 1995). Bronfenbrenner is a comparativist who is repeatedly reminded by his experience and research that the dynamics of human development display persistent variety over time and space. The observation of the persistence of variation and change led him to be, at heart, a multidisciplinary experimenter and interventionist. His awareness that societies are large natural experiments in the differential effects of resource allocation over the life course called his attention to the importance of social class within a society as a context for development. And he remained a firm believer in the resilience of individuals who have been deprived of essential social resources for development to be able to benefit from prosthetic and therapeutic interventions. Although Bronfenbrenner persistently emphasizes the importance of spatial location, his theoretical interests have never focused specifically on housing and living arrangements and only minimally on later life.

A complementary theoretical perspective is evident in the research of sociologist Aaron Antonovsky (1987). Like Bronfenbrenner, Antonovsky's intellectual interests remained at the margin of gerontology. But his construct of *sense of coherence* focused specifically on how any individual's development in time and space is affected by societal integration and social support and, in turn, affects comprehension of choices to be made; how the meaning and significance of alternatives are gauged; and how the availability of the resources essential to an effective response is assessed. Although Antonovsky does not relate his paradigm of coherence explicitly to later life or to housing and living arrangements, the construct adapts easily as an aspect of an individual's assessment of person–milieu fit. And the paradigm assessing the adequacy of this fit articulates well with the construct "successful aging" proposed by Paul and Margret Baltes (Baltes & Baltes, 1990) and by Margret Baltes (1996). The perspective of Baltes and Baltes provides a useful bridge between Bronfenbrenner's and Antonovsky's generic presentation of the ecology of human development and a specific application to late-life development, particularly as the risk of dependency increases.

Late life provides many illustrations of developmental continuities that result from the "successful aging" characteristic of the majority of older adults who retain essential functional capacities and socioeconomic resources. But what is the meaning of *success* in very late life when the probability of functional disability increases, often dramatically for a minority and eventually to some degree for most very old adults? The answer lies, Baltes and Baltes argue, both in the internal dynamic of selecting and maximizing personal capacities for adapting self and social expectations regarding behavior, and also of realistic assessment of expectations about potential prosthetic and therapeutic compensation from one's proximate milieu. Carp drew a similar conclusion several decades earlier. A critical variable in the dynamics of person–context transactions, therefore, becomes the design and intentions of social and spatial arrangements, such as housing and living arrangements, to anticipate and compensate for increasing personal disability. Margret Baltes (1996), moreover, in her cross-national research on nursing homes, has documented complementary evidence of the different ways caregivers in various care settings respond to disability in later life. From research in both Germany and the United States, she found that the probability is very high that nursing home caregivers, for example, tend to perceive residents as incompetent, not simply as frail, and to

reinforce in their interaction with residents a sense both that self-efficacy has been irrevocably lost and that total dependency is the inevitable outcome. Such milieus are not likely to counter increasing age-related disability with compensatory support to maximize functional independence and appropriate self-management.

Dependency, however, has proved to have "many faces" and one common face is dependency as a strategy in interpersonal relationships. Beyond the appearance of learned helplessness, dependency can be used to gain attention and negotiate compensatory assistance. Margret Baltes, like Bronfenbrenner in his optimism about the resilience of handicapped children, was confident about retaining a fundamental capacity for resilience among both frail older adults and their caregivers. Consequently, she demonstrated, through thoughtfully designed interventions, the capacity to stimulate both frail older persons and their caregivers to expect improvement in functional capacity. Resilient adaptation through "selective optimization with compensation" can be achieved, even for disabled older adults, in special housing contexts designed to provide compensatory care and social support without depriving individuals of choice.

In a reflective observation on the implications of the arguments and findings reported in *Examining Lives in Context* (Moen, Elder, & Lüscher, 1995), Bronfenbrenner (1995) offers several observations broadly relevant for "specifying ignorance" and designing research regarding housing as a developmental context for adults. He particularly stressed the importance of research on what he called "proximate processes," the observed transactions of individuals in time and space. Although his illustrations focused on the interactions of mothers and children in a home environment, one can easily extrapolate to the transactions of a frail older adult and caregivers in a nursing home or an assisted living facility. The key point is the emphasis on having longitudinal information for understanding transactional processes in time and space of the kind not available from cross-sectional survey evidence. Bronfenbrenner expands on this point with praise for the way in which Melvin Kohn's research, for example, illustrates how "causal chains" can be observed in the effects of work experience on the behavior of adults. As individuals live out significant portions of their lives in structured environments such as a workplace, evidence indicates that the particular patterning of person–context transactions tend to be consequential for future behavior. Kohn stressed particularly positive effects of the experience of autonomy in the workplace. (For a succinct summary of several decades of this research, see Kohn, 1995).

Kohn's initial focus in research on human development was the impact of social class location, first as reflected in child-rearing values of families; then, as reflected in young adulthood in educational aspirations and achievement; and eventually in the consequences of participation in workplaces that encourage autonomy and innovation. The differential structuring of work environments to maximize autonomy and encourage innovation proved to have two particularly significant outcomes—an enhanced sense of well-being and enhanced capacity and willingness to deal with change. An easy extrapolation moves one conceptually from curiosity about the developmental consequences of workplace structures among adults to the possibility of similar beneficial effects of the purposive structuring of housing and living arrangements to enhance autonomy and capacity to deal with change for adults in a special setting such as an ALH facility. This possible connection has in fact been made by Rudolf Moos in research that returns the focus on housing and living arrangements to the earlier interest in ecological theory.

Over two decades ago Moos (1976) wrote a treatise on "environment and man" that ranged broadly from the significance for development and behavior of natural and human-made physical environments, to population density, crowding, noise and pollution, to social environments and to the impact of organizational structure and change. A capstone concept of Moos's thought was "social climate"—"the 'personality' of the environment." His initial applications of this concept explored special therapeutic environments of hospitals and clinics and then the institutional learning environments of young adults in college. In time, special living environments of frail older adults became a logical extension of Moos's interest in the consequences of social climates of living environments for older adults. A Multiphasic Environmental Assessment Procedure (MEAP) (Moos & Lemke, 1994) was developed to characterize over 300 group residences—congregate, residential, sheltered environments, and nursing homes—with particular focus on explaining observed behavioral consequences. Regardless of the type of shelter, the MEAP has proved to be useful in characterizing residents and staff, physical and architectural features, the basic objectives of institutional policy and programs, and the social climate of various congregate living environments for disabled elderly. In research on group living facilities for elderly persons, structural features of residential facilities such as ownership, size, and level of care required by residents have been found to be useful predictors of outcomes for residents. But more important in determining behavioral outcomes for residents have been factors of *social climate* in which both autonomy and choice are legitimate and promoted; residents are involved in decisions about their community; and staff are committed to a milieu in which privacy, choice, and resident involvement are encouraged. Initial documentation indicates that a prochoice, pro-involvement social climate promotes well-being, better adaptation to change, and reduction of inappropriate use of facility care resources. These are outcomes reminiscent of Kohn's findings about the beneficial developmental effects of workplaces in which autonomy, innovativeness, and involvement are encouraged.

Further study of well-characterized older adults in well-characterized residential contexts begun by Moos and Lemke permit the kind of hypothesis development and theory building needed in research on housing and living arrangements if we are to move our understanding beyond routine characterization of housing stocks and their older inhabitants. This refocusing of interest returns our attention in research to the ecological perspective that prevailed when this handbook series was initiated almost three decades ago. Both theory and research suggest that positive dynamics of person–milieu transactions can be achieved for disabled elderly living environments designed to implement AHL ideals.

Moreover, housing and living arrangements provide strategic sites for exploring theories of behavioral ecology applied to caring environments, expanding the research of investigators like Moos with the organizational structural analysis of workplaces by investigators like Kohn. How are the promised benefits of ALH for residents achieved? The development and enhancement of a sense of self-efficacy, maintenance of appropriate autonomy, and enhancement of well-being even in the face of change are outcomes of particular interest in both work and housing settings. Specification of structured living environments that enhance and sustain a sense of autonomy also resonates with Bandura's research (1997)

on the development of a sense of self-efficacy, a construct referencing positive expectancy in regard to the outcomes of one's actions. Self-efficacy has proved to be one of the most powerful predictors of successful behavioral interventions with older adults (see, e.g., Kawachi, Kennedy, & Wilkinson, 1999, Part 3). And of particular interest in assessing the possible beneficial effects of ALH as a milieu providing reliable availability of appropriate care is the potential for the development not only of a sense of self-efficacy among residents but also, perhaps even more importantly, a sense of collective efficacy. Producing a living environment in which reliably available compensatory care can be a reasonable, shared expectation in a caring community. Collective efficacy refers, for example, to a shared expectation among members of a group sharing a space (a "community") in which objectives of the social group as a whole can on occasion have priority over individual objectives, and in which one can expect that the group will be appropriately responsive to the needs of individuals. It is just such a sense of the reliable availability of compensatory help that is an objective of a model ALH facility.

IV. Assisted Living Housing: A Strategic Site for a New Research Agenda

Overall, older Americans are the best housed citizens of a well-housed nation. This is the general conclusion drawn from the most recent (1995) evidence from the American Housing Survey (U.S. Department of Housing and Urban Development, 1999). Granted, this evidence indicates that housing sometimes costs too much, needs repairs, and presents problems of accessibility for a minority of disabled elderly. The findings of the AHS evidence, HUD concludes, call attention to a relatively unexplored dimension of housing—*appropriateness*—that should be added to the standard three of *affordability, adequacy,* and *accessibility*. The concept of *appropriateness* recognizes the diversity of the needs and preferences of older adults, including the dominant preference among older adults to *age in place* or in a setting that provides maximum independence and dignity without ignoring needs for physical and psychological security. But equally important for reestablishing interest in housing and living arrangements as issues of theoretical interest, *appropriateness* articulates particularly well with a transactional perspective of human adaptation and person–milieu fit. It is the potential benefit of achieving such a fit between declining functional capacity of individuals and reliable compensatory care of disabled older adults that makes ALH facilities potentially such attractive sites for gerontological research and theory.

Securing *affordable* housing that is also *appropriate* will remain a personal challenge for disabled and low-income elderly. Moreover, securing affordable, appropriate housing is also a problem for many very old persons (those 85 and older) who, in the long term, as Baltes and Baltes (1990) have observed, must anticipate the probability of reduced disability-free remaining years of life. For an aging population, ALH is clearly a prime site for exploring the potential and limits of designing a combination of housing with services capable of maximizing and maintaining functional capacity and a sense of well-being

In recent years, as the HUD report notes, both public and private sectors have begun to recognize and respond to the need for alternative housing that falls between shelter for those who remain totally independent and those who require near-total care. Such a continuum of need is not a new idea; it has been recognized and responded to effectively for many years (e.g., in the housing policy of Great Britain).

The author observed about three decades ago in Britain a policy debate about an adequate shelter policy in a society committed to governmental assistance in support of the public's welfare. In the period following the creation of the National Health Service in 1948, Britain tried to rationalize its procedures for determining how many hospital beds it should maintain per unit of population. The conclusion drawn was that a large minority (about 40%) of existing hospital beds were being used for social supportive services rather than for medically necessary therapy and that, therefore, the ratio of hospital beds required could possibly be reduced by 50% over a relatively few years (Maddox, 1972). This conclusion called attention to the values and preferences of both patients and the hospital staff that encouraged designing a better public shelter policy. If "bed blockers," as persons being "unnecessarily" sheltered in hospital beds came to be called, were removed from hospitals, where would they be housed? The British had developed a shelter policy to accommodate lower income but functionally independent persons with what was called Council Housing, reflecting the responsibilities of local governments to be involved in providing affordable shelter with some social and health services available. Sheltering disabled persons displaced from hospitals was an additional challenge that produced what came to be called Part III Accommodations. The prototype of these special accommodations was a domicilary shelter presided over by a warden who had the benefit of locally available general practitioners, visiting nurses, and social services as needed. The history and overall favorable experience with this type of shelter with services in Britain and more generally in Europe, particularly in the Nordic countries, can be found in Heumann and Boldy

(1993). In Britain, the complementary involvement of the private sector in provision of housing with services is illustrated by mature organizations specializing in shelter for frail older adults such as the Abbeyfield Society (www.amersham. freeuk.com) and Anchor Trust (www. anchor.org.uk/homepage.htm).

Until recently, shelter policy in the United States characteristically kept the provision of housing and services separate in policy and in financing. The current statement of policy intent in the noted HUD statement (1999), however, illustrates a decidedly different intent to recognize the potential benefits of integrating shelter and care services. HUD's new "Security Plan for Older Americans" embodies three goals:

1. To help older adults remain in their homes and connected to their families and communities
2. To expand affordable housing for low income older adults
3. To improve the range and coordination of affordable housing and supportive service combinations available to older adults

This Plan indicates an administrative intent to reestablish housing as an issue of theoretical interest by moving beyond counting units of adequate, affordable, and accessible housing toward exploring the beneficial behavioral consequences of focusing on the appropriateness of housing. Translating this intent into outcomes remains a future task for HUD and will require much more than noting the possible or probable significance of fitting the needs and wants of older adults to particular shelter environments from a large array of special environments such as domiciliary shelters, shared housing, adult care homes, and continuing care retirement communities. Bronfenbrenner's experience, as well as that of Carp earlier, suggests that adequate research on appropriate housing for very old adults will require longitudinal inquiry focused on "proximal processes" of adequately characterized residents interacting within clearly specified housing and living arrangement if we are to identify what works and what works most effectively. An illustration of such research is illustrated by Margret Baltes's monitored interventions with frail older adults dependent on care to compensate for reduced functional capacity (Baltes, 1996).

The progressive marginalization of theory in gerontological inquiry about housing and living arrangements has been reinforced in part by HUD's conclusion that the great majority of older adults in the United States are the best housed citizens in a well-housed nation. Beyond describing the cost, adequacy, and accessibility of housing, what is there to explain of interest to gerontologists? The recent declaration of interest by HUD in the appropriateness of housing reflects a new awareness of the large and increasing number of older adults who, although functionally disabled, expect and are expected to live in the community, to age in place successfully, rather than in special institutional settings. Appropriateness of housing is a concept that reestablishes the relevance of person–milieu fit as a question of theoretical interest and suggests the merits of a transactional perspective. A distinctive type of housing with services rooted in ecological and developmental theory, ALH has emerged partly in response to the widely shared personal and social preference of functionally disabled adults to live independently as long as possible in communities designed to provide the security of reliable availability of compensatory services as required.

What is so distinctive about ALH, and what prompts its choice for special focus in this chapter as a distinctive site for developing a new research agenda in housing, are its roots, implicitly and often explicitly, in communitarian values and in ecological and developmental theory. In its ideal manifestation, the ALH model promises a distinctive site for living arrangements structured to maximize quality of life for residents (not patients) who require, or are at risk of requiring, compensatory care. The promised structure is intended to encourage a sense of autonomy and the development of a sense of socially reinforced self-efficacy while at the same time assuring the reliable availability of compensatory care as needed (see, e.g., Hawes, Rose, & Phillips, 1999; Kane & Wilson, 1993; Wilson, 1996)

Regnier et al. (1995) list four basic concepts of a distinctive philosophy defining the core ideas of the ALH model: (a) creating a private place of one's own; (b) matching service to individual need, including around-the-clock capacity to respond to unscheduled care needs; (c) sharing responsibility among caretakers, family, and resident; and (d) providing residents with choice and control of their lives. Consumer demand has signaled that ALH is a very attractive housing option for individuals in an aging population (Pristin, 2000).

Although, in some sense, nursing homes might be considered to be assisted living facilities and their clients might be called, as they are, *residents*, they are, in the typical instance, quite different. Nursing home clients are more likely to be considered patients in a milieu that tends to minimize autonomy and maximize dependence on formal caregivers. A model ALH facility, designed to implement the ideals of this distinctive type of housing, provides for distinctly different person–milieu transactions.

Federal housing policy in the United States (in contrast to Great Britain, as noted previously) until recently reinforced the separation of housing and service provision in minimally regulated and supervised settings—such as old age, retirement, and board and care homes—by not funding such arrangements. Conse-

quently, ALH has remained an inadequately studied private-sector initiative. For an older population increasingly at risk for functional disability and that clearly has expressed its preference to age at home if possible, the prospect of a facility that invites residents to purchase with their housing levels of service appropriate to their assessed needs has been just what they wanted. Private-sector developers have been responsive to consumer demand, possibly overresponsive (e.g., see Pristin, 2000), in the 1990s. By 1998 there were at least 28,000 ALH facilities in the United States, with provision for over 612,000 residents (Mollica, 1998). Estimates of the numbers of residents accommodated in assisted living facilities ranged as high as 1.5 million (Citro & Hermanson, 1999; U.S. General Accounting Office, 1999). The level of investment in this market continues to be high; in the 1990s it increased by over 114%. Although the actual size of the potential ALH market is conjectural, it is undoubtedly large. And, as evidence of changing patterns of disability in an aging population and preferred sites for long-term care (e.g., Manton, Corder, & Stallard, 1997), nursing homes may be sought less frequently for management of late-life disability not requiring close medical or nursing supervision. Geographic variation in the development of the ALH market is also notable. Twenty-five percent of the available places for residents in assisted living facilities are in California, Florida, and Pennsylvania alone (Mollica, 1998). Continued growth of ALH in the long term can be reasonably expected.

Who are the elderly currently populating ALH facilities? Surveys indicate that the average older adult who has made the transition to an assisted living facility is an 83–year-old woman needing assistance with three activities of daily living. Almost 50% of these residents have some cognitive impairment (Mollica, 1998). A finding also reported in Mollica's survey of the characteristics of current ALH residents with important public policy implications is that, in 1997, the approximate annual income of residents was $31,000, and most residents (86%) received no public support. Since about 10% of older adults in the United States currently have incomes below the federal poverty line of $7,790 for individuals and $10,070 for a couple (U.S. Department of Housing and Urban Development, 1999) and one of the most powerful predictors of functional disability in adult populations is income (Maddox, 1999), a mismatch clearly exists between probable need for housing providing some compensatory care and the ability to pay for such housing out-of-pocket. Women living alone and minority individuals, who are at particularly high risk for functional disability, are among the most likely to have incomes below the poverty line.

Whether the political will to promote ALH as a federal or state policy priority so that low-income elderly can afford it remains to be determined but, in any case, it will depend in part on the demonstrated effectiveness as well as the cost and affordability of an ALH option. Affordability of ALH has effectively been demonstrated already for the large middle mass of older Americans. Demonstrating the effectiveness of ALH and comparing its cost effectiveness with alternative long-term care options will provide an essential component for future policy discussions. Our interest in this chapter, therefore, is to specify within the context of transactional theories of person–milieu interaction whether ALH modeled on the basic principles of autonomy, self-efficacy, and reliable availability of compensatory care has over the long term positive individual and community outcomes. The initial evidence from research in the tradition of social ecological, developmental, and organizational theory carried out in facilities that approximate ALH ideals has been affirmative (Moos

& Lemke, 1994). ALH appears, therefore, to be a strategic site for further explorations of the theories of Moos, Baltes, Kohn, and Bandura to this model as an effective strategy for minimizing functional dependency in later life.

The long-term-care facilities that reasonably approximate implementation of ALH principles identified by Moos and Lemke tend to confirm the hypothesized favorable outcomes for residents and the beneficial social climates of care facilities. Such evidence is consistent with prediction based on the theory and research of Bronfenbrenner, Antonovsky, Baltes and Baltes, Kohn, and Bandura. A pro-choice, pro-involvement social climate promotes a sense of well-being, better adaptation to change, and reduced inappropriate use of community care resources. Such outcomes are significant theoretically and lead to other important questions: What are the relative contributions of a positive social climate to the maintenance of functional competence? How does a positive social climate facilitate the modifiability of disability and activate the potential resilience of a disabled elderly person? What is the contribution of the key ALH variables, singly or in combination, to the creation and maintenance of a positive social climate and positive functional outcomes? Can cognitively impaired older adults benefit from ALH milieus?

At the organizational level, useful research questions can be posed: How often, and under what conditions do ALH facilities approximate model characteristics? Are culturally and socioeconomically homogeneous residents in an ALH facility more likely than residents in heterogeneous settings to experience favorable functional outcomes? Do ALH residents use health services in the facility and in the community less often and more appropriately than similarly disabled older adults in other housing settings? Do ALH facilities committed to the creation and maintenance of positive social climates tend also to generate distinctive commitments to the development of the social capital of ALH facilities? Although *social capital* is a marginal concept in gerontological theory, it is central to a substantial literature on income inequality and health relevant for assessing ALH outcomes (e.g., Kawachi et al., 1999, especially Part 3 on social cohesion and health). Both societies and social organizations tend to give attention to inequality of social resources distribution because of the known relationship between scarcity of resources and disability. But income inequality is typically not the only interest in the conceptualization and building of what might be called "competent communities"— communities that generate indicators of social capital such as civic trust, civic engagement, and a commitment to fairness and the expectation of reciprocity. Organizations and communities can and do promote and demonstrate models of trust, reciprocity, fairness, and engagement. One might reasonably expect a model AHL facility to focus on building a sense of collective efficacy that Baltes (1996) and Baltes and Baltes (1990) consider essential to an environment promising reliably available compensatory care for disabled elderly. And, beyond interest in resident–milieu fit, do ALH facilities generate milieus that attract and retain a workforce committed to develop and maintain ALH ideals?

The generation of interest in ALH as a major organizational initiative in a comprehensive system of long-term care is handicapped by the traditional indifference to planning a comprehensive system of long-term care in the United States. It is also inhibited by the continuing assumption that, to a large degree, except for the poor elderly, provision of long-term care is primarily a personal, not a societal problem.

Nonetheless, the rapidly emerging ALH industry that remains predominantly in the private sector eventually may develop and sustain a commitment to demonstrate the promised beneficial outcomes associated with appropriate housing for functionally disabled elderly who would benefit from an environment reliably providing compensatory care. ALH developers, for example, may conclude that appropriate care is probably both good business and in the public interest (Wylde & Zimmerman, 1999). And the gerontological research community may renew its interest in a transactional social ecological perspective as a useful mindset for future research on housing. ALH may be a promising, if not the most promising, site for exploring successful aging in very late life from the theoretical perspectives of human development, ecological, and organizational theory. Research on ALH, in sum, may revitalize theoretical interest in housing and living arrangements in gerontology.

As noted earlier, Kohn (1995), in an overview of his research on the effects of work environments on personality and behavior, has documented that the complexity of work environments and opportunities for personal involvement, autonomy, and mastery not only tends to produce a sense of well-being but also enhances the prospects for personal initiative and the willingness to take on and master the challenge of changing environments with greater confidence. By analogy, the complexities and opportunities of strategically designed care environments are critical ingredients in the transactions of persons with a milieu that enhances a sense of self-efficacy and that can be enhanced further by a sense of collective efficacy, to provide compensatory group and organizational support. Also of theoretical interest is how appropriately designed sheltered environments constitute strategic sites for exploring the Baltes and Baltes hypothesis of successful aging through selective optimization and compensation. This hypothesis suggests precisely what an optimal implementation of ALH is designed to produce for frail older adults. It is the prospect of achieving such positive outcomes that may drive the development of political will and social policy development in support of ALH as a realistic option for disabled low-income older adults who would benefit from such compensatory environments.

Furthermore, ALH facilities should be studied as the workplaces of care providers. For example, does a model AHL facility that produces positive outcomes for residents also produce positive outcomes for staff? Do such facilities invest in social capital (wages, education, development of supportive networks) that produces lower turnover, better professional performance, increased capacity to innovate, and higher job satisfaction?

The complexity of creating affordable assisted living environments and of doing theoretically significant research in such environments should not be underestimated. Assisted living facilities vary widely in the characteristics of residents, in the services provided, in the quality of care provided, and in the outcomes for residents (Hawes et al., 1999, U.S. General Accounting Office, 1999). But with better research tools for characterizing ALH residents and their special living environments, the opportunities for enhancing theory about beneficial transactions between older adults and their housing and living arrangements are available. Evidence that ALH can be made more affordable and represent value for money in providing appropriate shelter for a large population of older adults with functional disabilities will be a critical ingredient in stimulating serious consideration of ALH as a public commitment. If the United States were to follow Canada, Germany, or Japan in the development of a national long-term-care policy, ALH would be a likely component for inclusion. Short of that, as the United States responds to the changing patterns of functional disability among elderly persons and the diminished preference for nursing homes as a site for care, a portion of Medicaid dollars, now substantially directed toward nursing home care for low-income elderly persons, may well be better invested in improving the affordability of ALH.

References

Antonovsky, A. (1987). *Unraveling the mysteries of health: How people manage stress and stay well.* San Francisco: Jossey-Bass.

Baltes, M. (1996). *Many faces of dependency in old age.* Cambridge, UK: Cambridge University Press.

Baltes, P., & Baltes, M. (1990). Psychological perspectives on successful aging: The model of selective optimization with compensation. In P. Baltes & M. Baltes (Eds.), *Successful aging: Perspectives from the social sciences* (pp. 1–34). Cambridge, UK: Cambridge University Press.

Bandura, A. (1997). *Self-efficacy: The exercise of control.* New York: W. H. Freeman.

Bronfenbrenner, U. (1979). *The ecology of human development: Experiments by nature and design.* Cambridge, MA: Harvard University Press.

Bronfenbrenner, U. (1995). Developmental ecology through space and time: A future perspective. In P. Moen, G. Elder, & K. Luscher (Eds.), *Examining lives in context: Perspectives on the ecology of human development* (pp. 619–648). Washington, DC: American Psychological Association.

Carp, F. (1976). Housing and living environments of older people. In E. Shanas & R. H. Binstock (Eds.), *Handbook of aging and the social sciences* (pp. 244–271). New York: Van Nostrand Reinhold Company.

Carp, F. (1987). Environment and aging. In D. Stokols & I. Altman (Eds.), *Handbook of environmental psychology* (pp. 329–354). New York: John Wiley.

Citro, J., & Hermanson, S. (1999). *Assisted living in the United States.* Washington, DC: AARP.

Folts, E., & Yeats, D. (Eds.). (1994). *Housing and the aging population*. New York: Garland Publishing.

Geldersbloom, J., & Mullins, R. (1995). Elderly housing needs: Examination of the American Housing Survey. *International Journal of Aging and Human Development, 40*(1), pp. 57–72.

Hawes, C., Rose, M., & Phillips, C. D. (1999). *A national study of assisted living for the frail elderly: Results of a national survey of facilities*. Beachwood, OH: Myers Research Institute, Menorah Park Center for Senior Living.

Heumann, L., & Boldy, D. (Eds.). (1993). *Aging in place with dignity: International solutions relating to the low income and frail elderly*. Westport, CT: Praeger.

Kane, R. A., & Wilson, K. B. (1993). *Assisted living in the United States: A new paradigm for residential care for frail older persons?* Washington, DC: American Association of Retired Persons.

Kawachi, I., Kennedy, B., & Wikinson, R. (Eds.). (1999). *The society and population reader, Volume I*. New York: The New Press.

Kohn, M. (1995). Social structure and personality through time and space. In P. Moen, G. Elder, & K. Luscher (Eds.), *Examining lives in context. Perspectives on the ecology of human development* (pp. 141–169). Washington, DC: American Psychological Association.

Lawton, M. P. (2000). Chance and choice make a good life. In J. Birren and J. Schroots (Eds.), *A History of geropsychology in autobiography* (pp. 185–196). Washington, DC: American Psychological Association.

Lawton, M. P., & Nahemow, L. (1973). Ecology and the aging process. In C. Eisdorfer & P. Lawton (Eds.), *Psychology of adult development and aging* (pp. 464–488). Washington, DC: American Psychological Association.

Maddox, G. (1972). Muddling through: Planning health services in England. *Medical Care, 9*, 439–448.

Maddox, G. (1999). Sociology of aging. In W. Hazzard et al. (Eds.), *Principles of geriatrics and gerontology (4th ed.)* (pp. 231–238). New York: McGraw-Hill.

Maddox, G., & Lawton, P. (Eds.). (1993). *Kinship, aging and social change*. Annual review of gerontology and geriatrics (Vol. 13). New York: Springer Publishing Company.

Manton, K., Corder, L., & Stallard, E. (1997). Chronic disability trends in older United States populations: 1982–1994. *Proceedings of the National Academy of Sciences of the United States, 94* (6), 2593–2598.

Moen, P., Elder, G., & Lüscher, K. (Eds.). (1995). *Examining lives in context: Perspectives on the ecology of human development*. Washington, DC: American Psychological Association.

Mollica, R. (1998). *State assisted living policy, 1998*. Portland, ME: National Academy for State Health Policy.

Moos, R. (1976). *The Human context: Environmental determinants of behavior*. New York: John Wiley & Sons.

Moos, R., & Lemke, S. (1994). *Group residencies for older adults: Physical features, policies and social climate*. New York: Oxford University Press.

Myers, G. (1996). Research directions and unresolved issues. In R. H. Binstock & L.K. George (Eds.), *Handbook of aging and the social sciences* (4th ed.) (pp. 1–11). San Diego, CA: Academic Press.

O'Rand, A., & Campbell, R. (1999). On re-establishing the phenomenon and specifying ignorance: Theory development and research design in aging. In V.L. Bengtson & K.W. Schaie (Eds.), *Handbook of theories of aging* (pp. 59–80). New York: Springer Publishing Company.

Parmalee, P., & Lawton, P. (1990). The design of special environments for the aged. In J. E. Birren & K. W. Schaie (Eds.), *Handbook of the psychology of aging, 3rd edition* (pp. 464–488). San Diego, CA: Academic Press.

Pristin, T. (2000). Too much, too soon halts assisted-living boom. *New York Times, May 28, B 3*.

Pynoos, J., & Golant, S. (1996). Housing and living arrangements for the elderly. In R. H. Binstock & L. K. George (Eds.), *Handbook of aging and the social sciences* (4th ed.). (pp. 303–325). San Diego, CA: Academic Press.

Regnier, V., Hamilton, J., & Yatabe, S. (1995). *Assisted living for the aged: Innovations in design, management and financing*. New York: Columbia University Press.

Rosow. I. (1967). *Social integration of the aged*. New York: The Free Press.

Stone, R. I. (2001). Home- and community-based care: Toward a caring paradigm. In L. E. Cluff & R. H. Binstock (Eds.), *The lost art of caring: A challenge to health professionals, families, communities and society* (pp. 155–176). Baltimore, MD: Johns Hopkins University Press.

U.S. Department of Housing and Urban Development. (1999). *Housing our elders: A report card on housing conditions and needs of older Americans*. Washington, DC: USD HUD

U.S. General Accounting Office. (1999). *Assisted living: Quality of care and consumer protection issues*. Washington, DC: GAO.

Wilson, K. B. (1996). *Assisted living*. Washington, DC: American Association of Retired Persons.

Wylde, M., & Zimmerman, S. (1999). *A guide to research information for the long-term care industries: Assisted living communities and nursing homes*. Fairfax, VA: International Assisted Living Foundation.

Twenty-Four

The End of Life

Anne M. Wilkinson and Joanne Lynn

I. Introduction

Only a few generations ago, growing old was an unexpected phenomenon. Most people died earlier and mostly of illnesses that killed quickly—from infections, accidents, and serious untreatable diseases. Now, most people will grow old enough to face chronic conditions that worsen over time and lead to death. Such profound social change engenders confusion in language, social perceptions, and categories like "death and dying." The extension of life span, the increasing medicalization of health care, and the prominence of chronic illness in late life challenge society to meet new needs. Care at the end of life should enhance or maintain patient function, facilitate patient control and autonomy, encourage resolution of relationships, and provide family support before and after the death. It should assuage emotional and physical symptoms, facilitate spiritual growth, avoid family impoverishment, and generally support living a good life despite the shadow of death. Yet much of current medical practice and financing are inimical to the interests of persons with eventually fatal chronic diseases. Most health-care services, technology,

payments, and research focus on restoring health after acute illness. Society invests little in addressing the needs of the chronically ill and dying.

This chapter presents a conceptualization of the end of life that is much longer, more complex, and more commonplace than the narrow slice of time society now labels as "dying" or "terminally ill." This "last phase of life" spans most people's last months, or years, when chronic illness constrains daily activities and worsens despite treatment, eventually causing death. We will describe the main forces changing how people experience the end of their lives in the United States today, with an emphasis on epidemiological data, and recent insights from research, policy developments, education, and advocacy efforts, in order to describe how health care and social services might evolve in the coming years.

II. Changes in the Experience of "Dying" in the United States

A. Changing Demographics

Improved sanitation, better nutrition, immunization for communicable diseases,

Handbook of Aging and the Social Sciences, Fifth Edition

definitive treatment for infections, and therapeutic advances in clinical medicine have dramatically reduced mortality at younger ages and increased life expectancy. Whereas median life expectancy in 1900 was about 46 years, Americans can now expect to survive into their eighth decade (Field & Cassel, 1997). Average life expectancy at age 65 in 1900 was about 11.9 years (Guralnik, Fried, & Salive, 1996). By 1992, average life expectancy at age 65 reached 17.5 years (National Center for Health Statistics, 1992). Those over 65 years of age now account for about 13% of the total population. By 2030, when the entire baby boom cohort has entered old age, about 20% of the population will be over 65 (Friedland & Summer, 1999).

Large numbers of persons living into old age has led to long-term, chronic conditions associated with aging becoming the major pathway to disability and death. In one sense, this century's scientific, medical, and public health advances have made living easier and dying harder (Field & Cassel, 1997). Just a few generations ago, most people died at home. Today, Americans mostly die in hospitals or nursing homes surrounded by professionals, who are strangers, rather than family. Moreover, changes in family structure have meant that the elderly are now more physically and psychologically distant from their children and grandchildren. Not only does this indicate more isolation and less social support, but it also means that most Americans, even by middle age, have not lived with or cared for someone who was very sick and dying. Yet, we are now confronted with burgeoning numbers of individuals who will be seriously ill for a long period of time prior to their dying. These new facts about aging and the end of life will have to become more familiar to professionals and laypersons alike, and the myriad social service and health care arrangements currently available must change. Current family expectations and skills surrounding death and dying will also have to change.

B. The Relationship of Disability and Mortality

Although many chronic illnesses are not fatal (e.g., arthritis, hearing or vision losses), most fatalities now arise from chronic disease. Physical disability in older adults results primarily from chronic disease, and the prevalence of disability associated with chronic conditions rises substantially with increasing age (Fried & Guralnik, 1997). The continued growth in the number of elderly will mean a concomitant increase in the number of people affected by disability associated with chronic conditions. By 2040, the number of people in the United States with chronic conditions will increase by 60%, from about 99 million Americans in 1995 to approximately 158 million individuals in 2040 (Friedland & Summer, 1999).

Longitudinal epidemiological studies have demonstrated that age and disability are the strongest predictors of increased risk of future mortality, even after adjusting for demographic characteristics, behavioral risk factors such as smoking and weight status, and several chronic diseases (see Corti, Guralnik, Salive, & Sorkin, 1994; Manton, Corder, & Stallard, 1993). Two-year follow-up data from the National Long Term Care Survey (NLTCS) showed annual mortality rates rising from slightly over 15% in those with disability in instrumental activities of daily living (IADLs) to 21% for those with disability in one or two basic acitivities of daily living (ADLs), 24% for those with three or four ADLs, and 37% for those with five or six ADLs (Warren & Knight, 1982). Brock and Foley (1998), using data from the 1985 Survey of the Last Days of Life (a stratified sample of 1,500 decedents 65 years of age or older), found that three out of four decedents were nonambulatory on the day before death. Unlimited mobility fell from 59% 1 year before death to 30% 1 month before death and then to 13% on the day before death. The United States will face many challenges in providing appropriate and accessible care for persons with chronic conditions leading to death as the size of the older population grows and life expectancy continues to increase.

C. Timing, Trajectories, and the Misleading Reliance on Prognosis

Various authors have attempted to explain patterns of dying using terms such as the awareness of dying (Glaser & Strauss, 1965), trajectories of dying (Benoliel, 1987–1988; Glaser & Strauss, 1968), phases of dying (Pattison, 1978), stages of dying (Kubler-Ross, 1969), appropriateness (Weisman, 1984), and responses to challenges (Shneidman, 1977). Glaser and Strauss's (1968) concept of "trajectory of dying" illuminates patterns of patient experiences at the end of life. Trajectories have two important properties that define dying: duration, the time between onset of "dying" and the death; and shape, the course of the dying process. The combination of duration and shape can be graphed to represent an individual's or group's experience of dying. For example, some people die suddenly and unexpectedly (e.g., from a heart attack or accident), while others have forewarning with a slow, steady decline. The timing of some deaths can be anticipated, but for others it is ambiguous (perhaps involving remissions and relapses). For still others, there is no advance warning at all.

As exemplified in Figure 24.1, two broad groups can have substantial forewarning of death. One group has prolonged functional stability despite progressive illness, followed by a rapid decline over a few weeks or months before death (the classic example: lung cancer). The period of rapid decline is commonly labeled "terminal illness." Other people may have slowly progressive chronic illness with increasing disability, punctuated by medical crises, complications, and co-morbidities. For this group, any exacerbation can cause death rather suddenly (classic examples: congestive heart failure or chronic obstructive pulmonary disease) (Mor, Wilson, Rakowski, & Hiris, 1994; Wachtel,

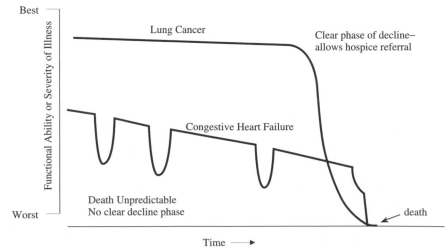

Figure 24.1 Illness impact trajectory. (Reproduced with permission from Skolnick, 1998. © 1998 American Medical Association.)

Allen-Masterson, Reuben, Goldberg, & Mor, 1989).

Only a few epidemiological studies describe the rates of these alternative trajectories. One population-based death-certificate follow-back study in La Crosse, WI, found about 17% of patients died suddenly without serious prior illness, 23% had a "terminal" phase, and 58% had a rather sudden demise in the context of serious chronic illness (Hammes & Rooney, 1998). A clear "terminal" phase is mostly associated in the popular mind with dying from cancer. However, the more common pathway is a rather sudden death while living with dementia, heart and lung failure, or strokes.

Thus, for most patients, the timing of death is not clear. Yet, health-care staff's behavior reflects their expectations about the timing and certainty of death (Glaser & Strauss, 1965). Moreover, our language, shared stories in popular movies and press, and public policy have all relied upon the "terminally ill" trajectory of cancer. For example, a clearly defined "terminal phase" of dying, as in some cancers, allows us to speak of a "transition from cure to care." This terminal phase allows enrollment in hospice and also signals patients, health care providers, and loved ones, to acknowledge that the person is dying and to prepare for the death. Because death from many chronic illnesses, such as congestive heart failure (CHF), occurs mostly from heart attacks, strokes, arrhythmias, or infections (all of which are quite sudden and unpredictable), the average chronic illness patient can never be classified as dying in the socially conventional (e.g., the cancer) model of death.

Examining patients' prognoses of survival on the days before death illuminates the inherent unpredictability of this more common course at the end of life. Lynn, and colleagues (Lynn et al., 1996; Lynn, Harrell, Cohn, Wagner, & Connors 1997) used data from the Study to Understand Prognosis and Preferences for Outcomes and Risks of Treatments (SUPPORT) (Connors et al., 1995), a prospective study of decision making in 9105 seriously ill patients in five teaching hospitals across the country conducted between 1989 and 1994, to estimate survival prognosis for the total sample of patients. In addition, the patients' physicians gave prognostic estimates during the same period (Lynn et al., Connors, 1996, 1997). For both methods, they used all prognoses that happened to lie within the 2 weeks before death.

The median SUPPORT patient had a 17% chance of living 2 months when prognoses were made 1 day ahead of death, and a 51% chance just 1 week ahead of death. Median physician estimates were similar: 10% chance of survival for 2 months when estimated 1 day ahead of death, and a 30% chance of surviving 2 months 1 week ahead of death. Although a prognosis of about 50% for 2 months is ominous, neither ordinary medical practice nor current social language would categorize individuals who have a "fifty-fifty" chance to live 2 months as "terminally ill" or as "dying." Yet, half of the patients who died in the SUPPORT study had prognoses of better than "fifty-fifty" just a week ahead of death.

Figure 24.2 presents the median prognoses by day before death for three classes of disease: lung cancer, acute renal failure or multiple organ system failure with sepsis, and congestive heart failure (Lynn, et al., 1997). Median prognoses varied substantially among diseases: lung cancer patients had a median prognosis of 17% to live 2 months on the day before death and 50% chance 1 week before death. Those with heart failure had a median prognosis of over 60% to live 2 months on the day before death and better than an 80% chance to live for 2 months, estimated 1 week before death.

Thus, most patients die within a very short time of having had quite ambiguous

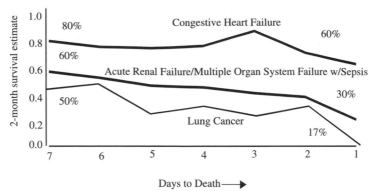

Figure 24.2 Median prognosis for 2-month survival by disease. (Reproduced with permission from Lynn et al., 1997. © 1997 Lippercott Williams & Wilkins.)

prognoses. Moreover, only a few patients will have a short, well-defined period that justifies special services or special attention because they are dying soon. Following social conventions, doctors and patients alike avoid describing patients as "dying" until they are unambiguously close to death. Consequently, most people with chronic illnesses never have a defined time in which to 'wrap up' their lives, plan for death, or consider hospice care.

If only a minority of the very seriously ill will have a period of "terminal illness," then current legal, social, and medical conceptualizations of hospice, palliative care, and other special programs will continue to fail to benefit most who face fatal disease. The dominant model of medical care delivery separates "aggressive" or life-extending care from "palliative" or death-accepting care, with an assumed "transition" between the two. This model of care does not match the physiological, social, psychological, spiritual, emotional, or the familial needs of patients dying from chronic illness. Another category and approach to care are needed in order to improve the situation for the large numbers of individuals who will die from serious chronic illness, but who will have a more sudden death.

III. Patients' and Families' Experience of Life at Its End

A. Psychological Experience

Dying is both a biological process and a psychological and social experience that occurs in a cultural context (Field & Cassel, 1997). Individuals develop their own repertoire of emotions in response to a terminal diagnosis. Kubler-Ross (1969) described dying as having five consecutive stages: denial, anger, bargaining, depression, and acceptance. Others have modified both the sequence and the elements of Kubler-Ross's staging system. For example, Buckman (1999) added fear of dying, guilt, humor, and the alternating emotions of hope and despair experienced almost on a cyclical basis.

An individual's attitudes toward death and dying, often measured as "death anxiety," are influenced by age, previous exposure to death, gender, and occupation, but *not* health status. In addition, strong intrinsic religious belief correlates with lower death anxiety, and higher death anxiety is associated with psychological maladjustment, particularly anxiety and depression (Neimeyer & Van Brunt, 1995). Moreover, some evidence suggests that people's fears of death are not easily altered, even by well-designed educational interventions (Durlak, 1994).

Death concern appears to shift across the life span. Kalish (1977) found that the elderly members of all ethnic groups thought about death more often than younger persons, but were less anxious about it. The relationship between age and death concern may not be linear, however. Gesser, Wong, and Reker (1987) found that general fear of death and dying was relatively high in the young, peaked in middle adulthood, and was minimal in old age. In addition, although nursing home residents may generally experience less fear of dying than younger persons, the older old (aged 75 and over) in such institutions may be come more death anxious than their young-old (aged 60–70) fellow residents (Devins, 1979; Mullins & Lopez, 1982). This resurgence of fear of death at advanced old age may reflect an exacerbation of anxieties about the pain involved in dying or about the subjective proximity of death rather than fear of the state of death per se, because death anxiety in this group was heightened for residents with diminished functional ability or subjective health (Neimeyer & Van Brunt, 1995).

Dying patients often experience clinical depression, delirium, anxiety, despair, helplessness, hopelessness, anticipatory grief (e.g., the preparation for the loss to come), and guilt. For example, 5 to 15% of the general cancer population and 23% of the National Hospice Study population experienced a major depression (Kathol, Mutgi, Williams, Clamon, & Noyes, 1990; Mor, Greer, & Kastenbaum, 1988). A similar rate (25%) afflicted end-stage renal disease patients awaiting transplants (Rodin & Voshart, 1987).

The prevalence of clinical depression increases with the severity of the illness, with active disease and inpatient status, with physical discomfort or limitations related to symptoms or treatment, and

with younger age (Vachon, 1999). Yet depression in dying patients is often dismissed as a natural reaction to knowing that one's life is ending. Although sadness and grief are normal, clinical depression is different. Cancer patients and elderly patients rarely receive antidepressants, although as many as 20% may be clinically depressed (Strouse, 1997). Left untreated, depression causes significant emotional harm and suffering, reduces patients' ability to participate fully in life and their ability to comply with medical treatments, and can contribute to other medical problems. Moreover, depression is the strongest risk factor for suicide (Moscicki, 1997).

Delirium is another common medical complication among dying patients, especially at the end stage of disease. A number of studies have found that from 15–75% of dying patients experienced delirium in the last year of life (e.g., Breitbart, Chochinov, & Passik, 1999; Farrell & Ganzini, 1995). Both depression and delirium are under-diagnosed in elderly patients but are treatable causes of suffering at the end of life.

B. Physiological Experience

No matter how good the care for other patients, cancer patients in the terminal phase suffer pain and other symptoms even when the necessary treatments were readily available. This inattention to symptoms was found for cancer patients dying at home, in hospitals, in nursing homes, and in cancer centers. International surveys describe similar rates of pain: 30–40% of cancer patients in active therapy and 70–90% of patients with advanced disease report pain (Foley, 1999).

Elderly patients have even less symptom management (Cleeland, 1998; Morley, Kraenzle, Bible, & Bundren, 1995). For example, Sengstaken and King (1993) reported that over 80 percent of nursing home cancer patients have pain. Bernabei and colleagues (1998) found that 26% of nursing home cancer patients reporting daily pain received no analgesics. In addition, patients older than 85 years of age were more likely to receive no analgesia, as were patients in minority groups. Although elderly patients have higher levels of untreated symptoms, there is a general lack of information on pain and opioid therapy in the elderly and old people are often excluded from research trials and studies.

Only a handful of studies address symptoms other than pain, and these typically involve cancer patients who are younger than the overall cancer population (Bruera, 1994). In addition, few studies have examined age relationships with symptoms and quality of life. The most definitive work on prevalence of symptoms at the end of life is that of Seale and Cartwright (1994) in Britain. They described the last year of life for everyone in a region in 1969 and again in 1987. Those dying in 1987 had the same sorts of symptoms as those dying in 1969. Symptoms in deaths from cancer versus death from other diseases were mostly similar, but cancer was associated with a higher rate of pain, vomiting, sleeplessness, loss of appetite, constipation, and skin breakdown. The number of reported symptoms increased with age, rising from 5.7 for those under age 65 to 7.4 for those aged 85 or older. Those dying at an older age had their symptoms for a longer period of time: 69% of the symptoms in people aged 85 or older had lasted for a year or more, compared with 39% for people under the age of 65 and 52% for those aged 64–84. Those dying at an older age were less likely to have found their symptoms "very distressing," a rate which fell from 50% for those under 55 years old to 31% of those aged 85 or older.

Pain and other symptoms often undermine the possibility of living well at the end of life. However, health-care providers routinely fail to evaluate or manage pain and other symptoms. Incorporating pain and symptom assessment and treatment into daily institutional routines can foster their effective treatment (Du Pen et al., 1999).

C. Spiritual Experience

Suffering goes beyond the physical dimensions of illness and impacts every aspect of a person's life (Cassell, 1982). For many, the approach of death inspires a search for meaning, peace, life closure, or transcendence that overcomes the fear and despair often associated with a terminal illness. A national survey (The George H. Gallup International Institute, 1997) asked what Americans thought would be important to them if they were dying. Most respondents said that human interaction would be important, 55% would want someone with whom to share their thoughts and fears, 54% would just want someone to be with them, 47% would want someone holding their hand or touching them, 50% would want the opportunity to pray alone, and 50% would want to have someone praying for them. When asked who they would turn to if they knew they were dying, 81% said they would turn to family, 61% said close friends, 36% said a member of the clergy, 30% said a doctor, and 21% said a nurse.

Despite the intellectual acceptance of "whole-person" care in medicine, the separation of mind and body continues to pervade clinical training. Suffering is conceptualized and treated primarily in terms of physical pain. Most physicians in current practice have had no formal education directed at human suffering, and very little training is directed toward the management of psychological or spiritual suffering in the terminal phase of illness (Byock, 1996). In addition, little research addresses religion or spirituality and end-of-life issues. The research that has been conducted has aimed to measure religiosity (the perception of one's beliefs and behaviors that express a sense of relatedness to spiritual dimensions or to something greater than the self), spirituality (a broader concept than religion or religiosity, including transcendence and the search for ultimate meaning and purpose in life), and well-being (sense of satisfaction with one's current life). However, the research methods and concepts used in this research have lacked precision. Comprehensive care of people who are at the end of life requires attention to the basic psychosocial needs of the individual, as a person. Dying well needs to be seen in terms of the potential for personal growth possible at the end of life, including an opportunity for providing a sense of meaning and a sense of completion.

D. Family Experience

Fatal illness adds a new dimension to families' experience, even for families who have faced years or decades of chronic illness. Not only do they have substantial economic and caregiving hardships, but they also face bereavement and loss. Family caregivers face the medical, psychological, and emotional experiences of illness and also often directly provide 24–hour care to patients. Studies in family caregiving to cancer patients show that approximately 70% of primary family caregivers are spouses, 20% are children (of which daughters or daughters-in-law are most frequent), and 10% are friends or more distant relatives (Ferrell, 1999). A study of terminally ill patients with various diseases and their caregivers (Emanuel et al., 1999) found that 87% of patients reported needing assistance in at least one activity, including transportation (62%), homemaking services (55%), nursing care (29%), and personal care (26%). Only 15% of patients requiring nonmedical assistance used paid caregivers. These patients were significantly

more likely to be unmarried, poor, and 65 years of age or older. Almost three-quarters of all care for these dying patients was provided by women. At the same time, women who needed care received less assistance from family members than men and were more likely to have to pay for that assistance. It appears that women are called on to provide care to dying family members but, as patients themselves, they must rely more on paid help.

Advances in cancer care now require that families manage complex medication regiments, parenteral infusion devices, and even parenteral and intraspinal medications. In addition, cancer treatments are increasingly being administered on an outpatient basis and may last for years. The physical and psychological complications of the disease and the intense treatment regimens are severe, protracted sources of stress for family caregivers. Siegel, Raveis, Houts, and Mor (1991) assessed the barriers to meeting advanced cancer outpatients' needs for services and found the most frequent reason for unmet needs was caregiver burden, with the caregiver increasingly overwhelmed by the progressively complex and demanding requirements of care.

Serious illness often causes economic hardship for patients' families. In the SUPPORT study (Connors, et al., 1995), one-third of patients required considerable caregiving assistance from a family member. In 20% of cases, a family member had to quit work or make another major life change to provide care for the patient. Loss of most or all of the family savings due to the illness affected 31% of families, and 29% reported the loss of the major source of family income. In addition, economic hardship for the family was associated with the preference to forego therapy (Covinsky, Goldman, et al., 1994; Covinsky, Landefeld, et al., 1994).

Patients suffering from progressive chronic illness, such as dementia, place added demands on caregivers (Biegel,

Sales, & Schulz, 1991; Pfeiffer, 1999). Alzheimer's disease is the most common dementia and accounts for two-thirds or more of all dementia cases. Despite the dehumanization that Alzheimer's disease and other dementias cause, loved ones maintain a human and humane desire to stay connected. As the disease progresses, patients lose their ability to talk, walk, or care for themselves and eventually become completely dependent on others, usually family members, and often frail elderly spouses. Even though all patients with dementia will die without having returned to health, and though most will die from the complications resulting from their dementia, patients with Alzheimer's may live with advanced stages of the disease for many years. The need for, as well as the burden of, therapeutic interventions also increase (Volicer, 1997). Demented patients may resist procedures. Caregivers are often in the position of having to make serious life-threatening decisions, for example whether to continue treatment by using physical or chemical restraints or if and when to place their loved one in a nursing home (Wackerbarth, 1999). At the same time, the therapeutic interventions may be less effective in dementia patients because of the recurrent nature of many problems and the continuing progression of the underlying disease (Volicer, 1997).

Moreover, caregivers for dementia patients find it difficult to recognize when a patient has reached a terminal stage of illness. One of the more difficult decisions for families is whether to withhold feeding tubes and intravenous (IV) hydration in response to a patient's inability to eat or drink. Families are often extremely conflicted about these decisions, especially if they do not know the type of care that their loved one would have wanted or if they view withholding or withdrawing treatment as euthanasia.

There is an extensive literature on caregiving to dementia patients (e.g., Mace, 1991; Rabins, Mace, & Lucas, 1982; Schulz, Visintainer, & Williamson, 1990), including a focus on interventions targeted to caregivers (i.e., Bourgeois, Schultz, & Burgio, 1996; Collins, Given, & Given, 1994). Many factors seem to influence how family caregivers respond to the demands of caregiving, and interventions for them typically include a wide range of services (e.g., individual and group counseling, information and referral, and coping, problem-solving, and skills development programs). However, Alzheimer's disease and other dementing illnesses continue to challenge the creativity and dedication of people who want to improve the quality of life for these patients.

IV. The Disjuncture between Current Health-Care Arrangements and the Needs of Elderly Dying Patients

A. Location at the Time of Death

Most people would prefer to die at home rather than in an institution (Fried, Van Doorn, O'Leary, Tinetti, & Drickamer, 1999; Mor & Hiris, 1983). Indeed, patients and professionals alike talk as if where one spends the end of life is largely a matter of choice. They speak of "deciding to put her in the hospital for evaluation," or "sending him home to die." But, in fact, most people do die in institutions. In 1949, 49.5% of all deaths in the United States occurred in institutions (39.5% in general hospitals and the rest in psychiatric and other kinds of hospitals and nursing homes). By 1958, the rate had risen to 60.9% (47.6% for general hospitals) (Corr, 1999). By 1980, 74% of deaths occurred in institutions (60.5% in hospitals) (Brock & Foley, 1998). In 1984, Medicare instituted a prospective payment system (PPS) to pay for hospital care with the consequence that hospitals began discharging patients more quickly and nursing home deaths increased, particularly for the oldest old (Sager, Easterling, Kindig, & Anderson, 1989). By 1992, about 57% of all deaths occurred in hospitals, 17% in nursing homes, 20% in residences (including hospice care), and 6% elsewhere (Field & Cassel, 1997).

Research indicates that use of institutional settings at death varies widely by diagnosis and socioeconomic factors (Wennberg & Cooper, 1996). Important factors related to higher rates of hospital or nursing home death include being over age 85 and living at home (before hospitalization), functional status and level of social support, physical disability and incontinence, and being an elderly (aged 85 or older) African American nursing home resident (Berry, Boughton, & McNamee, 1994; Fried, Pollack, Drickamer, & Tinetti, 1999; Merrill & Mor, 1989).

However, the strongest influence on the varying rates of hospital death across regions is regional patterns of care as expressed by institutional capacity. In the SUPPORT study of seriously ill patients in five teaching hospitals, the adjusted odds ratios of the likelihood of dying in the hospital varied nearly eight-fold (Pritchard et al., 1998). Patient preferences and sociodemographic or clinical characteristics did not explain much about the variations in place of death across sites. For Medicare beneficiaries in 1990, the percent dying in-hospital varied from 23 to 54% across U.S. hospital referral regions (Wennberg & Cooper, 1996). Patient level (SUPPORT) and national cross-sectional (Medicare) multivariable models produced consistent results: the risk of in-hospital death correlated closely with greater hospital bed availability and use. About 80% of the variation across regions lay with this factor. Other research supports this conclusion (Mor & Hiris, 1983). Thus, place of death is largely determined by characteristics of the local health system, not by

decisions being made by patients, families, and doctors at the time of facing serious illness.

B. Costs at the End of Life

Medicare beneficiaries account for between 80 and 85% of all deaths in the United States each year. Medicare payments during the last year of life averaged just over $26,000 (1997 dollars) between 1993 and 1998, six times the per-capita cost for beneficiaries who survived (Hogan et al., 2000). Although Medicare costs overall increased nearly fourfold between 1976 to 1988, Lubitz and Riley (1993) showed that dying patients have utilized the same relative share of Medicare expenses over these years, from 27 to 30%. More recently, Hogan et al. (2000) found that spending for the last year of life averaged 25% of total Medicare outlays between 1993 and 1998.

Inpatient hospital use is very high in the last 12 months of life, with more than three-quarters of decedents having at least one hospitalization in their last year (Hogan et al., 2000). Riley, Lubitz, Prihoda, and Rabey (1987) found substantial variation among diseases in costs at the end of life. Scitovsky (1998) showed that the costs of the final year may well be fairly constant across age groups, but that younger Medicare decedents had more of their costs borne within Medicare, whereas persons aged 85 and older had more of their costs in long-term care, which is largely covered by Medicaid, not Medicare. This was recently generally confirmed by Spillman and Lubitz (2000).

However, only a small proportion of beneficiaries have high expenses that would suggest persistently aggressive but futile care, and high-cost users are equally likely to survive as not (Scitovsky, 1994). Thus, the current rate of spending in the last year of life may well reflect a reasonable response to the decline in health status and function that occurs prior to an unpredictable time of death. Nevertheless, what is troubling is that patients, families, and even providers often find that the care now provided at the end of life is inappropriate or unwanted. In the SUPPORT study, patients and their physicians did not routinely make plans for the end-of-life care or for how to address predictable complications, nor did they discuss the overall course and aims of care. Despite long-term chronic illness with a predictably fatal course, physicians usually considered an order to forgo resuscitation only in the patient's last few days (Connors et al., 1995).

C. The Delivery of End-of-Life Care

Hospice is the only federal program for specialized end-of-life care (limited to patients with a prognosis of 6 months or less). Hospice began in the United States in the early 1970s as a grassroots movement to rescue dying cancer patients from aggressive treatment. The goal of the program was to provide palliative care (e.g., a focus on managing pain and other symptoms related to terminal illness instead of providing curative treatments) to terminally ill patients in their own home whenever possible. Within a decade of its beginning, hospice became a benefit under the Medicare program on November 1, 1983 (Kinzbrunner, 1998).

The hospice benefit consists of two 90–day election periods followed by an unlimited number of subsequent 60–day election periods. The patient must be certified as being terminally ill at the beginning of each election period. Medicare's hospice benefit includes services that are not generally covered in Medicare, such as home nursing care without homebound or skilled service requirements, on-call availability of providers for crises 24 hours a day and seven days a week, interdisciplinary team management for comprehensiveness and continuity, spiritual counseling, family support, treatment for pain/symptoms, medications, emergency acute medical care, bereavement care for survivors, and inpatient care when needed (e.g., for respite or symptom management). Hospice is widely perceived to have set the standard for good end-of-life care.

By 1997, the almost 3,000 hospice programs across the nation enrolled approximately 450,000 terminally ill patients a year (Kinzbrunner, 1998). Nearly half of Medicare cancer patients use some hospice benefits in the year prior to death, although hospice use for all other types of diseases is substantially lower (Hogan et al., 2000). Medicare pays a capitated, all-inclusive, prospectively set per diem (per day) payment for four categories of services reflecting different levels of care: routine home care, continuous home care (brief, crisis-oriented care), inpatient respite care, and general inpatient care. Routine home care accounted for 89% of all care delivered in Medicare hospice in 1998 (Gage, et al., 1999). The Medicare hospice benefit accounts for about 4% of the overall Medicare budget (Hogan et al., 2000).

Some evidence supports the widespread belief that home-care hospice patients are less costly than conventional care patients in the last year of life (Mor & Kidder, 1985; Mor & Masterson-Allen, 1987; Mor, Greer, & Kastenbaum, 1988). However, the research to date is marred by unmatched samples, differential time periods, lack of follow-up of those not enrolled, and other methodological shortcomings. A SUPPORT study analysis showed that investment in hospice in 1990 was having a small but significant effect in countervailing the influence of hospital bed use and supply (Pritchard et al., 1998).

However, the hospice benefit is restricted to people who have a terminal illness with a life expectancy of 6 months or less. This means that the vast majority of dying patients receiving hospice care enroll very late in their illness or not at all. The relatively predictable, brief final course of cancer is often suited to the regulatory prognostic limit and hospice model of care. Individuals dying with diseases other than cancer (e.g., those with heart and lung disease or dementia) generally do not have access to hospice, mostly because their illnesses do not have the clinically evident phase of overt decline in the last few months that qualifies them for hospice enrollment (see the prognosis/trajectory discussion above). In addition, the Medicare reimbursement requirement that 80% of care days be at home often makes hospice unavailable for those without family or others who can volunteer to provide needed personal assistance. Data from the National Hospice Study suggest that 70% of the care provided for "long stay" hospice patients was provided by informal caregivers (Mor & Masterson-Allen, 1987).

Furthermore, hospice only serves patients for a short period. Christakis and Escarce (1996) found the median survival time after enrollment for Medicare patients in 1990 was only 36 days. Almost 16% of patients died within 7 days, and over 28% died within 14 days of enrollment. Only 15% of Medicare patients enrolled in hospice were alive for 6 months or more. The average length of hospice stay in 1995 was 29 days (National Hospice Organization, 1999). While 80–85% of the dying population is 65 or older, only about 20% of patients of *all* ages who die in the United States receive hospice care (Health Care Financing Administration, 2000a; Hogan et al., 2000). Thus, hospice ends up serving a very small portion of the dying population for a short period of time. The prognostic and home care requirements, as well as psychological reasons for late referrals, pose substantial barriers to expanding hospice usage.

Fee-for-service, basic Medicare covers an array of acute-care services but does not cover important end-of-life services such as outpatient prescription drugs, "unskilled" supportive or custodial care, or interdisciplinary team management to cover urgent problems 24 hours a day with continuity across settings and time (see the chapter 21 by Feder, Komisar, & Niefeld, this volume). Incentives in fee-for-service Medicare are strongly oriented toward paying for medical treatments and procedures and institutionalization but not for long-term continuity and palliative services. Medicare managed care serves approximately 16% of the Medicare population (Health Care Financing Administration, 1999) and has both the flexibility and the direct financial incentive to establish integrated systems of management that provide cost-effective care and keep patients out of the hospital. Unfortunately, few regularized end-of-life programs exist in these systems (Lynn, Schall, Milne, Nolan, Kabcenell, 2000). Plans hesitate to develop model programs because a reputation for excellence in caring for very sick people creates a risk of skewing their membership toward increasing numbers of people needing expensive care. Thus, all managed care plans currently have an incentive to strive to enroll the healthy and avoid the sick. The Balanced Budget Act of 1997 (PL 105–33) (Health Care Financing Administration, 2000b) mandated risk adjustment in Medicare to mitigate the adverse selection problem (Iezzoni, Ayanian, Bates, & Burstin, 1998). However, even if the risk adjustment is adequate to pay for good programs, capitated plans may well be slow to move to encourage large numbers of high-cost patients to join.

V. The Direction of Current Reforms

Providing excellent, humane care to patients near the end of life, when cure is either no longer possible or no longer desired, is an essential part of health care (American Geriatrics Society, 2000). Too many people still suffer needlessly, both from errors of omission (when caregivers fail to provide palliative and supportive care known to be effective) and from errors of commission (when providers do what is known to be ineffective or even harmful). The current legal, organizational, and economic obstacles conspire against reliably excellent care at the end of life. For example, outdated and flawed drug-prescribing laws, regulations, and interpretations by state medical boards continue to intimidate physicians' prescribing practices for pain and symptom management. Fragmented organizational structures and financing often complicate coordination and continuity of care (see the chapter 22 by Kane & Kane, this volume). Medicare hospice benefits have made palliative care services available to a small segment of dying patients, but many more have illnesses that do not readily fit the traditional hospice model's services or meet the prognosis and other requirements for eligibility.

Traditional financing mechanisms continue to encourage the overuse of procedures and the underuse and poor coordination of needed services for the dying. Medicare is by far the dominant financier for end-of-life care, yet virtually none of its programs and methods of payment are conducive to good care. Expansion of hospice and other Medicare special programs (e.g., Program of All Inclusive Care for the Elderly [PACE]), risk-adjusted capitated care, or salaried arrangements (like the Veterans Administration) offer potential directions for innovations, demonstrations, and insight to shape reform (Wilkinson, Lynn, Cohn, & Jones, 1998).

Moreover, the education and training of physicians and other health-care professionals often do not attend to the appropriate attitudes, knowledge, and skills necessary to care well for dying patients. Biomedical and clinical research focuses almost exclusively on the acquisition of knowledge for the prevention, detection,

and cure of disease and not the understanding and management of complex, advanced, progressive illness. The major federal agencies responsible for health-care research and service delivery innovation have provided very little funding for end-of-life care issues. Finally, our culture has yet to discern how to talk realistically and thoughtfully about the end-of-life and how to value the period of "dying."

The Institute of Medicine (IOM) produced a report on death and dying and made seven recommendations designed to address the different deficiencies in care at the end of life (Field & Cassel, 1997). Their recommendations (pp. 7–13) state that people with advanced, potentially fatal illnesses and those close to them should be able to expect and receive reliable, skillful, and supportive care. In addition, physicians, nurses, social workers, and other health professionals must commit themselves to improving care for dying patients and to use existing knowledge effectively to prevent and relieve pain and other symptoms. Policy makers, consumer groups, and purchasers of health care should work with health-care practitioners, organizations, and researchers to (a) strengthen methods for measuring the quality of life and other outcomes of care for dying patients and those close to them; (b) develop better tools and strategies for improving the quality of care and holding health-care organizations accountable for care at the end of life; (c) revise mechanisms for financing care so that they encourage rather than impede good end-of-life care; and (d) reform drug prescription laws, burdensome regulations, and state medical board policies and practices that impede effective use of opioids to relieve pain and suffering.

The report also argued that educators and other health professionals should initiate changes in undergraduate, graduate, and continuing education to ensure that practitioners have relevant attitudes, knowledge, and skills to care well for dying patients and that palliative care should become a defined area of expertise, education, and research. Furthermore, the nation's research establishment should define and implement priorities for strengthening the knowledge base for end-of-life care. The IOM also suggested that public discussion on end-of-life issues would improve understanding of the modern experience of dying, the options available to patients and families, and the obligations of communities to those approaching death.

Much has been done or is in process to address these areas of need. A number of efforts are now underway to train professionals in end-of-life issues and palliative care. The American Medical Association has launched a profession-wide educational program, *Program to Educate Physicians in End-of-Life Care*, on how to provide quality advance care planning and comprehensive palliative care. The American Board of Internal Medicine (1996) has developed an educational resource document for physicians, *Caring for the Dying: Identification and Promotion of Physician Competency*, as part of a series of initiatives to promote physician competency in the care of dying patients during internal medicine residency and subspecialty training. The End of Life Physician Education Resource Center at the University of Wisconsin is collecting, evaluating, and disseminating curriculum materials. A group at Harvard and the Stanford Faculty Development Program are providing intensive training to palliative care professionals. The Center to Advance Palliative Care in Hospitals and Health Systems at Mount Sinai School of Medicine offers to support fledgling palliative care programs. The American Association of Colleges of Nursing has been funded by the Robert Wood Johnson Foundation (RWJF) to support a comprehensive, national education program to improve training in end-of-life care in nursing curricula.

Much research is also underway. The Project on Death in America and the RWJF have invested substantially in research projects, and the Agency for Healthcare Research and Quality (AHRQ) also has some projects underway. The National Institutes of Health issued a "request for proposals" in symptom research in 1999. The Institute for Healthcare Improvement has sponsored Breakthrough Collaboratives in quality improvement for end-of-life care, on advanced heart and lung disease, and on pain (Lynn et al., 2000). The Department of Veterans Affairs has initiated a series of innovations aimed at better care of advanced illness—pain as a fifth vital sign across the entire system, quality measures in advance care planning and pain management, faculty development, guidelines implementation, and others.

Humans have faced all manner of challenges over time. As things go, the challenge of having the opportunity to grow old and die slowly is not such a bad thing. However, it is a challenge. Society has simply never been in this position before. We have to work on language, categories, framing, meanings, rituals, habits, social organization, service delivery, financing, and community commitment. Much remains to be learned and done. The burgeoning numbers of persons living into old age and coming to the end-of-life makes the need for that learning and implementing all the more urgent.

References

American Board of Internal Medicine. (1996). *Caring for the dying: Identification and promotion of physician competency*. Philadelphia, PA: American Board of Internal Medicine.

American Geriatrics Society. (2000). *The care of dying Patients*. AGS position statement.[Online] Available: www.americangeriatrics. org/products/positionpapers.careold. shtml

Benoliel, J.Q. (1987–1988). Health care providers and dying patients: Critical issues in terminal care. *Omega, 18,* 341–369.

Bernabei, R., Gambassi, G., Lapane, K., Landi, F., Gatsonis, C., Dunlop, R., Lipsitz, L., Steel, K., & Mor, V., on behalf of The SAGE Study Group. (1998). Management of pain in elderly cancer patients. *JAMA, 279,* 1877–1882.

Berry D.E., Boughton, L., & McNamee, F. (1994). Patient and physician characteristics affecting the choice of home-based hospice, acute care inpatient hospice facility, or hospitals as last site of care for patients with cancer of the lung. *Hospital Journal, 9* (4), 21–38.

Biegel, D.E., Sales, E., & Schulz, R. (1991). *Family caregiving in chronic illness.* Newbury Park, UK: Sage Publications.

Bourgeois, M.S., Schulz, R., & Burgio, L. (1996). Interventions for caregivers of patients with Alzheimer's disease: A review and analysis of content, process, and outcomes. *International Journal of Aging and Human Development, 43* (1), 35–92.

Breitbart, W., Chochinov, H., & Passik, S. (1999). Psychiatric aspects of palliative care. In D. Doyle, G.W.C. Hanks, & N. MacDonald (Eds.), *Oxford textbook of palliative medicine* (2nd ed.) (pp. 933–954). New York: Oxford University Press.

Brock, D.B., & Foley, D. J. (1998). Demography and epidemiology of dying in the U.S., with emphasis on deaths of older persons. In J. K. Harrold & J. Lynn (Eds.), *A good dying: Shaping health care for the last months of life* (pp. 49–60). New York: Haworth Press.

Bruera, E. (1994). Research into symptoms other than pain. In D. Doyle, G.W.C. Hanks, & N. MacDonald (Eds.) *Oxford textbook of palliative medicine* (2nd ed.) (pp. 179–185). New York: Oxford University Press.

Buckman, R. (1999). Communication in palliative care: A practical guide. In D. Doyle, G. W. C. Hanks, & N. MacDonald (Eds.), *Oxford textbook of palliative medicine* (2nd ed.), (pp. 141–156). New York: Oxford University Press.

Byock, I.R. (1996). The nature of suffering and the nature of opportunity at the end of life. *Clinics in Geriatric Medicine, 12,* 237–252.

Cassell, E. (1982). The nature of suffering and the goals of medicine. *New England Journal of Medicine, 306,* 639–645.

Christakis, N.A., & Escarce, J.J. (1996). Survival of Medicare patients after enrollment in hospice programs. *New England Journal of Medicine, 335,* 172–178

Cleeland, C.S. (1998). Undertreatment of cancer pain in elderly patients. *Journal of the American Medical Association, 279,* 1914–1915.

Collins, C.E., Given B.A., & Given C.W. (1994). Interventions with family caregivers of persons with Alzheimer's disease. *Nursing Clinics of North America, 29* (1), 195–207

Connors, Jr., A.F, Dawson, N.V., Desbiens, N.A., Fulkerson, W.J., Goldman, L., Knaus, W.A., Lynn, J., & Oye, R.K., The SUPPORT Principal Investigators. (1995). A controlled trial to improve care for seriously ill hospitalized patients: The study to understand prognoses and preferences for outcomes and risks of treatments (SUPPORT). *Journal of the American Medical Association, 274,* 1591–1598.

Corr, C.A. (1999). Death in modern society. In D. Doyle, G.W.C. Hanks, & N. MacDonald (Eds.), *Oxford textbook of palliative medicine,* (2nd ed.) (pp. 31–40). New York: Oxford University Press.

Corti, M.C., Guralnik, J. M., Salive, M.E., & Sorkin, J.D. (1994). Serum albumin and physical disability as predictors of mortality in older persons. *Journal of the American Medical Association, 272,* 1036–42.

Covinsky, K.E., Goldman, L., Cook, E.F., Oye, R., et al. for the SUPPORT Investigators. (1994). The impact of serious illness on patients' families. *Journal of the American Medical Association, 272,* 1839–1844.

Covinsky, K.E., Landefeld, C.S., Teno, J., Connors Jr., A.F., et al. for the SUPPORT Investigators. (1994). Is economic hardship on the families of the seriously ill associated with patient and surrogate care preferences? *Archives of Internal Medicine, 156,* 1737–1741.

Devins, G. M. (1979). Death anxiety and voluntary passive euthanasia. *Journal of Consulting and Clinical Psychology, 47,* 301–309.

Du Pen, S.L., Du Pen, A.R., Polissar, N., Hansberry, J., Kraybill, B.M., Stillman, M., Panke,

J., Everly, R., & Syrjala, K. (1999). Implementing guidelines for cancer pain management: Results of a randomized controlled clinical trial. *Journal of Clinical Oncology,* 17, 361–370.

Durlak, J.A. (1994). Changing death attitudes through death education. In R. A. Neimeyer (Ed.), *Death anxiety handbook: Research, instrumentation, and application* (pp. 243–260). Washington, DC: Taylor & Francis.

Emanuel, E.J., Fairclough, D.L., Slutsman, J., Altert, H., Baldwin, D., & Emanuel, L. (1999). Assistance from family members, friends, paid care givers, and volunteers in the care of terminally ill patients. *New England Journal of Medicine,* 341, 956–963.

Farrell, K.R., & Ganzini, L. (1995). Misdiagnosing delirium as depression in medically ill elderly patients. *Archives of Internal Medicine,* 155, 2459–2464.

Ferrell, B.R. (1999). The family. In D. Doyle, G.W.C. Hanks, & N. MacDonald (Eds.), *Oxford textbook of palliative medicine* (pp. 909–917). New York: Oxford University Press.

Field, M.J., & Cassel, C.K. (Eds.). (1997). *Approaching death: Improving care at the end of life.* Washington, DC: National Academy Press.

Foley, K. (1999). Pain assessment and cancer pain syndromes In D. Doyle, G.W.C. Hanks, & N. MacDonald (Eds.), *Oxford textbook of palliative medicine* (pp. 310–331). New York. Oxford University Press.

Fried, L.P., & Guralnik, J.M. (1997) Disability in older adults: Evidence regarding significance, etiology, and risk. *Journal of the American Geriatrics Society,* 45, 92–100.

Fried, L.P., Pollack, D.M., Drickamer, M.A., & Tinetti, M.E. (1999). Who dies as home? Determinants of site of death. *Journal of the American Geriatrics Society,* 47, 25–29.

Fried, T.R., Van Doorn, C., O'Leary, J.R., Tinetti, M.E., & Drickamer, M.A. (1999) Older persons' preferences for site of terminal care. *Annals of Internal Medicine.* 131 (2), 109–112.

Friedland, R.B., & Summer, L. (1999). *Chronic conditions: A challenge for the 21st+ century.* Washington, DC: National Academy on an Aging Society.

Gage, B., Miller, S.C., Coppola, K., Laliberte, L., Mor, V., & Teno, J. (1999). *Important questions for hospice in the next century: A literature review of Medicare hospice.* Monograph. Washington, DC: The Urban Institute.

Glaser, B.G., & Strauss, A.L. (1965). *Awareness of dying.* Chicago: Aldine.

Glaser, B.G., & Strauss, A.L. (1968). *Time for dying.* Chicago: Aldine.

Guralnik, J.M., Fried, L.P., & Salive, M.E. (1996). Disability as a public health outcome in the aging population. *Annual Review of Public Health,* 17, 25–46.

Hammes, B.J., & Rooney, B.L. (1998). Death and end-of-life planning in one Midwestern community. *Archives of Internal Medicine,* 158, 383–390.

Health Care Financing Administration. (1999). *Protecting Medicare beneficiaries after HMO's withdrawal,* HCFA Fact Sheet, July 15, 1999. Baltimore, MD: Author. Available:www.hcfa.gov.

Health Care Financing Administration. (2000a). Transmittal No. A-98–34. Baltimore, MD. Author. Available: *www.hcfa. gov/pubforms.*

Health Care Financing Administration. (2000b). *Balanced Budget Act of 1997, PL 105–33.* Baltimore, MD: Author. Available: *www.hcfa.gov/regs/bbaupdat.htm.*

Hogan, C., Lynn, J., Gabel, J., Lunney, J., O'Mara, A. & Wilkinson, A. (2000). *Medicare beneficiaries' costs and use of care in the last year of life. Final report.* Washington, DC: Medicare Payment Advisory Commission.

Iezzoni, L.I., Ayanian, J.Z., Bates, D.W., & Burstin, H.R. (1998). Paying more fairly for Medicare capitated care. *New England Journal of Medicine,* 339, 1933–1938.

Kalish, R.A. (1977). The role of age in death attitudes. *Death Education,* 1 (2), 205–230.

Kathol, R.G., Mutgi, A., Williams, J., Clamon, G., & Noyes, R. (1990). Diagnosis of major depression in cancer patients according to four sets of criteria. *American Journal of Psychiatry,* 147, 1021–1024.

Kinzbrunner, B.M. (1998). Hospice: 15 years and beyond in the care of the dying. *Journal of Palliative Medicine,* 1 (2), 127–137.

Kubler-Ross, E. (1969). *On death and dying.* New York: Macmillan.

Lubitz, J.D., & Riley, G.F. (1993). Trends in Medicare payments in the last year of life.

New England Journal of Medicine, 328, 1092–1096.

Lynn, J., Harrell, Jr., F.E., Cohn, F., Hamel, M.B., Dawson, N. & Wu, A. (1996). Defining the "terminally ill": Insights from SUPPORT. *Duquesne Law Review, 35,* 311–336.

Lynn, J., Harrell, Jr., F.E., Cohn, F., Wagner, D., & Connors, Jr., A.F. (1997). Prognoses of seriously ill hospitalized patients on the days before death: Implications for patient care and public policy. *New Horizons, 5*(1), 56–61.

Lynn, J., Schall, M.W., Milne, C., Nolan, K.M., & Kabcenell, A. (2000). Quality Improvements in End of Life Care: Insights from two collaboratives. *Journal of Quality Improvement, 26,* 254–267.

Mace, N.L. (1991). *Dementia care: Patient, family, and community.* Baltimore, MD: The Johns Hopkins University Press.

Manton, K.G., Corder, L.S., & Stallard, E. (1993). Estimates of change in chronic disability and institutional incidence and prevalence rates in the U.S. elderly population from the 1982, 1984, and 1989 National Long Term Care Survey. *Journal of Gerontology: Social Sciences, 48* (4), S153–166.

Merrill, D.M., & Mor, V. (1989). Pathways to hospital death among the oldest old. *Journal of Aging and Health 5,* 516–535.

Mor V., Greer, D.S., & Kastenbaum, R. (Eds.). (1988). *The Hospice Experiment.* Baltimore, MD: The Johns Hopkins University Press.

Mor, V., & Hiris, J. (1983) Determinants of site of death among hospice cancer patients. *Journal of Health and Social Behavior, 24,* 375–385.

Mor, V., & Kidder, D. (1985). Cost saving in hospice: final results of the national hospice study. *Health Services Research, 20,* 407–422.

Mor, V., & Masterson-Allen, S. (1987). *Hospice care systems: Structure, process, costs and outcomes.* New York: Springer Publishing Company.

Mor, V., Wilson, V., Rakowski, W., & Hiris, J. (1994). Functional transitions among the elderly: Patterns, predictors, and related hospital use. *American Journal of Public Health, 84,* 1274–1280.

Morley, J.E., Kraenzle, D.M., Bible, B., & Bundren, B. (1995). Perception of quality of life by nursing home residents. *Nursing Home Medicine, 3* (8), 191–194.

Moscicki, E.K. (1997). Identification of suicide risk factors using epidemiologic studies. *Suicide, 20,* 506–509.

Mullins, L.C., & Lopez, M.A. (1982). Death anxiety among nursing home residents: a comparison of the young-old and the old-old. *Death Education, 6,* (1) 5–86.

National Center for Health Statistics. (1992). *Vital Statistics of the United States, 1989,* (2), Sect. 6, Life Tables. Washington, DC: U.S. Public Health Service.

National Hospice Organization (NHO). (1999) *Hospice fact sheet.* [On-line] Available: www.nho.org/facts.htm#a.

Neimeyer, R.A., & Van Brunt, D. (1995). Death anxiety. In H. Wass & R.A. Neimeyer (Eds.), *Dying: Facing the facts* (pp. 49–88). Washington, DC: Taylor and Francis.

Pattison, E.M. (1978). The living-dying process. In C. A. Garfield (Ed.), *Psychosocial care of the dying patient* (pp. 133–168). New York: McGraw-Hill.

Pfeiffer, E. (1999). Stages of caregiving. *American Journal of Alzheimer's Disease, 14,* 125–127.

Pritchard, R.S., Fisher, E.S., Teno, J.M., Sharp, S.M., Reding, D.J., Knaus, W.A., Wennberg, J.E., & Lynn, J. (1998). Influence of patient preferences and local health system characteristics on the place of death. *Journal of the American Geriatrics Society, 45,* 1242–1250.

Rabins, P.V., Mace N.L., & Lucas, M.J. (1982). The impact of dementia on the family. *Journal of the American Geriatrics Society, 248,* 333–335.

Riley, G.F., Lubitz, J.D., Prihoda, R., & Rabey, E. (1987). The use and costs of Medicare services by cause of death. *Inquiry 24,* 233–244.

Rodin, G., & Voshart, K. (1987). Depressive symptoms and functional impairment in the medically ill. *General Hospital Psychiatry, 9,* (4) 251–258.

Sager, M., Easterling, D.V., Kindig, D.A., & Anderson, O.W. (1989). Changes in the location of death after passage of Medicare's prospective payment system. *New England Journal of Medicine, 320,* 433–439.

Schulz, R., Visintainer, P., & Williamson, G.M. (1990). Psychiatric and physical morbidity effects of caregiving. *Journal of Gerontology, 45,* (5) 181–191.

Scitovsky, A.A. (1994). "The high cost of dying" revisited. *Milbank Quarterly*; 72, 561–591.

Seale, C., & Cartwright, A. (1994). *The year before death*. Brookfield, VT: Ashgale Publishing Company.

Sengstaken, E.A., & King, S.A. (1993). The problems of pain and its detection among geriatric nursing home residents. *Journal of the American Geriatrics Society*, 41, 541–544.

Shneidman, E.S. (1977). Aspects of the dying process. *Psychiatric Annals*, 8, 25–40.

Siegel, K., Raveis, V., Houts, P., & Mor, V. (1991). Caregiver burden and unmet patient needs. *Cancer*, 68, 1131–1140.

Skolnick, A.A. (1998). MediCaring Project to demonstrate, evaluate innovative end-of-life program for chronically ill. *Journal of the American Medical Association*, 279, 1511–1512.

Spillman, B.C., & Lubitz, J. (2000). The effect of longevity on spending for acute and long-term care. *New England Journal of Medicine*, 342, 1409–1415.

Strouse, T. (1997). Identifying and treating depression in women with cancer: A primary care approach. *Medscape Women's Health*, 2, (9). 3.

The George H. Gallup International Institute. (October, 1997). *Spiritual beliefs and the dying process: A report on a national study conducted for the Nathan Cummings Foundation and Fetzer Institute*. Princeton, NJ: The Gallup International Institute.

Vachon, M. (1999). The emotional problems of the patient. In D. Doyle, G.W.C. Hanks, & N. MacDonald (Eds.), *Oxford textbook of palliative medicine* (2nd ed.) (pp. 883–908). New York: Oxford University Press.

Volicer, L. (1997) Hospice care for dementia patients. *Journal of the American Geriatrics Society*, 45, 1147–1149

Wachtel, T., Allen-Masterson, S., Rueben, D., Goldberg, R., & Mor, V. (1989). The end stage cancer patient: terminal common pathway. *Hospice Journal*, 4, 43–80.

Wackerbarth, S. (1999). What decisions are made by family caregivers? *American Journal. of Alzheimer's Disease*, 14, 111–119.

Warren, M.D., & Knight, R. (1982). Mortality in relation to the functional capacities of people with disabilities living at home. *Journal Epidemiology and Community Health*, 36, 220–23.

Weisman, A.D. (1984). *The coping capacity: On the nature of being mortal*. New York: Sciences Press.

Wennberg, J.E., & Cooper, M.M., for the Dartmouth Atlas of Health Care Working Group. (1996). *The Dartmouth atlas of health care in the United States*. Chicago, IL: American Hospital Publishing, Inc.

Wilkinson, A.M., Lynn, J., Cohn, F., & Jones, S.B. (1998). End-of-life in managed care: Achieving excellence through MediCaring. In *Managed care: Making it work for older people* (pp. 40–55). Washington, DC: The Gerontological Society of America.

Twenty-Five

Emerging Social Trends

Stephen J. Cutler and Jon Hendricks

I. Introduction

Like generalizations, prognostications are fraught with uncertainties; the future is fickle. Nonetheless, our goal in this chapter is to identify some prominent trends likely to affect older people in the years ahead, couch them in terms of factors we can be sufficiently sure will be operative in coming decades, and hazard a guess about how events might unfold. Lacking crystal balls of our own, we rely on the best thinking of the gerontological community and then extrapolate in directions that seem reasonable. Based on these projections, we identify topics that ought to merit the attention of gerontological research and, where appropriate, point to implications for policy and practice.

A. The Forces of Change

The dawn of the new century found the world with three times the number of people it had at the beginning of the 20th century. Within little more than a decade of the publication of this book, another billion will be added, bringing the total to about 7 billion. Of that number, those aged 60 and older will account

for roughly 1.2 billion by 2025, almost 15% of the total. Another 800 million will enter the ranks of old age by midcentury (U.S. Bureau of the Census, 1999a). Suffice it to say, not only is the size and distribution of the population unprecedented, but the globalization of economic participation is a new consideration and will likely portend unanticipated consequences.

To make sense of what may come, it is important to point out three aspects of population gains. First, the highest percentage increases in the number of elderly people within nations in the next five decades will occur in less developed countries characterized by the lowest levels of economic affluence. Second, because the greatest increases will occur in regions least prepared economically to deal with them, aging will be a worldwide issue and the consequences will eddy across national boundaries. Third, demography in and of itself is not destiny, nor is even its meaning automatically apocalyptic—the numbers mean what we and our policy decisions say they mean. What the demographics do affirm is that growth of the older population is exponential, that people are living longer and remaining more vital, and that the decisions we make with regard to everything from public health, to employee and retirement benefits, and even to fertility issues are inseparably bound to the fabric of human life.

Technological change over the course of the twentieth century was staggering. From the invention of the modern bicycle as the century began, we have pushed the frontiers of knowledge past atoms to neutrinos, past germ theory to mapping of the human genome, stem cells, and other of life's mysteries. Technology has altered the way we work and helped prolong life and health even as it lessened the difficulties of travel or communicating with others through the information superhighway. In 1950, some 46% of older men were still on the job; today that number is more like 17%, yet they are living longer and in better health (U.S. Bureau of the Census, 1996). Technology, coupled with economic shifts, moved older men out of the workplace, even as life expectancy increased by half over the past 100 years.

But is technological change tantamount to progress? In the face of population growth, has technology helped preserve the environment or lessened the drudgery associated with mundane tasks for all segments of society? With energy derived from fossil fuels, has the demand for ever more energy, disproportionately in the industrialized world, degraded the environment? Energy consumption, economic prosperity, technology, and population growth are intertwined and will affect the way the future unfolds. The downside of technological innovation is that it is not spread equally across the world's population and some are left out. Inevitably, the explanation has been that there is a lag, and the promise has always been that with time, the effects of technological innovation will be diffused to benefit everyone. As several of the earlier chapters in this handbook make clear, certain segments of the population are still waiting to benefit. Worldwide, there is a disparity between resources and needs for large segments of the population. With declines in fertility and in mortality, the weight of responsibility for underwriting the social safety net will become more pronounced as the population pyramid comes to resemble an obelisk.

It has long been argued that technology, broadly defined, engenders social change by creating new opportunities but also new problems. The two are inexorably linked, mirror images of one another, and carry differential relative costs and benefits. There can be little doubt that technology and cultural values profoundly influence one another. Insofar as aging is concerned, one implication is immediately clear: technology has made it possible for people to live long enough to become politically problematic in terms of the allocation and distribution of resources. In other words, medical and work-related breakthroughs have increased life expectancy and, in so doing, created ever greater demands on medical, communal, and economic assets.

One certainty of technologically based knowledge is that the complexity of the instrumental aspects of learning tends to disenfranchise those who are not facile. Another is that as knowledge-based economics mature, those who represent previous ways of doing or knowing are depreciated in the eyes of those trained in the new technologies. Finally, though technologies in and of themselves are not solutions, neither are they problems. It is the meaning attached to them that creates disparities.

B. The Paradox of Progress

Increases in life expectancy and vitality have created the specter of generational conflict and the perception that old people are impediments to society's wellbeing. Equity discussions became de rigeur in the 1990s, often posed in terms of "What have you done for me lately?" with the answer implying what is fair or how governmental benefits should be distributed. It is ironic that those who helped fuel economic development now are asked to justify receipt of what was once promised to them. Although we should avoid using age as a proxy for being deserving, we must recognize that doing otherwise compounds the intricacies of policy decision making. One of the curiosities of the modern world is that the United States is alone among its industrialized counterparts in not providing universal health insurance, even while it spends a greater percentage of its gross domestic product on health care than does any other nation for the patchwork of benefits that are provided (Anderson & Poullier, 1999). Extrapolating from these patterns, societies are facing difficult decisions made even harder by the declining workforce undergirding Social Security and Medicare payroll tax withholdings. By 2025, the cost of Medicare alone will near $2 trillion dollars (U.S. House of Representatives, 1999).

II. Aging Baby Boomers Are Worldwide

Because the demography of aging is the focus of other chapters in this handbook, we summarize only briefly the major contours of population aging as it is occurring in both developed *and* developing nations. We also discuss two general phenomena, cohort norm formation and structural lag, associated with population aging that warrant gerontological attention.

A. Population Aging

Few trends have been singled out for closer scrutiny than the aging of the baby boom generation. Between 2000 and 2030, when the trailing edge of the boomer cohort will have reached old age (i.e., 65+), the size of the older population in the United States will nearly double (from 35 to 69 million persons) and the percentage of older persons will increase from about 13% to approximately 20% (U.S. Bureau of the Census, 1999a).[1] Other developed countries are even further along in the aging transition. Between 2000 and 2030, the percentage of persons 65 years of age and older in the developed nations as a whole will increase from 14 to 23%. At the same time, longer life expectancy and decreasing fertility will shift the age distribution of the older population itself. In the United States, the percentage of the 65+ population that is 80 years and older will increase from 26% in 2000 to 38% in 2050, and in the developed nations in general, from 22 to 37%.

Often overlooked, however, is the revolution in population aging occurring in developing regions. Persons aged 65 and older will increase in numbers from 249 million in 2000 to over 680 million in 2030, their percentage of the total population will increase from 5 to 10%, and the older populations of developing countries will also be aging. In 2000, persons 80 years and older make up about 13% of the population aged 65 and older, but by 2050 that percentage will nearly double, to 25%.

A distinguishing characteristic of the developing nations is the much larger population base on which aging will occur. Projections for mainland China, for example, show an increase in the size of the 65+ population from 87 million in 2000 to 224 million in 2030 (the *total* population of the United States in 1980 was 226 million). Another hallmark is the rapidity of population aging. In France, it took 115 years for the percentage of persons 65+ to double from 7 to 14% (1865–1980), in Sweden 85 years (1890–1975), but China's

---

1 Unless noted otherwise, data on population aging in this section are drawn from this source.

older population will double from 7 to 14% in a span of 27 years (2000–2027) (U. S. Bureau of the Census, 1992, Table 2–2).

B. The Gray Horizon and What It Will Bring

Regardless of the temporal dimensions of change, the outcome is a steady and rapid graying of the globe. Unquestionably, population aging will have widespread consequences. Two general phenomena are likely to have important implications for emergent social trends—cohort norm formation and structural lag.

1. Cohort Norm Formation

In unprecedented numbers over the past half century, older persons have been spending a major portion of their lives in a life-course stage referred to variously as the "retirement years," "the leisure years," and "the golden years." Normative expectations governing roles and contributions of older persons have been vague. That older persons were new to the roles and the roles new to them perpetuated some measure of cultural indeterminacy about appropriate responsibilities, obligations, and perquisites—thus explaining earlier gerontological concerns about whether age norms existed and whether an aged "subculture" was likely to develop. Several observers (e.g., Riley & Riley, 1986) believe the indeterminacy of the earlier era has not yet been resolved, but the rapid growth of the older population and its improved circumstances (in health, education, and finances) provide an opportunity for "cohort norm formation," for clarifying normative expectations about appropriate roles. In some areas, such norms do seem to be well established, as in norms of reciprocity (Gouldner, 1960) guiding the sequencing of intergenerational support or Ekerdt's (1986) notion of the "busy ethic," a set of norms and values giving legitimacy to activities pursued in retirement.

Cohort norm formation, however, takes us only so far. As studies of political behavior generally indicate, there are cross-cutting allegiances that may have higher priority than age. Even if favorable images of old age erode negative stereotypes and ageism becomes less rampant, large numbers of older persons will still not identify themselves as "old." The broad age range within the older population, regional and cross-cultural variations, and other manifestations of subcultural differences may mitigate the process of cohort norm formation. Still, the older population will be much larger, numerically and proportionately, increasing marketers' attention to this population's discretionary income and further highlighting age-related contentious political and economic issues. The growing visibility and prominence of older populations, the ways they see themselves, and the ways society views older persons call for attention by researchers to the promulgation of cohort norms, the form they take, and consequences associated with their emergence.

2. Structural Lag

Looked at another way, the increasing numbers and changing circumstances of the older population have taken place faster than societal structures can adapt—a phenomenon known as "structural lag" (Riley, Kahn, & Foner, 1994). As a result, there is a disjuncture between opportunity structures and the capabilities of older persons, between roles open to them and their potential contributions.

The notion of structural lag has had its widest application to aging populations in developed nations, but it is also relevant to changes in developing countries. Historically, the slower pace of population aging in developed nations enabled the creation and expansion of public support (imperfections aside) with time available for periodic fine-tuning and accommodations. Developing nations, however, must move quickly to implement appropriate infrastructures in the face of rapidly increasing longevity, changes in family structure, and shifts from rural-agrarian to urban-industrial economies.

Across the globe, structural lag brings pressure on social systems to adapt support and opportunity structures to the new realities of an older population. These pressures and how they are accommodated will vary considerably according to preexisting cultural, social, economic, and political systems. The role of older persons in responding to structural lag, whether reactive or proactive, may reflect and shape the process of cohort norm formation. The form these processes take in various social settings, how they are initiated, and with what consequences, are issues that warrant scrutiny.

III. Technology and the Shifting World of Work

Work has long been a defining characteristic of the human condition. During the course of the last century, work and retirement became formal institutions central to definitions of the life course and what it meant to be old in nearly all countries participating in the global economy. By the time the century ended, far-reaching changes in the nature of work and the workplace were altering what were normative standards. From the enactment of Social Security in 1935 to the end of the century, involvement in work-related activities marked sequential phases of adulthood, and detachment marked the onset of old age. By the end of the first quarter of the new century, less than one-fifth of the men and only about 10% of the women older than 65 will be in the U.S. labor force (Fullerton, 1999). Of course, those are averages, and distinctive patterns for subsegments of the popula-

tion will persist alongside various forms of age discrimination. Although age of eligibility for full Social Security will increase from 65 to 67 between 2003 and 2027, that does not necessarily mean the full complement of workers engaged in the labor force at age 55 will continue in it into their later 60s. The ways in which retirement will unfold for various segments of the population will reflect ways in which personal conditions coalesce with policy and economic factors.

Formerly, once policies were in place and personal attitudes or characteristics, such as health status, were congruent, local economies and demographics were significant as far as determining whether older workers remained in the labor force. Now, the import of local economies has been blurred by the globalization of productivity and the ability of corporations to shift production to virtually any spot on the globe. Incentives and disincentives are no longer determined locally or even nationally, as employers are not bound by local conditions. This is particularly anguishing for local workers because paid employment provides the vehicle by which retirement benefits and incomes are based and self-concept and public identity are couched. That continued employment is beyond either individual or local control is vexing to say the least.

A. Downsizing Our Expectations

Careers have long been thought of as passageways through the adult years leading to retirement. There were always exceptions to be sure. Women and minorities may have had a hard time identifying with the concept of a career trajectory when their work histories were anything but stable, orderly, or progressive. But the notion of career-like trajectories came to dominate conceptualizations of adulthood. Gerontologists have viewed life as a ladder, akin to an occupational trajectory, a series of changing statuses, yet with continuity.

We have also asserted that the primary rewards of work were either internal or external, with the former having the greater salience in terms of meaning and satisfaction. Because technology may well collapse occupational hierarchies into a very few broad categories as structured by information-processing mandates, it is debatable whether opportunities for autonomy will be any greater than has previously been the case, and the notion of intrinsic internal rewards providing the greatest source of meaning may need to be reconsidered. The notion of career tracks may also have to be modified, as a succession of entry-level or noncumulative positions becomes typical. As Henretta (1994) put it, working may be akin to participation in spot labor markets rather than a cherished career pathway. To the extent that organization of the life course has been ordained by the organization of work, familiar phases may change as the traditional constraints and opportunities associated with work are altered while the labor market shifts from manufacturing to the provision of services and contingent labor markets (Han & Moen, 1999). Of course, that does not inevitably mean that the work role is without value or that substitutions for work, including involvement in voluntary organizations, might not provide alternative meaning (Cutler & Hendricks, 2000).

Whenever resources become scarce, or the size of a cohort increases, volunteer opportunities proliferate. There is little doubt that voluntary participation provides significant rewards to those who participate and those who rely on volunteer contributions (Cutler & Hendricks, 2000). If work roles are attenuated or become less rewarding, there are also profound implications for how we think of education. With distance learning and other forms of technologically driven educational delivery increasing, middle-aged and older persons no longer have to travel to a campus to engage in mind-enhancing educational opportunities. In addition to lifelong learning for its own sake, basic skill levels need to be upgraded regularly for those who are to remain productive. Furthermore, if a country is to stay competitive in the global economy, its workers must provide and maintain skills that are current and globally relevant. For example, computational and information management skills must be refreshed at frequent intervals and encompass worldwide developments to retain their niche in the marketplace.

B. Globalization of Policies and Retirement

The rapid aging of the population in the early decades of the 21st century will result in considerable stress generated around domestic policies. Several issues loom large. First, movement into and out of the labor force is ongoing and flexible; it does not make sense to assume all people younger than age 65 are in the labor force and all those older are unproductive. At the same time, although revenues upon which taxes are drawn to support domestic decisions are usually localized within a country, the effects of those decisions are global, at least insofar as production sites can be situated virtually anyplace on the globe and ex parte decision-making processes frequently accompany emplacement in developing nations. The latter implies that the more affluent partner can stipulate the terms of placement.

Generally speaking, European countries, the United States, and many other industrialized nations can be characterized as having one or more of three types of income support models for their elderly populations. There is the familiar pay-as-you-go model, wherein taxes are collected from those of working age and given to those no longer able to work or care for themselves. Second, is a system of defined contributions, which does not transfer resources between generations but provides benefits contingent on previous contributions. Finally, there are defined-benefit models blending previous contributions with welfare-type support (Bovenberg & Van der Linden, 1997). To the extent that the World Bank promotes one type or another, most commonly a form resembling those in place in industrial nations, the less affluent trading partner may have to assume a greater tax and benefit burden than might otherwise be the case. As noted, the age distribution in many less developed countries is changing rapidly, and there is concern about the capacity of many nations to provide basic safety net assurances in the face of both the pace of change in market economies and the extent to which goods and services are obtained from up-market trading partners relative to demographic transitions to an aged population. Paradoxically, as developing nations implement social-insurance systems, they frequently model them after those in industrialized countries and in accord with stipulated guidelines embedded in loan policies of the World Bank (World Bank, 1995).

Likely as not, the press for successively older Social Security eligibility ages will spread, but so too will flexible retirement policies. Fiscal policies and benefit packages will reflect both factors. Yet, if the marketplace does not provide jobs for older workers, other changes will have diminished impact. To ensure that skill levels of older workers remain consonant with market needs, educational institutions will need to accelerate development of distance and continuing education options targeted at mature students. A related issue revolves around ageist and other negative stereotypes about what mature adults can learn and which skills they can master. Finally, colleges and other learning environments will have to facilitate age-integrated classrooms and student bodies in order to help blur the boundaries between segmented views of the life course.

C. Economics of Labor-Force Participation

As should be apparent, labor-force participation reflects an array of factors beyond human capital per se. Ageism is one dimension of the determination of whether individuals continue to work or not. With the graying of the baby boomers, it is debatable whether ageism will continue to be the "sleeper" issue it has been. On the one hand, the baby boom has managed to redefine every phase of life through which it has passed. On the other hand, when resources are scarce and needs are plentiful, denigration of persons or groups not considered essential to core concerns is common. Within the workplace, age-based divisions of labor frequently reflect the pace of technological innovation and congruence of the workforce with characteristics of customers. In addition, female and male labor-force participation rates and job assignments reflect a gendered decision-making process. Gender differentials in wage levels and occupational mobility are well documented in both developed and developing countries (Tzannatos, 1999). Local public policies tend to perpetuate comparable patterns so that, for example, unpaid household work or reproduction is not assigned economic value in the calculation of social welfare. As a consequence, women face a greater risk of poverty throughout life and especially in their later years (U.S. Bureau of the Census, 1996).

D. Consumerism as a Form of Productivity

Consumer spending is central to economic vitality, and spending among elderly persons is significant. Stereotypes notwithstanding, spending does not decline dramatically for many segments of the population after age 65 (Russell, 1997). With the graying of the baby boomers, the already substantial consumption pattern among older people is going to rise to unprecedented levels. According to the Bureau of Labor Statistics, consumers in the 55- to 64–year-old range spend 15% more than the national average, and in the cohort aged 45–54, the figure is approximately 17% above the average. Those figures portend what lies ahead for spending patterns among older persons. To illustrate, households in the age range of 55–64 spend 56% more than average for women's clothing and are second only to the next younger cohort in spending on transportation and entertainment. Those between ages 65 and 74 spend more in most categories than people in the 25- to 34–year-old range (Russell, 1997). With education levels among older persons climbing as new cohorts enter the ranks of old age, spending will likely follow suit, depending on employment and income histories.

The meaning of consumption is more portentous than its implications for household expenditures and business revenues suggest. The symbolic significance of consumption as a stanchion for self-concept and sense of identity will drive future expenditures. A person–object synthesis occurs as people vest themselves in their possessions, whether the latter are literal or figurative. Another aspect of consumption patterns links to participation in respected activities and to their status-defining characteristics—consumption as status symbol (Cutler & Hendricks, 1990). Depending on the viability of other sources of consensual validation, the symbolic relevance of consumption patterns may become increasingly salient.

IV. Biomedical Technology

Significant implications for emerging social trends will stem from developments and breakthroughs in biomedical technology. Advances that once seemed like science fiction are rapidly becoming reality and adding to the arsenal of procedures for treating disease. Illustrative of both opportunities and challenges are developments in molecular biology.

A. Mapping the Human Condition

The first phase of the Human Genome Project will be completed within the decade. A composite product of both public and private efforts, this project seeks no less than to map the entire human genetic structure. The potential consequences are far-reaching. For example, the ability to identify specific genes associated with a particular disease (e.g., Alzheimer's disease) will enable scientists to focus their research, thus enhancing the likelihood that successful interventions will be discovered. On the other hand, physicians will need to be better versed in genetics to use and interpret new diagnostic tests, and resources devoted to genetic counseling will need to be expanded (Holtzman & Watson, 1998). How knowledge of our genetic endowment will affect one's sense of self, make demands on decision making and agency, and alter the dynamics of family systems are among the many topics needing further study (Sobel & Cowan, 2000).

The prospect of targeted genetic intervention has implications for life expectancy. Estimates are that elimination of diseases of the heart would add 4.6 years to life expectancy and eradication of malignant neoplasms 3.4 years (Anderson, 1999, Table B). Even if complete elimination is unrealistic, there is evidence that one approach to gene therapy called angiogenesis can reverse deterioration accompanying coronary disease (Ware & Simons, 1999). The discovery of genes associated with higher breast cancer risk can lead both to greater self-vigilance and to prophylactic measures reducing risk (Wilfond, Rothenberg, Thomson, & Lerman, 1997). In other words, knowledge of genetic risk will permit preventive surveillance and interventions that will extend life expectancy.

Among the more robust findings in epidemiology has been the influence of lifestyle on late-life morbidity and mortality (Rowe & Kahn, 1998). Embeddedness in systems of social support is clearly a factor in late-life well-being. Lack of exercise, improper diet, smoking, excessive drinking, and stress are among lifestyle behaviors increasing morbidity and risk of death. If genes are found to play some role in behavioral aspects of lifestyle, this may provide another avenue by which genetic intervention might enhance late-life well-being (Conrad & Gabe, 1999).

A continuing concern is whether gains in life expectancy have been accompanied by gains in *active* life expectancy (Liao, McGee, Cao, & Cooper, 2000). In other words, is the period of late-life morbidity being compressed, the period characterized by frailties, infirmities, and functional limitations shortened? If developments in genetics add to life expectancy, will there be commensurate increases in years of functional well-being or perhaps an accelerated trend toward the rectangularization of vitality?

Apart from the relatively small number of cases of early-onset Alzheimer's disease having a clear genetic basis, the best symptomatic predictor is age. U.S. General Accounting Office (1998) estimates based on a meta-analysis of 18 studies suggest that the prevalence rises from 1.1% among persons 65 to 69 to 52.5% for persons 95+. This relationship between age and symptomatic onset might invite speculation that Alzheimer's will afflict everyone who has the good fortune

to live long enough, but available evidence suggests otherwise. Based on their studies of centenarians, Perls, Silver, and Lauerman (1999) concluded it is fallacious to assume a correlation between longevity and increasing probability of disease, including Alzheimer's. Their work suggests the presence of a demographic selection process, such that the longer one lives, the healthier one has been. Much like the racial crossover in mortality (Johnson, 2000), it appears that those persons surviving the longest will be the hardiest.

To some extent, the ultimate scientific achievement would be identification of biological mechanisms regulating aging processes. Some laboratories have shown that reducing caloric intake or genetic alterations can produce increased life spans in worms and rodents, but the evidence for genetic governance of the aging process remains questionable (Miller, 1999; Rowe & Kahn, 1998). Nevertheless, it is tempting to contemplate the consequences, as Seltzer (1995) has done, were it possible to slow the process of aging, prolong the period of youthful vitality, and extend the life span.

B. Technology for Old Age

There is every reason to believe that developments in molecular biology will lead to identification, treatment, and cure of diseases afflicting persons in middle and late life. Other advances in biomedical technology have already demonstrated their ability, depending on one's perspective, either to lengthen life or prolong the dying process. And a wide range of assistive devices is being used, resulting in higher levels of functioning among older persons (Manton, Corder, & Stallard, 1993). Yet, along with opportunities to enhance well-being, these developments present challenges and dilemmas.

Debates occasioned by the rapidity of change in biomedical technology are excellent examples of cultural lag, wherein norms and values are out of synch with technical options. The revolution in genetics has "met" the revolution in information technology, raising a host of issues about confidentiality, potential misuses of genetic information for insurability and employability, and genetic discrimination and selection (Holtzman & Watson, 1998). Discoveries of genetic correlates (i.e., APOE) of sporadic and late-onset Alzheimer's have raised questions about permissible uses of APOE testing and who should have access to the results. In view of their predictive limitations, should tests be used only for adjunct diagnostic purposes, or should individuals be allowed to request and receive their test results? Such questions bring the issues to the intersection of biomedicine and ethics (Post & Whitehouse, 1998). Can the debates be productively framed and resolved by invoking principles such as autonomy, beneficence, and the limits of positive rights?

C. The Paradox of Health Care

The delivery of health care in the United States is based on a model emphasizing acute conditions even though many illnesses that beset older persons are chronic and enduring. Thus, the structure of health-care delivery and financing is misaligned with the health-care needs of older people and the ability of individuals or families to pay for services (see chapter 21 by Feder, Komisar, & Niefeld, and chapter 22 by Kane & Kane, this volume). Furthermore, access to and use of health services are differentially distributed by wealth as a reflection of more general systems of inequality.

Who will pay for advances in biomedical technology? Surely, those who are well off are in a position to avoid problems of genetic discrimination by paying for tests out of pocket rather than using insurance coverage (Mehlman & Botkin,

1998). Asking who will pay also prompts examination of the politics behind allocation of economic resources and how the emergence of an aging society affects those decisions. Proposals for more explicit rationing of scarce and expensive health-care resources by age (e.g., Callahan, 1987) are likely to be seen. Debates about eligibility for programs and services, about whether access should be age based or means tested, and about the absence of universal health coverage will doubtless continue as advances in biomedical technology place continuing pressure on the financing of health care.

V. The Information Revolution

One of the more far-reaching developments in the last third of the 20 century was the transformation of communications and information processing. In a relatively brief period, computers became a pervasive and integral part of our lives. One need think only of the wide range of doomsday predictions associated with the Y2K rollover to understand how dependent we are on computing and data-processing technology. The advent of personal computers and related developments such as the Internet and World Wide Web are bringing the power, potential, and peril of the information revolution to the level of individual households regardless of age.

A. Connected to the World

The connectedness of elders to their social networks has been well documented (Soldo & Hill, 1993). Frequent interaction with family, friends, and neighbors is common, the bonds providing a wide range of support from these contacts. Developments in information technology promise new ways to maintain linkages. E-mail, now the most prevalent innovation, gives elders and their network partners an easy way to maintain contact. Information available through the World Wide Web and e-commerce has great potential, particularly when access to information resources or commercial transactions is difficult because of limited mobility. Although not yet widely utilized, the availability of voice technology and Webcams will add other communication modalities. Recognizing that communication is the primary use to which many persons put personal computers, manufacturers are configuring inexpensive systems targeted to that specific end.

An important development stemming from available technology has been the advent of on-line support groups. These not only have the advantage of being available at any hour but also are not limited by geographical boundaries. More research on who is involved in on-line support groups, the uses made of them, and the consequences of participation would be of considerable interest, especially in comparison with traditional support groups (e.g., Bass, McClendon, Brennan, & McCarthy, 1998).

Current cohorts of older persons are less likely to use personal computers because of expense, lack of interest, or fear (their own or that of others) that they are incapable of acquiring the necessary skills. Nevertheless, attitudes toward computer use and skills in using them are modifiable through exposure (Czaja & Sharit, 1993). Future cohorts of older persons will also be increasingly familiar with personal computers based on experience. How interaction through cyberspace will alter social networks, the support they provide, and even the nature of "communities" will be fertile topics for inquiry (Wellman & Hampton, 1999).

B. Housing and Transportation

Technological developments will have significant implications for the environments in which older persons live and for their mobility beyond the household. In regard to housing, for example, much has been made of the "smart house," a design concept incorporating information and communication technology to monitor the living space itself and the residents and capable of responding to changing needs. Labor-saving designs and home modifications grounded in the ergonomics of aging hold great promise for ameliorating increasing environmental demands often associated with aging processes (AARP and Stein Gerontological Institute, 1993).

As population aging brings an increase in the number of older persons and in their average age, the number and characteristics of older drivers will change also. Dependence on the automobile as the primary means of personal transportation will not diminish among persons whose residences are in suburban and rural areas ill serviced by public transportation, and among those for whom driving is a symbol of continuing independence. Common changes with aging in sensory modalities and in reaction time should be reflected in automobile design, in information presented to older drivers, and in roadway design and signage (Schaie & Pietrucha, 2000).

C. Future Prospects

The application of information and other technologies to the needs of older persons is certain to be a significant trend with implications for well-being. How accessibility, availability, and utilization of these advances are distributed among the aged, however, also bears examination. Although the technology associated with smart houses may foster independence, safety, and enjoyment, meeting more basic needs such as adequacy, affordability, and accessibility will continue to be problematic for significant numbers of older persons (U.S. Department of Housing and Urban Development, 1999).

As many commentators have noted, the transformation in communications technology has had the effect of creating a "global village." Communication throughout the world is nearly instantaneous, and events unfolding almost anywhere can be followed with little or no delay. Information on the widest range of topics is readily available through the World Wide Web. At the same time, such information contributes in powerful ways to the shaping, defining, and construction of problems. To paraphrase Marx, access to the "means of communication" can be used to perpetuate images, to define the deserving and undeserving needy, and to frame public policy debates. Access to and control over the information superhighway—that is, the "digital divide"—are factors in the distribution of power, status, and resources. From a political economy perspective, the ways older persons relate to communications, how they are portrayed by the content of that information, and how various forces such as population aging and cohort norm formation affect these processes are topics that warrant careful examination.

VI. Ethnicity and Cultural Participation

One perplexity of aging is that lifelong forms of social differentiation play out in the later years. All manner of social class, ethnic and racial divisions, not to mention gender differences, compounding throughout life, continue to shape life experiences in old age. Public policy is seldom designed to correct disparities but at most provides a safety net. Of course, under certain circumstances, what appears to pose hardships may be a source of strength and advantage. The much discussed demographic crossover is an example. Surely, to get to that point many

hazards must be surmounted. When they are, it should not be surprising that those who have faced disadvantage find much in their lives that is satisfying. Whether this is because subgroups of the population nurture values and beliefs emphasizing the positives in a long life and supportive networks and organizations, or is due to a sense of accomplishment at having beaten the odds, is difficult to say. The point is that older African Americans and certain other racial/ethnic subgroups of the population express greater satisfaction in old age than do whites, regardless of circumstances (Johnson, 2000).

A. Demographics of Minority Aging

The United States is becoming a nation of blended races. By midcentury, approximately 20% of the population will be of mixed ancestry. Among Asian Americans, perhaps as many as one-third or more will be able to identify mixed racial backgrounds, and among Hispanics as many as 30% are already marrying outside their racial or ethnic groups. With successive generations, the rates will likely be even higher. Beginning with the 2000 census, respondents were no longer limited to a single choice of racial or ethnic background. Still, one thing is certain, minorities will compose larger percentages of all age groups in the years ahead. At the end of the century, racial and ethic minorities were about 27% of the U.S. population; by 2015, they will make up one-third. Interestingly, foreign-born individuals now comprise 8% of the total population. Improvements in life expectancy are also making a difference. Although gaps between African-American and white life expectancy have endured, there have been significant relative improvements among Latinos (Pollard, 1999; Serow & Cowart, 1999).

African Americans are currently the largest single minority group, the next largest being Hispanics, followed by Asian and Pacific Islanders, then Native Americans and Native Alaskans. In little more than the next decade, Hispanics will likely be the largest minority group, and they will be located disproportionately in the West and Southwest, whereas African Americans will continue to be the most represented minority group in 24 states in the South, East, and Midwest—especially Ohio and Michigan. Population increases among minority elders will be dramatic. Hispanics older than 60 are expected to increase by over 300%, Asian Americans and Native Americans and Alaskans by over 280%, and older African Americans by nearly 120% (Serow & Cowart, 1999). The need to revisit public policies to accommodate the growth in the numbers of minority elderly will become increasingly clear.

B. Will Subordination Go Away?

Racial- and ethnic-based inequalities are divisive controversies facing society. Criticisms and responses often run hot and outstrip rational discussion. In the late 1990s, Mason (1997) asserted that differential job skills and human capital account for only two-thirds of the earnings differentials between minority workers and their white counterparts. He noted that approximately one-third remains unexplained by human capital variables, and other causes of the disparities must be investigated if discrimination is to be fully understood. If Mason's contentions are even approximately the case, it is likely Americans have some distance to go before discrimination and the accompanying inequalities are obliterated.

As Stoller and Gibson (2000) point out, one's position in various social hierarchies shapes one's worldview and how aging is experienced. Part of the heterogeneity among older persons in terms of well-being and status is a reflection

of society-wide patterns over the course of their lives. Privilege and disadvantage are cumulative statuses compounding with other factors, and each entails a number of cross-cutting themes that get painted most boldly during times of stress and national crisis. In other words, being poor is associated with gender, minority status, health conditions, and so on, such that not having economic resources implies more about quality of life than simply not having enough income. Therefore, economic disparities and other inequities have long-term consequences that play out in old age.

C. Effects on Aging and Policy

If long-established trends persist, all manner of public policy will be implicated. For example, lifelong patterns of lower incomes, less stable employment histories, and less education are all associated with impaired health status and precarious retirement incomes. Furthermore, because minorities are not spread equally across all states, specific areas will feel the impact of these unmet needs more than others. Consider also that certain chronic conditions are more prevalent in minority populations and low-income categories, and the effect on Medicare expenditures is likely to be substantial. Couple growth in the Hispanic population with what is currently a pattern of Hispanics being less likely to have health insurance—meaning they arrive in old age with a greater prevalence of chronic and untreated conditions that place them at greater risk—and the dimensions of the nation's healthcare picture can begin to be discerned. Further complicating the picture are cultural differences in accessing service programs (Serow & Cowart, 1999). Certainly the country is going to have to address some troublesome questions about targeting services and changing policies.

VII. Contributions of an Older Population

As noted elsewhere in the handbook and later in this chapter, a recurrent theme is concerns about the societal burdens imposed by population aging. Fears about the costs of programs supporting older persons, threats to the viability of Medicare and Social Security, and the presumed economic self-interest of the aged at the expense of young persons are often rooted in simplistic interpretations of dependency or support ratios (Hendricks, Hatch, & Cutler, 1999). However, a narrow focus on "old age" dependency ratios fails to recognize that the *overall* dependency ratio will be no higher in 2030 than it was in 1900 (U.S. Bureau of the Census, 1998). Such an excessively aggregated statistic also tends to portray members of the 18–64 age group as "independent" and persons 65 and older as "dependent," a view that assumes older adults are a drain on societal resources rather than productive contributors. Refuting this assumption are the significant contributions of older persons in many areas. Here, we broach volunteerism and intergenerational transfers, two areas in which emerging trends suggest the roles played by older adults will continue to increase.

A. Volunteerism

Productive activity, as Herzog and Morgan (1992) and others note, is not limited to paid work but occurs within a variety of nonpaid contexts, a major one being the volunteer sector. However, some have suggested that voluntary contributions overall and by older persons in particular will diminish over time. Putnam (1995), for one, has argued that there has been a decline in "civic" participation in recent decades. Other analyses support this contention in that the relationship between age and volunteerism is curvi-

linear: low at the younger ages, rising to a peak among middle-aged persons, and then declining with increasing age. Together, these perspectives imply that volunteerism among older persons is not only low but declining as part of the more general secular trend (Cutler & Hendricks, 2000). In contrast, Rotolo (1999) makes the case that civic participation in the form of voluntary association memberships has not declined from the mid-1970s to the mid-1990s. Other studies (e.g., Cutler & Hendricks, 2000) assert that the curvilinear pattern of age differences in association memberships is primarily an artifact of compositional differences that, when controlled, yield membership levels of older persons as high if not higher than those of younger and middle-aged persons.

Formal association affiliation is only one type of voluntaristic participation. As the example of participants in a "memory walk" suggests, one need not be an association member in order to contribute to civic, charitable, or other causes. A partial sense of the magnitude of voluntaristic contributions by older persons may also be gained from their participation in the three major programs operating within the Corporation for National Service's National Senior Service Corps. In 1996, over 490,000 persons aged 60 and older contributed 119 million hours through the Foster Grandparent Program, the Retired and Senior Volunteer Program, and the Senior Companion Program. Approximately 80,000 local nonprofit and public agencies had Senior Corps volunteers, whose contributions yielded an estimated value of $1.4 billion, a nearly 12–fold return on the federal investment in the three programs (U.S. Senate, 1998).

Voluntarism among older persons likely pays off in other ways, in that participation in volunteer activities appears to be associated with well-being and health. Researchers see an association between volunteer activity, physical health, depression (Herzog, Markus, Franks, & Holmberg, 1998), and lower mortality (Glass, de Leon, Marottoli, & Berkman, 1999). Such findings suggest that benefits accrue not only directly from contributions of volunteers but also indirectly from savings associated with better health.

B. Intergenerational Transfers

Related to voluntarism in terms of productivity are the contributions of older persons through a variety of intergenerational transfers, which operate at three levels: (a) within families and other proximate social networks, (b) through contributions to community programs targeted at younger persons, and (c) in terms of the allocation of societal resources between generations. In this section, we focus on the first of these. Programs contributing to the well-being of younger persons (e.g., Foster Grandparents) were noted in the previous section, and issues of "generational equity" and associated public policies and programs are considered in the next section.

Soldo and Hill (1993) identify three forms of intergenerational transfers that take place within families: (a) space, measured by coresidence; (b) time, or the provision of services; and (c) money, as in goods and services. Studies of intergenerational transfers consistently note that resources, assistance, and support flow in both directions. Coresidence with adult children and children-in-law may increase with advancing age and especially with frailty and widowhood (Crimmins & Ingegneri, 1990), but there has also been a growing tendency for younger persons to return to their parent's home in times of economic or social need (Goldscheider & Goldscheider, 1999). Older persons have long played an important role in the lives of their grandchildren, and an increasing number are raising their grandchildren (U.S. Bureau of the Census, 1999b).

Other forms of support flow freely from older parents to adult children, and there is agreement that the amount of affective and instrumental support flowing downward exceeds the amount of support flowing upward until fairly advanced ages (Morgan, Schuster, & Butler, 1991).

C. Emergent Trends

Current rates of volunteerism will be maintained in the coming decades, and the changing characteristics of older cohorts (higher levels of education and income, better health, more years spent in retirement or in part-time work) suggest their voluntaristic contributions may well increase. If resources allocated to social programs are cut in either absolute or relative terms, the implications of volunteerism for individual and societal benefits and for the roles and status of the older population bear special watching. Intergenerational transfers within the family also warrant close attention. Lower birth rates, the growing prevalence of four- and even five-generation families, and high rates of divorce, coupled with the growth of blended families, all may have implications for intergenerational transfers. Studies of how public policy affects the ability of families to provide intergenerational support are crucial since "third-way" policies have emerged in which relative responsibilities are assigned to families, markets, and governments. And although those in need were previously protected from market forces, the latter are now factored into public policies for needy populations (Myles & Quadagno, 2000).

VIII. Policy and the Future

There is no doubt tomorrow's older persons will be different from today's. The meaning of old age will be different, too, as successive cohorts have distinct experiences, reaching old age in different societal contexts. As generations, and especially the baby boom, pass in turn, they will alter social structures and the meanings that accrete to various age categories.

What is not in doubt is the impact public policy will play in shaping life chances of all segments of the population, including older people. Some policy mandates are directly age-based, whereas others are age-relevant, but in either embodiment the outcome shapes experience. Policy makers will continue to struggle with issues of universal access or coverage and needs-based provisions. Just as certain is that interest groups will continue to lobby for favored solutions. Should policies be targeted to low-income categories or be universal? After that decision is made, should benefits be flat-rate or means-tested? If the decision is made to predicate governmental programs for older people on means-tested criteria or other needs-based factors, it will likely be justified in terms of demographic imperatives and, not coincidentally, will fundamentally alter the nature of the existing social contract, even as the effects eddy throughout the economy and society (Hendricks et al., 1999; Korpi & Palme, 1998).

Likely as not, need and functional capabilities will be highlighted as criteria for defined eligibility and put forth as viable alternatives to historic age-based entitlements. At the same time, the provision of economic security will likely be at least partially privatized and decentralized. Questions of generational equity will get more problematic as the old-age cohort size grows, and the struggle will be intensified unless some unexpected economic boon materializes. It is quite likely that Social Security and Medicare will continue, even if transformed in piecemeal fashion. Absent a domestic crisis, changes will come slowly and will reflect economic viability (Binstock, 1999).

A. Generational Equity

Questions about distributive justice and fairness will be inevitable parts of future deliberations. There are many imponderables, but with a rising minority population, a declining wage base reflecting growth in service-sector employment patterns, and movement of many economic activities to off-shore sites, the debate about whether each generation is receiving its due is not going away. Instead, the level of distress is likely to increase for each of the three reasons mentioned above, and the specter of generational conflict is going to become ever more perceptible until policies are retrofitted or a gentler national ethic evolves. Terms of the debate are clear to those who care to look; the goal is to make certain that policy implementation does not exacerbate conflicts unnecessarily.

B. Worldwide Perspectives

Worldwide growth in the proportion of older persons and the globalization of economic shifts will require worldwide coordination and decision making. The danger of a demographic explosion has been utilized in current policy debates and alarms are often sounded. Simple-minded cross-national comparisons are not particularly enlightening, as it is too easy to misconstrue models and assume comparability. Still, there is little evidence that age-specific population growth has dire consequences in terms of impact on gross domestic product. When viewed with an unstinting analytic eye, many social insurance programs are found to be less costly than critics contend. Finally, behavioral changes may provide more compensatory responses than rewriting policies (Binstock, 2000).

Likely as not, worldwide increases in the age of eligibility for publicly funded retirement benefits will emerge as an effective means of dealing with rising program costs. Revisions will be justified not only in terms of the impact on the public coffers but in terms of functional capacity and improving life expectancies. Of course, there will be pockets and portions of the population left at serious disadvantage by such policies. Another tack may be to broaden the tax base from which entitlement programs draw revenues, as is being done in some industrialized countries that are locating such policies within the purview of general revenues, and perhaps means-tested contributions from older persons themselves will be implemented more extensively. With global economies and the worldwide movement of capital, it may be that debate will occur about whether revenues for entitlement programs must be earned within national boundaries, as is currently the case in large measure. There are numerous other possibilities, such as spreading and pooling risks across a broader number of participants, reforming social insurance programs to tighten eligibility requirements, emphasizing both public and individual savings programs and the composition of those savings. But one thing is certain: changes will not come quietly (Binstock, 1999; Bovenberg & Van der Linden, 1997). In order to make informed decisions on how best to fund domestic policies, changing birth rates and labor-force participation rates along with a range of other factors must be part of the equation. Finally, gender, racial, and ethnic issues will remain. Even though the lion's share of Social Security recipients in the United States will be women, they and minority workers have a history of lower wages and will have lower benefits. How we construct old age is debatable, but the major role that formal or implicit policy decisions play is not.

Acknowledgment

We thank Ann Donahue for her many contributions to the preparation of this chapter.

References

AARP and Stein Gerontological Institute. (1993). Life-span design of residential environments for an aging population. *Proceedings of the Universal Design of Residential Environments for an Aging Population.* Washington, DC: American Association of Retired Persons.

Anderson, G. F., & Poullier, J-P. (1999). Health spending, access, and outcomes: Trends in industrialized countries. *Health Affairs, 18,* 178–192.

Anderson, R. N. (1999). *U. S. decennial life tables for 1989–91, vol. 1, no. 4, United States life tables eliminating certain causes of death.* Hyattsville, MD: National Center for Health Statistics.

Bass, D. M., McClendon, M. J., Brennan, P. F., & McCarthy, C. (1998). The buffering effect of a computer support network on caregiver strain. *Journal of Aging and Health, 10,* 20–43.

Binstock, R. H. (1999). Challenges to United States policies on aging in the new millennium. *Hallym International Journal of Aging, 1,* 3–13.

Binstock, R. H. (2000). Healthcare costs around the world. In E. W. Markson & L. Hollis-Sawyer (Eds.), *Intersections of aging: Readings in social gerontology* (pp. 418–425). Los Angeles: Roxbury.

Bovenberg, L., & Van der Linden, A. (1997). Pension policies and the aging society. *OCED Observer, 205,* 10–15.

Callahan, D. (1987). *Setting limits: Medical goals in an aging society.* New York: Simon and Schuster.

Conrad, P., & Gabe, J. (Eds.) (1999). *Sociological perspectives on the new genetics.* Oxford: Blackwell.

Crimmins, E. M., & Ingegneri, D. G. (1990). Interaction and living arrangements of older parents and their children: Past trends, present determinants, future implications. *Research on Aging, 12,* 3–35.

Cutler, S. J., & Hendricks, J. (1990). Leisure and time use across the life course. In R. H. Binstock & L. K. George (Eds.), *Handbook of aging and the social sciences* (3rd ed.) (pp. 169–185). San Diego: Academic Press.

Cutler, S. J., & Hendricks, J. (2000). Age differences in voluntary association memberships: Fact or artifact. *Journal of Geron-tology: Social Sciences, 55B*, S98–S107.

Czaja, S. J., & Sharit, J. (1993). Age differences in the performance of computer-based work. *Psychology and Aging, 3*, 59–67.

Ekerdt, D. J. (1986). The busy ethic: Moral continuity between work and retirement. *The Gerontologist, 26*, 239–244.

Fullerton, H. N. (1999). Labor force participa-tion: 75 years of change, 1950–98 and 1998–2025. *Monthly Labor Review*, December, 3–12.

Glass, T. A., de Leon, M. C., Marottoli, R. A., & Berkman, L. F. (1999). Population based study of social and productive activities as predictors of survival among elderly Ameri-cans. *British Medical Journal, 319*, 478–483.

Goldscheider, F. K., & Goldscheider, C. (1999). *The changing transition to adulthood: Leav-ing and returning home.* Thousand Oaks, CA: Sage.

Gouldner, A. W. (1960). The norm of recipro-city: A preliminary statement. *American Sociological Review, 25*, 161–177.

Han, S K., & Moen, P. (1999). Clocking out: Temporal patterning of retirement. *Ameri-can Journal of Sociology, 105*, 191–236.

Hendricks, J., Hatch, L. R., & Cutler, S. J. (1999). Entitlements, social compacts, and the trend toward retrenchment in U.S. old-age programs. *Hallym International Journal of Aging, 1*, 14–32.

Henretta, J. (1994) Social structure and age-based careers. In M. W. Riley, R. L. Kahn, & A. Foner (Eds.), *Age and structural lag* (pp. 57–79). New York: Wiley.

Herzog, A. R., & Morgan, J. N. (1992). Age and gender differences in the value of productive activities. *Research on Aging, 14*, 169–198.

Herzog, A. R., Markus, H. R., Franks, M. M., & Holmberg, D. (1998). Activities and well-being in older age: Effects of self-concept and educational attainment. *Psychology and Aging, 13*, 179–185.

Holtzman, N. A., & Watson, M. S. (1998). *Pro-moting safe and effective genetic testing in the United States* (Final Report of the Task Force on Genetic Testing). Baltimore: The Johns Hopkins University Press.

Johnson, C. (2000). Adaptation of oldest old Black Americans. In E. W. Markson & L. Hollis-Sawyer (Eds.), *Intersections of aging: Readings in social gerontology* (pp. 133–141). Los Angeles: Roxbury.

Korpi, W., & Palme, J. (1998). The paradox of redistribution and strategies of equality: Welfare state institutions, inequality, and poverty in the western countries. *American Sociological Review, 63*, 661–687.

Liao, Y., McGee, D. L., Cao, G., & Cooper, R. S. (2000). Quality of the last years of life of older adults: 1986 vs. 1993. *Journal of the American Medical Association, 283*, 512–518.

Manton, K. G., Corder, L., & Stallard, E. (1993). Changes in the use of personal assist-ance and special equipment from 1982 to 1989: Results from the 1982 and 1989 NLTCS. *The Gerontologist, 33*, 168–176.

Mason, P. L. (1997). Race, culture, and skill: Interracial wage differences among African Americans, Latinos, and Whites. *Review of Black Political Economy, 25*, 5–39.

Mehlman, M. J., & Botkin, J. R. (1998). *Access to the genome: The challenge to equality.* Washington, DC: Georgetown University Press.

Miller, R. A. (1999). Are there genes for aging? *Journal of Gerontology: Biological Sciences, 54A*, B297–B307.

Morgan, D. L., Schuster, T. L., & Butler, E. W. (1991). Role reversals in the exchange of so-cial support. *Journal of Gerontology: Social Sciences, 46*, S278–S287.

Myles, J., & Quadagno, J. (2000). Envisioning a third way: The welfare state in the twenty-first century. *Contemporary Sociology, 29*, 156–167.

Perls, T. T., Silver, M. H., & Lauerman, J. F. (1999). *Living to 100: Lessons in living to your maximum potential at any age.* New York: Basic.

Pollard K. (1999, July/August). U.S. diversity in more than black and white. *Population Today*, p. 7.

Post, S. G., & Whitehouse, P. J. (Eds.) (1998). *Genetic testing for Alzheimer disease.* Bal-timore: The Johns Hopkins University Press.

Putnam, R. D. (1995). Bowling alone: Ameri-ca's declining social capital. *Journal of De-mocracy, 6*, 65–78.

Riley, M. W., & Riley, J. W. (1986). Longevity and social structure: The potential of the added years. In A. Pifer & L. Bronte (Eds.),

Our aging society: Paradox and promise (pp. 53–77). New York: Norton.

Riley, M. W., Kahn, R. L., & Foner, A. (Eds.) (1994). *Age and structural lag.* New York: Wiley.

Rowe, J. W., & Kahn, R. L. (1998). *Successful aging.* New York: Pantheon.

Rotolo, T. (1999). Trends in voluntary association participation. *Nonprofit and Voluntary Sector Quarterly, 28,* 199–212.

Russell, C. (1997). The ungraying of America. *American Demographics, 19* (7), 15–18.

Schaie, K. W., & Pietrucha, M. (Eds.) (2000). *Mobility and transportation in the elderly.* New York: Springer.

Seltzer, M. M. (Ed.) (1995). *The impact of increased life expectancy: Beyond the gray horizon.* New York: Springer.

Serow, W. J., & Cowart, M. E. (1999). Distributional changes in the American aged population, 1995–2025: Impact on entitlement programs for the elderly. *Hallym Journal of Aging, 1,* 26–34.

Sobel, S. K., & Cowan, D. B. (2000). Impact of genetic testing for Huntington disease on the family system. *American Journal of Medical Genetics, 90,* 49–59.

Soldo, B. J., & Hill, M. S. (1993). Intergenerational transfers: Economic, demographic, and social perspectives. In G. L. Maddox & M. P. Lawton (Eds.), *Annual review of gerontology and geriatrics: Focus on kinship, aging, and social change* (vol. 13, pp. 187–216). New York: Springer.

Stoller, E. P., & Gibson, R. C. (2000). *Worlds of difference* (3rd ed.). Thousand Oaks, CA: Pine Forge Press.

Tzannatos, Z. (1999). Women and labor market changes in the global economy: Growth helps, inequalities hurt, and public policy matters. *World Development, 27,* 551–569.

U.S. Bureau of the Census. (1992). An aging world II. *International Population Reports,* P25 (92–3). Washington, DC: U. S. Government Printing Office.

U.S. Bureau of the Census. (1996). 65+in the United States. *Current Population Reports,* P23 (190). Washington, DC: U. S. Government Printing Office.

U.S. Bureau of the Census. (1998). *Statistical abstract of the United States: 1998* (118th ed.). Washington, DC: Author.

U.S. Bureau of the Census (1999a). *International data base.* Washington, DC: Author. Available: www.census.gov/ipc/www/idbnew.html

U.S. Bureau of the Census. (1999b). Coresident grandparents and grandchildren. *Current Population Reports,* P23 (198). Washington, DC: Author.

U.S. Department of Housing and Urban Development. (1999). *Housing our elders: A report card on the housing conditions and needs of older Americans.* Washington, DC: Office of Policy Development and Research.

U.S. General Accounting Office. (1998). *Alzheimer's disease: Estimates of prevalence in the United States* (Report No. GAO/HEHS-98–16). Washington, DC: Author.

U.S. House of Representatives (1999, May 17). *Medicare and health care chartbook.* Washington, DC: U. S. Government Printing Office.

U.S. Senate. (1998). *Developments in aging: 1996* (Report 105–36 of the 105th Congress). Washington, DC: U. S. Government Printing Office.

Ware, J. A., & Simons, M. (Eds.) (1999). *Angiogenesis and cardiovascular disease.* New York: Oxford University Press.

Wellman, B., & Hampton, K. (1999). Living networked on and offline. *Contemporary Sociology, 28,* 648–654.

Wilfond, B. S., Rothenberg, K. H., Thomson, E. J., & Lerman, C. (1997). Cancer genetic susceptibility testing: Ethical and policy implications for future research and clinical practice. *Journal of Law, Medicine, & Ethics, 25,* 243–251.

World Bank. (1995). *Averting the old age crisis: Policies to protect the old and promote growth.* Washington, DC: The World Bank.

Author Index

Subject Index

503